# ECHOES OF BATTLE

## THE STRUGGLE FOR CHATTANOOGA

# ECHOES OF BATTLE

## THE STRUGGLE FOR CHATTANOOGA

AN ILLUSTRATED COLLECTION
OF UNION AND CONFEDERATE NARRATIVES

RICHARD A. BAUMGARTNER LARRY M. STRAYER

BLUE ACORN PRESS

Published by

**Blue Acorn Press**
**P.O. Box 2684**
**Huntington, W.Va. 25726**

ISBN 1-885033-16-8

Baumgartner, Richard A., 1953—
Strayer, Larry M., 1955—

Echoes of Battle: The Struggle for Chattanooga.
An illustrated compilation of Union and Confederate narratives detailing 1863's Tullahoma, Chickamauga and Chattanooga campaigns in Tennessee and Georgia.

Includes bibliographical references and index.

History — American Civil War

Manufactured in the United States of America

Design & typography by Richard A. Baumgartner

# Contents

# Timeline

## A brief summary of principal events

**June 23-July 7, 1863:** Tullahoma (Middle Tennessee) campaign.
**June 24-26:** Skirmishes at Hoover's Gap, Tenn.
**June 24-27:** Skirmishes at Liberty Gap, Tenn.
**June 27:** Federal forces occupy Manchester, Tenn.
**June 30:** Confederate Army of Tennessee under Gen. Braxton Bragg evacuates Tullahoma, Tenn., beginning retreat to Chattanooga. Bragg encamps there July 7.
**July 1:** Occupation of Tullahoma by Maj. Gen. W.S. Rosecrans' Army of the Cumberland.
**August 16-September 22:** Chickamauga campaign.
**August 16-October 19:** East Tennessee campaign.
**August 21:** Federal artillery begins shelling Chattanooga.
**September 7-9:** Confederates evacuate Chattanooga.
**September 9:** Federals enter and occupy Chattanooga.
**September 11-13:** Skirmishes at or near Davis' Crossroads, Ringgold, Rock Spring and Lee & Gordon's Mill, Ga.
**September 18:** Skirmishes at Pea Vine Ridge, Reed's and Alexander's bridges.
**September 19-20:** Battle of Chickamauga.
**September 21-22:** Army of the Cumberland retreats to Chattanooga.
**September 22-30:** Three XV Corps' divisions begin march to Chattanooga from Vicksburg, Miss. Second Division, XVII Corps, starts from Memphis on October 5.
**September 24-October 3:** Transfer of XI and XII corps from the Army of the Potomac to the Army of the Cumberland.
**September 30-October 17:** Wheeler/Roddey raids on Federal communications.
**October 16:** Creation of the Military Division of the Mississippi, with Maj. Gen. U.S. Grant assigned to command. Maj. Gen. G.H. Thomas ordered to command Department of the Cumberland, replacing Rosecrans.
**October 24:** Maj. Gen. W.T. Sherman assumes command of the Army of the Tennessee, replacing Grant.
**October 27:** Federal river expedition to Brown's Ferry reopens Tennessee River supply line.
**October 29:** Night fighting in Lookout Valley; battle of Wauhatchie.
**November 23:** Chattanooga campaign opens with assault and capture of Orchard and Bushy knobs.
**November 24:** Battle of Lookout Mountain.
**November 25:** Battle of Missionary Ridge.
**November 26:** Skirmishes at Chickamauga Station, Tenn., and near Graysville, Ga.
**November 27:** Battle of Ringgold Gap, Taylor's Ridge, Ga.
**November 28:** Federal pursuit of Bragg's troops ends; Confederates retreat to Dalton, Ga., where winter camps are established.
**December 2:** Lt. Gen. W.J. Hardee supersedes Bragg as Army of Tennessee commander, and is replaced in turn by Gen. J.E. Johnston on December 27.

"The fact that a hundred and fifty thousand men,
with all the appliances of war, have struggled
for the possession of these mountains, rivers,
and ridges, gives a solemn interest to the scene,
and renders it one of the most interesting,
as it is one of the grandest, in the world."

**Diary of**
**Brig. Gen. John Beatty**
**Missionary Ridge**
**January 1, 1864**

# Preface

## Fighting for Chattanooga: The common soldiers' struggle

On November 21, 1863, Sergeant Lewis E. Jones of Company B, 36th Ohio, sat in his quarters in besieged Chattanooga, Tenn., and penned a long letter home to a friend. "We contend with a powerful and stubborn foe," he observed, and "know that a well organised and powerful army still lays before us. When you hear that the Rebel armies are demoralized and disorganized — do not believe it. If you do you dishonor us. They have good armies. Ah, as good fighting men as ever the world produced. But whilst we hold Chattanooga we hold one of the most important places in the south."

Just four days after his ink dried, Jones' regiment scaled and clawed its way up Missionary Ridge east of town in one of the most dramatic and consequential battles of the Civil War. Gen. Braxton Bragg's two-month-long siege was decisively lifted, his army in full retreat. Few knew it at the time, but events transpiring around Chattanooga in late November 1863 marked a turning point in the war, and presaged the Southern Confederacy's collapse some 16 months later. Indeed, as Sergeant Jones wrote, Chattanooga was one of the South's most important places, and thousands died struggling for its possession.

Depicting the drama and everyday experiences of these dynamic months involved the review and selection of more than 450 narratives from Federal and Confederate eyewitnesses. Many of these accounts were drawn from contemporary sources — letters, diaries, journals and newspapers found in private and public collections across the country, including battle reports excerpted from the *Official Records of the Union and Confederate Armies.* Other sources included regimental histories and veterans' periodicals, primarily *The National Tribune, The Ohio Soldier* and *Confederate Veteran.* Pamphlets issued by the Military Order of the Loyal Legion of the United States (MOLLUS) and material published in *The Southern Bivouac* and the *Southern Historical Society Papers* proved valuable as well. Individual soldier memoirs and reminiscences, in both published and unpublished form, furnished many illuminating narratives.

Among nearly 1,000 accounts surveyed for this work, only those written in first-person style were selected for the chapter bodies — thus preserving an authentic flavor of the times. Shorter passages from these narratives were used in the chapter introductions and photograph/illustration captions.

Of perhaps greater importance are the photographs themselves. A majority of the 465 images chosen are published here for the first time. Relying on wartime portraits and landscapes to complement the first-person narratives continues a Blue Acorn Press standard unsurpassed in Civil War publishing. Exhaustive searches located many rare portraits, while others surfaced by means of uncanny, fortuitous circumstance. Wherever possible, unknown views or rarely seen poses were sought and used of recognizable personages, such as generals and field grade officers — a quest often fulfilled by the contributions of photography collectors in nearly two dozen states.

Some familiar photographs are captioned here correctly and with greater detail than their previous publication. These revisions reflect information gleaned through years of research. Many individual images were made months, even weeks, before the subject fell in battle. Among those of survivors, anguish and determination are often-seen expressions.

Twenty-six illustrations accompany the photographs, mostly engravings based on sketches by leading artists of the day. Chief among these were Theodore R. Davis, who also worked as a correspondent for *Harper's Weekly,* and Alfred R. Waud, whose portfolio is widely recognized for accuracy. Other sketches were composed on the spot by talented men in the ranks.

Nine maps specially drawn for this volume are based on cartography found in *The Official Military Atlas of the Civil War* and *Map of the Battlefields of Chattanooga and Wauhatchie,* prepared in 1896 by the Chickamauga and Chattanooga National Park Commission.

As best as can be determined, all ranks listed in the text, sidebars and photograph captions are those held by individuals at the specific time, verified through regimental rosters, army registers, adjutant general reports, and compiled service and pension records.

***Echoes of Battle: The Struggle for Chattanooga*** chronologically dovetails into our previous compilation ***Echoes of Battle: The Atlanta Campaign,*** following similar format and design. Like its predecessor, this volume does not attempt to detail or analyze strategy, military operations or command decisions in the region between June and December 1863.

Coverage of the Tullahoma campaign and Chickamauga battle should be viewed as introductory chapters to the book's primary focus, and are not intended to relate the full story of those events. Selections for the Chickamauga chapter highlight salient moments of that bloody two-day battle, which set the stage for what transpired within the shadows of Lookout Mountain and Missionary Ridge. The Knoxville-East Tennessee campaign, while occurring simultaneously with operations around Chattanooga, falls outside the book's parameters and receives marginal attention.

Following the war, a non-commissioned officer who served in the 4th Texas Infantry wrote: "A soldier of the line in a great army ... if he is at all observant, sees a great deal in camp, on the march, and on the picket and skirmish line. But in a great battle, as a general rule, he sees but little after he fairly gets into it. In fact, he is in big luck if he can keep in touch with his file leader and hear the commands of his officers."

Keeping this rule in mind, only a collection as assembled here can accurately portray the vast panorama of the common soldiers' struggle for Chattanooga. Of the ordinary men who shouldered muskets and the officers who led them, the echoes remain ...

Richard A. Baumgartner
Huntington, W.Va.

Larry M. Strayer
Dayton, Ohio

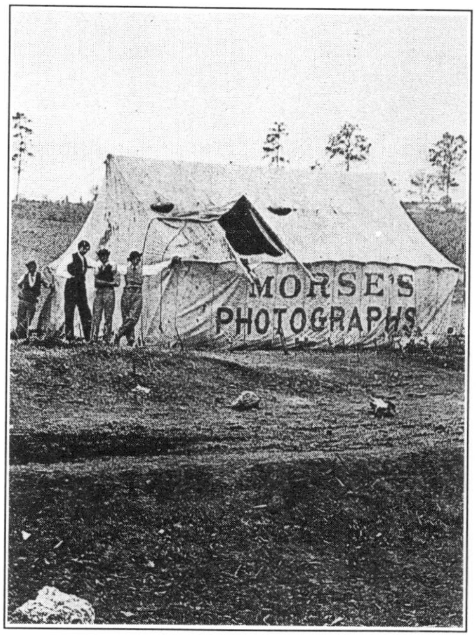


■ Field gallery of A.S. Morse, official photographer for the Department of the Cumberland. With headquarters in Nashville, Morse operated a branch location in Huntsville, Ala., and also made commercial portraits of soldiers. Taking cameras directly to the troops, as seen in this Chattanooga scene, he is best known among many unsung photographers who collectively created a thriving business in Army of the Cumberland camps. The surviving body of their work preserves a historical legacy of the men they photographed. Their own legacy, as seen by the names below, is far less familiar:

Brigham Bishop, who joined with J.W. Campbell, XX Army Corps, to form Campbell & Bishop; I.H. Butler, Bonsall & Company; M. Carpenter, army photographer; Cressey, Adams & Company, headquarters, who also shared a partnership under Perry & Cressey; H. Goldsticker; Greenwall & Stringham; Hannay, 2nd Brigade, 1st Division, IV Army Corps; Nixon & Dunn, Chattanooga; Peck's Place, Chattanooga; S.D. Phillips, 3rd Division, XIV Army Corps; and Schwing & Rudd, Army of the Cumberland.

CHAPTER 1

# A rat in a barrel with the bunghole closed

## Tullahoma Campaign: Rosecrans ousts Bragg from his Middle Tennessee stronghold

Confederate General Braxton Bragg knew he was in deep trouble on June 30, 1863. Just 10 miles northeast of his headquarters at Tullahoma, Tenn., the bulk of three Federal infantry corps was poised to strike Bragg's right flank, push behind his defenses and cut off the Army of Tennessee from its only line of escape by rail. The prospect was shocking and unexpected, but the situation confronting the Southern army during the previous week was plain to see, even by the lowest privates. Their commander had been completely outgeneraled. Within 24 hours, his orders sent them marching away in disheartening retreat — a tramp that did not end until they reached the safety of Chattanooga.

In 11 days at a cost of 570 casualties, "we had dislodged the enemy from two strongly entrenched camps, and driven him out of Middle Tennessee," wrote the Federal commander, Maj. Gen. William S. Rosecrans. The Tullahoma campaign further rocked Confederate hopes when coupled with simultaneous Southern defeats in early July at Gettysburg, Pa., Vicksburg, Miss. and Port Hudson, La., and was hailed within the Army of the Cumberland as a "brilliant success." In reviewing the operation, Rosecrans attested that "no adequate idea can be had of this campaign without taking into consideration the character of the country over which the corps were obliged to move, and the fearful condition of the weather. It was the hardest march ever made by the Army of the Cumberland."

For nearly six months Rosecrans' army had been encamped around Murfreesboro, following the drawn battle of Stone River. Bragg, his opponent, lay stretched to the south in a wide arc from Columbia to McMinnville, with two corps of infantry under Gens. Leonidas Polk and William Hardee entrenched just north of the Duck River at Shelbyville and Wartrace, respectively. Fronting the Confederate infantry positions was a range of rough hills through whose gaps the main roads passed to the south. In Polk's sector, these gaps were held by strong detachments with heavy columns within sup-

# 'The men are busy as bees'

Fresh from picket duty, Capt. John H. Phillips of Company D, 22nd Illinois, poses with the usual overnight equipment carried by Federal officers to lonely posts and reserves, which supported the ever-watchful sentinels. Suspended from his left shoulder are an army-issue canteen and haversack; from his right shoulder hangs a bedding roll, which included the recently issued shelter-tent, a rubberized ground sheet and woolen blanket. The photograph was taken May 26, 1863 at Murfreesboro, Tenn.

Earlier in May, Ohio corporal Bliss Morse described the military post at Murfreesboro, following an absence of three months: "I hardly knew the place. The forests were cut down and cleared off around the town, sawmills in use, store houses are [rising], forts and a magazine. They have built strong forts of heavy timber and some are covered with the same. Some of the trenches and forts are laid up with large bundles of brush of cedar bound by strong wire and are laid very solid. They serve as bales of cotton for breast works. Our men are busy as bees and it is one vast camp for miles around. The picket line around the camp is seventeen miles. The hills and valleys are dotted with tents, horses and wagons. At the depot are very large stores of food. You do not know how strong 'Old Rosa' has got fortified."

During the weeks preceding the summer campaigning in Middle Tennessee, both Union and Confederate pickets and cavalry patrols eagerly sought information about the enemy's disposition and movements. More often than not, this duty proved uneventful and boring. False alarms were frequent, as related by 1st Lieut. Chesley A. Mosman of Company D, 59th Illinois: "Last night [June 4] our cavalry was ordered to halt, but didn't. The picket fired away and yells 'Now, God damn you, can't you halt?' They did."

# 'A stranger to his men'

Although Gen. Braxton Bragg commanded the Army of Tennessee longer than anyone else, he never gained popular stature among his men.

"While Bragg was an able man," wrote Col. William Preston Johnston, an aide to President Jefferson Davis, "he was too rigid and narrow to be a great one. He was very harsh and intolerant where he once imbibed a prejudice, and he was not slow, nor always just, in assuming his conclusions. He was always a partisan, and merciless toward those who resisted him, even when his acts were clearly arbitrary. He did not inspire love or reverence, but he commanded respect and fear. He trusted too much those who agreed with him, and was apt to undervalue those who held aloof from or offended him. But if this rugged outline seems too much the likeness of a military despot, it should be added that his purposes were great, pure and unselfish, and his aspirations high."

The native North Carolinian and 1837 West Point graduate "was a stranger to his men to the last," wrote Private Philip D. Stephenson of the 13th Arkansas. "Soon after assuming command he had a man shot for stealing a chicken. This has been denied, but ... it was believed universally by the men. Austere, morose, rarely showing himself, known only to his men by his military orders, the feeling toward him grew into positive dislike. And yet that army followed him, followed and obeyed him, endured hunger, hardships, rags and nakedness for him, fought repeated battles for him ... and yet *in* all and *through* all, with no love for *him* and little confidence *in him.*"

In the 10 weeks prior to his dismissal on November 30, 1863, Bragg was the target of caustic comments. A Tennessee brigade staff officer, Capt. John W. Harris (killed the following May), wrote: "Every one here curses Bragg. It [the Confederate victory at Chickamauga] is the only good thing we have had during the war and through Braggs imbecility we have thrown it away ... Nearly every General Officer here asking [President Jefferson Davis] to remove Bragg ... I hope that it will be done for it will put our troops in much better spirits."

This portrait of Bragg was taken by R. Wearn at the Premium Photographic Gallery in Columbia, S.C.

porting distance. "Such was the strength of the position at Shelbyville," recalled a Federal officer, "that General Rosecrans anticipated stubborn resistance should he attack it, and in the event of success in assaults, the enemy could cover his retreat, having a route to his rear easily defended. He therefore proposed to turn General Bragg's right, and, avoiding his entrenchments at Shelbyville altogether, provoke a battle on ground of his own selection, or force him to retreat on a disadvantageous line."

Rosecrans' corps and division commanders, however, were universally opposed to moving forward just then. Confidentially polled on June 8, 15 of them believed an immediate advance was inadvisable, and 11 shared the opinion that the Confederates, if threatened, would fall back behind the Tennessee River and refuse battle. Four days later, the army's chief of staff, Brig. Gen. James A. Garfield, summarized for Rosecrans their primary reasons for deferring an attack:

1. With the Army of the Potomac defeated in Virginia at Chancellorsville, and Federal forces bending all their energies in a yet undecided struggle at Vicksburg, it is bad policy to risk our only reserve army to the chances of a general engagement. A failure here would have most disastrous effects on our lines of communication and on politics in the loyal states.

2. We should be compelled to fight the enemy on his own ground or follow him in a fruitless, stern chase, or if we attempted to outflank him and turn his position we should expose our line of communication and run the risk of being pushed back into a rough country well known to the enemy and little known to ourselves.

3. In case the enemy should fall back without accepting battle he could make our advance very slow, and, with a comparatively small force posted in the gaps of the mountains, could hold us back while he crossed the Tennessee River, where he would be measurably secure and free to send reinforcements to [Gen. Joseph E.] Johnston. His forces in East Tennessee could seriously harrass our left flank and constantly disturb our communications.

Estimating that Rosecrans' effective force outnumbered Bragg's by nearly 24,000 men (the figure actually was closer to 19,000 on June 10), Garfield instead *urged* an immediate offensive move — citing nine points of argument to his commander:

1st. Bragg's army is now weaker than it has been since the Battle of Stone River or is likely to be again for the present; while our army has reached its maximum strength, and we have no right to expect reinforcements for several months, if at all.

2nd. Whatever be the result at Vicksburg, the determination of its fate will give large reinforcements to Bragg. If Grant is successful his army will require many weeks to recover from the shock and strain of his late campaign, while Johnston will send back to Bragg a force sufficient to insure the safety of Tennessee. If Grant fails, the same result will inevitably follow so far as Bragg's army is concerned.

3rd. No man can predict with certainty the result of any battle however great the disparity in numbers. Such results are in the hand of God. But viewing the question in the light of human calculation, I refuse to entertain a doubt that this army which in January last defeated Bragg's superior numbers, cannot overwhelm his present greatly inferior forces.

4th. The most unfavorable course for us that Bragg could take would be to face back without giving us battle; but this would be very disastrous to him. Besides the loss of material of war and the abandonment of the rich and abundant harvest now nearly ripe in Central Tennessee, he would lose heavily by desertion. It is well known that a widespread dissatisfaction exists among his Kentucky and Tennessee troops. They are already deserting in large numbers. A retreat would greatly increase both the desire and the opportunity for desertion and would very materially reduce his physical and moral strength.

While it would lengthen our communications it would give us the possession of McMinnville and enable us to threaten Chattanooga and East Tennessee, and it

■ Maj. Gen. Earl Van Dorn commanded the Confederate cavalry corps in Middle Tennessee early in 1863 — his veteran troopers instilling fear in many of their opponents. On March 5 at Thompson's Station, 25 miles south of Nashville, four of Van Dorn's brigades overwhelmed a reinforced Federal brigade and an 80-wagon forage train. Forty-three percent of the Union expedition's 2,837-man force was captured after a stiff fight, while another 200 were killed or wounded.

Marched to Tullahoma, the prisoners were packed into freight cars bound for Chattanooga. Their commander, Col. John Coburn, 33rd Indiana, later recalled the departure: "All overcoats, leggings, knapsacks and extra clothing were taken from men and officers. I demanded to know by whose order. The reply was, 'By order of General Bragg, in retaliation for an order of General Rosecrans, stripping Federal uniforms from our soldiers.' I answered, 'Strip off any rebel uniform found on us,' adding that 'this was a cowardly and barbarous act, and the men engaged in it deserved hanging.' I demanded an interview with General Bragg. This was refused. The men, shivering, half-starved, without sleep or rest, were then crowded into box-cars, without a seat, and started for Chattanooga. They were denied the privilege of getting sticks of wood at Tullahoma for seats in the cars. The floor of the one I was in was covered with wet manure."

After nearly two months spent in Richmond's Libby Prison, Coburn's command was exchanged on May 8 — the day after Van Dorn was murdered near the site of his March victory.

would not be unreasonable to expect an early occupation of the former place.

**5th.** But the chances are more than even that a sudden and rapid movement would compel a general engagement, and the defeat of Bragg would be in the highest degree disastrous to the rebellion.

**6th.** The turbulent aspects of politics in the loyal states renders a decisive blow against the enemy, at this time, of the highest importance to the success of the Government at the polls and in the enforcement of the Conscription Act.

**7th.** The Government and the War Department believe that this army ought to move upon the enemy. The army desires it and the country is anxiously hoping for it.

**8th.** Our true objective point is the rebel army whose last reserves are substantially in the field, and an effective blow will crush the shell and soon be followed by the collapse of the rebel Government.

**9th.** You have, in my judgment, wisely delayed a general movement hitherto till your army could be massed and your cavalry could be mounted. Your mobile force can now be concentrated in twenty-four hours and your cavalry, not equal in numerical strength to that of the enemy, is greatly superior in efficiency and morale.

**With Maj. Gen. Ulysses S. Grant tightening the noose around Vicksburg's beleagured defenders in Mississippi, and Maj. Gen. Ambrose E. Burnside's small army about to march for Knoxville in East Tennessee, Rosecrans' 65,000 men struck tents at Murfreesboro on June 23 and 24. Their chief's strategy was simple: While Maj. Gen. Gordon Granger's Reserve Corps and the majority of Maj. Gen. David S. Stanley's Cavalry Corps feigned an attack on Bragg's left, the corps of Maj. Gens. George H. Thomas (XIV), Alexander McD. McCook (XX) and Thomas L. Crittenden (XXI) would deliver the main blow against the Rebel right, defended by Hardee. But even before the echoes of cannon and rifle fire reverberated through the rugged hills on June 24, the skies above Middle Tennessee darkened and began to rain. Foul weather persisted during the entire campaign and turned every line of march and bivouac into a vast, oozing mud-bog.**

**"The roads are in terrible condition," wrote Sergeant Michael S. Bright of Company B, 77th Pennsylvania, on June 30. "We have had more rain during the last week than we had all winter. My pencil is so badly soaked with water that it wont make a mark."**

**Capt. Robert P. Findley of Company K, 74th Ohio, remembered that "the rain descend[ed] in torrents, and the clayey mud adhered to our feet, rendering the march peculiarly laborious. Long before our halt for the night, which came an hour after darkness fell, the boys were cured of their desire for the experiences of the field, and pined for the comfortable bunks they had so long enjoyed ... It was long after we filed into camp before the last man had retired to sleep. My own bed had been made in a hollow, which gathered the water, and when I was awakened at daylight I was half submerged."**

**Another company commander, Capt. Daniel W. Howe of Company I, 79th Indiana, was part of a detail convoying a large, heavily loaded ammunition train 30 miles from Murfreesboro to Manchester. The wearying journey took four days, which Howe described in a letter to his mother: "The roads were badly cut up before we started. We were in consequence as much delayed by the stalling and breaking down of wagons. I saw a great many all along the road and many had to throw out a portion of their load to get along at all. The boys have a model way of making mules pull. Whenever a**

■ 1st Lieut. William Murphy, adjutant of the 6th Kentucky Cavalry. Throughout the winter and spring of 1863, Rosecrans, concerned with the state of his understrength, under-equipped cavalry forces, badgered government authorities for a plethora of supplies — especially horses, mules and weapons. The requisitions were filled at snail-like pace, if at all. On May 21, the army's Cavalry Corps had some 2,000 troopers lacking mounts, and an exasperated Rosecrans pleaded with Washington for help. "The price and the rigorous inspection [of horses] at Louisville prevents rapid purchases," he opined. "The quartermaster there telegraphed a few days ago that he was averaging but 9 per day."

Considered one of the best regiments in the Cavalry Corps' 1st Division, the 6th Kentucky skirmished with Confederate cavalry while reconnoitering near University Depot, Tenn., on July 4. In this action, Adjutant Murphy was shot and killed.

# 'No trifling minutiae escaped him'

■ Maj. Gen. William S. Rosecrans

Maj. Gen. William Starke Rosecrans assumed command of the Department of the Cumberland on October 30, 1862, and led the army of the same name for 10 days shy of a year. Like Bragg, he was a talented strategist possessed of a quick temper and odd eccentricities. Unlike his Confederate adversary, Rosecrans enjoyed the goodwill of a majority of his troops, who affectionately referred to the native Ohioan as "Old Rosy" and "Old Starkey."

"Every time I see him I like him the more," observed Illinois Corporal Tighlman H. Jones in late spring 1863. "He is a plain strait forward man, good size, rather large head, high forehead, a very mild even countenance. He has a word for every one of his boys and likes to talk with them. He is ardent and insisting and if there is a man in the army that is devoted to his country it is General Rosecrans."

Following a brigade inspection and flag presentation in Murfreesboro three months earlier, Corporal Mead Holmes Jr. of Company K, 21st Wisconsin, informed his parents: "A speech from 'Old Starkey' brought tears to many eyes unused to weep ... We love to hear 'Old Starkey's' thunder-voice; it stirs our souls. There is of course a tendency to low spirits, and it seems good to have some one speak to us."

"The soldiers were satisfied that their commander took an interest in their welfare," noted Cincinnati *Daily Commercial* correspondent William D. Bickham. At reviews, "he examined the equipments of the men with exacting scrutiny. No trifling minutiae escaped him. Everything to which the soldier was entitled was important. A private without his canteen instantly evoked a volley of searching inquiries. 'Where is your canteen? How did you lose it? When — where? Why don't you get another?' "

Writing of the general after the war, Gen. Jacob D. Cox recalled Rosecrans' nervous energy and manner of speaking, "which was apt to grow hurried, almost to stammering, when he was excited," especially under stress. "His impulsiveness was plain to all who approached him; his irritation quickly flashed out in words when he was crossed, [but] he was fond of conviviality, loved to banter good-humoredly his staff officers and intimates, and was altogether an attractive and companionable man, with intellectual activity enough to make his society stimulating and full of lively discussion. His standard of soldierly excellence was high, and he was earnest in insisting that his brigadiers and his staff officers should co-operate vigorously in trying to attain it."

An amusing anecdote of a Presbyterian minister's visit to Rosecrans' Murfreesboro headquarters early in 1863 was related to Cox by the clergyman: "He called on General Rosecrans," Cox wrote, "and among others met there Father [Patrick] Treacy, the general's chaplain, a Roman Catholic priest [Rosecrans had converted to Catholicism while at West Point two decades earlier]. During the visit Rosecrans was called aside by a staff officer to receive information about a spy who had been caught within the lines. The general got quite excited over the information, talked loudly and hurriedly in giving directions concerning the matter, using some profane language. It seemed suddenly to occur to him that the clergymen were present, and from the opposite side of the room he turned toward them, exclaiming apologetically, 'Gentlemen, I sometimes *swear,* but I never *blaspheme!*' "

■ Capt. J. Monroe Stookey of Company E, 59th Illinois, was his regiment's ranking line officer and acting major in mid-1863. Describing incidents of the campaign to his brother, he wrote: "We had rain every day since we left Murfreesboro ... perhaps you [can] imagine we felt any ways nice after being thoughorly drenched every day & very short rations & the broad canopy of the heavens for our roof at night & hard marches with heavy loads, occasionally [pulling] out a wagon that was mired in mud. The privates they have the hard times but I heard no complaints. [On the 26th] there was a cracking of Musketry kept up by the skirmishers on both sides. They would talk & laugh and yell all kinds of Way's at each other that day but nothing transpired of importance."

Stookey's friend, 1st Lieut. Chesley A. Mosman of Company D, noted this verbal sparring in his diary: "Skirmishers yell, 'Whats the calibre of your gun?' Reb, 'Yankee calibre.' 'You shoot too high.' 'Little lower.' 'So that will do.' 'Got Vicksburg yet?' The Rebs are accurate shots. Tonight one Reb says, 'How do you like Jeff Davis?' and another shot at our Jeff. Yank, 'Hold a candle for that man to see to shoot by' and nearly struck him."

**team stalls, they all get around and at a given signal some whip, some pry and the balance yell like a pack of savages. The last seems to have more effect than anything else."**

## 'Wet to the skin'

### 2nd Lieut. Charles C. Briant
### Company K
### 6th Indiana Volunteer Infantry

We left Murfreesboro and started the 24th day of June soon after dinner. We had gone only a short distance when it began to rain, and it not only rained every day, but it seemed to me every hour from that time on up until about the third day of July. It rained so much and so hard that we ceased to regard it a matter of any consequence, and simply stood up and took it, without attempting to seek shelter or screen ourselves in the least. Why should we, when we were already wet to the skin? Shelter was a matter of impossibility, except the few "dog tents" which only a part of the boys had, and they could only be used at night, and even then they only covered a part of us, for our feet and legs up to our knees always took the weather as it came, no matter whether it was wet or dry; and during this nine or ten days, no man attempted to remove a particle of his clothing. He simply went to bed like a horse, with his shoes on.

The incessant rain had filled every little stream and gulch to overflowing, while the water was rushing down the sides of the mountains in great sluices, and had filled the stream, up which we came, and along which passes the only road that allows any possible chance to escape, until it was full from bank to bank, rushing and tumbling along down the rough, rugged and rocky channel, thick with mud, foaming and frothing, and roaring in a most threatening manner.

We were now at the very head of this long, deep gap, and about six miles from its mouth, waiting for orders to "follow Thomas" by way of Beech Grove, which would compel us to pass down this angry stream, and one among the many strange things is that such orders should reach us at 8 o'clock at night, and by 9 o'clock the whole division was on its way, splashing along down the muddy stream. Dark as the bottomless pit, and raining straight down; splash, splash, splash, splash, sometimes knee deep, sometimes waist deep, and always in water; slop, slop, slop, slop, here we go, sometimes in the road, and sometimes stumbling over logs and stones. Every once in a while you could hear someone call out, "Where are you, Bill?" "Here, what the thunder are you doing away out there?" Pretty soon it would be, "Where are you, Company A?" or, "Where are you, Company K?" This was the only possible way for the different companies to keep anywhere near together.

But still we go, splash, splash, down the muddy stream until, I think, it was 3 o'clock in the morning, the bugle blew halt and soon word came back for us to turn in for the night. Turn in where? Mud and water were all around us. It was so dark we could not see an object beyond an arm's length. The companies were all mixed up, or, in other words, there was simply nothing

■ Officers of Rosecrans' staff, spring 1863. Captioned "Our Mess," the photograph probably was made at Murfreesboro and shows, from left: Major William McMichael (assistant adjutant general), 1st Lieut. William L. Porter (aide-de-camp), Lt. Col. Arthur C. Ducat (assistant inspector general), Capt. Henry Thrall (assistant adjutant general, who died September 18, 1863), 1st Lieut. James K. Reynolds (acting aide-de-camp), and Capt. John H. Young (chief commissary of musters).

Rosecrans relied heavily upon his staff to coordinate movements of his widespread columns during the Tullahoma operations.

like order or organization among the companies or regiments, and when the order to "turn in" was received, it was "every fellow for himself" from that time until daylight.

It was curious to see the boys getting together next morning. But after a hurried breakfast the bugle again blows the "fall in" and away we go for Beech Grove. We soon strike the Manchester pike, and another day is put in amidst mud and rain.

A short halt at noon for coffee and on we go. Another short halt at supper time for coffee, and again we move on. Dark sets in, and still we press forward. About 9 o'clock at night a very heavy thunder storm came up, and for a change the most terrific storm of thunder and lightning prevailed, while the rain came down in torrents, but still we move on. The lightning was so vivid and thunder so rapid as it played among the treetops which slashed each other as their branches met over the narrow, muddy road along which we still followed as best we could in the inky darkness, that it seemed to me that Satan himself had been turned loose. Ten o'clock comes, and still we are plodding along in the dark and mud, while the lightning is still darting livid streams of fire among the treetops, and in a sporting way would now and then hit some old scraggy rock on the mountains a whack just to see the slivers fly. Eleven o'clock comes and still we press forward,

■ Drummer Theophilus E. Hill of Company I, 34th Illinois. The regiment's sergeant major, Lyman S. Widney, captured the feelings of many Federal soldiers on the eve of the campaign. "At last we see preparations for the advance of our Army," Widney wrote on June 22, "and we expect stirring events after our prolonged season of inactivity. It is high time for the Army of the Cumberland to do something for the good of our Country."

The following day he continued: "The possibilities of the campaign before us engrossed all our thoughts. As usual there were privates ready to inform us of every movement in advance, but as these self appointed commanders of imaginary Brigades and Divisions failed to inform us in our last campaign that the enemy would surprise us before breakfast, we lacked confidence in their predictions."

In this late-war portrait, Hill, recently promoted to corporal, wears a XIV Corps acorn pin fastened to his blouse.

wet to the skin and mud to the knees, while it was with difficulty that I could lift my feet out of the deep mud. I stagger as I walk. Merciful father, give us strength to endure these hardships, that we may not fall and perish by the wayside.

Half past eleven and we have reached the top of the mountain. Hark! The bugle sounds the halt, and amidst the pelting rain and roaring thunder we receive orders to "turn in" for the night. My partner of last night [1st Lieut. George B. Green, Company K, who was killed four months later at Brown's Ferry] was nowhere near me, nor did I take the trouble to look him up. Again it is a case of self-preservation, and on my own hook I began to cast about for a resting place for the night. By the aid of the flashing lightning I made my way to a rail fence nearby, and securing a couple of rails, I placed one end of them on a log while the other end rested on the ground, turning the hard edges in, then with my haversack placed on the log between the rails for a pillow, I stretch myself between the rails, place my hat over my face, and under an oil-cloth covering me from head to feet, I folded my arms across my breast and was soon unconscious of past troubles.

**The first fighting of consequence during the campaign took place north of Wartrace at Liberty and Hoover gaps. Troops of McCook's XX Corps met Hardee's men at Liberty Gap, which was held by two Arkansas regiments and a section of artillery belonging to Maj. Gen. Patrick R. Cleburne's division. Stubborn resistance slowed the Federal advance for a time, inflicting 261 casualties, but opposition eventually melted away in the rain when both Confederate flanks in the defile were enveloped, and a subsequent counterattack was repulsed. Five days later, Sergeant Bright of the 77th Pennsylvania informed a relative back home: "We flanked their position on both sides, and some places [in the gap] were so steep we had to pull ourselves up holding on to the trees and bushes. They kept up a lively fire, but it went mostly over our heads and we got to the top at last and chased them about a mile down the other side. On the afternoon of the 25th at Liberty gap we had about as hot a fight as the Old 77th has been in yet. We had to charge about 500 yards across a muddy corn field. The Rebels were drawn up in three lines on the Hill in front of us and their Artillery on the Right. In a very short time our Regt lost more than one fifth of its men in killed and wounded. By the time we got across the field our ammunition was about gone, but then an Indiana regt and an Illinois regt came up and got the Rebels cleared off the Hill."**

## 'The picture of desolation'

### Journal of
### Sergeant Major Lyman Widney
### 34th Illinois Volunteer Infantry

**Wednesday June 24 —** All preparations having been made during the night we were ready early this morning when orders came to advance upon the enemy ... Once in line we moved over the [Shelbyville] turnpike like a huge serpent with its head to-

# 'An air of decisive command'

Lt. Gen. William Joseph Hardee commanded a corps in the Army of Tennessee. This photograph, believed to be previously unpublished, was taken in Bowling Green, Ky., by C.R. Edwards soon after Hardee's troops entered the town in early October 1861. (Promoted to major general on October 21, 1861, Hardee still wears here the uniform of a Confederate brigadier general).

His arrival in Bowling Green stirred up public interest, the citizens turning out to see him and "his brave and daring toothpick boys." A reporter for the Nashville *Republican Banner* described Hardee as "about fifty years old [he actually turned 46 on October 12, 1861], has strong marked features, and possesses an air of decisive command ... His manner, though stern, is restless ... He is about medium size, with a singularly fine muscular development, which can withstand the varying vicissitudes of any sort of a campaign."

Hardee's corps anchored the Confederate right when the Federals advanced from Murfreesboro on June 24, 1863 to open the Tullahoma campaign. He felt the rebel troops were too scattered geographically, and disagreed with Bragg's selection of Tullahoma as the backbone of the Army of Tennessee's defenses. Within two weeks of Tullahoma's abandonment on June 30, the Confederates — many badly demoralized by the retreat, and news of the twin defeats at Gettysburg and Vicksburg — were in Chattanooga. While the rank and file grumbled and seriously questioned Bragg's competence, Hardee remained in high esteem. "He never denies himself," wrote Jason M. Fairbanks, Hardee's secretary, "not even to the humblest private in the Ranks, and by consequence he is very much beloved by all the soldiers, high and low, and can count on them with confidence ..."

■ Brig. Gen. St. John R. Liddell's four Arkansas regiments suffered 120 casualties defending Liberty Gap, half of them in the 2nd Arkansas Infantry which ran out of ammunition and lost its flag on June 25. "Our soldiers were exceedingly eager and excited, and gallantly maintained the contest for some time," Liddell reported. "There was some difficulty, however, in getting the ammunition [brought up], on account of the boggy nature of the ground, caused by so much rain. Two color-bearers of the Second were killed, and the third, standing on a declivity of the hill, was fatally struck, and falling forward headlong, cast his colors toward the base, in close proximity to the line of the enemy. The colors were not missed until the regiment had retired over the crest of the hill, and having now no ammunition, it was useless to renew the attack for their recovery. This is a source of great mortification to the regiment as well as the brigade."

When Liddell's men reached Tullahoma on June 28, 300 of them were without shoes.

wards the enemy, its outspreading fangs represented by a line of skirmishers ready to strike the object lying across its path.

We had not proceeded very far until the irregular snapping of musketry announced that the enemy's pickets were opposing our advance but they retired slowly saluting us from every point of cover with persistent valor which delayed but did not arrest our progress. Six miles from camp ... our Division headed towards Liberty Gap. As we advanced the enemy gathered strength until our skirmishers encountered a resistance too vigorous to be dispelled. Willich's Brigade then deployed on both sides of the road while ours [commanded by Col. John F. Miller] moved up to support it. We found a Brigade of the enemy under General Liddle[sic] before us and our skirmishers had to be heavily reinforced to dislodge and press him back to the entrance of Liberty Gap where he held his position at the close of the day. We passed through Liddle's camp which was occupied by his troops last night and for sometime previous. Evidently we had deprived them of comfortable quarters at a very inopportune time as rain fell steadily all day drenching Blue and Gray alike.

Our engagement did not permit us the privilege of a camp nor could we allow it to the enemy. When darkness approached our Brigade bivouacked on a hillside minus every article of baggage not carried on our backs. Rain fell incessantly and wood being scarce we kept fires alive with difficulty. It was my good fortune to secure a boulder partly imbedded in the mud near our fire where I might sit with my chin resting on my knees; lying down was out of the question. A rubber blanket partially protected my body from the cold rain. In this position I tried to find consolation in the belief that I would either be killed or cured of a slow fever that had tormented me for more than a week.

**Thursday June 25 —** The morning light disclosed a wretched camp occupied by dripping dispirited soldiers searching blindly for the missing requisites of a warm breakfast. As for my slow fever the rain washed it entirely out of my system during the night, leaving only a damp, hungry feeling. Although a narrow valley only separated us from the enemy and all signs indicated that we would be called to cross it before the day was over yet our present discomforts were so immediate and pressing that our thoughts dwelt more upon them than the contingencies of battle.

About noon Willich's Brigade attempted to dislodge the enemy from the entrance of Liberty Gap but did not meet with success. We were held in readiness to support this attack until 3 p.m. when an order came for a portion of our Brigade including our Regiment to advance which we did promptly. Rushing down the hillside we passed around a spur at the foot and found before us a level field of growing corn nearly waist high and beyond it the hills on either side of the Gap where the enemy concealed his numbers in the brush. Our appearance on the scene attracted the enemy's fire while we were forming for the charge. It was not our purpose to waste time in making a show so before we had time to consider what were our surroundings the order was given and over the fence we clambered into the midst of the young corn which toppled over before us as grain before the reaper while behind us it lay crushed into the soft mud that reached our shoe tops. Not tender stalks of corn alone toppled over as we advanced — blue forms here and there were seen to fall and rich red blood added its color to the picture of desolation into which that peaceful cornfield had been so speedily transformed.

We who wrought this destruction gave little heed to the doleful picture at our backs as we struggled forward. Our eyes were fixed upon the brush beyond the field where the flash and smoke of musketry disclosed the danger line. The sooner we reach it and dislodge the enemy the fewer of our number will be left writhing in the muddy field. As we emerge from the field the smoke clears away before our eyes and we enter the cover unopposed. Our enemy is retreating towards the southern end of the Gap while we prepare to bivouac on the hillside of the stronghold we have won. But first comes the duty of looking after our comrades who fell with the toppling corn. Three of our Regiment lie dead upon the field and twenty-six are wounded while the loss in our Division is two hundred and thirty-one, including our Brigade Commander seriously wounded. It was my sad duty to search in the darkness for the body of a dead comrade and help to bear it saturated with a frightful mixture of blood and mud to the hillside where we consigned it to a hastily dug grave.

**At Hoover's Gap, meanwhile, Thomas' XIV Corps was spearheaded by the mounted infantry brigade of Col. John T. Wilder, whose 1,900 Indiana and Illinois troopers carried new magazine-fed, seven-shot Spencer rifles. His firepower further was augmented by the attached 18th Indiana Battery of Capt. Eli Lilly, whose oversized command consisted of six 10-pounder Rodman guns and four mountain howitzers. Considered an energetic and enterprising officer, Wilder was anxious to prove what his soldiers already believed — that they were equal to two or three times their number of men armed with muzzle-loading guns.**

**"The instructions Colonel Wilder received were to move out, drive the enemy's outposts and get within striking distance for the next day [June 25]," recalled Corporal George S. Wilson of Company C, 17th Indiana. "But he determined to do more. Ten miles from Murfreesboro we struck the rebel pickets, and immediately put spurs to our horses and drove them back on their supports, and, without halting, pushed their whole outpost force back at a gallop; following so closely and rapidly that before the alarm reached the rebel camp we had ridden through the whole length of the gap. Now the enemy's chosen ground for defense lay behind us; while we took our position at the southern entrance to the gap with the same defensive advantages to us that he would have had in holding the northern entrance. Thus by a dash, rapid and bold, and wholly unexpected, not only by the enemy but by his own superiors, Wilder had gained one of the most important positions on General Rosecrans' whole line. The next question was, could we hold the ground until the infantry, now miles back, could get up?"**

## 'The responsibility to disobey orders'

### Col. John T. Wilder
### Commander
### 1st Brigade, 4th Division, XIV Corps

At 3 o'clock on the morning of June 24th [my] brigade passed

■ Capt. Hiram Chance of Company A, 49th Ohio, commanded skirmishers protecting his regiment's right flank during Willich's assault at Liberty Gap on June 24. While driving a disorganized group of Confederates up a slope late in the day, he was shot in the chest and expired soon after, just as the 49th ran out of ammunition. "He was a young man of culture, free from every vice, a citizen loved for his virtues," lamented Col. William H. Gibson six days later. "He died as he had lived ... and his last words were 'Oh, my mother! Oh, my country! How I love thee!' "

Upon gaining the slope's summit, "we found the Camp of the 15th Arkansas regiment whom we had been fighting on the hill," noted diarist Francis Kiene, a private in Company I. "They had left most of their Tents sitting and meny knapsacks were left. A table was left setting that was set for supper."

■ Private John Munson of Company F, 72nd Indiana, personified the attributes of speed, mobility and rapid firepower in this rare quarter-plate tintype, perhaps the only known photograph of a member of Wilder's Lightning brigade taken in the field. Equipped with Spencer rifle and astride a horse nicknamed "Col. John Mosby," Munson was wounded slightly in the left hip near Rock Springs, Ga., on September 12, 1863. After recovering, he rejoined the 72nd and served until muster-out in July 1865.

south through Murfreesboro and took the advance of the Fourteenth Corps, with General J.J. Reynolds following as the advanced division of Thomas' infantry. The mounted infantry moved forward at a quick walk toward Hoover's Gap, ten miles south of Murfreesboro, where a brigade of cavalry stood guard to prevent the passage of our forces. Hoover's Gap was a narrow valley through a line of lumpy hills, some four miles in extent and about three hundred feet high, the hills being wooded and thickly grown with underbrush and green briers, making it impracticable for cavalry. The turnpike, a good macadamized road, wound through this narrow pass some four miles in extent, following a little brook, one of the headwaters of Stone River.

Our advance guard, consisting of five companies of the Seventy-second Indiana and twenty-five brigade scouts, all under Lieutenant-Colonel [Samuel C.] Kirkpatrick, Seventy-second Indiana, came suddenly on the enemy's pickets about a mile north of the entrance to the gap. We at once charged them at a gallop in a column of fours, surprising and dispersing [the Confederate] command, who were in bivouac at the gap, routing them in disorder, without even time to saddle or mount their horses, and the brigade pushed on through the gap, and not even a scout or messenger of the enemy being ahead of us to give the alarm to the enemy's infantry, under General [William B.] Bate, supposed to be at the summit of the gap where the turnpike descends to the valley of the Garrison fork of Duck River, running west at right angles to the line of Hoover's Gap.

I decided to move rapidly on, intending to surprise the enemy's infantry the same as we had surprised and dispersed their cavalry. Judge of my astonishment, when we reached their supposed position, to find no force there. Looking down the valley to the village of Beech Grove, two miles to the west, down the valley of the Garrison fork, we could see the tents of an encampment. I at once halted the command, dismounted and deployed three regiments of my force in a line across the road and gap, with the flanks retired, keeping the Ninety-eighth Illinois in reserve, and put the Eighteenth Indiana Battery in position to cover any advance of the enemy, and sent Lieutenant-Colonel Kirkpatrick with his five companies and the scouts to stir up the enemy, which they did in fine style.

General Bate commanded the brigade, which belonged to General A.P. Stewart's division of four brigades of infantry, placed along the valley of Garrison fork, and seemed to be entirely unaware of our advance. Many of the officers of Bate's brigade were at a spring holding a Masonic picnic in honor of St. John, it being the 24th of June, St. John's day. Colonel Kirkpatrick rode into their camp and had time to take seven wagons loaded with tobacco out with him and bring them back to our men, who had "tobacco to burn." General Bate, supposing it to be a cavalry dash, aroused his men and came speedily up to attack us. We allowed him to come within about one hundred yards up a gentle slope in front of our line when we opened a terrific fire from our Spencer rifles, and Captain Lilly poured double-shotted canister from his ten-pound Rodman guns into their lines, which staggered and repulsed them with severe loss. Bate's Twentieth Tennessee Infantry tried to turn the right flank of the Seventeenth Indiana in the forest at our right, when the Ninety-eighth Illinois quickly moved up the hill and doubled them up by a charge on their left, hurling them back in confusion out of reach, and they were compelled to retreat beyond reach of our fire, and other troops were sent to their assistance. Then they came up more cautiously and opened on us with two batteries at a distance of about half a mile, with a rapid fire, which did little execution.

While this was going on, Captain [Alexander A.] Rice, Adjutant-General of the division, came riding speedily to the front with orders from General Reynolds to me to fall back immediately, as the division was six or eight miles in our rear, having stopped to repair a bridge without letting me know of it. I told him I would hold this position against any force, and to tell General Reynolds to come on without hurrying, as there was no danger of our being driven out of the position. Captain Rice repeated his order for me to fall back, and I told him I would take the responsibility of remaining where I was, and that if General Reynolds were on the ground he would not give such an order. Captain Rice said that he had no discretion in the matter, and that if I did not obey the order he would put me in arrest and give the command to Colonel Miller [Abram O. Miller, 72nd Indiana], who would fall back as ordered.

I declined to obey the order of arrest, and requested Captain Rice to return to General Reynolds and tell him we had driven their force back, and could not be driven by any forces that could

■ Col. John T. Wilder's mounted infantry brigade, attached to Thomas' XIV Corps during the Tullahoma campaign, consisted of the 17th Indiana, 72nd Indiana, 98th Illinois, 123rd Illinois and the 18th Indiana Battery. After the war Wilder claimed that the Army of the Cumberland's cavalry commander, David S. Stanley, lacked full confidence in the Hoosier's troopers on the eve of the Hoover's Gap fight. He recalled: "General Stanley seemed anxious to send a cavalry brigade with General Thomas, as he said, to take care of my 'tadpole' cavalry, as he called us, fearing I would rush into the enemy and get captured, and Stanley would have those magazine guns [Spencer rifles] to fight. General Thomas assured General Rosecrans that if my brigade were captured there would be no need for cavalry about."

■ Private William N. Rogers of Company C, 98th Illinois, proudly displays the Spencer rifle issued to Wilder's troops in mid-May 1863. Hoover's Gap "was the first battle where the Spencer repeating rifles had ever been used," Wilder later wrote, "and in my estimation they were better weapons than has yet taken their place, being strong and not easily injured by the rough usage of army movements, and carrying a projectile [.52-caliber one-ounce bullet] that disabled any man who was unlucky enough to be hit by it."

One of Rogers' brigade comrades testified that the Spencer "never got out of repair. It would shoot a mile just as accurately as the finest rifle in the world. It was the easiest gun to handle in the manual of arms drill I have ever seen. It could be taken all to pieces to clean, and hence was little trouble to keep in order — quite an item to lazy soldiers."

When issued new cavalry jackets in March 1863, Wilder's men promptly removed the yellow taping, underscoring their dislike of cavalrymen and a desire to remain distinctive as mounted infantry. Rogers' jacket, above, reflects this alteration.

come at us. He then left just as the second attack was being made. This move was repulsed without difficulty, and when the enemy had fallen back out of range, General Rosecrans, with General Thomas and General Garfield, came riding up with their staff and escort. General Rosecrans came up to me and asked what we had done, and I told him in a few words, and also told him I had taken the responsibility of disobeying the order of General Reynolds to fall back, knowing that we could hold the position, and also felt sure that General Reynolds would not order us to retire if he were present.

General Rosecrans took off his hat and handed it to an orderly, and grasped my hand in both of his, saying: "You took the responsibility to disobey orders, did you? Thank God for your decision. It would have cost us two thousand lives to have taken this position if you had given it up."

General Reynolds just then came riding up in advance of his forces, and General Rosecrans said to him: "Wilder has done right. Promote him, promote him," and General Reynolds, after looking over the position, said to me: "You did right, and should be promoted and not censured."

The next morning an order was read at the head of every regiment of the Fourteenth Corps describing the attack of my command, saying that the conduct of the brigade should be emulated by all, and recommended my promotion as a Brigadier-General, and directing that the command should thereafter be known as Wilder's Lightning Brigade.

**With the loss of the gaps and his right flank dangerously imperiled, Bragg, hampered by a number of physical ailments, decided on June 30 to evacuate Tullahoma and withdraw the Army of Tennessee across the Elk River. "At Tullahoma Gen. Bragg summoned a council of war of corps commanders for the object of having their views on the situation," recalled 1st Lieut. W.N. Mercer Otey, the army's chief signal officer. "Gen. Bragg was pacing up and down the piazza of his headquarters nervously twitching his beard. I could see that matters were critical, and his indecision was finally determined by the advice given by Gen. Polk to the effect that expediency required our retiring to Chattanooga, as to remain where we were would place us in the position of a rat in a barrel with the bunghole closed, the bung in this case being the [railroad] tunnels in our rear, through which our subsistence must necessarily be transported. With this condition confronting him, no prudent general like Rosecrans would attack when he could flank us and destroy the line of communication in our rear. Chattanooga, in an air line, was sixty miles away, with the Cumberland Mountains and Tennessee River to cross. This decision determined upon, the army was put in motion ..."**

**Three Federal divisions marched into Tullahoma at noon on July 1. Many in the ranks were relieved to find that the Confederate withdrawal negated a costly assault against the town's formidable defenses. Private Solomon M. Deacon of Company K, 87th Indiana, wrote to his brother: "I was one of the first to enter. It is well fortified. A large fort commands all entrances from the north and outside of this and completely encircling the town are rifle pits and breastworks. In front of these the rebels had fallen trees for a distance of half a mile**

**which would [have] made our progress very slow with a large force, for they would have pepered us pretty lively I expect if they had made a stand. I could not help admiring our boys as they were skirmishing across this fallen timber before they knew that the rebs were gone. I could see them in a long line leaping over logs and when they had got about half way across they commenced to shout and double quick as fast as possible. Each man vied with the other to see which should reach the fortifications first. But old Bragg had vamoosed."***

## 'Fighting rear-guard actions day after day'

### Private John A. Wyeth
### Company I
### 4th Alabama Volunteer Cavalry

There was to be no great battle at Tullahoma, where behind formidable intrenchments Bragg's army had for months been sheltered, and upon which Rosecrans was now advancing. When we arrived the wagon-trains had had a four days' start along the awful roads to Chattanooga. The artillery went next, then the long lines of infantry floundered through the mud, and last of all we brought up the rear.

Nothing so depresses an army as a retreat; no duty is so harrowing and demoralizing as that of fighting rear-guard actions day after day. South of Tullahoma, with the regular installment of rain, we stood off the aggresive Union cavalry until we cleared the half-barren post-oak and black-jack plateau, from the summit of which we descended to cross Elk River on a planked-over railroad-bridge, and at dark on July 1st found ourselves posted to oppose the enemy at the crossing of this river known as Morris' Ford.

On the morning of July 2, we were up early and were congratulating ourselves on having a short rest. It was clear, and as soon as the sun rose we turned our saddles bottom side up to dry, and while some of the men were busy getting breakfast a number of us went down to the river to indulge in the luxury of a swim. As we were finishing our simple breakfast of corn-bread and bacon the videttes left half a mile from the ford on the north side of the stream fired at a squadron of the Fourth Ohio Cavalry, which chased them into the river. As soon as the guns were heard we were ordered to rush to the ford and hold the enemy back. Some of us (sixteen in all) were fortunate enough to reach a small thicket near the crossing, where we ensconced ourselves in a gully. Others lay down behind a worm-fence, with nothing but that and the light fringe of bushes for protection.

We had barely reached our places when the Federals opened on us with a heavy fire of small arms and two pieces of artillery. This fire raked the bivouac on the open hillside behind us — excepting the small number who had already succeeded in sheltering themselves close along the bank — back over the crest of the

■ Private John A. Wyeth of Company I, 4th Alabama Cavalry. When the 4th fell back to Chattanooga during the last few days of August, Wyeth recalled, "an attempt was made to collect all the carbines and most modern and effective guns in the regiment and give them to the two flanking companies. I had bought my Burnside carbine with fifty dollars given me by my married sister, and I resented the order to turn it in for a long and heavy Austrian rifle. It so happened that a dear friend was ordnance officer, and when the inspection was made he allowed me to retain my carbine."

This portrait was taken in 1861 while Wyeth was a cadet at La Grange Military Academy in Franklin, Ala.

* On November 25, 1863, Deacon was killed on the crest of Missionary Ridge when a bullet struck him in the forehead. He is buried in Chattanooga National Cemetery.

■ Private Nathaniel Delzell of Company D, 17th Tennessee, was taken prisoner on July 3 near Tullahoma, only six miles from his home. With the Confederates retreating to Chattanooga, Delzell was treated as a deserter by Federal authorities, for he took an oath of allegiance and was paroled just six days later.

One month after Tullahoma's abandonment, another Tennessean, Private William H. Davis, wrote to his sister from Chattanooga: "We have had some few Dessertions since we reached this place but those that desert us in the hour of adversity will be Remembered in the days of prosperity. We can spaire them very well, for they are Nothing but a nuisance to us. A dead Expense."

hill fully a half-mile away. As we had no artillery, our position was not to be envied. To try to escape exposed us at close range to the fire from small arms, and to grape and canister for fully four hundred yards of open hillside. Realizing that we were in for it, we prepared for rapid loading by laying our cartridges and caps in rows on the ground and concentrated our fire on the narrow roadway which led into the stream from the other side.

After having driven everybody else away, the enemy gave their undivided attention to us, and for nearly three hours there was the liveliest firing I ever heard. They were so near we could distinctly hear every command given in an ordinary tone of voice. Those of our men who were lying behind the old fence suffered severely, and a number were killed or wounded (we could hear their groans), and long before the fight was over no resistance was offered anywhere except by our small squad of sixteen men.

Finally they tried volley-firing, concentrating all their small arms and both cannon loaded with grape or canister on our thicket, an area not larger than half an acre. Our fire must have been effective, for we kept their two guns and them back in the undergrowth, where they could not aim with accuracy. Our heads alone were exposed, and after the first volley we ducked into the gully to avoid the others, for we distinctly heard the guns being loaded and knew about when they were going to pull the lanyards. The missiles crashed in showers through the bushes or plowed up the dirt over us, but we were unhurt. They seemed coming thick enough to mow the saplings down, and but for the gully we would all have been killed.

Being informed of our situation, General [Joseph] Wheeler had hurried back two Parrott guns, which at this moment were unlimbering on the crest of the ridge behind us where we could not see them, but were in plain view of the Federals. The roar of these guns, the whizzing of the shells as they passed not far above our heads, and their explosion in the timber across the river was the most welcome sound I ever heard, for the Yankees scampered away as fast as our men had earlier in the day. Then when all was clear we ventured out and rejoined our company, to be publicly commended by our good colonel for what we really couldn't help doing.

Little of interest occurred for the next few days; and, worn out with the constant marching and fighting, loss of sleep, and daily rains which kept us wet and chilled, we proceeded at leisure down Big Wills [Lookout] Valley to a recruiting camp near Alexandria, Alabama.

## 'Green apples and an occasional ear of corn'

### Private James Turner
### Company G
### 6th Texas Volunteer Infantry

Slowly we retreated in the rain back to Tullahoma where we arrived at about noon on [June 30], completely worn out and covered with mud. Rations of corn meal and bacon were issued to us, and having no cooking utensils we baked our bread on flat fence rails turned up to the fire, making the well known johnny cakes, and we cooked our bacon on forked sticks. We enjoyed the feast

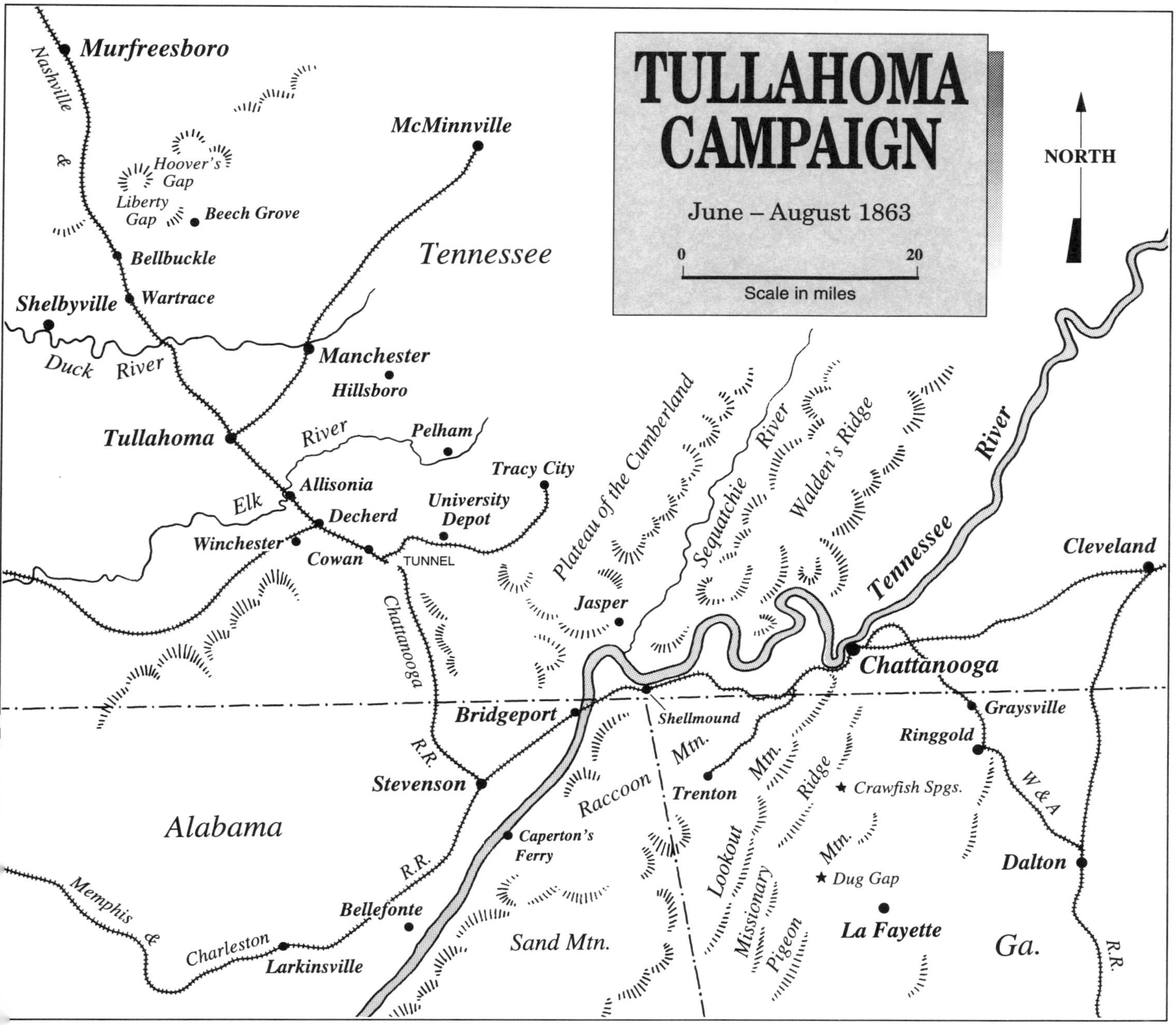


for we had been without food since leaving Wartrace. We remained in line at Tullahoma until night, thinking we would make a stand at that point, for the place was fortified, but after dark the order to march was given and the retreat to Chattanooga began.

Our brigade acted as rear guard and on the next day we halted at Bethpage Bridge on Elk River, near the town of Allisonia, where we held the enemy in check until our retreating army could get well started over the bridge, which was immediately burned, and fell back to the foot of the mountains where we remained in line until the following evening when we, too, started over the mountains.

We retreated down the Sequatia[sic] Valley, crossed the Tennessee River on a pontoon bridge and went into camp near Tiners [Tyner's] Station, about nine miles east of Chattanooga. As we

■ Maj. Gen. Alexander McD. McCook, center, poses near Winchester, Tenn., with his XX Corps headquarters flag and staff members. From left: Lt. Col. Horace Fisher (assistant inspector general), Lt. Col. Gates P. Thruston (assistant adjutant general), Capt. Frank J. Jones (aide-de-camp), McCook, Capt. Alexander C. McClurg (ordnance officer), Major Caleb Bates (aide-de-camp), and Lt. Col. George W. Burton (assistant commissary of subsistence).

A native Ohioan whose seven brothers also served in the war, McCook was considered an affable but poor field commander by many subordinate officers. Wrote one Federal brigadier in July 1863, the same month this photograph was taken: "He looks, if possible, more like a blockhead than ever, and it is astonishing to me that he should be permitted to retain command of a corps for a single hour."

had had nothing to eat since leaving Tullahoma except green apples and an occasional ear of corn picked up in the road, we were somewhat hungry and were glad to get the green corn issued to us on our arrival.

All of our tents having been burnt up at Tullahoma, we built brush arbors for shelter and made ourselves as comfortable as possible. The great quantity of commissary stores which Bragg had been collecting for so many months at Tullahoma had also been burned up to keep them from falling into the hands of the enemy, so we had to live for a week or more on green corn, which soon became tiresome, and we were delighted to receive the corn meal and bacon which finally came to us, and we came near eating up a week's rations at one meal.

**With Bragg now behind the Tennessee River and fortifying Chattanooga, Rosecrans, harried by a stream of War Department telegrams to keep moving, prepared for a new operation. "A campaign like that of Tullahoma always means a battle at some other point," wrote 1st Lieut. Henry M. Cist of Rosecrans' staff. "The fact that these two armies were yet somewhere to meet and engage in deadly strife was apparent to the commanders of both armies. Where and when that meeting was to be was the problem ..."**

**Chattanooga was the objective. The so-called gateway to the Deep South was an important railway hub, ironmaking center and the key to an advance into Georgia, Alabama and East Tennessee. Asserted Cist: "At that time this place was of the utmost importance to each of the contending forces, and the highest prize in a military point of view that the Army of the Cumberland ever contended for." To reach Bragg, Rosecrans first had to traverse the Cumberland Mountains — a rugged, heavily timbered range with little water or forage — before crossing the Tennessee River. The Federal commander intended to flank the Confederates out of Chattanooga instead of attempting a direct attack on the town. His plan necessitated stockpiling an immense amount of provisions and other stores, and repairing the Nashville & Chattanooga Railroad to serve as the army's critical supply line. All this took time, something the impatient authorities in Washington felt Rosecrans had taken too much of already. On August 12, Private George W. Williams of Company E, 121st Ohio, wrote to his parents: "I believe that Rosecrans army is or soon will bee on the move again, and I would not care how soon if the weather was cooler. But it is so very hot I dont believe we could stand it to march now."**

**In spite of stifling temperatures, the Federals set forth on August 16. In general lines of march, Crittenden's XXI Corps headed toward Chattanooga via Sequatchie Valley and Walden's Ridge; McCook's XX Corps moved on the opposite flank in the direction of Stevenson-Bellefonte, Ala.; and Thomas' XIV Corps advanced in the center toward Bridgeport.**

## 'Experiences of the night'

### Capt. Robert P. Findley
### Company K
### 74th Ohio Volunteer Infantry

On the 16th of August we again took up our line of march and crossed the Cumberland Mountains. The road was narrow and precipitous, and the sun beat down unmercifully upon us. Our brigade halted for the night at the base of the mountain, our regiment camping some little distance up its side. We constructed beds of rails, on which we spread green corn cut from the fields.

On in the night, as I lay awake, I heard a strange sound as of some large body sliding down the mountain. I sat up and looked in the direction of the noise. I soon saw what I thought to be a large bear, and it was heading directly for me. As it came nearer I discovered that it was a cow, and as the declivity was steep it was sliding down on its hind legs. It passed within a foot or so of me, and, becoming frightened by my movement, began to run along the line on which the regiment was sleeping. As it ran it stepped on the men who were lying along its track. They awoke alarmed, and that increased the fright of the beast, which ran at full speed, bellowing. The men tried to drive her away, but she was evidently following a trail usual to her, and she kept on in her mad dash. Men were knocked down by her horns and hoofs, and some were severely hurt. The screaming of the men and the bellowing of the cow aroused the pickets and the sentinels, who fired their guns, the long roll was beaten, the brigade was called into line, and not

■ Chaplain Charles T. Quintard, 1st Tennessee, served on Gen. Leonidas Polk's staff during the Tullahoma and Chickamauga campaigns. After the evacuation of Tullahoma, Quintard found himself "in full retreat. I rode to Cowan [Tenn.], where I found General Bragg and his staff, and General Polk and his staff. I rode up to them and said to General Bragg: 'My dear General, I am afraid you are thoroughly outdone.'

" 'Yes,' he said, 'I am utterly broken down.' And then leaning over his saddle he spoke of the loss of Middle Tennessee and whispered: 'This is a great disaster.' "

## Soldiers Three

**In one of the most revealing portraits of officers "in the field" to emerge during the war, three lieutenants of the 105th Ohio, XIV Corps, pose at right for an army photographer at Jasper, Tenn., August 27, 1863. For William Wallace (left) of Company I, Reuben G. Morgaridge (center) of Company C, and Albion W. Tourgee, Company G, the campaign look is striking: opened coats and shirt collars, lack of vests, broad-brimmed regulation army hats (issued to the 105th on August 24) — all adaptations aimed at beating Tennessee's summer heat. Kersey trousers are worn without rank piping; Wallace appears to be wearing infantry boots, while Morgaridge and Tourgee favor army brogans.**

**Each lieutenant also wears his accoutrements: commercial haversacks, issue canteens and sword belts without straps. Holstered revolvers of different calibers and cap boxes are attached to their belts, as would be their M1850 Foot Officers swords (Tourgee cradles an 1850 Staff and Field model). Wallace's sword rests on his shoulder, a popular way of carrying it on the march.**

**While Wallace and Morgaridge wear no rank insignia, close examination shows two lieutenant's bars on Tourgee's shoulders, reflecting recommendations of a July 1863 general order, which reads in part:**

*To prevent the disorganization of the army by its officers being picked off by the enemy's sharpshooters ... officers of all grades are authorized to wear single breasted blouses, with the distinctive badge of rank on each shoulder ... The rectangle of the shoulder-strap being too conspicuous on the field of battle, need not be worn.*

**Also noteworthy is the absence of knapsacks or blanket rolls. The omission could have been an oversight of the photo staging, or a reflection of the officers' practice of not personally carrying these items when campaigning. Another Ohio officer, writing from Manchester, Tenn., on June 30, observed: "Yesterday all knapsacks and baggage not actully needed, were ordered to be sent back. The men were not allowed to carry more than 'one blanket, either woolen or rubber.' All chose the rubber, and you may rest assured that many a poor fellow in this army has reason to bless the one who introduced them."**

until the commanding officers were assured of the cause of the disturbance did they permit us to return to our beds. The next morning there were many amusing and strange stories related of the experiences of the night. A number of the men were willing to make oath it was a bear they had seen.

With the first blink of dawn we arose, prepared our repast and marched at six o'clock. Our journey today was not unlike the movements of large armies generally — half double-quick a few hundred yards, then a halt just long enough to procure a comfortable seat; then another dash and another halt — nothing more wearying. However, jokes passed freely, and everyone seemed joyful. Our speeches and actions little indicated the terrible mission in which we were engaged.

**The mountain crossing consumed four days, and on August 21 the artillerists of Wilder's Lightning brigade (accompanying Crittenden) began throwing shells into Chattanooga. "Prisoners say we will get cut all to pieces if we undertake to take the place, and as we intend to take it I suppose we are to be cut up soon," wrote Private Alva C. Griest of Company B, 72nd Indiana, in his diary. "Our advance opened on the city across the [Tennessee] River and for awhile cannonading was heavy."**

**The following day, Capt. John S. McGraw of Company B,**

57th Indiana, wrote to his wife from atop Walden's Ridge: "I had a glass and could see the city quite plain and see horsemen riding through the streets, and see their camps of which they seem to have quite a number. This is an important point and they will endeavor to hold it as long as they can ... Wilder is down in the valley with his brigade of mounted infantry and one battery. He went down to the river on Friday and destroyed two steamboats right under their noses that they had running in the river. It stirred them up — a perfect hornets nest. They opened on him with their guns a cross the river and were hurrying to and fro with their troops. I guess they thought the whole yankee army was on them."

In Chattanooga, the 24th Alabama's colonel, Newton N. Davis, described the bedlam in a letter home: "The Yanks made their appearance very suddenly on the opposite side of the River and commenced shelling the town. The streets are always crowded with soldiers & citizens, men, women & children. You never saw such skidadling in all your life. Shop Keepers, Peach & apple venders, and speculators of all descriptions, both Jews & Gentiles commenced running in every direction. The shelling was kept up nearly all day. I understand that four persons were killed and some seven or eight wounded, mostly citizens. One lady was killed and a little Girl had her thigh broken. All the floating population, camp followers, are leaving on the trains as fast as they can get off. We

■ In a photograph believed taken August 29 or 30, 1863, soldiers of the 1st Michigan Engineers lay a log-trestle and pontoon bridge across the Tennessee River at Bridgeport, Ala. Two weeks earlier, the Confederates burned the Nashville & Chattanooga Railroad bridge (background) just ahead of pursuing Federals belonging to Maj. Gen. Philip H. Sheridan's XX Corps' division. An eyewitness, Private Amandus Silsby of Company A, 24th Wisconsin, wrote to his father: "Being previously tarred, it blazed up almost as soon as they set the match to it. The whole landscape brightened up, as if 'lit' by gas lights. Two of our batteries began to throw shells at the rebs. It looked splendid in the night time. Some of the shells would burst prematurely, high up over the river and ill fated bridge. Finally came a tremendous crash & all was over."

■ Capt. Lucius H. Drury, 3rd Wisconsin Battery, assumed an unusual job in Chattanooga not long after its Confederate abandonment. "Nearly all the material of war had been removed," wrote an Indiana officer, "but among other things left in the hurry of departure was the type and presses of the Chattanooga *Rebel,* edited by Henry Watterson and Charles Faxon of Gov. Isham Harris' staff. Watterson had been editor of the Nashville *Banner* and Faxon of the Clarksville *Chronicle,* until the vicissitudes of war drove them from home ... The type and press of the *Rebel* were put in order under charge of Capt. Drury, of a Wisconsin battery, and soon we had a spicy newspaper with volunteer editors and compositors."

**will have hot work here before many days I think. The Yanks are in large force on the opposite side of the River and doubtless will make a desperate effort to cross the River at some point. Every thing is in readiness to give them a warm reception whenever the attempt is made."**

**A "warm reception" never materialized. The appearance of blue uniforms in Sequatchie Valley and opposite Chattanooga, coupled with Burnside's arrival at Knoxville, contributed greatly to Bragg's misinterpretation of Rosecrans' strategy. Believing the Federals intended to cross the Tennessee at and above the town, the still-ailing Confederate commander could offer no resistance one week after Wilder's bombardment began to the *real* passages downriver between Shellmound, Tenn., and Caperton's Ferry in Alabama. The movements of Thomas' and McCook's corps soon showed Bragg that his opponent was maneuvering to cross Lookout Mountain through several gaps. If successful in concentrating his forces once over the heights, Rosecrans could cut Confederate communications and the line of retreat south. After two frustrating days of weighing options, Bragg ordered Chattanooga abandoned late on September 7. In the early morning hours of September 9, three enlisted men belonging to the 97th Ohio paddled across the Tennessee River in a canoe. They were the first Union soldiers to enter the town.**

## 'We took possession of the town'

### Sergeant Asbury L. Kerwood
### Company F
### 57th Indiana Volunteer Infantry

[The Confederates] withdrew the last of their forces on the 9th, and our brigade [George D. Wagner's, XXI Corps] immediately took possession. A horse ferry-boat, left by the enemy, was used in crossing the river, and before night the colors of the 97th Ohio were planted on a fort near Cameron Hill. The other regiments soon followed, and at night our command bivouacked on the green close to the river. Movements then in progress by McCook's corps endangered their rear and caused the withdrawal, which gave us possession of the long-wished-for stronghold, Chattanooga.

On the following morning the soldiers engaged in a general stroll over the town. Many of the citizens had gone away, but there were some loyal people and these remained at their homes. Others, who had heretofore engaged in the cause of the rebellion, were unwilling to follow the fortunes of the now crumbling Confederacy, and sought protection inside the Union lines.

As soon as I had finished my breakfast I started in search of the office where a noted rebel sheet, called the *Chattanooga Rebel,* had recently been published. After making inquiry of several citizens, I was directed to the place and found the vacated apartments of the late rebel quill-driver in the second story of a building on the west side of Main Street. Upon entering, I found the press still standing. Ink, type, books, manuscripts, &c., lay scattered about the floor. Copies of rebel sheets from various parts of the South were to be found in large numbers. A large box setting in one corner was partly filled with books, and had been

abandoned when the work was less than half done, as if the retreat had been made with the greatest haste. Gathering an armload of papers and various other trophies, I returned toward camp.

Business houses along the street, which had been closed by their late occupants, were broken open by the soldiers, who rarely found anything except raw peanuts, of which there was an abundance. Some of the boys made their way to the express office and found a quantity of tobacco, together with hundreds of letters which the agent, a Tennessee doctor, had neglected in his haste to take with him. In one bundle, containing sixteen letters, was a correspondence between the doctor and a young lady of Philadelphia, Pennsylvania, with whom he seemed to have been on the most intimate terms until the breaking out of the war, when she informed him that as he "defended southern interests," she claimed the privilege of defending the interests of the North, and that they must then and "forever be as strangers and enemies." During my long stay in the South I had the privilege of perusing many captured letters, mostly written by Southern ladies, but the correspondence above mentioned, for intelligence and ability, far surpassed anything of the kind I ever read.

Wagner's brigade, being small in numbers, was assigned to garrison duty in Chattanooga. Col. [George W.] Lennard was appointed provost-marshal; the 57th was assigned to duty as provost-guards, and the other regiments to picket and fatigue duty. Order was restored soon after we took possession of the

■ Four regiments of Gen. George D. Wagner's brigade, XXI Corps, constituted the Post of Chattanooga after the town's occupation on September 9. That morning, three non-commissioned officers of Company C, 97th Ohio, crossed the Tennessee River by canoe and commandeered a small ferryboat, which was employed to transport Wagner's 1,700 infantrymen from the north shore.

Lookout Mountain looms beyond Chattanooga in this view taken by George N. Barnard about six months later. At far left are the First Presbyterian Church and the Nashville & Chattanooga Railroad barn. Immediately right of the rail barn's roof are the multiple chimneys of the Crutchfield House hotel. In the middle distance at center is Academy Hill, topped with whitewashed buildings erected by the Confederates and known as Bragg Hospital. Many of these wooden structures were razed and replaced with warehouses to supply Gen. William T. Sherman's 1864 invasion of Georgia.

■ Brig. Gen. John Beatty's XIV Corps' brigade saved Negley's and Baird's divisional trains of 400 wagons from capture on September 11 and 12. An inveterate diarist, Beatty noted on the 12th: "We expected an attack this morning, but, reinforcements arriving, the enemy retired. I am writing this in the woods, where we are bivouacking for the night. For nearly two weeks now, I have not had my clothes off; and for perhaps not more than two nights of the time have I had my boots and spurs off. I have arisen at three o'clock in the morning and not lain down until ten or eleven at night. Last night my horse fell down with me, and on me, but strange to say only injured himself.

"Our army is divided — Crittenden on the left, our corps (Thomas) in the center, and McCook far to the right. The greatest danger we need apprehend is that the enemy may concentrate rapidly and fight our widely separated corps in detail. Our transportation, necessarily large in any case, but unnecessarily large in this, impedes us very much. The roads up and down [Lookout] mountain are extremely bad; our progress has therefore been slow and the march a tedious one. The brigade lies in the open field before me in battle line. The boys have had no time to rest during the day and have done much night work, but they hold up well."

town. Trains commenced bringing supplies from Bridgeport. Prisoners and deserters arrived almost daily from the front, who invariably concurred in the opinion that the rebel army would continue its retreat as far south as Rome, Georgia.

## 'A direct ascent up the mountain side'

### Capt. Francis W. Perry
### Company I
### 10th Wisconsin Volunteer Infantry

On the evening of September 4, 1863, the bugle sounded the advance and General Thomas' corps was soon moving across the river, and on the 5th, with the mountains towering almost perpendicularly above our heads, camped near Spring Cave.

A road must be constructed up an inclined plane on the mountain side from foot to summit, winding around bluffs and boulders, cutting and rooting up trees, filling gullies, dislodging rocks and leveling earth until a track could be cut wide enough to permit artillery and baggage-wagons to pass up. Each brigade had been provided with shovels and picks sufficient to supply at least one regiment in each brigade. As each regiment detailed for that purpose was armed and equipped with a shovel or pick, they slung their guns over their shoulders and marched up the mountain side, taking their places at intervals, stacked their arms and, with cheers and jovial good spirits, made an attack, charging (with picks in advance) upon trees, rocks and dirt.

At first it seemed a hopeless job, but stout hearts and determined wills soon overcame every obstacle, and a way was cleared ready for advance. Then came another detail of regiments, stationed at each steep grade — in fact, lined both sides of the entire ascent — ready to assist each struggling team and help roll the wheels where the exhausted and discouraged animals failed to move the load. Men armed with blocks of wood followed each wagon to block the wheels at each stop, and so, by main strength, the loads were rolled and carried up the mountain side.

In the space of three days' hard labor we had constructed our roads up, across and down the mountain sides into the valley beyond. I shall never forget the laborious and hazardous march as we approached the southern declivity and commenced the descent. It was the day for our brigade to march in the rear of the division. The night was dark and, as we commenced the descent, the valley was one expanse of impenetrable darkness, except the camp-fires of advanced regiments dotting this darkness hundreds of feet below, like so many stars scattered along the valley, forming a most grand and beautiful sight.

The descent was hazardous for heavy teams. Wheels were chained, fires or other lights placed at every dangerous angle, and every precaution taken for safety. Yet, some loads became unmanageable and went over the precipices below to meet destruction, or broke down to be rolled out of the way for others to follow. But woe to a sutler's cart and his goods if such an accident should happen to him. By orders, no sutlers' teams were to be permitted in the line of the baggage train. Little sympathy, therefore, would he get from the generals if the soldiers did appropriate a pocket full of cigars or tobacco — and it takes but a few regiments to carry off the goods of a well-stocked sutler's tent in their pockets. Nor would guilt greatly harass the soldier's conscience, for in value it would be but a small fraction of what the sutlers had exacted of him in extortionate prices.

The mountain peaks had been gained by the signal corps and flags were telegraphing directions to different parts of the army. News was received that General Bragg had gained information of our movements and was retreating from Chattanooga, destroying the railroad and bridges behind him.

Leaving Trenton to our left, our corps was pushed forward in the direction of Dalton and Ringgold, hoping to strike Bragg's retreating columns. The Lookout range of mountains still lay between us and Bragg's line of retreat. To climb and pass this mountain range seemed a greater task that what we had already accomplished. Its summit was still higher, and the perpendicular rock-crested top far more formidable than the steep sides of the range just passed.

Miles to the south and west of us was a break in this shining wall of granite, where a pass might be effected. We could only climb it by a direct ascent up the mountain side, too steep for our heavy ordnance and baggage train; and a zigzag road must be cut, first to the right, then to the left, by short, steep inclined planes, until the summit could be reached. Each turn from one direction to another being too short for long teams to exert their full strength, the heavy loads had to be rolled up by men at the wheels, a task requiring the muscle and strength of every man. As each load was carried around one bend and over the inclined plane to the next, it was again seized by the next gang of men, and so on to the top, a continuous toil until the whole army train had reached the summit, taking several days to accomplish the task. The advance, having climbed the ascent, camped at the top for the night, to move on early the next morning to prepare a new means of descent into the valley. On the opposite side we found a more feasible passway, and before night the First Division [commanded by Maj. Gen. James S. Negley] made its descent and camped in [McLemore's Cove]. The following morning, hoping to overtake Bragg's retreating forces, two divisions were advanced without waiting for the remainder of the corps to pass the mountain.

At Dug Gap in Pigeon Ridge, we encountered what we supposed to be Bragg's rear guard, but soon found a heavy force in our front. Forming a hasty line to contest a passage of the gap, we held our position until afternoon, when a cavalry force attempted to turn our left flank and cut us off from the remainder of the corps still on the mountain, forcing us to retreat back to the mountain, around the gap, to protect the descent of those not yet over, where we threw up temporary breastworks and rifle-pits, and remained until the balance of the corps could descend, occupying two nights and days. In the meantime our scouts had ascertained that Bragg's entire army was again marching [toward] Chattanooga to cut us off from our reserve corps crossing the river at that place, and thus force us to recross the mountains or be cut to pieces in detail.

To reach the junction of Chickamauga and Lookout valleys [sic] at the head of Pigeon Ridge, and place our corps in conjunction with Crittenden's, between Bragg's army and Chattanooga, and

■ Capt. Robert H. Spencer of Company H, 10th Wisconsin, marched with Thomas' corps as it hurried to consolidate with Crittenden. Fellow company commander Capt. Francis W. Perry recalled the critical movements of mid-September: "Each regiment or brigade had its own peculiar experiences. It was more of a race than a march. Fires were built along the roadside, from every available material, and left in our rear as a show of a general camping for the night by our forces, while every leg was put upon its best muscle to out-reach the advance of General Bragg's army moving in the same direction on the opposite side of Pigeon Ridge. The long lines of fires were designed to serve a double purpose: first, to deceive Bragg as to our actual position and lead him to suppose that we were slumbering by our camp-fires, giving him ample time to reach and cut us off with extra exertion; and second, to deceive him as to our actual numbers and strength."

At Chickamauga on September 20, Perry and Spencer were both captured, along with 43 others from their companies. Spencer remained a prisoner until war's end.

# 'A wretched fiasco'

Maj. Gen. James S. Negley's 2nd Division, XIV Corps, barely escaped disaster on September 11 near Pigeon Mountain's Dug Gap. After debouching from Lookout Mountain into McLemore's Cove on the 9th, Negley learned that strong enemy columns were within easy distance to envelop and pounce on his three brigades. "Bragg impatiently urged attack by Hindman's Division from the north side or mouth of the cove, but it was somehow unaccountably delayed," recalled a Confederate brigadier. "The enemy, finding himself in great danger, skillfully maneuvered with a bold front to gain time. Then, to the surprise of all, he suddenly withdrew from our front to Lookout Mountain, [and] thus was Bragg completely foiled."

The Confederate commander angrily blamed Hindman (later wounded at Chickamauga) for failing to destroy Negley, while ignoring a stream of his own confusing communications and orders that served to stymie the operation. Analyzing the incident after the war, Federal Gen. John B. Turchin wrote: "Looking at the matter from a military standpoint, it must be acknowledged that it was a wretched fiasco, in which Hindman bore the most prominent part. It showed also, that it was not enough to originate a plan; it required the capacity to execute it, and of that there was a lamentable deficiency."

■ Maj. Gen. Thomas C. Hindman

The above photograph of Negley (third from left, leaning on sapling) and staff members has been captioned for decades as 2nd Division headquarters on Pigeon Mountain. As battle appeared imminent, however, it is highly unlikely that a photographer was present at McLemore's Cove or Dug Gap on September 10 and 11. The image probably was taken earlier in the month or in late August. Officers in the view include Major James A. Lowrie, Capt. Alfred L. Hough, Capt. Charles T. Wing, Capt. Gilbert M.L. Johnson, Capt. John H. Young and 2nd Lieut. William W. Barker.

hold him in check until McCook's corps could arrive, was the only chance for the safety of our scattered army. Now commenced a hot race between the two contending forces which should first gain that point.

**Bragg determined to meet Rosecrans as the Federal columns to his west debouched from the mountain defiles. Taking up positions from Lee & Gordon's Mill on West Chickamauga Creek south to LaFayette, Ga., the Confederate commander correctly interpreted that a hurried pursuit was being made after his army, under the idea that he was in full retreat. Rosecrans' widely separated corps, Bragg reasoned, could be attacked and defeated in detail. But an attempt on September 11 to smash two isolated XIV Corps' divisions in McLemore's Cove nine miles northwest of LaFayette was botched, as was another on the 13th against Crittenden's divided corps near Lee & Gordon's. Angered by the lost opportunities, Bragg ordered his commanders to concentrate along the east bank of Chickamauga Creek, where they would wait for expected reinforcements to arrive from Virginia before giving battle.**

**These movements forced Rosecrans to completely alter his original plan. With his own left now threatened, he ordered Thomas and McCook to move north and effect a "life and death" linkup with Crittenden. Marching, countermarching and occasionally skirmishing under broiling skies between September 13 and 17, both armies were coated with dust. Writing home on the 16th, Major James A. Connolly, 123rd Illinois, told his wife of the campaign's harsh but hardening effects:**

**"If you could see me in my rags and dirt as I am now, you would laugh immensely, and if my dear mother could see me she would laugh first and then cry to see me looking so much like a beggar man; my coat is out at the elbows and all the lining torn out, my vest is lost, my shirts all gone but two, and they so small they wont button anywhere, my boots with huge shiny legs but soles 'gone up,' and my hat the very picture of misery and delapidation, but my boots will hold my spurs, and I have a fine horse and saddle and my regiment a good reputation, and that's sufficient, for I can look the 'brass and blue' ornamental fellows squarely in the face and feel proud of the rags I have won in my country's service. I would wear better clothes if I could get them, but I am dressed as well as the rest of our brigade, and we are so constantly moving that we can't get time to 'go to town' to get anything better. But it doesn't make any difference in the field, for a fine uniform does not make a soldier."**

**Before descending the heights west of Chickamauga Creek, the 74th Ohio's Capt. Robert Findley looked out over a nighttime bivouac of troops belonging to Thomas' XIV Corps. "The fires had died down and stillness reigned," he wrote. "I meditated on war. Here was a large body of men whose duty it was to kill their fellows, and the more successfully they fulfilled that duty the more their glory. They were marching like lambs to the slaughter. They knew that in a very few days at least they would be engaged in deadly strife, and many must die ..."**

■ 1st Lieut. Henry M. Cist of Rosecrans' staff regarded the Tullahoma campaign and subsequent maneuvers forcing the Confederate evacuation of Chattanooga as "the most brilliant one[s] of the war, made in the face of the strong column of the enemy, whose business it was to watch every movement, and as far as possible to retard and cripple the advance. Rosecrans ... in every instance deceived his opponent down to the withdrawal of Bragg from Chattanooga. Bragg never intended his withdrawal to be permanent; all the indications he left behind him pointed that way. None of the bridges were destroyed as he retired. All storehouses, hospitals and other buildings used by his army were left standing, and Rosecrans' mistake was in construing Bragg's withdrawal to be a demoralized retreat and in ordering his army to pursue before this was definitely determined."

CHAPTER 2

# Like the mighty roar of a dozen Niagaras

Three weeks of maneuvering end in bloody carnage along Chickamauga Creek

Just before midnight on September 18, a train carrying sleeping Confederates lurched to a halt in a cornfield near Catoosa Springs, Ga. Aboard were the veteran infantrymen of Gen. Joseph B. Kershaw's South Carolina brigade. Shouted orders to disembark rang through the crisp, chilled air, and the drowsy Palmetto State soldiers clad in new uniforms jumped to the track's ballast in ill-humor. One of them, John T. Coxe, a teen-aged private in Company B, 2nd South Carolina, recalled his regiment's arrival:

"In any army, there are always plenty of men 'cocked and primed' for shooting off 'tongue bombs.' So while getting out of the cars many not very choice expressions were heard, such as: 'I'm damned hungry,' 'I wish Abe Lincoln was in hell,' and many others of like import. I noticed a group of officers standing at a short distance, and to the surprise of all we heard the stentorian but perfectly cool voice of General Kershaw say: 'That is lovely language to be coming from the mouths of South Carolina gentlemen!' And that was all he said. And it was quite enough, because after that one could have 'heard a pin drop' while we were crossing that cornfield."

Kershaw's brigade was the latest of five from Robert E. Lee's army in Virginia to come to the aid of Bragg. The reinforcements were commanded by Lee's "Old Warhorse," Lt. Gen. James Longstreet, who for weeks had advocated sending support to the Army of Tennessee. Other reinforcements bolstered Bragg's ranks from Mississippi, as part of Gens. William H.T. Walker's corps and John C. Breckinridge's division arrived just before Chattanooga's evacuation. Maj. Gen. Simon B. Buckner's troops in East Tennessee and Maj. Gen. Nathan Bedford Forrest's hard-fighting cavalry joined Bragg shortly afterward, as did two more brigades from Mississippi.

As Longstreet's troop trains chugged and jolted to Georgia, Southern morale lifted. Capt. D. Augustus Dickert, a 3rd

South Carolina Infantry company commander, described the boisterous, patriotic displays:

"Long trains of box cars had been ordered up from Richmond and the troops were loaded by one company being put inside and the next on top, so one-half of the corps made the long four days' journey on the top of box cars. The cars on all railroads in which troops were transported were little more than skeleton cars; the weather being warm, the troops cut all but the frame work loose with knives and axes. They furthermore wished to see outside and witness the fine country and delightful scenery that lay along the route; nor could those inside bear the idea of being shut up in a box while their comrades on top were cheering and yelling themselves hoarse at the waving of handkerchiefs and flags in the hands of the pretty women and the hats thrown in the air by the old men and boys along the roadside as the trains sped through the towns, villages and hamlets of the Carolinas and Georgia. No, the exuberant spirits of the Southern soldier were too great to allow him to hear yelling going on and not yell himself. He yelled at everything he saw, from an ox-cart to a pretty woman ... The news of our coming had preceded us, and at every station and road-crossing the people of the surrounding country, without regard to sex or age, crowded to see us pass, and gave us their blessings. Our whole trip was one grand ovation."

In the meantime, Bragg's plan to turn Rosecrans' left flank continued taking shape. Both commanders shifted troops

■ Illustration by Alfred R. Waud showing Longstreet's troops disembarking near Catoosa Station, Ga., on September 18. Five brigades from the Army of Northern Virginia arrived in time to fight at Chickamauga, among them the veteran Texas Brigade commanded by Gen. Jerome B. Robertson. During the trip, "the old brigade fell in love with South Carolina's hospitality," wrote Private John C. West of Company E, 4th Texas, to his brother. "At every depot and station throughout the state the ladies, old and young, flocked in loaded with baskets of provisions, fruits and delicacies of every character which these scant times afford, which were offered amid smiles and tears and expressions of congratulations and encouragement to every soldier."

■ Maj. Gen. Simon B. Buckner, commanded the Department of East Tennessee since May 1863. He evacuated Knoxville on August 25 in the face of Burnside's approaching army, and abandoned immense stores and supplies. Buckner's corps of two divisions eventually reached LaFayette, Ga., marching for Chickamauga Valley on September 16. Four days later, his troops formed part of Longstreet's left wing at Chickamauga where, one participant observed, Buckner was "as thoughtless of danger as if he were out on an equestrian pleasure excursion."

Bucker's presence with the Army of Tennessee as a corps commander was augmented by the arrival in July of Lt. Gen. Daniel Harvey Hill, who was given Hardee's corps. On July 15, Hardee received orders from the Confederate War Department to join Gen. Joseph E. Johnston in Mississippi. Six weeks later at Enterprise, Miss., he assumed command of paroled prisoners from the Vicksburg garrison — duty that ended in late October when Hardee was transferred back to Bragg's army.

**based on scraps of information gleaned from scouts and cavalry reconaissance. For the enlisted men, the seemingly interminable tramping parched already dry throats. With no rain in weeks, the roads and trails of northwest Georgia became ribbons of orange dust. "We have been marching and countermarching in almost every direction," wrote Col. Newton N. Davis, 24th Alabama, to his wife on September 16. "Several times we have marched all night long without any rest or sleep. The heat and dust has been almost intolerable. At times the dust would rise so thick as to become almost suffocating. But strange to say our men have stood it finely. I have just as many men in my Regiment now as I had the day we left our camp near Chattanooga. The men seem to be perfectly hardened to it and are now able to stand almost any amount of exposure and fatigue."**

**While Davis praised his men's stamina, the Tennesseans of Maj. Gen. Benjamin F. Cheatham's division were exhausted. One of them later recalled a ludicrous moment near Rock Spring Church after a fatiguing all-night march:**

## 'The nearest semblance of pandemonium'

### Private William W. Stokey
### Company C
### 11th Tennessee Volunteer Infantry

About 4 o'clock in the morning we halted, and most of the men, being very tired, lay right down wherever they halted, many of them in the middle of the road. Our Brigadier General [Preston Smith], as we halted that night, informed us that we might expect a battle before daylight, and commanded that we not straggle nor leave approximately our respective places as he and all of us expected a fight at any moment. As it happened I sat leaning and sleeping against a tree some little distance from the road, and because of this precaution was able to see much of the fun which happened later on.

It seemed that we had hardly fallen asleep when we were aroused by the nearest semblance to our ideas of pandemonium that we ever heard before or since, accompanied by the wild shouting of our comrades who were nearest the noise and knew what it was, yelling to us, "Look out! The artillery is stampeded and is running away!" From my vantage point, being on the far side of an old stake and rider fence, to which I ran with an unseemly speed at the first outbreak of the inferno, I could see the other boys less fortunate and only half awake in their frantic efforts to get out of the way of what we all at first thought was a Yankee artillery or cavalry charge. I laugh till this day whenever I think of some of the ludicrous things I saw that night. I saw some of the boys climb impossible trees with the agility, accuracy and speed of squirrels, while others struggled ten deep for the protection of a slender sapling trunk. One poor fellow ran his cheek into one of the sharp projecting rails of the old stake and rider fence, and with extraordinary good fortune missed inflicting upon himself serious injury.

Another amusing little incident was a conversation I overheard between two of my comrades several feet away from me, behind a small tree trunk. One of them, my cousin, D.W. Street, it appeared from the argument which carried to me above the tumult, had been the first to reach the tree aforesaid, and the other fellow, whose name I have forgotten, had the incomparable gall to make a successful tackle and separate my cousin from first place at the sapling. It was then that I heard my cousin tell the other fellow, in no uncertain words, to "fade" (or words to that effect); that this was his tree, and immediately thereafter I saw the unknown hurled aside as my cousin resumed his position in a loving, embracing attitude next to the tree. At the same time I saw Lieut. Sandy Brown of Company E tear through a puddle of muddy water waist deep, he thinking that the water was only white sand — there being several patches of this close about — and climb a tree with the agility of a monkey.

**With ominous signs of Confederate concentration against his left growing, Rosecrans urged his XIV and XX corps commanders to hurry their scattered commands to consolidate with Crittenden's troops near Lee and Gordon's Mill on Chickamauga Creek. In spite of wearying exertions, many Federal soldiers marvelled at the mountainous countryside as they marched north. "The scene was one of beauty and splendor almost insurpassable," observed 2nd Lieut. Leroy S. Mayfield, a diarist in Company I, 22nd Indiana. Fellow Hoosier Peter Keegan, an Irish sergeant in Company C, 87th Indiana, was impressed by cornfields hacked out of the heavily timbered terrain between Stevens' Gap and Crawfish Springs. He noted in his diary: "There seems to be an abundance of [corn] along this Chickamauga, all of a first class article. Saw corn stalks 18 feet high. The country thro' which we passed is splendid. The land is of good quality. There seems to be a good deal of attention paid to the raising of fruit. We passed Crawfish Springs, but I did not have a chance to see them. I am told they excel anything in the Spring line that we have seen yet."**

## 'A perfect song came from a thousand men'

### 1st Lieut. Alfred Pirtle
### Aide-de-camp
### Lytle's Brigade, 3rd Division, XX Corps

Early on the morning of the 17th, orders came to march, which we soon found were to again climb Lookout Mountain, taking a route along towards the north, evidencing that we were retiring towards Chattanooga. The news spread soon that Rosecrans was doing everything he could to unite his forces, for Bragg had received reinforcements and taken the offensive. The men were not frightened, but seemed to be resolved to do their best to aid their commanding officers to retrieve the mistakes and to drive back the enemy.

There had been no rain for weeks, making a dust that clung to every object it touched, and some times was at least six inches deep. Through this we waded until about four o'clock [when] we halted and bivouacked, it being seen that we were likely to re-

■ Lt. Gen. James Longstreet arrived at Catoosa Station during mid-afternoon of September 19, and with two staff officers immediately rode west in a frustrating search for Gen. Bragg. Lt. Col. G. Moxley Sorrel, Longstreet's assistant adjutant general, recalled: "[Bragg] should surely have had guides to meet and conduct us to the conference on which so much depended ... But we were left to shift for ourselves, and wandered by various roads and across small streams through the growing darkness of the Georgia forest ... At one point in our hunt for him we narrowly escaped capture, being almost in the very center of a strong picket of the enemy before our danger was discovered ... Another road was taken for Bragg, about whom by this time some hard words were passing." Late that night, the trio finally found Bragg's camp and the commanding general asleep in an ambulance.

Before leaving Virginia, Longstreet bade Gen. Robert E. Lee goodbye and later wrote of their parting: "As my foot was in the stirrup he said again, 'Now, general, you must beat those people out in the West.' Withdrawing my foot to respectful position I promised, 'If I live; but I would not give a single man of my command for a fruitless victory.' "

■ 1st Lieut. Alfred Pirtle, an aide on Gen. William H. Lytle's brigade staff, recalled an unusual incident occurring on the eve of battle: "In August I had received from our sutler a gold seal ring with my initials engraved in script upon a beautiful piece of bloodstone. Though the ring was rather larger than my finger, I managed to use it, for it was then great fashion for the officers to sport seal rings.

"The night of September 18th I was wearing gauntlets as I rode with Gen. Lytle at the head of the Brigade, marching half asleep along the sandy road. I put my right hand into my back right-hand pocket for some article, but as I drew it out I felt the ring drop from my finger. Instantly, in a loud voice, I gave the command 'Halt.' Reaching ground, I felt in my haversack for a short piece of candle which I habitually carried. The instant I had felt the ring slipping from my finger I dropped the gauntlet into the dust, and it lay before me. Every horse and man was worn out, remaining perfectly still right in their tracks where they had stopped at my order to 'Halt.'

"I found the candle, lit it, and there in the dust shone the oval shadow of the ring, showing in the dust right by the gauntlet. I seized it, dust and all, and gave the command to 'Forward' and the march was resumed. Gen. Lytle asked why I so suddenly assumed the authority to stop the column, which gave me a chance to tell him the story in full, to which he said, 'A man who can drop a ring in six inches of dust at the head of a column, in such a scene as this, and find it, is not going to be hit in the coming battle.' "

sume the march at any moment. We took what rest we could until about nine o'clock when we resumed the road, making about two miles an hour and then resting awhile. There was, in addition to the heat and dust, the smoke of a thousand tiny fires which had been made by other troops who had preceded us in the forced marches, converging on Chattanooga. This was now plain to everybody and passed without discussion, save to make guesses how many would unite before Bragg met them on the road. All the couriers who reached Brigade Headquarters reported that, as far as they knew, the corps were making good time, and it looked as if Rosecrans would join all his men on the night of Friday [September 18].

About one in the morning of the 18th we were marching in dead silence along the dusty, smoke-laden road, when a fine baritone singer broke the stillness with the well-known tones and words of the war song "John Brown's Body Lies Moldering in the Ground," to which everyone listened with perfect quiet, and when the chorus came, a perfect song came from a thousand men who were keeping time with the cadence of the song. The second verse was given by the same voice, and with more effect, as he seemed to be filled with the aroused feelings of his hearers who hung upon every word, ready to join in the mighty volume of song which sprang from the throats of all. And the same might have been said of the third verse.

Along about two o'clock we went into bivouac, when all but the camp guards at once fell asleep. Although it was so late, the guard whose relief was supposed to be on post, under the orders of the Commander of the Guard, established the posts and surrounded the sleeping hundreds with vigilant men, and in a very short time only those whose duties kept them awake were in charge.

The camps were not awakened by any bugle calls for strategic reasons. But the guard going off duty demanded their reliefs at the regular hour so that the camps were astir about eight o'clock, though marching orders from Division Headquarters did not come as early as usual; yet we marched on the northern route before ten o'clock, halting for a rest about noon, and went into camp along about four. After resting some hours, we resumed our march (now forced), seeing more signs from time to time of other commands having been over the same roads [although] we did not overtake another command. The bivouac halt came as usual, late in the afternoon, of which all availed themselves as much as possible. This road on top of Lookout Mountin was only a way cut through the monotonous woods, just wide enough for a vehicle to move upon. The dust was deep, making it hard on man and beast in marching. Water was not to be had when on the route of the march, making it even harder on the animals.

## 'Through stifling smoke and scorching heat'

**Private John T. Booth**
**Company G**
**36th Ohio Volunteer Infantry**

The miles marched by us that night [September 18-19] were most toilsome and wearisome ones; the almost entire line of march, where we passed through lanes, both sides were illuminated by burning fences, while in the forest the fire ran among the leaves, writhing, twisting and turning as it wended its serpentine way along where there was but little upon which to feed, then fleetly sweeping and surging on in crackling flames as more abundant material was reached; now spitting and hissing as within its capacious maw was embraced and consumed the thicker undergrowth and fallen timber, then frolicking or playfully dallying at foot, then climbing in whole embrace, or skipping or darting in fiery jets, now creeping, now climbing higher, on and up in trailing lines still higher, or racing with speed from root to topmost branch, fed and led in its ascent by the dry and tinderlike bark of the dead and standing timber; tongues of flame could be seen leaping from bough to bough, from tree to tree, gyrating with eddying swirl among, licking with flaming touch, devouring with scorching breath from within, from nether to loftiest tip, the branches of many of the hoary, gigantic monarchs of those forests. Utterly beyond human control was that fiery holocaust of garnered harvests, fences, copse and forests; not a single fence, I believe, along the entire line of march escaping; destruction seemed rife on every hand. It was only now and again as the cold, eddying wind of that sharp, frosty September night lifted the heavy, dark pall of smoke that enveloped us, that we could get a glimpse of the stars as they twinkled dimly from out of a reddish sky illuminated with a lurid glare from below.

There were evidences of grim, stern visaged war on every hand, columns of smoke and pillars of fire around and about us. We marched through stifling smoke and scorching heat at times, while from the road over which we tramped and our trains were passing, covered as it was with pulverized earth shoe-top deep, there arose a cloud of dust that enveloped us completely, its finer particles permeating our clothing, penetrating the ears, eyes, nostrils and mouths of the moving troops, causing exquisite suffering to man and beast. This toilsome march continued during the entire night, interspersed with an occasional short halt, of which I availed myself to obtain, upon each occasion, despite the bleak night winds, a few moments of much needed rest and sleep.

## 'Marching made with a broken step'

### Brig. Gen. John B. Turchin
### Brigade commander
### 4th Division, XIV Corps

The divisions commenced to move, but there was more halting than moving. Although the supply trains were sent by the Chattanooga Valley road toward Chattanooga and separate from the troops, yet the ammunition train was moving with the troops by the same road behind each division. The night was dark and foggy; the fences along the road were set on fire wherever farms were, and the smoke filling the air made it heavy and oppressive. A wagon delayed by broken harness or some other trifling cause, detained the whole division for an hour. Sometimes an ammunition wagon would approach dangerously close to the burning fence, and occasionally one would dart over the burning rails scattered on the ground. It was a wonder that some fearful explosion

■ Orderly Sergeant Thomas J. Stanley of Company G, 36th Ohio, was a veteran of the regiment's earlier service at 2nd Manassas, South Mountain and Antietam. As part of Turchin's XIV Corps' brigade in September 1863, the regiment "on the 18th [was] under arms all day near Pond Springs, occasionally skirmishing with the enemy," wrote Sergeant Alfred R. Phillips of Company E. "The troops that had formed the right wing (McCook's 20th Corps) were rapidly marching north past us. When night came we were withdrawn and followed in rapid march toward Chattanooga, our line of march illuminated by the blaze of burning fences, set on fire by the marching troops. The march lasted all night and it was not till 9 o'clock a.m. on the 19th that we arrived on the field."

Stanley was killed eight months later at the battle of Cloyd's Mountain, Va. His father, James Stanley, was a captain in the regiment.

■ Private Lorenzo C. Glenn of Company C, 17th Tennessee, marched on September 18 in the van of Bushrod Johnson's provisional division, which was ordered from Ringgold to cross Chickamauga Creek at Reed's Bridge, pivot left and sweep toward Lee and Gordon's Mill. Before reaching the Chickamauga, Federal vedettes from Minty's cavalry brigade were encountered at Pea Vine Creek and Glenn's comrades fired some of the first Confederate shots of the battle. Covering as skirmishers, Capt. George W. McDonald's Company K killed four troopers 300 yards ahead of the regiment. Only one man of the 17th was lost during the day, when 2nd Lieut. Joseph Hastings was severely wounded at Reed's Bridge by an artillery shell.

did not happen. The dull rumbling of wheels on the dusty roads, the occasional snorting of animals, the clinking of arms, and the subdued voices of tens of thousands of men gathered in close proximity, presaged the gathering of force that would soon burst in a storm of battle.

The night marches of large bodies of troops are necessarily slow because, in the first place, men and trains have to follow only the road, hence the column becomes exceedingly long, and the marching made with a broken step, now halting and again hurrying in order to close up. In the second place, every obstacle, however trifling and easily overcome in daytime, appears magnified and insuperable in the night. If troops had to make a speedy march in the daytime they could have given the road to artillery and trains and marched themselves on the sides of the road and in closer order; but in the night time it is impossible to do so.

**The opening shots of the battle of Chickamauga were fired about 10:30 a.m. on September 18. Moving from Ringgold to effect a lodgment west of Chickamauga Creek, Brig. Gen. Bushrod R. Johnson's provisional division ran into Federal cavalry pickets and brisk skirmishing echoed from Pea Vine Creek to Reed's Bridge on the Chickamauga. That afternoon, Wilder's mounted infantry held off a Mississippi brigade for three hours at Alexander's Bridge. By 4 p.m., five Confederate brigades were across the creek, but Bragg's well-conceived plan to attack and smash Crittenden's corps was frustrated by subordinates' delays and unexpected Federal opposition. Alert to the grave danger, Rosecrans managed to rush Thomas' corps to Crittenden's left, but no commander on the field knew the exact position of either army as day broke on September 19.**

**Amid heavy forest, tangled underbrush, fields and scattered farm lots 10 miles south of Chattanooga, the next 40 hours witnessed a herculean slugging match that was unparalleled in ferocity during the entire war. The opposing sides gained no decided advantage on the first day, in spite of tremendous casualties. But late in the morning of September 20, a division moved in error from the Federal defensive line created a gap at the precise point where Longstreet, commanding the Confederate left wing, launched an assault with 11,000 men. The onslaught pierced the Union center and drove back Rosecrans' right, shattering two XX Corps' divisions. Unable to rally fleeing troops and believing the army destroyed, Rosecrans, McCook and Crittenden fell back to Chattanooga. Thomas, reinforced at a critical moment by two brigades from Granger's Reserve Corps, remained on the field with parts of seven divisions, and fought until nightfall. For survivors, the battle left indelible impressions.**

**"It required military genius to move a mighty army across great rivers and over mountain ranges in the face of a vigilant foe," wrote an Ohio private. "But to face the pitiless storm of bullet and shell that rained down upon the volunteer soldiers at Chickamauga required something that was never obtained at West Point, and qualities which far out-rank military genius. The battle was unlike any other engagement in which I took part during the war. Divisions were taken from one corps and sent to another. Brigades were broken up by send-**

ing regiments hither and thither as the changes of battle developed the position and strength of the enemy."

Another Buckeye soldier, Private Jacob H. Allspaugh of Company H, 31st Ohio, recalled: "On the part of the XIV Corps, at least, the battle of Chickamauga was fought on empty stomachs and with dry canteens dangling at our hips. All night long before the battle of the 19th we were under arms or marching, and reached the left only in time to go without breakfast, and help to spoil Bragg's plan of cutting us off from Chattanooga; and though munching dry crackers during the intervals between charge and counter-charge may have kept our stomachs from open rebellion on Saturday, it illy prepared our worn bodies for the work of the following day. Hunger and thirst, next to a desire to do duty, reigned supreme."

Perhaps a Confederate participant, Sergeant Valerius C. Giles of Company B, 4th Texas, summed up best when he wrote: "Soldiers in pictures who stand up in unbroken lines and fire by platoons don't represent the soldiers who fought [at] Chickamauga. As [it] was a battle in the wilderness, such battle formation was an utter impossibility. Chickamauga was a desperate battle — full of dramatic features, where no favors were asked and none offered."

■ Sergeant Isaac Skinner of Company I, 4th Michigan Cavalry, epitomized the veteran troopers of Col. Robert H.G. Minty's brigade, whose skirmishers first encountered advancing Confederates east of Pea Vine Ridge early on September 18. Outnumbered six to one, Minty's cavalrymen and cannoneers of the Chicago Board of Trade Battery gamely delayed Bushrod Johnson's division for seven hours, until driven back to Reed's Bridge across West Chickamauga Creek. The frail structure was traversed with only minutes to spare, as Minty wrote: "Before the first squadron had time to cross, the head of a rebel column, carrying their arms at right shoulder shift, and moving at the double-quick as steadily as if at drill, came through the gap not 500 yards from the bridge. One squadron of the Fourth Michigan ... was cut off by the rapid advance of the rebels. They made a gallant resistance and eventually swam the creek without the loss of a man."

# September 19

## 'Fix bayonets, forward, double-quick, charge!'

### Capt. Israel B. Webster
### Company I
### 10th Kentucky Volunteer Infantry

At break of day, Sept. 19, 1863, the order came down the line, "Halt! Close up; front; stack arms and prepare and eat breakfast as rapidly as possible." This was the morning succeeding the memorable night of Sept. 18, during a great part of which the whole heavens were lighted up by the fires kindled along the line of march. The halt was made near a running brook, and in a very short space of time many little fires were burning, around each of which were gathered small groups of men eagerly watching the coffee boiling while they toasted slices of bacon on the end of a stick.

Just at this inopportune moment, boom! boom!! boom!!! came the sound of cannon from the direction in which we had been marching, and at no great distance from us. As if by instinct, every man abandoned his coffee, disposed of his bacon, either by putting it in his mouth or his haversack, and rushed for his gun. When the command "Attention!" came, every man was ready to take arms promptly at the word. "Shoulder arms! Right face! Forward, march!" quickly followed, and we were again on the move.

The grand rush now made by those who had abandoned their coffee-boilers to regain possession of them, and secure the benefit of the much needed stimulant, was enlivening. To see the attempts made to swallow the hot beverage while marching over the

■ Col. John T. Croxton's brigade of the 3rd Division, XIV Corps, became the first Federal infantry command engaged at Chickamauga. On the morning of September 19 he was ordered to capture a Confederate brigade presumed to be cut off near Jay's Mill. Croxton's five regiments — the 4th and 10th Kentucky, 10th and 74th Indiana, and 14th Ohio — ran into troopers of Forrest's cavalry, who retreated after absorbing one withering volley. The incident caused more troops on both sides to be funnelled into the fight, which quickly escalated in fury. Falling back under intense pressure, three of Croxton's regimental commanders were wounded, one of them mortally. The following day, Croxton himself received a serious flesh wound in the leg.

In July 1864 he was promoted brigadier general and commanded a cavalry brigade until war's end. A particular favorite of Gen. George H. Thomas, Croxton was called by that officer "the best soldier Kentucky has furnished to the war."

rough road was ludicrous in the extreme. I was one of the party that went through the experience of trying to eat hardtack and bacon, and drinking hot coffee, while marching over rough ground. Many among our regiment went into the Chickamauga battle with both hands full of something to eat or drink.

We had not far to go to find the enemy. The Major of our regiment rode down the line, and in a confidential manner said to me: "Captain, we have a soft snap here. A rebel brigade has crossed the creek to this side and our forces have destroyed the bridge behind them, and we are now going in to gobble them up." With that he rode off. Company A (Capt. Charles W. McKay), 10th Ky., was sent to the front after our line of battle had been formed, and deployed as skirmishers to cover the front of the 10th Ky. and 14th Ohio. Company A was not out very long before it was forced back to us in a hurry; and to use Capt. McKay's expression when asked the why of his sudden return, "It was too hot out there."

Our line remained as first formed and prepared to meet the anticipated attack of the approaching enemy. For a short space of time an ominous silence prevailed in that place, broken occasionally by the sound of a musket-shot in the woods in front of us, followed by the peculiar and indescribable sound made by a minie-ball rushing through the air. These "silence interrupters" were few and far between at first, but they rapidly increased in frequency, so much so that the timid and weak-hearted were anxiously searching with their eyes for some safe place, such as a friendly tree (size unimportant) or a rise in the ground behind which they could, at the last moment, retire.

Here at this time and at this place fell the first soldier [of the regiment], mortally wounded. His name was [Daniel] Stewart, a private in Company D. I heard the thud when the bullet hit him, followed almost immediately by the most inhuman sound that ever escaped from the vocal organs of a man. Never will that cry be erased from the memory of all who heard it. His arms went up, his gun flew far from him, and he fell in his place with a death wound in his groin.

Just at this time Capt. [John T.] Milburn of Company B (extreme left company) notified Col. [William H.] Hays that a large force was approaching our left flank at exactly right angles to us. The orders to "Left face, forward; double-quick, file left," came in rapid succession, and away we went to meet the new attack. This movement was too late to prevent a heavy loss in Cos. B and K, for the enemy detected our move to change front and poured a heavy volley into our left, which those two companies caught. We soon hustled the "Confeds" away from there, and then took our wounded off the field. We had no time to care for the dead because of the advance of the enemy upon what at first was our right, but just then was our rear.

The command now came, "Right face, forward, double-quick, file right, march," which sent us flying across the field; the line at right angles with our first line, where we met the foe advancing from that direction. We soon cleared that part of the field and for a short time were at rest. Now again they advanced upon the first ground that we had met them, and where Stewart had been killed. Of course, we must again change front, by the left flank, filing left, to meet this new attack. And thus were we attacked, and thus did we meet them for I know not how many hours, nor did we get any relief until our cartridge-boxes were empty, and we were sent to the rear for ammunition while a brigade of Regulars took our place in the field. Up to this time the men had worn or carried all the baggage they usually marched with. The orders to lay off knapsacks and fill cartridge-boxes were obeyed with alacrity, and not any too soon. All had not secured a full supply of ammunition when the word "Attention!" rang out, and "Fall in, 10th Ky." immediately followed. The line was quickly formed and began moving in the direction of the ground first taken by us in line of battle.

We had thus advanced but a short distance when "Halt! Lie down!" came. We promptly obeyed. The brigade sent to relieve us had been routed and was making tracks to the rear at a lively gait, closely followed by the Johnnies in hot pursuit. Over our prostrate line went the blue-coats like a mob without form, in squads of from one to half a dozen. When nearly all had passed over us, "Attention!" rang out, which brought every man to his feet. The pursuing grays, seeing us come up out of the ground, as it were, stopped from their mad run and poured a volley into us. Their aim was not good, as little damage was done, but Private Richard Roaler of my company received a mortal wound just as he straightened up.

"Fix bayonets, forward, double-quick, charge!" was now the order, and away we went in full chase of the Johnnies, who, but a few moments before, were rushing over the same ground in mad pursuit of the flying "Feds." In this second race the "un-Feds" showed up well as racers, for when our commander at the proper time called a halt not a Johnny Reb could be seen. When we came to a stand-still our line presented a curious formation. The center had advanced far ahead of the flanks, making an inverted V-shaped line. "Dress on the colors" necessitated the advancing of the flanks.

While this was going on I saw, some distance in advance of us, what appeared to be a full battery. The horses were lying down, and not a man was to be seen around there. I immediately called Col. Hays' attention to it, and suggested that we "go for it" and take it off the field. He shook his head, but said nothing. I returned to my place. The next moment I heard a voice in front, and looking in the direction of it saw the Adjutant of the 14th Ohio sitting upon his horse a short distance in front of the line, calling attention to the battery. The 14th Ohio was formed on our left, and the Adjutant was in front of the junction of these two regiments. Col. Hays observed what was going on, and seeing a disposition on the part of the men to take that battery, he called out: "If you want it, go for it," and we were soon moving toward it.

At a proper distance we halted, and Company I was ordered to advance and deploy to cover the whole line to prevent a surprise while the guns were being hauled off to the rear. This skirmish-line was many yards from the main line, and when this order was completed the skirmish-line was very thin, as the company was not numerically large and had considerable ground to cover.

When all was ready men from both regiments were detailed to do the work. As they neared the battery a cry came from away beyond — a cry of distress, an appeal for help, a boyish voice crying to be saved. It was a cry that went to the hearts of the men of the detail there present, and I said to one of them: "Go to his relief, and I will protect you with my guns."

Away he sped, closely followed by a dozen pair of eyes. Sud-

■ 1st Lieut. Joseph B. Newton, adjutant of the 14th Ohio. Only three other Federal regiments at Chickamauga suffered more total casualties than the 14th, which lost 54 percent of 449 officers and men engaged. "Loss heavy," Newton tersely wrote in his diary on September 19. "Fought about four hours during the day. Fought superior numbers all the time. Charged the rebels and drove them about 200 yards. Outflanked. Fell back."

On the 20th he continued: "Morning very foggy. Broke away about 9 a.m. Soon the fighting [began] till dark but lost ground. Most desperate fighting. I have no desire to pass another day as this has been. Our cause is still dear, but oh, the cost of work like this."

■ Assistant Surgeon Charles H. Stocking, 10th Kentucky, barely escaped capture on September 19 while tending a wounded man on the battlefield. By nightfall, only one road was open to the army's main hospital at Crawfish Springs — four miles from the day's fighting. Surgeon Glover Perin, Army of the Cumberland medical director, reported that "this movement made the removal of the wounded a task of considerable magnitude, as our loss in wounded on Saturday afternoon [the 19th] was very severe, being, as nearly as I could estimate, about 4,500. Every effort was made to place the men under shelter ... When this could not be done the men were arranged in rows near each other and lines of camp fires built at their feet."

Perin further reported that, once Chattanooga was occupied by Federal troops, "over 200 bales of cotton were found secreted in various places, which were seized, carefully guarded and reserved for mattresses. Had it not been for this fortunate circumstance the sufferings of our wounded would have been much greater, as it was impossible to have procured straw, and the supply of blankets was limited. About 150 upholsterers, tailors and saddlers were detailed to make mattresses, so that by [September 30] every severely wounded man was provided with a comfortable bed."

denly he was lost to view. For a time great uneasiness prevailed among our little squad. Each man was straining his eyes to catch a sight of the rescuer, while a deep silence reigned in our midst. At length he was seen returning, and as he neared us we observed that he had something in his arms. That something proved to be a lad, apparently some 12 or 14 years of age, who had received a wound of some kind that had crippled him, and he was unable to get off the field without help. His rescuer carried him to the rear, and as he passed me he said: "This is my boy from now henceforth," while great tears rolled down his cheeks and his voice trembled with emotion. I have never heard of this boy since, neither do I know who the rescuer was. I believe he was of the 14th Ohio.

This little incident did not consume much time, nor did it interfere with the work at hand. The balance of the detail was doing its best to get the dead horses detached from the battery. One of the men borrowed a knife of me to cut the harness with. We succeeded in hauling off five guns, when an interruption of a startling nature stopped the work. Rapid musket-firing suddenly commenced on our right and in our rear. What did it mean? We had been so engrossed with our work that we had taken no note of what was going on behind us. We had been sent to watch the front, while the others were protecting our rear. This heavy musketry in the rear meant danger to us — either death or capture.

On looking around to the place where we left the line when we were sent forward as skirmishers, not a living person was to be seen. All had gone. For a moment I was startled, but having full confidence in our field officers I was soon myself again, and ordered my men to hold the line intact and slowly fall back. After several yards to the rear had been gained, I called a halt and looked anxiously back for some order as to where I ought to go. There were more or less woods on this part of the field, which prevented my seeing any distance. Not many minutes passed when I saw our regiment double-quick immediately across our rear from left to right of the field by right flank, going toward the musketry then so heavy. As yet I had received no orders and did not feel justified in abandoning my position without them.

As I continued to watch all points I discovered the Colonel's orderly coming toward me. When he saw I was watching him he beckoned with his hand for me to come off the ground we then held. I understood, and called for a "rally on the right," which call was responded to with a will by each man. When all were gathered I took my place beside the Orderly-Sergeant [Thomas J. Brown, severely wounded on September 20], instructed my Lieutenant [1st Lieut. William E. Kelley, wounded and captured on September 20] to keep the men in their places, and follow me. By the right flank we moved toward the firing, which all this time was rapid. We had covered more than half the distance when I discovered on the right of us a fallen tree, in the lap of which was our [Assistant] Surgeon, Dr. [Charles H.] Stocking, dressing the wound of a soldier. I notified him that I was the last of our troops off the field and it would be well enough for him to take note of it, and I passed along. The next time I saw the Surgeon he told me I had saved him, as he had not been thinking of anything except what he was doing at that time and he made a narrow escape from capture. He expressed his gratitude to me for calling his attention to the danger of his position.

About this time the boys in blue were getting away pretty fast. They left one at a time at first, then by twos and threes, then in larger squads until it seemed that none would be left to keep up the fight. All this time Company I was making good time to the rescue. A staff officer came riding along, and suggested to me that I halt and give the enemy a volley. It was plain to be seen that our brigade, or at least a portion of it, had been routed, for the men were coming off the field very rapidly, every man for himself. The rebs were closely following, shouting as they came, their bullets sounding unpleasantly near, now and then hitting some retreating form.

The ground where this officer made his suggestion did not suit me. It was descending into a hollow, beyond which was rising ground which I thought better. So bearing off a little more to the right I struck out for the higher ground. Soon after crossing the hollow and while climbing the rise, Lieut. Col. Wharton, 10th Ky., came walking along, why not mounted I never knew, and accosted me thus: "Where are you going, Captain? Halt, and give them a volley."

"I will as soon as I get on a little higher ground," I said. But I doubt if he heard me, for he had hurried on past.

When the brow of the rise was reached I ordered "Halt, about face!" and to load and fire as fast as possible. I instructed the Lieutenants to hold the men to the work. I then fell back from the line thus formed, just far enough from the noise of the firing to be heard, and with my voice and the brandishing of my sword I attracted the attention of the retreating men. In the course of a few moments I soon had quite a number of such to join my company, and in an incredibly short time my little company had grown to about 300.

Capt. F[ranklin] S. Hill, Company F, 10th Ky., came along, and when he saw my success he began to rally a line on my right, and soon had a goodly number of men pouring cold lead into the advancing rebs. We were never routed from this point by the Johnnies. In fact, they were checked right there and we remained upon this impromptu line until relieved by other troops, which occurred soon after, they passing in our front unmolested. Our brigade left the field in good shape, all intact, excepting the killed and wounded.

## 'Piles of knapsacks were scattered everywhere'

### Private George W. Miller
### Company I
### 31st Ohio Volunteer Infantry

The regiment marched all of the night of the 18th, and at daylight halted for breakfast. Fires were kindled, the coffee pounded as fine as possible with bayonets, and by the time it was boiling the report of artillery sounded on the air in our front, seemingly quite near. We swallowed the hot coffee in a hurry and were soon on the way up the road to the scene of action. A brisk musketry fire was going on in front on the right of the road; orders came to double-quick, which was kept up till the regiment filed right into the woods.

■ Lt. Col. Gabriel C. Wharton, 10th Kentucky. The regiment entered the battle with 421 effectives and suffered 166 casualties over two days. Company B alone lost 20 men in less than an hour on September 19. Wharton assumed command of the 10th the following day on Horseshoe Ridge, his Kentuckians helping to repulse three separate assaults before their ammunition ran out. "It seemed two or three times it would be impossible to hold our position," he wrote, "so overwhelming was the force of the enemy, but our troops, being partially screened by rails, poured volley after volley into their masses ... Several of [the 10th's officers] took the guns of their wounded men and shot away every cartridge in their boxes."

J.H. Van Stavoren of Nashville took this portrait of Wharton holding a straw hat with black silk headband.

■ Private Oscar N. Wheeler of Company K, 31st Ohio. Detached from its own brigade, the 517-man regiment supported Croxton about mid-morning of September 19. Prior to engagement, Wheeler and his comrades unslung knapsacks, marched into a pine woods reeking of burned powder, dressed ranks and lay down adjacent to the 10th Kentucky. Listening to gunfire ahead, the Ohioans were seized with anxiety, as recounted by Private Samuel A. McNeil of Company F:

"As we lay waiting ... I took note of the blanched faces nearby, yet it did not occur to me that my own face was perhaps a trifle paler than those about me. Though I had served at the front for two years and been under fire many times, fidelity to truth compels me to say it required a great effort to hold my own under the terrible strain brought to bear upon us for 20 minutes in that Georgia forest."

The following day Wheeler was captured. Later exchanged, he reenlisted and was appointed orderly sergeant of Company E, 184th Ohio, as shown in this 1865 photograph.

After going some distance the regiment halted, and orders were given to unsling knapsacks. A guard was appointed from each company to look after the knapsacks, and little did we think that we would never see either knapsacks or guards again. They were captured by the rebels later on.

We took up the line of march, soon coming to the place where the skirmish of a few minutes before had occurred. The firing had ceased, the rebels falling back out of range, and all was quiet. The wounded were being collected, and the sight was not a very encouraging one to the boys, who expected to be plunged into battle any moment. The regiment halted here, changed front, and marched through the timber for quite a distance. Piles of knapsacks were scattered everywhere, showing that troops were ahead of us.

Firing now commenced in our front. The bullets were singing among the trees, scaling the bark from the trunks. We were ordered to lie down. Thoughts of home came rushing through our brains. A few days before we had been jubilant at the thought of meeting the enemy soon, but now the *zip* and *whiz* of the bullets coming so near dampened our ardor very decidedly. Visions of contraband chickens we had appropriated for the good of the service floated before our eyes and we wondered who would eat them if we didn't.

The regiment in our front, having exhausted its ammunition, fell back to our rear. We were now the front line, with nothing between us and the enemy but some brush which the rebels had taken possession of and were making our location a very unhealthy place. But our minie balls gave them as good as they sent, and Lieut.-Col. F[rederick] W. Lister in command, ordering us to fix bayonets and charge, the rebels fell back and soon melted away out of sight in the distance. In making this charge our regiment had taken an advanced position, and was in great danger of being cut off from the main line, so we fell back and were finally relieved and sent to the rear. We lost several wounded in the fight and our color bearer was killed.

## 'Just five minutes time to pray'

### Chaplain William W. Lyle
### 11th Ohio Volunteer Infantry

At eight o'clock our regiment formed in line of battle and took position on the brow of a hill about two miles north of Gordon's Mills, and near the Chattanooga road. By this time the engagement had become general, and troops were rushing forward rapidly. Feeling anxious to have one more opportunity of speaking a word of encouragement to the soldiers who were about to enter into the very jaws of death, and many of whom, perhaps, would never hear words of prayer upon earth again, I rode up to Colonel Lane and asked just five minutes time to pray with them before going into action. "Certainly," was his instant reply. "I wish you would have services; I think there will be time."

Another pen must describe the scene as witnessed by others on the morning of that eventful day. Says a [newspaper] correspondent:

"General Turchin's brigade of Reynolds' division, Thomas' corps, consisting of the Eleventh Ohio, Colonel Lane; the Thirty-sixth Ohio, Colonel Jones; the Ninety-second Ohio, Colonel Fearing, and the Eighteenth Kentucky, Lieut. Col. Milward, took position on a low spur of the ridge near the Chattanooga road, and in the rear of [a] tannery. Before the skirmishers were deployed, a scene occurred with the Eleventh, which, for sublimity and moving power, has been seldom surpassed. The chaplain rode up in front of the line, and the colonel gave an order which, on being executed, formed the regiment in two divisions, with the chaplain in the center. Without dismounting, he addressed the troops in a clear, loud voice that sounded strangely amid the loud explosions of the artillery and the rattle of musketry.

"'It is but little I can do for you,' said he, 'in the hour of battle, but there is one thing I will do — I will pray for you. And there are thousands all over the land praying for you this morning, and God will hear them. You must now pray, too; for God is a hearer of prayer. And if this is the last time I shall ever speak to you, or if these are the last words of Christian comfort you will ever hear, I want to tell you, dear comrades, that God loves you. I pray God to cover your heads today in the battle-storm. I pray that he may give you brave hearts and strong hands today. Be brave, be manly! Remember the dear old flag, and what it covers. And if any of you feel uncertain as to your future, look to the Savior who died for you; and, if any of you fall this day in battle, may you not only die as brave soldiers for your country, but die as soldiers of the Lord Jesus Christ. Let us pray.'

"Instantly every head was uncovered and bowed in reverence, while hands were clasped on rifles, the bayonets on which were gleaming in the morning sun. The flag, pierced and rent on a dozen battlefields, was drooped, and, strange but glorious sound on a battlefield, the voice of prayer was heard. When the chaplain closed, he raised himself in his saddle, waved his hat two or three times around his head, exclaiming, 'God bless you today, dear comrades, and make you strong and brave. Strike for Liberty and Union! Strike for God and humanity! And may our battle-torn flag lead to victory this day! God's presence be with you, comrades!'

"A low, murmuring Amen was heard from the ranks as the chaplain closed. Major-General Reynolds and staff passed along the lines during the services, but halted when they came to the Eleventh. With uncovered head the General rode up close to the regiment and remained till the conclusion of the brief services. At the moment they were concluded he uttered a hearty Amen, which had a thrilling effect. Grasping the chaplain's hand and shaking it warmly, while a tear glistened on his cheek, he was heard to exclaim, 'Sir, I am glad I was here to join with you!' and instantly rode off, followed by his staff. This acknowledgment of religious principle on the part of General Reynolds had a very happy effect."

Scarcely five minutes elapsed till the entire brigade moved forward and engaged the enemy.

## 'We can't save the battery'

### 1st Lieut. Lucius G. Marshall
### Section commander
### Carnes' (Tennessee) Battery

On the night of the 18th the battery bivouacked on the east side of West Chickamauga Creek, about three miles south of Lee and Gordon's mill and about eleven miles from Chattanooga. The fire of skirmishers had been heard all day, and at dark the forage-wagons came into camp with several dead soldiers loaded on top

■ Chaplain William W. Lyle, a Presbyterian minister, served with the 11th Ohio Infantry. In 1865 he recorded his impressions of the Chickamauga fighting: "In many places the battle-lines could be distinguished only by dense clouds of dust that rose up in long, reddish lines, and by white, vapory smoke that rolled in great clouds through the woods, or rose above the forest trees, and rolled along the sharp ridges and sweeping hill-sides. Sometimes the long lines of dust and the wreathing, rolling smoke from artillery would recede or advance, be thrown suddenly into sharp angles or formed gradually into swelling curves, indicating the ebb and flow of the fearful, mighty tide-wave of battle. I had heard the roar of battle at Bull Run, had felt the earth quiver under the fierce conflicts of South Mountain and Antietam, but the incessant roar of artillery and musketry on this terrible day seemed to exceed all three battlefields combined. The musketry was neither in distinct shots nor in repeated volleys, but for hours it was one mighty, fearful, continuous roll, which, added to the shouts of the combatants as they charged to and fro, together with the loud, deep booming and crashing of the artillery, seemed more like the mighty roar of a dozen Niagaras than anything merely human."

■ Capt. William W. Carnes, one of the youngest battery commanders in Confederate service, marked his 22nd birthday on September 18. After his battery's destruction the following day, he was given first choice from nearly 60 Federal guns captured at Chickamauga to rebuild the battery, and then was promoted to artillery battalion command. A fellow Tennessean later recalled that "one of his great friends and admirers was Colonel [Hypolite] Oladowski, General Bragg's chief of ordnance. From the battle of Perryville on through its career, Carnes' Battery used large quantities of canister shot at close quarters. This accorded so well with Colonel Oladowski's notions that he called Carnes his 'canister shot captain' and was ready to sound his praises on all occasions."

Early in 1864 Carnes transferred to the Confederate Navy, a decision based on his antebellum service as a U.S. Naval Academy midshipman. He was appointed executive officer of the ironclad *Savannah* and later commanded the steamer *Samson.*

of the corn. The greatest battle of the West was at hand.

Early on the morning of the 19th picket-firing began, sometimes rising almost to a roar. The battery was ready and expectant. About nine o'clock the order came to move to the west side of the creek, the crossing of which was made at Hunt's Ford, some two miles above Alexander's bridge, and not more than a mile from the camping-ground of the previous night. Across the creek the battery proceeded down the west side, at a trot where practicable, over not a very smooth road, till it passed beyond Alexander's bridge, a march of about two miles. On both sides of the road sat the soldiers of Longstreet's corps, who had just reached the ground from Dalton, where they arrived early that morning by rail. The soldiers of Longstreet's corps were splendid-looking men, healthy, clean and well dressed. As the battery, accompanied by [Marcus J.] Wright's brigade, thundered rapidly over the rough road between the rows of Eastern veterans, the latter fixed a gaze of astonishment upon these, the first Western Army men they had yet seen. The Virginians [sic] were excusable. The Army of Tennessee never looked worse, while at the same time it was never in better fighting order. But three weeks of maneuvering in the densest dust without washing had conferred the same uninteresting color upon everything — man, beast and material.

The battery moved on at a trot with Wright's brigade, and inadvertently going too far to the right, ground had to be taken to the left, the column at the same time nearing the enemy's front but approaching it diagonally. The Federal artillery was doing its best, and the open forest was filled with missiles from which [W.H.T.] Walker's [corps] had just fled, leaving a gap which Cheatham's brigades were now to occupy. Wright's brigade, at a double-quick the last four hundred yards, approached within perhaps three hundred yards of the enemy's works, and swiftly drew into line of battle, not leaving room for the battery to form in the center of their line as they should have done.

Capt. Carnes halted the battery a moment in line close behind the brigade, presuming the usual situation would be accorded the artillery for the protection of its flanks; but the heavy, devastating fire of the enemy forbade the brigade to attend to the rights of the battery. After three of the cannoneers were killed in this awkward situation — two of them being young men of Augusta, Ga., who had been recently enrolled — the Captain, on his own responsibility, ordered the battery forward till it should pass the left flank of Wright's brigade, a movement which was executed at a trot, all in plain sight of the enemy's artillery and infantry who had been in position there since daylight. The command happened to make this movement left in front — or, better stated, celerity of execution demanded that the left should precede the right — so that, as the fire was to be to the right, the teams had merely to wheel to the left when the whole had passed the brigade, and then the battery was in line. A minute or two was thus saved in getting ready to fire.

The order to unlimber (which was done by simply unhooking and dropping the trails without reversing the teams) and commence firing was obeyed in much less time than I take to relate it, and that too by every piece simultaneously except the right, the ammunition of whose limber-chest had become fast and for a few seconds resisted all efforts to extricate the cartridges. The

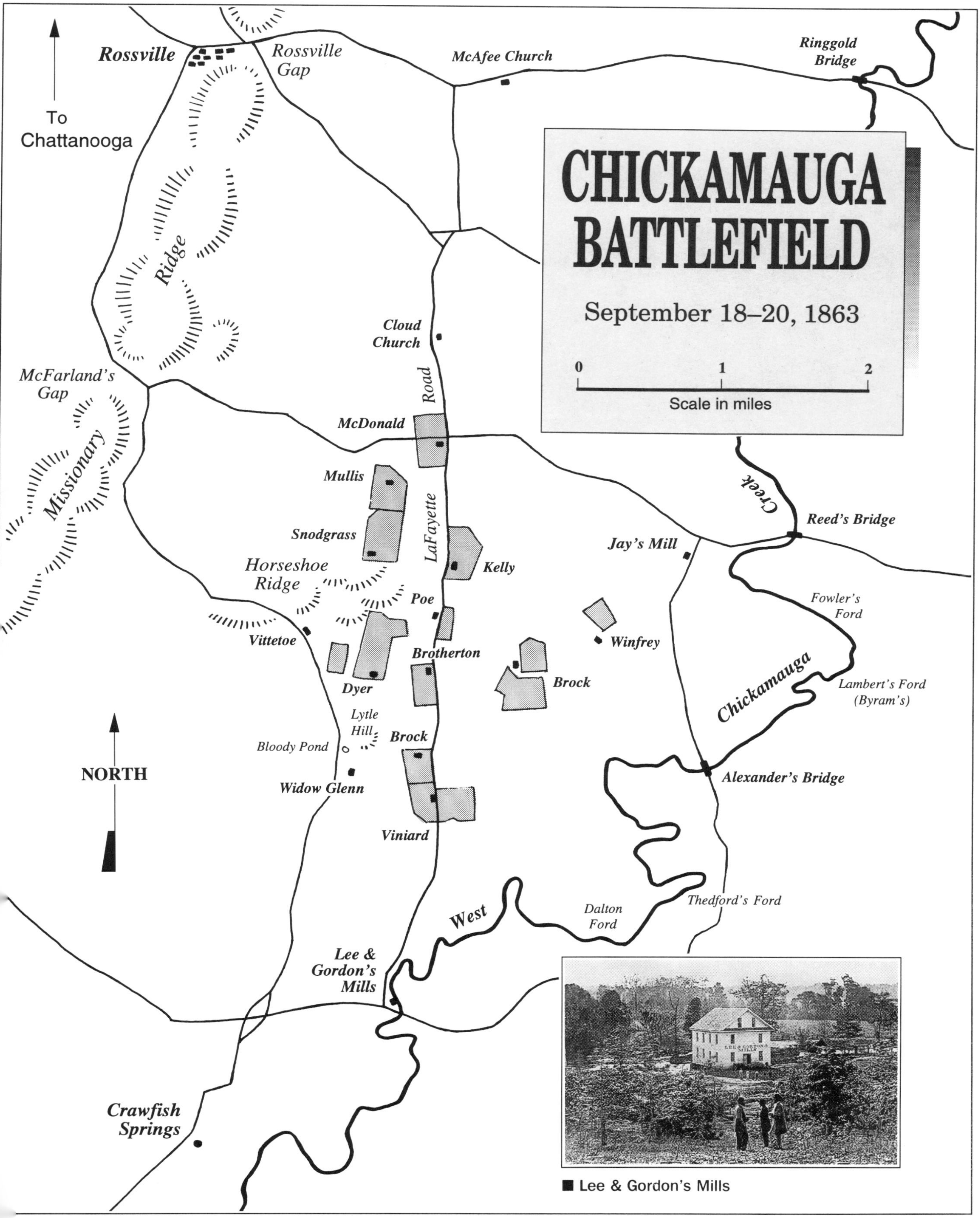
CHICKAMAUGA BATTLEFIELD
September 18–20, 1863
0 1 2
Scale in miles
Rossville
Rossville Gap
McAfee Church
Ringgold Bridge
To Chattanooga
Ridge
Cloud Church
McFarland's Gap
Missionary
Road
McDonald
Mullis
Snodgrass
LaFayette
Kelly
Creek
Reed's Bridge
Jay's Mill
Horseshoe Ridge
Poe
Fowler's Ford
Vittetoe
Winfrey
Brotherton
Brock
Dyer
Chickamauga
Lambert's Ford (Byram's)
Lytle Hill
Bloody Pond
Brock
NORTH
Alexander's Bridge
Widow Glenn
Viniard
Thedford's Ford
Dalton Ford
West
Lee & Gordon's Mills
Crawfish Springs
■ Lee & Gordon's Mills

■ Confederate gunners at Chickamauga seldom had open fields of fire like the one illustrated above. Capt. Thomas L. Massenburg, a Georgia battery commander, described the destruction of Carnes' battery: "The woods through which they advanced were so dense with undergrowth that it was almost impossible to keep the battery up with the infantry line. The infantry struck the enemy first, and as soon as Carnes could clear the ground of undergrowth, which he had to do with a detail of men armed with axes, he put his battery in position, and opened on the advancing Federals with canister. Of the left gun detachment, the Captain informed me that only one man besides himself was known to have gotten out, and he (a German corporal) was so badly wounded as to be permanently disabled. The terrible slaughter in and around Carnes' battery was the talk of the army, and I, with many others, visited the spot and saw the men and horses lying dead about the guns. In one place there were 13 horses touching one another."

limber-chest standing open, and the team not having been reversed, the white pine of the unclosed cover raised vertically attracted hundreds of hostile infantry shots, which, passing through the wood and puncturing the outside tin, made the chest resemble a huge grater. Three or four men were endeavoring to loosen the ammunition at the same time with their heads over the chest, but strangely enough not one of them was then hit. All the horses of the piece, however, expect the wheel-team, were killed before the gun was discharged. The wheel-team were hit, and, springing over the roots of a large tree, turned the limber bottom upward, scattering the ammunition on the ground like a load of apples. The driver, Mathews, thinking the situation desperate, urged on the two wheel-horses, and their speed at once righted the empty limber. Mathews, with his team, escaped further casualties and crossed Alexander's bridge, thus saving the only two horses belonging to the battery that survived the battle.

Four times a minute for the first three or four minutes, at least, each gun was discharged at very short range, probably two hundred yards; but the battery was a target for the concentrated fire of both the adverse artillery and infantry, since Wright's brigade had disappeared from the right flank, though it had rallied long enough to stand one volley after the battery went into action. But now — that is, eight or ten minutes after the artillery was in line — the whole brigade was out of sight. Probably they did right to leave, for otherwise they would have been annihilated. As it was, they left the ground strewn with their wounded and dead. The battery now stood alone, with no support in sight either on the right or on the left; in fact, there had at no time been any support on the left.

Col. John C. Carter of the Thirty-eighth Tennessee refused to leave the line with his regiment, and, finding himself alone, came walking into the battery as if for a social visit. His lavish display of coolness and his intrepidity were indeed admirable. The enemy, easily perceiving the odd exposure of the artillery, jumped over their works, ran behind a large fallen tree about a hundred yards farther to the left, lying at right angles to the line of the guns, and, resting their muskets on the fallen tree, poured a heavy fire right across the battery from flank to flank. The left piece, under the personal direction of the Captain, wheeled and gave them several shots, mainly to cover the retreat of the battery men not killed, for it was now evident that the place was untenable.

Lieut. James M. Cockrill was serving the guns of his section effectively, though only two or three men remained to each detachment. The right section was playing squarely to the front under my command. I was on foot assisting, for by this time only two of the detachment of the right piece had escaped death or severe wounds. The battery was clearly overpowered. Nineteen of the men were killed dead in their places, and upward of twenty men were wounded, most of whom never resumed service in the artillery. Forty-nine horses were killed in harness.

The situation was held about ten minutes after the infantry left us. About the eighth minute Orderly Sergeant [Finis E.] White hurriedly announced to me that the enemy were flanking the battery, alluding to the ambush behind the fallen tree before mentioned. I told him to report to the Captain, but the latter was fully cognizant of the fact, and was at that moment training the left piece against the flankers. Lieut. A. Vanvleck received several severe wounds at the Captain's side, and while the infirmary corps were trying to bear him to the rear — an additional member being added by the Captain's order to assist, as Vanvleck was a heavy man — he was shot through the breast from side to side, and killed him thus in the hands of the litter-bearers. The same shot that killed Vanvleck broke the arm of the man ordered to assist. Sergeant John Thompson was killed by the side of his gun. Private [John] Lane, a Mexican war veteran, was also killed while making his way to the rear badly wounded.

When all the horses had fallen except one of the teams of the right section, the Captain gave orders to limber up the right piece and get away. The team came forward under the gallant drivers in the midst of a storm of all sorts of shot, but the six horses fell in a heap, the lead-team with their heads on the trail of the piece they were going to save. The Captain then said: "We can't save the battery. Let the men leave as quick as possible."

The guns were now silent. The men were all lying on the ground, whether dead, wounded or unhurt, and occupying as little space as possible. I called to my section to rise and follow, when I mounted my horse which stood near hitched to a swinging limb. I mounted not very hastily, for the act seemed to challenge the enemy's fire. The latter, however, were intent on felling at first all the artillery-horses they could, and besides they were at the moment extending their flanking enterprise and were now somewhat

■ Col. John C. Carter, 38th Tennessee, fought for three hours September 19 on the immediate right of Carnes' battery. The artillerists and Carter's men shared a long and close association which engendered good-natured taunting, as recalled by Musician Davis Biggs of Company D: "Carnes' battery was often near us in camp, on the march and in the fight. It was an inspiration to see them dash up into position, wheel around like a flash, and, with machine-like precision, begin to load and fire. [Once] we had been travelling about a week on a freight train ... stopping occasionally to cook and warm over fat pine and rosin fires. The weather had been cold and soap and water scarce, and when we began to unload opposite their camp, one of the batterymen yelled out: 'Hello, boys! Here's one of them nigger regiments Jeff Davis called out.' "

Carter, promoted to brigadier general in July 1864, was mortally wounded at the battle of Franklin and died December 10.

# Like 'driftwood in a squall'

■ 1st Lieut. Bromfield L. Ridley

■ 1st Lieut. J.D. Richardson

Two of the youngest Confederate officers to fight at Chickamauga were good friends — 1st Lieut. James D. Richardson, adjutant of the 45th Tennessee, and 1st Lieut. Bromfield L. Ridley, aide-de-camp to Maj. Gen. Alexander P. Stewart. Both were 18 years old in September 1863.

On September 19, Stewart's three brigades under Gens. H.D. Clayton, W.B. Bate and J.C. Brown attacked the Federal center in order to rescue the just-captured battery of Capt. W.W. Carnes. Clayton was thrown in first.

"Did you ever witness driftwood in a squall?" Ridley later wrote. "Such was the havoc upon Clayton. Four hundred of his little band were mown down. It was his first baptism of fire but he stayed there until out of ammunition. General Brown [whose command included the 45th Tennessee] then went in and was greeted like Clayton. The booming of the cannon, the thinning of the ranks, the thickness of dead men, the groaning of the dying — all were overcome to recapture that battery. Forty-eight horses of Carnes' had been shot down, and amid their writhings the close quarters had set the woods on fire. But Brown ... got Carnes' battery out of the cyclone. Then Bate came into the arena. He rescued the colors of the Fifty-first Tennessee and captured several pieces of artillery. Added to the horror of the galling fire, the generals and staffs encountered a number of yellow jackets' nests and the kicking of the horses and their ungovernable actions came near breaking up one of the lines. Blue jackets in front of us, yellow jackets upon us, and death missiles around and about us."

Ridley's friend Richardson barely survived the battle. During desperate fighting on the 20th, their paths crossed briefly. "His remark to me, 'This is hot, isn't it?' impressed me as very cool and deliberate," Ridley continued. A short time later, "near one of the trees behind which several were sheltered, a soldier came up. Richardson and S.H. Mitchell [a private in Company C] asked his command. The soldier uttered, 'Thirty-eighth Ala——,' and before completing the word Alabama, a cannon ball took half his head off, the blood spattering them."

in rear of the battery. These two circumstances probably saved the survivors, for it was at that time quite in the power of the enemy, without danger, to pick off every one of the battery men who left the place. Only thirty-five men followed the Captain and Lieutenants from the terrible spot.

The little party, instead of going to the rear, had to travel for two hundred yards across the line of the enemy's fire, as the battery was nearly surrounded before we started. But no casualties occurred except the loss of the Captain's beautiful dark-bay, called Prince, which received five shots in the fight. The Captain shouldered his saddle, and all the remnants moved away toward the banks of the Chickamauga about a mile distant. Even here the enemy's shot fell thick, and an improvised field hospital had to be moved over the creek. While moving to the rear Capt. Carnes met Gen. Preston Smith, who informed him of the loss of his battery commander, Lieut. [John H.] Marsh, then commanding Scott's battery, and offered to put Carnes in his place. The Captain accepted, and was soon in command of Scott's battery, which command he retained till Sunday morning, September 20.

As to our battery, the enemy rushed in, chopped down the limbers and dragged the gun-carriages by hand about one hundred and fifty yards toward their line before [A.P.] Stewart's division, then approaching double-quick, could open fire. At the first volley, however, the enemy abandoned the guns where they were and returned to a line of works in rear of the first. To insure the early restoration of the battery, Col. [H.W.] Walter of Bragg's staff, a friend of Capt. Carnes, invited the General to the ground to see the evidences of the desperate fight made on the spot. Stewart's division had made a fight of perhaps three hours over the ground before it was recovered, and thus the heaps of dead were somewhat greater than were due to the battery. Bragg said he would like to sell Rosecrans some more batteries at the same price as this. His orders were positive to restore everything as the Captain desired and prescribed. As a compliment, the new guns were inscribed "Chickamauga, Sept. 19, 1863."

■ 1st Lieut. Terry H. Cahal of Company K, 45th Tennessee, served on Gen. Alexander P. Stewart's staff. Near dawn of September 20, while riding over the field where Stewart's division was heavily engaged, Cahal discovered the body of a longtime friend. "He had fallen," Cahal wrote 10 days later, "in attempting to rally his comrades when they were broken and driven back on the evening before. I had parted with him as he went into the fight, and as he clasped my hand and bid me adieu, he repeated his motto to me, which he said should animate him in the coming fight. It was the last six lines of Lochul's reply to the seer before going into the battle of Culloden. I buried him and marked the sacred spot with a piece of board, writing his name and company upon it, beneath the epitaph of 'Dead upon the Field of Honor.' And as I laid him in his last resting place I made an oath above his grave to avenge his death."

## 'Picked off one by one'

### 2nd Lieut. James F. Meline
### Company H
### 6th Ohio Volunteer Infantry

About 9 a.m. [September 19] we came across Baird's division ... when a heavy musketry fire was opened in the direction of his advanced brigade. Our brigade was formed in line, ready to assist him if necessary; but the firing subsiding, we retraced our steps toward our own division. On our way back we met great numbers of Thomas' troops going to the left, and wondered what it meant. We had scarcely retaken our places with the division when we were ordered back to the left. Our brigade was formed in two lines — our right resting on Reynolds' division, and our left on Cruft's brigade; the Twenty-fourth Ohio and Thirty-sixth Indiana forming the first line, the Twenty-third Kentucky and Eighty-fourth Illinois the second, and our regiment as reserve

■ Capt. Henry H. Tinker of Company H, 6th Ohio Infantry, was seriously wounded on September 19 during the regiment's unsuccessful effort supporting the 19th Indiana Battery on Brotherton's ridge. As the Alabamians of Clayton's brigade threatened to turn the 6th's right flank, Tinker "was shot through both legs, near the knees, and in terrible suffering, was removed to the field hospital of [Palmer's] division, which the shifting of the lines next morning made it necessary to abandon. He was left in a dying condition, as was supposed, with not more than twenty minutes to live, the surgeon said."

Taken captive on September 20, Tinker survived and was paroled with other wounded Federal prisoners nine days later. Recalled regimental historian Ebenezer Hannaford: "Captain Tinker reappeared, clad in a dirty suit of mingled blue and gray, and weak as a child from intense suffering. His old comrades greeted him almost as one risen from the dead."

behind the battery.

The first line had been engaged but a few minutes when the rebels began flanking us on the right, and the Sixth Ohio, with the battery, was ordered to extend the front line in that direction. As soon as we were formed the rebels made their appearance, advancing against us in two columns. The battery promptly opened with canister; at the same time our regiment met them with such deadly volleys that they were soon driven from the field. They returned, but with no better success than before. The regiment remained some time after all its ammunition was expended, and, on being relieved by another one, was complimented by General Palmer for its gallantry and steadiness. By him we were ordered to a position in the rear of the Nineteenth Indiana Battery, where we could get ammunition, and, having refilled our cartridge-boxes, were again ready for action.

General Reynolds was at the battery, and, as Colonel Anderson moved our regiment to re-occupy its original position, he asked the colonel to remain and support it, but Anderson replied that his orders required him to report again to General Palmer, and we kept on. Reynolds said he feared he would lose the battery as it was entirely unsupported, and all his own regiments were in action. We had just entered the woods on our way back to the first line when we saw our troops giving way; and one of Reynolds' aides just then galloping up to the colonel and begging him to come and save the battery, the regiment was about-faced and double-quicked back. Before we got fairly into position, the battery became engaged, and I saw the rebels advancing upon it in four columns. The men at the guns worked well, but fired somewhat too high. I watched the cannoneers and horses fall, picked off one by one by the unerring shots of rebel sharpshooters, and saw that, as the regiments on our right were broken, there was nothing to prevent us from being flanked. The last round of shot was fired and we heard the command, "Limber to the front!" but still we lay there, determined to save those guns. The rebels had nearly surrounded us, but the battery — all except one piece — was safely retreating, when we received the order to raise and fire. We did so, and checked the charging enemy for a short minute, and then "changed front to the rear on the tenth company," and fired a volley in that direction. We were now flanked on both sides, while the rebels were bearing down upon us in front. Things looked desperate, and I began to think of Libby [Prison]. Reynolds, who still remained with us, had his horse shot under him, and at last ordered us to retreat double-quick.

As soon as we got out of this box we reformed behind a rail fence, and soon afterward were joined by the Ninth Indiana, a splendid fighting regiment, from our own division. Reynolds then ordered us forward, and forward we went in fine style, assisted by the Ninth Indiana. Our advance was short, however, for we no sooner cleared a little stretch of woodland than we were met by a most murderous fire from both flank and front, and were obliged to fall back in some confusion. Rallying, however, as soon as we could, we fell back slowly, firing at every step. Here our loss was heavy — many privates killed and wounded, Colonel Anderson, Captain Tinker (my captain) and Captain [Jules J.] Montagnier wounded, and Lieutenant [Jonathan B.] Holmes captured. It was now nearly dark. We were relieved by Jeff. C. Davis' division, received General Reynolds' thanks for what we had done, and by his orders then reported to our own division, which we found badly used up. How we suffered that night no one knows. Water could not be found; the rebels had possession of the Chickamauga and we had to do without. Few of us had blankets, and the night was very cold. All looked with anxiety for the coming of dawn; for although we had given the enemy a rough handling, he had certainly used us very hard.

## 'Tomorrow would be a bloody day'

### Orderly Sergeant James L. Cooper
### Company C
### 20th Tennessee Volunteer Infantry

On the morning of the 19th, Saturday, we were put in motion about sun rise, and both armies made preparation for the day. The day was bright and beautiful, and the world never seemed half so attractive before, now that there was a good chance for leaving it soon. Every thing was quiet until about eight or nine o'clock when light skirmishing began on our right. It was tolerably light for half an hour when the battle commenced in earnest, and from that time till dark there was a continuous roar of small arms and artillery that made the very leaves on the trees quiver. I never heard such a crashing of small arms before, and I hope I never will again.

Our division, [Gen. Alexander P. Stewart's] was moved to the right by slow degrees, so that by midday we were directly in rear of the heaviest firing. Our Corps (Buckner's) had been engaged some time when our division was ordered into action. We were sent in by brigades, and two brigades, Clayton's and Brown's had preceded us. We saw them both repulsed, and moving to the front were soon under a very heavy fire. We pressed steadily forward unchecked by the murderous discharges of their small howitzers, loaded with canister and grape, and drove the first line from their position. Here occurred the prettiest fighting during the whole war. We rushed up on a little hill, and the enemy were just below us, all crowded together in a deep hollow. Our rifles were in prime condition and our ammunition so good that I really enjoyed the fight. The enemy's reserve was soon brought up and then we had hard work to hold our position. Finally near dark we were driven back some distance, when night put an end to the conflict.

We slept on our arms that night [and] prepared to renew the battle at early dawn. Nothing decisive had been done but the enemy were very much alarmed. We had captured a good many guns from him, and driven him from several strong positions. All night long the Yankees were busy arranging their lines, and the clatter of thousands of axes, fortifying, and the rolling of artillery to positions told us that tomorrow would be a bloody day. Numbers of wounded had been left between the lines, and their cries for help were heart-rending.

Just at day break we sprang to our feet and prepared for the expected attack. It did not come, however, for the Yankees had had enough of us the preceding day. Everything was so quiet this beautiful Sabbath morning that for several hours all thought there would be no fighting. About nine o'clock the terrible slaughter commenced again ...

■ Orderly Sergeant James L. Cooper of Company C, 20th Tennessee. On September 19 his depleted and nearly exhausted regiment lost 98 officers and men out of 162 engaged. In his journal Cooper wrote: "We were exposed to a very heavy fire of artillery, for two or more hours. We were lying down in the grass, and numbers of the men actually went to sleep while the shells were bursting all around them. I had been in great danger several times during this battle. Men were shot down all around me, but I was not touched. My right hand man received two bullets before he could get away from his first wound."

Two months later Cooper was wounded at Missionary Ridge, and suffered further wounds in 1864 at Resaca, Ga. and Franklin, Tenn.

## 'Our eyes and ears open all night, and our fingers on the trigger'

**In fighting for the Brotherton Farm on September 19, Major John P. McGuire, 32nd Tennessee, had his horse shot dead beneath him. After darkness enveloped the surrounding woods, McGuire found the battlefield eerily surreal:**

That night was one never to be forgotten, especially by those of our regiment who were on the skirmish line. It was my lot to command the skirmishers covering Brown's brigade and our regiment that night. We stood at the muzzle of the enemy's muskets, so to speak, and they stood at the muzzle of ours; so that the *least* noise never failed to provoke a shot. We therefore learned to be *very quiet.*

Our army lay upon arms, and as all were worn and tired with the day's work, all were soon asleep. Of course we skirmishers and pickets had to keep our eyes and ears open all night, and our fingers on the trigger. We happened to occupy a portion of the field near a farm-house, in and around which large numbers of Federal wounded had been gathered during the day, and near which a very large number of animals in harness were left by the retreating and beaten enemy. Some of these animals were dead, some wounded, some parts of a train unhurt, but could not escape on account of some of the others of the train being either dead or disabled.

As the night grew old the monotony was heavy, and the stillness intense and painful; yet often, in the midst of this, wounded soldiers about the house could be heard begging piteously for water; another and another would shriek with pain as if a dagger was at his heart; then the groaning of the wounded animals, or the neighing of a sound horse, would appear to be a signal for the rest of the animals to make their complaints and efforts to be released from their confinement; they would break forth in the most hideous and unearthly yells and groans imaginable, which seemed to be taken up from the signal point and would run all along the line, sometimes lasting a minute or two; yet no one dared move to offer relief.

# September 20

## 'Inch by inch — sullenly, doggedly'

**Private Lewellyn A. Shaver**
**Company A**
**1st Alabama Battalion (Hilliard's Legion)**

What soldier does not remember how, on the eve or in the midst of a battle, his thoughts have turned to his dear native bowers and the loved ones whom he left behind him. It was with thoughts of this character, and deep solicitude for the issue of the severe struggle pending in their immediate front, that the men of the Legion passed the 19th of September 1863.

At length night came, and the storm grew less violent — *grew less violent, but did not cease.* All through the night a sharp fire was kept up between the pickets, and, ever and anon, the booming of a cannon, startling us in our troubled slumber, reminded of the carnage of the past day and the coming horrors of the morrow. After nightfall, too, the shrieks and groans of the wounded lying on the battle-field between the two lines were more clearly heard. Add to all this the facts, that the night was cold, our supply of blankets and clothing scanty, and the orders prohibited fires, and you will readily understand that "tired nature's sweet restorer, balmy sleep," visited but few eyelids in the Legion for any length of time during the night of that stirring day.

So passed the night.

The storm revived — the smoldering fires of battle were rekindled — fresh fuel was added, and the flames burst forth anew.

The fighting this day was less fitful — more continuous. The Confederates bore steadily forward; the Federal masses gave back, inch by inch — sullenly, doggedly.

Until about 3½ p.m. the Legion advanced with the advancing army, encountering a constant stream of wounded who bore witness to the sharpness of the conflict, and also to the cheering fact that the Confederate flag was being borne onward in triumph. Their march this day was through the theatre of the previous and the present day's battle. On all sides round they viewed heaps of silent slain — friend and foe, man and beast, in one promiscuous slumber. At length, at about 3½ p.m., the banner of the Legion was unfurled for the first time in battle, the command "Forward, double-quick!" was given by the gallant Gracie, and the brigade rushed impetuously into action.

## 'Our canister hurled them back'

**Private Sherman Hendricks**
**Battery C**
**1st Ohio Light Artillery**

We parked on a hill at 10 p.m. and rested until 3 a.m. of the 20th, when we went to the front. Our flanking pieces were 12-pounder Napoleons, the rest six-pounder rifles, all brass pieces.

The two Napoleons were placed on the front line where the infantry had built a small breastwork of logs and brush about two feet high, so the muzzles of the guns would just clear the top. Soon the tide of battle, which had been muttering all the morning on the left, rolled toward the right, and the artillery kept up a continual roar until it reached our two pieces. The rebels were hurled backward before our charges of canister.

During this fight Sergt. [George M.] Salkeld stood upon the works watching the approaching enemy and telling his gunner where to fire. As the other four pieces lay back in the woods waiting orders and taking all the back fire, I could not find a tree big enough to cover me, but as soon as the first charge was repulsed and we were ordered to the front I forgot my fears and felt strong enough to carry a cannon all alone. The remaining pieces of the right and left sections took places next to the Napoleons on their right, while the center section took the extreme right of the battery. About half an hour of quiet was all that was given us in which to take our places at the front, when the roar of artillery was heard again on the left, and it came toward us in a manner that made us feel rather shaky again. We were all watching for the approaching foe, and soon saw them, their bayonets glistening in the morning sun, when we were ordered to commence firing.

They charged up to within six rods of our muzzles when our canister hurled them back. We had lots of canister but no grape, although I notice that infantrymen always speak of grape and canister. The second charge they came nearer and we mowed them down in windrows. We could keep our front clear as long as our flanks were protected and the canister held out. A third time they came on. Between the second and third charge Gen. Wood made that unaccountable blunder of withdrawing his division from the front line and passed to our rear [Brig. Gen. John M. Brannan's division, XIV Corps] to the support of Reynolds on our left. We had not much more than begun our morning operations against this third charge when we noticed bullets coming from our right. We turned our guns in that direction. When we fired our last charge the rebels were not two rods away. Our section was badly cut to pieces in this flank charge.

I was number two on our gun (called the Ashtabula gun), and Daniel Horton was number four. He was shot down and did not move after he fell. Then, B[arnhart] Reichart, number three, acted for both. Albert LeClere was number one. He had just said to me that he could not hold out much longer, and I was thinking of taking hold to help him when he was wounded in the head, dropped the sponge staff and turned away. I sprang across the muzzle of the gun and picked up the sponge staff to take his place, when Amos Austin of the Madison gun came up with his staff in hand and said: "Let me act; our gun is disabled. Gunner Haskell is badly wounded." I at once resumed my own post. We fired perhaps half a dozen times more, then were ordered to limber up, and Austin returned to help save his own piece. As we were running off our gun I was wounded, and there were not men enough left to get the gun through to the brush. Sergt. [Theodore] Stoughton and Reichart dismounted it, however, and escaped just as the Johnnies were on the point of laying hands on them. How they came off alive I do not know. Stoughton came out with the gun limber and three horses, ridden by [Privates Andrew C.] Johnson and [Theodore] Ingersoll, and picked me up, so I rode off the field

■ Corporal Joseph J. Landram of Company A, 4th Kentucky Infantry. On September 19 this regiment supported Battery C, 1st Ohio Light Artillery, but unfavorable terrain prevented the Buckeyes from engaging. When the Federal center was pierced the following day, the Kentuckians broke and streamed to the rear, leaving the cannoneers isolated. Battery C commander 1st Lieut. Marco B. Gary ordered the brass guns double-shotted with canister as the Confederates advanced within 100 yards of his right piece. With support gone and casualties mounting, Gary, too, decided to leave the position. He reported: "So great was the loss of horses [25 killed] that several of the pieces had to be drawn far to the rear by hand, and the only piece lost in the engagement was abandoned after being dismounted and the linch-pins thrown away 200 yards to the rear, the men becoming too much exhausted to drag it farther by hand."

Landram survived the battle, which cost the 4th Kentucky 191 officers and men — a loss in Croxton's brigade only exceeded by the 14th Ohio.

■ Detail from an albumen photograph showing three 6-pounder James guns and crews of Capt. Wilbur Goodspeed's Battery A, 1st Ohio Light Artillery, taken by the Nashville firm of A.S. Morse. On the afternoon of September 20, recalled battery historian Henry M. Davidson, "our artillery, which had been placed about 600 yards in rear of the works, had not yet opened its fire. At last, after due preparation, the rebels advanced ... The signal was given and the thunder of cannon rolled along the whole line from one end to the other, in one terrible billow of sound. On, on they pushed, heedless of their falling comrades, whom our gunners at every shot were sweeping down by hundreds. Braver men never fought in any cause; but despite their iron courage, the carnage was too fearful for endurance."

About dusk, "I attached the prolonges to my pieces and retreated firing," Goodspeed recalled. "The enemy closed in from three sides, and his batteries came so near that we fired at each other with canister. Under orders I limbered up ... and brought into camp my battery complete." Battery losses included 40 horses — 15 to wounds, and 25 to hardship and "not unharnessing for six days."

on the gun limber. The Madison gun was brought off by [Corporal] John Austin with his wheelers. All the other horses were either killed or wounded and had to be cut out. The other two sections lost two or three caissons and several horses.

The battery, being so badly disabled, was sent off the field toward Chattanooga. We did not lose near as many men in proportion as our infantry supports in the two days' fighting. Wilkinson, Gilbert, Horton and Harris were killed; Chapman, LeClere, Haskell, Childs, St. John, Belknap and myself were all seriously wounded.*

## 'Many a blanched face did I see'

### Capt. Israel B. Webster
### Company I
### 10th Kentucky Volunteer Infantry

About 3 o'clock a.m. Sept. 20 we were aroused, ordered into line and soon took up the march, destined for we knew not where nor for what. However, we did not travel far until a line of battle was formed. Everything was shrouded in darkness. The morning air was cold, and the grass and foliage damp with the heavy dew of night, causing great discomfort. Fires were not allowed, and very few of us had blankets and none had overcoats. From that time

* Privates O.H. Haskell, Leroy St. John and C.H. Belknap died of their wounds before the end of the year. Privates Joseph Chapman and Silas M. Childs transferred to the Veteran Reserve Corps in 1864.

until daylight seemed very long and felt very uncomfortable.

All was silent after our line was formed. The men huddled together in little groups upon the ground for comfort and company, conversing in whispers about the previous day's fight. Otherwise, deep silence prevailed. It was an anxious time for all. None of us knew why we were there, but all surmised it meant a battle. About the moment of the first appearance of dawn the report of a gun fired immediately in our front was heard. Every man was awake and peering anxiously into the darkness, which was now fast becoming less opaque. As objects became visible our first discovery was a line of soldiers in our front behind a light breastwork of rails and logs, hastily thrown up in a very imperfect manner. We were then occupying a second line. We were instructed to fall back a short distance to a dry ravine where we lay down. The line in our front was attacked [about 9 o'clock], and for a long time the missiles of death came very fast.

All these missiles did not stop at the first line. Hundreds of them reached our line. Several of our men got shot in the top of the shoulder as they lay hugging close down in the little ravine with their heads toward the front and their heels high up on the other side of the ravine. Some got shot in the leg as they thus lay. It was a trying time to us of the second line. There was a sparse growth of trees scattered here and there, and many a leaf fell among us as we lay there, cut off the parent stem by the passing bullets, while one could see the little blades of grass that were being moved by the wind, just near his head, fall upon the ground, cut down by a flying missile. We dared not move from there. Neither could we return the fire on account of the first line, fearing we might hit the men in it. All we could do was closely embrace Mother Earth and wish the enemy would quit throwing such ugly things at us. How long we lay thus I cannot say, but probably not so long as it seemed.

When the firing began the intervals between were quite long. These grew shorter and shorter each moment, until at the end of 15 or 20 minutes there was continuous musketry, interspersed with the boom of cannon, and getting nearer to us each moment. At the proper time our first line began firing; then the roar of the musketry was something terrible to the listener, and after a time many feet could be heard making tracks to the rear, running over us as we lay there. We were ordered up and to the front, but could make little headway on account of meeting so many retreating, and particularly on account of such dense smoke as filled the air. Nothing could be seen for it. It appeared that by some means the rail and log breastwork had caught fire, and before we could advance any distance the fire was under good headway, and we were forced to fall back to prevent being burned up or suffocated by the smoke. Our line was halted in due time, and the enemy had not yet passed the breastworks when we felt an enfilading fire from our right rear. Our attention was called in that direction, and we saw coming through a cornfield a large body of men marching in good form in line of battle with colors flying, apparently as unconcerned as though passing in review. The word passed down the line that the colors were Gen. McCook's battleflag. We were ready to believe this, as they were just in rear of our line, and only a few moments before Gen. Baird had ridden up to and instructed one of our commanders to remain where they were and not change position. His words were, "Not yet; not yet,"

■ Capt. Israel B. Webster of Company I, 10th Kentucky, barely emerged unscathed from the furious late-afternoon fighting on Horseshoe Ridge, as he recalled: "A single bullet went singing along and struck some object with a thud. It seemed a long time before anyone had any idea where it struck. Suddenly a soldier standing at my side threw up his right hand, and the sight which met the eyes was sickening. The ball had struck the back of the hand, passing through it and destroying it. His hand and mine were nearly touching each other at the time, and my escape was very close."

■ 2nd Lieut. Orville T. Chamberlain of Company G, 74th Indiana. This regiment of Croxton's brigade received 60 additional rounds early on September 20, and twice blunted Confederate assaults north of Dyer Field while sheltered behind hurriedly built breastworks of logs and fence rails. Georgians of Henry Benning's brigade loudly advanced to within 70 yards, when the Hoosiers stood up and began pouring deliberately aimed volleys into the single gray line. The intense fire staggered Benning's men, but soon depleted the 74th's extra cartridges. Chamberlain volunteered to fetch more. Thirty-three years later he was given the Medal of Honor, the citation reading: "While exposed to a galling fire, [Chamberlain] went in seach of another regiment, found its location, procured ammunition from the men thereof, and returned with the ammunition to his own company."

and he soon left our vicinity.

A short time afterward a mounted officer rode up to me and said: "Captain, do not let your men shoot down there (pointing toward the cornfield). Those are our men." He wore the uniform of a Federal officer, and I did not doubt him for a moment. I went among the men and reported his orders to them. As I did so, one of my company turned around and responded very promptly: "Captain, they are shooting at us." I then told them to give it to them thick and fast.

In the meantime I gave my attention to the party who had shown so much concern for the safety of that approaching column. It appears that he mistrusted that his identity had been discovered, as I saw him riding at a breakneck speed to the cornfield. He did not go very far, however. His Confederate friends caught the horse bearing only an empty saddle.

Closely following this incident was another of considerable interest. Four men were seen coming into our lines, each having hold of one corner of a blanket. The contents were apparently heavy, as the men labored hard in their efforts to carry it. They succeeded in reaching and passing through our line immediately by where I was standing. I looked at the object in the blanket. There lay as fine a specimen of physical manhood as one need to look upon. I glanced at his features to learn if I had ever known him. No, I never saw him before. There was every evidence of suffering upon his countenance and, as his glance met mine, I shall never forget the deep frown which swept over his face. Great furrows sank deep into his brow, and scorn is no name for the expression he gave me as he was borne along in his helpless condition. Who was this man, and why this frown? I only had time to inquire as to the first; the latter I surmised. I was told by his bearers that it was Gen. [Daniel W.] Adams of the Confederate army, and that he was seriously wounded. He was brought into our lines by mistake, his bearers supposing they were going to their rear until it was too late to correct the error.

As he was borne away my attention reverted to our surroundings, and I found the forces of the enemy were fast getting into our rear, turning our right flank and doubling us up like an elbow, shortening the angle at every moment, thus enabling them to fire upon us from three directions. We were nearly annihilated when instructed to "come out of that," which we lost no time in doing. Our loss here was considerable. Capt. Seth Beville of Company E, 10th Ky., received a mortal wound from which he died [on September 21]. Second Lieut. John H. Myers, Company I, was killed instantly and several others were killed.

As we came out of this trap we were marched over a small hill, upon the top of which were a few pieces of artillery supported by some infantry. We passed over the hill, descended into the valley, halted beyond for a short rest and, if possible, to gather our scattered forces. We were wonderfully reduced in numbers, but at the end of a short time we were rejoiced to see some of the missing ones come in.

Gen. Thomas sat upon his horse about half way up the hill behind which we were, intently watching the events as they occurred. Several attempts were made by the Confederates to take this hill, but failed. Staff officers were constantly reporting to

■ Gen. George H. Thomas observes the fighting on September 20 and issues orders to staff officers. His calm presence raised morale on Snodgrass Hill and Horseshoe Ridge, as related by an Ohio enlisted man: " 'For God's sake, hurry up that ammunition; they are coming again,' was the word that was passed back from those in front, and the frequent click of a bayonet as it found its way over the muzzle of an empty musket gave emphasis to the demand. Just at this crisis there appeared, only a few paces in rear of our part of the line, the man who of all others could do the most good in that emergency; and as the cries for ammunition increased, mingled with curses and threats from the more impatient, a few of us then and there heard our first, last and only oral command from Gen. Thomas: 'Give them the cold steel.' How it thrilled us! That command of 'Pap' Thomas seemed to transform men into whole platoons."

Gen. Thomas from other portions of the field. In doing so, they were obliged to ride up the hill through a space about 20 yards wide in full range of the enemy's sharpshooters. We knew they were there because we heard the music of the little missiles as they passed harmlessly by. Gen. Thomas seemed to know about their presence, or he bore a charmed life, as he just kept out of the range; but these staff officers, as they rode up to him, had to pass over the ground covered by them. Many a blanched face did I see cross this dangerous ground.

After several attempts of the rebs to take this hill it seems they had determined to have it, for they came again with an increased force, and apparently were on the verge of success. Our artillery support gave way and came scampering down on our side of the hill. Gen. Thomas had not ceased his vigilance. He saw it all, and in a moment he drew his sword, rose in his stirrups and rode among his men, shouting to them: "Go back! Go back! This hill must be held at all hazards!"

Riding on up to the top with his sword flashing in the light, and his face expressive of determination, his words acted like magic. The men turned again to the front and with shouts regained their positions. Like an avalanche they swept down upon the advancing and almost victorious enemy, and drove them back. Thus this important position was saved. I was told that the infantry sup-

■ Brig. Gen. James B. Steedman's Reserve Corps' division of mostly untried troops lost one-fifth its strength in 20 minutes of fighting after arriving on Horseshoe Ridge about 2 p.m. "This havoc and destruction lasted a short time only," recalled Private Frank W. Gates of Company K, 115th Illinois, "when we fell back to the top and a little way over the crest of the ridge. [Then] another charge of the enemy had to be resisted. Comrade after comrade went down. A third and lastly a fourth charge were resisted. In rallying the lines for the last stand Gen. Steedman displayed the most splendid bravery, riding up and down the lines, telling the boys in the most positive terms the position must be held at all hazards, even at the point of the bayonet."

Col. John G. Mitchell, the division's 2nd Brigade commander, was less complimentary of Steedman. "Save for the fight," Mitchell asserted, "no more worthless man ever commanded men. He had no idea of the needs of his men, no thought of their food and clothing or comforts ... His devotion to cards and whiskey and women filled the measure of his delight except when under fire and then he was a lion."

porting the battery was composed of stragglers, men who had become separated from their commands during the day. They were unofficered and strangers to each other, and while they respected officers in general, there was no one who would wade in deep except for "Pap" Thomas. It was he, and he alone, who saved that point at that time.

When our line was formed we were posted upon the ridge in the rear of where Gen. Thomas was, and ordered to hold it. This was late in the afternoon of the second day, Sept. 20. Hundreds of men had become separated from their commands and knew not where to find them. Thus it was that I had some 20 men in my company whom I never saw before, and who were entire strangers to all of us.

On the top of the hill we were ordered to lie down and keep silent. We knew a rebel battery was in our front for we heard the boom of the guns. Every moment we expected to see the rebels coming up the other side of the ridge. This ridge was covered with woods, and on the rebels' side was a thick growth of underbrush that prevented our seeing 10 steps in our front. No one can imagine the intensity of our feeling while looking for evidence of an unseen enemy. We knew that he was approaching us. While we lay there under these exciting circumstances we were startled by the boom of a big gun, seemingly much nearer to us than the other had been. The missile went flying through the air, cutting off the small limbs of the trees as it climbed over the ridge. It passed over and struck a large tree in our rear with such force as to shatter it. The racket was terrible, and the effect upon our men was electric. Nearly every man sprang to his feet, took a long and earnest look in the direction of the noise, and then at each other. Not a word was spoken. In a moment my 20 "strays" sprang as one man to the rear and went scampering down the hill. I never saw or heard of them after that race of theirs down the hill. Our own men, after the first shock was over, resumed their recumbent position, calmly watching events in silence.

The moments passed; no noise in front to give us an idea of where the enemy was or what he was doing. The silence was painful. One could hear the heart of his neighbor throb — all was so still. At last a faint sound. Soldiers exchanged inquisitive glances, seeming to ask: "What is that?" The sound increased. It came nearer. It was in our rear. "Look, see those clouds? What is it?" The clouds thickened and rolled this way. Anxiously watching, we saw the clouds were of dust. What caused the dust in such immense quantities? We did not know, but in a short space of time all mystery was cleared up. It was Gen. Steedman (first Colonel of the 14th Ohio) coming to our relief. He was riding in front, leading his command by the right flank until our whole rear was covered, when the command "By the left flank" was given, and without a halt his whole line moved up the hill, passed over us and descended the rebel side into the thicket, out of our sight in a twinkling. There was no confusion, no talking or cheering. It seemed as though every man thought he had a special errand down there, and it behooved him to get there as soon as possible. For a few moments all was still. Then broke out a fusilade of musketry that was terrific.

Once more our little handful was called upon to go to the front. This time it was to hold a narrow space on the same hill, considerably nearer to Gen. Thomas' position, and to the left of where Gen. Steedman went over. On the very top of the hill at this new position was an old-style rail fence, up to which the men went, and getting close to the ground could see some distance in the front by peeping between the rails. No enemy could be seen in front, but rebel bullets kept coming in our direction which was anything but pleasant. There was not space very close to the fence for all of us, and it was dangerous to be far back from it unless very close to the ground. Thus the same sharpshooters who had the range on Gen. Thomas' position also had the range on us, by firing to their left. Josh Able [Private Joshua J. Abel] of Company I was struck by a flying bullet just below the knee-cap of both legs. Lieut. W.E. Kelley was struck in the same way, only in a different part of the body. I took them both to a house nearby where other wounded had been taken. There was a large number of them there at that time.

It was sundown when I left Lieut. Kelley. When I passed along I saw what I knew must be a rebel force coming up through the cornfield (for we were still near the cornfield of the morning). Considering this important, I began looking for the commanding officer to whom I might impart the information. I found Gen. Wood, and told him what I had seen. His reply was: "Let them come. We can only receive them with cold steel. Our ammunition is expended."

It was now growing dark and I was astray from my command. While trying to locate it I saw a line moving to the rear and approached it for information. I could learn nothing, and determined to wait until all had passed and then fall in with the men. By this determination I was relieved of further worry, for my command was a part of that column.

We marched along in a narrow pass for quite a distance, and about 10 o'clock we halted and remained there during the night. Thus ended the second day's fighting. All our wounded, who were left at the house before mentioned, were captured the next day.

## 'We pursued the flying enemy'

### 1st Lieut. James H. Fraser
### Company B
### 50th Alabama Volunteer Infantry

A little before sundown [of the 19th] we reached the battlefield. The ground in many places was actually covered with the yankee dead, but they still held a strong position, and we knew they would make fight again on the morrow ...

The night was quiet as if there were no enemy within ten miles. Our fires were bright and blazed high, and though the dead men were thick under the stacks yet the men were gay and lively, as full of hope and confident of victory as ever. We all knew that we would fight in the morning, and we all felt that we would whip the enemy. We could not be sad. We had longed and wished for an opportunity to meet the foe again; now it was granted us. Gen. Bragg had just issued an address to the army telling us that we had "twice thwarted the attempt of the enemy to flank us; that we had been largely reinforced, and that now we must force him

## 'I belong on the other side'

**Among the fragments of retreating Federal regiments seeking safety on Horseshoe Ridge was a group from the 31st Ohio, whose ranks stampeded in the face of Longstreet's midday assault. Private Jacob H. Allspaugh of Company H recounted the following incident, which allegedly occurred somewhere between Dyer Field and the ridge:**

At points in the wood the fighting had almost been hand to hand, yet was but a prelude to the struggle that awaited us for the possession of the barricades on Horse Shoe Ridge that long, eventful Sabbath afternoon. But this place of close work was not destitute of its amusing scenes.

At one point, in a countercharge, we occupied a position held a few moments before by the enemy, which brought their skulkers and killed and wounded in the rear of or mixed up with our irregular line. Seeing a fine-looking young soldier dressed in a neat suit of dark blue, unarmed, and standing behind a tree for protection, a pompous Colonel inquired why he was not firing like the others.

"Why, I'm a color-bearer," said the soldier, hugging the tree still closer and exhibiting his color-belt.

"Well, then, where is your flag?" said the Colonel, who liked to carry a point.

"I lost it in that close work back there," said the soldier.

"Well, pick up a gun and go to work like the other men," said the officer, thinking he had added one more soldier to our depleted ranks.

"Why, Colonel," said the soldier with a kind of foolish look getting possession of his face. "I belong on the other side." And sure enough it was one of Longstreet's men [who wore dark blue-gray uniforms] that the Colonel had been trying to force into our ranks. Just then was no time to care for straggling prisoners, and as the enemy occupied the ground a short time after, the young color-bearer probably rejoined his regiment.

■ Brig. Gen. Zachariah C. Deas' command of five Alabama regiments and battalion of sharpshooters paid dearly for its success on September 20 — suffering the most casualties in any brigade of Longstreet's left wing. After routing Col. Bernard Laiboldt's Illinois and Missouri troops of Sheridan's division, Deas momentarily was checked west of the Glenn-Kelly Road by the hurried arrival of Sheridan's 1st Brigade, under Gen. William H. Lytle. In the 22nd Alabama, which lost four color bearers, half its officers and nearly 190 enlisted men during the day, regimental command devolved upon Capt. Harry T. Toulmin of Company H.

"Moving ... amid a destructive fire of shot and shell, some 200 yards across an open field, the regiment became engaged with [Lytle's troops]," Toulmin reported. "Here took place a terrible conflict, which lasted about 20 minutes. When re-enforcements came to our support [we] pushed forward with a yell and drove the enemy in dismay from his strong position."

Wrote Deas: "On Sunday afternoon I passed over some ten or a dozen ordnance wagons filled with ordnance stores, three or four pieces of artillery and caissons, many ambulances, and one or two supply wagons, and a dozen or more mules and horses. There had evidently been a stampede here and these were the fruits left for us."

to the issue." We had nothing to discourage us. And more than all, Longstreet had driven them more than two miles that day, and we could not bear the idea for him to come from Virginia and gain all the glory of whipping "Rosy."

Early in the morning, Sunday the 20th, we were called to attention, the roll was called, and every man answered "here" loud and lively. At sunrise we advanced in line of battle, but soon halted on the ground that our troops had occupied last on the evening before. Here we remained until nearly eleven o'clock. The battle had opened on our right about sunrise. Gen. Deas said that he was ordered to take it up as soon as it came down the line. There was but little or no skirmishing in our immediate front, but up on the right of the brigade they were cracking away at each other frequently.

Presently, Generals Longstreet and Buckner rode down the line. Longstreet is the boldest and bravest looking man I ever saw. I don't think he would dodge if a shell were to burst under his chin. Gen. Deas said, "Gen. Longstreet, I presume."

"Yes, sir," said Gen. L.

Gen. Deas then told him his own name and said he was ready to advance with his brigade. Gen. Longstreet told him where to go and where he thought he would meet the enemy. Gen. Deas called the brigade to attention, and commanded "Forward." I think it could have been heard at least three miles.

We moved along, first at slow time, then quick, then double quick, and as we came in sight the boys all took the run, and everyone shouted and shot as fast as he could. Their first line gave way like nothing; so did their second and third. Our charge was irresistable. We actually cut the yankee line in two halves. One went one way and the other went another. They were scattered to the four winds. A great many of them were so cowardly that they did not shoot as we advanced on them but stuck their heads behind logs and waited for us to pass them. It was the quickest and prettiest fight I ever saw.

Dixon Allen and Corporal Harvey were killed in the charge. Capt. Richardson and Lieut. Blair were wounded. Two bullets passed through my clothes, one through my boot leg just above the ankle. I had my boots outside my pants, and the bullet went through my boot, pants and cut clear through the sock, carrying a part of it out with it, but it did not hurt me and I did not mind it. We pursued the flying enemy for more than a mile and a half, and when at last we were ordered to halt by our generals we were tired, scattered and exhausted.

A few minutes were allowed us to rest ourselves and to reform. The enemy were so much discouraged that they did not get into action again until nearly 4 o'clock in the evening, but we were not resting all the time. It was ascertained that he had massed all his forces between two high hills that could not be flanked, and to be carried must be stormed. We were ordered to charge one of these hills. Everyone felt that it was almost certain death to go up, but it was ordered and we obeyed the order, advancing steadily and slowly. The ground was so steep that we could not go with a rush until we reached the top of the hill. As soon as our heads were visible above the crest of the hill we were met with a terrible volley of grape and canister and minie bullets not more than 80 yards distant. The men could go no further; death reigned on every side; the grape and canister swept the earth. The brigade gave way, rallied and came back, again we were driven back, and again we came to the charge. [With other troops coming] to our relief again the shout of victory rose high. The enemy was beaten and took advantage of the night to hide himself.

## 'Hold this ridge for Gen. Sheridan's sake!'

### Corporal Austin E. Stebbins
### Company D
### 88th Illinois Volunteer Infantry

During the night [of September 19] Bragg moved his army to the north, or to his right and our left. Our division moved two miles north at daylight and formed line of battle. Hard fighting commenced on our left at 10 a.m. We could see rebel troops across a cornfield in our front moving north.

About noon we were ordered to double-quick up the road north. We had gone about a quarter of a mile as hard as we could run when we were halted and ordered to right face. Looking up on a hill 30 or 40 rods away we saw a battery unlimbering. The underbrush was so thick we could not see which way the guns were pointing. They had bay horses, the same as the 11th Indiana, so we supposed it was our battery and we were going up to support it. What further confirmed us in that belief [was that] Rosecrans, McCook and Crittenden came riding right down from the direction of the battery, and were not more than 10 or 15 rods from it when it went into position.

Rosecrans rode through our regiment and came up to the rear of our colors. I was so close to him I could have put my hand on his horse. He gave the command in person to our regiment to charge. When he said "Fix bayonets, forward, double-quick, charge!" the line moved forward in fine shape. When we got within about 10 rods of the battery it opened on us with grape and canister. We were hurled back, and on reaching the road the bugle sounded the halt; the line was again formed, and again we were ordered to charge, only to be driven back again. This was repeated four times. The last charge every man seemed to be determined to take that battery, and I believe we would have done so. But when we had gotten within four or five rods of it a line of infantry opened on us. They were lying in front of the cannons. Our men fell like grain before the sickle. Our beloved Gen. Lytle, commanding our brigade, fell mortally wounded. What was left of our regiment fell back across the road and up on the ridge to the west.

Halfway up the ridge I saw many men tugging at a rope, trying to pull a cannon. They had run against a dead tree, with the tree between the gun and the wheel. I caught hold of the wheel with several others and tried to back it up. We called to the men on the rope to slack up, but in the noise of battle they could not be made to understand, and kept on pulling. We clung to the wheels until the rebs were within 100 feet of us and continuously firing; several balls struck the wheel I had hold of. We abandoned the gun and it was captured.

On reaching the top of the ridge we began to form a new line. Rosecrans came riding up the ridge from the south, and cried:

■ Private William J. Phillips of Company H, 19th Alabama, was among 469 riflemen of his regiment to assault the left flank of Lytle's brigade. According to the 19th's commander, Col. Samuel K. McSpadden, the Federals were found on "an elevated skirt of heavy open woods, where we came upon him and drove him in utter confusion from two pieces of artillery and other breastworks. We continued to pursue the enemy for some distance across fields, woods, roads and hills ... and found we had utterly cut the enemy's lines asunder."

The Alabamians' successful charge cost the regiment 43 percent casualties. Thirty-four officers and men were killed, including Phillips' younger brother as well as their company commander, 1st Lieut. Joseph B. High. Two months later Phillips was captured on Missionary Ridge and imprisoned at Rock Island, Ill., for the rest of the war.

■ Lt. Col. Theodore S. West's 24th Wisconsin formed the left center of Lytle's brigade line, which was assailed shortly before noon by Deas' and Patton Anderson's Confederate brigades. When the neighboring 36th Illinois buckled and began streaming rearward, the 24th's left flank suddenly was exposed to an enfilading fire that felled West with a serious wound. Unable to quit the field, he soon was taken prisoner.

Assuming command, Major Carl von Baumbach reported: "We here lost Brig. Gen. W.H. Lytle, who was shot down while in the rear of the center of our regiment encouraging the men. Our two left companies were swung to the rear and poured effective fire into their ranks, but they still moving up in overwhelming numbers, we were at last forced to give way. We retreated in some disorder ..."

"Form a line! Don't fall back! Make a stand here. Hold this ridge for Gen. Sheridan's sake."

He rode on north along the ridge, and we began and had formed nearly our whole regiment in line when Sheridan came up on his black horse from the south, the same as Gen. Rosecrans had, and said: "Fall back, boys! Fall back!" His keen eyes had seen off to the left, north of us, what Gen. Rosecrans could not have seen 15 minutes before, because they were not there then, in an open field not more than a quarter of a mile away — 15,000 or 20,000 rebel troops marching to cut us off. It was a grand sight, a score of battle-flags floating triumphantly on the breeze. This was Longstreet's Corps, flushed with victory. They were marching rapidly to the west.

We fell back to the road, halted and reorganized our division. It took some time to get into shape. We started then to join Thomas on the left, having to march around by way of Rossville. When we came up in the rear of Thomas' right wing it was away after dark, and we were ordered into camp at Rossville about midnight.

Our loss in the charge on the battery was heavy, in our company particularly. We went in with 45 men and came out with 22; the others lay dead and wounded — not one taken prisoner unless wounded on the field. Sergt. John C. Crattz was the highest officer in the company. All the commissioned officers lay wounded with Gen. Lytle on the hill.

## 'Let us die right here'

### 1st Lieut. Alfred Pirtle
### Aide-de-camp
### Lytle's Brigade, 3rd Division, XX Corps

The sounds of warfare rolled away northward as we again took the road [from Crawfish Springs] in the same direction, while we saw signs of a battle having been there not long before. Along about the time we had been halting for the night, we came to Lee & Gordon's mill and went into bivouac, expecting orders to move to the front at any minute. The afternoon [of September 19] was about half gone when Brig. Gen'l Lytle got orders to take half of his brigade, and guided by the messenger, take the road for a position on the battlefield.

The General immediately selected the regiments that were to fill the order, directed Capt. Grover, the Adjutant of the Brigade, to remain at Lee & Gordon's mill, assisted by me, to stay in camp and carry out, as far as possible, such orders as might come, and soon marched towards the sound of firing. After nightfall, Grover remarked to me that he knew I would keep awake, and therefore he would turn the Headquarters over to me while he got a short nap, promising to give me relief when I was so sleepy that I could not stand it another minute. Even if I had been about dead for sleep, I felt the weight of actually being responsible for the care of the whole camp — so heavy that I sat outside the tent listening for anything that [might] happen. But all was quiet at midnight [when] I woke Grover to let me snatch a few minutes' sleep.

The galloping up of a courier broke my nap, as he said at once that we were to leave as soon as we could and he was to guide us to our destination. Therefore we issued the required orders in the name of General Lytle to break camp and follow Headquarters, which were soon on the road leading to the neighborhood of the Widow Glenn's. In a march of about an hour and a half we reported to General Lytle. The remainder of the Brigade [was] in bivouac near a small log cabin, which we were told was the Headquarters of Maj. Gen'l Rosecrans. Being almost dead for sleep, I threw myself on a blanket near Gen'l Lytle and was at once asleep, awakened only by the noise of the camp which was roused at break of day, to find that the very cool air that ushered in the dawn had made such a dense fog over the waters of Chickamauga Creek that all movements were almost impossible.

Couriers were sent from Army Headquarters just as soon as one could see. Before we had disposed of a snatched breakfast, prisoners under heavy escort arrived on the march to Chattanooga, among whom a bright and brave lieutenant boastingly announced that the men were from Longstreet's Corps, and he spoke it with decided pride: "You fellers will catch hell this morning." This was the first intimation that the men learned of the joining of men from Virginia. This did not worry the rank and file, for we set to work at once to raise breastworks in our front at the Widow Glenn's, commanding our front for quite a distance. As soon as the fog began lifting, firing broke out a long distance to our left, indicating that both armies had begun to push towards Chattanooga.

When the timber breastworks in our front were finished, Gen'l Lytle laid down on a bear skin that Joe Guthrie, a citizen groom, had laid at the foot of a tree in a spot Gen'l Lytle chose as his Headquarters, where he would be convenient to all that was going on. When I returned to his side after carrying some orders, he was at full length on the bear skin, resting all he could, since he had slept almost none the past night. He took out his watch and said, "Just at this time, eleven o'clock, our good sisters are going to church to pray for us, who need their prayers."

We saw Gen'l McCook and his staff gallop away after a brief stop at Army Headquarters, to be soon followed by Maj. Gen'l Philip H. Sheridan and his staff on a like visit. Gen'l Sheridan came to our spot and told us that we would very likely be under fire very soon, because Gen'l Longstreet had joined Bragg late in the afternoon of Saturday, and the enemy was pushing things all along the line. Gen'l Sheridan marched towards the left with the [other] brigades of his Division, just as soon as the word came that they were ready, leaving only our Brigade. Our Gen'l gave orders to his staff to warn the Colonels to have their men ready to march to the left the moment the order came, directing me at the same moment to give the same warning to the Battery of the Brigade, which he had put under my direct care, particularly on the march to this battle.

When I returned to the Widow Glenn's after bearing this order, the Brigade was marching in column of fours rapidly towards the north on the road that ran past the spot. I hurried to the Battery and saw it take the road, then galloped on the side of the road amid clouds of dust towards the right of the command, which was now double-quicking. The head [of column] turned off to the right-hand side of the simple, sandy road, making for the fighting.

The battle seemed to be right with us, for as the regiment I was

■ Brig. Gen. William H. Lytle, commanding the 1st Brigade of Sheridan's division, "was killed, shot in the head while gallantly leading us up the hill to charge the enemy," one of his men lamented. "He was a brave and good man, an accomplished gentleman, and a good Gen. He had by his kindness won the affection of the officers and men of this brigade. He was one of the few of our generals which seemed to realize that soldiers are men. He always treated us as such, reserving only to himself the power which his rank conferred."

In this Bridgeport, Ala. portrait taken a few weeks before his death, Lytle wears a medal designed "in the shape of a Maltese cross of gold, studded with diamonds and emeralds." His former regiment, the 10th Ohio Infantry, made the medal presentation in a "picturesque valley among the Alabama hills, surrounded by his present and his old command, ladies and officers of rank."

■ 2nd Lieut. Charles W. Eaton

■ 1st Lieut. Charles T. Boal

■ 1st Lieut. John M. Turnbull

■ Col. James Findlay Harrison

**Although their commander was killed, every member of Lytle's brigade staff survived Chickamauga and was lauded for "usefulness and recklessness of danger in the performance of duty." Of the four pictured here, Col. J. Findlay Harrison served as a volunteer aide, 2nd Lieut. Charles W. Eaton as aide-de-camp, 1st Lieut. Charles T. Boal as topographical engineer, and 1st Lieut. John M. Turnbull as assistant inspector general. The portraits of Harrison, Eaton and Turnbull were taken in Bridgeport, Ala., just three weeks before the battle by Schwing & Rudd, Army of the Cumberland photographers.**

**In the wake of the brigade's rout, wrote Chaplain William H. Haigh, 36th Illinois, Turnbull desperately tried to rally fleeing comrades. "The lieutenant, after executing Lytle's last order to form a second line, had his horse shot under him. He made all haste to procure another, then rode back to the ridge where we saw him [undertaking] to organize by pressing into the ranks every person that came to the rear. Lieut. Turnbull with his co-workers had gathered two or three hundred men, and it was not long before Gen. Sheridan had quite a force ready and willing to follow him anywhere."**

**While reconnoitering an enemy skirmish line eight months later near Dallas, Ga., Turnbull was shot through the left knee, losing the leg to amputation.**

accompanying debouched from the line of the road, men began falling under the enemy's fire while making the change of formation from column of fours to "company into line." Level space extended a short distance and then the ground rose sharply for a few yards to the break of a hill, that at this moment was occupied by a part of our Brigade, resisting a heavy fire from the enemy. To our left was a level field, from which rose another part of the same ridge we were holding. As soon as I could separate myself from the column, I made my way among the fragments of companies to a point on the ridge held by us, where I saw Gen'l Lytle and most of his staff.

The line was in front of us as we sat on our horses, but it was thin and losing men momentarily, giving our commander increasing anxiety. He sent one of his staff to urge the colonel of a regiment still at the foot of the slight rise to bring up his men. He directed another to bring up a section of the Battery, and place it by hand in the line. This was done, diminishing the fire at once in our front, which had been bad enough — the men only being held in their alignment by the presence of Gen'l Lytle; for if he could stay, they were ashamed to retreat. I have heard that a moment before the fire opened on the men who first formed the line on the ridge, he had said: "Men, we must make a stand right here. We can die but once. Let us die right here." It would seem, if this was true, and I did not hear it, that he felt someone had "blundered," and it was their duty to hold on. Every man must have felt as I did, that we were fighting desperate odds. And yet those men stayed as if every man had grasped the meaning of their General.

The fire reopened, and looking at one of us he said, "For God's sake, bring up another regiment." I thought he was looking at Lieut. Boal, but Boal must not have heard him, and he looked at me, near him. He had just a moment before said to me, as he leaned towards me, "Pirtle, I am hit."

"Are you hit hard, General?" My heart was in my mouth, and I was hardly able to speak.

"In the spine. If I have to leave here, you stay and see that all goes right."

I answered, "I will."

Then came his call for another regiment, as I have said. Lieut. Boal, evidently not having heard the order, I looked at the General and, saluting with my sword, galloped down the hill where Col. Silas Miller of the 36th Illinois was trying very hard while on foot to rally his men, in order to lead them up the slope to reinforce the line there. I found he had better success in making the men understand him dismounted, and I did likewise, rallying the men in groups, starting them towards the front that was very hotly engaged and wavering. The officers as well as the men were doing their best, for everyone realized the enemy were making a desperate attempt to take our position.

Doing all I could to help Col. Miller, I held my horse's bridle in my left hand, urging the soldiers forward by all arguments at my disposal. Amid the increasing confusion, timed shells exploded almost simultaneously by my horse's side, making him frantic, perhaps wounding him, because he reared and broke loose from me, and galloped out of sight in the melee. Just at this instant I saw the big sorrel horse the General had been seated on, rush riderless down the slope, and I knew the General had fallen from

■ Col. Silas Miller, 36th Illinois, succeeded to command of Lytle's brigade amidst the chaotic retreat west toward Missionary Ridge. Taking stock of the brigade's casualties, he found that 55 were killed, 321 wounded and 84 captured or missing. The 21st Michigan's colonel and lieutenant colonel both lost their lives. Miller's own regiment, entering the fight on September 20 with 370 effectives, suffered 20 killed, 101 wounded (15 of these mortally) and 20 missing, while all three field officers had their horses shot beneath them. Rankled by criticism directed at Sheridan's division, he wrote shortly after the battle: "[Sheridan] held his position till he would have been a murderer to have asked [his troops] to try to do so longer."

Nine months later at Kennesaw Mountain, Ga., Miller was wounded in the right shoulder and arm. Taken to a Nashville hospital, he died of gangrene poisoning on July 27, 1864.

■ Rev. William T. O'Higgins, chaplain of the largely Irish Catholic 10th Ohio (two companies were composed of Germans), celebrated Mass in Lytle's honor after his body was returned to Chattanooga. Well known to many Confederate officers for his published poetry, Lytle was removed from the battlefield by men of Deas' brigade and initially interred behind Southern lines. In a letter to Bragg sent October 9, Rosecrans personally requested the body's return. Bragg consented, and his assistant inspector general, Col. Joseph P. Jones, accompanied the uniformless remains to the exchange site on the LaFayette Road. Under a flag of truce, Jones met a small Federal delegation on October 12, turning over a package of Lytle's personal effects and a certificate of identity before an ambulance carried the general away.

him and was dead. I started towards the spot where I had left him, making my ascent in that direction, but the men gave way in a crowd and carried me along with them, so that I knew my commander was gone.

The tide rolled down the little hill, officers and men mingled in great confusion. An officer of our staff, Col. Findlay Harrison, passed me riding the best he could in the mass of retiring men and saw me. To him I shouted in the rush, "Tell my father you saw me, and my address will be Libby Prison!"

"Not by a damned sight," he said as he stopped, dismounted and raised me to the saddle, and ran along going faster than his horse, which had just been wounded. We kept on and reached the foot of the hill, which rose quite a distance above us. As I looked back at this moment I saw the infantry of the enemy had gained some little on us as we scrambled across the bed of a stream, firing as they came, but making no casualties. At the moment I looked again, a squad of them fired at me, being a good mark — a man on horseback. I have always thought that seventeen fired at me. There may not have been so many, but I thought there was, for one ball clipped the mane in front of my left hand, another's wind was felt by my left leg, and a third cut hairs from the horse in front of my legs. And then they walked back and disappeared in the forest. Col. Harrison ran on, soon joining a number of troops resting on the grass, for the chase was over. My horse lasted up to the summit, but very likely died from his wounds.

Gen'l Sheridan, commander of our division, and part of his staff were in the rapidly increasing group of soldiers of the various commands that had been driven from the front. Gen'l Sheridan did not say a word of chiding, directing all to rest, and then to find their companies or regiments right there on the ridge. He handsomely expressed his sympathy for me in the loss of my General, offering me a position as Aide to him until the fate of the Army was settled. Orders were sent to each Brigade to reform where they were, reporting to Division Headquarters as soon as possible, but to rest quietly as they were. The result was that by three o'clock, there were thousands of men ready to take up the march, which we did, following northwardly, proceeding towards Ross[ville] Gap, which we passed through late in the afternoon in perfect military order, [creating the impression that] reinforcements, passing through the Gap, were on the road to the battle still raging. We kept the road and before sundown, reached Cloud's house where the column halted and rested in place for a long time. We then retraced our steps back through Ross' Gap, and went quite a distance out on the flat lands westward, going into bivouac long after dark.

---

The body of Brigadier General Lytle was buried by the enemy with great care, because he had been acquainted for years with many of the Rebel officers. Soon after the Army had become settled in Chattanooga, communication was had with the enemy in regard to sending his body to his friends, yet weeks passed before the arrangements were concluded.

When it was known that the flag of truce was to be sent out, the 10th Ohio Vol. Inf., of which Lytle had been the first Colonel, made preparations to take charge of the remains. They procured a

large hospital tent, leveled off the ground, hung mourning emblems for decorations and erected an altar for the Mass that Father [William T.]O'Higgins, chaplain of the regiment, would say in the presence of the dead. Colonel Joseph W. Burke had selected Lt. [Joseph] Donahue [of Company D], four sergeants and ten men for a Guard of Honor to take charge of the casket, as long as it was unburied. The Guard met the escort at the entrance of the camp of the 10th Ohio and took charge, which they did not relinquish for a moment, night or day, until the casket was placed in Christ Church the noon of the funeral in Cincinnati. The dais on which the casket lay in the tent at Chattanooga had been made by carpenters in the regiment, covered in white, in the center of the tent, but with one of the Guard of Honor on duty over it.

It was very soon known throughout the Army that the remains were in camp, which brought crowds of those who thus showed their estimate of the dead, though they knew the casket was still sealed. The next morning at an early hour, Rev. Father O'Higgins offered Mass in the tent which was crowded, for the 10th Ohio held many Catholics. Appropriate ceremonies attended by a great crowd were later held in the tent, and then the body was formally given in charge of the Guard of Honor.

I had been given ten days' leave of absence from the regiment to accompany the escort to Cincinnati, to represent the General's staff at the funeral. Consequently, I left with the party and went with it to its destination. It was always the case that one of the officers, guards or myself had the casket in sight.

■ Field and staff officers of the 10th Ohio mingle with regimental color bearers in Chattanooga. Recruited entirely from greater Cincinnati, the regiment earned the nickname "Bloody Tinth" during 1861's western Virginia campaigns. After suffering 50 percent casualties at Perryville in October 1862, Rosecrans assigned it to duty as his headquarters and provost guard, where it "rendered efficient and valuable services," at Chickamauga on September 20 "in covering the movement of retiring trains on the Dry Valley Road, and stopping stragglers from the fight." Following Rosecrans' removal a month later, the 10th served at Thomas' headquarters until it mustered out in June 1864.

Col. Joseph W. Burke (fourth from right) assumed regimental command after Lytle's promotion to brigadier general. Burke posed with (from left) Lt. Col. William W. Ward, Adjutant Thomas Patterson, Quartermaster Luke Murrin and Major John E. Hudson. Lieuts. Daniel Twohig and Peter Gepner are at far right.

■ The Lytle Guard of Honor, photographed October 21, 1863 at the Cincinnati gallery of Hoag & Quick's. The escort was composed of an enlisted man from each company of the 10th Ohio, and was accompanied by the general's servant Joseph Guthrie (far left). Lieuts. Joseph Donahue (seated at left) and Alfred Pirtle were jointly in command. Displayed in the background are the 10th's colors with regimental streamer.

Pirtle later recalled: "The Guard of Honor was mounted the moment they came into the rotunda at the Court House, one at the head and one at the foot [of the coffin], each at 'Parade Rest' with his rifle with bayonet fixed, and remaining so motionless until relieved at the end of half an hour, that persons were seen to touch them to see if they were men."

The remains taken from the tent were carefully deposited in a heavy, stong army wagon, because of the dreadful road all the way to Stevenson, Ala., where it was expected the railroad to Nashville would be reached, by which we were to go through that city to Louisville. The old Carnifex colors used by the 10th Ohio at Carnifex, Va., in September 1861 were placed on the casket by the Guard of Honor. The regiment in full equipment was already in line and wheeled into column of companies, the left in front, and took the march for the wharf on the Tennessee River. The band of the 10th Ohio led by Sergeant O'Grady [Principal Musician John O'Gready], Gen'l Lytle's bugler in the old 17th Brigade in 1862, headed the procession; then the regiment with "reversed arms" next; the wagon next surrounded by the Guard of Honor; then followed a horse with mourning housings, and I came on foot, the only member of the staff who could be spared from duty — a solitary mourner. Arriving at the wharf, the regiment wheeled into line, halted and as the wagon passed, presented arms, the colors drooped, the drums rolled — and the "Bloody Tenth" bade goodbye forever to all that was earthly of their beloved commander.

The journey by wagon and rail [passed] in dreadful weather until we reached Nashville Oct. 18th. The Adams Express Company provided here a special car for the party, in which they made the ride to Louisville, where they arrived after dark and were quartered under the direction of Lt. Donahue, while I went to my home at my father's. The remains were housed by an undertaker on 7th Street near Market Street, guarded by the Guard of Honor.

The next morning at a very early hour, Dr. [Nathaniel] Foster [Lytle's brother-in-law] and I went to the spot where the remains lay. They had been undisturbed since they had been disinterred near the Military Hospital at Chattanooga. But we had a two-fold duty to perform, for it had become necessary to change them into the massive and elegant casket sent by the family from the home of the General in Cincinnati. When the moment came to handle the army casket, everybody in the room was sent out save Dr. Foster, myself and the Englishman, Joe Guthrie, who had been the body servant of Lytle for years. We held a close inspection, when we unitedly felt that it was the late General Lytle before us in his underwear that he wore on September 20th, for Guthrie and I had known it well. After a consultation it was agreed that I should order that the final casket would now be used, which was not to be opened again under any circumstances.

Col. Marc Mundy [commanding Post of Louisville] honored us by his proffer of an escort to the boat which was to take us to Cincinnati. Therefore we placed the body in the coffin and thence in a hearse, left the undertaker's, joined the escort and proceeded to the wharf. Dr. Foster, Lt. Donahue and I, occupying a carriage, followed the hearse guarded in military style by the Guard of Honor. The agents of the Adams Express Company met us at the boat, the *Nightingale,* and provided us with the national colors with which to drape the coffin. We placed the honored dead on the forecastle of the boat, stacked the arms of the Guard of Honor at the head and foot, and spread the old Carnifex colors across them. The flag of the steamer was lowered to half mast as the band softly played. We moved slowly from the shore, and for the last time the noble and gallant Lytle left Kentucky, the state he so much loved and where he is so deeply mourned.

## 'Shot through my right wrist'

### Private Thompson P. Freeman
### Company F
### 113th Ohio Volunteer Infantry

At Chickamauga, September 20, Company F, of which I was a member, was on the picket line. Captain Levi T. Nichols was in command, and we were advancing through a cornfield, when "zip, zip" came the bullets from the left, striking the cornstalks on every hand. We were nearing some timber, and by the time we reached it the cannon shots of the enemy were coming from our front, striking the ground sometimes and bounding high in the air, or go crashing through the timber at a dangerous rate. While we lay for a brief time crouched behind trees to cover us from the

■ Lt. Col. Gates P. Thruston, XX Corps' chief of staff, later wrote of the Federal right wing's disintegration: "With a wild yell the Confederates swept on. They seemed everywhere victorious. Rosecrans was borne back in the retreat. Fugitives, wounded, caissons, escort, ambulances thronged the narrow pathways. He concluded that our whole line had given way, that the day was lost, that the next stand must be made at Chattanooga ...

"Riding on, I struck the Dry Valley road running along the east slope of [Missionary] Ridge. Nearby I found Sheridan and [Gen. Jefferson C.] Davis with the remnants of their five brigades. General Phil was furious, *swearing* mad. No wonder he was angry. The devoted Lytle and the truest and bravest had fallen in vain resistance around him. His splendid fighting qualities and his fine soldiers had not had half a chance. He had lost faith ...

"I tried to halt the rear of the column, but without success. The miseries of a mounted officer trying to pass marching infantry on a narrow roadway can be well imagined. Time was precious. I rode furiously through the thicket, alongside, and appealed to officers. 'See Jeff, Colonel?' they said; 'See Phil?' Some old trudger in the ranks called out, 'We'll talk to you, my son, when we get to the Ohio River!' "

■ Members of Company D, 113th Ohio, entered the fight on Horseshoe Ridge as unbloodied troops, like many in Steedman's division. Sergeant Jasper N. Hall, Company E, recalled the carnage: "Reaching the summit, we met the enemy in overwhelming numbers. Now came the tug of war. Grape, canister, shot, shell and other death-dealing projectiles made of our ranks a harvest of death. Shells and cannonballs were doing their deadly work, cutting trees and large branches which, in their fall, sent consternation and sometimes death into our ranks. One limb in its fall killed two men. Our division was occupying the brow of a hill, with orders to hold it to the very last moment. The men hugged the ground, loading and firing continually, each man as fast as he could. We held our position till nearly sundown. Nearly half the men in our company and the regiment were killed, wounded or missing."

enemy, more than one incident took place among the men of the company. One of them, whose reputation for bravery had been below par, shook as with a chill, and whimpered: "I never thought I would come to this; how I wish I was at home." In subsequent actions he distinguished himself for bravery and soldierly bearing.

The cannonading ceased, and our company resumed its place in the regiment, capturing two prisoners who had hid in a hollow. After we returned and had taken our place, the troops in front of us were ordered to charge the enemy in our front, while our line was ordered to lie down at the foot of the hill. Almost immediately we were ordered to charge over the same ground, and, as we advanced on double quick, we met the first line falling back, having been overpowered by the enemy. Many of these were falling as they came, and it seemed to me they were being killed by our fire.

I determined not to fire until I got a fair view of a Johnnie. I waited but a moment, for off to the left oblique I saw a rebel step from behind a tree, at the distance of twenty-five or thirty yards, and point his gun in the direction where I stood. I drew up my gun, aiming at his whole body, intending to hit him somewhere, but my gun snapped and refused to fire. I tried a second cap, and it snapped. Seeing that my left-hand comrade was shot, I took up his gun and discharged it at the rebel at the tree.

Presently I observed that there was no one at my immediate left, and was on the point of turning back, thinking I was alone, when I heard Lieutenant [James L.] Wheelock give the command:

"Stand up to them, boys; don't give an inch!" Turning to my right, I found the rest of the company completely in line and doing desperate work. I now began to reload my gun, and in doing so I received a musket shot through my right wrist, completely disabling me from further duty. Lieutenant Wheelock was shot through the lungs about the same time, from the effects of which he died the next day.

I now attempted to leave the field, dragging my gun with me with my left hand. I at length abandoned my gun, and went to the rear to find a surgeon. I soon found one, and was about speaking to him, when a shell of the enemy exploded uncomfortably near us. He suggested that we had better get beyond the range of those guns, and I agreed with him. We hurried off, crossing a ravine and halting behind a tree. Having two handkerchiefs, I bound one tightly around my wrist and made the other into a sling to support my wounded arm. I made an effort to go on and find an ambulance, but in doing so I fainted and fell. The fall, together with the voice of a comrade near by, revived me so that I got up, and, standing against a tree, soon recovered so as to be able to go on in search of an ambulance. I was advised to go to the field hospital, but after a fruitless effort to find it, I set out to return to our former camp, which I reached about sundown. I had walked seven miles and was exhausted from fatigue and loss of blood.

Going to a spring near by, I sat down with the intention of bathing and dressing my wound, when a couple of Indiana soldiers came along, and, learning that I was wounded, one of them bathed and dressed my wound quite skillfully, and I then learned for the first time the dangerous character of my injury. The hand was almost severed from the arm by a minnie ball. At the regiment to which these two men belonged I drank some coffee and felt much refreshed.*

■ Private George Weber of Company C, 113th Ohio, fell wounded on Horseshoe Ridge but managed to escape capture. One of his comrades, Private Francis M. McAdams, Company E, wrote in his journal: "We advanced and fell back by turns until sundown, when our ammunition becoming exhausted, we were compelled to quit the field and leave many of our dead and wounded in the hands of our enemy. The air was thick with smoke, and the trees seemed to bend and reel before the storm of lead and iron. Under all this we stood as sheep before the slaughter, only yielding when ammunition was out. Our regiment's loss is: killed, 27; wounded, 98; missing, 66. We fell back ... pretty well fagged out. When we left the field our Company numbered only eight men."

Weber recovered and transferred to the Veteran Reserve Corps in April 1864.

## 'Our double shots of canister'

### Unknown enlisted man
### Battery M
### 1st Illinois Light Artillery

We reached the field about 6 p.m. on the 19th, going on the trot and gallop a portion of the way from Rossville. We put our guns in position in some heavy timber on a slight hill, guns pointing to the northwest about in the direction of Chattanooga.

A little after sunrise of the 20th the infantry about us advanced into the bush to the northeast, and we followed. After traveling about for some time we finally emerged from the woods and halted at a corner of a field. A more pleasant, tranquil morning, sky more clear, I cannot recall. The men amused themselves by cracking walnuts, writing and playing cards, until just at 9 o'clock we

* Freeman escaped capture and four days after the battle entered Cumberland Hospital in Nashville. Two months later he returned home to Ohio to convalesce, and was discharged April 25, 1864. Despite several diagnoses recommending amputation, his hand was saved.

■ 2nd Lieut. A. Piatt Andrew III, 21st Indiana Battery, commanded a section of two Napoleon guns on September 20 that helped repel a late-morning assault by part of Maj. Gen. Patrick R. Cleburne's division just south of the Kelly Field. Nearby, Andrew's cousin, an 87th Indiana lieutenant, was shot through the head and killed. Shortly after the battle, the artillery officer wrote home: "I passed through both days' fight without a scratch. Indeed, I cannot boast of even a hole in my clothes. Several balls passed as close as was agreeable to have them, but they had sufficient respect not to touch me. Joking aside, I am satisfied never to see another battle. Descriptions can give you no idea of the misery which one witnesses in such a place. And yet, so soon does one become hardened to such sights, one scarcely notices the dead and dying. In some instances, I had to be continually on the watch, lest in our movings the wheels should crush some dead or dying friend or foe. So frequently were such scenes presented, that they excited no feeling. No time, too, was allowed *for feeling.*"

heard a sudden roar of musketry to the east and southeast, apparently about a mile distant. There were no distinct, separate shots. It was a sheet, solid at that, of roaring noise. In half a minute the belching of cannon was heard, and in less than a minute that too became a solid roar.

In a few minutes Gen. Gordon Granger, who was near our battery, gave the command to move forward. As we advanced and halted by turns we saw a column of cavalry to the northeast marching to the east, as we were. It was about a mile distant. I spoke to Gen. Granger about it, telling him it was rebel cavalry, but the General said it must be ours; but the truth was disclosed when, about 11 a.m., shells came in very lively from the north where the cavalry had entered the timber. Gen. Granger had us take position on a slight elevation on open ground and train our guns on the battery, which was so far back in the underbrush that we could only locate it by the smoke as it arose above the brush. They had splendid range on our position, and every shell came as close as we desired. One passed through the horse of our orderly sergeant on the instant he dismounted. Gen. Granger sighted one of our guns, but as he did so a shell passed only a few inches above his head. He mounted his horse and said: "Follow me. I have work for you in another place."

We limbered up and followed him along the edge of the brush to the westward for about a quarter of a mile, when we halted on quite an elevated plateau, the ground to the east being about 40 feet lower and cleared for over half a mile. Off to the east in the opening we could see a few of our men walking over the field, and there were patches of smoke as though many men had been engaged clearing a field and had been burning many piles of logs. One log house was also on fire. There was no firing going on, and we lay about on the ground until, precisely at 2 o'clock, Gen. Steedman gave the command to stand to arms and then started up the slightly inclining ridge, going southward into heavy timber, but the trees were so far apart that we had no trouble in moving freely along with our guns and caissons.

The infantry straggled along on both sides and among our guns. The rebels gave an unearthly yell and came charging toward us from the east over another rise of ground. There was a little underbrush among the trees, but not enough to obscure the view or obstruct free action. Our infantry immediately, as if by magic, were in line and countercharging. Gen. Steedman, who was at the head of the column, wheeled his horse and came flashing back, yelling as loud as he could: "Halt! Halt! For God's sake, men, halt!"

He swung his black hat and swayed his body as he urged his horse on through the men until he reached a flag, which he grabbed, and wheeling his horse, facing to the west, waved the flag frantically, continually yelling "Halt!" Finally the infantry halted, and he ordered them to right face and marched them calmly up the ridge until we reached the end of it, where our battery took position, the 121st Ohio, Col. [Henry B.] Banning commanding, supporting us on the left flank.

Seven times [Longstreet's] men charged up to and a little over the summit of the ridge next to us that afternoon; but even his men could not stand up against our double shots of canister, and we held the ridge until dusk — two of our guns being out of ammunition a portion of the time.

## 'The earth trembled beneath our feet'

**Private Henry H. Eby**
**Company C**
**7th Illinois Cavalry**
**Staff orderly**
**Palmer's Division, XIV Corps**

By the evening of the 19th the battle was well under way, and during the night many changes were made in our lines. Gen. [John M.] Palmer's division took position in the woods on a long, low ridge extending north and south, and a short distance east from the Kelly field, which also extended north and south. During the night of the 19th a line of temporary defenses was constructed with old logs, trees and stones, or anything that would answer the purpose. These breastworks were from two to three feet in height, making very good protection for the infantry while they were lying down.

During the morning [of the 20th], when the battle was momentarily expected to open, Gen. Palmer was standing in rear of the temporary defenses, inspecting them, and the infantry were lying on the ground behind them awaiting the attack, when some of them were peering over the top of a log which composed the upper portion of the defenses looking in the direction of the enemy, trying to discover their position. Everything was as still as death, when an enemy's bullet struck the log, knocking off a large splinter and sending it whizzing through the air. The General, seeing what happened, cried out, "Down with your head, my man, you have got only one head and you may want to use that in a minute." In an instant several more bullets came over, passing

■ A ragged Confederate battle line in the woods at Chickamauga. When provided with fields of fire, Federal artillery cut great swaths in assaulting infantry, as recorded by two Southern officers who survived horrible wounds on September 20. "Every officer and man in my company who went into the fight was killed, wounded or struck with a ball," wrote Capt. John H. Martin of Company D, 17th Georgia. "While trying to capture a flag I was shot through my under jaw, the bones of both sides being crushed, from the effects of which I never recovered."

Far worse off was Capt. John M. Sloan of Company G, 45th Mississippi, who recalled: "When in command of my company in front of the enemy's lines, and under a heavy fire of shot and shell, I had the misfortune of having my under jaw, upper teeth and part of my tongue shot away, and my face terribly mutilated by the explosion of a shell." At Ringgold three days later, Sloan's chin was removed and his nose sewn back to his face. Unable to chew, for the next 30 years he was fed fluids while lying on his back.

■ Maj. Gen. John M. Palmer commanded the 2nd Division of Crittenden's XXI Corps. Ordered to retire from the Kelly Field shortly before 5 p.m. on September 20, Palmer watched the systematic withdrawal of his 1st Brigade. He later wrote: "I saw the Rebels cross from our late defenses, and, to my regret, a Rebel battery approached within four hundred yards of where I sat on my horse, at the foot of a large dead pine tree. As the Rebel fire seemed aimed at [the brigade's] flank, I expected that soon a shot would enfilade [its] line with terrible slaughter. While completely absorbed in the scene before me ... my horse sunk to the ground, and I fell at the foot of the tree. I was at once conscious that my hat had fallen off, and that my hair, mouth, eyes and collar were filled with some soft substance, but what it was I could not, for a moment, blinded as I was, even guess. I arose to my feet, cleared my eyes and then found that a shot from the Rebel battery had struck the dead pine, a piece from the tree had probably fallen upon my horse and prostrated him, and had, at the same time, covered me with the soft, rotten wood."

through the folds of the General's pants. One of the boys seeing what took place looked at the General and said: "General, down with your legs, you have only one pair of them and you may want to use them in a minute." In an instant all was confusion, and the bullets were coming over almost as thick as hail, and I think there was use for heads and legs.

The battle in our front began in the morning about nine o'clock, and raged fiercely at intervals during nearly the whole day and along Snodgrass Hill until after dark. The Confederates charged Palmer's front repeatedly, but were as often repulsed. Some parts of the Union lines were broken by the enemy during the day and our prospects for success appeared rather discouraging.

During the day, while Gen. Palmer and myself were riding from one part of the line to another, his horse was struck just over one eye by a bullet, which stunned him and he fell to the ground. The General, being in a hurry to reach another part of our line, asked me to let him ride my horse, to which I consented and remained with his, which soon recovered, regained his feet, and apparently was all right again. The General returned and gave me my horse, and we mounted and rode away to another part of the line, where he wished to give some directions. The infantry were lying behind their low breastworks, and the gunners of the artillery were alert near their guns awaiting the attack. The General had just dismounted in rear of the line of battle, and I was on my horse near by waiting for orders, when the enemy made another terrific movement on our line. Immediately our artillery bellowed with a deafening roar, sending forth its terrible missiles of destruction among the enemy, who when coming within rifle range received also the fire from our infantry, from whose long lines burst forth a sheet of flame; and the Confederates were repulsed with heavy loss. Their bullets came over at a fearful rate; at times it seemed as though they came as thick as if one would take a handful of shelled corn and scatter it broadcast. The roar of firearms from friend and foe was deafening, and it seemed as if the earth trembled beneath our feet.

The General was standing, talking to some of the officers. He turned toward me, saying: "Eby, you should not expose yourself unnecessarily. You would better dismount and step behind a tree while you are waiting for orders." I immediately obeyed the General's suggestion with a good will. The firing in our front ceased at times, but we could hear the incessant roar of musketry and artillery off at our right and rear, we being on the left. It seemed to move off farther and farther, until it sounded as though it were a mile away. Then in a few moments it would begin again nearer to us, and again roll off gradually in the distance. Thus the afternoon wore slowly away ...

Late in the afternoon the heaviest firing seemed to be shifting toward that part of the line of battle adjacent to Snodgrass Hill, where the enemy was concentrating its best forces, trying hard to turn our right flank and get possession of the road leading to Chattanooga. They could thereby sever our communications with the latter place and the North, and they came very near accomplishing their object. They attacked Gen. Thomas' line repeatedly and as often were repulsed with heavy loss, Gen. Thomas holding his position.

Being a mounted orderly on Gen. Palmer's staff, my duties were

■ Four batteries were attached to Palmer's division at Chickamauga, two of them belonging to the 4th U.S. Artillery and commanded by the officers pictured here. Above, 1st Lieut. Harry C. Cushing, Battery H, was heavily engaged on both days of the battle, his four Napoleon guns and two 12-pounder howitzers moving frequently to support brigades in three different divisions. Battery M, consisting of four 24-pounder howitzers under 1st Lieut. Francis L.D. Russell (left), fought wheel-to-wheel with Battery H for a while near the Brotherton House on September 19. Combined, Cushing's and Russell's men expended 1,271 rounds during the battle, much of it canister and short-fused case shot fired at close range.

One of Palmer's brigade commanders, Col. William Grose, praised both young officers in his after-action report: "Those lieutenants, although they look like mere boys, yet for bravery and effective service they are not excelled if equalled in efficiency by any artillerists in the army. They have the credit of being in the last of the fighting, and then retiring with but the loss of one piece of Lieutenant Cushing's that had been disabled during the engagement."

A Maryland native, Cushing remained in the Regular Army and retired as a major in 1895. Russell, who early in the war served as a private in Duryee's 5th New York Zouaves, died May 11, 1864.

■ 1st Lieut. John M. Sutphen commanded Company D, 90th Ohio, during the withdrawal of Palmer's division from Kelly Field. Being the last of Gen. Charles Cruft's brigade to leave, the regiment soon absorbed Confederate musketry in its rear and artillery fire in the flank. Victory-flushed Southerners jumped over the just-vacated breastworks and rushed for the vulnerable Ohioans. When shells began screaming over and into the column, many in the 90th broke and ran, although a good percentage of the projectiles failed to explode. Still, 15 members of the regiment were captured, the adjutant and a company commander were killed, and Sutphen was slightly wounded. Cited by the 90th's colonel for "coolness, fortitude and bravery," he was promoted captain of Company D to date from New Year's Day 1864.

to go where ordered, carrying messages from one part of the army to another. Gen. Palmer's division held its position during the day, and just about the time that the battle closed, which was near the close of the day, it was withdrawn. A short time before its withdrawal Gen. Palmer and staff, including myself and two other members of Co. C, rode away from the line of battle across the Kelly field toward the woods beyond. But before reaching the woods we came to an old-fashioned rail fence, and just as the fence was reached a heavy artillery fire was opened upon us. The shots struck nearly lengthwise of the fence, cutting and splintering the rails and throwing the pieces about us in every direction, frightening our horses so that we were prevented from crossing the fence as soon as we desired.

I had no objection to rails but preferred to have them remain in the fence. The General and staff managed to cross the fence in advance just about the time that the battery opened fire upon us, and rode into the woods, where we lost sight of them. Two other comrades and myself were yet at the fence, trying to cross and follow the rest of the group, which was our duty to do. We finally succeeded, and also rode into the woods in search of the General but he had gained some distance on us and we failed to find him. We continued the search until, becoming somewhat discouraged and night closing in upon us, we stopped and held a council of war, trying to determine in which direction to go. My two comrades started off in a different direction from the one taken by myself, and reached the Union lines in safety. I went in the direction in which I expected to find Palmer's division, thinking that I would be all right.

It had now become quite dark, and I soon arrived at the place where I expected to find Palmer's troops, and suddenly came to a long line of stacked guns, which could be seen by the aid of some small camp-fires beyond, and on approaching them saw some men between myself and the fire, near the guns. Some were standing, some sitting and others lying on the ground. I learned I was now inside the main line of the Confederate army.

It being nighttime I was unable to see distinctly what was before me and the reader can imagine my predicament. As I proceeded on farther a voice near me called out "Halt!" which I obeyed. I was able to see some object just ahead of my horse, but was unable to tell what it was. In a few seconds I discovered two men near my horse's head. One called out, "Surrender, here, get off your horse," which I proceeded to do, as they had the muzzles of their guns uncomfortably close to my face. And now my goose was cooked.

I never obeyed orders more promptly, and did not stop to argue the case with them nor ask whether their guns were loaded. There was not the smallest chance to escape, as I now found myself surrounded by quite a number of the enemy, about ten to one. The two Confederates who captured me quarreled, each claiming my sabre and revolver. My sabre was one we had captured from a Confederate lieutenant at the battle of Stone River, and was a beauty.

Little did I care which one got them. I was a prisoner of war under guard and obliged to comply with all orders, no matter what they were. In a few moments I was conducted under guard

to some commissioned officer's headquarters for inspection. Before starting I took my pup tent from my saddle, hung it over my shoulder, and bade good-bye to my faithful horse, rubbing my hand down over her honest face as we parted. But now at our final separation came over me a more piercing sense of the loss of my honest four-footed friend, that was always so willing and ready to do her duty. We had endured together [for two years] the perils of the battle, the scout, the outpost picket and the skirmish; also the hardships of the march through mud and slush, the courier service, and many gripings of hunger which we had shared together. Now at last our paths separated. I was retired from actual service to become a prisoner, and she bore her new rider away to battle against her old friends. It was a sad parting. *

■ An early post-war view of the Kelly House and cornfield, looking slightly north of east from the Lafayette Road. About 5 p.m. on September 20, just as two of Palmer's brigades began extricating themselves from breastworks at the background tree line, Henry D. Clayton's Alabama brigade charged north through the corn stubble. Half of Palmer's troops retired in good order; those closest to the Confederates, according to Clayton, were sent "fleeing in wild disorder across [the] large open field ... many taking refuge in and around a hospital (Kelly's house)."

The 38th Alabama, under fire for the first time at Chickamauga, captured 200 Federals besides those found wounded at the house. Over the two-day fight, nearly 1,250 muskets, 640 sets of accouterments and 20,000 cartridges were picked up from the battlefield by Clayton's men.

* Gen. Palmer commended Eby, the only enlisted man mentioned by name, in his lengthy report 10 days after the battle: "Private Eby, Seventh Illinois Cavalry, remained with me all day as orderly, but at the close of the battle on Sunday was wounded[sic] and fell into the hands of the enemy." Eby was confined at Libby and Belle Isle prisons in Richmond, Va., before being taken to Danville, Va., where he escaped on January 22, 1864. Recaptured a week later, he was returned to Belle Isle and exchanged on March 14, 1864. He rejoined his regiment at Memphis, Tenn., in late May.

■ Private John T. Coxe of Company B, 2nd South Carolina Infantry, enlisted six months to the day before his regiment's fight on September 20. Soon after the last volleys died away, he joined comrades feasting on captured rations, and recalled: "We were very hungry and tired, and at once went for the full haversacks and knapsacks of the Federals. They were full of such 'goodies' as ground old government Java coffee, crackers, ham, sugar, canned beef and other good things. We ate ravenously of everything right away ... It is hardly to be believed that we could sit there around blazing fires consuming those welcome provisions and talking about various ordinary matters while the dead and dying lay all about us, but such was the actual case."

## 'We raised a great Rebel shout'

### Private John T. Coxe
### Company B
### 2nd South Carolina Volunteer Infantry

Sunday, September 20, 1863, [was] a lovely day, though cold and frosty in the early morning. Everything was quiet till about 8 a.m., when the ball of battle opened suddenly on the wooded heights beyond the river, and immediately we began to cross the river on the debris of the burned [Alexander's] bridge. The fire of both armies was continuous and very heavy. Clearing the river our brigade, in column, continued in the old road up grade with cleared land on both sides up to the Alexander dwelling house, where we halted a little while. In the bottom land to the right, along and down the river on that side, we saw a large body of cavalry maneuvering and were told they were Forrest's men.

We were at the foot of the hill on which the battle was raging. Here our column turned sharply to the left on a road going around the Alexander house, marched a quarter mile, halted and right faced in line of battle. Then pretty soon our line was ordered forward through thick woods up the hill. The great thunder of battle was heard higher up the hill in our front and left front. We rushed along and soon met many Federal prisoners and our own wounded going to the rear. We heard much cheering, and the noise of battle seemed to be receding on the left. We also saw some captured artillery going to the rear. Coming to a road with a house and field on our left, we saw many evidences of recent fighting. Here some of Longstreet's mounted officers slightly changed our course to the right. Advancing still in line of battle through the woods, we soon came in contact with some of Hood's men, who told us that they had been fighting hard since early morning and that Hood had been killed. This was a mistake; he was severely wounded, losing a leg, but survived.

After awhile we came to a long and wide field, and to the left we saw some of our batteries in the same field firing into a hill in their front. We also saw the smoke of a burning house in the woods on our right front. Here in the edge of the woods we changed front north, got under fire and then left-flanked into the big field. As we did so, we met about two captured Federal batteries and caissons coming down from the wooded ground on the opposite side of the field. The Federal prisoners captured with the guns were still mounted and driving the batteries and caissons off the field under Confederate guards.

It was about noon when we flanked into the field and heard from a party of jubilant officers that the center and right wing of the Federal army had been smashed and driven from the field. Although our throats were parched, we raised a great Rebel shout. But when we got well into the field and faced north, we saw something that looked ugly. There, facing us, was a Federal line of battle much longer than our own line. We could see no other Confederate troops near us, although we knew [Brig. Gen. Benjamin] Humphreys' brigade of our division was somewhere to our right in the woods. But we lost no time. Gen. Kershaw gave immediate orders to advance and attack the Federals in our front, and the whole brigade did so enthusiastically. After one volley the

Federals gave way and fell back up a sort of knob, which was the north end of the field. The top of this knob was covered by dense woods, which went back a short distance to a depression, on the bottom of which an old road ran east and west. From the north side of the old road another and higher wooded hill rose up, and this we learned afterwards was called "Snodgrass Hill," famous as being the scene of the hardest, longest and most bloody part of the battle of Chickamauga.

The brigade lost several men in this field, including Private [Elias F.] Beacham of our company, severely wounded. The Federals rallied and reformed at the edge of the woods on the top of the knob and waved their flags at us as if to say: "Come on." We were already going on with cheers. My regiment, the 2nd, was on the left of the brigade, and as we rushed up the slope in a shower of bullets, we saw a ravine on the left as if it ran around to the rear of the knob. Seeing this, Lieutenant Colonel [Franklin] Gaillard, then in command, flanked our regiment into and up the ravine at double quick, at the same time saying: "Let us get behind those fellows up there and capture them." But the Federals were too alert for the success of our effort, and when we rejoined the other regiments a little beyond the knob we saw the Federal line double quicking in full retreat up the south face of Snodgrass Hill. We charged right after them through the woods and drove them back to the top of the ridge, where we found they were protected by fallen timber. They launched a withering fire of grape and canister and rifle balls against us from behind the logs, and then we withdrew half way back down the hill to the depressed road. Thus protected from the terrific fire from the top of the hill, we lay down in the road.

Meanwhile the battle was raging to right and left, and for awhile we enjoyed a nice breeze passing through the woods, now and then blowing from the trees bunches of yellow leaves, which gently sailed down and settled on the ground among us. In my mind I compared these falling leaves to the falling men on that battle field. But we did not enjoy the protection of that depressed old road for long, because the Federals launched a charge down the hill against, or rather upon us. But we had sufficient notice of their coming to be ready for them. Our officers commanded us to hold our fire till they got in short range and then "give it to them." Here they came armed with Colt repeating rifles and a shout. They were allowed to get within twenty yards of our position in the thick undergrowth along the road, then, before they visualized our presence, we rose up as one man and poured into them such a volley from our faithful Enfields as to make many of them bite the dust for the last time, while many more fell badly wounded. The remnant staggered back up the hill as we closely pursued them with the hope of breaking up and capturing their line at the top. But we were met by such a terrific fire of grape, canister and spherical case from their cannon and bullets from their quick-firing rifles from behind log fortifications, that we ourselves were compelled to fall back over the brow of the hill for protection, though we didn't go back all the way to the old road. Neither did the Federals dare sally out from their works any more.

Meanwhile, reinforcements were steadily arriving on both sides, and a crashing fire was kept up on both sides for some time. Then

■ Private George T. Eisele of Company B, 10th Mississippi, was cited by his regimental commander for conspicuous bravery during a mid-afternoon assault aimed at the 21st Ohio on Horseshoe Ridge. Covered by artillery fire and smoke from brushfires ignited by the bursting shells, Eisele and his comrades twice charged uphill — the second time to within 15 yards of the Federal battle line — before reeling back in the face of the Ohioans' Colt's rifles. Their firepower caused Lt. Col. James Barr to report in error that the Mississippians were "compelled to retire by vastly superior numbers." Before running out of ammunition, Barr's own muskets became "so choked the men were compelled to force the balls home by hammering the ends of their ramrods against trees."

■ Capt. Isaac Cusac of Company G, 21st Ohio, was wounded in the left hand shortly before dusk on Horseshoe Ridge. In the confusion preceding the regiment's surrender, Cusac's outnumbered comrades heard voices calling from the hillside below their position, followed by volleys and wild cheering. "During one of these close encounters," recalled Private Abel Comstock of Company C, "a great, long, lank Johnnie in a butternut suit threw down his gun, threw up his hands and ran into our line yelling, 'I surrender! Don't shoot! I surrender!' I should say he was a man of thirty or thirty-five years of age, dark and swarthy ...

"This man turned and looked over our line in great surprise and said: 'Good God! Whar's all yo men?' He was told he could see for himself; he then said, 'If they all knew how few we were, yo all wouldn't last five minutes; they all think there is a whole division massed on this line.' "

we looked to the left and, at a little distance, saw another brigade in line of battle advancing up the same ridge. Then our brigade was shifted to the left so as to connect with this other advancing brigade, and at the same time other troops shifted from the right and took our place. Then our brigade and that on our left charged up the hill. We were met by a heavy fire of both arms, but held our ground. Many of our men fell here, including one of my messmates, John Pickett, badly wounded in the head by a piece of bursting shell. Soon after this we saw that the brigade on our left began to fall back down the hill, and the firing on our front practically ceased for awhile; but to the right and left we could still hear the thunder of battle.

The sun was getting near the setting point, but our immediate fight went on, though in a desultory way, because it was then known that the Federal force on the hill was so surrounded that it could not escape. The battle was already won on all other parts of the field, where the Federal center had been pierced and his right wing crushed, and the main Federal army was in full retreat back toward Chattanooga. At dusk we dropped down to our first position on the old road, and soon after dark the Federals above us "threw in the sponge," surrendered without terms, and as prisoners of war were marched down through our lines, where already bright fires were burning and lighting up the wooded hill and the pale and bloody forms of the dead and dying of both sides. It turned out that we had killed more of the Federals than we thought we had.

## 'Our Colt Revolving Rifles repulsed every attack'

### Capt. Isaac Cusac
### Company G
### 21st Ohio Volunteer Infantry

In the night of the 20th the Confederates had moved to the left, and there appeared to be no enemy in our front. It was some time after sunrise before we had any orders, then we were ordered to move to the rear and to the left. The brigade moved to the rear until it reached the Dyer farm, and there formed in close columns by companies and marched to the left, or north, through the farm until we reached what is known as the Snodgrass house, at the east end of the ridge. The house is a small one, and there were several peach trees standing near. A road passes through this farm on the east side of the house, running in a northwest direction. The 21st Regiment was deployed on this road, directly east of this house, with the right reaching to the south end of the lane and near the woods.

At that time there was severe fighting going on between three and four hundred yards to the southeast of our line. We could see the Federal troops moving to the left, and we were expecting to have to fight where we were at that time. We threw down the fences on the east of us and placed the rails so as to protect us from the balls of the enemy. Soon after we had arranged the fence to suit us, we were ordered away from our position (and were detached from our brigade), and saw no more of the brigade that day. We were marched by the right flank out of the lane and moved in a southwesterly direction in the woods, about one-fourth of a mile southwest of the Snodgrass house. There we met, as we supposed, a part of Brannan's division retreating in great disorder.

The first man I saw that I recognized was Colonel [Moses B.] Walker of the 31st Regiment O.V.I., who was making a great effort to stop the broken lines. As he noticed the 21st move in, he rode up to us and said, "21st stand firm and adamant. This line must be stopped right here." We remained there but a short time and then moved to the south, down the slope of the ridge to a flat, or low piece of ground at the foot of said ridge. Although we had to fight our way down the ridge, the enemy appeared very careful and slow to attack us, as though they did not know what was in their front. Our position in the flat not being a very good one, we fell back on the ridge in good order and formed our line along the south crest of the ridge. It was now about eleven o'clock. We saw no Union troops on that part of the ridge at that time, except a part of a battery that was placed near us on our left.

We had been on the ridge but a short time when the enemy made a desperate attack on us, but was repulsed. Again and again did they attempt to drive us from the ridge, but we were not to be moved by lead or demon-like yells, but we lay close to the ground and with our Colt Revolving Rifles repelled and repulsed every attack. About one o'clock p.m. some troops came in on our right, and the 22d Michigan charged over us as we lay on the ground, but only remained in front of us a short time when they fell back over us. The enemy then followed up and made a desperate effort to break through our lines. The enemy's loss must have been very heavy as they came near us, and we kept up a constant and terrific fire on them, compelling them to fall back. About this time a regiment formed on our left and did some good work, but later in the day they disappeared.

Sometime in the afternoon a regiment came in our rear and laid down and began firing over us, their balls passing very near our men. We feared they would kill some of our men. I requested those in the rear of my company to cease firing, or else to raise up and fire.

The 21st held [its] position amidst showers of bullets, shot and shell, until sundown, when we were out of ammunition and could not get any. The regiment then moved to the rear a few rods into a hollow, where we were then secure from the fire of the enemy. While in this position I was standing in front of the regiment, when a Colonel (whom I was unable to recognize) rode up to me somewhat excited, saying to me, "Move those men up on the line." I said to him, "Colonel, we have no more ammunition." His reply to me was, "It does not make a God damn bit of difference. Have the men fix bayonets and hold that line."

The language and the manner that the command was given in stirred up my "Irish" blood, and I said to him, "Go and talk with the officer in command." He then rode to the rear of the regiment where Major [Arnold] McMahon was, and gave him the same orders, though not in the same language. Then the Major gave orders to fix bayonets, which was promptly obeyed, but when the order was given to "forward march," not a man moved. About that time some of the men on our right shouted, "Boys, do not leave us!" and when the second command was given, every man moved forward on double quick, and was met by a most murderous fire

■ Sergeant Isaac N. Dunafin of Company E, 21st Ohio, yielded to overwhelming numbers after his comrades ran out of cartridges. Their Confederate captors, wrote another Ohio prisoner, soon "commenced an active trade with our boys for canteens, haversacks, &c., which was kept up all along the road until we stopped for the night. Our boys and the rebs were immediately on the best of terms recounting to each other their various adventures during the fight. Although hungry, thirsty and tired, we were marched from one headquarters to another until midnight, when we came to Chickamauga creek. Here we were allowed to satisfy our thirst, and wash the caked powder from our lips and faces. Up to this time it would have been hard to tell whether we were not some of 'Uncle Sam's' contrabands."

Dunafin never returned to his regiment. His death as a prisoner remains unrecorded.

■ Major Arnold McMahon, 21st Ohio, assumed regimental command after Lt. Col. Dwella M. Stoughton was shot through the shoulder by a sharpshooter during the afternoon of September 20. Ordered to hold his position at all hazards, McMahon was remembered by his men as a strict disciplinarian who knew no fear.

Twenty years after the battle, he repaid the tribute: "The private soldier who obeyed orders (all did not) and stood there to be shot down, with an empty gun in his hand, when there was seemingly no reason in such a cause, is the equal of any officer in courage and discipline. No men could have done better than the ten line officers who under the most discouraging circumstances held the few soldiers who remained at the last in line of battle until they were crushed out together and captured (only one officer disobeyed orders and left his company and ran away before the last grand charge was made). An empty gun and an empty belly and a thirsty mouth are not promoters of courage. Backbone will accomplish a good deal and our men must have had it to remain on that field as they did."

# 'Our ammunition began to fail'

**Colt's revolving rifles played a critical role in the defense of Horseshoe Ridge on the afternoon of September 20. A five-chambered cylinder in these rifles gave many in the 21st Ohio a rapid-fire advantage over their Confederate adversaries, which enabled them to hold largely superior numbers at bay until ammunition was exhausted.**

**Private Elbridge G. Wetmore of Company K recalled: "The 21st Ohio went into battle that morning with 517 men, 24 officers and 12 non-combatants; 342 men were armed with revolving rifles [caliber .56], 175 men were armed with Enfield rifles [caliber .577]; there were 43,550 rounds of ammunition expended — 90 rounds each to the revolving rifles and nearly 75 rounds each to the Enfields."**

**Another member of the 21st wrote: "Later on in the afternoon, our ammunition began to fail. The cartridge boxes of the dead and wounded were searched, and even the Enfield cartridges were tried, but proved too large."**

**Major Arnold McMahon pointed out a serious disadvantage of the Colt's. "The diversity of calibers in our arms caused us great trouble in that battle," he remembered. "Attempts to use cartridges caliber .58 in rifles caliber .57 burst the gun. Cartridges caliber .57 burst Colt's revolving rifle caliber .56. The continued firing without means to clean Colt's rifle choked the cylinder so that it would not revolve. It was no uncommon thing for the men to clean their guns with their own urine. This might not be called cleaning. However, the moisture removed the burnt powder so that the guns would work."**

■ Private Joseph Harding of Company H, 31st Ohio, poses defiantly with a Colt's rifle, characterized by its revolving cylinder. Never issued to his regiment, the Colt's probably was acquired by Harding at his own expense.

which killed and wounded many of our men, myself being wounded in my left hand.

When we reached the line on the ridge a short distance to the right of where we were at sundown, we fell to the ground and remained in that position until dark. The enemy could have undoubtedly driven us from the ridge at any time after sundown, as the three regiments that held that part of the line were all out of ammunition. But they had a better thing on us by lying still in front, while a part of their forces swung around to the rear of us, shutting us in. This they did in good shape, taking in the 22d Michigan, the 89th Ohio and the 21st Ohio, all except a few on the left of the 21st.

The enemy that came in our rear did not quite cover our left company, and when they ordered us to lay down our arms, Lieutenant [Thomas B.] Lamb, followed by several others, ran to the left and made their escape, the enemy firing at them as they ran but without effect. Those who were taken prisoners gave up their arms, and while standing in line, the enemy in our front fired a volley at us at short range, but very badly aimed, as I know of no one being hit. A rebel officer near me shouted to them to cease firing, and informed them who they were. That was the last firing I heard that night.

■ Major William M. Owen, Washington Artillery of New Orleans, served as Preston's divisional artillery chief on September 20. He later wrote of encountering Gens. Longstreet and Buckner, seated on a log while eating lunch that afternoon: "Gen. Longstreet hailed me and asked for a pipeful of tobacco. I produced my little bag, and he filled his meerschaum pipe. I then asked him what he thought of the battle; was the enemy beaten or not? 'Yes,' he said, 'all along his line. If we had had our Virginia army here, we could have whipped them in half the time. By the by, don't you want some guns for your command? I think my men must have captured fifty today. You can have as many as you want.' "

When the major asked to have the order in writing, Longstreet laughed and instructed his assistant adjutant general to comply. According to Owen, "the General then said, 'I think there must be some horses too; I certainly saw some go by with the guns.' 'Oh!' I said, 'include the horses by all means,' and the horses were added to the order."

## 'Go ahead, General! We are not whipped yet!'

### Major William M. Owen
### Chief of Artillery
### Preston's Division, Buckner's Corps

It was now 4 o'clock, and the remnant of the Federal army still stubbornly held the Horseshoe Ridge, although during the day they had been assaulted by Breckinridge, Bushrod Johnson, Patton Anderson, Hindman, and lastly by Kershaw, and all had lost heavily. Longstreet determined to take the ridge, and sends to Bragg for some of the troops of the right wing, but Bragg says, "they have been fought out and can do him no good."

The position held by the enemy is a very Gibraltar, its sides precipitous and difficult to climb, but the day is wearing away and no time should be lost. Longstreet determines to put in his Tenth Legion, [William] Preston's 5,000, and sends for the General and orders an immediate advance. "It shall be done," replies Preston, and the command Attention! is given down the lines of the three brigades. The young troops spring to their arms; it is their baptism of fire, and if they are whipped they won't know it.

The lines are dressed, and at the commands Forward! Forward! the 5,000 move on in beautiful order. The enemy opens a terrific fire, but up the hill our men advance; now the enemy's bullets begin to tell upon the lines, and men fall to the right and left, dead and wounded, but the rest move on undismayed, firing rapidly as they advance. But the artillery and infantry fire is too hot for them, although they have fought most gallantly, and, halting under the crest where some protection is had, the lines are dressed and General Preston, reassuring them by his presence, rides down the lines and cooly examines each man's cartridge box, and says, "Men, we must use the bayonet — the bayonet — we will give them the bayonet!" The men, one and all, cry out, "Go

■ Brig. Gen. William Preston, a native Kentuckian, Harvard graduate and former minister to Spain, assumed command of his division in Buckner's corps just four weeks prior to Chickamauga. His three brigades under Gracie, Trigg and Kelly took 4,100 infantrymen into the battle on September 20, losing 1,275 killed and wounded.

During the division's march from Knoxville to Georgia earlier that month, newly appointed staff member Major William M. Owen found Preston to be "a most interesting travelling companion as well as polished gentleman. He is chock-full of anecdote, and many an hour have I listened to his experiences ... As we jog along, he on his Kentucky thorough-bred, he tells me of his French cook and the attaches of his [Spanish] palace; how the former was brought from Paris regardless of expense, and what dinners he served for state occasions. And when we halted in some patch of woods to bivouac in the open air, and partake of our slice of bacon and dip our crackers in the grease, he would give a sigh of satisfaction, and say, 'Ah! Owen, this is just as good. Now we are *greased* for another day.' "

ahead, General! We are not whipped yet!" Confidence restored by the General's cool demeanor, and with the enthusiasm of the troops raised to the highest pitch, Preston rides to the front and centre of his line, and leads the way with splendid dash and bravery, waving his cap above his head, his gray hair floating in the breeze.

With fierce yells and shouts the troops advance — Gracie on the right, Kelly the centre, and Trigg the left. It is a brave sight. Gracie and Kelly meet a determined resistance; but Trigg, who had been pushed to the enemy's right in the hope of overlapping and flanking him, sweeps down on his flank and rear, capturing 500 prisoners, the colors of the Twenty-first Ohio, the Twenty-second Michigan, and of two regiments unknown, together with Colonels Lefebvre[sic] and Carlton, and Lieut.-Col. Glenn. The enemy, assailed on front and flank, falls back, and the battle-flags of Preston's division are planted upon the summit of Horseshoe Ridge ...

## 'A most treacherous act'

### Capt. Isaac H. Bailey
### Company B
### 58th North Carolina Volunteer Infantry

On the morning of the 19th, at a very early hour, just as soon as you could distinguish the blue from the gray, the whole army was put in position as far as we could see. Our brigade was formed at the upper side of a wheat field, forty yards below the fence and woods that ran parallel with our division. After remaining in line about forty-five minutes the command was given: "Unfurl your banners." At this moment the sun broke forth, dispelling the fog, and as our banners floated out on the breeze the Federals commenced playing "Yankee Doodle" and to move out eastward on an almost parallel line with ours. Almost immediately we were ordered to march in a parallel direction, the enemy inclining to the right and to the left.

There was soon a terrible cannonading around us, but with little damage — none to the Fifty-eighth North Carolina. Very soon after this we captured a battery of artillery on a round eminence in a corn field, and greatly hoped to get to guard them, but by the time we had exchanged a few chews of tobacco we were ordered away. For the balance of the day, with the rest of the brigade, we were held in reserve.

At about 7 o'clock Sunday morning, the 20th, the two flanking companies, A and B, commanded by Captain Tobey and myself [respectively], of the Fifty-eighth North Carolina Volunteers, together with five companies from the other [brigade] regiments, were put under the command of Lieutenant-Colonel Edmund Kirby of the Fifty-eighth, and ordered in the direction of Alexander's bridge across the west prong of Chickamauga river as skirmishers to feel the strength of the enemy in that direction.

We proceeded about one and a fourth miles when we came to an open field lying along the Chickamauga river some three fourths of a mile in length and about the same in breadth. When we had gone nearly half way down through the field, we could see fortifications all up and down the river the full length of the field and about twenty-five yards from the river bank.

Notwithstanding we knew that the enemy was behind the breastworks, we had to advance to feel his strength. So we slowly advanced until we came to the fortifications of fence rails leaning from our advance in the direction of the river to where the enemy had fallen back to and under the bank of the river to draw us over, then to fire on us as we would have to retreat over the fortifications just passed. As soon as the line of skirmishers had passed over the fortifications, the enemy fired from their ranks, three or four men deep, a most galling and enfilading fire into our ranks. We had now ascertained by sad and painful experience what we had been sent out to do. We were then obliged to retreat through the rail fortifications upon the woods and across the old fields of broom straw waving in the melancholy wind, and over a number of our most loved comrades left dead on the field.

The battle was raging furiously all day long from end to end of the field and for five or six miles up and down the Chickamauga. Charge after charge was made by the Confederate and Federal lines, each in turn, while the shells from the opposing batteries lumbered and burst over our heads. At about 3:30 p.m. we regained our regiment.

The Fifty-eighth North Carolina, the Sixty-third Virginia and the Fifth Kentucky, in order named, moved to the front and formed in line of battle, the left resting on the Chattanooga road. The enemy occupied a range of ridges, from which they had repulsed no less than seven assaults made by our troops. The approach to these ridges was along spurs and where ridges intersected ridges and through intervening depressions or hollows, all more or less wooded, but more open and exposed opposite the right of the brigade. One of the assaults had been made by General [James Patton] Anderson's brigade. Before we could reach him in such a way as to successfully relieve, he had been repulsed.

The line being again formed, the Fifty-eighth North Carolina, which was on the right, moved with steadiness through this comparatively open space till the extreme right arrived within ten or twelve feet of the enemy. The line of the brigade formed with the line of the enemy at an angle of perhaps 24 degrees, the right of the Fifty-eighth being at the angle. After exchanging fire with the enemy for about one and three fourths of an hour, we attempted to dislodge him by assault, and for this purpose the Fifty-eighth was transferred from the right to the left of the line, and moved forward, swinging somewhat to the right. When we arrived at the base of the hill, the enemy was heard to cry: "We surrender! We surrender!"

Colonel John H. Kelly, Eighth Arkansas Regiment, was in command of the brigade. He immediately stepped to the front, two horses having been shot from under him within the past few minutes, and called upon the officer who seemed to be in command and demanded that if he proposed to surrender he should lay down his arms.

He came to the front saying: "Wait a moment!"

Kelly replied: "No, sir! Lay down your arms instantly, or I will fire upon you," and turned to give his command, but before he could give the command "Ready," the enemy poured upon us a terrific fire, with a loud exclamation: "You are firing upon your

■ Capt. Isaac H. Bailey of Company H, 58th North Carolina, was struck in the leg, side and head on Horseshoe Ridge's slope, which was strewn with 160 dead and wounded Tar Heels from his regiment. "My men were engaged in their first battle," reported Col. John B. Palmer, who was hit slightly himself. "The list of casualties tells of their endurance and terrible exposure. Every field and staff officer and one-half of the balance of the regiment killed or wounded indicates the nature of the conflict. My acting lieutenant colonel (Edmund Kirby) was killed early in the action. With the words 'Drive them, boys! Drive them!' on his lips he fell, pierced by four balls, while leading my right wing."

■ Sergeant John L. Clem of Company C, 22nd Michigan, strikes a bemused pose a few months after his well publicized exploit on Horseshoe Ridge, where he allegedly shot a Confederate officer from his horse. According to Clem, he was ordered to "Halt! Surrender! you damned little Yankee son of a bitch," just before he shot the Rebel. Feigning death during the twilight confusion of September 20, Clem made his way safely to Chattanooga, only to be captured by Confederate cavalry early in October during a wagon train raid. While a prisoner at Gen. Joseph Wheeler's headquarters, Clem proudly was displayed by the general as his "fighting Yankee baby" until his exchange two months later. Travelling to Ohio, Clem's age and war stories caught the attention of news reporters, who dubbed him the "Drummer Boy of Chickamauga." Promotion and assignment as orderly to Gen. Thomas quickly followed.

"Johnny is a boy of twelve, and was born at Newark, Ohio," wrote Chaplain Alonzo H. Quint, 2nd Massachusetts. "He measures four feet and one inch in height. He has a frank, pleasant, firm face, with light eyes and hair. He dresses neatly, sports his sergeant's chevrons and a pistol. Johnny is really a manly looking little fellow; is self-possessed, but modest. He used to drink whiskey and swear, but he has been taught better, he says."

friends." Having discovered that no friends were in advance, but that it was a most treacherous act on the part of the enemy, firing was continued with vigor. A deadly fire was, and had been ever since we came within range, poured into our ranks by the foe.

In this action the regiment lost about half of its numbers, by official report of Colonel Kelly, commanding the brigade. Company A, Captain Tobey, started on the charge with thirty-four muskets and reached the top of the hill with only twelve, losing twenty-two. In conjunction with Colonel R.C. Trigg, Fifty-fourth Virginia, commanding another brigade, we captured three regiments of the enemy, which surrendered to Colonel Trigg. As the column commenced moving with the prisoners a volley was fired into our ranks, causing a good deal of confusion, it then being dark.

Early in the action Lieutenant-Colonel Kirby, while cheering his men, fell pierced by four bullets. Major Dula was wounded [and] Colonel [John B.] Palmer, the only field officer then with the regiment, also was wounded, but still continued in command. I, too, fell, almost mortally wounded — left leg broken, shot through the right side and one ear almost severed from my head. Thirteen commissioned officers, including the adjutant, had been killed and wounded; two-thirds of the right flanking company, Captain Tobey's, were killed and wounded, as were about seven-tenths of the left flanking company, my own.

## 'The whole color guard was shot down'

### 1st Lieut. William B. Hamilton
### Company F
### 22nd Michigan Volunteer Infantry

About noon on September 20, the 22d Michigan was on its way from McAfee's church with eighty rounds of cartridges per man, and about four hundred and fifty strong. One company, B, was left at Granger's headquarters as guard. Much of the way we went double-quick in the direction of heavy firing — both artillery and rifle. When we had arrived within about half or three-fourths of a mile of the line of smoke, there was some delay while the other regiments of Steedman's Division came up and the division was deployed.

At this point there was a large open space extending east and south from the main ridge (which was close on our right), for nearly half a mile. Down through this opening the division advanced — brigade front — in splendid order up toward the line of fire on Horseshoe Ridge, with Steedman riding ahead. There were three lines, [with] the 22d Michigan in the second line. Much of this space was obstructed by fallen timber and the regiment had to perform some evolutions to avoid it. A Confederate battery on our left kept the ground ploughed and the air filled with shot and shell as we advanced. When we reached the firing-line there was a move made to form a line of battle in a cornfield facing us to the east. Then came a sudden change of action and the 22d was rushed into the woods to the west in column of fours by the right flank. This could not have been much after 2 o'clock p.m.

We had advanced perhaps sixty or eighty rods when we were

halted and faced to the left in line of battle. Then the order to advance was given, and as we began the ascent, Lieutenant-Colonel [William] Sanborn shouted, "Fix bayonets!" With the rattle of the steel the men began to yell, and in the next two minutes they were over the ridge and chasing the Confederates down the south slope. But here we met a sudden check. A terrific fire was poured into us from front and flank, and in the few minutes we stood there endeavoring to return the fire about one-third of our brave fellows went down, killed or wounded. Our lieutenant colonel was shot through the foot and ankle. Captain William A. Smith, Company H, was mortally wounded. The whole color guard was shot down; four or five of them killed. All this during the ten or fifteen minutes we tried to hold the position.

While attending to some wounded men, the next thing I knew our men had faced about and were slowly retiring up the hill. Colonel LeFavour was riding back and forth along the line straightening out some confusion. I was one of the last to reach the ridge and had a good chance to look around. I could see no regiment to the west of us at that time. There was a lull in the firing as we fell back, reaching the ridge again somewhere about three o'clock, where LeFavour promptly faced us about and ordered us to lie down or shelter ourselves as best we could and stay there.

■ Col. Heber LeFavour (seated far left), 22nd Michigan, commanded a demi-brigade of his own regiment and the 89th Ohio on September 20. Both repulsed repeated Confederate assaults, eventually exhausting their ammunition until ordered to fix bayonets to empty muskets. Five color bearers in the 22nd were successively shot down before the regiment was overwhelmed at dark by Trigg's brigade. With more than 135 dead and wounded Michiganders lying in their midst, LeFavour ordered his men to stop fighting. He and 261 members of the 22nd were taken prisoner.

In this photograph, LeFavour (paroled on May 7, 1864, and showing the scar from his facial wound) was joined by regimental Surgeon Abram P. McConnell (seated center), Adjutant Louis A. Allor (seated far right), Quartermaster Charles J. Bockius (standing center), and two unidentified first lieutenants.

■ Col. Jesse J. Finley's 6th Florida of Trigg's brigade received its baptism of fire on September 19. Finley wrote that his men "purchased whatever reputation they may have won at a fearful cost of life and blood." Caught unsupported east of the LaFayette Road on the Viniard Farm, the Floridians' ranks were raked by two Federal batteries, cutting down 165 officers and men. Their losses the next day on Horseshoe Ridge were trifling by comparison — only one man killed and six wounded.

Finley, serving as a cavalry captain in the Second Seminole War, and mayor of Memphis in 1845, was promoted brigadier general on November 16, 1863, assuming command of the Army of Tennessee's Florida brigade. In 1864 he suffered wounds at Resaca and Jonesboro, Ga.

The order of companies when charging over that hill was the usual one, as follows, from left to right, G, K, E, H, C, I, D, F, A. I was then the left file closer of my Company, F, next to A Company on the flank. I saw only what seemed to be a thin skirmish line extending along the ridge, lying down facing south and said to be the 21st Ohio. Soon after we settled down on the summit I saw a regiment fall in on the right of our position. It must have been the 89th Ohio. Its line extended to the southwest by west toward the main ridge.

About sunset it became apparent to Colonel LeFavour that the remainder of our division had withdrawn, leaving our flank in the air. He accordingly ordered us to march toward the rear for the purpose of rejoining our division. We marched down the hill till halted by an officer on horseback in Federal uniform. He said, "The orders are to hold the hill at all hazards; use the cold steel if necessary; reinforcements and ammunition will be here soon." I heard no general's name mentioned as giving the order, though I stood within thirty feet and heard all that was said.

[The colonel] faced us about again and marched us back to the identical spot we had left ten or twelve minutes before. We found it still unoccupied, and in less than twenty minutes we were prisoners. The sun had gone down and the full moon was just rising.

## 'Stack your arms, or I'll cut you to pieces!'

### Private J. M. Weiser
### 54th Virginia Volunteer Infantry

Chickamauga was one of the greatest and most spectacular battles of the war. Its roar, on account of the length of the lines of battle in action at the same time, was deafening, and said to have been heard at one point one hundred and sixty-eight miles in an airline. I saw a twenty-pounder Parrott, the report from which, by itself, would carry for twenty miles, repeatedly discharged, saw the flash and recoil of the gun, and yet could not distinguish its individual sound in the tremendous roar of musketry, and I was probably much less than a hundred yards away.

The part taken by Trigg's Brigade I think worth recording. We belonged to Bragg's third battle line, his reserve. We were called upon late in the afternoon of the 20th to attack the Federal line, which had stood firmly up to that time against the assaults of Longstreet. As we passed over his line, one of his men remarked: "Boys, you're going to catch hell now." He spoke truly, as the loss in our own regiment, the 54th Virginia, of over one hundred men proved, but we gave more than we caught and swept on in a magnificent charge carrying everything before us till we were halted suddenly just as we were about to take possession of a battery which had no defenders left, all either shot down or put to flight.

Without orders, we began fixing bayonets. Colonel Trigg came riding along the front. "Let us go get that battery," we were shouting. It was already ours, but we wished to demonstrate our ownership by laying our paws on it. But we were astonished by the order, "About face!" Then we saw in our rear a line of blue closing up the gap in the Federal line which we had made in our impetuous charge. Colonel Trigg rode a hundred yards in front of his advancing line, where he could easily have been riddled with bullets, and in a stentorian voice, but clear as a silver bell, which made itself clearly heard above the then subsiding din of battle, shouted: "Stack your arms and lie down, or I'll cut you all to pieces!"

The boys in blue, who had not yet closed the line behind us, lay down, but did not stack their loaded and bayonetted rifles, but awaited our advance with orders, as they afterwards told us, to wait for the command to fire and then use the bayonet. But Colonel Trigg wheeled his left wing so as to enfilade the end of the incompleted Federal line, and we steadily advanced, guns loaded, bayonets fixed, fingers on triggers, and thumbs ready to cock our guns in a fraction of a second.

When perhaps fifteen or twenty feet from the enemy, a nervous Confederate inconsiderately, or accidentally, discharged his musket. Instantly came the deadliest, most menacing sound I have ever heard — the click of cocking locks of both lines — while the boys in blue jumped up and, with guns at their shoulders and fingers pressing triggers, awaited the command to fire, which was not given, their officers realizing the futility of the slaughter which would have followed. We advanced slowly, repeating "Surrender, boys, we've got you." Our opponents finally began lowering their guns, which we took and threw behind us. Then at once we became friends and began a frenzied trading of tobacco for coffee.

## 'It's all up with us now'

### Journal of
### 2nd Lieut. Edward S. Scott
### Company G
### 89th Ohio Volunteer Infantry

**September 20th** — Soon after sunrise, we retired to a better position some two hundred yards in our rear, behind a fence on the edge of some woods. We lay here till nine or ten o'clock. The firing was renewed soon after sunrise, and the roar of battle was tremendous on our right near what seemed the center. The order to move came just as we were issuing two days' rations; so that our company had to issue a box of crackers while on the march. We marched across the country till we struck the Mission Ridge road, which we followed till we came near the scene of conflict, the firing being right in front. We stopped here for a little while in a sort of hollow, but were soon ordered forward marching part of the time by line-of-battle. The firing had ceased in our front by this time, and we continued marching bearing toward the right, through the woods most of the time for, I suppose, about two miles.

Just after we left our first stopping place on the Mission Ridge road, we had a splendid view. We were moving up a slope just to the right of the road; just to the left of the road was a large plain, part of it planted in corn. Scattered over this was about a division of infantry marching in line-of-battle with their skirmishers out, while away beyond we could occasionally see rebel cavalry between the scattered trees. After we left this and had gone pretty

■ Col. Robert C. Trigg, 54th Virginia. Three of four regiments in the brigade he commanded ascended Horseshoe Ridge as darkness fell, and managed to interpose themselves on the right flank and rear of the weakened Union line. "Wrapped in the fog, they looked like so many phantoms on a ghostly brigade drill," recalled a 21st Ohio officer, who was unable to distinguish the oncoming troops' identity. Moments later, Trigg's Virginians and Floridians overwhelmed the surprised, tired Federals nearest them — capturing most of the 21st Ohio, 89th Ohio, 22nd Michigan and five stand of colors.

In spite of his success, Trigg was not wholly satisfied. In his after-action report he lamented: "Before beginning the movement I requested two brigades which were in my rear to form on my left and co-operate with me. They declined for want of ammunition. It is greatly to be regretted that they were not in a condition to give me assistance. Had they formed on my left our line would have extended nearly, if not quite, to the [LaFayette] road, and being in rear of the enemy, all his forces occupying the ridge would have been completely cut off."

■ Field musicians of the 89th Ohio, photographed in Chattanooga shortly after the battle of Chickamauga. Differing from regimental brass bands, field music consisted of fifes, drums and bugles — instruments used to communicate commands to regimental formations in camp and field. These musicians wear distinctive sky-blue colored jackets, similar to the pattern adopted by the Veteran Reserve Corps.

In five hours of fighting on September 20, the 89th lost its national color and suffered casualties amounting to 19 killed, 63 wounded and 171 missing or captured.

near a mile, we came upon a large open field which was commanded by the rebel artillery and were shelling it pretty briskly. We lay down just before we got in range. While we were lying here, one of our batteries got into position and replied with what effect we could not tell, as we were soon ordered forward on the "double-quick" which we kept up till we were out of range. The shells made the boys dodge considerable. It was rather amusing to see them. They would be going along on the "double-quick" when a shell would come howling along just above them & down they would go, flat on the ground till it had passed, then jump up and trot along on the "double-quick" again. No one was hurt, although some of them came pretty close.

A little farther on we came to another open field, where they appeared to be massing troops; we stopped here for five or ten minutes when the troops were all put in motion again. This movement was pretty hard on the men, it was very dusty, quite warm, and no water, and they got scattered considerable while on the "double-quick." They nearly all came up, however, while we stopped in the field. We moved on with the rest of the troops and soon got into hot work.

We were marching along in line-of-battle behind another line. The line in front ascended a hill and going down the other side were heavily engaged from the time they left the crest of the hill, as we could tell by the roar of musketry. We ascended the hill and lay down on the crest. We were under a very hot fire here, the air above us seemed literally filled with missiles of all sorts. We had been lying here but a few minutes when the line in front consisting of the 115th Ills., I think, commenced falling back, and as the enemy continued driving them, retreated right over our Regt which immediately commenced firing. The rebels for some reason did not follow up their advantage. Our Regt continued firing for some time down the hill in front, which was covered with bushes and undergrowth, lest they might come on us under the cover of the bushes. Pretty soon Gen. Steadman[sic] came along in front of our line on foot, calling to the boys to cease firing.

There were some twenty-five wounded but none killed in this

engagement. None were hurt in our company. Roll-call showed forty-two men present. Billy T[hacker] was struck by a spent ball in the shoulder but not hurt. The Col. [Caleb H. Carlton's] horse was shot under him. Capt. [William C.] Russell, A.A.G. on Gen. Granger's staff, was killed just to the right of our Regt. Not three minutes before, he had delivered an order to our Col. saying "that he thought Gen. Steadman had asked for us to hold that position, and that he had better stay there." He was a fine looking officer.

The line that had fallen back over our Regt had rallied and gone away some place, so that we were left in front without any support in our rear. It was a trying time for our Regt when the line in front fell back over it, but it stood nobly. After a short time of quiet, firing commenced again on our right. It was tremendous, almost deafening. The roar of musketry was incessant and at intervals of two or three seconds it was increased by the roar of cannon. The conflict here was terrific; first one side driving then the other. At last the rebels began to get the advantage and slowly drove our men back. As the line on our right gave way, they began to come on us and at last came on us with full force. Our Regt was lying rather too far back on the crest of the hill, I think, so that we could not see them till they were pretty near on to us. Their first onset was so impetuous and our line on the right falling back enabled them to come in on our right and pour in an enfilading fire so that our Regt gave way a little and the right had to swing around to meet the enfilading fire. We stood here for some time when the rebels came on with such force that we were obliged to retire; we fell back slowly till we reached a sort of hollow which ran up and down the hill. The 22d Michigan was on our left, more toward the top of the hill. Here we stopped and from which we made charge after charge, but were driven back to it each time by superior numbers. The question was now anxiously asked by every one, "Why don't we get reinforcements?"

The 89th & 21st Ohio, and 22d Mich. seemed to have been forgotten and left without support or assistance, and I don't suppose our whole force amounted to 500 men. In our Regiment our men were nearly half killed or wounded and our ammunition nearly gone; in some of the companies, entirely gone, and they were taking the cartridges out of the boxes of the killed and wounded. It was a fearful place; the musketry fire was terrible. We were exposed to very little cannonading. In our last charge they fired one round of grape at us. Those who had been in several heavy fights say that they never saw the musketry so heavy as it was here.

We had now been in the fight some three hours. Our men were becoming discouraged & disheartened, and night or reinforcements were more than anxiously looked and prayed for; the more so as it was pretty generally thought that we were surrounded. A column of men had been seen to go through the hollow at the bottom of the hill we were on, but the smoke was so thick we could not tell whether they were our men or rebels; now it was pretty generally thought they were rebels. I myself thought they were our men.

It was after sunset and pretty nearly dark and the firing had nearly stopped when we could hear a column of men halt in the hollow at the bottom of the hill & brought to the front. Just at this moment the 21st Ohio which was on the left of the 22d Mich-

■ Col. Caleb H. Carlton led the 89th Ohio at Horseshoe Ridge, and was among 13 officers of the regiment taken prisoner there. "Nothing stands out so prominently in my memory," related Orderly Sergeant Joseph C. Oliver of Company G, "as the figure of Colonel Carlton sitting [on] his horse and smoking his pipe in the midst of the storm of bullets which were decimating our ranks." Carlton, an 1854 West Point graduate who assumed command of the 89th only two months before, briefly eluded his captors in the dark but could not bluff his way past Confederates of the 5th Kentucky Infantry. Sent to Richmond's Libby Prison, he was exchanged several months later.

2nd Lieut. Edward S. Scott of Company G also was sent to Libby, where he escaped in February 1864. After the war he wrote: "I have always been of the opinion that we were deliberately left [on Horseshoe Ridge], since we were 'orphans' away from our regular command, in order to facilitate the withdrawal of other troops."

■ 1st Lieut. Stephen V. Walker, commanding 31 men of Company D, 89th Ohio, fell September 20 on Horseshoe Ridge. One of his sergeants described Walker's death soon after the battle: "During the second charge on Sunday he was, sword in hand, rallying some of our men who had for the moment given way, when a musket shot struck him down, entering his heart. 2nd Lt. [John V.] Baird caught him as he fell, asked him if he was much hurt. He slowly opened his eyes, closed them again, and as brave an officer as ever drew sword had gone from among us. They tried to conceal his death from the company, but he soon was missed, and when his death was whispered around, gloom settled on every face in our company. All felt they had lost a friend and a brother."

Of 15 men from Walker's company captured at Chickamauga, 11 died in 1864 in prison camps at Andersonville, Ga. and Danville, Va.

igan came down the hill and the Col. told the Major to go to our right as he was afraid they were trying to flank us. They had no more than got there when we could hear the command "forward!" in the hollow and the soldiers commenced coming up the hill. We did not know who they were. Our men were ordered to lay down. This was a moment of intense excitement; we did not know who they were and were fearful to fire on them lest they were our own men coming to reinforce us, and fearful if they saw us they would think we were rebels and fire on us. Our men were almost out of ammunition; half of them had no cartridges. They had been discouraged and disconsolate by the fearful slaughter, lack of reinforcements and with the idea that we were surrounded.

As soon as we discovered this body of men coming up the hill the men were ordered to fix bayonets and lay down in the hollow to which we had fallen back. And now commenced a scene which under other circumstances might have been amusing. As they began to approach us the men from both sides commenced singing out "Halt, Halt!" and "Who are you?" etc.; they to keep us from firing or retreating and us to keep them from firing while we tried to find out who they were. Once, the 21st Ohio broke but they were brought back.

I could not help but think they were our men till they got within ten feet of us, when through the smoke of battle and the growing darkness I could see their gray uniforms and I knew then that they were *rebels!* I turned round to Capt. [Wesley R.] Adams who thought also that they were our men and said, "It's all up with us now." The rebels were advancing in a fine line — a whole brigade, Kelley's — with their guns all at a "ready." We then saw that resistance would be useless in our condition and against such superior numbers and they soon surrounded us and made preparation to take us away, amid shouts of "don't fire!" and "throw down your guns!" etc. Gen. Kelley [Col. John H. Kelly] rode up to Col. Carlton and said something which I did not understand, to which the Col. ans[wered:] "I'll not do it, sir, till I know what I'm about." I then heard him say, "I'm Col. Carlton of the 89th Ohio; do you wish my sword, sir?" Gen. Kelley told him to keep his sword.

While all this was going on, and soon after we were taken, another body of rebels came up in our rear on top of the hill and for some reason or another, fired a volley into us, rebels and all. The rebels scattered like sheep at this volley, hiding behind trees, logs. I piled with the rest behind a big tree in the middle of the hollow; the mass were piled three or four deep. I was a fool for not trying to get away. Quite a number did take advantage of this and escaped, my cousin Wm. Thacker among the number. The Col. and Lt. Col. [William H. Glenn] put spurs to their horses and had it but they were stopped when the rebels rallied again. The rebels on the hill only fired one volley at us, when I suppose they found out their mistake. It proved, however, that resistance here would have been useless as we were completely surrounded. Gen. Kelley testified to our bravery by saying that "We charged that hill three times and every time there was a *fresh brigade* of yankees there." Our brigade of two small regiments was the only one there.

After our capture we were marched to the rear, part of the time over the battlefield of Saturday and the morning, till we reached the road when we were countermarched back & forth, losing the way, cutting across country, through fields etc., passing by rebel camps, batteries, etc., till we were brought up at Gen. Bragg's headquarters. Here we lay for some time.

The boys, after they were taken, destroyed a good deal of their equipments, cutting up their cartridge boxes, etc. Just a little while after we were taken a captain came up to me & wanted my sword. I refused to give it up to him. He tried very hard to get it. I told him I didn't think he was the proper authority, that I wouldn't give it up till I was compelled by one of his field officers. By some means he found out my name & after we had gone some four or five miles I heard my name called during a short halt, & going out side of the column found this capt. with the major of the regt (54th Va.) The capt. told him this was the man he was speaking about. His major asked to see my sword. He then told me "he would take my sword," and ordered me to "take it off." I did so. The two officers then had quite a dispute as to who should have it, ending with the major taking it at last. I regretted very much to give this sword up, but it is the fortunes of war.

My company suffered very severely in the battle, more so than any other in the Regt. Lieut. [Granville] Jackson was killed instantly, also Joseph C. Smith, Theodore N. Vaughan, Corporal Silas Weaver and David Morrison. There were some eight or ten wounded besides, more or less severely. O, it was a fearful day. I regret very much that I did not get to take Jackson's watch. He was killed while we were falling back the first time. I with part of my company were some what advanced & did not know they were falling back till I looked around and saw them some distance down the hill. As I was going down I saw Jackson, lying sort of doubled up, his head resting on his right arm. I saw as soon as I looked at him that he was dead; but I could not stop then, and did not get an opportunity afterward to see him. Those that saw him when he was shot say he was struck in the face ... The company, all with perhaps one or two exceptions, did splendid, went into the action with 42 men and came out with 19. There were perhaps three or four that escaped capture.

After we left Gen. Bragg's H.Q. we marched for some time when we changed guards. The 54th Virginia had been very gentlemanly to us. We kept on under our new escort. After midnight, we halted in one corner of a field on what had been an old straw pile, where we were formed in close order, and stopped for the night. We built up fires for it was quite cold. I laid down & tried to sleep but did not do much of it on account of the cold & I had no blanket.

■ Private Theodore T. Fogle of Company G, 2nd Georgia Infantry, wasted no time after the battle to inform his parents of its outcome: "I am now writing at nine o'clock at night by a fire built of Yankee ammunition boxes; this is Yankee paper & I have a Yankee portfolio full of the same sort. We have so far gained a splendid victory & I am safe, never was touched ... But our poor little regiment has suffered awfully. I dont know how many we lost today but yesterday we lost 88 men and 8 officers killed & wounded. My company has only four men & two officers left. My brigade captured two lines of breastworks & 7 pieces of artillery. I had my hands on one of the guns just as we drove the Yankees from it. Gen. [Henry L.] Benning had a horse killed under him yesterday & today he rushed right up with us & cut a Yankee artillery horse out of the harness, put a saddle on him & rode him out, the balls were flying thick as hail all the time.

"Thank God we have worsted old Rosecrans this time, he will probably retreat to Chattanooga tonight. If he does we will pursue him, he cant fight much now for we whipped his reserves this afternoon & I just now hear that we have taken a great many prisoners."

Elected first lieutenant of his company early in 1864, Fogle was killed May 6 at the battle of the Wilderness.

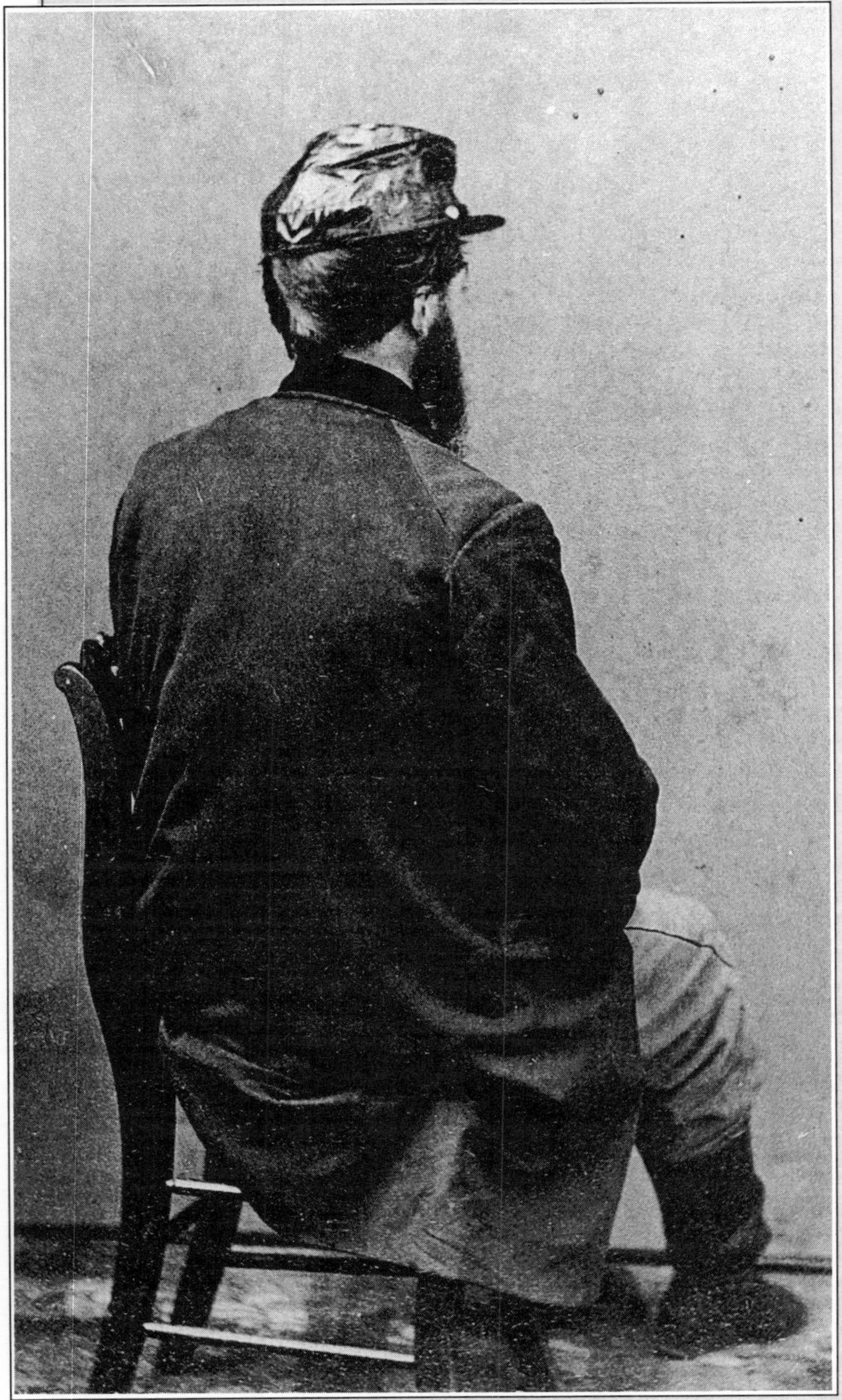

■ 1st Lieut. Orison Smith of Company E, 36th Illinois, was killed in the fight for Lytle's Hill on September 20. As a non-commissioned officer at Stone River, he was wounded, captured and incarcerated in Richmond's Libby Prison until exchanged in the spring of 1863. This unusual portrait was taken by the photographic firm of Dawson & Freeman in Elgin, Ill.

# 'Such priceless, fruitless sacrifice'

Chickamauga was one of the war's bloodiest battles. Of roughly 120,000 combined troops engaged, 28 percent were killed, wounded, captured or missing — a statistic as coldly impersonal as the iron and lead used to create the human carnage. But every casualty possessed a name, a home, a life history. For nearly 4,000 of these, life ended in the fields, ravines and tangled woods 10 miles south of Chattanooga.

"What a miserable night [September 19] was for me," wrote Private Robert H. Hannaford of Company C, 93rd Ohio, who was shot in the thigh. "I lay there thinking of all my friends and those I loved and was never likely to see again. I was wounded, tired, hungry, cold and dirty, and worst of all a prisoner ... My companion was a poor fellow, a married man with a family, continuously talking about his wife and children. He said he hoped his life would be spared to get home to see them once more. But his wish was not to be gratified on earth. Several days later his leg had to be amputated and he died the next day."

For Private Lewellyn Shaver, the night of September 20 was a somber one. His 1st Alabama Battalion was mauled in its first fight, losing 24 killed and 144 wounded out of 238. "I stood in one spot and witnessed many death scenes occurring simultaneously," Shaver reflected. "On my left lay Zeno Gayle, breathing his last; on my right was young Richard Bibb, expiring in the arms of a comrade. The list might be extended indefinitely, but it is painful to recall the memory of such priceless and apparently fruitless sacrifice ... The remnant of the 1st Battalion — now a mere squad — huddled around a single fire. Each face was powder-stained and haggard to the last degree. There was but little talking; our thoughts were of our fallen comrades."

Casualty lists, like the one at right from the *Cincinnati Daily Commercial,* appeared in newspapers North and South for weeks following the battle. There were faces behind the names printed in small type, column after column. A few of them are shown on the subsequent pages.

NATI DAILY COM

CINCINNATI, THURSDAY MORNING, OCTOBER 8, 1863.

# CASUALTY LIST.

## BATTLE OF CHICKAMAUGA.

### 14th Ohio.

OFFICERS WOUNDED.

Captain Pomeroy, severely, ankle.
Lieut. Cobb, Co A, side.
Lieutenant H W Bigelow, flesh, right leg.
Captain Albert Moore, slightly, head.
Lieutenant McBride wounded and missing. This officer was wounded while attempting to rescue a rebel from the fire in some bushes near by; in doing this, another wounded rebel near by shot him.
Lieutenant Bennet, Co. E, leg.
Captain W P Pugh, slightly by spent ball, leg.
Lieutenant Van Meter.

NON-COMMISSIONED OFFICERS AND PRIVATES.

Company A.—Killed—Wm Anderson, John Hoars, John Hepp

Wounded—Corporal Geo Dodd, Corporal A D Tarbox, Ephraim James, Sergeant John Gilliman, seriously, Corporal G B Hanford, Francis M Seagur, L S Warner, Wm Burns, Sergeant James M Perrin, C M Williams, mortally, F O Burns, Jarrard Jolly, Henry Nel's, slightly.

Missing—Samuel T Wood, Henry L Waldron.

Supposed wounded and prisoners—Andrew Glenn, Eli Burchfield, Jacob Ha.bauer, F W Bonior.

Company C—Killed—Sergt Frank Brumhoffer, James B Burton, Geo W Horton.

Wounded—Lyman Ball, mortally; Gilbert Applegate, A J Martin, Alfred Isbell, Jas Burwell, Moses Cenisino, Jacob Curgett, Horace M Dibble, Philip Ensfield, Michael Kingsley, Jacob Kane, James McKay, slightly; C J Prince, Thos L Phillips, Kil Robedeauz, J Sullivan, Richard Skhan, Charles Upel, Henry J Wilson.

Missing—George E Church George R Morris, John Albison, Thomas Foley, Michael Lutes, John Lancelott.

Taken Prisoners—John Venan.

Company D—Killed—James Wells, L B Clemens, John Miller.

Wounded—Geo Cyfang, mortally; G B Hartman, Lewis Cramer, mortally; Henry Andrix, Thos Burke, S B Butterfield, mortally; S H Bates, Wm Casteel, Wm Edsell, Smith Knowles, Wm B Morse, mortally; Bass Mirice, Daniel Marsh, Samuel Overmire, Thos Patten, Allen Rich, C P Russell, Peter Shasteen, Fred Speiglee, A F Thatcher.

Missing—John Booker, Geo Brubaker.

Company F—Killed—Adelbert Knapp reported, Eleakim Munson, corp C A O'Callaghan.

Wounded—Alfred W Hinds, Albert Fox, seriously, Jacob Sarbeak, Wm Cooper, Chas Dennis, David M Thorpe, Francis G Ward, Wm Farley slightly, (now on duty,) Alvah J Ingersoll, Wm B Kitchel, Aaron Rulapaugh, Chas Van Orman slightly, Joseph Hardee, Henry Gifford slightly, Sergt Chas G Tibbitts, corp Wilson Olathrop slightly, A L Smith.

Company G—Killed—Miles J Osborn, David Balsinger, Barney Smith, corp B F Doring, corp Christopher Brunnig, Edwin T Tenant.

Wounded—David Pice, John M Bunks, David Roger, Geo Balsinger, David S Beadle, Geo A Byers, Geo W Coffist, Wm Hoover, Levi Lichty, Elias McCalla, Thos Murphy, Christopher Smith.

Missing—John A Eckles, D F Pond, corp — Conrad, Henry A Brown.

Company H—Killed—Corp Kanomer and Anthony Feinelspech.

Wounded—Carr, Lyman Carpenter lost right arm, Wm Bergan, Conrad Poe, Sergt Moore, Sergt Croxton, John Nicholson, Samuel Spencer, — Weizel, Leonard Engele, corp Salto, Joseph Varkl and Wm Liverman.

Missing—Corp John Beeley, — Lathrop, Sergt Hathway, corp Brown and corp Miller.

Company I—Killed—Sergt Geo Smith and Mason Fessy.

Wounded—Sergt J T Pray, Chas Birch, Edward Burrs, John Oahle, Benedict Geesback, Chas Hanford, supposed mortally; Benj Huttle, supposed mortally; Lucas Kerr, Osias Smith, Geo Sweitzer, supposed mortally; Rufus Trumbull, Henry Van Fleet, James Ward, John Welch, Wm Walfinger and Geo Yager.

Missing—Sergt Edward Sly, Corp Matthew Scott, Corp Anson A Reed, Corp Wm Garnet, Peter Bater-n, Noah Coder, Frank French, Edgar T Potter and Jacob Hipp.

Company K—Killed—Sergt B O Leasure, Corp W K ...ck, Corp O Ogelvie, Corp W Belford, Corp W Flem-...; Corp Perry Burton, John Featheringall, H ...lin, Abner Killin, Benj Louis, Louis Ogelin, supposed killed; Wm Scott, Francis Bowen, supposed ...ed; Wm Coun.

right thigh; First Sergt S P Snider, wounded in left arm; Sergt J Meredith, wounded in head, slight; corp John Bartlett, killed; John Bailey, finger shot off on left hand; Harrison Clark, wounded in right leg, slight; Zeno Hakes, wounded in left hand, slight; Junius Hopkins, wounded in left shoulder; James Shaw, wounded in right arm; Wm Taylor, wounded in left foot; Calvin Hudson, missing; Harvey Wheeler, missing; Wm Thompson, either killed or taken prisoner.

Company E—First Lieut W F Hinman, wounded in right arm; First Sergt John Cooper, killed; Sergt Chas Nickerson, missing; corp Lewis Schneider, killed; corp W F Hulett, killed; John Shadrew killed; Jacob Keeler, killed; Jas O Pague, wounded in left thigh; Louis Worden, wounded in left side; Peter Gesner, wounded in left side; Thomas Kelley, missing; John Yarham, wounded and missing.

Company F—Corporal H Bertel, killed; corp Jacob Spellman, wounded in right arm, amputated; corp J R Rowley, wounded in right arm; corp Chas Jennings, wounded in right thigh; corp Saml Shirts, missing; corp J Funk (color guard), wounded in breast, slight; Geo Low, wounded in left shoulder; E McCormac, wounded in left hand; Charles Bay, wounded in finger; E Carnehan, missing.

Company G—First Lieut Nelson Smith, killed; Sergt Oliver Evans, wounded in right thigh; corp H Helliker, in right arm; corp Jas Delano, in left foot; corp C O Hess (color guard), missing; J Atterholt, wounded in hand; Jacob Gharst, in right shoulder; Henry Leidky, right thigh broken; A Lyon, wounded in left shoulder and leg; Peter Sharp, wounded in leg; Jacob Binhamer, Peter Clemens, David Grubaugh, missing.

Company H—Second Lieut Otho Shipley, wounded in right hip; Sergt J Paisley, disabled by a horse running over him; corp Wm George, wounded in arm; J R Greneltch, killed; S Lent, wounded in right shoulder, slightly; Wm Taylor, left thigh broken; Moses Stockdale, wounded in ankle; B M Stockdale, in hip, slightly; William Orr, thigh broken by a caisson.

Company I—First Lieut J P Brown, wounded in right ear and neck; Sergt J Jones, in left leg; corp John Sims, killed: Thos Baldwin, wounded in right shoulder; Chas Medker, in left hand; Fred Coonrad, in left foot; Henry Vallely, in left hand; Jacob Welson, in head, slightly; C Waller, missing.

Company K—Sergt H Lazenby, wounded in left arm; corp N W Fitzsig, in arm; ... Wolf, in right arm; W L Taylor, wounded or killed; John Bowers, killed; N Edwards, killed; J E F... wounded in left arm; Henry Elliott, in foot; ... in left leg; R Loicher, in head; W... zig, N Laer, B F Luby, J F Berg... Joseph Mulle... missing; B O Raudebaugh, kill...

Those reported as missing were among the bravest soldiers, and it is supposed that most of them, at least, were wounded and unable to get off the field.

### 124th Ohio.

Colonel O H Payne, Chas D Hammer, wounded.

Company A—Henry Kenfield, Adam Sipe, killed. Sergt Wm B Sclover, sergt Geo W Wing, sergt Alex Cepsky, corp Chas C Leonard, corp Geo Foster, corp John H Yerler, corp Eben W Gauzee, corp George Miner, Ed Brainerd, Ed Bartlett, Jacob Fritz, Ed Gates, Chas Gibbs, Isaac Hardy, James Williams, Wm Clague, Daniel Herr, John W Gould, Wm Losey, wounded. 1st sergt H F Henry, Wm Bryan, Wm Emerson, Henry Scheener, Jonathan Wyeth, missing.

Company B—Corp W J Atkins, killed. 2d Lieut. Chas M Stedman, 1st sergt Geo E Jeffries, sergt Orson Vanderhof, sergt Loyd, A Marsh, corp Moses Fuller, Andrew J Lovy, Lyman F Dougherty, Ed Earick, Jackson Young, T N McCoy, Arthur Butloug, Nathan Miller, Seth Oakley, wounded. George Benton, missing.

Company C—Corp Chas Walsh, John Flannigan, Jacob Mooney, Henry Mathews, Jacob Rye, Pat Welch, wounded Sergt Dexter, Lane, James McDonald, Melvin Shepard, Allison Gibson, missing.

Company D—Jacob Bath, Henry Daniel, Peter Dath, Wendel Kunstle, Peter Moss, George March, Henry Miller, John Shelt, Pet Fulk, Samuel Wertey, Corporal Mat Mourn, wounded; Sylvester Donley, missing.

Company E—Corporl Ira Wade, killed; Corporal Lucius E Cole, wounded; Albert Alleman, James Benson, John Crew, Charles Cordes, Alonzo Emmons, James Larkin, William Lawless, Isaac Warren, John Miller, wounded; Corporal Matthew J Plunkett, Matthew Chandler, Johnson Lucas, Henry W Lewis, missing.

Company F—First Sergeant ...

John Burchell, John Smothers, First Lieut Kelley, J J Able and Henry Taylor.

Slightly Wounded—John T Rose, Sergt W... dis, Silas Mundy, Wm B Harrison.

Missing—Josiah Brown.

Company C—Capt Ed Hilpp, commanding—Jas P Thurman.

Seriously Wounded—Geo Meese, Martin M... Mike McNamara.

Slightly Wounded—J M Buckman, Ord Se... Martin, John Hoagland A T Andrews, Secon... J E Sallee, Capt John Craig.

Missing—B B Sapp

Company H—Capt W T Shively, comma...

Killed—None.

Mortally Wounded—Michael Welsh.

Severely Wounded—John Sluder, Addison Zach Eads, Moses Campbell, Second Lieut W ...low.

Slightly Wounded—D A Shirely, D E Rice.

Missing—Wm Roots

Company E—Capt S E Berill, commanding—E John Fowler, E M Adams, Jas Hundley.

Mortally Wounded—Capt S P Berill, (since Geo W Ensor, Geo Noe, Wm Adams, Richard Lo... Philip Corcoran, and John Campbell.

Severely Wounded—Alex Spraggins, Jno L D... Jack Thompson, and Wm A Myers.

Slightly Wounded—Jack Waters, Geo Nix, P... Sullivan, Joseph Jeans, Thos Malley, Jno W Cou... Wm Edwards, and W H Dodson.

Missing—Robert Walker, E A Thompson, and Fields.

Company K, Capt Henry Walker, comma... Killed—Edward Wilkins, D Campbell, D Mallon; L M Male.

Severely Wounded—Richard Welsh, and R Rhea

Slightly Wounded—Charles Garvy, Tobias R... Adam Molin, Wm McVeigh, M Cady, and Wi... Rose.

Company G, Capt Jas M Davenport, comman...

Killed—None

Mortally wounded—Joseph Ballard, James Wa... and John M Clark.

Severely wounded—Capt J M Davenport, Tho... Peck, William Hayden, Lemuel Ferrell, and Edw... Avis.

Slightly wounded—Jas Blandford and Miles Ko...

Company B, John T Milburn commandin... Killed—Ord Serg't Philip McGrath, Serg't Ja... Scott, George Fenwick, Joseph S Mattingly, Rob Blandford, T J Paterson and J T Blair.

Mortally wounded—Thomas Miles.

Severely wounded—Serg't William Harding, Fra... Green, Thomas Fenwick, Ed Blandford, C H Mi... Wm Whitfield, Wm Fogle and Wm Butler.

Slightly wounded—David Blair, Walter Matting... E A Llewellen, James Sanders and Capt J T Milbu...

Missing—John Miles.

Chaplain R C Nash was severely wounded.

RECAPITULATION.

Killed, 21; Mortally wounded, 15; Severely wounded, 52; Slightly wounded, 65; Missing, 12: Total, 1...

### 15th Kentucky.

Topographical Engineer Staff of General Beatty. Capt Isaac H LeFevre, 88th Indiana Volunteers, mortally wounded and a prisoner; Lieutenant Caulkins, 104th Illinois, slight wound and a prisoner, A A D Staff

Corporal Jas Teahan, Geo Stills, Geo Ewing, company F, Philip Schneider, I, James Moore, H, killed Henry C Field, A, John D Baker Serg J A Headley Lazarus Hoffman, J W Stewart, B Serg J T Williams, B I Smith, G R Ewing, John Fogle, John Lafollette Jas B Cook, C, J R Shaddick, Mike McDonald, A Christ, Jas Burnett, A C Hornbeck, D, Geo Williams, John Cunningham, John Burk, Thos Chillor, E, Serg Jas A Turner, corporals John H Middleton and John W Bule Frank Appleton, Milton Davis, F, wounded; C Miller, I, wounded and missing; A Michael, F Koening, I, John Motz, John Smith, N Weaver, H, Serg Jos Gallagher, Chas Sweeney, James McLaughlin, Pat Donahue, Danl McConnelly, Hugh McGrady, G, Jacob Smith, J H McClure, Jas Pait, K, Wm Campton, Jas Tully, K, wounded; Orderly Serg Wm H Beatty, John H Tucker, A, James Beady, Fred Koberg, First Lieut R F Schaffer, E, J H Conner, F, W Kirchler, I, A Seibert, Otto Laspe, John Harding, H, Jas Curry, Pat Crawly, G, John E, McGranahan, Hugh Gravis, C Harrington, K, missing. Killed, 5; wounded, 42; missing, 15. Total, 62.

### 88th Indiana.

Killed—Corporal ...

■ Corporal Cornelius A. O'Callaghan (right) of Company F, 14th Ohio, was shot dead on September 19. The regiment's 54 percent loss rate, among the Army of the Cumberland's highest at Chickamauga, was expressed by another corporal, Alonzo H. Wood of Company A: "On Saturday morning we had 52 men at roll-call in our company and at the roll-call on Monday there was 25 men in line."

■ Lt. Col. Elhannon M. Mast (below), commanding 304 men of the 13th Ohio, was killed on the Brotherton Farm September 19 when the regiment was flanked by superior numbers and forced to retreat.

■ Col. Julius A. Andrews, 32nd Texas Cavalry, was wounded on September 19 while his regiment fought as infantry in Gen. Matthew D. Ector's brigade.

■ The Army of the Cumberland's Regular Brigade suffered heavily at Chickamauga. Among the wounded was young Drummer James Doyle (left) of Company B, 1st Battalion, 18th U.S. Infantry. Major Sidney Coolidge (below), commanding the 16th U.S. Infantry's 1st Battalion, took 308 effectives into the battle, losing 241. Eighty-five percent of these were captured or missing. Coolidge was killed on September 19, and Battery Coolidge, later built on a spur of Cameron Hill in Chattanooga, was named for him.

■ Lt. Col. James D. Tillman, 41st Tennessee, was severely wounded in the shoulder September 20 during an unsuccessful assault on Horseshoe Ridge. He recovered in time to lead the 41st as colonel in 1864, and on April 18, 1865 was placed in command of the remnants of 10 different Tennessee regiments.

■ Col. Hans C. Heg, 15th Wisconsin, commanded the 3rd Brigade, 1st Division, XX Corps. On September 18, the 33-year-old native Norwegian wrote his wife that his command was "ready for anything. The Rebels are in our front and we may have to fight him a Battle — if we do it will be apt to be a big one. Do not feel uneasy for me. I am well and in good spirits — and trusting to my usual good luck. I shall use all the caution and courage I am capable of and leave the rest to take care of itself."

After four hours of ferocious fighting near the Viniard Farm the next day, a sharpshooter's bullet slammed into Heg's bowels as he rode among his brigade's shattered ranks. "He did not stagger or fall," wrote Capt. Albert Skofstad of Heg's regiment. "But even when death stared him in the face ... he once more rallied his men, and rode on for about a quarter of a mile. Loss of blood enfeebled him, and he was obliged to give up his command. He was taken to a hospital, where he passed the weary night in suffering ... but he uttered no complaint." Shortly before noon on September 20, Heg expired — one of four Federal brigade commanders to lose his life at Chickamauga.

■ 2nd Lieut. William A. Rhodes of Company G, 36th Ohio, was shot September 19 by an Alabamian of Hood's command, and died of his wound three weeks later.

■ Capt. John W. Spink of Company D, 89th Illinois, was fatally wounded by canister fire September 19 west of the Winfrey House.

■ Major James Leighton, 42nd Illinois, was killed near sundown September 19 in the Viniard Farm's east field. The charge in which he fell recaptured six guns belonging to the 8th Indiana Battery, lost earlier in the day.

■ Capt. Reuben V. Kidd (below) of Company A, 4th Alabama Infantry, was shot through the heart on September 19. That night he was buried on the battlefield under an oak tree — notched for future identification by Kidd's black servant using the officer's own sword. "I have a beautiful sword presented me by the company," Kidd wrote earlier in the war, "which if I am killed and the Yanks don't get, I wish sent home." The sword and scabbard reached his sister in Selma, and three years later she initiated a search for Kidd's grave. After two days the tree was found but the grave was empty. Kidd's final resting place remains unknown.

■ Private Green L. Sheppard (above) of Company C, 1st Battalion Georgia Sharpshooters, was mortally wounded near the Winfrey Field early on September 19. Carried to a field hospital, he died of pneumonia four days later. Sheppard's brigade commander, Col. Claudius C. Wilson, reported losses of 99 killed, 426 wounded and 80 missing out of 1,200 effectives taken into the battle.

■ With Capt. William L. Scott absent sick, 1st Lieut. John H. Marsh (below) commanded Scott's battery on September 19. Supporting Gen. Preston Smith's brigade during the afternoon, the Tennessee artillerists were firing spherical case and canister at Federals only 350 yards away when Marsh's left arm was shattered by a minie ball, and he was carried from the field. Resuming command the following day, Scott later wrote of his friend: "He refused to have [the arm] amputated, although this was urged by the Surgeon in charge. So severely was he wounded that he remained confined in the hospital at Marietta for six months, having been for six weeks in the field-hospital before his removal to Marietta. At the end of that time, although his wounds were unhealed, he returned to his command."

In 1864, Marsh turned down a disability discharge offered by Gen. Joseph E. Johnston in order to continue active field service on Gen. Otho F. Strahl's brigade staff. At the battle of Franklin on November 30, Marsh accompanied the ill-fated Confederate assault mounted. His horse was shot dead under him, and a few moments later he, too, was killed.

■ Brig. Gen. Preston Smith led his Tennessee brigade into woods south of the Winfrey House on September 19, during an ill-timed night assault of Cheatham's and Cleburne's divisions. After twice admonishing skulkers from another brigade ahead of him, Smith and an aide, Capt. Thomas H. King, rode forward in the darkness to ascertain a third delay caused by troops halted in their immediate front. When the line was reached, Smith, unsure of the soldiers' identity, inquired who was in command. The troops proved to be Federals, who fired a point-blank volley at the two officers. Capt. King was instantly killed. One bullet struck the 39-year-old Smith in the chest, smashing a gold watch carried in a pocket over his heart before the missile was diverted internally. He died less than an hour later.

Smith's successor, Col. Alfred J. Vaughan Jr., narrowly escaped the same fate when he, too, rode ahead and was discovered to be a Confederate officer. A shot fired at him missed, but killed another member of Smith's staff riding at Vaughan's side. The colonel immediately ordered nearby riflemen of the 12th Tennessee to shoot, and in the ensuing confusion scores of enlisted men from the 77th Pennsylvania surrendered, turning over a stand of colors to Vaughan.

■ Major George T. Perkins was wounded in the thigh September 20 while commanding the 105th Ohio during a bayonet charge.

■ Corporal Gustavus A. Wood of Company A, 36th Ohio, arrived home one month after the battle. The *Marietta Register* reported: "He is still suffering from his serious wound received at Chickamauga. The ball struck him in the face, passing around the cheekbone, and out near the middle of the back of the neck. He was seriously wounded a little over a year before at Antietam, the ball then striking his chin, producing an ugly wound [seen here], and lodging under his tongue."

■ Capt. Ezra Ricketts of Company F, 17th Ohio, was killed September 20 east of the Dyer Field when his regiment stampeded in the face of Longstreet's late-morning wing assault.

■ Brig. Gen. John Gregg, commanding six regiments in Bushrod Johnson's provisional division, was shot in the neck while reconnoitering September 19. "[He] was in advance of the line when he was wounded," wrote Private W.J. Davidson of Company C, 41st Tennessee, "and was left in the hands of the enemy for awhile, who rifled him of his sword, money and watch, and were taking him off the field when he feigned death and was left on the ground." A Confederate charge rescued the general shortly afterward. Near Richmond in October 1864, Gregg again was struck in the neck, this time fatally.

■ Maj. Gen. John Bell Hood (right), whose left arm was mangled by shrapnel at Gettysburg and remained in a sling, was placed in command of Longstreet's corps on September 18. At the height of the Confederate breakthrough in Dyer Field, a minie ball plowed into Hood's upper right leg, fracturing the femur. He slid from his horse and was carried by members of his old Texas Brigade to a field hospital. There, the leg was amputated about six inches below the hip joint. After recovery, Hood rejoined the Army of Tennessee, becoming its commander in July 1864.

Corporals Jackson E. Webster (left) and John Doughty of Company D, 10th Wisconsin.

■ During the Federal withdrawal from Kelly Field near dusk on September 20, a simultaneous Rebel assault caught the 10th Wisconsin in the open, routing the regiment. Lt. Col. John H. Ely (above) was felled by a bullet, captured and died in Confederate hands two weeks later. More than 140 officers and men of the 10th were captured, including Corporals Jackson Webster and John Doughty (at left) of Company D. Doughty died in captivity at Danville, Va. in July 1864, while Webster remained a prisoner until paroled the following December.

Another member of Company D, Private William W. Day, recalled: "Three times that day did we repel the charge of the enemy, but the fourth time they came in such numbers and with such impetuosity that they fairly lifted us out of our line. When we broke for the rear I was encumbered with knapsack, gun and accoutrements." Day dropped his pack, but soon was stopped by a Rebel soldier aiming a rifle point-blank at his chest. "I was surprised and indignant. He had the drop on me [so] I handed him my gun and he threw it into a clump of bushes." Day remained a prisoner for the rest of the war.

■ Col. Daniel H. Gilmer (left), 38th Illinois, was shot down September 20 when his brigade was routed in the Confederate breakthrough between the Brotherton and Brock farms. Private William E. Patterson of Company K, wounded the previous day and later captured, recorded in his diary: "[Jefferson C.] Davis' division was attacked and the left flank turned, swinging the line around like a door. They retreated and again rallied behind some breastworks that had been thrown up some time previously. The rebels again advanced upon them and were about to surround them and they again retreated, the 38th leaving their fearless Colonel Daniel Gilmer dead on the field."

■ 2nd Lieut. Robert A. Moore of Company G, 17th Mississippi, was killed September 20 between the Dyer Field and Snodgrass Hill. Promoted from private only six weeks before, the 25-year-old farmer's burial site remains unknown. The regiment lost 12 killed and 75 wounded before its brigade commander, believing an attempt would cost half his men, deferred assaulting Snodgrass Hill.

■ Private William R. Smith of Company D, 4th Texas, was killed on September 20. A comrade, Sergeant Valerius Giles of Company B, recalled the carnage: "Men [were] staggering and stumbling to the rear covered with blood, some swearing and some calling on God to protect them in their blind endeavor to find shelter from the storm of iron hail. [It] made me feel like the world was coming to an end then and there."

■ 2nd Lieut. William W. Calkins of Company E, 104th Illinois, served as an aide to Gen. John Beatty. While carrying ammunition to the crest of Horseshoe Ridge, he was wounded in the right leg and captured. He successfully escaped from prison at Columbia, S.C. in November 1864.

■ Capt. Stephen B. Espy of Company G, 115th Illinois, was brigade commissary of subsistence for Gen. W.C. Whitaker. Advised to remain behind at Rossville with the wagons, Espy instead rode to Horseshoe Ridge where he helped rally his regiment until killed.

■ Capt. Charles E. Rowan (left) of Company F, 96th Illinois, also served on Whitaker's staff. On September 20, while carrying orders on the ridge, he mistakenly rode into a Confederate battle line and was taken prisoner after two bullets ripped through his clothing. Rowan escaped near Atlanta and bluffed his way to within 25 miles of Chattanooga, when he was recaptured by Confederate cavalry. Moved to Libby Prison, he was among 108 Federal officers to escape there in February 1864.

■ Private Daniel L. Sower of Company G, 49th Ohio, was wounded and among 30 soldiers from his regiment captured on September 20. "I was in both days of the battle of Chickamauga," he later wrote, 'and wounded in both hands by a cannon ball, which caused me to be taken prisoner just at dark the second day. I remained on the battlefield that night, by an old farmhouse where hundreds of dead and wounded were laying. The next morning I was taken with other prisoners back over the battle ground and witnessed a scene of horror that was most dreadful."

Sower was transported to Richmond and remained in captivity until May 8, 1864, when he and 300 other Federals were exchanged aboard two ships in the James River. "An attempt to cheer was made," he continued, "but our emotion was too great to be expressed in words, and was more generally manifested in tears." After spending six weeks in an Annapolis, Md. parole camp, Sower reached his Ohio home on July 4. He returned to his company on January 6, 1865.

■ 2nd Lieut. Robert F. Fleming of Company I and Private William D. Bailey (left) of Company H, 121st Ohio, were both killed on Horseshoe Ridge. Engaged in only its second battle, the regiment fought hand to hand on September 20, capturing the 22nd Alabama's colors while suffering 99 casualties. It belonged to the Reserve Corps' brigade of Col. John G. Mitchell, who reported total losses of 461 officers and men — one-third of his command.

■ 2nd Lieut. Isaac P. Rule (left) of Company I, 101st Ohio, was struck down September 19 in the east Viniard Field. His fate was described by Corporal Joseph Raymond in a letter written the following month to Rule's brother, Daniel:

"Your much loved brother Isaac is no more. He received a mortal wound Saturday, the 19th, about three or four o'clock, in the abdomen, the ball lodging in his right hip. I was near him when he fell, and immediately ran to him, but could render him no assistance alone, the Regiment at the moment having been slightly driven back ... He felt from the first that his wound was fatal, and expressed himself so to one or two of his friends as we were carrying him in. He seemed perfectly calm and resigned ... I did not talk with him upon the subject of his departure, thinking he would speak of it himself, but his sufferings would not permit him to talk much.

"I had some hope that he might get better, until Sunday afternoon, when he began failing fast. He died at six o'clock [September 20], just as a Regiment of rebel cavalry rode up to the hospital, which was surrendered to them. Monday we buried him, with about twenty others who had died at the hospital. I marked his grave with a piece of plank, on which I carved his name in full, and should every outward mark be obliterated, I think I could find his grave. I have his effects that he had about his person ... You have the most deep and heart-felt sympathy of every member of the 101st Regiment, who have learned to love and value your lamented brother ..."

Front and rear views of Lieut. I.P. Rule's headboard, carved and placed on his battlefield grave by one of his corporals.

# CHAPTER 3

# Starvation stared us in the face

## Chattanooga under siege: Hunger and privation sorely test opposing armies

Quartermaster Sergeant John Snow was lucky at Chickamauga. While his Alabama battery under Capt. Charles L. Lumsden was hotly engaged supporting Bushrod Johnson's division on September 20, Snow was assigned to the battery wagons two miles to the rear. The next day he rejoined his command — and discovered a gruesome spectacle.

"On the 21st we camped on the battle field as the Yankees had retreated," Snow wrote to his sister. "I witnessed such a scene as I hope never to see again. There was a twenty acre grove near us which was fitted with tents and used as a hospital. The night before it was crowded with our wounded and dying soldiers, but the next morning, cold, and the ground covered with a heavy frost showed three hundred stark & cold [bodies] laid side by side in an edge of the wood. I rode over the battle field, which can only be described as a world of bloody and mangled corpses, some with the sweet smile of resignation to death mantling their faces, others with the distorted features that would be produced by bodily pain or remorse of conscience. Some fell with their muskets firmly clenched in their hands against the breastworks which they charged with success, but with the expense of their own lives. On the evening of the 21st I saw dead bodies which had been killed on the 19th lying in the broiling sun, and their faces as black as ebony, and they were then just beginning to bury the dead. I was glad to leave this scene ..."

Other Confederates found the battlefield equally horrifying. "In a big oak was a Yank hanging by one arm, dead," wrote Private William R. Talley of Havis' Georgia Battery. "He had climbed the tree, tied himself to a limb so as to shoot over a hill at our boys and some one of our sharpshooters saw him and killed him."

In Longstreet's corps, Private O.T. Hanks of Company K, 1st Texas, wrote: "Some of my comrades and myself are detailed to bury the dead. The first thing done, we dig a trench about

■ **Left:** This well-preserved locket tintype of a Federal cavalryman was found wrapped in cloth under a rock on Missionary Ridge 122 years after the battle of Chickamauga.

**six or eight feet long, as the case requires, six feet wide, about twenty inches deep. Now the solemn rite of collecting them to the grace side. This done, we spread articles of clothing and blankets on the bottom and lay them tenderly side by side. All are collected that we know of except one. Not far distant lies a corpse with every rag of clothing burnt off, and was burnt beyond recognition. His company mate said the last he saw of him he was behind that oak tree. The tree was decayed and probably caught on fire from the blaze from the muzzles of the guns. He remarked that if it was him he had six half dollars in his pocket, and suggested we scratch in the ashes and find it. It was only a second until out came one piece, until the whole amount was brought out. We bore him tenderly to the grave on two ramrods which were plentiful, laid him beside the others, spread clothing, blankets, etc. over them, then covered them with soil, that being their last resting place."**

**"For days our men were busy burying the dead, caring for the wounded that remained on the field and gathering up the guns, blankets, swords, broken caissons and broken ambulances," recalled Chief Musician William J. Worsham of the**

■ Lookout Mountain looms over the nearly flat expanse of Chattanooga Valley just below the city. On September 21, Rosecrans stationed the Federal 6th Tennessee Infantry at a bridge spanning Chattanooga Creek to stop all Union soldiers below the rank of major general. The Tennesseans' brigade commander, James G. Spears, reported about 10,000 officers and men were halted and sent to the front on the 22nd. The 6th later moved to the top of Lookout, where Private Nicholas B. Grant of Company F watched the Confederate vanguard move in below. "Every dog has his day," he wrote, and "our day will be by-and-by. The Rebels intended to cut off our retreat, but we beat them." Early on the 24th, Grant's regiment withdrew — the last Federals to leave Lookout Mountain before Confederate occupation.

■ Capt. James P. Kirkman of Company E, 10th Tennessee. With its rolls filled almost entirely with men of Irish descent, the "Bloody Tinth" suffered 48 casualties at Chickamauga. Two of Kirkman's fellow company commanders were killed, as was his first lieutenant and four privates — the most fatalities for any company in the regiment.

After the battle, frustration caused by the severe fighting and subsequent lack of confidence in the army's leadership further reduced the 10th's ranks. Between September 21 and November 12, 38 men deserted, leaving the regiment with only 104 effectives.

**19th Tennessee. "Dead men and dead horses lay thick all over the field. It would be useless to attempt a description of the scene of suffering. The crazed condition of those poor fellows, many whose brains had been plowed by the deadly bullet, both Federal and Confederate, yet living, but unable to tell of their suffering was a pitiable spectacle indeed."**

**And another Tennesseean, Private Sam R. Watkins of Company H, 1st Tennessee, graphically wrote: "The Confederate and Federal dead, wounded, and dying were everywhere scattered over the battlefield. Men were lying where they fell, shot in every conceivable part of the body. Some with their entrails torn out and still hanging to them and piled up on the ground beside them, and they still alive. Some with their under jaw torn off, and hanging by a fragment of skin to their cheeks, with their tongues lolling from their mouth, and they trying to talk. Some with both eyes shot out, with one eye hanging down on their cheek. In fact, you might walk over the battlefield and find men shot from the crown of the head to the tip end of the toe."**

**On the Federal side, Col. Benjamin F. Scribner, 38th Indiana, commanded a XIV Corps brigade and wrote: "I once again passed through a fiery ordeal with but little damage. I have the wear and tear which my good constitution is able to bear. I was hit four times; a spent ball on my shoulder tore my arm a little, a slight scrape on the cheek and two grazes on the legs comprise the damage. My poor little gray horse had one of his legs shot off, and he carried me along for some time before I observed it ... The bloody 1st Brigade has been terribly abused. My loss has been very heavy. I have lost more than half the brigade in killed, wounded and missing. I hope it will not turn out so bad when the smoke clears off."**

**Another Hoosier, Corporal William B. Miller of Company K, 75th Indiana, suffered two painful wounds on September 19. Shot through the right thigh, the minie ball lodged in Miller's left thigh; using a forked chestnut branch as a crutch he hobbled through the battle, barely eluding capture.**

**"We got along very well but I am very sore and loss of blood has weakened me," Miller wrote in his journal September 20. "The road was full of wagons and ambulances going to Chattanooga and there are all kinds of reports as to our defeat. Some think our army will be annihilated but I dont fear any such result. If we was so terribly defeated our army would retreat faster. I think our forces will hold Chattanooga any way and that it will be our base for another campaign."**

## 'The loneliness seemed almost suffocating'

### Sergeant Augustus C. Ford
### Company A
### 31st Indiana Volunteer Infantry

The army had dropped into a heap, so to speak, behind Mission Ridge, and in and around McFarland Gap and Rossville, after leaving the field of Chickamauga on the night of September 20, 1863, with little care for aught but rest — only rest. If victory had not perched upon the banners of the South, it was not *then* claimed that she had rested from her uncertain flight upon ours,

# 'Armstrong, let's give them a dare'

**Brig. Gen. Nathan Bedford Forrest was incredulous when Bragg neglected to press the retreating Federals to Chattanooga. Early on September 21, Forrest himself pushed almost to Rossville, accompanied by Brig. Gen. Frank C. Armstrong and 400 of Armstrong's cavalrymen. Armstrong's account of the following episode that day was related by Forrest biographer J.A. Wyeth:**

When nearing Rossville they came upon a rear guard of Federal cavalry, seeing which Forrest remarked, "Armstrong, let's give them a dare." He immediately ordered a charge, and the two generals, at the head of some four hundred Confederate cavalry, at full speed rode down upon the Union troopers, who fired a volley and fled in the direction of Chattanooga. Forrest's horse was fatally wounded by this volley, a Minie ball passing through his neck and severing one of the large arteries. The blood spurted from the divided vessel, seeing which Forrest leaned forward from the saddle, inserted the index finger of his hand into the wound, and thus, stanching the hemorrhage, the animal was still able to carry his rider onward with the troops pursuing the Federals. As soon as the field was cleared, Forrest, removing his finger from the wound, dismounted when his noble charger sank to the earth and was soon lifeless.

**A week later Bragg ordered Forrest to turn his command over to Gen. Joseph Wheeler — which threw Forrest into a violent rage. In a scathing letter followed by a personal visit to Army of Tennessee headquarters, he called Bragg "a damned scoundrel," and that if Bragg ever again tried to interfere with him it would be at the peril of his life. With President Jefferson Davis' intervention, Forrest soon received a new, independent cavalry command in Mississippi and West Tennessee. His old division was given to Armstrong.**

■ Brig. Gen. Nathan Bedford Forrest

■ Brig. Gen. Frank C. Armstrong

■ Lt. Col. George E. Flynt, XIV Corps assistant adjutant general. A message he sent to Rosecrans' headquarters late on September 21 from Rossville reflected the confusion and wild rumors running rampant during the army's retreat: "An intelligent contraband, belonging to [the] quartermaster of Cheatham's division, states that the enemy's advance is about 3 miles from here. Says he heard them say they numbered 100,000 men ... Generals Hood, Gregg, Smith and Adams reported killed. Says the Virginia rebels say they never saw such fighting; to yell only makes the Yankees pitch in. Says the rebels say they are bound to go to Kentucky and Tennessee for the purpose of getting bacon, &c..."

Nine hours later, Rosecrans wired the War Department that "the mass of this army is intact and in good spirits ... Retired on Rossville, which we held yesterday; then retired on Chattanooga. Our position is a strong one. Think we can hold out several days, and if re-enforcements come up soon everything will come out right."

■ 2nd Lieut. Francis M. Hatfield of Company H, 31st Indiana, distinguished himself in battle at Stone River and again for cool and efficient service at Chickamauga. The battle cost this 380-man Hoosier regiment 83 aggregate casualties, including a company commander and color sergeant killed. Chaplain Hiram Gillmore, whose horse was shot beneath him, remained "constantly on the field attending to wounded, much exposed."

and the hour for hope had gone.

But the dawn of light on the morning of the 21st brought fresh hope with power to endure. No army ever more cheerfully marched to new duties than the Army of the Cumberland that bright September morning. The Twenty-First Corps climbed to the top of Mission Ridge and stretched its length along the crest to the north, from Rossville to about the point since known as Bragg's headquarters.

The day wore away and the attack that had been hourly expected was not made. Busy and willing hands had been building from early dawn until after nightfall.

At 10 o'clock when all was quiet as the sick chamber, and we lay sleeping behind the barricade, a whispered order came to be ready to march in ten minutes and without a word being spoken aloud. Standing in line, awaiting orders to move, an order was received for a company from our brigade to be left deployed along the entire line of our works. Company A, Thirty-first Indiana was detailed, and stepping a pace or two out of line we stood at "attention" while the command marched away, the officers stepping from their places in line to take a hurried leave of their associates, while the soldiers whispered jocular messages to General Bragg, or made requests for souvenirs from Belle Isle or Libby prison.

We stood in perfect silence until the last sound of the marching columns died away in the valley to the west. The loneliness that followed seemed almost suffocating, but recovering from the stupefying influences of the situation we proceeded to obey our orders by deploying the little command at intervals sufficient to cover the ridge occupied by our command during the day. The enemy — Polk's Corps — was in position in our front, and so near that all night long we could plainly hear every loud word spoken in their camp, the marching of their columns into position and the rattling of their artillery over the rough grounds, while we stood looking steadily into the impenetrable darkness of the deep gulch and forest between us. Neither orders to rejoin our command, nor the morning, it seemed, would ever come.

Suddenly hoofbeats of an approaching horseman were heard in the distance, but owing to the peculiar echoing of sound the direction could not be determined. A mounted soldier rode into our line from its right — south — flank and was brought between two bayonets to the company commander. To learn that he did not bring orders ending our lonely watch was a severe disappointment, but it had its compensation. He claimed he had been sent from corps headquarters with a bottle of whiskey to the chief of artillery, under whose direction empty caissons had been rattling over the rough hills away to our right all night long. How he had ridden into our lines it puzzled him to know, and he was greatly distressed at being a prisoner. We dismounted him and relieved him of his arms and munitions of war, and gave him assurance that although he would be unable to reach his alleged chief of artillery immediate arrangements would be made for the disposition of the burden of his errand.

With a command of not more than fifty men, on a lonely mountain ridge, miles away from the army to which we belonged, and but a few hundred yards from a powerful enemy, I remember a thought came into my mind that this perhaps was the opportunity to do something that would make report of our service worthy the attention of our country — a youthful ambition as commendable as hopeless. But a courier that came crashing through the brush and over fallen timbers from the foot of the mountain, stopped indulgence in the illusions of a foolish hope, and we hurriedly "rallied on the center," and followed while the courier led the way down to the valley and on to the Rossville road a mile or more away. A hurried march of half an hour brought us inside the cavalry vidette, three miles or more out from Chattanooga. We dropped to the ground for a moment's rest just as the morning sunlight was touching the tallest pines on Mission Ridge. Almost instantly all were asleep.

Awakening suddenly I saw standing before me, with his hand grasping the rein of his horse, and still between two bayoneted guns, our prisoner of a few hours before, who was as much delighted that our uniforms, which looked gray by starlight, were blue, as I was surprised that he wore the same color.

Resuming our march, as we drew nearer our lines that ran from the foot of Lookout Mountain around to the Tennessee River on the north, we beheld an army playing at the game of war with "spades" as trumps. Far around to the northward, on the high ground since known as Fort Wood, we saw a squad of soldiers standing on the half-made works looking intently at our little moving column, and we directed our course toward them. Climbing over the works where they stood and receiving congratulations at our unexpected return, we stacked our arms and followed suit by also playing "spades" from the quartermaster's deal, while distracted women and children stood stupefied and overwhelmed at the destruction of their beautiful suburban homes that a few hours before had been the pride and ornament of Chattanooga.

For hours after we were safely within the new line of works we heard the roar of the enemy's cannon and saw the puffs of smoke from bursting shells over the works we had left, and on which we finally saw hundreds of the enemy standing looking down upon us in our place of safety.

Attempts were made to throw shells into our lines, which were by that time well formed and fortified, from batteries on Mission Ridge, but the effect, in most part, was more to our amusement than danger.

## 'Corn cobs covered the earth'

### Capt. D. Augustus Dickert
### Company H
### 3rd South Carolina Volunteer Infantry

Early on the morning of the 22nd we were ordered forward towards Chattanooga, the right wing having gone the day before. On nearing the city, we were shelled by batteries posted on the heights along the way and from the breastworks and forts around the city. It was during one of the heavy engagements between our advanced skirmish lines and the rear guard of the enemy that one of the negro cooks, by some means, got lost between the lines, and as heavy firing began, bullets flying by him in every direction, he rushed towards the rear, and raising his hands in an entreating position, cried out, "Stop, white folks, stop! In the name of God

■ Lt. Col. William D. Gale served as a volunteer aide to his father-in-law, Lt. Gen. Leonidas Polk, commander of the Confederate right wing at Chickamauga. Polk incurred Bragg's wrath for failing to launch a daybreak assault on September 20. Nine days later he was suspended from command and ordered to Atlanta, where Polk resumed a letter-writing campaign to President Jefferson Davis pleading for Bragg's removal. He assailed Bragg for squandering the initiative won after the battle, and noted that army morale was slipping because of delay and indecision — views shared at the time by many officers, including Gale.

"General Bragg refused to believe that he had won a victory," Gale bitterly wrote later. "I can forgive Mr. Davis for all the blunders he made & persisted in during the war — except the infernal sin he committed in placing Bragg at the head of the army of Tenn & keeping him there, as he did. Bragg was," Gale concluded, "a bantam in success & a dunghill in disaster."

# 'His leg had to be taken off'

**For weeks after Chickamauga hundreds of soldiers wrote home telling sad tales of the deaths or wounds of comrades. The following letter by a Wisconsin officer was written to the father of one of his men.**

Dear Sir;

Corporal Edward Glenn wishes me to write you a few lines, thinking you will be interested in his welfare. I take pleasure in acceeding to his wish, but knowing you will be pained and saddened at the misfortunes that befell him ...

No braver boy went into that bloody fight of Sunday than "Sandy" Glenn. When we commenced falling back, bourne down by swarms of the cursed Rebels, "Sandy" was struck by a bullet in the wrist of the right hand and as he was retreating he heard Colonel McCreery of the 21st Michigan calling for assistance to help him carry the body of General Lytle from the field, and he stopped to help him; but the Col. was shot down and Sandy received a wound in the right side. He now found that if he staid longer he would be taken prisoner and he made an effort to escape but was shot through the right leg below the knee — shattering the bone all to pieces.

The Rebels took him prisoner and paroled him there but left him where he fell for six days and seven nights, without dressing his wounds. What little he got to eat or drink was given him by a few humane rebels. Sandy was brought into our lines under a flag of truce Friday the 26th and his wounds were dressed but his leg had to be taken off below the knee. The Surgeon told me that he would be able to be home in a month or six weeks. He feels very anxious about how he is to get along in the future, but I assured him that he would be looked after and something done for him for he deserved it if any one of our noble soldiers ever did.

I remain yours, Thos. T. Keith
2nd Lieut. Co. D 24th Wis. Vols.

**Seven months later, Keith himself was killed in battle at Adairsville, Ga., during the Atlanta campaign.**

Almighty, stop and argy!"

In moving along, near the city we came to a great sink in the ground, caused by nature's upheaval at some remote period, covering an acre or two of space. It seemed to have been a feeding place for hogs from time immemorial, for corn cobs covered the earth for a foot or more in depth. In this place some of our troops were posted to avoid the shells, the enemy having an exact range of this position. They began throwing shells right and left and bursting them just over our heads, the fragments flying in every direction. At every discharge, and before the shell reached us, the men would cling to the sides of the slooping sink, or burrow deeper in the cobs, until they had their bodies almost covered.

A little man of my company, while a good soldier, had a perfect aversion to cannon shot, and as a shell would burst just overhead his body was seen to scringe, tremble and go still deeper among the cobs. Some mischievous comrade took advantage of his position, seized a good sound cob, then just as a shell bursted overhead, the trembling little fellow all flattened out, he struck him a stunning blow on the back. Such a yell as he set up was scarcely ever heard. Throwing the cobs in every direction, he cried out, "Oh! I am killed; I am killed! Ambulance corps! Ambulance corps!" But the laugh of the men soon convinced him his wound was more imaginary than real, so he turned over and commenced to burrow again like a mole.

Rosecrans having withdrawn his entire force within the fortifications around Chattanooga, our troops were placed in camp, surrounding the enemy in a semi-circle, and began to fortify. [We were] stationed around a large dwelling in a grove, just in front of Chattanooga, and something over a mile distant from the city, but in plain view.

**It took four full days for Bragg's army to catch up with the Federals in Chattanooga. Believing Rosecrans would evacuate, Bragg did not vigorously pursue, despite entreaties by Gens. Longstreet, Nathan B. Forrest and others. Early evidence suggested the Federals *were* leaving; a steady stream of wagons and ambulances crossed north over a hastily constructed pontoon bridge on the Tennessee River. But what some Confederates perceived to be a panic-driven withdrawal never materialized. As Bragg's equally weary soldiers settled into a vast arc of positions from Missionary Ridge to Lookout Valley, the Federals traded muskets for axes, picks and shovels, and began to dig in.**

**"We were so completely whipped and cowed at Chickamauga," wrote Private Francis M. Carlisle of Company D, 42nd Indiana, "that our most dashing Generals such as Rousseau and Jeff. C. Davis were up and down our lines constantly giving us good cheering news, and would make bright and encouraging speeches to us, and sent out barrels of whiskey to stimulate the boys. If Bragg had known that we were so badly whipped he could have destroyed our whole Army at that time; but in two days we had our works so strong that it was out of the question to move us out."**

**"Rosy has thrown up fortifications all around Chattanooga and if he can keep his lines of communication open to the rear, he *can* hold the town," Private Aurelius M. Willoughby of Company H, 39th Indiana Mounted Infantry, boasted in his**

# An officer's successful masquerade

**When the 33rd Ohio fell back to Chattanooga on September 22, the men found their ranks depleted by more than a third. Nearly 80 officers and men were surrounded and captured two days earlier at Chickamauga, when a shouted order to retire could not be heard above the din of battle.**

**Numbered among the regiment's dead was Major Ephraim J. Ellis, killed by a Confederate sharpshooter and hurriedly buried on the field. His loss was keenly felt in the 33rd, perhaps most by 2nd Lieut. Charles R. Pomeroy (left) of Company I, who immediately went to Col. Oscar F. Moore with a request for a special mission. His story was related by the regimental adjutant, 1st Lieut. Angus L. Waddle:**

On our arrival at Chattanooga Lieutenant Pomeroy asked permission from the colonel to return to the battlefield and secure possession of the body of Major Ellis, whose grave he had marked that he might recognize it. The colonel, knowing the almost certainty of his being captured, was not disposed to give the permission, but the lieutenant was so persuasive and so confident that he finally yielded and provided him with an ambulance. A soldier volunteered as driver and thus equipped he passed through our lines. They had not proceeded far before they were picked up and taken before a confederate general officer, to whom the lieutenant represented himself as a surgeon and stated his errand. His appearance was well calculated to sustain the character assumed. Of rather tall, slender build and wearing glasses, which added somewhat to his naturally intellectual countenance, his story seemed a plausible one — so much so that, after making a prisoner of the driver and conficating the ambulance and mules, he was placed in a hospital to assist in caring for the wounded.

He managed to sustain his assumed character in this trying place and in a few weeks was forwarded to Richmond, where, as surgeons were not held as prisoners of war, he was released and returned to his command — soon, alas, to meet the fate of the friend for whom he had been willing to sacrifice his liberty.

**Less than 11 months later, Pomeroy was killed outside Atlanta leading Company A in an assault on Confederate skirmishers near Utoy Creek.**

■ Sergeant Levi A. Ross of Company K, 86th Illinois, was made acting sergeant major on September 20 at Chickamauga. "I saw veteran soldiers," Ross wrote, "who had survived the storms of Donelson, Shiloh, Fort Henry, Corinth, Perryville and Stone River, and all said this Sunday [at] Chickamauga was the hottest and bloodiest of all. After listening all day to the roar of cannon and the incessant and most terrific rattle and roll of musketry it is a wonder that every man in both armies is not in eternity."

Ross, pictured here at war's end, was promoted to captain of Company K on April 20, 1865.

**diary. "Our regiment has dismounted itself and their horses are sent to the north side of the River with their train. Our boys have thrown up splendid works in front of the town. Genl Willich rode up to where our boys were at work and said — 'Ah! what regiment is this working with *spurs* on their heels?' "**

**Rosecrans' besieged soldiers turned Chattanooga into an impregnable fortress. The Confederates entrenched as well, and the opposing armies stared at each other over the next two months.**

**"The impression gains ground," 1st Lieut. George W. Rouse, adjutant of the 100th Illinois, wrote on September 27, "that the rebels will not attack our entrenchments, though the hills and valleys along our entire front are nightly lit up by the camp fires of the enemy, who were promised on the evacuation of this place, that we should be speedily driven back across the Tennessee or annihilated. They know too well the strength of the position and our fighting qualities to make an attack. Rumors are current of a flank movement by the rebels, but it is not much feared."**

**"Our Pickett duty is Pretty hard," wrote Private Hezekiah Rabb of the 33rd Alabama. "Some days we are allowed to talk & exchange Papers with the Yanks & other days we have to shoot at almost Every noise we hear. We are Tolerably well fortified & the Yanks are much better I think. Some think it likely we may stay here all the winter."**

## 'Sergeant-Major, we are whipped like hell'

### Journal of
### Acting Sergeant Major Levi A. Ross
### 86th Illinois Volunteer Infantry

At 9 p.m. [on September 20] we silently withdrew from the sanguinary field of Chickamauga, leaving our dead and wounded in the hands of the enemy. When we arrived at Rossville we found that the whole army had fallen back to the mountain ridge overlooking the valley of Chattanooga. Even Gen. Thomas, who had stood all day as a wall, hurling back superior numbers, was here. This Sabbath day, so fraught with human suffering and all the tragic scenes of grim-visaged war, will ever be remembered ...

**Sept. 21st.** Rebels attacked us about 2 p.m. Our position was very advantageous. Occasionally a shell would burst around us killing and wounding a few. We all lay flat on our faces. While the batteries were firing the skirmishers kept up a sharp and constant racket, but they did not attack us with any considerable force, feeling their way cautiously. The loss in the 86th for the three days [September 19-21] was only 8 killed and 15 wounded. This is nothing compared to those regiments that had but a corporal's guard left.

During the progress of the battle I took note of the effect of danger on the different boys. If ever a man ought to have a serious thought it is when his companions are falling around him with the chance that the next ball will pass through his own heart and send him to his long home. Our boys who habitually swore, cursed and swore as profanely and foolishly as they ever did in the quiet safety of the camp.

At 8 o'clock p.m. all firing ceased, and again the commanding General found it expedient to shorten his lines by concentrating all his forces around Chattanooga. Accordingly, we commenced to fall back as noiselessly as possible. The wheels of the batteries and caissons were all wrapped with wool blankets and drawn from their positions by the troops, and every man in line crept down the mountain side speechless, as if his life depended on the issue of noise or no noise. As we descended into the valley and were once more in our little Rossville, the Adjutant rode up to me and said: "Sergeant-Major, we are whipped like hell, and the Army of the Cumberland is on a grand retreat to Nashville." I could not agree with our desponding Adjutant. Passing up the line our Captain locked arms in mine and said: "My God, Ross, we are whipped." This was the general impression among officers and men, and none of us liked the idea of falling back before a victorious foe. I felt more hopeful and that all would end well though we were forced to assume the defensive.

**Sept. 22nd.** Up on the Rossville road the Johnnies made a charge today, but were repulsed with loss by a brigade of Regulars, [though] as a rule the Regular soldiers are less efficient and reliable than the volunteers.

**Sept. 23rd.** Genl. Rosecrans and staff rode around the lines this morning and, as is ever the case when a commanding general appears, the troops loudly cheered. But we feel more like cheering Rosecrans' chief of staff, Gen. James A. Garfield who planned the concentration of Rosecrans' scattered corps, and Gen. George H. Thomas, called "Pop" Thomas by his loving boys, than to offer our approving cheers to Rosecrans himself, who, had it not been for the ability of a cool-headed Garfield to plan and an imperturbable, well-poised, clear-headed, self-reliant Thomas to execute, the Army of the Cumberland would have been literally annihilated by Bragg's overwhelming force, in detail.

## 'Thronged with ambulances and wagons'

### 2nd Lieut. Isaac H.C. Royse
### Company E
### 115th Illinois Volunteer Infantry

I had been wounded in the left shoulder by a fragment of a shell [on September 20], but continued with my company until the next morning. Colonel Moore then observed my wound and ordered me to Chattanooga, and while the regiment was moving out on Missionary Ridge on the 21st I was on my way over the dusty road towards the city. The whole country between Rossville and Chattanooga had been tramped and worn by the thousands of troops and army wagons till the road seemed a very wide one. Wide as it was, it was thronged that day with ambulances and wagons, and wounded men on foot and on horseback — all very anxious to get to a place of safety.

Being able to care for myself, after a night's lodging in a house filled with wounded, on the morning of the 22nd I went to the church a short distance north of the old Crutchfield house, where I found Surgeon Garner H. Bane busy with important surgical operations. The surgeon informed me that he had neither eaten

■ 2nd Lieut. Isaac H.C. Royse of Company E, 115th Illinois, was wounded in the left shoulder by a shell fragment at Chickamauga and walked to Chattanooga on September 21 for medical treatment. "All the churches and other public buildings and many dwellings in Chattanooga were converted into hospitals," he wrote. "Many of the wounded had no shelter of any kind, but were left lying on the ground in the front yards of residences or wherever most convenient to unload them ...

"After a night's lodging in a house filled with wounded, on the morning of the 22nd I went to the church a short distance north of the old Crutchfield House, where I found Surgeon Garner H. Bane busy with important surgical operations. The surgeon informed me that he had neither eaten nor slept since the battle, but with many other surgeons had constantly worked day and night, being sustained by the excitement and an occasional sip of brandy."

■ 1st Lieut. Joseph Gore of Company A, 115th Illinois, was captured on September 24 while in command of a 40-man detail attempting to recover a ferryboat stranded in the Tennessee River. One of Gore's men, Private J. M. Waddle of Company E, recalled:

"As we neared Lookout Mountain, a regiment of Longstreet's men arose and poured a volley of bullets into our boat. The first volley wounded our mules and some of our men. A few who were good swimmers leaped into the river and attempted to swim to the opposite shore, but a fierce fire was kept up at those in the water. Our boat, being disabled, turned round and round and rapidly drifted to the shore. The rebels then ordered us to jump off and tie the boat, and we were then taken to Longstreet's headquarters. Henry Roberts of Company E, who had deserted from the rebel army and joined us at Normandy, Tenn., in August previous, was among our party. When they took our names he gave his nickname, 'John Wilder.' They then marched us farther up the mountain, soon passing a line of battle. As we came near them Roberts remarked, 'There is my old regiment.' I told him to draw down his hat over his eyes. He did so, but they recognized him and immediately called to the officers, who handcuffed him and marched him away. We learned from the rebels that he was shot a short time afterwards. After marching us to Bragg's headquarters and taking our rubber blankets and other equipments from us, they started us on our journey southward."

nor slept since the battle, but with many other surgeons had constantly worked day and night, being sustained by the excitement and an occasional sip of brandy.

The siege was on at once. Very soon the Confederates had taken position on Missionary Ridge, with their advance line extending across the valley to Lookout Mountain, threateningly near our works. The Union forces were working night and day putting the old rebel forts in order, building new ones, digging trenches and throwing up earthworks. The whole place was on "rush orders." As early as the 24th the Confederates were on Lookout Mountain and had taken possession of the road to Bridgeport. Thus our lines of communication to Nashville were cut off, except the very difficult one over Walden's Ridge and down Sequatchie Valley, a distance of seventy-five miles of little used mountain roads to Stevenson, Ala.

The difficulty of securing supplies for such a large army was at once apparent, and the danger that the Confederates who were daily receiving large reenforcements would attempt to take the place by storm, made it imperative that all the wounded who were able to travel should be sent to the rear. The danger of the situation becoming known to the wounded through the excited surgeons and nurses, what was very nearly a stampede to the North began on the 23rd. Every man at all capable for the journey, and very many so badly wounded that to attempt it was at the imminent risk of life, scrambled for a chance to get away. All the ambulances and wagons available were soon filled. Hundreds with arms and legs bandaged, and many more or less severely wounded but whose wounds had received no attention, took to the road afoot. And thus the crowds streamed over the pontoon bridge and up the slopes of Walden's Ridge. The jolting of the ambulances and wagons was excruciating to the badly wounded, but regardless of the cries of pain the procession moved on. A dozen or more died that night and were buried in rude graves, without coffins or ceremony, on the summit of the ridge.

The next day's march brought them down into the Sequatchie Valley, and late on the third day they were at Bridgeport, Ala. Then there was a long wait, some of the men in field hospitals and many more on the ground without shelter, till railroad transportation could be provided to take them to Nashville to the hospitals.

An incident of this march of the wounded over Walden's Ridge may be worth mentioning. W.G. Henry of Company E, who was so badly wounded that he could not help himself, was lying on a bed of straw in a big government wagon, the most comfortable transportation at his command. Five or six others, less severely injured, occupied it with him. All went fairly well, though it may be imagined the jolting over stones and ruts was not particularly soothing to the wounds, till a turn was reached in the descent to Sequatchie Valley.

There the road was cut out of rock and was barely wide enough for one team to pass. A perpendicular wall of rock rose at one side, while on the other was a precipice nearly as steep, perhaps three hundred feet to the bottom. This dangerous situation was enhanced by the fact that the roadbed inclined from the mountain wall towards the precipice at a pretty steep grade. As this particular wagon reached the narrowest place, the rear wheels began

■ 1st Lieut. Samuel C. Alexander (seated at far right) with enlisted men of Company K, 115th Illinois. Col. Jesse H. Moore, regimental commander, wrote in an October letter home: "There are no better disciplined men in the army, none more obedient to orders, none more patient amidst the scenes of suffering. They have not had a blanket, or even a shelter tent since we left Bridgeport, September 12th. As serious as these privations may seem to the friends at home who sit around cheerful fires, sleep on soft beds and gratify their appetites with the choicest productions of a land of plenty, I am persuaded that you could find nowhere a merrier or more cheerful crowd than can be seen every day in my camp."

sliding towards the edge until it was almost within the breadth of a tire of going over, when the wagon was brought to a stand. Soon all who could help themselves were out, but poor Billy Henry was left to the chance of a whirl down the mountain. He could not get out of the wagon, and there were not well men enough in the party to lift him out. Imagine, if you please, his state of mind as his wounded companions and the driver discussed ways and means for holding the wagon from going over till the narrow place should be passed, and what a relief it was to all when it was safely over.

While the wounded were traveling over the mountain, the remnant of the 115th was going into camp opposite Brown's Ferry, a little below the ball of the foot on the "Moccasin" opposite Lookout Mountain. The 96th Illinois, 84th Indiana and 40th Ohio went into camp opposite the mountain.

On the 24th the regiment met a severe loss in the killing and capture of a detail that was taking an old ferry-boat down the river past the mountain. Lieut. Joseph Gore of Company A was in charge of a detail from the various companies, in all some forty men, who were ordered to get the boat off a reef some distance above the point of Lookout where it had lodged, and bring it down to Brown's Ferry.

They got the boat loose at 10 a.m. on that day, and at 1 p.m. started down stream. The boat was propelled by mule power and all went well till opposite the point of Lookout Mountain. Although the rebels had as yet made no demonstration on the mountain, Lieutenant Gore was apprehensive of danger and was taking all possible precaution against an attack, while fearlessly obeying his orders. As they passed the narrows opposite Point Lookout, the rebels opened on them. One of the mules was killed at the first volley and the boat was disabled. In its helpless condition the boat was rapidly carried by the current to the mountain side of the river. Seven or eight of the men jumped overboard and tried to swim ashore, but all were killed or drowned excepting a man from Company F. All the others were made prisoners.

■ Brig. Gen. James A. Garfield, future president of the United States, served as Rosecrans' chief of staff from January to October 10, 1863. Rosecrans had great respect for Garfield and paid him a glowing tribute for his contributions in the Tullahoma campaign. "I feel much indebted to him for both counsel and assistance in the administration of this army," Rosecrans wrote. "He possesses the instinct and energy of a great commander."

Garfield's buoyant mood before Chickamauga turned to melancholy after the battle, as viewed in letters home to his wife, Lucretia, in late September. From Chattanooga on the 23rd he wrote: "We must ... save ourselves if saved at all. If calamity befalls us you may be sure we shall sell ourselves as dearly as possible. Keep up a brave cheerful heart. The country will triumph if we do not."

## 'The moon hung in a cloudless sky'

### Private George Barkhamer
### Company K
### 19th Ohio Volunteer Infantry

On the second night after the Army of the Cumberland had stacked arms on its defensive line in front of Chattanooga, I was down in the valley on picket duty, possibly a half mile or more from our line of works. The night was a magnificent one. The moon hung high in a cloudless sky over the rebel camps. We had but just returned from Chickamauga and expected a renewal of the struggle at any moment. The lines were still very sensitive, and early in the evening the enemy commenced feeling our skirmish line, and as the hours advanced became more and more aggressive. Heavy supply and ammunition trains were heard moving over our pontoon bridge across the Tennessee at Chattanooga, and this undoubtedly led the enemy to believe that our army was evacuating the city.

At 9 p.m. I went out on post, my station being a large oak tree standing almost in the center of a wagon road that passed on either side of the tree. To my right the line stretched across a field out through the open country beyond, where the heaviest fighting was going on, and plunged into a dark forest immediately to my left. The rebels did very little shooting where we were, and we probably did still less, as we were expecting them to advance. To my right a rail fence ran parallel with the road out into their lines, and here I imagined that a whole rebel division might move up under cover. Back in front of our line of works huge fires sprang up as if by magic, showing that our men on the line of battle were on the alert and ready for work, while high up above the river on the other side the signal lights were bowing and nodding their messages from Moccasin Point.

Presently a brigade of infantry and a battery drew out of our works and came down into the valley, soon convincing our Southern friends that we had no intention whatever of evacuating the city that night. The condition of the air permitted sounds to be heard clearly and at great distances, and the stern commands mingled with the shouts and curses from the opposing pickets were plainly audible amid the crackle and din of the fire along the lines.

Some of the rebels deserted their skirmish line that night, and I saw several in the field to my right, running into our lines with loud cries to our men not to shoot. One rose up on the inside of the fence, not over ten rods in front of me, and stooping over with shouts of "Don't fire, don't fire! I surrender!" rushed past within a few feet of my post, barely escaping the shots from our pickets in the field to my right. He kept straight on as long as I could see him. This deserting of rebels, while on outpost duty in the night, grew to be a common thing afterwards, and I do not believe there was a night during the two months and over that the two armies confronted each other at Chattanooga in which from five to fifteen Johnnies did not leave their outposts and come into our lines as deserters; of course, the deserters were most frequent from the regiments organized in territory afterwards occupied by our army.*

It must have been about 11 o'clock that night when my attention was drawn to a noise as of cavalry moving within the enemy's lines. This was only what was expected by us down on the left that night, and our instructions had looked to a probable advance by that road. The cavalry, indeed, held the first place in my imagination that night, and several times I had thought I detected troopers deploying in front, but found it a mere delusion. This time, however, there was no mistake. Cavalry were surely in motion and approaching on the very road I was posted on. Once they stopped, but soon I could hear them again coming toward me and distinguish clearly the "tic, tic" of their arms as the momentum of the cavalry horses' measured stride brought the canteens, tin cups and equipments into sharp contact.

Presently, the men on my right discharged their guns and this kindled up the line to my left in the woods, and in turn drew forth a blaze from the rebel line in front. But with a wild rush the cavalry came up, and, having fired down the road in their direction, I ran into the woods. The troopers bending low in their saddles swept past like the wind, and when a moment later, I reached the reserves who had started to support the picket line, and were already close up, I found them standing in line and the commander in loud conversation with a captain of cavalry, who, with his company or squadron of mounted men, were protesting with many oaths that they were Union soldiers.

And so they actually proved to be. Having been detached to destroy some bridge in the direction of Cleveland [Tenn.], they had been unable to rejoin the army before its withdrawal to Chattanooga, and as the Confederate right rested opposite to our left on the Tennessee River, they had found themselves completely shut out and in the rear of the rebel army. Waiting until quite late in the evening so that their uniforms would not reveal their identity, they had started boldly up from the rebel rear, and answering all inquiries as to their business with the statement that they were ordered out to reconnoiter in front, they successfully

■ Corporal Ambrose B. Balmont of Company I, 19th Ohio, twice witnessed his regiment scatter in confusion at Chickamauga. On September 20 it fought most of the day broken into squads with fragments of other regiments, and was not rallied and reorganized until late that night near Rossville. Ninety casualties, more than one-fourth of them captured or missing, were reported by the 19th's commander, while six of seven members of the color guard were wounded. Falling back to Chattanooga, the regiment hurriedly entrenched during the next two days in the town's eastern outskirts.

On July 9, 1864, Balmont was killed by a sharpshooter along the Chattahoochee River above Atlanta.

* On October 8, 1st Lieut. John D. Floyd of Company A, 17th Tennessee, wrote to his wife concerning Confederate desertions: "I have much that I would like to communicate to you but prudence under present state of affairs forbids; I hope though before many weeks have passed to see you as I confidently believe our army will reoccupy Middle Tennessee. Many whom I had looked upon as warm supporters of our cause on leaving Tennessee became discouraged and deserted. They must have been very despondent indeed or feared the results of a battle very much to be willing to bear the disgrace of desertion, in preference to staying with us. But we have lost nothing as the men we have with us now are reliable. My faith in our success is unshaken and my determination to continue to fight against the Yankees until the last is firm as ever."

■ Nurse Kate Cumming traveled to the front a week after Chickamauga, and described what she found in the Confederate hospitals at Ringgold, Ga.: "Wounded men, wrapped in their blankets, were lying on the balcony. I went into a room which was filled with others in the same state, some of whom were suffering for want of water. They all seemed perfectly resigned; the more so as we had been victorious. How they seemed to glory in it!

"We could see the wagon trains come in with their precious burdens. As many as fifty came in at one time. We rolled bandages until the afternoon, and could scarcely supply the demand. The surgeons were getting the wounded men ready to send off on the train. I was rejoiced when we were told we had rolled enough for that day. There had been no rain for some time, and the wagons raised the dust in clouds, and when the men were taken out of them they were almost as black as negroes."

made their way through the rebel camps, passed the picket reserves on the road and the rebel picket line, and then, bending down on their horses' necks, had started on a gallop for our lines, rushing headlong into them in the way I described without, as far as I knew, sustaining any casualties whatever. It was certainly a wild and daring undertaking.

After the scare was over, we hastened back to our places on the line. I took my post at the tree on the road again, and there was considerable firing kept up on the picket line from then on until daylight.

The post next to me in the woods to my left was patrolled by a farmer's boy from Stark County, Ohio — a member of Company I of our regiment. I had become much interested in him, as through the long hours of picket duty of the day he related to me his experiences at Chickamauga, where upon the disruption of the right-center of the army, on Sunday, he had joined that part which maintained its position under General Thomas and fought as a free-lance until evening. He now was taking great pride in polishing up a very superior gun that he had secured on the battlefield on Sunday.

At daybreak I was relieved from my post, but before the morning moon had paled and slipped from sight back of the Cumberland Mountain range, and ere the new-born day had flushed the hostile brow of Missionary Ridge in our front, Death, on his grand rounds, had relieved the picket on my left forever. He was found at his post in the morning, shot in the face and stark and stiff, but still clutching his gun.

## 'Gazed at each other like grim monsters'

### Chief Musician William J. Worsham
### 19th Tennessee Volunteer Infantry

Bragg and Rosecrans settled down to work with pick and spade, directly under each others' guns with all their might as if preparing a grave each one for the other. Bragg kept pushing the enemy's lines in on the city until he held the river from Lookout Point to about half way to the city and from Sherman Heights to the river above. For days the videttes of each army stood in two hundred yards of and gazed at each other like grim monsters. The valley out and around Chattanooga was literally blockaded with breast works and plowed up with rifle pits. The crest of Mission Ridge, its base and sides were furrowed with rifle pits and covered with cannon. Every now and then from the summit of Lookout Mountain were sent savage, hissing shells which would fall and burst in the camp of the enemy. For days the pickets of each army sat in their "Gopher Pits" cracking jokes with each other, while from the top of Mission Ridge and the rocky peak of Lookout went shrieking messengers of death over their heads unnoticed and uncared for by them, and the signal flags from the mountain tops talk with each other in their silent way over the enemy's camp.

A peculiar scene is here presented in the two encampments of supposed hostile foes; both armies were under the range of a single shot; the bands of each played for the entertainment of the other; while the sweet notes of "Dixie" were wafted towards the city over the encampment of the enemy, they were met by those of "Yankee Doodle" coming over to us. Another uncommon feature of these two encampments was while the enemy could plainly see the men and officers moving around Bragg's headquarters, we in turn from the top of Lookout and the ridge with glasses could see what the Yankees had for dinner.

## 'The grandest scene my eyes ever beheld'

### Major Clinton M. Winkler
### 4th Texas Volunteer Infantry

Camp near Chattanooga
September 27, 1863.

For three days and nights we have been in line of battle in front of the enemy; during the day, except an occasional boom of the cannon, we have been quiet, but every night we have skirmishing in front of our line, and the troops in readiness for action at any moment. Today, Sabbath as it is, our situation is unchanged. Officers are riding round, subordinates and men are lying in the shade, some writing letters on paper taken from the Federals in the recent fight; the working parties, meanwhile, busily engaged in strengthening our position.

On Friday last a party, of which I was one, obtained permission to visit Lookout Mountain, and about noon, the day being beautiful, set out and, in the course of an hour, had ascended as far as our horses could carry us, and dismounting, were climbing up its steep and rugged sides, when I disengaged myself from the balance of the party and sat down upon a shelving rock, to contemplate the grandest scene my eyes ever beheld.

Looking away to the northward, the Tennessee River could be seen winding its way through the mountain range southward, until it seemed to empty itself into the foot of the mountain where I sat, it being so high and steep, as seemingly, to overhang and exclude from view the river sweeping its base. The town of Chattanooga, situated on the east side some half mile from the river, is plainly seen, together with the large depot and railroad creeping down the valley, while across a large horse-shoe bend of the river, in which the town is located, may be traced the line of fortifications some time since evacuated by General Bragg, and within which Rosecrans has taken shelter since his defeat at Chickamauga. The enemy's encampment, along and within the heavy works, are plainly visible to the naked eye, and viewed through a glass presented a scene of life and bustle, interesting to contemplate, especially when we consider them our mortal enemies.

Their batteries are planted and frowning down upon us, their long lines of bayonets glistening in the sun, their rows of tents, the cloud of dust that is constantly ascending as they move to and fro, as officers dash along the lines, or their trains of wagons passing down to the pontoon bridge, and crossing the river, lose themselves among the mountains to the right, the whole surrounded and surmounted by mountains grand and gloomy, and as I gazed in amazement at the scene I thought of the exclamation of Bascomb at the falls of Niagara: "God of grandeur, what a sight!" — almost bewildered by the beauty spread out before me.

I do not believe it is the intention of our general to make an-

■ Major Clinton M. Winkler, 4th Texas. After little more than a month's service with Bragg's army, he wrote to his wife on October 22: "Our connection with the army of Virginia, I fear, is at an end, but if we can better serve our country here, we ought to cheerfully submit, though the feeling is unanimous among those who have served uner General Lee in preferring that army to this. Next to going home, every one would prefer going back to the Old Dominion [than] remaining here, or soldiering anywhere else in the Confederacy.

"During the time of high waters, last week, we were almost without provisions for four days. The rains, however, have ceased, and we have our usual supply. Our principal article of bread-stuff is the coarsest kind of corn meal. Stuff it is, and no mistake. Occasionally we get flour, some rice, and, once in a while, can purchase Irish potatoes; but this is an exhausted, mountainous, poor country."

■ Private Theodore C. Howard, nicknamed "Doc" by comrades in Parker's Battery, was known as a "loquacious and rascally little fellow" proficient in the art of foraging. On October 5, the battery spent its first full day on top of Lookout Mountain, firing nearly 500 rounds into Chattanooga and surrounding Federal camps. Calling army service "the best and happiest days of my life," Howard was a lucky campaigner. At Chancellorsville five months earlier, a shell fragment carried away part of his right ear — nearly hitting him square in the face.

other direct attack at present, but to cut off Rosecrans' supplies and compel him to come out of his stronghold and give us a fair fight in an open field.

We have greatly strengthened our position by throwing up earth-works, behind which we are safe from any shelling the enemy may honor us with. The opinion prevails that when our artillery opens upon the place, Chattanooga will become too warm for the cold blood of the North, but I have no confidence in shelling them out. I believe, unless we interrupt their communication, so as to compel them to withdraw, we will be compelled to storm their works to get at them. There is little likelihood that General Rosecrans will attack now that we are fortified. I fear we have been too tardy in our movements; we should have followed up the victory of the 20th, before the enemy had time to recover from the shock of defeat.

## 'Cannoneers to the wheels!'

### Private Royal W. Figg
### Parker's Virginia Battery

Arriving in front of Chattanooga, we halted behind Missionary Ridge. Here the drought was followed by excessive rains so that, together with insufficient clothing and food, some of our boys got sick and had to be sent back to the hospitals at Rome and other places in Georgia. When the frequent rains at last retreated we saw Lookout Mountain, tall and lonely, standing as a sentinel among the hills. Before many days the Parker battery, having light three-inch rifled pieces, was ordered to ascend it, and from thence to shell the enemy.

On one side Lookout Mountain rises almost precipitously to a height of fifteen hundred feet, its base being washed by the Tennessee river. The ascent, even by the regular road, was difficult; and the command, "Cannoneers to the wheels!" was frequently given — the men having to assist the horses in their arduous task. As we toiled up the steep road glimpses of scenery of surpassing beauty were afforded here and there. Picturesque valleys suddenly opened far below, while beetling rocks above seemed ready to topple on us. Add to the emotions naturally produced by such scenes the fact that we were marching to fight a brave and skilful enemy, who might fire on us at any moment from an opposite elevation, and you can imagine that the boys were very much interested!

A halt was ordered on a plateau when we were as yet far below the top of the mountain. Opposite, and within easy range, was a Federal battery, which we called the "Moccasin," from the resemblance of the hill it occupied to a shoe. The Yanks were well entrenched there and had been troubling our infantry with too many salutes. The Parker guns now opened on the "Moccasin" battery, and pretty soon convinced it that it had better let our infantry alone.

The next morning the ascent of the mountain was resumed. Our eyes were feasted with sights of the grand and beautiful as we toiled upward, but these scarcely prepared us for the glory of the view from the summit. It seemed almost limitless. In front, to the right, to the left, mountain on mountain loomed tall and blue as

far as vision might extend, while the Tennessee river, winding gracefully among them, gleamed out here and there in bright relief.

There is a jutting rock, facing Chattanooga, on which I have often stood as a sentinel during the witching hours of the night. It juts from the mountain-side several yards. From thence every fire in the Federal army might be seen, while the outer line, like a flaming crescent, marked its limits. Then an intervening dark space, and the opposite Confederate fires glared against the sky.

What weird thoughts coursed through my brain during some of those sentinel hours on that jutting rock! Away down in the valleys it might be calm, but there, almost every night, the winds would rise and seemed not voiceless in their unrest. The trees swayed to and fro and rustled their leaves; but it was not simply sound — there was sympathy expressed: "Poor, insane humanity," seemed saying the moaning winds, "poor, warring humanity! Look to the everlasting hills for your help — even above thee — for the Right and the True!" The sharp report of a picket gun startles the valley below; the winds moan drearily; the clouds descend upon the mountain and cling to the trees, weeping that the voice is not heard.

The "Moccasin" battery returned the first shots that we fired from our lofty position, and one shell narrowly missed General Bragg, who was with us at the time; but they did not seem to know that they could reach us and seldom or never replied to us afterwards. Every morning, about nine o'clock, our business-like firing commenced, and was generally kept up in leisurely style until night.

■ The tangled, rock-strewn slope of Lookout Mountain's nose is plainly evident in this photograph showing Moccasin Point, the Tennessee River and part of Chattanooga in the distance. "Most of the soldiers took the opportunity of visiting Lookout Mountain and feasting their eyes upon the finest scenery of the South," wrote Capt. D. Augustus Dickert of Company H, 3rd South Carolina. A winding wagon road led to the mountain's brow, as did a footpath which "had to be climbed hundreds of feet, perpendicularly, by means of ladders fastened to its sides. Some of the boldest climbers took this route to reach the summit, but after climbing the first ladder and looking back towards the gorge below, I concluded it was safer and more pleasant to take the 'longer way round.' Looking from the top of Lookout Mountain — its position, its surroundings, its natural fortresses — this would have made an old feudal lord die of envy."

■ Major Augustus B. Bonnafon, in charge of the 78th Pennsylvania's skirmishers at Chickamauga, temporarily commanded the regiment in place of Lt. Col. Archibald Blakeley after the battle. Both men felt the sting of army regulations when they arrived in Chattanooga — a result of Blakeley's verbal order on September 20 excusing two footsore and shoeless non-commissioned officers from duty. Written permission from a regimental commander was required by the provost marshal to prevent such soldiers from being arrested, but Blakeley had neither pencil nor paper at hand to comply while standing in line of battle. As it happened, the sergeant and corporal *were* arrested, and Blakeley, too, was placed in confinement a few days later for disobedience. He recalled: "I explained the matter to Major Bonnafon, who took command, and I went to quarters. I had not thought of them repeating the command to Major Bonnafon, but they did and the Major refused, and he came to quarters in arrest a few hours later than I did. We were court martialed and fined a month's pay, but, thank God, they never got [the sergeant and corporal] and I was well pleased with the result."

## 'A matter of interest and amusement'

### Sergeant Joseph T. Gibson
### Company A
### 78th Pennsylvania Volunteer Infantry

By [September] 25th, instead of being a matter of apprehension, the average soldier would have been very glad to have had the Condeferates make an attack, for we felt able to resist successfully any assault that might be made on us. The Confederates planted their batteries along the side of Lookout Mountain, bringing two heavy guns to the point of the mountain. These two "84 pounders," as we called them, very soon came to be a matter of curiosity rather than apprehension, for they scarcely interferred with our work as we fortified the place. The 78th Pennsylvania helped to build what afterwards came to be known as Fort Negley, which soon grew to be one of the strongest forts on the right wing of our Army.

During all this time the Confederate artillery threw shells into our camp but did very little damage, and we came to regard their firing on us from the point of Lookout Mountain and elsewhere as a matter of interest and amusement rather than alarm or danger. We measured our distances by an air line from the point of Lookout Mountain every day by counting the seconds from the time we saw the smoke rising on the point of the mountain indicating the discharge of an "84 pounder" until we heard the sound. Knowing that sound travels at the rate of about 1,100 feet per second, we could easily measure the distance. We also discovered that shells traveled for that distance at about the same rate that the sound traveled, for simultaneously with the sound of the discharge of the gun on the mountain we could see and hear the explosion of the shell in the neighborhood of the camp. There were a few casualties and some narrow escapes, but these only helped to keep our interest.

The pickets of the two armies along Chattanooga Creek were not more than from seventy-five to one hundred feet apart, and they were on the best of terms, and conversed frequently on various subjects. The Confederate pickets had the impression that we were pretty hard up for rations, but, in answer to their inquiries, they always found the pickets on the Union line ready to fling a cracker across the little stream that separated them.

Nevertheless no words can adequately describe the suffering of the soldiers. The topic of conversation every day and every hour during the weeks that preceded the opening of communication was the practical question as to when General Hooker would arrive with commissary stores. When the horses were eating their corn it was necessary to guard them to prevent the soldiers from appropriating the corn to their own use. Soldiers often paid twenty-five cents an ear for corn, parched it, ground it and made gruel of it in order to satisfy their hunger. The coarsest food was relished as we never had relished the choicest and daintiest morsels provided by the most skillful cooks. During all this time a great majority of the soldiers did not grumble or complain; they only compared notes and kept up the conversation in order to keep their courage up, and stimulate their hopes.

## 'Go to hell! I have been there'

### Private Thomas J. McCall
### Company H
### 15th Pennsylvania Cavalry

When the rebels had thrown their lines around us at Chattanooga, and starvation stared us in the face, we welcomed the news that there was plenty of corn and vegetables in Sequatchie Valley. I for one rejoiced when Sergeant Yerkes [Orderly Sergeant George S. Yerkes, Company H] came to my tent and told me that I was one of three detailed from our company to go with the detachment from the Regiment, then in camp on the west side of Cameron Hill. The detail was composed of Abel Turner, Robert Kincaid and myself, of Company H. We were to meet the detachment at the pontoon bridge at 5 o'clock next morning, which we did, and found Captain McAllister of Company G in command.

With the wagon train we crossed the Tennessee River and went up the road on the east side of Walden's Ridge. Owing to the starved condition of horses and mules our progress was slow. We understood that we were to go into the valley via Poe's crossroads. On arriving at the place we should have turned up the mountain, but for some reason the Captain intended to go up to the head of the run and cross the divide into the Tennessee Valley, about thirty miles above Chattanooga. We went about six miles and camped for the night. In the morning the Captain received information that General Wheeler with a division of Confederate cavalry was in the Tennessee Valley, and we countermarched and went up the mountain. It began to rain — a drizzling, cold October rain — and continued until after 2 o'clock. About 3:30 we had crossed the plateau on top of the mountain to where the road came up from the Robinson house in the valley.

Just there we met the head of the wagon train coming up from the valley, and as the road was narrow we had to wait until they passed before we could go down. They were driving as fast as they could and were considerably excited, and on inquiry they told us that Wheeler's cavalry was in the valley. Captain McAllister discredited the story, and said, "I will go down and drive them out," so we went down to the Robinson house. Company G occupied the large house where the road we went down intersected with one leading from the head of the Sequatchie River on down to the Bridgeport road, several miles down. Captain McAllister and Lieutenant Lingle occupied a small house just across the road. We parked the train about 100 yards below in a field. We had, I think, twenty-five wagons and 150 mules.

Turner, Kincaid and I slept in a wagon. After supper we went to the house to talk to the boys, and while there one of the citizens from up the valley sent a colored man to Captain McAllister and told him that Wheeler was camped four miles above, and he told me the same story.

My comrades and I were anxious to get a mess of sweet potatoes, and got out earlier than the boys at the house. We rode up to the house and there another colored man met us, and said that his mistress had sent him down to tell us to get out of the valley; that told of their loyalty.

Lieutenant Lingle made a remark about the pickets, when Cap-

■ 1st Lieut. Harvey S. Lingle of Company G, 15th Pennsylvania Cavalry, was appointed acting regimental adjutant following the Sequatchie Valley fighting. On December 29, 1863, he was shot during a mounted charge on Confederate cavalry at Mossy Creek in East Tennessee. Private William M. Palmer of Company L, whose hip was shattered by a bullet in the same engagement, described Lingle's last hours in a makeshift hospital: "The wounded from the various commands kept coming in and took up every available place in the church. I was placed on the floor, near the pulpit steps. In a short time Adjutant Lingle was brought in, wounded through the body. He was laid alongside of me. He was a brave and efficient officer and one of the most lovable comrades in the Regiment. All night long the surgeons were kept busy, amputating limbs and dressing wounds. About 4 a.m. Dr. [James W.] Alexander visited Adjutant Lingle, who seemed to be unconscious. He shook him, whereupon he opened his eyes, but remained silent. When the doctor asked him if he was aware that he could not live much longer, he undertook to reply, but in a few minutes he calmly passed away. I laid alongside of him for some two hours before he was removed for burial in the cemetery adjoining the church."

■ 1st Lieut. Comley J. Mather of Company F, 15th Pennsylvania Cavalry. Being an independent command, his regiment reported directly to the department commander and did not serve as a complete body during the siege — whole companies as well as individuals being detailed for specialized duty. A number of well educated enlisted men were selected for clerical work; one of these, Private John Tweedale, was considered by Gen. Thomas to be the best clerk in the Army of the Cumberland.

Companies B, H and K served as Rosecrans' and Thomas' headquarters escort during the Tullahoma, Chickamauga and Chattanooga campaigns. "One of our duties was to inform ourselves and keep posted on the positions held by our troops at all times, in camp or on the march," wrote Corporal T.H. Smith of Company K. "Our duties covered a wide scope, from acting as ordinary soldiers on the skirmish line to riding in state behind the General who commanded the army."

tain McAllister said he had called them in to get their breakfast. My two comrades and I went on out the road leading up the valley, about 200 yards, into the edge of the woods, and on the bank and a dozen paces to the right stood a darkey cabin. We rode up to the door and asked where there was a sweet-potato patch. The old mammy said, "I done had some in de garden, but fo' de Lawd, de sojer boys ober to de house done got them all."

Just then the advance of Wheeler's cavalry came around the bend of the road less than 100 yards from us. I raised my carbine, and the officer in command called out, "Don't shoot!" The carbine, a Sharps, had been in an open wagon the day before and the cartridge was wet and missed fire. I told Kincaid to get out of that, for he was mounted on a mule. I then fired my pistol and they fired at us. There were only five on the advance. I saw the head of the column just as Turner and I broke for the rear, and when we got to the house there was lively work among the boys getting ready to leave before the rebels got there. Fortunately, as I afterward learned, the rebels stopped to inquire of the old woman at the cabin about our strength. She, in blissful ignorance, magnified it to such an extent that they advanced slowly, and by that time the most of our men had mounted and began firing.

I finally got the cartridge out of my carbine by striking the butt on the pommel of my saddle. John Crum gave me a package of cartridges. By that time all the boys except Henry Sayres and Jack Pugh had mounted. Pugh had led his horse in between the picket fence and the house and had to back him past the gate to get him out, and by that time the road up the valley was full of Johnnies. The officers were commanding them to close up briskly. Firing was going on from both sides. Just then one of their men dismounted about forty yards from us, laid his long gun on the fence, blazed away and then threw down the fence. They began to pour through the gap to cut us off, and then our boys broke for the mountain.

I had held back for Pugh, and just as he mounted a Johnnie rode around the house and called out to halt. Pugh yelled out to him, "Go to hell! I have been there." I believe he had been a prisoner at Belle Isle.

The company had now quite a start on us. One man was a couple of lengths from me and Pugh was far to the rear. The Johnnie beat us to the fence, but, thank the Lord! it was about the best stake-and-rider fence I ever saw down South. They yelled out, "Halt, you damned Yankees!" But we did not stop. There must have been twenty-five or thirty of them. They fired, but never hit man or horse.

We dashed to Company G about seventy-five yards farther on. They were in a bunch and Lieutenant Lingle commanded the men to scatter out, as he said that the rebels would concentrate their fire and kill some of us. We obeyed at once. Just then comrade Over's horse was shot in the neck, and he barely got off before the horse fell dead. Jim took his bridle, halter and saddlebags off, cut the girth of the saddle, gave his saber and other things to some of the company, shouldered his carbine and footed it up the mountain.

A short time after, as we were going up the mountain, a detachment made a dash after us, but we turned around and drove them down again. We then filed off to the left, threw down a fence, went into a corn field and watched them burn our train. We

# Surfeited vith the good hings to eat'

**Immediately after Wheeler's cavalry ft Sequatchie Valley, most of Col. illiam J. Palmer's 15th Pennsylvania ivalry, including Private Jeremiah elwicks (right, wearing the regiment's stinctively piped jacket) of Company was positioned at several sites ong Walden's Ridge. Palmer reported October 4:**

"The loss of the rebels in the fight ear Anderson's was 120 killed and ounded (sixty killed, chiefly with saber) id eighty-seven prisoners ... The rebels t very drunk on the liquor they ptured; some of them must be clothed tirely in our uniform now. I saw lids of ixes on the mountain marked 'uniform, ousers,' etc. We have no wagons left to ul forage ... My men have no bsistence, but are living on the untry. We had but one day's rations in iattanooga when ordered out, and uld not take three as directed."

**The situation soon improved, as called by Adjutant William F. Colton:**

"That to every evil that comes to us ere is a blessing attached was emplified when General Wheeler irned up our wagons in Sequatchie illey, and the Regiment was sent over ere ... to see how he did it. iattanooga when we left it was just itering on its starvation campaign, with ly quarter rations for the infantry, and good deal less than that for the orses. Sequatchie was rich, every other eld was a corn field, and thousands of gs and many cattle covered her hills id valleys. Poultry and potatoes could had with the usual hunt for them, and nile our comrades of the infantry iffered and were hungry in iattanooga, we in Sequatchie were irfeited with the good things to eat, and ould have grown fat if Colonel Palmer id only allowed us to get lazy, but that as not his way. Our horses enjoyed it, o."

■ Wheeler's horsemen attack a Federal wagon train in Sequatchie Valley on October 2. The Confederates then spent several hours looting and burning well-stocked wagons until Union cavalry appeared, forcing their withdrawal. "There was a delicious quota of sutlers' wagons filled with good things to eat and wear," wrote Col. Isaac W. Avery, 4th Georgia Cavalry, who was cited by Wheeler for gallantry that day. "And the hungry and soiled Confederates went after the unwonted luxuries with a gusto born of long deprivation."

turned sorrowfully toward Chattanooga, arriving in due time, much disheartened. Henry Sayres was captured and paroled with the teamsters.

I dreamed of the capture of our train the night after Sergeant Yerkes detailed me to go with it. I saw the scene of our attack, where he halted in a bunch, heard Lieutenant Lingle give the command to scatter out and saw him as plainly as I ever did. Then imagine my surprise in the morning when I met him at the pontoon bridge. The dream was repeated just as vividly the following night. I told the boys about it, but they did not believe it would come true, but the second morning I saw it fulfilled. This was the only dream I ever had that came true.

## 'Like so many African elephants'

**1st Lieut. George B. Guild**
**Adjutant**
**4th Tennessee Cavalry C.S.A.**

In the latter part of September 1863, just after the battle of Chickamauga, by order of General Bragg, General Wheeler was sent into Middle Tennessee with his cavalry corps. He moved up the Cleveland Road to Red Clay, and forded the Tennessee River at or near Cottonport, some thirty miles above Chattanooga. The object of the raid was to cut off all supplies from the North for

Rosecrans' army, then at Chattanooga. The Nashville & Chattanooga Railroad from Bridgeport to Chattanooga was then in possession of the Confederates.

The opposite bank of the Tennessee was closely picketed by the enemy, and the command was to keep as still as possible so as not to draw their attention until after we had crossed. We reached the ford after a night's ride and rested there till daylight. I can never forget the beauty and picturesqueness of the scene that was presented that moonlit night when four or five thousand cavalry forded the beautiful Tennessee. It happened that the Fourth Tennessee Regiment was in front; and, headed by a single guide, we descended the banks and dropped into the river, and then the line swung down the stream across the silvery surface of the broad waters like the windings of a huge dark serpent.

As we reached the opposite shore the gray dawn of a bright September morning was breaking upon us. About one-half of the regiment was dismounted and silently moved up the bank. But a few moments had elapsed before the bang of a solitary gun was heard, and in another second bang! bang! bang! went the guns, and then a perfect fusillade. All were now wide awake, and the stillness of the scene was suddenly transformed into busy preparation for a fight. Another regiment was hurried forward and thundered down the road leading from the river in the direction of the firing. A few more shots were heard, and all was still again. A large picket of mounted men had been driven off with the loss of several men and some prisoners. The remainder of the command moved out from the river as they came over, and in due time all were safely over. The trail of the ford was a devious one and very deep in places. One would reasonably suppose that many mishaps would have occurred, but nothing of a serious character happened.

The command then moved toward Middle Tennessee across the mountains into the Sequatchie Valley, where we went into camp for the night at a crossroads. Nothing of note occurred during the day. About daylight the following morning we were aroused by an order to saddle up and mount our horses, as the bugle sounded "boots and saddles." In a few moments more we were moving down the valley at a rapid rate, not knowing at the time what was up.

A few miles away we commenced overhauling Federal wagons, partially plundered; then the cry of a wagon train was raised. As the pace quickened, these captures thickened along the way, and after going ten or twelve miles down the valley to the vicinity of Jasper, there opened the richest scene that the eye of a cavalryman can behold. Along the side of the mountain hundreds of large Federal wagons were standing, with their big white covers on them like so many African elephants, solemn in their stately grandeur. They had been rushed up there by the teamsters and abandoned.

This was too rich a bonanza to be left without an escort; and in a few minutes the rifles sounded from the mountain sides, indicating that we would have to do some fighting for such booty. Men were dismounted in haste and hurried to the right and left. A vigorous fire was kept up for a while when the enemy, seeing that they were greatly outnumbered, surrendered after some casualties on both sides. The escort numbered 1,200, with many drivers of the wagons. Some of them had escaped by cutting loose

■ 1st Lieut. George B. Guild, adjutant of the 4th Tennessee Cavalry. Following Wheeler's raid into middle Tennessee, his regiment in late October was ordered to Trenton, Ga., to picket gaps in Lookout Mountain as far as 20 miles below Chattanooga. "I suppose they were sent out there," Guild later wrote, "from the fact that a good many members of Company H lived at Bridgeport, Ala. [as well as Hamilton County, Tenn.], and were familiar with the country and railroad track from there to Chattanooga. These same men ... had been highly complimented by General Bragg on their scouts and the information they had given him."

# 'A tempting piece of cheese and

■ Private William W. Cavender (left) of Company K, 1st Georgia Cavalry, was reputed to be an excellent pistol shot and one of Wheeler's most trusted scouts. Private John S. Broyles (above) of Company H, 5th Tennessee Cavalry, enlisted seven months before the raid.

**Maj. Gen. Joseph Wheeler's report of his Sequatchie Valley raid was short and unembellished. After initially capturing and destroying 32 six-mule wagons, his command of 1,500 men approached Anderson's Crossroads and drove off a body of Union cavalry. "We here found a large train of wagons," Wheeler wrote, "which proved to extend from the top of Walden's Ridge for a distance of 10 miles toward Jasper. This train was heavily loaded with ordnance, quartermaster's and commissary stores. The number of wagons was variously estimated at from 800 to 1,500. No one saw, perhaps, more than half the train. The quartermaster in charge of the train, as well as other employees, stated that there were 800 six-mule wagons, besides a great number of sutler wagons.**

**After a warm fight, the guards were defeated and driven off, leaving the entire train in our possession. After selecting such mules and wagons as we needed, we then destroyed the train by burning the wagons and sabering or shooting the mules."**

**One of Wheeler's troopers, 18-year-old Private John A. Wyeth of Company I, 4th Alabama Cavalry, was more descriptive in recounting the episode:**

Early on the morning of October 2d, [we] encountered the advance guard of an infantry escort to an enormous wagon train loaded with supplies for the army in Chattanooga. Parts of two regiments under Colonel John T. Morgan were ordered to charge the escort of the train, which they did, but were repulsed and came back in disorder. I was standing near Colonel A.A. Russell who commanded the Fourth Alabama Cavalry, when General Wheeler rode up and ordered him to lead his regiment in. As soon as our line could be formed, we rode forward at full speed, and receiving a volley at close quarters, were successful in riding over and capturing the entire escort within a few minutes. We found ourselves in possession of an enormous wagon train, and such a scene of panic and confusion I had never witnessed.

Our appearance directly in the rear of Rosecrans' army, which was not more than twenty miles away, was wholly unexpected. As a matter of precaution, the Federal general had directed Colonel E.M. McCook with a division of cavalry, then near Bridgeport, to move up the Sequatchie valley and be within supporting distance of this train, but he failed to be in position at the critical moment.

When the fighting with the escort began, the teamsters had turned about in the hope of escape in the direction of Bridgeport. As we came nearer, they became panic-stricken and took to their heels for safety, leaving their uncontrolled teams to run wild. Some of the wagons were overturned, blocking the road in places with anywhere from ten to fifty teams, some of the mules still standing, some fallen and tangled in the harness, and all in inextricable confusion. For six or eight miles we followed this line of wagons, with every half-mile or so a repetition of this scene. As

# crackers'

ve proceeded, men were detailed o set fire to the wagons and to kill the mules, since it was mpossible to escape with the ivestock.

After a run of six or seven niles, I ventured to stop for a few ninutes to help myself to a empting piece of cheese and some rackers which I saw in one of the wagons. Filling my haversack, I was on the point of remounting when General Wheeler galloped up, sword in hand, and said to ne, "Get in your saddle and go on after the enemy." As he and I were the only Confederates in sight just then, I said, "All right, General. Have some cheese," and he private and the major-general rode on side by side down the Sequatchie Valley road "after the enemy" and munching cheese and crackers.

By this time the smoke of the burning train was visible for many miles, and soon the explosions of fixed ammunition, with which a number of wagons were loaded, sounded along the valley road, not unlike the firing of artillery in action.

The capture and destruction of this immense train was one of the greatest achievements of General Wheeler's cavalry. Its loss was keenly felt by the Federals, for it added to the precarious situation of the army in Chattanooga, and reduced rations to a cracker a day per man for several days in succession.

■ Maj. Gen. Joseph Wheeler

■ Brig. Gen. William T. Martin commanded a division in Wheeler's corps during the October raid into Middle Tennessee. The native Kentuckian turned Mississippi lawyer was commended by Wheeler for "gallant assistance in the capture and destruction of the wagon train," and for covering the Confederate retirement near Anderson's Crossroads the evening of October 2 and morning of October 3. Martin's troopers tangled with pursuing cavalrymen from the 2nd and 4th Indiana and 1st Wisconsin regiments, losing 105 officers and men as prisoners. These included Martin's assistant inspector general and the commander of his personal escort.

This portrait was made by the Richmond, Va. photographic firm of C.R. Rees in 1862, when Martin served under J.E.B. Stuart as lieutenant colonel of the Jeff Davis Legion.

the mules and mounting them.

We knew that there was a large infantry force not many miles away, and we set to work destroying everything at once. Orders were given that no plunder was to be carried off. This, however, was but partially enforced. The wagons were loaded with all manner of clothing and rations for the army of General Rosecrans. Among the wagons were a number belonging to sutlers, with rich stores of all kinds. The result of the capture was seven hundred and fifty wagons, twenty-six hundred fat mules and twelve hundred prisoners. The wagons, or the most of them, were loaded with rations for the army. The enemy was afraid to risk railroad transportation, and was endeavoring to provision their army at Chattanooga by means of wagons from McMinnville. It had rained the night before and left the roads so slippery that the wagons could not go over the steep mountain pass.

Such of the mules as we could not take off were destroyed. The wagons and the greater part of their contents were destroyed on the spot, the debris covering acres of ground. I was particularly struck with the fine harness that had been stripped from the mules, as it lay chin-deep over ten acres of ground. Such a calamity as this would have been most seriously felt by us, and would have retarded movements for months; but with "Uncle Sam," with all the world at his back, it made no perceptible difference. If it created a ripple of discomfort anywhere, we never had the satisfaction of knowing it.

## 'A camp kettle full of whiskey'

### Private Theodore Petzoldt
### Company C
### 17th Indiana Mounted Infantry

On October 1, as a part of General Crook's command, we crossed the Tennessee River and started in pursuit of General Wheeler whose command had been destroying some of our wagon trains in the Sequatchie Valley. On the 3d we attacked Crew's Rebel brigade at Thompson's Cove and routed them, capturing a number of arms and the battle flag of the 2d Kentucky Cavalry, presented to them by the ladies of Elizabethtown, Ky.

Along toward evening, as we were riding toward Thompson's Cove, we passed General Crook's headquarters. As we came opposite he came out. We were halted and he asked what regiment it was and who was in command.

When told that it was the 17th Indiana Mounted Infantry, Major [William T.] Jones in command, he gave us the order to carefully proceed into the valley ahead and dislodge a Rebel force which was stationed there.

We rode forward for quite a while and were then ordered to dismount and proceed carefully on foot. It soon grew quite dark as we moved slowly and silently forward through the trees. Suddenly a short distance ahead of us I heard someone call out in the darkness: "Halt! Who goes there?"

Instantly we all halted and made ready for action.

"Yankeelike," replied Major Jones, desiring to parley with him and gain time.

"Come over here, Yank," ordered the Rebel sentry.

Major Jones' reply was the command ringing out in the darkness — "Forward march, double-quick! Fire! Charge!"

We fired and rushed forward, but the Rebels fled before we could reach them. After pursuing them a short distance we halted and made ready for any night attack that might be made against us. We took up our position in a dry wash without lights or fires.

It was very dark. Sometime during the night we heard someone approaching. Instantly all was attention. Soon we discerned a lone horseman slowly approaching. As he got almost among us someone called "Halt!"

He instantly stopped and Bill Davis took him prisoner, and after trying to get out of him where the rest of his company was, which he claimed that he did not know, he was sent back to General Crook's headquarters. The man had probably been away from the other men on some business and was returning, not knowing that the rest of the command had fallen back. Thus he fell into a trap.

The next morning we found one dead Rebel. Where the Rebels had had their horses tied they had cut the halters in their haste to get away.

Soon after this the Rebels made a raid in our rear, and on October 4 we went to McMinnville, Tenn., about 50 miles northwest of Chattanooga. Here we had a fight with some of the Rebels and succeeded in driving them out of McMinnville, losing two killed and four wounded, but none of them were in our company.

We then went southwest and when beyond Shelbyville, October 7, at Farmington, attacked the Rebels. As we were following them up they suddenly switched out of the road and up a hill, thinking that we would pass them by and not observe what they had done, when they could attack us in the rear. But our commander had observed what they had done, and when we were even with them he ordered a charge up the hill. The Rebels fell back a short distance and made a stand. We followed up and made another charge and the Rebels fell back again. As they were getting ready to retreat Captain [Jesse] Goad saw the Rebel gunners bringing up their horses to take the cannon away. He gave the order to shoot the horses. After we had shot some of them the gunners surrendered and we took them prisoners with two cannon. Our company had no casualties in this fight, but Company E lost 14 killed.

We captured two barrels of whiskey this day that the Rebels had taken at Shelbyville the day before. After we went into camp that evening the sergeant went around with a camp kettle full of whiskey and in a tin cup that he carried he gave each of us some to drink.

Among the prisoners we took was an old acquaintance of Captain Goad. They had both run on boats on the Ohio River before the war. As we were marching along to our camp for the night they walked arm in arm talking of the old times. Our regiment lost 48 killed and wounded in this engagement, including three commissioned officers. We captured 300 prisoners.

After crossing the Tennessee River at Lamb's Ferry October 9, further pursuit of General Wheeler was abandoned and we returned to Chattanooga and from thence moved to Huntsville, Ala.,

■ Col. Edward M. McCook, 2nd Indiana Cavalry, commanded the 1st Cavalry Division's pursuit of Wheeler. While wagons burned on October 2, McCook's regiment and the 1st Wisconsin Cavalry charged Wheeler's rearguard, slashing with their sabers. A five-hour running fight over eight miles finally ended at dusk. The Federals recovered a number of prisoners, several hundred mules and a few wagons.

McCook claimed bagging 93 Confederate troopers and 12 officers — including Major Duff Green Reed, Wheeler's assistant adjutant general. "Many of the rebels captured were wholly or partially clothed in our uniforms," McCook reported, "and nearly all loaded with plunder taken from our train and people. Major Reed was not present at this time; he was lying in a state of such helpless intoxication that I had not even deemed it necessary to place a guard over him. Most of [the rebels] had a full supply of whisky."

■ Maj. Gen. Alexander McD. McCook, XX Corps commander, was relieved of duty October 9 following his corps' rout on the Federal right at Chickamauga. Former newspaper editor and Assistant Secretary of War Charles A. Dana, who bombarded the War Department with blunt, often caustic, and sometimes erroneous reports from Chattanooga and Nashville after the battle, wrote on September 30 that McCook had lost favor with his troops: "... the same conviction pervades all ranks; in fact, I was myself aware that the soldiers believed victory to be impossible so long as McCook commands [an] army corps. The other day, as General Rosecrans was making one of those little speeches to a group of men which it is his constant practice to deliver as he passes among them, a soldier asked him if General McCook still commanded the Twentieth Army Corps. 'Yes,' was the answer. 'Then the right will be licked again,' said the man; and all the others agreed with him."

A court of inquiry early in 1864 exonerated McCook of misconduct at Chickamauga, but he held no further position of high field command during the war.

from where on October 12 we started in pursuit of the Rebels under Forrest, Roddey, Wharton and others.*

## 'My sense of the injustice'

### Maj. Gen. John M. Palmer
### Division commander
### XXI Corps, Army of the Cumberland

The loss of the battle of Chickamauga by our army was followed by false reports, which were published in the newspapers of the North, and produced great excitement throughout the country, and reports were made to the war department by the assistant secretary of war, Mr. [Charles] Dana, who was on the battlefield with Rosecrans, and left the field with the general, and was with him in Chattanooga hours before the struggle was over, and I have always believed that Garfield took no pains to make the actual conduct of the officers and soldiers known to the president or the secretary of war.

The newspapers were filled with the most false and extravagant reports of the battle, and of the conduct of the troops of different commands. One of the reports published in a Cincinnati paper was that Crittenden's command broke and fled, etc., while the truth was, that Crittenden's corps, either from the accidents of the first day's separations or from the practice of Rosecrans, which was to issue orders directly to any officer of any rank whose services he needed, in disregard of all immediate officers, was broken up on both days of the battle, and Crittenden and McCook were left without a command ... The result of the misrepresentations and the clamor which followed the battle of Chickamauga led the war department to perpetrate acts of the most signal injustice to officers and men.

Rosecrans was relieved from the command of the army, and the 20th and 21st Corps were broken up, and McCook and Crittenden ordered before a court of inquiry. My division was attached to the 4th Corps, the command of which was given to General Gordon Granger. I disliked Granger, and submitted to that part of the arrangement only as a matter of duty, and I felt indignant that the 21st Corps, to which my division belonged, should be broken up in the face of the enemy.

Military men are often accused of egotism, and perhaps there may be some grounds for the accusation, but at the same time no man can successfully command soldiers who does not maintain his full claim to respect. The spirit which prompts men to be jealous of the honor of the organization to which they are attached is one to be cultivated, within reasonable limits, and nothing more dishonors a commander in the estimation of his officers and soldiers than a belief that he is insensible to his own honor or theirs.

I felt constrained by these considerations to emphasize my sense of the injustice of the order which relieved Crittenden, and blotted the 21st Corps out of existence, by tendering my resigna-

* Petzoldt, a German immigrant from Russwein, Saxony, came to the United States in July 1860.

tion, which I did in the following letter, addressed to the adjutant-general:

Headquarters 2d Division 21st Army Corps
Chattanooga, Tenn., *October 8, 1863.*

SIR — I respectfully tender the resignation of my commission as major-general of volunteers in the army of the United States. I am not indebted to the United States; I have no public property in my possession; there are no charges against me. I was last paid up to and including June 30, 1863, by Major N.M. Knapp, paymaster.

I tender my resignation because the late order of the war department, which abolishes the 21st Army Corps, and orders its late commander, Major-General Crittenden, before a court of inquiry, implies, and will be understood by the country as implying, the severest censure upon the conduct of the officers and men lately composing the corps.

The order is, in its circumstances, without example in the military history of the country. No corps, before this, has been deprived of its commander, and stricken out of existence within a few days after a great battle, in the midst of important military operations, and in the face of the enemy. By this sudden, decisive, sweeping order, the government has given to the misrepresentations of the fugitives from the battlefield the weight of its own apparent indorsement, slander is dignified into history, and henceforth refutation is impossible.

I did not enter the service of the country for this reward, nor can I by remaining in the army give effect and force to the imputation which the order implies upon the memory of the dead, and the character of my comrades who survived the battle of Chickamauga.

I respectfully urge that my resignation be at once accepted. I would not willingly separate myself from the Army of the Cumberland until it is again ready to assume the offensive, but I hope to receive notice of the acceptance of my resignation speedily, and that it will by that time be ready to move forward.

Respectfully,
JOHN M. PALMER, *Maj.-Gen. Vols.*

It is due to General Rosecrans to say that he was no party to the injustice which I resented, and he, in his indorsement on my letter of resignation, attempted to secure for us justice. He informed me that he had forwarded my resignation to the adjutant-general. I copy his indorsement in full, as it carries with it the refutation of one of the calumnies that is even now sometimes reproduced by careless historians:

Headquarters of Dep't of the Cumberland,
Chattanooga, *October 9, 1863.*

Respectfully forwarded, wholly disapproving the acceptance of the resignation of this prudent, brave and valuable officer, which would be a serious injury to the service. I also disagree with him in his opinion that the consolidation of the corps implies a censure on the officers and men composing it. I doubt not the war department will as promptly vindicate these officers and men, as I most certainly shall in my report of their magnificent fighting in the battle of Chickamauga.

W.S. ROSECRANS, *Major-General.*

Notwithstanding this indorsement by General Rosecrans, I was notified of the acceptance of my resignation, and I prepared to quit the army. I left Chattanooga, on the 14th day of October, by a steamboat which was plied between that place and Bridgeport, where I expected to take the railroad for Nashville. I was greatly surprised, on my arrival at Bridgeport, to be overtaken by a courier, with an order from the adjutant-general setting aside the acceptance of my resignation, with directions to resume my command at Chattanooga.

When I returned, I found General George H. Thomas in command of the Army of the Cumberland, and I succeeded him in command of the 14th Army Corps. I confess this promotion gratified me, and the more so, as I felt that I owed it in a great measure to the good opinion of General Thomas, under whose eyes I had fought at Chickamauga.

■ Maj. Gen. Thomas L. Crittenden was relieved of XXI Corps command on October 9, a victim, like McCook, of questionable conduct at Chickamauga and the pen of Assistant Secretary of War Charles A. Dana. One week after the battle Dana wrote to Edwin M. Stanton in Washington: "The feeling in the case ... toward Crittenden is relieved somewhat by consideration for his excellent heart, general good sense, and charming social qualities. Against these, however, is balanced the fact, which I can testify to from my own observation, that he is constantly wanting in attention to the duties of his command, never rides his lines, or exercises any special care for the well-being and safety of his troops, and, in fact, discharges no other function than that of a medium for the transmission of orders."

A native Kentuckian whose older brother George served as a Confederate general, Crittenden was absolved of guilt by a court of inquiry, and briefly commanded an Army of the Potomac division in 1864. He resigned his commission that year on December 13.

■ Maj. Gen. George H. Thomas, nicknamed "the Rock of Chickamauga" for his stand at Snodgrass Hill on September 20, took command of the Army of the Cumberland on October 19, replacing Rosecrans. The change was applauded widely in Chattanooga, as expressed by a member of the 78th Pennsylvania: "General Thomas was too good and great a soldier to embarrass the Government by finally refusing to take the command. Had any other general than Thomas been put in General Rosecrans' place the Army would probably have been displeased, but General Thomas was held in such high esteem that all were satisfied. The soldiers of the 78th Pennsylvania, having been with General Thomas at Stone River, as well as at Chickamauga, were delighted, for they regarded him as one of the greatest commanders in the Union Army."

Thomas established his Chattanooga headquarters in the house above, located at the corner of Third and Walnut streets.

The corps was composed of three divisions, the first commanded by Brigadier-General Richard W. Johnson, the second by Brigadier-General Jefferson C. Davis, and the third by Brigadier-General Absalom Baird. Each of the divisions consisted of three brigades, with the usual proportion of artillery; the whole amounting to about fourteen thousand men. The division commanders all belonged to the regular army. General Johnson and General Baird were graduates of the military academy at West Point, and General Davis was appointed from civil life for his services in the Mexican war. I think these officers were not pleased that a volunteer officer was appointed to the command of the corps, but we soon became excellent friends, and cooperated with the utmost good feeling.

## 'A very sad fact in the presence of the enemy'

### Brig. Gen. William W. Mackall
### Chief of Staff
### Army of Tennessee

October 5, 1863.

We opened our guns on the enemy this morning about ten. It is nearly three now and as I expected made a big noise and nothing more. Last night we found out that there was a petition to the President to relieve General Bragg, circulating among the General Officers. It gave Bragg much distress and mortification. I do believe he thought himself popular. I feel sincerely sorry for him. He has labored with great industry and great zeal. I do not see any good to result from relieving him, as the President won't use the only useful man — Johnston. They have telegraphed the President to come on. I suppose we will hear tonight.

October 9, 1863.

Mr. D. comes this evening ... Bragg thinks now that he will triumph, but he was very despondent yesterday, and is as blind as a bat to the circumstances surrounding him. He ought not to command this army unless his enemies are taken away, for he is vindictive and cannot do justice.

October 10, 1863.

The President, three aides including Custus Lee [sic], Colonel Preston Johnston and General [John C.] Pemberton arrived last evening ... I heard yesterday that Longstreet had signed the petition for the removal of Bragg, and if he has not, at all events he is talking about him in a way to destroy all his usefulness. Bragg is in fine humor today, evidently thinking he has the President on his side, but Mr. Davis is as wily as a serpent and Bragg has yet to discover whether he is as harmless as a dove ...

The President is riding around the lines this morning and the troops are hurrahing, which I am glad of for the common good. I am satisfied that Bragg cannot usefully command this army and that I can do no good, for if Mr. D. sustains him, he will be too elated to listen to reason. I do not know a single contented general in this army; a very sad fact in the presence of the enemy. I do not believe that Mr. Davis could do as much good by sending ten thousand men to this army as by putting Lee or Johnston

■ Brig. Gen. William W. Mackall resigned as Bragg's chief of staff on October 16, less than three days after President Davis' visit to the Army of Tennessee. Mackall's son William later wrote of his father's decision: "He felt that his usefulness in that army was at an end. His views as to the conduct of the campaign were at variance with those of General Bragg and he had no confidence in the latter's Generalship and felt assured that if he remained in command of the army, disaster to the country would follow ... He was always just to General Bragg and gave him full credit for his loyalty and earnestness, but he considered that he was lacking in many of the attributes essential to the make-up of a great captain."

Mackall became Gen. Joseph E. Johnston's chief of staff in January 1864, serving in that capacity until Johnston's removal as Army of Tennessee commander on July 18, 1864.

■ President Jefferson Davis left Richmond by train on October 6 to confer with Bragg and his generals. After a three-day journey Davis inspected the Army of Tennessee on the 10th, and briefly spoke to troops from Pulpit Rock on Lookout Mountain. In his diary, newly promoted 2nd Lieut. Edwin H. Rennolds of Company K, 5th Tennessee, recorded his impressions of the Confederate president: "Jeff Davis passed along the lines to-day and the troops were formed in line to receive him. I had a good look at him and found him better looking than I had expected. He was dressed in citizens black. Three cheers were given for him and also Gen. Bragg, who accompanied him."

Wrote Private T.T. Fogle of Company G, 2nd Georgia: "President Davis looked better than I ever saw him but at best he looks like the God of famine. He is a dried up specimen of humanity. He was attended by all the Generals & their staff officers, it was as brilliant a cavalcade as I have seen since the war commenced. Gen. Longstreet was the fat man of the party; something is in the wind for he seemed to be in a good humor."

here, and I do not think he can do anything but mischief by putting any other. If Longstreet, this will be very acceptable to the corps, but all the others will say: "We don't know him, and we know that Bragg is careful of us, doesn't fight unless he has a good chance, and he has never been beaten exactly, and this time has beaten Rosencrantz badly."

October 12, 1863.

Mr. Davis has just gone to see the [Chickamauga] battlefield. It amuses me to look on and see the ways of the world. Two nights ago Bragg was denouncing ——; yesterday dined with him; everything is made Couleur de rose ...

A band came up to serenade Mr. Davis and then they called on him for a speech. I only heard from my tent that the people in the ranks were the heroes and future nobles of the land. Then they called for Bragg who made one, but I heard nothing of it. Then they called for Pemberton, who I think only told them that he never made a speech in his life. Since I began to write they called out Davis again, who has just closed, and Bragg is at it again ... In his speech this evening, the President told the audience that he had ridden over the battlefield and that the General who could drive a foe from such a field, the hardest he had ever seen, was worthy of all confidence and the shafts of malice had been hurled harmlessly against him. The mob shouted, of course, and they would have shouted just as loud if he had told them that their comrades' lives had been uselessly sacrificed and he would send them a better General. Poor man, he is an enigma to himself.

The President has now been here two days and I believe has decided to sustain Bragg. Under the circumstances of the troubles in the army, I am in doubt what to do. Should I quit my position now, it might look as though I were wanting to add to the troubles, and to stay is very disagreeable. I will take time and reflect earnestly, and if God assists decide rightly. I want success, by whom it comes I care not, but I don't want for my children's sake to lose all reward of labor. I do not want them sneering at me in future years.

## 'Our weary way through rain and mud'

### Diary of
### Sergeant George W. Holmes
### Company G
### 100th Illinois Volunteer Infantry

**Oct. 1st.** It rained nearly all night; we got up to stand at arms at 5 o'clock. The clouds have passed off, and the air is clear and pure. We can see the rebel camps quite plain, and we see a force marching to the right, for what purpose we do not know. I am detailed to go with a party to pile up brush in front of our breastworks to frustrate the enemy if they should attack us. We also stretch a wire along in front, so that they will be thrown down if they should come up in the dark. Several of our own men, myself included, forgetting about it, have got several falls from it.

**Oct. 3d.** Stood at arms from four to six. Orderly Sergeant Thomas Bleber and I got a pass to go down town and see the wounded boys. Found them in good spirits. L.L. Warren, my messmate before the [Chickamauga] battle, was wounded in the leg near the ankle. He walks with crutches. John C. Batterman looks bad. He was wounded under the right arm, a ball passing through his body and coming out near the spine. Frank Lafayette was wounded in the arm, shattering the bone, but is in good spirits. We hear that a long train was burned by the rebs in Sequatchie Valley.

**Oct. 5th.** Some deserters came in to-day. The rebs began to throw shell about four o'clock, but they do not reach us. We send them some in reply, but cannot tell the effect, but hope they will be hard to digest. The cannonading is kept up slowly all day.

**Oct. 7th.** Here we are in sight of the rebels. The two armies lie within gun shot all the time. The pickets talk with each other and exchange papers. At night we look to the south, and there all along on what is called Mission Ridge, we see their camp fires. This ridge extends from Lookout Mountain around to the Tennessee, forming a kind of far off boundary to the city, I judge about four miles distant. The most of the rebel army are on the top. But there is a portion on this side, and their pickets extend down to within less than a mile from our camp, and about sixty rods of our picket line.

This evening along comes Ord. Serg't. Tom Bleber and says, "Serg't. Holmes, report to go to Stevenson right off, don't wait for anything." So I start for brigade headquarters and there find 1st Lieut. Lines, who has charge of twelve men and three non coms. from our regiment. There is a similar detachment from each regiment in the division. Those from our brigade are in command of Captain Potter, of the 26th Ohio. The whole are in command of the lieutenant colonel of the 26th Ohio. We march down town and report ourselves. The colonel reports to corps headquarters, and then takes us over the river on a pontoon bridge, where we camp for the night.

**Thursday, Oct. 8th.** Get up at five and march at seven. We go about a mile and then halt at the field hospital. I run over and look at the boys, and find them all snug and comfortable in good tents and beds. The wagons in our train take along all that are able to go to Stevenson. L.L. Warren goes along.

After an hour's halt we go on, taking the road for Walden's Ridge by way of Anderson's Crossing. But the order is changed and we take the river road. After a march of about seven miles we are fired upon by the rebels from across the river. They keep themselves concealed so that we could get but few shots at them, while we are entirely exposed. They killed three and wounded seven of our men, and killed and wounded twenty mules. This was mostly done while we were going over a little bare hill where our drivers stopped to lock the wheels. They soon stopped that and let the wheels take care of themselves, and drove down the hill at full speed. One driver got his wagon upset. A battalion of the pioneer brigade was in camp near. So we left our "casualties" with them and went on. After marching some time we took a road which leads up Walden's Ridge, and with some difficulty reached the top and found ourselves on "Bob White's farm."

**Friday, Oct. 9th.** Started on this morning, road very uneven. We are out of rations so I step out and run on ahead down the mountain, and come to the house of a Mr. Knox, and ask them if they have anything cooked. The old lady goes to the table and breaks off a piece of corn bread. I also got my canteen filled with

■ Capt. Rodney S. Bowen of Company A, 100th Illinois, kept a detailed journal during his service, and noted on October 27 the issue of some eagerly awaited food: "And now comes into our camp four companies of the 31st Indiana that have been to Stephenson[sic] to guard a supply train, and it has taken 20 days to make the trip, a distance of 60 miles as they have to go. With such difficulties has the army to be supplied with rations. As a result of this arrival, an orderly makes his appearance and asks: 'Is this the headquarters of the 100th Ills?' To which the reply is quickly made: 'It is, sir.' 'I am ordered to report to you with two days' rations for 312 men.' 'Very good, sir.' Then the hungry tigers of the 100th set up a shout long and hearty, for although there has been no grumbling, it has been pretty hard to satisfy a soldier's appetite on half a cracker and corn foraged from the poor mules."

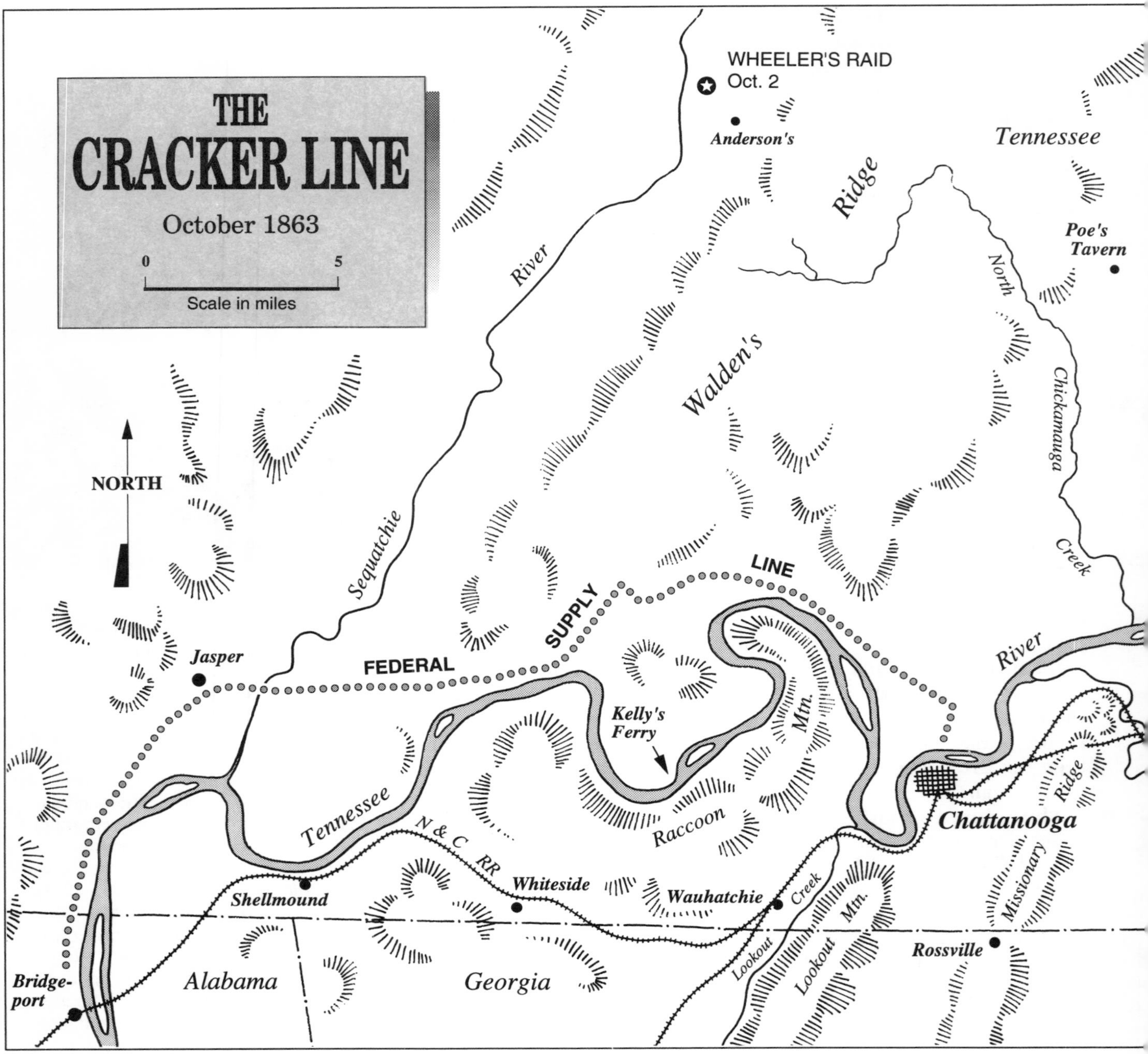


some milk and pay the woman twenty cents.

Went on a short distance and as it was a hot day, I went upon a little hill and lay down to sleep. When I woke up the train had all gone by, so I hurry on and overtake them about four miles from Jasper. After resting a short time, start on for Jasper. Luckily, the sutler of the 115th Illinois overtakes me and I ride with him to Jasper. Here I go to a bake shop and buy two pies and two loaves of bread, and eat them, and am still hungry. Going along a little further I find Prince, our old sutler, who is here with a stock of goods. I get some cakes and maple sugar. By this time the train comes up and the boys empty every bake shop and every other eating establishment in the town. I get into a forage wagon and ride to Battle Creek, where we camp for the night.

**Saturday, Oct. 10th.** On the move again early and go on to

Stevenson, which is a small place on the railroad with a tavern and a few dwelling houses. L.L. Warren and the rest of the wounded boys are deposited in a Sibley tent, expecting soon to go on to Nashville. We drew three days' rations — to last six.

**Sunday, Oct. 11th.** The train loads up with hard-tack, sow belly, coffee, etc., and a little after noon takes the back track. Get to Jasper about noon of the 12th. We press on, and the rain comes on, and we go into camp after dark.

**Oct. 13th.** On our weary way through rain and mud, and reach the foot of the mountain on the 14th, about a mile and a half further up than where we came over, and go into camp. Here we are detained by trains ahead of us. Here we see the remains of a train burned by the rebels. A brigade of the reserve corps are now in camp here, and the rebels keep their distance.

**Oct. 15th.** After the rear train had got up we start on. After a while we have to stop for a mountain stream — swollen by the rain — to subside; so we build fires and camp for the night.

**Oct. 16th.** The stream having run down, we go on to the edge of the mountain. Here the view is most splendid. Way down below us the trees look like shrubs; off in the distance is the Tennessee river with its many windings, a waving line of silver in the landscape; and there to the right is Old Lookout standing out in bold relief against the sky; farther to the left is the city of Chattanooga scattered on the opposite bank of the Tennessee. The road here goes down by the side of the peak, and turns short around it and down on the other side. The descent is very difficult. We had two wagons upset while going down. After getting down the road is good and we hurry on. In time we get back to the hospital. Here we met Capt. Elwood who has resigned and is going, as he says, to start for "God's land" (meaning Joliet!) in the morning. We reach the bank of the river and have to wait for repairs on the pontoon bridge. Towards night we go over. It is not often you see a happier set of fellows than we are at getting home.*

## 'Our gunners had splendid practice'

### Corporal David G. Blodgett
### 10th Indiana Battery

The evening after the battle of Chickamauga our battery was ordered across the Tennessee River. We went down to the extreme point of Moccasin, opposite Lookout Mountain. The next morning the enemy opened on us with artillery. In our position we were unable to do them any damage, and so moved back out of range to choose position — Captain Naylor, our battery commander, having the choice. My section, Lieutenant L. Cox commanding, took the highest point where it could command all the territory from Lookout to Mission Ridge. Lieutenant Alf Cosner took position to our right about two hundred yards distant. We immediately commenced fortifying under charge of the engineer corps, our men cutting down all the timber in our front. The Twenty-second Michigan Infantry took position between our two sections on a

■ Major Michael H. Fitch, 21st Wisconsin, served at Chattanooga on the division staffs of Gens. Richard W. Johnson and Absalom Baird, XIV Corps. During the siege Fitch's letters were filled with sarcasm born of the army's plight. "The want of sleep and sustenance and the excessive dust put me into a half comatose state," he wrote on September 27. "But I am now 'caught up' and feel remarkably well. I go out to the picket line occasionally and get shot at merely to keep up a healthy state of the system and a proper realization of our situation."

On October 22, Fitch wrote: "It is very likely some fine morning this army will wake up to find the commissary exhausted, and all the trains stuck in the mud between here and Stevenson, the nearest depot. But then we can live a long time on the horses and mules, together with white-oak bark. I sent one of my horses back to Stevenson to subsist him while the little chestnut is living here on dead grass and wagon wheels. I take him out on the picket line every day to let him have a whiff of the rebel army, merely to keep him well aware of the great cause which requires so great a sacrifice of corn and oats on his part."

* Holmes, a native of Green Garden, Ill., was killed at Rocky Face Ridge, Ga., on May 10, 1864.

■ Brig. Gen. John M. Brannan, commander of the XIV Corps' 3rd Division, was named the Army of the Cumberland's chief of artillery on October 10. Five days later, Rosecrans and Thomas praised Brannan for "magnificent" fighting at Chickamauga, where his division lost 2,191 killed, wounded and captured — the highest casualty count of any Federal division in the battle.

Brannan's artillery field service dated back to 1841, the year he graduated from West Point. During the Mexican War he was appointed adjutant of the 1st U.S. Artillery, whose commissioned roster at that time included Joseph Hooker, Irvin McDowell, John B. Magruder, A.P. Hill and Thomas J. Jackson — all becoming distinguished general officers.

natural ridge. The Forty-eighth Indiana was on our right and rear. In a few days our works were in condition to commence operations.

Lieutenant Cox ordered us to open fire on the enemy and see if we could draw them out. We succeeded admirably, and had a very nice little artillery duel. Nobody was hurt on our side, though the rebel shot exploded and struck all around us. Some of the finest shots we made while on Moccasin Point were made with shells thrown at us by the enemy. We dug them up, re-primed them and sent them back. We fired more or less every day.

Having a signal corps with us, we had to telegraph to headquarters in Chattanooga the cause and effect. Our gunners had splendid practice and got the exact range of every point. No body of men or any object could move without our gunners giving them a dose. Often when the pickets came in they would say that the Johnnies' pickets had complained in this manner: "Why don't that damned Tenth Indiana battery fight the artillery? We are not disturbing them." Our orders were to fire at anything we thought suspicious.

We practiced throwing over Lookout Mountain, and could see the shells go way over, but as we could not see through the mountain we could not see their effect. There was a road leading to the top of the mountain, and about half way up was an open space of the length of a six-mule team. We tipped over many a one there, until they were afraid to make the attempt in daylight.

One day several men were over from town to see us. While they were there, the enemy moved quite a force out to an open field to our left front and about opposite Fort Negley, and it looked as if they intended an advance. We opened on them with shell, the gunners doing splendidly, and shattered the ranks of the enemy as they retired, leaving a number of dead and wounded. Our men were complimented very highly. We left one tree in our works, using it as a look-out — a non-commissioned officer being detailed to watch with a powerful glass the movements of the enemy. Whenever he reported a battery being placed in position our boys would make the rebel position too hot, and they would seek a change of climate. Nearly every move the enemy made was exposed, and then they would be shelled out.

## 'This nightly serenade'

### Capt. George T. Todd
### Company A
### 1st Texas Volunteer Infantry

[On September 21] we drew rations and advanced the day after, and formed at the foot of Lookout Mountain in full view of Chattanooga, and went into a regular siege of that city. We staid there besieging the town two months. The federals erected a battery across the river on Moccasin Point, made by a bend in the Tennessee River, and every night, when they knew we had left the trenches and were asleep in our dog tents exposed to their fire, opened on some portion of our lines which formed a crescent around the city. In this way they killed and crippled some confederates before they could get under cover of the works. We became so accustomed to this nightly serenade that we only opened one ear to see what part of the line was selected, and if not near us went to sleep again.

One night, however, this scribe has cause never to forget. As Captain of Company A, with one of the men, J.L. Allen, I was in sound sleep in my little tent 20 feet from the "bomb-proof," when a shell from the federal battery burst in Company K adjoining us. The cries of a wounded man aroused Allen, and he woke me and said we had better "git" to cover. I answered that we had better wait for the next shot before getting up, but he insisted, and I rose to a sitting position, and was pulling on my boots when the next shot came striking the tent at my side, and passing across my knapsack where my head was resting the minute before, struck the ground between Allen's feet as he stepped from the tent, and without exploding entered the earth. We didn't wait any longer before rushing for our "bomb-proof." Next morning the boys dug up a ten-pound steel-pointed parrott shell at a depth of 8 feet. This was only one instance of many narrow escapes from sudden death.

## 'A run of the gauntlet'

### Private James R. Maxwell<br>Lumsden's Alabama Battery

[In October] the weather was stormy, rains came in deluges and bridges between camp and Chickamauga Station were washed away, cutting off our supplies. Forage getting short, Capt. Lumsden detailed perhaps 20 men to go on horses over into Wills Valley to the west side of Lookout Mountain. The road to be traveled was the dirt road skirting the base of the cliff about half way up the mountain, above the Tennessee river opposite the Moccasin bend. The Federals had a battery entrenched on Moccasin Point just across the river.

The detail left before day and passed the danger point before it was light enough to be seen. By mid-day sufficient forage of corn and fodder had been obtained. Each horse and mule resembled a perambulating haystack, for they were loaded with two big sacks filled with corn on each side and as many bundles of fodder as could be tied on with ropes.

Sergeant John Little had charge of the squad, containing among others Alex Dearing, Ed King, Rufe Prince and Dave Jones. It was a sort of picnic. The men bought chicken, butter and buttermilk and got the farmers' women to cook for them. Dave Jones bought a bee gum of honey and had a time getting out the honey, with all the crowd assisting. Then again it was good for sore eyes to loaf around in a farmer's front yard and see his wife and daughters flitting about, and every now and then get to talk to them a little. Calico dresses and sun bonnets perhaps, but they were a treat to the soldiers who were tired of seeing nothing but men for so long.

The detail put off having to pass the front of that battery so long as they could and had their frolic out. But they had to pass that point in daylight in order to have time to get over the balance of the mountain road, with each animal loaded in the manner it was. There was no way of dodging it. There were rocks and

■ Private James R. Maxwell joined Capt. Charles L. Lumsden's Alabama Battery on October 15, 1863, after spending 18 months with the 34th Alabama. "On being transferred to this command," recalled Maxwell, "I had with me a negro body servant named Jim Bobbett, taken from my father's plantation, whence he left a wife but no children. He was allowed to come at his own request, and had been with me from the time I entered service [April 1862]. There were perhaps a dozen or more servants connected with the Battery, some belonging to commissioned officers, others to privates. Without any legislation or orders of army commanders, such servants were part and parcel of the commands to which their owners belonged, and cheerfully did their part in connection with the commissaries of their commands, being utilized largely as company cooks. For such service they were welcomed by the commissary department and got their share of the rations ... As a rule they were liked by all, and were glad to assist any and all soldiers for small rewards and even for personal thanks. They were great foragers, for their masters first, and next for their own and their master's friends."

■ Private Francis Messinger
Battery F, 1st Ohio Light Artillery

# Behind the guns

By November 25, 1863, at least 58 field artillery batteries and one company of heavy artillery bolstered Chattanooga's defenses and guarded Federal supply depots. Some batteries in Chattanooga proper were sadly understrength. In the 3rd Wisconsin Battery, only one field piece remained (the other five and 33 battery horses were lost at Chickamauga).

Siege conditions further reduced the animal population as feed and forage in town critically dwindled. The Army of the Cumberland's chief of artillery, Brig. Gen. John M. Brannan, wrote in frustration: "The battery horses of the Department of the Cumberland either died, or [became] so emaciated from starvation as to render but few of them fit for service." Brannan and his subordinat officers also complained of defective powder, time-fuses and projectiles, especially shells furnished for the heavy 4½-inch Rodman guns mounted in Fort Wood and Battery Rousseau.

But not all batteries shared the same privations. Bugler William G. Putney, whose Battery I, 2nd Illinois Light Artillery, was stationed *outside* Chattanooga above the mouth of North Chickamauga Creek, actually found life comfortable. He later wrot

"Foraging parties went out every week up the Sequatchie valley, and after being gone two or three days would return loaded with forage for the horses, and beef, hogs, chickens and whatever could be found in the way of provisions, which proved very acceptable to both men and horses The men cooped up in Chattanooga had a pretty hard time, while the battery boys had more than enough Battery I was in splendid condition, though every other battery in the Army of the Cumberland was utterly unable to move for want of horses, most of them having died of starvation."

■ Private Jonathan Stafford
Battery C, 1st Ohio Light Artillery

■ Private Marquis D. Flint
Battery I, 1st Illinois Light Artillery

■ **Above:** 1st Lieut. Aaron P. Baldwin, 6th Ohio Battery, poses in an unidentified camp with one of his 10-pounder Parrott rifles (note caissons and Sibley tents). Baldwin assumed command of the battery on July 6, 1864, when Capt. Oliver H.P. Ayres was killed by a sharpshooter at the Chattahoochee River.

■ A view of Fort Wood, sketched by soldier-artist Alfred E. Matthews of Company I, 31st Ohio, and refined by illustrator Edwin J. Meeker. Strong fortifications and breastworks built in the weeks after Chickamauga convinced Federal commanders — and many Confederates — that Chattanooga was impregnable to frontal assault. Soldiers joked about the digging, as recorded October 2 in the diary of Private P. Turner Vaughan of Company C, 4th Alabama:

"Our line of battle now touches the river on the extreme right and left enclosing Chattanooga and its host of Yankees. They make the air noisy day and night with the sound of busy axes, picks and shovels. We advanced our picket line several nights ago and dug our rifle pits within a few hundred yards of the Yankee breast works. The next morning a Yank cried out 'Hello boys! What did you dig them holes for?' 'Come over,' said a Rebel, 'and see, and now tell us what have you thrown up all that dirt and piled up all those logs for?' 'Oh,' said he, 'we did that for a shade.' "

wood and cuts in the road that would protect on each side, but sight in front of the battery for perhaps forty yards or more on the road was cut out of the precipice, and for that distance it was a "run of the gauntlet." Arriving at the place, the men crowded the cut on the west side. Each man on his animal made ready and as his name was called, at perhaps 30-yard interval, he made his rush as fast as he could persuade his animal to go.

The enemy could only take pot shots at one animal and not at a crowd. Those Yankees surely had sport, but they did not get to fire each of their four guns many times before all were past the bald place without the loss of man or animal. They yelled and we yelled back that they could not shoot worth "shucks." They shelled the woods along the route, but our men were out of sight and did not tarry till each reached some cover, when we halted for them to ease up, which they soon did, not being able to see anything to shoot at. They had their fun target shooting. Our boys had the fun of dodging. As there were no casualties, it could always be looked back upon with a sportsman point of view as one of our funny episodes.

A few days thereafter camp was moved over beyond the top of Missionary Ridge, about Oct. 23rd, into a woodland location with plenty of spring and creek water nearby. To soldiers in camp a living spring was a blessing, as it was the only security against contamination and consequent disease.

On the march or while the army was in the trenches, rations were issued, cooked, the bread being baked and the beef boiled. Bacon or salt pork was issued raw, the soldiers eating it raw or boiled on coals, if convenient, and the meat not too scant. In permanent camp, the soldiers drew the rations raw or cooked, as they preferred. Almost always each mess preferred to do its own cooking.

With us Confederates, bread was mostly corn pone, sometimes biscuits, sometimes hard-tack. Cold cornbread or hard-tack crumbled into a tin can and boiled with perhaps a few scraps of meat was "cush," and "cush" tasted good, hot off the coals, after a hard day's marching or fighting.

At one time the Confederate government experimented with a mixture of cowpea flour and wheat flour, for the making of a nourishing hard-tack. Doubtless it was nourishing enough when there was plenty of time to boil them soft enough to eat, but most men's teeth were not able to grind them. It took a hatchet or ax to break them up and the broken pieces resembled shiny pieces of flint rock. They were not so great a success for the soldier on the march as the inventor expected.

## 'A handful of cracker dust'

### Private Esau Beaumont
### 3rd Battery
### Wisconsin Light Artillery

The day after the destruction of the battery,* the only piece saved (a howitzer) was posted on the left near the Tennessee River facing Missionary Ridge. On the 22nd a line of earthworks was laid out and entrenching began and a lunette was thrown up. This was afterwards Fort Wood; our lone howitzer occupied it first. Afterward siege guns were placed therein. This day the last foraging was done; a load of corn was brought in from ground quickly occupied by the rebels. The men worked like beavers and by nightfall a line of works was built, too strong for assault by weary men.

Immediately our horse feed became scarce and grazing was soon used up. Some of the boys would crawl through the lines and pull grass for feed while they would be in the shelter of anything to screen them from sharpshooters. They would put the grass in corn sacks and drag them in behind themselves to our own lines. The rebels were within short range but never shot anyone, undoubtedly thinking it was surrender or starvation in a short time. The little corn soon disappeared and the horses in the best condition were sent to Bridgeport to save their lives. Many had already died tied to trees or posts, which they gnawed as long as they had strength. During the siege 10,000 horses and mules died of starvation.

All this time the besieged were throwing up entrenchments and continually strengthening the lines, heavier guns were placed in position and we were drawn into the outskirts of the town. The great problem now was how little a man could subsist on. It was really pitiful to see the men scratch over the ground where the mules had been fed to find a kernel of corn that might be trod in the mud (a horse does not look over ground closer or make cleaner

■ Quartermaster Sergeant John D. Galloway, 3rd Wisconsin Battery, found his duties lightened immediately after Chickamauga where the battery lost five of six guns and most of its horse equipage. Still, he shared the siege's hardships with his surviving comrades, one of whom recalled: "Some of the boxes of crackers passed over to the battery had got wet and were spoiled — a sour, mushy lot of dough utterly unfit for food, yet this stuff was eagerly sorted over, the dry and sound pieces separated from slush while crowds of half-starved wretches stood around and clawed, and almost fought over the sticky mess to get an inch of sound cracker out of it. This stage of the siege was the darkest period of our lives."

* On September 20 at Chickamauga, the 3rd Wisconsin Battery lost five of its six guns captured, and suffered casualties of 26 men and 33 horses.

# 'Like so many beavers felling timber'

**On October 27, after three months of hard campaigning, the 92nd Illinois Mounted Infantry left its Tennessee River camp at Harrison's Landing to rest and re-fit at Bridgeport, Ala. The journey over Walden's Ridge and through the Sequatchie Valley rivaled the regiment's toughest service, and taxed the men and mounts to the extreme. Early in November, one trooper wrote home about their animals' voracious appetites:**

Our object, or rather the object of General Thomas, in ordering us to this point, is for the purpose of giving us a more complete outfit; and at present writing Colonel Atkins [Smith D. Atkins], with one hundred and thirty men and officers, is at Nashville, procuring Spencers, horses and saddles, and all the traps pertaining to completeness. The remainder of the Regiment are to recruit up the animals on hand, that have of late become magnificently transparent. We have them tied to the trees with trace-chains and such, for the reason that they have eaten up all the picket ropes and halters, and have turned in to eating each other's manes and tails. The mules have fared some better than the horses, but not much; not having any tails or manes, they have lost their ears, ornaments indispensable to a mule's beauty.

There is not a tree within a mile of this camp that the horses or mules have not gnawed off the bark; they work at it like so many beavers felling timber. Last night, they all commenced gnawing the trees at once; and the Chief of Scouts said: "The cars are coming; don't you hear them?" "No," said I, "that is the horses and mules grinding bark." "Why," he said, "what are we grinding bark for?" I replied, "Going to tan the hides of them animals before spring." And the Chief of Scouts replied, "Oh, oh, I see it."

"If he dies, I'll tan his skin —
And if he don't, I'll ride him again."

■ Private Carleton Smith of Company B, 92nd Illinois, poses armed with a holstered revolver and Spencer repeating rifle.

work of a dirt pile). Many of the mules had to be sent to bring crackers over the mountains by packing. Others were being used to carry the wounded over the same mountains from the camp across the Tennessee, opposite Chattanooga, where the poor fellows were without food. Those who survived the trip were landed at Stevenson, Ala., only to receive a handful of cracker dust — not a very satisfying amount of food after riding in an army wagon over sixty miles of all sized stones.

We suffered with cold as the weather became severe. All stumps and shade trees to be found were dug up to burn. A large raft of logs was sent down the Tennessee river to destroy our pontoon bridge but our boys captured it, saved the bridge and made firewood of the logs.

Our rations kept diminishing, and we received but a pint of corn for three days' rations. We parched the corn, ground it in coffee mills and made a porridge of it. Frequently while preparing this dish, children of the miserably poor and destitute natives would drift into our camp and after wistfully gazing upon it would say, "I like cohn." Such pathetic appeals always resulted in their receiving a portion of the coarse and scant supply. A corn loaf of unsifted meal, baked in a common sized bake kettle, would be cut into 26 parts, and would sell for 50 cents a piece. Cow's heads divested of meat would bring $1. For soup purposes, animal tripes were eagerly eaten after a homely preparation.

■ 1st Lieut. Michael J. Kelly (far right above), 4th U.S. Cavalry, was the Army of the Cumberland's chief of couriers. "In many places where the signal officer cannot work [Kelly's] excellent arrangement known as 'the courier line' is invaluable," reported *Harper's Weekly* correspondent Theodore R. Davis, who sketched couriers at a relay station at left. "The stations are distant from each other five miles. In many places the line is a mere trace or trail through the forest. At each station a fresh courier is ever ready to mount as the arriving one is seen approaching, and taking his dispatches he dashes off at a gallop to the next station." Couriers left Bridgeport every two hours, carrying with them 10-pound sacks of nails to supply pontoon-boat building and other construction work in Chattanooga.

Seated at Kelly's right is Capt. Henry Stone, a member of Rosecrans' staff.

■ Capt. Charles C. Aleshire, 18th Ohio Battery, commanded the crews of six 3-inch ordnance rifles positioned with Capt. William A. Naylor's 10th Indiana Battery on Moccasin Point. Both batteries targeted Lookout Mountain, paying particular attention to the Cravens House, artillery emplacements and a signal station on the summit. On October 9, their brigade commander described the day's shooting results: "Several shots were fired at the white [Cravens] house; I think it was struck twice. It is a kind of palatial resort for rebels. They have been seen around thick until our shells made it rather hazardous for comfort.

"Aleshire has the signal station on Lookout under range. Yesterday his third shot gave a double-quick impetus to what was left of the signal party. Today his second shot imparted similar action. Both shells were percussion and exploded direct on the point. This was done at a 6-degree elevation. I had been advised by the chief of artillery that a shell could not be sent there. I was skeptic enough to think otherwise."

## 'The nearer the bone the sweeter the meat'

### Private Alexander R. Thain
### Company D
### 96th Illinois Volunteer Infantry

Our brigade withdrew from Missionary Ridge on the night of September 21, and on the 22d we marched through Chattanooga, crossed to the north bank of the river and encamped on Moccasin Point. This memorable piece of ground lies within a loop of the Tennessee at the northern extremity of Lookout Mountain, its shape bearing some resemblance to an Indian moccasin, the tow being thrust between Lookout and Chattanooga and the heel lying down toward Brown's Ferry.

The side of the point which lies next to the mountain is low and fertile, and prior to our occupancy had been covered with a fine crop of corn and beans which, fortunately for us, had been somewhat carelessly harvested. Our camp was situated several hundred yards from the river, nearly opposite the northern base of the mountain, and a little distance behind the camp rose a considerable ridge — the instep of the moccasined foot — on which was posted the 18th Ohio Battery. This loud-mouthed neighbor occasioned us a good deal of anxiety during our stay on the point. As soon as it was securely sheltered by strong works it began to talk to the mountain in a very emphatic way, and Lookout wrinkled its rocky brows and began to talk back. These occasional dialogues would not have troubled us in the least if the principal parties had kept the conversation exclusively to themselves, but the Boanerges who held forth from behind Pulpit Rock on the crest of Lookout had an inconvenient way at times of talking at large to the whole camp. At such times he had many listeners who paid very close attention to his remarks, but who fervently wished that he would bring his fire-and-brimstone preaching to a speedy close. The northeast side of a tree was the favorite point for listening, and a puff of smoke on the point of the mountain was the signal that a monosyllabic remark, in the shape of a shell, would, in a few seconds, utter itself somewhere on the point, and the question was — *where!*

Gen. Bragg had decided to force Gen. Rosecrans out of Chattanooga by the gradual process of cutting off his supplies, maintaining in the meantime as close a siege as possible, with the expectation that we must soon abandon the place to avoid starvation. The pretense of a siege was little more than a farce; but the question of how to obtain a sufficiency of supplies in the face of a watchful enemy who held our direct line of communication soon became serious enough.

During the early part of this period trains passed along the river road, but at great peril, several men being wounded and the mules killed, so that a blockade was created. On one occasion, First Assistant Surgeon Moses Evans of the Ninety-Sixth accompanied an ambulance train of wounded. While passing "The Narrows," he was wounded by a bullet which cut his ankle, but was not seriously injured.

The daily ration issued to the men was reduced, not to point of starvation, but to such a degree that we hung on the edge of hun-

# 'Sacrifices made and toils endured'

**During the siege, as food, clothing and other staples grew scarce in Federal camps, many Confederates found their own supplies equally poor, or worse.**

**1st Sergeant James L. Cooper**
**Company C, 20th Tennessee Vol. Inf.**

October 1863. We were almost starved during this month. The rations were very scant at best, and then sometimes, the railroad would not come up to time. Then it was dreadful. One occasion I well remember, when for three days, in place of our meat ration of three quarters of a pound of beef, or one sixth of a pound of bacon, we drew one spoonful of sugar daily. We were constrained to add to our allowance by "charging sutlers" and eating corn, beef guts, and all other kinds of trash that came our way.

**Private Joseph Brigham**
**Company B, 50th Tennessee Vol. Inf.**

Sis, I want you to send me some socks the first chance for I cant get any for love or money ... If there was any possible chance to get anything from home I would like to have a good overcoat for this winter — I am ashamed to ask for anything from home but such things as overcoats & yarn socks cannot be got here."

**Capt. H.W. Henry**
**Company K, 22nd Alabama Vol. Inf.**

While we were encamped on Missionary Ridge, rations were unusually scarce. The artillery horses near us were guarded to prevent the men from stealing their feed, and whenever the position of a battery was changed the men could be seen gathering up the scattered corn and washing, parching and eating it. Shortly after pay day some wagons came into camp loaded with iron-clad pies and other foodstuff, which, of course, went like hot cakes. Our men had just been paid off in Confederate currency — $22 for two months' service. Passing by my quarters I noticed one of my men with a stack of twenty-two iron-clads piled up in his arms, while he was taking generous bites from the topmost one. As he went to his quarters I asked: "What are you going to do with all those pies?" Scarcely stopping, between mouthfuls he replied: "Gwine to eat 'em."

**Private John C. West**
**Company E, 4th Texas Vol. Inf.**

There are so few chances of buying anything that I really have no use for money. Most of us spend money for tobacco, but I use so little that it does not amount to an item in my expenses, and when we are out of rations nothing to eat can be purchased within ten miles of us ...

You have no idea what a comfort it is to stand in mud to the ankle, on an empty stomach, and read a line from sympathizers at home. Newspapers may exhaust their stereotyped phrases, and correspondents may discourse eloquently about the sufferings of the "poor soldier" until the phrase becomes a by-word and fails to excite an emotion of pity, much less a tear, but I will say now (for perhaps I may not live to say it face to face in the better days to come), that the sacrifice made and the toils endured by the *private soldier* in the service of the Confederate States cannot be appreciated or expressed in words, nor will they ever be known except to those who have shared them. Not even the officers of infantry, whose duties are almost as arduous, can tell the tale of hardships which fall to the lot of the man in the ranks. He is the lowest mud sill in this structure which is being reared, and when the edifice totters all the props and braces must be placed upon his shoulders. My thoughts are all the news I have — we seldom get a paper here. We have been in the mud for over a month in an almost continuous rain, and are not allowed to send to Richmond for blankets and overcoats, which many of us have there, because it will not be thought of until the hospitals are filled with pneumonia and pleurisy.

# 'It is darkest just before day'

**Medical personnel in both armies were taxed to their limits tending thousands of soldiers wounded at Chickamauga. But when free from duty, acting hospital steward Joseph Whitney, 96th Illinois, composed letters to his wife Mary. In two of these from October, Whitney described aspects of his life under siege:**

After the fight I went to Bridgeport with an ambulance train to take care of the wounded. Going and coming back was five days, a distance of 120 miles. The rebs are just across the river from [Moccasin Point] where our regiment is. We are shooting at one another about half the time, no great damage done on either side. The only fears are of our communications being cut off by the rebels. They have captured one train of wagons and our knapsacks. For us it is a great loss. Some of the boys lost their knapsacks with all their blankets. When we left Bridgeport to reinforce General Thomas we were ordered not to take anything but our rubber blankets ...

It has rained for four days and four nights [October 12-15] without ever ceasing. Night before last our tent fell down and it was raining very fast. The rain wet us and our beds, so that we could wring water out of our beds and clothing. We had to lay wet for the rest of the night and last night, ditto. No end to wet feet. I wish I had a pair of boots but the prospect is rather poor of getting them from home. Boxes do not come through any more on account of the railroad being out of repair.

I wish I had some good apples from home. I get pretty hungry sometimes. All we have to eat is sow belly and hard tack and quarter rations at that. We parch corn and eat that, and for a change we grate it and make pudding. I do not know when I shall be paid. I wish I had some money to send to you now for Mother. I have but five cents and am out of tobacco and have no postage stamps, so you see I am pretty hard up. I do not feel discouraged yet about the war, although things look rather dark in this quarter. It is an old saying you know, "It is darkest just before day." I hope that the day will dawn on us soon.

ger for a number of weeks, and sometimes dropped over the edge, and found great difficulty in climbing back again. The field of corn on the point delayed this result in our camp for a time, a large ear of corn being about equal to the daily ration then issued to us. But soon the vast hunger of the mules stripped the fields so bare that one might search for hours and be rewarded with only a few poor "nubbins." Corn near the bank of the river was worth its weight in Rebel lead.

The members of the regiment usually alluded to this camp as "Starvation Point" in after months. At no other time during our entire period of service were the rations as low as here. On one occasion soap, candles, pepper and vinegar comprised the bill of fare. The comments made upon this occasion would be entertaining could they be reproduced. Later, corn alone was issued on a few occasions, and the men would ask the officer issuing it, in a semi-serious way, how they could be expected to eat corn without any soap or candles, or if they would not prefer to keep the corn and give them some pepper and vinegar. But notwithstanding the short rations, the lack of blankets and clothing, the continuous exposure, the constant danger and the anxiety, felt if not expressed, lest retreat should become necessary, and disaster to the army and the cause result, the men were cheerful and uttered few complaints. They were by no means discouraged, but each had an abiding faith that help would come from some source, and that the army would succeed in driving from the strongholds in their front the then exultant enemy.

The following episode took place at the hungriest point of the quarter-ration period. Two members of Company D were on guard in the woods some distance north of our camp. They were very hungry and had not between them so much as a grain of parched corn. Inspired by hunger, their imaginations made out endless bills of fare, and their memories recalled the many appetizing things which they had eaten before leaving home.

When by these mental exercises they had whetted their appetites to a keenness which was almost unbearable, they saw, to their great joy, a quadruped approaching through the bushes. It was one of those long, lean, hound-like Southern hogs which were known among the soldiers as "wussers." It looked like the genius of starvation, wearing a swine-like form. But how to secure such shadowy game was a difficult question. As well attempt to catch a greyhound by direct chase; and a bullet, though aimed with the greatest skill, might easily miss an object which was so thin that you had to look twice before you could see it. But something must be done, and done quickly; and so one of the soldiers shot at the shadow and hit it — at the junction of the jaws, and then began a chase. The lower jaw of the pig dropped square down, but otherwise it held its forces well together; and with a continuous squeal issuing from its throat it started through the bushes at a high rate of speed, followed by the comrades in hard pursuit.

At last one of the pursuers seized a large iron bolt which had fortunately been dropped by some passing wagon, and threw it with such strength and skill that the porcine prize soon lay at their feet. Panting and triumphant, they bore it to the picket post; skinned it, roasted it bit by bit at their fire, and ate it all at one meal. But then they were very hungry, and it was very lean. If the proverb "The nearer the bone the sweeter the meat" is true, that was the sweetest meat, as it averaged, ever eaten by man.

## 'The stomachs to forage'

### Capt. James R. Carnahan
### Company I
### 86th Indiana Volunteer Infantry

All through the first month of the siege the troops were called out frequently during the night into the trenches to be ready to repel threatened attacks. These calls at night with heavy skirmish duties, fatigue duty, short rations, thinly clad and illy supplied with blankets for the cold frosty nights, made the service at this time anything but play. The army had stored its winter wearing apparel and blankets, and was therefore poorly prepared to endure bad weather. Rations daily grew more scarce and the mules grew weaker, thousands dying from overwork and starvation. The long trips over the rough mountain roads compelled them to perform extraordinary labors. The army mule should be voted a badge of honor for services rendered.

Day by day the men came to understand the situation and to see with a clearer vision the difficulties of their environment.

On the rebel skirmish line at the east side of a small field, across which the Second Brigade skirmish line extended, was a log cabin in which there was daily posted a rebel sharpshooter who made good use of his opportunities. A picket detail was his special delight, and many a picket marching out to duty was disabled by his unerring rifle. And a soldier going outside of the entrenchments for any purpose was a fair mark. Next to a picket detail he seemed to delight in having a crack at soldiers going out for wood. But wood was necessary, even if it took blood. At length the timber was all cleared away, much of it having been cut and carried to camp on the boys' backs after night. The sharpshooter wounded a number of the Eighty-sixth when going out to the skirmish line. To fire at the cabin was useless and he was left undisturbed. Once or twice a gun from Fort Wood was turned upon the cabin and a few shots would quiet him for a time, but he soon resumed his vocation.

On the 30th of September, some members of the Eighty-sixth were on duty on the skirmish line. Two or three of them, tired of sharpshooting, crept out along the bank of Citico Creek to a concealed place and gave him a few shots that annoyed him. He at once stopped shooting and began swearing. For a time now it was a war of words instead of bullets, and it was difficult to decide which side was the more fluent and vicious. The Eighty-sixth boys returned to the reserve and the heathen rebel rested from his labors. They came off the line at 3 a.m., returned to the reserve and tried to sleep. They had just got soundly asleep when a heavy shower came up suddenly, and when they awoke they were in water up to their necks — lying down, of course. This little incident gives one some idea of the trials of a soldier's life. It was useless of course to try to sleep on the ground in such a deluge of rain.

On the night of October 1 it continued to rain, accompanied by a wind storm, blowing down tents and scattering numerous necessary articles in various directions. Many tents blew down a second time. Add this to all other things which the men endured at Chattanooga — hunger, fatigue, dangers and trying vigils — proved to

■ 1st Lieut. Littleton V. Ream of Company G, 86th Indiana, wears a metallic IV Corps badge in this late-war portrait. The equilateral triangle officially was adopted as a symbol in April 1864, seven months after the corps was created by reassigning regiments from Crittenden's and McCook's old corps. Maj. Gen. Gordon Granger commanded the IV Corps during the Chattanooga and Knoxville operations.

■ Six privates of Company G, 27th Illinois, from left: Amisa G. Wood, Garrett Debaun, Ed Castle, John Webber, Joshua F. Thornton (killed in 1864 at Kennesaw Mountain) and Frank Wood.

On October 16, 2nd Lieut. Henry M.F. Weiss of Company F wrote to his wife: "[We] lay around in the mud, exposed to all kinds of weather, until the ground for our new Camp was ready, for 3 days, during which the tardy motions of our superiors were damned up hill and down dale ... For the last month we have been on ½ and ¼ Rations, officers and men alike; the other day officers could only obtain one pound of flour, two ounces of coffee and sugar for two days. Some times the men are an entire day without a bite to eat. Rather tough is it not? There is prospect of better things today. God grant it! Something to eat is a great event just now!"

be an exhausting strain upon the whole physical system. Many finally broke down who seemingly bore it fairly well at the time. The siege dragged on.

The best road left open to Rosecrans' trains wound around along the north bank of the river, being cut into the terminal cliffs of Walden's Ridge as they jutted up close to the bank of the river. The enemy's pickets patrolling the river bank acted as sharpshooters at "the Suck," a bend of the river around the north end of Raccoon Mountain, where the trains were forced near them and killed many mules, drivers and train guards. They maintained constant watch and fire, and rendered the road so dangerous that it had to be abandoned, the trains going over Walden's Ridge further north. This necessitated many more miles of travel, and far more difficult mountain roads to be used, to convey the hard tack and bacon to the famishing soldiers in the beleagured town. The longer trips and more difficult roads required greater time, when time was an element of much importance. The mules on account of their extraordinary exertion and lack of forage were daily growing more feeble and less able to work. Bad weather set in and added deep mud to the rough and execrable mountain roads. Daily, rations grew scarcer until, as the boys jocosely remarked, it was only river water with a very faint suspicion of coffee about it.

On the afternoon of [October] 7th, the Eighty-sixth received orders to be ready to start on foraging duty at a moment's notice. The lieutenant colonel sent word that his command could not go on account of not having any rations. The information was returned that rations would be provided.

The following morning at 9 o'clock the Eighty-sixth was ordered to fall in, and it marched through town and across the river where rations were issued. The guards of the trains were veterans from the ranks of the besieged army. They knew the situation. They did not see anything wrong in famishing men supplying themselves.

The expedition proved to be foraging duty beyond a doubt; for if ever a regiment of Hoosiers had the stomachs to forage it was on coming out of Chattanooga after what appeared to be a three weeks' fast. The purpose of the expedition was to secure corn and corn-fodder as forage for the mules and horses, but it also gave the Eighty-sixth, acting as guards, an excellent opportunity to turn the occasion to good account for themselves. The duties of the trip were many and various, such as loading wagons, catching chickens, ducks and pigs, standing guard and doing picket duty when the place of bivouac was reached at night.

On the afternoon of the 9th, having reached a point some thirty or forty miles northeast of Chattanooga, about thirty of the wagons were loaded with forage. Besides securing forage for the animals, the boys caught the chickens, geese and turkeys of the mountaineers, killed their hogs, cattle and sheep, went into the houses and ate the biscuits on the table, carried off their beehives, and destroyed quite as much in getting what they may have needed as they themselves consumed. Looking back upon this conduct one cannot but pronounce it a brutal destruction and waste. The passions of the soldiers had been aroused to their highest pitch by their suffering while besieged in Chattanooga, and they stopped not to think of the suffering they might inflict on innocent non-combatants. The foraging was continued during a part of the 10th when the train and guards started on their return trip, and reached camp between 3 and 4 o'clock on the 11th.

Rations were drawn on the 12th, what purported to be for three days. On the 13th the men were eating parched corn again, so scant was the supply drawn the day before.

The greatest suffering of the Eighty-sixth on account of scant rations occurred from the 20th of October to the 9th of November. A member of the regiment who kept a diary has this record for the 20th: "The boys are all out of rations and swearing about starving." In the record for the 25th it is found that he was on picket and this note is made: "I only had one cracker for dinner." On the 26th he wrote: "We ate our last cracker for dinner. We drew about a tinful, supposed to be a pint, of flour for a day's rations of bread-stuff. The boys are all grumbling about the scarcity of rations. This is the shortest rations we have yet drawn."

In the record for the 27th he made this note: "We had to do without any dinner as we could not get anything to eat. The boys are furious about the rations, as most of them have had nothing to eat since breakfast, all day. Toward evening we drew a little beef." After this record was made, somewhat later in the evening other rations came, and this man's journal says: "We received three crackers and one pound of flour as a ration for two men for one day. We also drew a few grains of coffee." On November 2 this is the record: "Brother and I ate half a cracker and a little bacon for breakfast. The boys are grumbling a good deal to-day about rations. We drew a little beef this forenoon and had that for dinner. Late in the evening we drew, what purported to be, one day's

■ Capt. William Strawn of Company F, 104th Illinois, found privations in Chattanooga were experienced universally. "During the siege, officers, privates and the poor dumb brutes alike suffered for want of food," he wrote. "Where the skinny cattle were slaughtered, heads sold for two dollars and a half apiece. These were scalded like a hog's, so that even the hide was not wasted. The paunch was soused in the river and being prepared was considered an especially dainty morsel. I have eaten portions of about every part of a beef, except the horns and hoofs, and all was good. The days seemed longer and grew more monotonous. The uppermost thought was how to get something to eat."

# 'Resigned to my fate'

**At Chickamauga, Corporal Merritt J. Simonds of Company K, 42nd Illinois, had his right leg shattered and laid on the battlefield with other casualties for nearly a week. Following a truce, some 100 Federal ambulances were allowed through Confederate lines to evacuate the wounded to Chattanooga. Simonds was among them. On October 8 he wrote home:**

Dear Father:

I write to you in different circumstances than ever before. I have been severely wounded in the right leg just above the knee in the fierce battle of the Chickamauga, which was fought on the 19th and 20th of last month. I was wounded on Sunday the 20th about noon and remained on the field until the next Saturday night when I was taken off about four miles to a hospital. I suffered considerable for want of care. The rebs helped me some for the first four days, then they let one of our doctors and some of our men come to see us. They dressed our wounds a little, gave us something to eat, etc. Still we did not get off the field until nearly the end of the seventh day. We could have but little care then as there were so many of us and we drew nothing but corn meal and a little beef from the rebs. The next Wednesday we were taken in ambulances to our present place, which was very hard for us being a rough road of thirteen miles.

I have as good care as can be taken of me here. I have had a fever nearly every day since I was wounded. It has brought me down pretty low and weak. The doctor thinks he has broken it now. The doctor says my leg will be stiff when it gets well. I am resigned to abide the kind will of our heavenly Father. I read my testament and pray to Him that whether I live or die I may yield to his glory. Pray for me. Sherwin was killed instantly on the battle field near me. I shall write often and let you know how I am. Give my love to all enquiring friends. If we never should meet again on this earth may we meet in Heaven is the prayer of your unworthy son.

■ This photograph of Simonds was taken on August 29, 1863 in Bridgeport, Ala., exactly two months before his death.

**On October 27, Simonds wrote home what proved to be his last letter:**

Dear Father:

Since I last wrote I have been growing worse. My leg is now mortifying above the knee and the doctors say I cannot live more than two days at the longest. You must not take this to heart but look to a higher source for comfort, for it is God's will and I feel resigned to my fate. I hope to meet you all in a better world.

I would like to have my body taken home and buried beside my mother. I am comparatively comfortable at present. There is no pain in my leg. I have some things which I authorize William Mott to take home and some others I authorize George Wright to sell and send the money to you. I owe Sherwin King two dollars. Will you please pay his father as poor Sherwin is no more.

Father, my mare and colt I wish you to keep in remembrance of me. My love to all my family and connections. Tell them I would have written to many of them if I had thought sooner. I now bid you all a kind good bye.

M.J. Simonds

**Three days later, Private George Wright sent the following letter to Simonds' father:**

Dear sir:

I am sorry to inform you of the sad intelligence that your much beloved son Merritt is no more. He died last night. I cannot make it seem that he is dead. Poor boy! How much he anticipated and hoped to enjoy himself on returning to his dear friends at home after the close of the conflict. But his conflicts are all over, and I trust he is now in the enjoyment of perfect bliss. It seems hard to give him up, and yet we must not murmur. Although we cannot see him again in this world we can prepare to meet him in another and better world. Merritt was a good soldier. He always done his duty cheerfully and as a brave soldier. We will bury his remains tomorrow and mark his grave distinctly so that they could be found if wanted.

Yours with respect,
George H. Wright

**Simonds never realized his wish to be taken home to DeKalb, Ill., and buried next to his mother. His remains today lie in Chattanooga National Cemetery.**

rations of hard tack to do us four meals." On November 5: "We drew six small crackers to the man to do one day and a half."

These are facts — a correct account of the actual rations drawn, noted at the time, by the members of the Eighty-sixth. Nor is it believed that the Eighty-sixth suffered for the want of rations more than other regiments of the Army of the Cumberland. The assertion is here made that no regiment within the lines of the beleagured town at any time during the siege ever received full rations of even three articles of the ration list.

## 'Down to Hell's half acre'

### 1st Lieut. R.M. Collins
### Company B
### 15th Texas Cavalry (Dismounted)

Being in the immediate presence of the enemy, we beat the Confederacy out of about six weeks' drilling. We put in a part of September, October and a part of November in guard duty. [My] brigade was near the center of the line. Guard duty was pretty trying; our line of pickets was about two hundred yards from the Federal line. We could see their pickets plainly, and when no big officer on either side was near we would sometimes get up a tem-

## Brothers unto death

Brothers William W. (left) and Gurden R.B. Dunbar served as privates in Company K, 38th Ohio. Gurden, younger by a year, poses with a Colt's revolving rifle while William holds a .69-caliber smoothbore musket. William died of disease in Chattanooga on November 18, 1863, and his remains lie today in Section C, Grave 495, Chattanooga National Cemetery.

"As the days and weeks wore on," recalled 1st Lieut. Wilbur F. Hinman of the 65th Ohio, "supplies grew less and less. Hundreds, gaunt from hunger and worn by toil and watching, gave out entirely and thronged the hospitals, whence many were daily borne to the city of the dead."

Nine months after William's death, Gurden was killed during an assault on Confederate works near Jonesboro, Ga.

Corporal Bliss Morse of Company D, 105th Ohio, bitterly noted the fate of yet another soldier who fell sick during the siege:

"Benjamin Lamport of our Co. died yesterday [October 22]; he has been unwell for a long time with chronic diarrhea, and died through neglect — and want of care on the part of Doctors. It was through the influence of our boys, officers and Doc. that he was sent to the Hospital one week ago. He was in the Pioneer Corps and was exposed to all this rainy weather in one of these dog tents. Yet he was a 'private' and of no consequence while an officer [2nd Lieut. Alonzo Chubb, also of Company D] not sick half as long nor near as bad off can resign and go home and will be a well man in one month."

■ With an unidentified battery's guns and limbers parked in the foreground, the hutted camp of the 57th Indiana appears at right. From September 9 until late October, the 57th served as the town's provost guard. Wrote regimental historian Asbury L. Kerwood: "As the season advanced the weather became quite inclement, and the troops set about building comfortable quarters. Plank and boards, wherever found, were appropriated, and on some portions of the lines, where there was timber suitable, clapboards were made by the men. Our regiment being in town, and more convenient to building material, were not long in providing themselves with comfortable houses of plank, many of them being covered by shingle roofs and had brick chimneys. Our only dependence for fire-wood was what we could find inside our own lines, and we remained so long at Chattanooga that our resources became very meager. Trees, stumps, logs, rails and everything suitable for wood, inside the beaten path of our sentinels, was used, and yet the supply was insufficient to the demand. Each day our men went to the front and cut wood, and the wagons came out in full view of the rebel pickets to load."

porary armistice, lay down our arms and meet on half way grounds and have a nice friendly chat, swapping our flat tobacco for Lincoln coffee, or our little 8x10 newspaper, *The Chattanooga Rebel,* for their big blanket-sheet dailies, such as the *New York Herald, Tribune, Cincinnati Times* and *Louisville Journal.*

Sometimes we would strike Federals on duty who would have none of us; these were generally Pennsylvania troops. We could always get along with Ohio and other western troops, but those first named and all other eastern troops always seemed to have a big red mad on.

Our bill of fare was pretty tough; corn-bread and poor beef was about all we had as a rule, and when the rule was suspended it was generally by a day's ration of bacon. The writer's mess consisted of Capt. J.A. Farmwalt and Lieut. Jerry Johnson; Lieut. John Willingham belonged to it but he was generally at regimental headquarters acting as adjutant. We kept a cook hired by the name of Ad Huffstuttler, at $30.00 per month in Confederate money; guess he was a Dutchman by his name, anyway he could forage and cook like one. He would prowl around the butcher pen, get beef heads, feet, liver, brains, sweet-breads, marrow, gut and other parts that we had always seen thrown away, and make up messes nice enough for a king. He also done our washing and mending.

[Sometimes] Capt. Farmwalt would be our head cook. He would fry the grease out of the bacon, and with our corn-bread, water and the grease, make a dish he called "cush;" this with some of the corn-bread burned to a black crisp, out of which we made coffee, was fine living. However, we "reckon" the hard exercises each day and the total absence of anything like dyspepsia or indigestion was what made it all go down so well.

It doubtless seems to the reader that the same routine of duty each day and night would get to be distressingly monotonous, but not so — there was something to be done every day, or some news going the rounds, and when not on guard duty, or on the fatigue party list, or putting some finishing touch in making our quarters more comfortable, and not writing letters home or to two or three Georgia girls at the same time, we could go down to Hell's half acre.

Now this was a place in front of and near the center of our main line, and just in rear of our picket line, it being some three quarters of a mile in front of our line of battle. Here the thugs, thumpers and gamblers from our army as well as from Atlanta and other cities collected to gamble, and you could get a square up and whack at any kind of game from faro, monte, draw-poker and seven-up down to thimble ring poker-dice and three-card monte. I don't know where the boys got the money, but they had stacks of gold, silver, greenbacks and Confederate. The place should have been called Hell's whole acre, for they had about that much ground worn as slick as glass, and more gambling going on than I have ever seen at one time since; and more hard-looking characters — the Five Points of New York City could not beat it even in its palmiest days.

## 'Damned if I feel like shooting you fellows'

### Private Chauncey C. Baker
### Company C
### 1st Wisconsin Heavy Artillery

The armies were pretty near to each other, and both had pickets out watching every movement of the enemy.

One day we were perfectly astonished by the sight of a little child toddling toward our lines. She was such a little innocent, unafraid creature, entirely unconscious of any danger. She came from the direction of the Rebel army, and, needless to say, we surrendered to her without the firing of a gun. When she reached a place within our lines, hundreds of our men gathered around her. Apparently she was perfectly at home as she stood looking at us with wide-open eyes in which shone perfect trust and confidence.

The boys began to ply her with questions as to what her name was and where she came from, but she could give no satisfactory answer. One of the men asked her to whom she belonged, and she lisped: "Uncle Jim." Then we asked her who Uncle Jim was, and she pointed toward the Confederate lines, by which we knew that she must have strayed away from Uncle Jim and in some mysterious manner made her way through both picket lines into the Yankee army.

Every man wanted to take her in his arms and kiss her, and how they did wish they had some candy or cakes to give her, but army rations afforded nothing of this kind. Then some of the men thought of sugar and each wanted to give her some, of which they had a plentiful supply. So we loaded her down with big lumps of the sweet stuff, and one boy happened to remember that he had a string of beads which he brought and placed around her white neck. Another had a silk handkerchief, which he tied about her throat, while the other boys, not to be outdone, searched among the keepsakes which their sisters and sweethearts had sent them and found handkerchiefs and ribbons, which they tied on her small person.

■ Officers of Company C, 1st Wisconsin Heavy Artillery. Seated at left is Capt. John R. Davis, while the others are 1st Lieut. Ezra R. Lisk, 2nd Lieut. Frederick Ullmann and 2nd Lieut. Benjamin F. Parker. Formed during July-September 1863, this company became operational at Chattanooga's Fort Wood by mid-October as part of the 2nd Division, Artillery Reserve. Armed with two 30-pounder Parrotts and four 4½-inch Rodman guns, the Badger State artillerists became part of the city's permanent garrison at the end of November, when two 3-inch ordnance rifles and two 12-pounder Napoleons were added.

# A 'fight' on equal terms

**Brig. Gen. Walter C. Whitaker, a native of Shelbyville, Ky., commanded a brigade of Illinois, Indiana, Ohio and Kentucky troops in the 1st Division, IV Corps. Early on November 1 the 84th Indiana and 115th Illinois of the brigade broke camp on Moccasin Point near Brown's Ferry and crossed the Tennessee River. There they began a laborious 15-mile march to Shellmound, Tenn. to guard supplies at the railroad station.**

**2nd Lieut. Isaac Royse, acting adjutant of the 115th Illinois, was among those tramping the rough mountainous roads. He later wrote:**

"The 115th moved off at the head of the column, across the pontoon bridge and over the hills beyond. Very soon an obstacle was met in Lookout Creek too deep to ford. Colonel [George P.] Buell was quickly on the scene with a detachment of the pioneer brigade, and at once began the construction of a temporary bridge.

"General Whitaker was impatient at the seeming slow progress and offered to Colonel Buell a company of men to help in the work, which, being accepted, the general called on Colonel Moore for a detail and I promptly reported the leading company for the work. Not content with that, General Whitaker began ordering the men about much as a boss would at a house raising. Colonel Buell resented that as an interference with his duty and called on the general to get out of his way. That was too much for General Whitaker's Kentucky blood, and he proposed settling the matter in Kentucky fashion. Colonel Buell said, 'You are a brigadier general and I only a colonel. We are not on equal terms.'

"Instantly the general took off his coat and threw it on the ground, saying, 'There is the brigadier general; here is Walter C. Whitaker ready to fight you on equal terms.'

"Buell replied, 'My duty is to build this bridge. After that is done I will talk to you,' and went on with his work. Very soon the bridge was done and the column moved on without further incident."

■ Brig. Gen. Walter C. Whitaker

■ Col. George P. Buell

One produced a rosette of red, white and blue ribbon, which he pinned on her dress. Another found a small silk flag, and that also was pinned on her; all of which she enjoyed immensely and seemed to think it was all "in the play."

I saw tears come into eyes that had not been wet since they left their mothers, wives and sweethearts in the far-away North. Our captain took the child in his arms and, while he pressed her close to his heart, said: "Boys, I've got a little girl at home about the age of this little one. O God! I wonder if I shall ever see her again?"

At this every man removed his hat and stood silently at attention, but if you had asked them why they did so they could not have told you.

And then the question was raised, what shall we do with her? For obviously, we could not keep the child in such circumstances of impending danger. The problem was solved by one of the men removing the ramrod from his gun and tying a white handkerchief upon the end, then, after obtaining permission from the captain, he took the child and her gifts in his arms and started toward the Rebel lines.

Bob Chambers, one of the biggest devils in our company, called to him to hold on a minute; he wanted to send "Uncle Jim" some coffee. "I'll bet he hasn't had a good cup of coffee since the war began," he said. So he filled a small bag with the precious grains and gave it to the little girl, saying: "Take this to your Uncle Jim."

The boys all shouted a good-bye as they started for the Rebel lines, the little girl still holding high the flag of truce. As they neared the Confederate lines several men came forward to meet them, among whom was Uncle Jim who was searching for his little girl in every direction.

# Narrow winding passages & immense auditoriums

**Early in November, Sergeant Isaac C. Doan of Company B, 40th Ohio, enjoyed an unusual diversion from duty during the siege: subterranean exploration.**

Under the mountain on the west of our camp "Nickajack," about two miles south of Shellmound, was Nickajack cave, the largest in this region. Upon the mountain above is the point where Georgia and Alabama join upon the south line of Tennessee, so that within the darksome winding passages of the cavern you can become a tenant at will of either of the three states. A good place to dodge the sheriff.

About a dozen of us got leave of absence for a day, provided ourselves with candles, provisions and hatchets, and set out for this cave. Near its mouth was an old saltpetre manufactory, dismantled by the rebels when compelled to abandon it. The nitre was obtained from a brown earth brought from the cave, said to be very rich. This cave is provided with the inevitable stream of water running through it, and the obvious inference is that this is the active agent in producing the cave — the stream providing itself a channel through the heart of the mountain by finding and dissolving out the softer portions.

We entered a long flat boat and were wafted by push poles some half mile into the cave where we found our stream issuing from beneath some rocks too low for exploration as our limited time would allow. The cavity divides and subdivides into a vast number of passages which cross and recross each other, forming a network of dark alleys that are very bewildering. Some of them are said to be over five miles in length.

We selected one and followed it to the end, marking with our hatchets each branch or cross road, so that we might return the same way without getting lost. Judging by the time consumed we must have traveled about three miles. In places the ceiling came so low that we had to lie down and walk like a snake a short distance, emerging into a vast hall, perhaps fifty by two hundred feet and from ten to thirty feet high. The countless beads of moisture hanging from the stone ceiling would flash back our lights with a sparkle suggestive of a cave of diamonds.

Our route alternated between narrow winding passages and immense auditoriums, where an ordinary tone would be exaggerated into a roar. In many of these the ceiling was hung with stalactites, resembling an inverted forest, varying from the smallest quill-like pendant through all gradations of size to those that would weigh hundreds of pounds, which when struck sharply with a hammer would sing out in tones like a cathedral bell. I gathered a fine stalactite about the size and length of an ordinary lead pencil, a perfect cylinder in shape, pure white and hollow for half its length. I tried hard to preserve it, but it was very frail and did not survive the fortunes of war.

We arrived at the end of our passage about noon and there we ate our dinner in a magnificent stone dining hall, in which a regiment could eat without crowding. It was shady and cool.

Not far from where we dined was bat headquarters, where about a bushel of these nocturnal birds had their rendezvous. Some were hanging to the ceiling, others hanging to them, and others to them, &c., an inverted cone of acro-bats. We took a can we had just emptied of peaches, and filled it with bats and took them into camp as living witnesses of our visit to their home. The first and last time I was ever engaged in the canning of meats.

And now we turn our faces toward the outer world. We turn our backs upon the weird shadows, the damps and chills, the hanging forests of stalactite creeping down slowly and surely, their brethren of the stalagmite persuasion as slowly and surely creeping up, promising a meeting which we cannot stay to witness. Never before did the day burst upon me with such splendor. Emerging suddenly from our six hours of constant groping among the shadows of old night, and of wrestling with the powers of darkness into the golden glory of a Southern day; the brightness exaggerated by the contrast almost blinded us — and I realized as never before how blind we are to the beauty and the grandeur of this old world of ours.

■ Col. John G. Parkhurst, 9th Michigan, was appointed Post of Chattanooga commander on November 7, policing the town with the 15th Kentucky, 44th Indiana and his own regiment. In addition to his XIV Corps provost marshal duties, he interrogated Confederate prisoners and deserters, and investigated reports of the army's own scouts and spies. As post commander he selected the site for burying Federal dead; this plot later became part of the Chattanooga National Cemetery. In February 1864, Parkhurst's duties were expanded to include the entire Department of the Cumberland.

Ed Avery, who was carrying the child, learned from Uncle Jim that the child's father had been killed at the battle of Chickamauga, and that her mother had since died, leaving the child to the care of Uncle Jim, who was waiting for a chance to send her to his home in the Southland.

Tightly holding the baby in his arms and looking fondly at her, Uncle Jim said: "Boys, I am going to get permission to take her to my home, and maybe while I am gone this battle will come off. I hope it will, for damned if I feel like shooting at you fellows after this — at least, for some time to come," he added with a smile upon his weather-beaten features.

And as the gray-clad men around him grasped his meaning, a regular Rebel yell went up from each throat, which was echoed from the blue-clad lines as they witnessed the dramatic scene, and both sounds blended into whispering echoes from the rugged sides of Lookout Mountain.

## 'This state of affairs cannot last much longer'

### Capt. Daniel O'Leary
### Company K
### 15th Kentucky Volunteer Infantry

Chattanooga, Tenn.
Oct. 24th 1863

My dear wife,

Your welcome letter of the 18th arrived to-day and it is needless for me to say that it gave me great satisfaction to learn that all the loved ones at home were well. I must also acknowledge the receipt of another letter from you on the 19th and was unable to answer it before this in consequence of changing camp just at that time.

We moved close to the river near lookout mountain about two miles from where we were. I was on picket yesterday and could see the enemy as plain as could be, a small creek only dividing us. We live very peaceably getting water out of the same creek when on picket. There is an understanding that they are not to fire on each other unless when attempting to advance the lines. All communication is forbidden on both sides but some of the boys will violate orders sometimes.

It rained very heavy yesterday and they were not watched quite so close as usual and the consequence was an exchange of coffee for cornbread and apples. It was all done without uttering a word on either side. When the reb got the coffee he raised his hat and with a polite and graceful bow disappeared among the bushes. Then the fellow called out "I say Yank, does it rain over there?" "Yes, but I don't get wet." Our man had a good gum blanket and perhaps the reb was wishing it was his. They seem to be happy. They were either whistling or singing during the day.

You can form an idea of our situation here when I inform you that our men are living on half rations, and according to reports of deserters from the enemies ranks they were faring much worse. This state of affairs cannot last much longer. If we do not succeed in opening rail road communication we will either have to suffer or evacuate, and that will be the last resort as we are fortifying all the time. Gen'l Grant who now commands arrived here today

# 'Busy at the water's edge'

**During the siege even officers participated in the lively picket trading conducted between the lines. 1st Lieut. Spillard F. Horrall of Company G, 42nd Indiana, related the following incident:**

As brigade inspector, [I] always had charge of the picket line in our brigade front. For days and days the pickets of the two armies were exactly on opposite banks of Chattanooga creek; and not fifty yards apart for at least one-half of the brigade line.

On visiting the pickets for inspection one day, and on approaching a sentinel on one of the posts, it was observed that he had no gun in hand, and was unarmed at the edge of the water in the creek. It was likewise noticed that the rebel sentinel on the opposite side of the stream was unarmed, and in the same way was busy at something at the water's edge. Surprised beyond measure at such hazardous business while on duty by a sentinel, in the face of the enemy, this writer quickened his steps, and by all the authority at command demanded of the sentry: "What in thunder are you doing or daring to try to do?"

■ 1st Lieut. Spillard F. Horrall

*Sentry* (very coolly): "Opening up trade and commerce with a foreign country."

"But I don't understand you, sir."

*Sentry* (composedly): "Well, you see this small piece of plank? This is our ship. We have named her 'Peace.' Now 'we'uns' on this side, as 'they all' say on that side, discovered that 'they all' on the other side had plenty of tobacco. Now 'we all' on this side have plenty of coffee, but 'they all' have none; and 'we all' no tobacco. Now we declared an armistice, established this line of communication, and, Lieutenant, see how it works?"

Saying this the comrade's ship was given the necessary propelling power, and the ship touched port on the other side, its cargo of coffee was unloaded, the ship reloaded with tobacco, and safely landed in port whence it started. The sentinel as he unloaded the tobacco triumphantly said:

"You see, Lieutenant, it is the simplest thing in the world. *'Reciprocity.'* See? Take a chew?"

Then shouldering his gun and bringing it to a "present," he resumed his duty, as the corporal of the guard bore away the tobacco to the "reserve."

and I would not be surprised if something was to turn up soon. There has been a great many changes in the army here lately. We were changed back to our old division again. As you may like to know I will inform you that we are the 1st brigade in the 1st division of the 14th Army Corps.

Affairs have been very quiet here lately, but the weather has been wet and cold. And we are not well provided with the comforts of life as usual, and it is impossible to get anything sent through at present. So you need not attempt to send me any of the many articles of clothing I now require, having lost most of what I had in the late movements. But I can get along very well for some time to come ...

I remain ever your
loving husband

Daniel

CHAPTER 4

# Knocking the cover off the cracker-box

## Brown's Ferry: Surprise river expedition opens Chattanooga's supply line

Opening river and rail lines to the stockpiles of supplies at Bridgeport, Stevenson and Nashville was the key to ending Chattanooga's siege. Finding a successful solution to this problem was top priority at Army of the Cumberland headquarters by mid-October. Before his replacement by George H. Thomas on the 20th, Rosecrans began formulating plans to open the so-called "Cracker Line," and designated the army's new chief engineer, Brig. Gen. William F. "Baldy" Smith, to work out the details.

Smith immediately reconnoitered the Tennessee River from Williams Island upriver to a range of hills on the opposite bank, where a narrow gorge ran south into the valley between Raccoon and Lookout mountains. He deemed this site, known as Brown's Ferry, suitable for effecting a bridgehead that would provide access to the road to Kelly's Ferry. Such a lodgment would seriously interrupt Confederate communications up Lookout Valley and eliminate Rebel picket forces down to the river on Raccoon Mountain. Wrote Smith: "The ridge seemed thinly picketed, and the evidences were against the occupation of that part of the valley by a large force of the enemy, and it seemed quite possible to take by surprise what could not have been carried by assault. The major-general commanding the department visited with me the ferry a few days after this reconnaissance ... and I was directed to make the necessary arrangements for the expedition."

Smith was referring to 41-year-old Ulysses S. Grant, who arrived in Chattanooga on October 23 as the newly appointed commander of the Military Division of the Mississippi, comprising the Departments of the Ohio, the Cumberland and the Tennessee. Grant's first task was to ask Thomas and his staff officers for an assessment of the military situation. When Smith's turn came, Grant's attention was aroused by the chief engineer's ideas to forge a new supply line. On the 25th, Smith was given the responsibility to make the attempt at Brown's Ferry within the next two days.

■ Brig. Gen. William F. "Baldy" Smith (right), the Army of the Cumberland's recently appointed chief engineer. For the Brown's Ferry operation he ordered preparation of 50 pontoons and two flatboats to carry 1,500 selected troops from Chattanooga down the Tennessee River and past Confederate pickets to the landing site (above). "It was deemed better to take this risk," he wrote, "than to attempt to launch the boats near the ferry, because they would move more rapidly than intelligence could be taken by infantry pickets, and, in addition, though the enemy might be alarmed, he would not know where the landing was to be attempted, and therefore could not concentrate with certainty against us." Two "hogback" ridges (below) frame the Brown's Ferry gap with Raccoon Mountain in the distance.

■ Brig. Gen. William B. Hazen, commanding a brigade in Wood's division, IV Corps, led the Federal waterborne assault at Brown's Ferry on October 27. "The success of this expedition was complete to the minutest detail," Hazen later wrote. "It was a misty night, with that peculiar stillness felt only just before day, and our progress with the current was in absolute silence. I was in the fourth boat, and landed at the signal-station to direct the boats to their proper landing places ..."

Hazen's troops stayed in Lookout Valley for the next week. "We found in the valley a large bin of corn, some cattle and a mill," he continued. "We first began to issue the corn by the ear (five ears a day to each man); and by splitting their canteens and perforating them, the men would grate the corn into meal and make a coarse but palatable bread. But a neighboring mill was soon running; and our additional supplies, with fresh new camps, and the knowledge of the good work we had done made us all very happy."

## 'The flotilla moved noiselessly out'

### Brig. Gen. William B. Hazen
### Brigade commander
### 3rd Division, IV Corps

Almost immediately after General Thomas assumed command, I was directed to report to General Baldy Smith. Smith told me his plan for opening the line of the river, and informed me that I had been selected for the delicate duty of carrying my brigade in boats at night down the river past the enemy's pickets to Brown's Ferry, nine miles from Chattanooga, there to effect a landing on the south bank, which would be fortified and held as a *tete de pont.* This would enable Hooker's command — the Eleventh and Twelfth Corps, then at Bridgeport — to come up on the south side of the river, make a junction there and hold Lookout Valley with a bridge secured across the river, without which it would not be safe to bring troops into that valley.

The river makes a long bend below Chattanooga so that, by marching directly across the neck from the town, Brown's Ferry was only two miles away. We rode across that neck, and Smith pointed out the precise spot he had already chosen for the landing, made plain at night by a gap in the hills which lined the south bank of the river. I was to take thirteen hundred [later increased to 1,600] picked men of my brigade, in fifty-two parties in that number of boats, each under the command of a well-known and tried leader. The remainder of the brigade, about an equal number, under command of Colonel Bassett Langdon, First Ohio, joined by Turchin's brigade, were to march to Brown's Ferry across the neck, and as the boats unloaded, be ferried over in them as rapidly as possible.

It was desired that I should land and occupy the two hills to the left of [a nearby] house. There was a picket post at this point, and also one in the depression between the two hills. It was thought best to organize a party of seventy-five men who should be the first to land, and at once push out on the road that comes in at the house, clearing and holding it, while half the organized force should be landed simultaneously at each of two gorges, who should immediately push up the hills, inclining to the left, and following the crests until they were wholly occupied. Each party of twenty-five was to carry two axes; as soon as the crest should be reached, a strong line of skirmishers was to be pushed out, and all the axes put to work at once felling a thick abatis. Positions were also selected for building signal-fires to guide us in landing.

I afterward selected tried and distinguished officers to lead the four distinct commands, who, in addition to being fully instructed as to the part they were to take, were themselves taken to the spot, and every feature of the bank and landings made familiar to them. They, in turn, just before night [of October 26] called together the leaders of squads, and each was clearly instructed as to his duties; for they were of such a nature that each had in a great degree to act independently, but strictly in accordance with instructions. At twelve o'clock at night the command was awakened and marched to the landing, and quietly embarked under the superintendence of Colonel Stanley, of the Eighteenth Ohio Volun-

# 'Gaining a proper ascendancy'

**Recently promoted to command the newly created Military Division of the Mississippi, Ulysses S. Grant's arrival in Chattanooga on October 23 was anything but auspicious. Maj. Gen. Oliver O. Howard, XI Corps commander, recalled his first impressions of Grant:**

On the 21st of October I visited General Hooker at Stevenson, Ala., and during the interview he told me that General Grant was on the train coming south from Nashville. Hooker had made preparations to receive the general and have him conducted to his own quarters. Grant was at that time very lame, and suffering from injuries occasioned by the falling of his horse a short time before in New Orleans. Hooker sent a spring wagon and a staff officer to the depot, but for some reason he did not go himself.

As I must take the same train southward bound to get back to Bridgeport before dark, its arrival found me at the station in waiting. I presumed that General Grant would remain overnight with General Hooker, but this presumption was not correct. Several acquaintances among the officers who were on the train met me as I stepped into the forward part of the car. General Grant, sitting near the rear, was pointed out to me, and I passed on at once, as was proper, to pay my respects to him.

Imagine my surprise when I saw him. He had been for some time before the public, the successful commander in important battles; the newspapers had said much for him, and several virulent sheets had said much against him; and so, judging by the accounts, I had conceived him to be of very large size and rough appearance. The actual man was quite different; not larger than McClellan, at the time rather thin in flesh and very pale in complexion, and noticeably self-contained and retiring.

Without rising he extended his hand as I was presented, smiled pleasantly and signified very briefly that it gave him pleasure to meet me. He then permitted me to continue the conversation.

General Hooker's staff officer came with the tender of conveyance and offer of hospitality. The quick reply, made with some emphasis, at the time astonished me: "If General Hooker wishes to see me he will find me on this train." I hardly need say that Hooker very soon presented himself and offered his courtesies in person to his new commander.

■ Maj. Gen. Ulysses S. Grant

I wondered at the contrast between these two men, and pondered upon the manner of their meeting. Grant evidently took this first occasion to assert himself. He never left the necessity for gaining a proper ascendancy over subordinate generals, where it was likely to be questioned, to a second interview. Yet he manifested only a quiet firmness.

Declining Hooker's kind hospitality, Grant and staff went on with me to Bridgeport, where ... Grant and I shared a common wall-tent between us. He had a humorous expression which I noticed as his eye fell upon a liquor flask hanging against the tent within. "That flask is not mine," I quickly said. "It was left here by an officer, to be returned to Chattanooga. I never drink." "Neither do I," was his prompt reply.

■ Col. Timothy R. Stanley, 18th Ohio, was chosen by Gen. W.F. Smith to organize and superintend the Brown's Ferry operation. After the expedition's specially selected troops were assembled, Stanley assigned their duties. "I directed boats' crews to consist of 1 corporal and 4 men," he wrote, "and each two boats to be under command of a sergeant, each detail to be under command of a commissioned officer. I afterward added a large flat [boat], in which I carried 60 men. The pontoons each carried 25 men besides the boats' crews, making in the whole fleet fifty-two boats and 1,600 men. I had provided one of the flats for General Hazen ... and in that I took passage with General Hazen and staff."

teer Infantry, each squad in its own boat.

At precisely three o'clock a.m. the flotilla moved noiselessly out. I desired to reach the landing at a little before daylight, and soon learned that the current would enable me to do so without using the oars. After moving three miles we came under the guns of the enemy's pickets, but, keeping well under the opposite shore, were not discovered until the first boat was within ten feet of the landing, when the enemy's pickets fired a volley harmlessly over the heads of my men. The disembarkation was effected rapidly and in perfect order, each party performing correctly the part assigned it with so little loss of time that the entire crest was occupied, my skirmish lines out and the axes working, before the reinforcements of the enemy, a little beyond the hill, came forward to drive us back.

At this time they came boldly up along nearly our entire front, but particularly strong along the road, gained the hill to the right of it, and would have caused harm to the party on the road had not Colonel Langdon, who commanded the remaining portion of the brigade, arrived with his men at this moment. After a gallant but short engagement he drove the enemy well over into the valley, and also gained and occupied the right-hand hill. The enemy made a stubborn fight all along the hill, but were easily driven away with loss. General Turchin's command now came over, and took position on the hills to the right. My troops were all brought to the left of the road.

Our losses were five killed, twenty-one wounded and nine missing. We buried six of the enemy, and a large number were known to be wounded, including the colonel commanding [William C. Oates, 15th Alabama]. We captured a few prisoners, their camp, twenty beeves, six pontoons, a barge and several thousand bushels of corn.

## 'To act as sharpshooters'

### 1st Lieut. Robert T. Coles
### Adjutant
### 4th Alabama Volunteer Infantry

[On] the 8th of October, the 4th Alabama, alone, was ordered across the mountain into Lookout Valley. The object being to act as sharpshooters, the men ensconced along the overhanging bluffs of the Tennessee River on Raccoon Mountain, the River there being about three hundred yards wide, to shoot down the mules of the wagon trains of the enemy which were compelled to pass, after crossing over from Chattanooga, along the narrow road between the bluff and River, on the opposite side. We held the Railway on the South Side from Lookout Valley to nearly opposite Bridgeport, thus forcing the Union Army to secure their supplies by wagon train from Bridgeport and Stevenson, their nearest bases.

The day after reaching the Valley we were re-enforced by the 15th Alabama, Colonel Oates in command. He brought over with him a section of Barrett's Battery, which he had great difficulty in getting up and over the mountain into the valley. Colonel Oates deployed his men and picketed from Brown's Ferry, which is nine miles by the River below Chattanooga, down to our line. His posi-

■ *Harper's Weekly* **illustration captioned "Longstreet's sharp-shooters firing on a Federal supply-train." These riflemen belonged to the 4th Alabama of Law's brigade and created havoc for several days by shooting mule teams across the Tennessee River. Private Turner Vaughan of Company C recorded the episode in his diary:**

***Oct. 11th. Sunday.*** Halted last night at the base of Raccoon mountain, moved again early this morning to the banks of the Tenn. One of the roads by which Rosecrans supplied his army runs along the opposite bank of the river. Our object coming here is to blockade this road. Two companies of our regiment have been sent out and are now actively engaged in firing into their wagon trains. The companies on picket have done considerable execution — stopped the wagon train and killed a number of mules. The drivers left their teams and took to the woods as soon as the firing commenced. The road is very narrow and the wagons could not be turned around so they have been standing still since morning, the mules being exposed to a continuous fire from our picket lines.

***Oct. 14th. Wednesday.*** It has been raining without cessation for 2 nights & days. We are now most unpleasantly situated. Our picket duty is very heavy & rations are scarce. For meat we kill what sheep & hogs we can find, but bread is very *hard* to get. Looking for a supply today. There is no wagon road across the mountain to where we are and rations have to be brought to us on pack mules. The Yankees have not tried to run the gauntlet with another train. They cross the mountain higher up on pack mules."

tion was principally along the River bank, ours up among the bluffs. The line occupied by the two regiments extended about five miles. It was understood that the other regiments of the brigade, the "fortycans," as we called them, would be sent over to support us. We secured sufficient supplies for our needs in the valley and were progressing very well in our isolated retreat, shooting mules to our hearts' content, and enjoying the sport immensely, until we had reduced the Union Army to half rations by forcing it to secure supplies by a more difficult and circuitous mountain road.

On the 25th of October we were very much surprised to learn that the rest of the brigade — 44th, 47th and 48th Alabama — which had been ordered over to support us, had been ordered back across the mountain to the main army. We were perfectly aware that we were inflicting great damage on the enemy, and that we would not be permitted to remain there much longer without an effort on the part of the enemy to dispossess us.

We had brought our Whitworth rifles from Virginia with us. These were placed down the River on our extreme left to shoot down the front teams, which after being done, the road was entirely blocked and we then proceeded in a leisurely manner to use our English rifles. The road was too narrow between the bluff and River for the teams to turn around or escape in any manner, and were compelled to stand until all were shot down. I saw one of the Whitworth rifles, an English gun with globe sight carrying a large ball, a few of which ran the blockade, in the hands of one of our sharpshooters, kill two mules at one shot — the heavy missile passing through their necks.

The bend in the Tennessee River below Chattanooga begins at that city and curves around in the shape of a horse shoe, Chat-

■ **1st Lieut. Robert T. Coles**

# 'We were left alone to our own resources'

**1st Lieut. Robert T. Coles served as adjutant of the 4th Alabama from March 1862 until the end of the war. He sharply criticized Confederate commanders for scant attention paid to the strategic Southern left flank between Raccoon and Lookout mountains. Coles later wrote:**

"General Grant, with his unlimited resources, was not long in taking advantage of the weak and frivolous attempts made by General Bragg, and the half-hearted manner of General Longstreet of conducting affairs on the left, which was entrusted to his care. It was plainly apparent to all in the regiment that General Longstreet, who had distinguished himself by the able manner in which he handled the left wing of Bragg's army in the Battle of Chickamauga, that his interest, after this battle, began to wane, as it did before the battle of Gettysburg. If he was ever over on our side of the mountain while we were on duty there, no one of the regiment saw him. We were left alone and to our own resources. Of the General officers, General Law was the only one who studied, kept in touch with, and understood thoroughly the perilous position in which we were placed, and he was perfectly ignored by those higher in authority.

"For the irreparable loss of Lookout Valley, General Bragg attributed it to General Longstreet and he in turn to General Bragg. This disaffection and want of cooperation — it matters not upon whom the burden of blame should fall, whether upon one or both — was deplorable, when concert of action by those highest in authority was so essential to the success of our arms."

tanooga being at the heel of the shoe at its upper end, and Brown's Ferry exactly opposite at the lower heel. It is only a short distance, about two miles, across the heel from Chattanooga to the Ferry, but nine miles around by the River. The scenery in the vicinity of Raccoon Mountain is grand and wild. The bluffs on both sides of the River, which almost approach the water's edge, loom up hundreds of feet perpendicularly, while the River winds its turbulent and tortuous way through them.

At Brown's Ferry is a series of ridges running parallel with the River, the road from that point running through a gap in the ridge up Lookout Valley, crossing the railway at Wauhatchie. Extending back from the river up the valley for three or four miles and dividing the valley near about its center for some distance, is a succession of hills about two hundred feet high, with precipitous and very thickly timbered slopes — what we termed "hogbacks" — one after another, with very narrow crests, in many places not over two to six feet across.

The position of the 4th Alabama was different from that of the 15th Alabama. Being up among the bluffs on Raccoon Mountain, no direct attack could be made upon it from the River. The only way to get us out was by a flank movement of the enemy. Our duties, summed up in a few words by Colonel Oates, were: "Law sent the 4th Alabama to do this perilous and all-important work down to the point of Raccoon Mountain, to act as sharpshooters, and prevent the use of the River and the wagon road on the other side of the River; and the 15th Alabama to picket the River from the right of the 4th Alabama, up to Brown's Ferry."

These were the only instructions received by the 4th Alabama.

The transportation of [our regiment] consisted of one poor old pack mule, which we kept busy packing supplies up the mountain. We surrounded ourselves with a strong picket line day and night. Sampey of E Company fired his gun one night and called the Corporal of the guard and created thereby, among the few of us not on duty, no little consternation and uneasiness. When the Corporal reached the post he was informed by Sampey that, hearing someone approaching, and not obeying his challenge, he fired, and was positive he had killed a "Yankee," for he heard him struggling in the dry leaves. He and the Corporal then made an examination and found that Sampey had shot a large coon squarely through the head.

One cool frosty morning, October 27, 1863, just before daylight when the fog was hanging low and heavy along the Tennessee River, picket firing was heard up above us among Colonel Oates' men. As the firing continued for some time, we became very apprehensive that the enemy was forcing a crossing in Colonel Oates' front at Brown's Ferry. The firing had scarcely ceased when our pickets from the extreme right came running in and stated that the 15th Alabama pickets, after making a gallant resistance against a large force, had been driven out and that Colonel Oates was brought out badly wounded.

At that time most of the men of the 4th Alabama were off duty; D and I Companies were the only companies on picket. We hastily called in the nearest and sent messages to the others to get out the best they could. Our cooking utensils were quickly strapped on our mule and we were soon ready to evacuate Raccoon Mountain. From some cause the mule, in the confusion, not placing our utensils on his back to exactly suit his fancy, got away from the

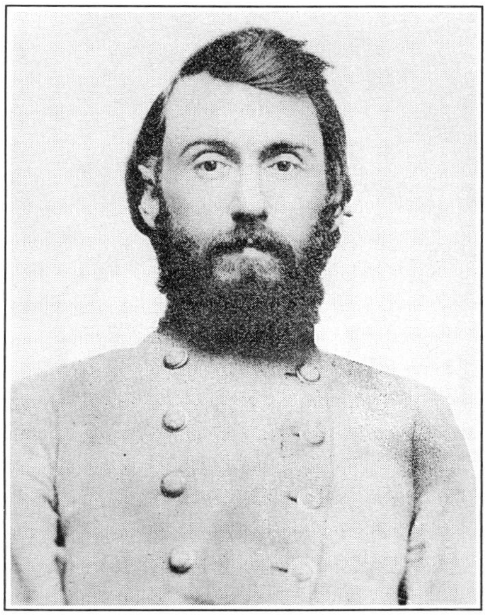

■ Lt. Col. Lawrence H. Scruggs alternately commanded the 4th Alabama with Col. Pinckney D. Bowles during 1863 and 1864. While captain of Company I, Scruggs led the regiment at Malvern Hill and Antietam, where he was shot in the leg. Convalescing at his Huntsville, Ala. home, he was promoted to field grade and recruited for the 4th hobbling on crutches. After recovery he commanded the regiment at Gettysburg.

On the rail trip to Georgia 10 days before Chickamauga, Scruggs' men stopped in Raleigh, N.C., where a mob of soldiers and citizens had just destroyed two city newspaper offices. In quelling the riot on September 11, North Carolina Governor Zebulon B. Vance wrote to President Davis: "I rode with all speed to the depot and got a Colonel Scruggs to march a detachment into town and restrain [the rioting soldiers] before they had done any damage."

■ Brig. Gen. Evander M. Law commanded a brigade of five Alabama regiments in Jenkins' (Hood's) division, Longstreet's corps. Five hours after the Brown's Ferry pontoon bridge was laid, Law's scouts informed him that Hooker's force, moving from Shellmound toward Chattanooga, was only eight to 10 miles from his Lookout Valley position. Law's report to Jenkins late on October 27 analyzed the situation: "My views, as thus communicated, were that it was probably not the intention of the enemy to attack Lookout Mountain at present, but to take possession of the railroad as far as the Trenton junction, 2 miles from the foot of Lookout Mountain, and by holding Lookout Valley to obtain supplies by running wagon trains from the junction across the bridge above Brown's Ferry to Chattanooga."

man leading him and went braying and kicking down the mountain trail, the boys laughing and yelling and picking up scattered utensils.

We flanked around, crossed the road from Brown's Ferry to Wauhatchie, and safely got over the "hogback" ridges next to Lookout Mountain. On our left, as we retreated, the enemy was seen on the ridges with axes busy felling trees and making breastworks. After getting in the valley we surrounded our mule and succeeded in capturing him, after he had kicked off everything except one skillet handle. Out of breath, we fell back slowly across the bridge which spanned Lookout Creek and retired under the crest of Lookout Mountain, where we found Oates' reserves and the section of Barrett's Battery, the latter firing an occasional shot at the enemy fortifying on the ridges.

General Law came over, and brought back our other three regiments and our friends the Texans and 3rd Arkansas that evening. That night D Company came in. Of Company I, four failed to get out and were captured; this was our only loss. The 15th Alabama pickets also got out and came in that night.

## 'Don't bring that nasty rebel into my house'

### Col. William C. Oates
### 15th Alabama Volunteer Infantry

Just after dark on the 26th of October a courier ... brought me a message in purport that a heavy force of the enemy, infantry and artillery, were attempting to cross the river south of the Raccoon Mountain, near Bridgeport, and that when they did so and advanced to the east end and turned Raccoon they would cut off my retreat and capture my command. A reenforcement of two army corps had been sent from the Army of the Potomac under "Fighting Joe" Hooker. These were the troops which were reported as in the act of crossing at Bridgeport, south of the Raccoon.

On receiving the message I wrote it, together with the grounds of my apprehension that an attack on me that night, or early the next morning, was imminent, and sent it to General Longstreet with a request to send reenforcements without delay; that he send me at least one more regiment that night. The courier returned before midnight and stated that he had delivered my communication to General Longstreet, as I had directed, and had a receipt for it. No other response came, and I lay down and tried to sleep.

Some time before day I dropped off into a doze, when I was aroused by William C. Jordan, a private in Company B, who was on the horse of the courier stationed with that company at my upper picket post at Brown's Ferry. The courier was asleep when the enemy landed. They crowded Captain Feagin so that he directed Jordan to mount the courier's horse and go for me. Jordan obeyed with alacrity, but did not have time to get saddle or bridle, and rode bareback, guiding the horse by the rope with which he was tied.

Jordan informed me that the Yankees were crossing the river and had driven Captain Feagin and his company away from Brown's Ferry. I asked how many he saw, and he replied, "Some seventy-five or one hundred." I had the long roll beaten and gave orders for the men to leave their knapsacks in camp and their little tent flies standing. Leaving one or two sick men to guard the camp, I mounted my horse and we moved off as rapidly as possible.

Along the river at Brown's Ferry there is a ridge or little mountain. The gap through this leads to the ferry. Just before reaching the gap and when within twenty steps of them, I heard the invaders at work building breastworks. I came near riding into them. I turned and rode down my line, telling the captains in a whisper to about face. We were marching left in front, and when we got about one hundred yards to the rear, countermarched. I then detailed two companies, Captains Shaaff and Waddell, and ordered them to deploy their men at one pace apart and instruct them to walk right up to the foe, and for every man to place the muzzle of his rifle against the body of a Yankee when he fired. Away they went in the darkness.

I could hear nothing more than the enemy's hammering and a stick crack here and there. I waited in breathless silence for them to fire, a much longer time than I thought was necessary; but when they did fire it must have done terrible execution, judging from the confusion of the enemy which followed. I could hear some running through the woods, others crying out, "We surrender, we surrender!" and some of the officers, I suppose, crying, "Halt! halt! Where are you going, you damned cowards?"

My companies got inside their works and drove them, capturing eleven prisoners. But the Federal line to my right fired on us heavily, and to meet that I deployed in like manner Company K and put it into the action. Their fire still outflanked me on the right. I put in one company after another, until all six of my reserves were into it, and still I could not cover the enemy's front. Company F — Captain Williams — was the last one I put in. The three left companies got inside the enemy's log defenses which they were constructing and drove them toward the river, capturing the ridge west of the gap; but my other three could not drive the Yankees from their position.

Company E, Lieutenant Glover of Company B commanding, had five men killed — all shot through the head, one right after another. I had a bullet pass through my left coat sleeve and my horse was shot. Captain Terrell, of Law's staff, arrived, and I sent him for the Fourth Alabama to withdraw and bring it to my assistance. I next sent a courier down the river to withdraw my other five companies and to bring them as speedily as possible, as I then knew that I was contending with a force greatly superior to my own. The fight continued. I went to the right company, as I could not see the officers, and it was not moving forward.

Day was then breaking and lighting up the woods so that I could see men twenty or thirty steps distant. I saw Sergt. Wilson Greenway of Company F step forward, crying, "Come on, men; it is a shame to lie back this way!" and he fell severely wounded. I rushed in among the men and ordered them forward and went forward myself, and when within about thirty steps of the enemy (I could see their heads as they fired from behind some logs) I was shot through my right hip and thigh, the ball striking the thigh bone one inch below the hip joint, slightly fracturing it, ran around it and passed through eight inches of flesh. It struck a blow as though a brick had been hurled against me, and hurt so badly that I started to curse as I fell, and said "God d——," when thinking that possibly I was killed, and that it would not seem

■ Col. William C. Oates, 15th Alabama, commanded a riverine operation of his own the night of October 25 when he led 40 volunteers in skiffs to attempt capturing several Federal infantry companies camped on Williams Island in the Tennessee River. However, when the lead boat landed a Union sentinel stationed at the river's edge fired his rifle nearly point-blank at the closest man to him — Sergeant Patrick O'Conner of Company K — but missed.

"With that a line of pickets at close distance along the bank opened fire," Oates recalled. "I called to the men in advance to fall back and drift with the current. I saw that my project was at an end and the thing to do then was to make a successful retreat. The balls chugged into the water all around and among us. One shot passed through the side of my boat between my legs as I sat on the side of it, but within a minute the reserve companies returned the compliment with such vigor and precision that the fire of our enemies ceased, and I fortunately succeeded in getting back without loss or injury of a single man, notwithstanding several of the boats were struck."

■ Company A, 18th Ohio, gathered for this informal portrait shortly before muster-out at Chattanooga in November 1864. The regiment hailed from southeastern Ohio and many of its members were experienced river and canal boatmen. These same men largely manned the oars and guided Hazen's flotilla downstream.

In recognition of the 18th's unique background, it was assigned to the Army of the Cumberland's engineer brigade for the remainder of its service.

well for a man to die with an oath in his mouth, I cut it off at that d—— and did not finish the sentence.

All this flashed through my mind as I fell. I tried to move my foot, but could not; I could only work my toes a little. M.E. Meredith, a playmate of my early boyhood, came and raised me up in a sitting position. I saw another man whom I had known from boyhood — Jeff Hussey — sitting behind a stump, and it occurred to me that he was there through fear, and charging him with cowardice, accompanied by unparliamentary language (I had forgotten my recent conversion), I ordered him to come out from behind that stump and help me. His response was an eloquent one. He held up one of his arms, which was bleeding profusely. I told him that I took back what I had said, but that he ought to be away from there as well as myself, and he could help me with the other arm, which he did.

As I hopped off on my left leg, with my arms around the shoulders of these two men, I expected at every step that some of us would catch in the back one of the many balls that were flying around us, but fortunately we escaped. They took me to a little house where many of our wounded had been collected in the yard, and laid me down among them. I told Hussey to get out and take care of himself and how to go to avoid capture. Meredith I ordered to return to his company, and to tell Captain Shaaff that he was in command and to use his best judgment, but not to lose the artillery which was then firing from an apple orchard one hundred yards from the little house.

Soon after he left me the balls from the enemy were striking the fence, or in the yard, ricochetting, and then hitting the house. The only inmates were two ladies. I was bleeding copiously and became very thirsty. I begged the ladies for a drink of water. One of them came to the door with a dipper of water, when a shot struck the house or fence and she jumped back and shrieked with fright. Seeing that there was no other chance to get the water, and my thirst now being almost unendurable, I crawled and dragged my wounded limb through the dirt of the yard to the doorsteps, when the ladies took me by the arms, helped me into the house and gave me water — God bless them! My men, poor fellows, lay scattered over the yard, bleeding and begging for water with no one to help them. The litter-bearers were busy bringing back the wounded. The ladies gave me another cold draught, and never did water taste sweeter.

But a few minutes elapsed before little Joe Rushing, my orderly, brought my other horse. I told him to go out and call two of the artillerymen to come and put me on him, which was done. I thanked the frightened ladies as I was carried from their house. Just as I mounted, my man Jordan, before mentioned, came up with eleven prisoners. This was about sunrise. I told him to return, that I would take charge of them. I gave my pistol to Rushing and told him, in their hearing, to walk just ahead of my horse with the prisoners in front, and if one of them looked back to shoot him. I told them to take the road ahead of us. We went a round-about way, a distance of about four miles, to reach the bridge on Lookout Creek, to avoid interception and capture, which by the direct road was but little over half that distance.

I came very near fainting more than once. My boot was running over with blood, and the wound made it very painful for me to ride. I would have fainted, but we crossed several bright little streams, at some of which I made the prisoners halt. The hindmost man had a tin cup, and I made him give me water and then let him give drink to his comrades.

Just before we reached the bridge, and right in front of a house, I met Doctor Hudson, the brigade surgeon. He made the prisoners lift me off my horse and started to lay me on the piazza, when a stout-looking woman appeared in the doorway, and with the look of a female hyena and the delectable voice of a sand-hill crane, shouted, "Don't bring that nasty rebel into my house; I forbid it!"

Doctor Hudson told the men to take me in, and turning to her he said, "Madam, get me some old linen to bind up this man's wound, and be damned quick about it or I will have your house laid in ashes!" Her manner changed, and she complied with the doctor's request in less than a minute. He had me laid on the floor on the veranda, gave me a drink of whiskey — which I very much enjoyed, as every wounded man does — and bound up my wound so as to stop the blood.

A member of the regiment, James M. Williams, came up and I turned over the prisoners to him, directing him to take them across the mountain to the provost guard. I directed him to search them for concealed weapons before starting. He did so, and took from their pockets several packages of cartridges. Some of these were carelessly laid upon the floor, and two of the prisoners slyly took up a package each and put them back into their coat pockets. After Williams had started and proceeded some distance with them, a straggling soldier who was present, having stopped to see what was going on, inquired, "I wonder what them prisoners

■ Private William H. Surles (left, holding guidon staff) of Company G, 2nd Ohio Infantry, served as an expedition oarsman. His friend Thomas J. Bond recalled: "The order came to our regiment to furnish three men from each company that were acquainted with river life. Surles, Alex Abrams and myself were detailed from Co. G ... We started for the landing, and on the way stopped at a large warehouse and were ordered to pick up an oar 12 feet long. On our arrival at the landing we found quite a number of pontoon boats, and we were ordered to practice rowing for about two hours. An officer stepped up to our boat and asked what regiment we belonged to, and to hold our boat for Gen. Hazen's staff, and to go to our regiment and get rations (which was very easily done, as we did not have any to get). We reported back at midnight, and found the wharf covered with troops loading the boats. We then crossed the river and rowed the boats down [to Brown's Ferry]."

Surles, whose older brother Alexander was killed at Chickamauga, had been a cabin boy aboard the steamer *Poland* plying the Ohio and Cumberland rivers when war broke out. In 1891 he received the Medal of Honor for gallantry at the battle of Perryville.

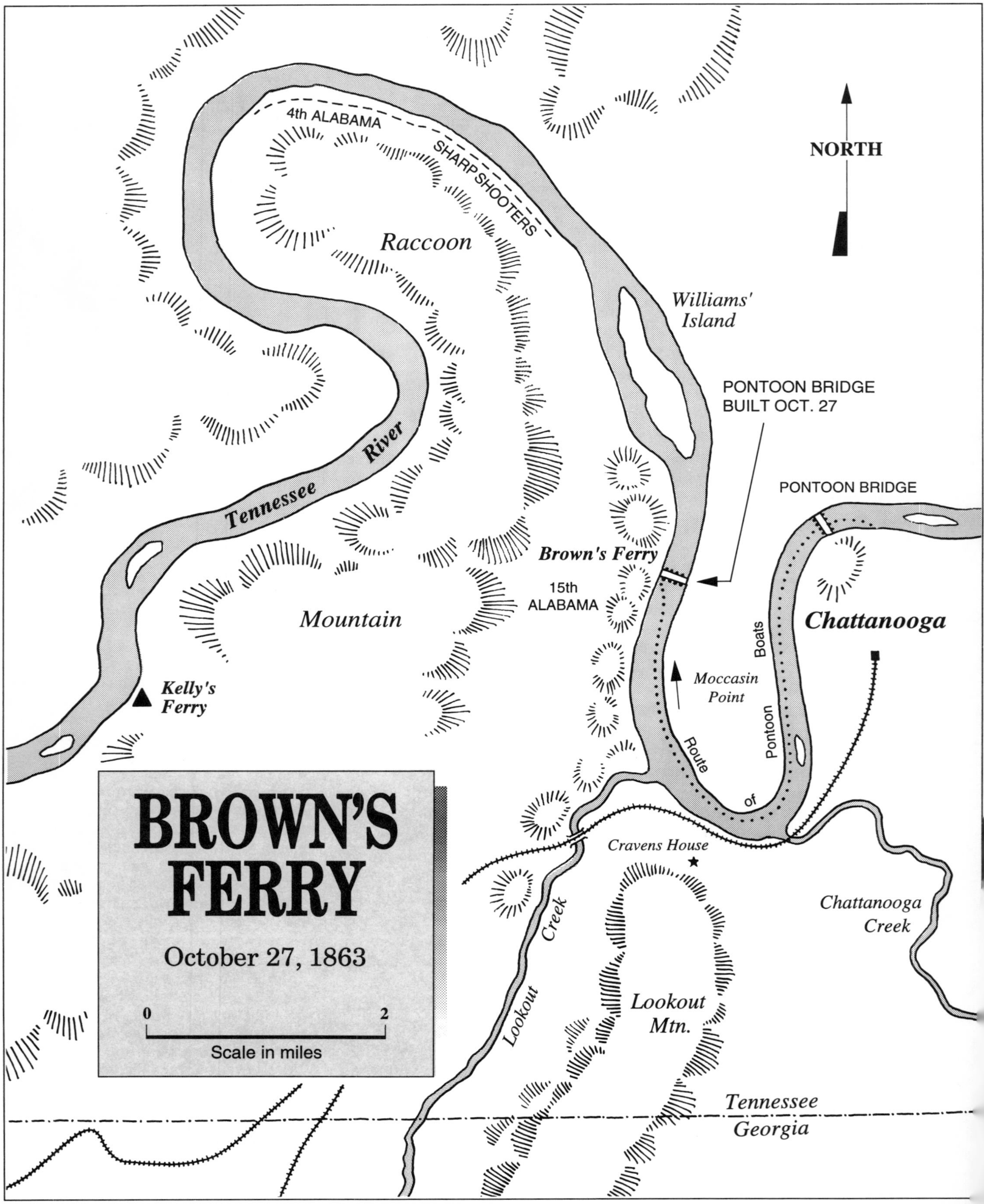
BROWN'S FERRY
October 27, 1863
0
2
Scale in miles
NORTH
4th ALABAMA SHARP SHOOTERS
Raccoon
Mountain
Tennessee River
Williams' Island
PONTOON BRIDGE BUILT OCT. 27
PONTOON BRIDGE
Brown's Ferry
15th ALABAMA
Chattanooga
Moccasin Point
Route of Pontoon Boats
Kelly's Ferry
Cravens House
Lookout Creek
Lookout Mtn.
Chattanooga Creek
Tennessee
Georgia

wanted with them cartridges? I saw two of them pick up a package each and put them in their pockets."

I immediately had him call to Williams to bring them back. He did so, and I told him to search again, which he did, and found the cartridges. They intended to take his gun, kill him and make their escape. In the light of reason we cannot blame them; but at the time I felt very much like firing on them with my pistol.

It was yet early in the morning, the sun being but little over one hour high. About this time General Law arrived with the other three regiments of his brigade and the Texas Brigade. He halted and came in to see me and to learn the situation in the valley. I told him that he was too late, in my opinion, to accomplish anything; that a heavy force had already crossed the river. I suggested that he ride up on an eminence near, from which he could overlook the river to Williams' Island and the greater part of the valley, although it is a valley full of hills and small valleys. He went up but soon returned, and said I was quite right; that they had laid a pontoon bridge and had then at least a corps in the valley.

Four Alabamians and four Texans were detailed, by General Law's order, to carry me on a litter over Lookout Mountain, and they did so — over the highest part to avoid the battery on Moccasin Point, several shells from which exploded near us and some went entirely over the mountain. I arrived at our field hospital just before night, where I found Doctor Davis, the accomplished surgeon of the Fifteenth Alabama, who probed and dressed my wound and made me as comfortable as possible during the night.

General Law reported back to Longstreet, or Jenkins, the situation and placed his troops in a position to aid the Fourth Alabama and my five companies which were on picket to get out. They retreated eastward along the Raccoon Mountain and got out late that afternoon without loss. Captain Shaaff also succeeded in getting out with the six companies which had been engaged and the artillery. At one time the gunners abandoned one piece and one caisson, but the Fifteenth Alabama men compelled the batterymen to carry them out, and both guns and caissons were thus saved from capture; but the men who were too badly wounded to travel afoot, our dead, our camp and baggage, with all of the men's blankets and clothing, except what they had on, and a considerable quantity of supplies, were unavoidably left to the enemy.

## 'Get up, boys! Yankees are coming!'

### Private William C. Jordan
### Company B
### 15th Alabama Volunteer Infantry

The Fourth and Fifteenth Alabama were sent over to the river across Lookout, the only troops in all that extensive territory north and northwest of Lookout Mountain, and between it and the Tennessee River. Surely a great mistake was made, as that was the key to Missionary Ridge. There should have been at least a division stationed in said territory. The Fifteenth Alabama, commanded by Colonel Oates, was on the right near Chattanooga, and the Fourth Alabama, commanded by Colonel Bowles, on our

■ Col. Aquila Wiley, 41st Ohio, was in charge of four regimental detachments totaling 575 officers and men during the Brown's Ferry operation. Transported downriver in 24 pontoons, Wiley's command occupied a "razorback" hill left of the landing — 150 men of his own regiment stationed at the beachhead's far left, two companies thrown out as skirmishers. He reported: "At the first sound of the axes [Confederate] skirmishers advanced up the hill and engaged ours vigorously ... Encouraged by the shouts of their officers to 'drive the Yankees into the river,' [they] only gave way when within a few yards of our own line."

Near Orchard Knob the following month, Wiley had a horse shot dead beneath him. In the Missionary Ridge assault two days later, one of his legs was shattered by a shell fragment, forcing its amputation and ending his military service.

■ Capt. Thomas Quirk commanded an independent company of scouts belonging to Brig. Gen. John H. Morgan's Confederate cavalry division. Some 500 troopers, including Quirk's scouts, remained of Morgan's command after his ill-fated Indiana-Ohio raid of July 1863, and performed duty at Chickamauga and Chattanooga.

Quirk, who earlier served as a private in the 2nd Kentucky Cavalry, was described by one of his men as "a dare-devil Blue Grass Irishman" who "attracted attention by his tireless activity and indifference to danger. His bravery was unquestioned, but he did not possess other qualities which make a capable and successful leader. A blue coat to him was like a red flag to a mad bull, and he went at it on all occasions without regard to anything or anybody. Nonetheless every man in his company liked him and followed him without hesitation. I emphasize 'followed' because this wild Irishman never let anyone get ahead of him in going into a fight, and he didn't know how to quit and retire gracefully."

left. We had about half of the regiment on picket on the river. Our picket line was about ten miles long, from three to five men at a post, at intervals from two hundred to four hundred yards apart.

The post that myself and two others were watching, as we only had three guns, was Brown's old ferry below Chattanooga, a very important position. There was a narrow pass that led down to said ferry place, steep abrupt mountains on each side of the pass. Five of the companies of my regiment were on picket. Colonel Oates had six companies in reserve with him about one mile from us. It was about a fourth of a mile through the pass, with rather a dim road through it. The enemy had a road on the other side of the river that they used for transporting supplies, etc., but it had been obstructed with dead mules caused by the bullets of the Confederates. When I was on picket we had become quiet and comparatively friendly and would talk to each other across the river.

One evening a negro came to me, sent from home, and brought me some provisions and clothing. We had a little cabin on the bank of the river to cook and sleep in, and I had made a pot of lye hominy that day, the day that Frank, the negro, came to me. Frank brought me a turkey, ham, some biscuits, eggs and cake, also a large bed spread that my mother gave me; my wife sent it to me as she could not get a blanket suitable. She also sent me securely in the basket a bottle of brandy. The articles above enumerated Frank brought to me that evening and left the balance south of Lookout Mountain with our quartermaster. Frank stayed the night before with the Forty-fifth Alabama, with a party from my neighborhood. Consequently there was not a drop of brandy left in the bottle, though well corked and tied in the basket. My good friends and neighbors in the Forty-fifth had emptied it, no doubt, with a quill. I told Frank that this was no place for him, to go back to the quartermaster and stay there until ordered otherwise.

We were quite friendly and communicative with the Federals that evening. Our boys would tease them about hardtacks and they would guy us about corndodgers. I stepped out with a pan of eggs and told them to come over, that we had everything that a heart could wish. I took my empty bottle and handed it around to the boys, and all went through the blank motion of drinking. One Yank said, "I believe that fellow has got spirits." I heard what he said and told him to come over. He said he would the next morning and exchange papers and swap coffee for tobacco, if his colonel would let him and provided we would not take him prisoner. We told him that we would deal fairly and honorably with him.

One of General [John Hunt] Morgan's lieutenants and a private were there with their horses to act as couriers in the event anything should occur. The lieutenant's horse was hitched on the bank of the river with the saddle off. The private had a calico-colored pony (Spanish), tied to a tree with a line around his neck, without bridle, with saddle on.

There was a great deal of growth of bushes on the bank of the river. The moon was shining brightly which cast a shadow for some distance in the water on the south bank of the river. I stood vidette from 12 to 2 o'clock that night. Soon after I went on vidette post I heard a splash in the water, but heard it no more. I was very watchful and vigilant the entire time until I was relieved. I told Mr. Payne, the man that relieved me, about the splash in the water. I supposed that it was a large fish that had made the noise.

I went to the little cabin, smoked my pipe, pulled off my shoes and jacket, and went to bed as though all right. I don't know when I had made such preparations before for sleeping. My canteen was hung on a nail in the cabin and I put my pipe on the mantle.

About the time that Mr. Payne had stood watch about two hours he came running in about 4 a.m., saying, "Get up, boys! Get up! Yankees are coming!" Our Captain, N.B. Feagin, was also at this post. We had only three guns. I told one of the men to take my gun as there were several there without guns, and the two cavalrymen had no guns. I put on my shoes and jacket as quickly as I could, threw my bed spread into the basket helter skelter with the remnant of ham, turkey bones, eggs, biscuits, cake, etc. I ran to the bank of the river as quick as I could, took my gun and began firing as rapidly as I could reload.

About one dozen dugouts or batteaus containing about ten or twelve men apiece were landing at the old ferry. The Yanks were shooting as they were landing, saying, "Get out, boys! Get out, boys!" We had to get back up the pass. I ran into the cabin and got my basket, leaving my canteen and pipe. There was a little light in the cabin, and I saw the door darkened with blue jackets immediately after I retreated from the cabin up the pass. The cabin was repeatedly struck by their rifle balls. The lieutenant got his horse out but left his saddle.

The little cavalry private got his pony out with a line around his neck, but lost his bridle. He saved his saddle. Captain Feagin ordered the little private to go after Colonel Oates but the fellow did not know the way. Captain Feagin said, "You go, Billy." I mounted the private's pony without bridle, gave him my gun and said to Captain Feagin, "Give me my basket, Noah," but the pony having a sore back and being excited from the firing of guns, and having no means of checking him, I missed my basket and the pony ran up the pass with me at full speed. Before getting through the pass, however, by pulling the line that was around his neck, and talking to him and patting him on the neck, I had him under fairly good training.

As soon as I got through the pass there was a very dim road that turned to the right and led to Colonel Oates' quarters. I found him up on the alert [for] he had heard the firing at Brown's Ferry place. I reported to him the situation and condition of affairs; he started immediately with his six reserve companies to the scene, being in such a hurry that he went without his hat, as he could not readily find it. He took Dr. Wilson's hat and told Wilson to get his. I went with Colonel Oates; he was riding his mare and I the Spanish pony without bridle.

The enemy by this time had placed trees to obstruct the Confederates, and with great rapidity Colonel Oates deployed his six companies and charged the enemy about twilight. I, as stated, started in with him without gun or bridle on the pony. The bullets were so thick and numerous that I expected to be shot off the pony every instant. I got off of him as it was right to protect myself as best I could under the circumstances. I had no gun, was doing no good and might be spared for another time.

While sitting on the ground, expecting to see the pony shot down any minute, William Holly of Company C brought in three prisoners with their guns. I ordered them to put their guns down

■ Private George B. Payne, a member of Morgan's command, served as a mounted courier during the Chattanooga siege. Born in June 1848, Payne was 14 years old when he enlisted in the 4th Kentucky Cavalry. Note the distinctive tam-o'-shanter worn in this 1862 portrait.

■ Theodore R. Davis sketched the Brown's Ferry landing in this engraving published in *Harper's Weekly.* The artist incorrectly depicted the Kentuckians and Ohioans aboard the lead pontoons with bayonets affixed to muskets. In reality, the expedition's troops carried only their weapons and absolutely essential equipment. Other potentially noisy items were left behind.

and took one myself. Shortly the Yanks said to me, "This is a very dangerous place, had we not better move?" I replied that I did not think we could improve on it at that time. The firing soon abated, and I mounted the pony and ordered the prisoners to march in front of me. After I had gone about 300 yards I saw Colonel Oates coming on his mare, bent over on the horn of his saddle with a slightly wounded man leading the mare, and another had hold of his leg. I waited for him for orders. Oates, considerably exasperated, said, "Jordan, give me my pistol." I replied, "Colonel, I would not do that." He then ordered me to march them in front of him, which I did. He then ordered me to go and relieve our five companies that were on picket on the river, and tell them to fall back to Lookout Mountain. He said, "Jordan, you know the situation, and know what to say to the pickets."

I left him and passed through our camps, and found Captain Richardson with his company who had come from the nearest picket line to the camps. The tents were all as they were when Colonel Oates left them that morning. Captain Richardson had heard the racket, but did not know what it meant. I told him in as short a way as I could the orders of Colonel Oates. Major Hill also was there with Captain Richardson. He said, "Jordan, I will go with you to relieve the pickets." I told him that was all right. When we got to the nearest company Major Hill said he would relieve that company and for me to relieve the others. I had to dismount and lead the pony as the country was so mountainous and rough. I finally succeeded in getting to Lieutenant Thornton, who was commanding Company D. He sent a man on foot to relieve the last company on the extreme left.

I came back through our camp, the tents still standing. Captain Richardson and company had left. Some old women were taking articles of clothing, cooking utensils, etc. I told them to wait, that everything was uncertain; that I hoped that it might turn out so that the boys would return to the camps and they would need the articles they were taking.

Everything was still and quiet, no noise of guns and artillery. I decided that I would bear to the right and come by the way of a little mill. After I came about one mile I overtook Captain Richardson and his company. He stopped and appeared to be bewildered, and told me that he did not know what to do; that he was afraid our boys had been captured as everything was so quiet and still. He said he wished he had someone to go over to see Captain Park and get orders.

I went through a large copse of woods and came across a Mr. Williams who owned the island below Chattanooga, skedaddling and trying to hide his horses. I told him to fall back to Lookout Mountain as quickly as possible. I then rode up to a plantation, keeping along a fence until I came to a lane, started down it and saw some Yankees about 300 yards from me. I quietly turned my pony, expecting to be shot at, but was not. I thought the white marks on the pony looked very large at the time.

I returned to where I had left Captain Richardson, but he had left. I put out through the valley for Lookout Mountain. I finally saw troops moving to my left about half a mile off. I could not tell at that distance whether they were the enemy or our men. I cautiously and gradually got nearer and found that it was a part of our regiment. They stopped and waited until I rode to them. I turned the pony over to his owner, about which he had been very uneasy. I had a nice bright gun that I kept, which one of the prisoners had that was in my possession that morning.

We recrossed the creek at the foot of Lookout Mountain about 8 a.m., established a line of battle and went to work on breastworks. The company that I relieved that morning came in about 10 p.m. They were cut off and had to take to the mountains. They walked about thirty miles that day, flanking around to avoid capture.

## 'We glided by Lookout Mountain'

### Corporal Launcelot L. Scott
### Company G
### 18th Ohio Volunteer Infantry

In October 1863, the 18th Ohio was withdrawn from the front line at Chattanooga and quartered near the river landing to handle the water craft. It furnished a crew for the steamboat *Paint Rock* and also worked the swinging ferry.

I had very pleasant duty for many weeks. I was stationed with a corporal's squad at the head of Chattanooga Island to catch the rafts that the enemy were sending down from Chickamauga Creek to break our pontoon bridge. We had a good skiff, and in it

■ Corporal Launcelot L. Scott of Company G, 18th Ohio. One of his comrades, Corporal Charles M. Heaton of Company D, was in charge of the third pontoon's oarsmen. Heaton recalled: "My coxwain's name was James Gardiner, who met with an accident while we were hugging the shore opposite the rebel batteries and pickets which lined the southwest shore of the river. He stood up in the boat in order to not lose sight of the boat in his immediate front. While in this position we passed under a long sycamore limb which was just high enough above the water to miss those of us sitting down. It caught Gardiner below the shoulders and swept him from the boat. He luckily caught the limb as he fell, which kept his head above water. While in that position he did not forget our strict orders not to speak above a whisper. He was rescued from his perilous situation by comrades in the boat following."

■ Capt. Charles A. Cable of Company G, 18th Ohio. Assisted by Capt. Ebenezer Grosvenor of Company H, Cable was placed in charge of 100 men from his regiment (many of them former Ohio River boatmen) to serve as unarmed crews for about 20 of the pontoons used on October 27. Even with the landing's completion at Brown's Ferry, Cable's important work was far from finished, as related by the 18th Ohio's commander, Col. Timothy R. Stanley: "I ordered breakfast for most of the men, keeping, however, a sufficient number of boats running to carry officers' messages, and gave directions to Captain Cable to fit up [a] ferry-flat, and cross two pieces of artillery, which he did, taking command in person under fire of the enemy's artillery. While going over with the first piece of artillery, a shell passed a few feet over their heads; a little farther on another plowed the waters just above and passed under the boat, but neither the enemy's fire nor fatigue detained them from their work. Much of the success which characterizes the expedition is owing to [his] efforts."

a long, slender, very strong rope called a whale line, such as were used in the whale fishery. We would hitch to the raft or drift and run ashore and snub around a tree and swing our catch into the bank. It would then be floated to the landing and cut up for firewood, of which there was a woeful lack in the camps. As the rafts were always sent down at night, we sometimes missed them. Then part of the bridge would be torn out, but other guards below would catch the wreckage.

In the evening of Oct. 26 all of the regiment not on special duty were ordered on an expedition without arms. At 10 o'clock we marched to the landing and found 50 new pontoons and two small flatboats in the water, and that we were to row them seven or eight miles down the river, full of armed men, to Brown's Ferry. We could not muster enough rowers, and details had been made from other Ohio regiments to make up the crews. The troops came, and at 2 o'clock we took our places and the loading began. There were 25 armed men and five of a crew in each boat, making a total of 1,600 in the expedition.

At 3 o'clock all were ready, and we started from the landing. A section of the pontoon bridge had been dropped out and a steamboat fire basket blazed on either side as a guide. We passed through the bridge, rowed to the north shore and then floated silently down. When we glided by Lookout Mountain and the enemy's lines we kept very silent indeed.

The night was clear. A bright moon hung in the west and we could see the rebel pickets standing on their bank of the river. They could not see us. The vapor that rises from a river on clear autumn nights effectually hid us from their sight. When we rounded Moccasin Point the current threw the boats toward them, but by quietly rowing all regained the north bank without an alarm.

Just at daybreak we neared Brown's Ferry and our colonel [Timothy R. Stanley], in a low tone, ordered us to slant across the river and land just below the boat ahead. As we approached the landing the rebel pickets there fired in our faces and retreated to the hills. The current was swift, the boats close together, and in a moment we had poured a line of men upon the shore.

The small opening was not large enough for all the boats, and some of them crashed into the trees overhanging the river below, but all of the fighters got ashore safely and we rowed to the north bank for another load of men who had marched overland and lay hidden in the woods until their time came. By the time we were crossing with our second load the rebel force had formed on the river hills, and while they fired at the men we had landed, yet they overshot and their bullets struck amongst us on the river.

One of our boatmen was killed and several wounded, but we persevered, and by sunrise had some thousands across and the position was secured. The enemy annoyed us very much by their artillery up the river near Lookout. They had a fair range, and the shells bursting between the river hills made a deafening report that fairly stunned us. When the enemy had been driven from the first hills we cut a road down the north bank, and crossed some field pieces in the larger flatboat, and then lined up our pontoons for a bridge. By noon our work was done. Hooker's army had come up, the enemy had been driven to the foot of Lookout, and we reached our quarters by dark thoroughly exhausted.

## 'Night attacks are notoriously uncertain'

### Surgeon Albert G. Hart
### 41st Ohio Volunteer Infantry

Tennessee River,
nine miles below Chattanooga,
Tuesday morning, October 27, 1863.

My Dear Boys:

I write you from the river-bank, with my hospital knapsack my writing-desk. But this morning is the fastest in military matters which I have ever known since I have been in the army, and I must sketch it to you just as it is before me ...

About five o'clock yesterday afternoon I received an order from Brigade Headquarters that "One surgeon or assistant surgeon will accompany each regiment in the march to-night." It was dark when 175 men out of our regiment, who on some pretense had been previously detailed, and ordered to have cartridge-boxes filled up to sixty rounds, were ordered to be ready to go on a march without blankets. No intimation was given as to the nature of the service. As the night wore on, it became known that a boat expedition was afoot.

I was called up at 1 o'clock a.m. and found a detail from each regiment in our brigade waiting to march. It was 2 o'clock a.m. when we got down to the river. Here a flotilla of pontoon boats awaited us, and slowly we got on board. The boats were twenty-five to thirty feet long, and about seven feet wide, but shallow. On board of each twenty-five men embarked, with five rowers and a steersman to each boat.

It is a moonlight night, but fortunately cloudy, and we gladly see the fog, which hangs over the river, thicken, and the dark shadow of the forest, skirting the right or north bank of the river, widening and throwing its friendly protection out to shield us even partially from observation. We are 1600 strong, bold, resolute, daring men, with enough electric fire among officers and men to kindle enthusiasm for any required deed of danger or daring. But night attacks are notoriously uncertain, and ours is no exception. I think it all over in quiet reflection as we float down, and make up my mind that some of us are pretty sure to sink in the waters of the Tennessee before the expedition is over.

It is understood that after we have descended two miles, or two and a half, the rebels hold the south side of the river with their pickets, and that we are liable to be fired upon at any point below that. Perfect silence is enjoined. I sit beside one of our captains, facing the south bank, and waiting for the first gun from the enemy. After two miles our oarsmen ceased rowing, and we floated still and silent down the rapid stream.

One of the boats near me struck a snag on the shore, a man is caught by the collar of his blouse, lifted out of the boat and dropped into the river. From the boat comes a sharp cry for help. We push for the spot, but the man has already reached the shore. "Go along with your old boat; I'm not half drowned yet." A quiet "All right," and again with muffled stroke we move on.

General Hazen is in the van, directing in barely intelligible voice, and calling out clear and low, "Close up! Close up!" For the boats are straggling as they move at different speed, and when we

■ Sergeant Major Robert A. Gault, 41st Ohio, was among the first in his regiment to learn of the Brown's Ferry operation when he copied the order detailing 25 selected men from each company and delivered the copies to their respective commanders. "Gen. Hazen was our first Colonel," Gault reflected, "[and] some of our boys thought that Hazen was much inclined to place the 41st in the front in important movements. The movement now to be made was considered to be a very hazardous one. The night of October 27 the detail was marched in regimental order over to the north side of the river, where pontoons were anchored. The soldiers were ordered to be strictly quiet, not to say a loud word. The 10 companies of our regiment were lettered in the following order, beginning at the right: A, F, D, I, C, H, E, K, G and B. I was with Co. F. Each pontoon was loaded in the order lettered above, with the 25 soldiers and their commanding officer."

Gault was promoted to captain of Company G in March 1865, a short time before this photograph was taken.

■ Corporal Otis A. Shattuck of Company G, 41st Ohio, traveled downriver near the expedition's van. A regimental comrade in the second boat later wrote: "As the leading pontoons were shoved close to the shore and our soldiers were about to land, the Confederate picket at that point, seeing or hearing what was coming, fired his gun, which aroused the reserve guard, who very hurriedly sprang up, fired a volley and ran back beyond the rugged hills. We were close to the river bank and they overshot us. Our leading companies landed so promptly and were so quickly in line that it seemed no time before we were climbing up the steep ridges, so steep that we were obliged to grasp the rocks and bushes to aid us in our advance."

make our landing our boats should be together that we may not be beaten in detail. My head drops down upon my arm; I find room between the legs of the oarsmen, drop upon the bottom of the boat, and sleep sweetly and soundly.

We have descended nine miles by the river in just two hours. There is the sharp rattle of musketry as we turn toward the left bank. I fully awaken only after several shots are fired from the shore, to find the balls whizzing over and around, and striking the water close to our boat. "Push for the shore! Push for the shore!" The oarsmen pull heavily at the oars. Our boats have dropped a little below our intended landing, but we reach the bank and leap ashore as we may. The company in our boat is formed instantly and rushes up along the bank to reach our proper position. Day is just beginning to break, but objects are confused at a short distance.

We are at Brown's Ferry. A few feet above the water there is a narrow bench of level ground 100 to 150 feet wide, above which towers a hill ascending at an angle of forty-five degrees. At this landing a ravine terminates, which cuts through the ridge, and a road comes down along it to the water's edge. On each side of this road is the high hill. In going back along the road 500 yards, you come out upon the broad valley beyond.

Stopping to dress a wounded man I get behind the regiment. I had not gone up more than two hundred yards, when I came upon a squad of sixty men of the 23d Kentucky holding the road, and although ten minutes had hardly elapsed since the landing, they were already cutting down trees to build a breastwork. I had only ascended a little distance when a fierce fight began at the point I had just left. I could not see it in the gloom, but I could hear the short, shrill yells of the rebs, so different from the cheer which our men use. Crack upon crack came the musketry. I could hear our men falling rapidly back; the rebels had got upon the opposite hill, and as our men retreated, the rebel shots crossed the road and came thick and fast around us. Our men threw out skirmishers to the right along the precipitous side of the hill to the right of the ravine, and the whole force pressed forward with furious cheers and moved up over the rocks, and up the almost perpendicular hill down which the rebels in the same order were advancing but a moment before. No man could guess what force the rebels had, or how soon we might run upon a line of battle which would sweep us down the hill like chaff. But the officers, who had been made fully aware of the ground to be gone over, pressed on the best speed they could make, and in a few minutes more they reached the top of the ridge on this hill.

Meanwhile our detachment of 600 men with which I had landed had moved up the precipitous path and reached the top of the hill on the left. The perpendicular ascent was not less than 300 feet. Great boulders, rocks, rubbish and underbrush were in their way. Along this ridge, or razor-back, a few feet wide, our men were posted when I reached them. Our regiment with Colonel Wiley is in the advance; the 6th and 124th O.V.I. and 5th Kentucky follow. The top is scarcely two yards wide, and in front again descends rapidly, but it is not so steep as on the river side. Our skirmishers form and push down the hill through the trees and underbrush. The rebels form rapidly, and, probably imagining our force to be small, make a furious effort to take back from us the ground we have gained. Our skirmishers fall back for a moment, but soon drive back the enemy, who, as the daylight advances, are to be plainly seen in the broad valley below, and can be heard giving orders for a rapid retreat. The day is won. But to secure ourselves in our position, our men throw up quickly a breastwork of small trees hastily cut down, loose stones and earth scratched up with their tin plates.

As soon as the position was secured, another act began. As I sat fronting the ferry, a crowd of men appeared on the opposite shore. At half-past 8 a.m. a pontoon bridge, made with the boats which carried us down, started from the bank. As it was pushed into the river, straight as an arrow, I thought how savage Indians of the olden time, watching its progress from the shore, would have thought it some wondrous animal, pushing itself across the water and bearing upon its broad back a thousand strange and unknown men, coming to drive them from their hunting-grounds. At 4 p.m. I crossed the river upon this bridge, capable of ferrying over a great army.

## 'We charged on them through the darkness'

### Corporal Arnold Brandley
### Company H
### 23rd Kentucky Volunteer Infantry

At about noon of [October 26] the 23d Kentucky, belonging to Gen. Hazen's brigade, was called in ranks by companies. The officer of my company, Capt. [Claudius] Tifft, informed us that there was to be a detail made from the regiment consisting of a certain number of men (amounting to 50), and that Co. H was to furnish six of this number; that he would at once choose his quota, which he did by calling the names of the ones desired, each man stepping forward as his name was called.

Those selected were: Sergt. William Johnson, First Sergt. James Jackson, Corporal Arnold Brandley, Privates James McKiernan, Charles Frazier and John Shiederly. The last named one did not go because [Redman D.] Buffington, a member of Company B, urgently requested Capt. Tifft to take him in Shiederly's place, stating that he was waiting for an opportunity to be killed and he thought this was his chance. Shiederly consented, and Mr. Buffington was installed in his place.

We were ordered to report for duty on the parade ground at dusk, and informed that we were about to undertake a dangerous task. What this was we were not told. At 6 o'clock that evening we met as ordered. The entire detail of the regiment was placed in line. After counting off we found we numbered 48 in ranks, commanded by Col. James Foy of the 23d Kentucky, Capt. Tifft and Lieut. [Thomas W.] Hardiman of Co. G. We were marched through the town of Chattanooga to the Tennessee River. There we boarded an old scow manned by two soldiers of the 18th Ohio (Col. Stanley's regiment), they having charge of the pontoon boats at that time. As soon as we were all on board Col. Foy requested us to remain perfectly quiet — not to speak above a whisper, and under no circumstances to fire a shot without orders. We then shoved off and steered for the north bank of the river, then floated

■ Lt. Col. Robert L. Kimberly, 41st Ohio, described his men's disposal of food found shortly after the fighting ended at Brown's Ferry: "In front of the Forty-first as it lay on the ridge after the enemy had gone, was a farmhouse a few yards from the base of the ridge. There was a corncrib near the house, and its contents were quickly distributed. As the men sat about their little fires, a savory odor was observed coming from a kettle in one of the men's messes. A little crowd was attracted by the grateful smell, and it was explained that two of the men had caught a couple of rabbits down by the farmhouse. There were many hungry sniffs of the odors from that little kettle. An hour afterward, two elderly maiden ladies, occupants of the farmhouse, came up to complain that 'you'uns have carried off our cats.' Well, they smelled as good as rabbits while they were cooking.

"Not many hours afterward there was an issue of fresh beef — an earnest of the good things coming in the wake of Hooker's men. By all odds, it was the finest and best-flavored beef ever issued to hungry soldiers."

■ Lt. Col. James C. Foy, 23rd Kentucky, commanded the expedition's lead barge carrying 52 men to Brown's Ferry. As the barge began to pass the ferry, Gen. Hazen shouted excitedly, "Pull in, Foy! Pull in!" thus alerting Confederate pickets. Immediately advancing 500 yards from the water, Foy's three squads began building breastworks behind a thin line of skirmishers. They were the first to absorb an enemy counterattack, losing two men killed and eight wounded.

"I could distinctly hear [Confederate officers] giving orders," Foy wrote. "In little time they were upon us, they adopting their usual plan of cheering and firing at the same time. We readily returned their fire, and soon had to fire nearly to our right. I knew by the report of their guns that they outnumbered us nearly four to one."

Ordering his men to fall back, Foy soon was reinforced by troops of the 6th Indiana and 1st Ohio. At daylight the threat ended and the Confederates withdrew, leaving the front-line Federals unmolested except for periodic, ineffective artillery shelling.

down with the current.

All went well until we passed undr a tree that had fallen out from the bank and was still hanging by the roots just high enough to allow the boat to pass under; the order was whispered, "Everybody down." Sergt. Reeves (afterward Captain) of Co. G attempted to leap over the tree, but he was not quick enough and was caught by the branches and swept into the cold stream. We could not stop the boat or assist him, not daring to make a noise; neither did Reeves cry for help, and we passed on in doubt of whether we would ever again see our comrade.

On, on we floated until we observed a single picket-fire on the south bank. Col. Foy then hallooed to the boat in our rear, if he should land. Then Gen. Hazen sent the word to steer for that light, which we did hurriedly. We all raised to our feet. Gen. Hazen's order was heard by the rebel picket, who gave the alarm to "Fall in, the Yanks are coming!" I heard the officer of the guard give the command, "Ready, aim, fire!" One of the oarsmen, an 18th Ohio boy, dropped his oar with a rebel bullet in his arm. We were thoroughly aroused and anxious to fire back, but we remembered our orders. When the rebels fired their volley we were not more than 30 feet from shore. With one of our oars being gone, the boat swung around as if on a pivot. Capt. Tifft jumped to the front and luckily reached some willows, which he firmly grasped, thereby saving the boat from floating away. We leaped from the boat on to a pile of drift wood. Here we found the bank very high above us, but by the assistance of roots, brush, etc., we reached the top.

When I got up the bank I found four of our men ahead of me; one of them was Capt. Hardiman. I asked him what to do. He said lay down and wait for the balance of the boys. The rebs were in and about a log house at the edge of what is known as Brown's Gap; there was no chinking between the logs, and we could see their movements very plainly. They were trying to organize, but before they were able to do so we charged on them through the darkness, firing as we went. We followed them on through the Gap to an open field. Here Col. Foy ordered us to throw up a barricade of fence-rails, logs, etc. Before this could, however, be completed the rebels were re-inforced and charged us. Our squad was scattered hunting material for the barricade; thus it became an easy matter to force us back to the starting point — the Tennessee River. Capt. Tifft called loudly for us to rally on the reserve, hoping thereby to deceive the enemy in our numbers.

We halted but a few moments on the edge of the Gap, when Col. Foy gave the order to charge, which we did in good style, driving the enemy once more through the Gap to an opening where they were cooking a large kettle of beef. Daylight had made its appearance by this time, and right here at this kettle of beef, in an old log house, we halted. Grabbing for the beef — running hands and bayonets into the hot water, gobbling up the delicious pieces of half-done beef — and around this old kettle the battle of Brown's Ferry and the charge of the first boat's crew ended.

Out of our boat's 48 men, 17 were killed and wounded. Volunteer Buffington's wishes were gratified, he being about the first man killed. Col. Foy was shot through his new hat. He lamented very much that he did not bring his old hat in place of this one.

■ Under long-range fire from guns atop Lookout Mountain, troops of the 1st Michigan Engineers lay the pontoon bridge at Brown's Ferry. "The bridge itself was a frail affair," wrote 1st Lieut. Charles E. Belknap of Company H, 21st Michigan. "Very soon after construction of the bridge, the enemy began sending down rafts of timber, which lodged against the pontoons in the rapid stream, causing many breaks ... Fastening ropes to these rafts, they were towed to the shores and made fast to trees. Many of the rafts were rigged with torpedoes, so arranged as to explode when striking any obstacle."

## 'Our Johnny friends made a dash'

### 1st Lieut. William A. Morgan
### Company E
### 23rd Kentucky Volunteer Infantry

About three o'clock the boats started following the large flatboat, my squad being in the last or fifty-second boat. So far as I know, the only instructions imparted to the commanders of the squads was that at the proper time we would receive orders from the right-hand side of the river, and in the shadow of the timber along the bank, as possible. I was also informed that the nature of the expedition was such that each squad might have to act independently of the others, in a great degree, until other orders were received.

The moon went down just before we started and although a light fog fell, we were able to distinguish the preceding boat. As we were crossing the river to pass through the opening made for us in the pontoon bridge that reached from Chattanooga to the north side, one of my boys remarked: "This reminds me of a picture I once saw of Washington crossing the Alps." His mixed history caused a general laugh, which was quickly suppressed by a voice from the boat ahead, in a kind a stage whisper: "Shut up, you damned fools! Do you think this is a regatta?"

■ An unidentified orderly sergeant, 21st Michigan, holds his felt hat with engineer's insignia, signifying the regiment's later assignment to the Engineer Brigade. By 8 a.m. on October 27, the 1st Michigan Engineers of Companies C, D and K, under Capt. Perrin V. Fox, unloaded equipment wagons on the bank opposite Brown's Ferry and commenced work on the pontoon bridge. As boats finished ferrying troops of Turchin's and Hazen's brigades from Moccasin Bend across the Tennessee River, the 21st Michigan helped to place them in line and construct a roadway. The pontoons then were anchored, connected by stringers and covered with green-pine planking. One pontoon in midstream was struck by Confederate artillery fire, the shell penetrating the boat's bottom and letting in a gush of water. Private Adrian Musty of Company D, 1st Michigan Engineers, quickly pulled off his blouse and cap, stuffed them into the hole and prevented the boat from sinking until it could be repaired.

The Michiganders completed the bridge within 10 hours.

Scarcely a mile was passed when we heard a splash ahead which told us that someone was overboard, and soon a man who had been swept overboard by a projecting limb was picked up. Silently we floated, using the oars only sufficient to get steerage way. Just before reaching Lookout Mountain we discovered the enemy's pickets, in groups of two or three, so utterly unconscious of our proximity that they appeard to be chatting with each other. At one post two pickets, made visible by the faint flicker of a fire, sat facing each other, astride of a log, and one, with lips puckered, was evidently teaching the other to whistle a tune, an occasional note of which we could hear. We soon passed another group who, from their actions, had evidently heard something, as they were intently listening and looking toward us.

Thus the time passed when suddenly the sharp crack of a rifle was heard away ahead, then another. My first thought was that the leading boat had been discovered and by the time the fifty-second boat reached that point the enemy would have a whole brigade lined up shooting at us. The noise ahead indicated that speed was the thing now and our oursmen bent to their work. In a few minutes a voice from the right bank, scarcely loud enough for us to hear, called out: "Pull across the river, go up the ridge, picket your front, and fortify." (Each squad had been furnished two axes for that purpose.) Quickly turning the boat in that direction, we soon reached the shore, which proved to be a steep hill about 200 feet high and very difficult to climb, at least where we landed. As soon as the boat was empty, the men in charge shoved out and pulled for the other shore. "What does that mean?" asked one of the boys as we slowly toiled upward. "That means," answered another, "fight and be damned to you." The fact was, although we did not know it then, that the balance of the brigade (under the command of Colonel Langdon, of the 1st Ohio) and Turchin's brigade had marched across the neck of land and were waiting at the ferry to be ferried over to our support.

Upon gaining the summit we discovered that the top of the ridge varied from two to six feet in width, and by laying down on the river side it made as good a breastwork as we wanted. By this time the musketry fire, about a half-mile on our right, which proved to be at the gap in the ridge leading to the ferry, was very heavy. Daylight was beginning to light up the tops of the hills, but it was still dark in the valley and Raccoon Mountain, about a mile across the valley, had the appearance of being surrounded by water. So far as I could see or hear, there was no enemy in our front. I at once deployed six men along the top of the ridge to the left and six more at the foot of the hill in the valley. After waiting a few minutes, the firing on our right indicated an increase in the enemy's forces (although the echo from Raccoon Mountain probably made it sound heavier than it really was) admonished me of the danger to our forces at the ferry, upon the success of whom the safety of all the others depended.

The squads on my immediate right, like my own, had nothing in their front apparently (although there might be some of the enemy in the valley, it was too foggy down there to see), and were standing idle, waiting for something to turn up. We had performed all that we had been ordered to do, but remembering the admonition that "each squad might have to act independently of the others," I concluded to make a demonstration in my front, hoping that by doing so I might be able to draw the partial attention of the enemy from our forces at the ferry. So I moved my six men at the base of the hill out into the valley, passing a small farm-house, until we reached a road which afterward proved to lead from the ferry to Lookout Mountain, and I judged we were one-third, or nearly so, from the ferry, between these two points.

As yet we had met none of the enemy, and although we could see nothing to shoot at, I directed the men to fire their muskets at intervals, as if skirmishing. This "monkey business" did not continue long. Then the report of the artillery in the vicinity of the ferry reached us, and before many minutes we could hear the enemy coming toward us from the right. Fearing we might be cut off from the hill, the rapidity with which we got back to and partly up the hill-side would be excruciatingly funny to an impartial observer. Calling the boys from the hill-top, I deployed the entire squad as skirmishers and again advanced.

The boats having abandoned us to our fate, as we supposed, the boys were pretty determined, and we soon struck a fairly strong skirmish-line of the enemy and started them going back until we again passed the small house, after which our "Johnny" friends made a dash and sent us whirling back almost to the hill. Then the musketry fire began along the hill-top and again we were able to advance within sight of the small house, from which we saw a wounded man carried, but we could advance no farther. The enemy was too much for us, and again we were compelled to retire and did not stop until we reached the hill-top, although the enemy did not follow us very far. By this time it was light in the valley and we could see the valley road occupied by a moving column of the enemy's infantry and two pieces of artillery, going to our left, in the direction of Lookout Mountain, at a fast walk, with flankers out, until they disappeared in the woods a half-mile or more away, where they halted long enough to fire a few shells at us and then resumed their march. The firing had ceased along our line and we could see the boats carrying troops from the north side of the river to the ferry, from which they were being moved up on the hill, strengthening our line.

About this time General Hazen came along and informed us that we had "knocked the cover off the cracker-box and plenty to eat was in sight if we would hold the ground we had gained." The enemy made no effort to regain the position, and later in the day General Hazen issued a circular congratulating the troops on their success, and as a recognition of their gallantry he ordered two ears of corn issued to each soldier and two ears to each officer on his personal requisition. (Hazen was methodical if he was anything). Two ears of corn as a reward of bravery may seem like a joke, but had the option of a medal of honor or two ears of corn been given the troops, very few would have accepted the medal.

Late the next day ... a steamboat passed up on the way to Chattanooga loaded with hard bread, bacon and coffee. When the troops near the river saw the steamboat and realized the fact that "the cracker line" flowed unvexed to Chattanooga, they broke forth in wild and vociferous cheers, which started some of us to inquiring the cause. One soldier rushed to the river and inquired of another: "Has Grant come?"

"Grant be damned!" said the other. "A boat-load of rations has come."

■ Brig. Gen. John B. Turchin, Russian-born commander of the 1st Brigade, 3rd Division, XIV Corps. His Ohio and Indiana troops were ferried across the Tennessee River from Moccasin Bend in pontoons after Hazen's landing, whose positions they reinforced. The meaning of the successful undertaking was not lost on Turchin's enlisted men. Wrote Private Thomas D. Osborne of Company B, 17th Ohio: "We remained there until Gen. Hooker's men came in sight [on October 28], bearing the old Stars and Stripes, on the skirmish line. We all yelled when we saw it coming, as we knew we would get full rations once more and a new pair of shoes, of which we were very much in need. I killed a cow on top of the hill and treated the whole skirmish line to beef — the first square meal we had had since the battle of Chickamauga. Gen. Turchin came along and told us to keep a close lookout for the rebels."

CHAPTER
5

# Splitting underbrush and moonshine wide open

## The battle of Wauhatchie: Courageous and costly night assaults in Lookout Valley

Before the last pontoons were anchored in the Tennessee River, Federal forces moved to reinforce the Brown's Ferry bridgehead. Word soon filtered through the ranks of Hazen's and Turchin's brigades that Maj. Gen. Joseph Hooker was on the way from Bridgeport, Ala., with his "Potomac boys" — two divisions of the XI Corps and another from the XII Corps — to open the so-called cracker line. By late afternoon on October 28, Maj. Gen. Oliver O. Howard's XI Corps troops bivouacked a mile from Brown's Ferry.

The Westerners were quick to initiate a heated rivalry with their Eastern counterparts, who traded epithets and invective with equal vigor. After passing through a XI Corps camp near Bridgeport, a trooper in the 92nd Illinois Mounted Infantry found the newly-arrived soldiers "well dressed, all with corps badges and paper collars, and much style. The horses of the Ninety-Second could scarcely crawl along — empty corn-cribs! The men were unwell from their lack of rations and hard duty, and their clothing worn out and ragged. Some thoughtless Potomac soldiers commenced to jibe the men of the Ninety-Second, and it required an effort on the part of the officers to keep the boys from replying with their Spencers. Men who are ragged from hard service, and emaciated for the want of food, do not like to be jibed."

Lt. Col. Robert L. Kimberly, 41st Ohio: "One of the incidents of [the Brown's Ferry] expedition was the meeting for the first time with troops from the East — Hooker's men. What was particularly noticeable about these men was the completeness of their outfit; beside the scantier outfit of the western troops, they looked something like walking museums of buttons and brass plates and ornaments. Some of their furnishings had never been dreamed of by the western soldiers. Everything, too, was fresh and in good condition — a contrast not relished by the men whose campaigns had been over long distances, taking them far from the base of supplies and compelling the

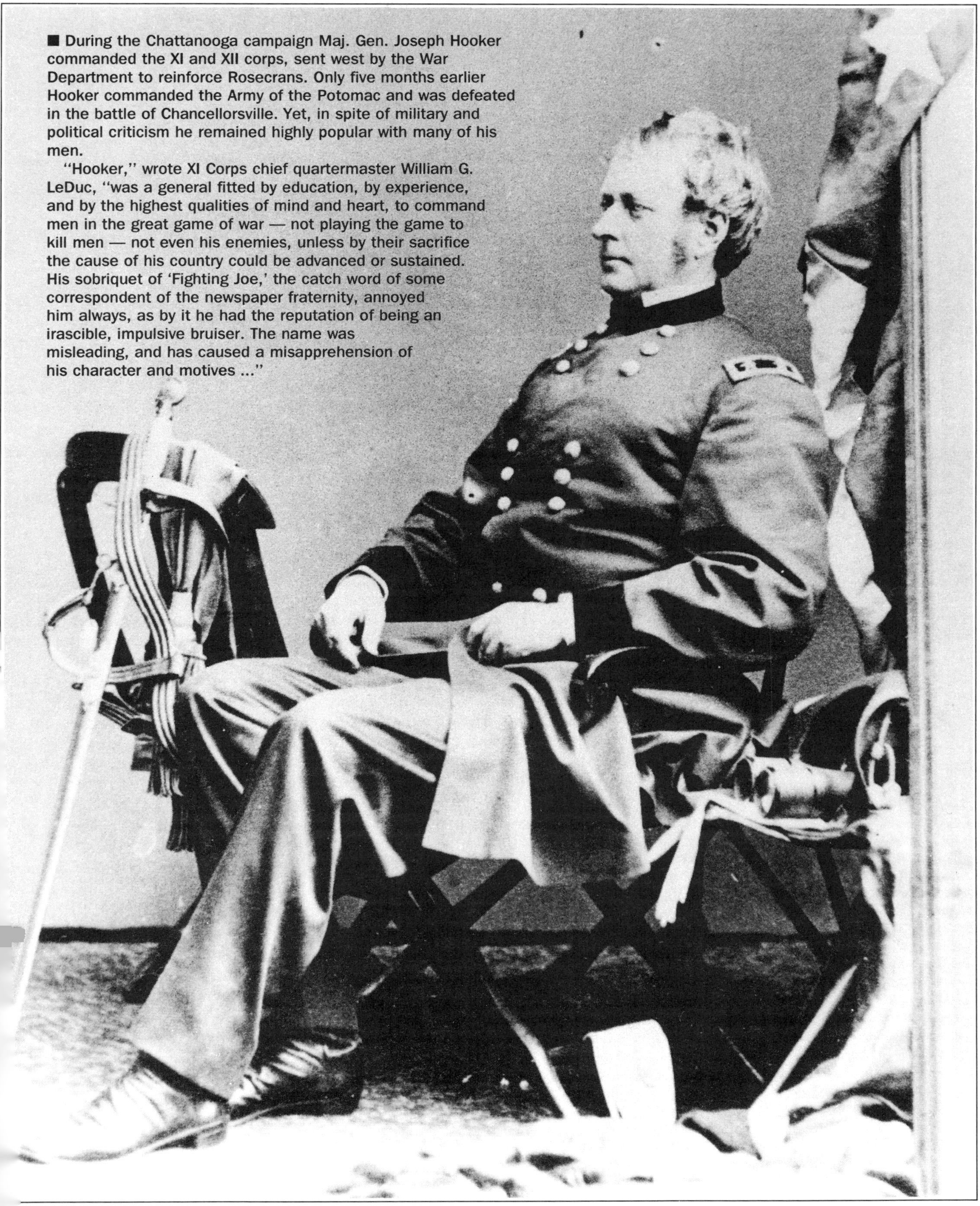

■ During the Chattanooga campaign Maj. Gen. Joseph Hooker commanded the XI and XII corps, sent west by the War Department to reinforce Rosecrans. Only five months earlier Hooker commanded the Army of the Potomac and was defeated in the battle of Chancellorsville. Yet, in spite of military and political criticism he remained highly popular with many of his men.

"Hooker," wrote XI Corps chief quartermaster William G. LeDuc, "was a general fitted by education, by experience, and by the highest qualities of mind and heart, to command men in the great game of war — not playing the game to kill men — not even his enemies, unless by their sacrifice the cause of his country could be advanced or sustained. His sobriquet of 'Fighting Joe,' the catch word of some correspondent of the newspaper fraternity, annoyed him always, as by it he had the reputation of being an irascible, impulsive bruiser. The name was misleading, and has caused a misapprehension of his character and motives ..."

■ Col. Horace Boughton commanded the 143rd New York. This regiment was among the first of Howard's XI Corps to reach Bridgeport after an eight-day rail trip from Virginia. "The 143rd Regiment was packed in freight and cattle cars, some of the men riding on the roofs of the cars because of their crowded condition," wrote a member of Company A. "When within a few miles of Bridgeport the train carrying the 143rd, while rounding a curve in a deep cut, met another train, and a head-on collision was the outcome. The impact was such that one locomotive was partly mounted on the other, and the two front cars of the train were telescoped about half their length. A number of soldiers were hurt, but fortunately none were killed. The train was abandoned and the journey completed in true soldier fashion with no more collisions."

Boughton was made a brevet brigadier general on March 11, 1865.

wearing of wornout articles for months at a time. The advantages of campaigning on short lines and near the seat of government was apparent enough in this case."

Capt. Henry Nourse, Company H, 55th Illinois: "There was invariably a lively sharpening of wits when the free and easy Western men chanced to come in contact with the brass-mounted troops of the Potomac. We pretended to sympathize deeply with our compatriots from beyond the Alleghenies, in their grievous separation from good society and the luxuries to which they had been accustomed. We volunteered our condolences because they could no longer draw from the quartermaster rye straw for their beds and Day & Martin's blacking for their shoes. We expressed our earnest hope that they might not be compelled to eat their hardtack without butter. We said to each other, with simulated admiration, 'What elegant corpses they'll make in those good clothes!' "

Private William Bakhaus, Company G, 47th Ohio: "In striking contrast to our appearance were Hooker's men, all dressed up as if for parade, in short neat looking jackets and paper collars. They had stars on their caps, on their coats, on their tents, on their flags, on their wagons. Everything they had seemed to be a brigadier general. We, at that time, did not know that the star was their corps badge, having never heard of such a thing before. We all commenced laughing at them and their paper collars, and each regiment as it came along took up the laugh, until at last matters became so serious that we actually came to blows ..."

"As the boys wore paper collars, had their shoes blacked and presented an orderly appearance, in marked contrast to the Westerners, they sneeringly dubbed them 'Paper-collar soldiers,' " wrote 1st Lieut. George K. Collins of Company I, 149th New York. "From the first it was evident that the men in the 11th and 12th Corps had not the respect of the Western troops, and there was no end of ways in which they manifested their contempt for them ... At this time in the West the general impression prevailed that the Army of the Potomac did not amount to much, and while its tactical knowledge was admitted, the Western men said, 'It was all very well, but fuss and feathers didn't count much when you come to fighting.' In other words, the Eastern troops were underestimated as fighters."

Surgeon Robert Hubbard, XI Corps assistant medical director: "The Western Department is, so far as my observation goes, less efficient, more disorderly and more corrupt than the Eastern, and I am disposed much to doubt the superior fighting qualities with which they are credited by so many ... I do not like this Department. It does not compare in its appointments with the Army of the Potomac. The men you come in contact with are wild and rough and form a kind of barbarous society for which I have no taste."

The War Department ordered the two Army of the Potomac corps west to help relieve Rosecrans' besieged troops after his defeat at Chickamauga. Hooker, defeated himself that May at Chancellorsville, Va., was given command of the 20,000-man force whose lead elements arrived by rail in Bridgeport only six days after leaving Washington on September 25. Among

# 'Fight or no fight, we must reopen this road'

As darkness fell on October 27, 1863, a train carrying the 147th Pennsylvania pulled into the station at Bridgeport, Ala. The Keystone soldiers quickly found a dramatic change from the familiar surroundings of Virginia. "We are in a Mountainous region," wrote Commissary Sergeant William M. Clark to his sister the following day. "The Cumberland, Blue & Alleghanies appear to culminate in this section, hence we have one confused mass of Hills, peaks, etc. Climate is quite mild, trees are mostly green. Grasshoppers are still thick down here, grass growing wherever it has a chance ...

"I am here with some dozen men, guarding regimental baggage. I have a Wall Tent for myself, plenty to eat, but as poor as a *Church Mouse,* not a *red!* We should have been paid before we left the Army of the Potomac. I am satisfied money is of no use here, save to purchase a little of the weed once in a while. I still smoke a pipe.

"This is the main Depot of the Army of the Cumberland; from here Stores are taken to the Army by wagons. Owing to the Mountains, and [Tennessee] River, our trains have to travel some 60 miles before they reach Chattanooga. Efforts are being made to open the road from here. Yesterday morning Gen'l Hooker and Geary crossed the River and advanced some 9 miles finding but few of the Enemy. Our Regiment crossed at Sunrise this morning, rumors are that a battle will take place. Fight or no fight, we must reopen this road, or we will have to evacuate Chattanooga."

One of the 147th's officers marching toward Lookout Valley that morning was Capt. H.H. Wilson, right, former commander of Company D, who served on Geary's staff as ordnance officer. The black plume worn on Wilson's hat was an object of widespread, derisive joking in the Army of the Cumberland.

■ An unidentified private belonging to Company C, 29th Pennsylvania, proudly displays three star badges on his cap and commercially purchased sack coat. As the emblem of the 2nd Division, XII Corps, the white stars worn by Geary's soldiers immediately caught the attention of western troops who mused that an entire division of brigadier generals had arrived. Sergeant George W. Holmes of Company G, 100th Illinois, wrote of his first impression: "[Hooker's] soldiers, especially the officers, look as though they had just come out of a band box, and they carry very heavy knapsacks loaded with extra clothing and blankets, pup tent, etc., enough to load a mule."

**the XII Corps troops traveling to this new assignment was a young Pennsylvanian whose journal gives a vivid account of the journey:**

## 'Where did all the Brigadier Generals come from?'

### Private David Monat
### Company G
### 29th Pennsylvania Volunteer Infantry

**Sept. 28, 1863 —** Our Regiment embarked and after they had passed through Alexandria [Va.] I heard of it and learned that our Corps & the 11th were ordered to join [Rosecrans'] army at Chattanooga, Tenn. Along with Jim Schall of the 109th Penna. we left the hospital and went into Alexandria. The only money I had was an old 2 dollar bank note of a town in Vermont. We had great fun in visiting the different saloons and after getting our liquor we would offer the note but no one would take it. We got feeling rather lively and came near being arrested by the Provost guard.

After our Brigade had gone through the city we took the following train, passed through Washington and over the Baltimore & Ohio Road to Benwood near Wheeling where we left the cars and crossed the Ohio River on a Pontoon bridge to Bellaire, Ohio. Here I caught up with the Regiment and reported for duty. We again took the cars and passed through Ohio & Indiana where at every station we stopped. The people crowded to the cars with baskets filled with pies, cakes and cans of coffee, and on leaving wishing us Godspeed and success. They all seemed in great distress and anxiety on account of having so many relatives and friends with the army about Chattanooga and they had had no reliable news from them since the fight at Chickamauga.

We arrived at Indianapolis, Indiana, where we changed cars and went to Jeffersonville and crossed the Ohio River on ferry boats to Louisville, Ky. and took cars for Nashville, Tennessee.

When we arrived here Jack MacLauchlan, Dan Kane, Aleck McAleer, Ben Benner and I concluded to leave the cars and see the city. We started up through the place — McAleer loaning us each 5 dollars & we left all our accoutrements in the car with the company and took only our canteens. We soon managed to buy some whiskey from an old woman. We travelled all over the city and had a number of growls with the Provost guards, who when they saw us would want to know "Where all the Brigadier Generals came from," alluding to our white star badge. They slurred us about not knowing how to fight and that the Army of the Potomac never got outside of Washington, and that all the Western army wanted us to do was to guard the Rail Roads so they could get rations and that they would do all the fighting.

As the trains going through stopped at Nashville some more of the fellows of our Corps got off and it was not long before the town had quite a crowd of the 12th Corps in it, and the growling with the Provost guard got hotter. It was reported that night some of our fellows got into a fight in the theatre and one of our Corps threw a Provost guard over the railing into the pit of the theatre. Next morning the Provost Marshal issued an order, ordering all the 12th Corps men out of the city or else they would be arrested and placed in the chain gang and be made to sweep the streets with a ball and chain on them.

As soon as we heard of the order we all rushed for the Depot and took the first train leaving and found our Regiment at Murfreesboro [where it arrived October 5], getting ready for inspection.

**Oct. 7, 1863** — As we had left our guns and accoutrements in the cars they got lost or some of the lads who had lost theirs confiscated ours — except my knapsack which an old school mate, Sam McFadden of Company D, found and returned to me. As our Captain was short in his accounts of several guns our 1st Sergeant told us he would give us guns and charge us with them. We kicked at this and as luck was with us we found a lot of guns and accoutrements at the depot in charge of the Post Quartermaster. It was not long before we were all equipped and had the guns apart getting ready for inspection. When we fell into line with the Company all ready our Captain looked at us pretty hard but said nothing. We did not care much as I know we were not charged with extra guns.

**Oct. 21, 1863** — We received orders to take cars and report to Stevenson, Alabama. When we reached Wartrace the trains were stopped to allow a special train with Gen'l Grant who was on his way to take command at Chattanooga. While we lay here a countryman came in with a wagon load of apples. As the post sutler at the place had been selling the boys beer and hard cider we were feeling pretty well and lively, so it did not take long for someone to suggest a raid on the apples and the countryman was sold out before he knew it.

After Grant's train had passed we moved on and after passing through a very long tunnel the train was ordered back to a siding to allow a freight train to pass. As Stevenson lay at the foot of the mountain our Colonel decided to march there. We left the cars and marched to the town and went into camp.

**Oct. 26, 1863** — Started on the move and after travelling about 14 miles halted at Bridgeport on the Tennessee River, where we rejoined our Brigade.

**Oct. 27, 1863** — After drawing 3 days rations and extra ammunition we crossed the River on a Pontoon bridge and after a march of 7 miles halted at Shell Mound near the Nick Jack cave from where it was said the Rebs procured a great deal of saltpetre. It was also reported that there was a creek in the cave and that no one had ever been able to explore to the end of it.

**Oct. 28, 1863** — Moved on through the Whiteside Valley and along the Tennessee River. We passed the boundary point of Alabama, Georgia & Tennessee and after marching 17 miles went into camp at a place called Wauhatchie at the foot of Lookout Mountain where the Railroad from Trenton, Ga. met the Nashville & Chattanooga Rail Road. Before we reached here and when we entered the valley we could see the Reb signal corps on the Point of Lookout Mountain, and when we reached Wauhatchie we could see the Johnnies camp on the slope of Lookout Mountain and heard they belonged to Longstreet's Corps, and that he was in command.

■ Lt. Col. Samuel M. Zulich, 29th Pennsylvania. Following his regiment's rail trip from Nashville to Bridgeport, he was detailed on October 27 to superintend working parties building a pontoon bridge at Shellmound and several roads leading to it. When fighting erupted the next night at Wauhatchie, he immediately left his post and hurried toward the sound of gunfire — arriving in time to play a major role in the battle. "The enemy having turned the left flank," wrote Col. William Rickards Jr. of the 29th, "captured our wagon train, which was recaptured by Lieutenant-Colonel Zulich of this regiment, who, having collected and organized a number of loose men, drove off the enemy and brought it safely to the rear."

■ Maj. Gen. Henry W. Slocum

■ Brig. Gen. Alpheus S. Williams

# 'The responsibility is immense'

When Maj. Gen. Henry W. Slocum learned that his XII Corps was being placed under Hooker's command, he immediately sent a letter of resignation to President Lincoln on September 25. Slocum and Hooker disliked each other intensely. "Our relations are such that it would be degrading in me to accept any position under him," Slocum wrote to Lincoln. The president, however, would not accept his resignation and the potentially volatile situation was muted when Slocum and a large portion of the XII Corps were assigned guard duty along the Nashville & Chattanooga Railroad in Tennessee.

During the train journey west, Slocum — greatly respected by his troops — carefully monitored their progress and well-being. At one station he was approached politely by a young Indiana soldier who desired a one-day furlough to stop at his hometown. Slocum replied that he could not give anyone a furlough just then, but told the youthful veteran: "If I had served in your regiment over two years without being home once, or absent from duty a single day, and was passing through my own hometown, I would certainly stop for just a little while on my own responsibility. And I will say this much, if you conclude to do so, and should get into trouble over it, I will do all I can to help you out."

Once in Tennessee, Slocum's men were strung out guarding Murfreesboro and the railroad between Nashville and Stevenson, Ala. Supervising their protection against marauding Confederate cavalry and bands of bushwhackers was frustrating, tedious duty for Slocum's 1st Division commander, Brig. Gen. Alpheus S. Williams.

"The responsibility is immense, without any possible credit," Williams wrote from Tullahoma on November 20. "On this long road, bridged over mountain streams and trestled across mountain valleys and ravines for two or three hundred miles, the whole Army of the Cumberland now in and about Chattanooga must get its supplies for man and beast. The country is full of guerrilla parties and the Rebel cavalry are always menacing right and left to pounce in upon a weak point ... I am obliged to have a guard at every bridge, culvert, tank and trestle on the railroad for over ninety miles. So I am kept going up and down to see how they are placed, what defense works, whether patrols are kept up, and generally if the railroad is as well guarded as possible. If important bridges are lost the whole army goes up ..."

**As the Federals entered Lookout Valley on October 28, their movements were watched intently by Confederate signalers on top of Lookout Mountain. Gen. Bragg, greatly angered by the rout at Brown's Ferry, summoned Longstreet to the mountain. While there, both witnessed the arrival of part of Brig. Gen. John W. Geary's XII Corps' division at Wauhatchie, three miles south of Brown's Ferry. As Geary's Pennsylvanians and New Yorkers bivouacked for the night, Longstreet planned to attack them with Hood's division, now commanded by Brig. Gen. Micah Jenkins.**

**Orders for the night assault — a rare occurrence during the war — were hurriedly dispatched to the four brigades responsible for the undertaking. Troops of Evander M. Law and Jerome B. Robertson were assigned to occupy a series of small ridges between Wauhatchie and Howard's XI Corps camps, thus enfilading any reinforcements sent to Geary through Lookout Valley. Brig. Gen. Henry L. Benning's Georgia brigade was to reinforce Law's left and act as a reserve. Col. John Bratton, placed in command of Jenkins' South Carolina brigade, was chosen to lead the direct attack upon Geary.**

**Just after midnight on October 29, the shock of battle crashed for miles through the tangled woods and steep hills of Lookout Valley.**

■ Col. E. Porter Alexander commanded the artillery of Longstreet's corps. On October 28 he watched from atop Lookout Mountain the Federal advance into Lookout Valley. "I can recall, very vividly, the appearance of the marching columns down the valley," he wrote, "& the fun I had that afternoon with their advanced troops & my rifled guns which were up on the mountain. The range was too great to do them any very serious harm, but just far enough to give my gunners an excellent chance & excuse for an afternoon of target practice during which we put in a few very pretty shots, & had all the fun to ourselves, for they did not attempt to reply. A little before sundown, the main body, which seemed to be a division of three brigades, stopped & went into camp near Wauhatchie & about a mile beyond our range. Gen. Longstreet was on the mountain with us, with Gen. Jenkins, & it was at once determined to make a night attack upon the encampment."

## 'One of the most foolhardy adventures'

### Col. Edward Porter Alexander
### Chief of Artillery
### Longstreet's Corps

Night attacks are specially valuable against troops who have been defeated and are retreating. They are of little value under any other circumstances. The war, too, had now reached a stage where men had become impossible to replace in the Confederate ranks. Nothing could be more injudicious than to sacrifice them, even for a success, which would have no effect upon the campaign.

That was the case in this instance. Near at hand, the Federals had double or treble the force of the Confederates, and the camp to be attacked was two miles within the Federal lines. The attack must be made, the fruit of it be gathered, and withdrawal accomplished before the light of dawn; for with the dawn, or even before it, an overwhelming force of the enemy would cut off the withdrawal.

The only troops available for the attack were four brigades of Hood's division, under Jenkins, which had been brought around the high toe of Lookout Mountain. This road was exposed to batteries on the north side of the river and could only be used at night. Three of the brigades, Law, Benning and Robertson, had suffered severely, both at Gettysburg and Chickamauga, and scarcely averaged 700 men each. These brigades were ordered to cross Lookout Creek, and seize the road between Hooker's camp near Brown's Ferry and the camp of Geary to be attacked. The remaining brigade was Jenkins' own, now under Bratton, and was about 1,800 strong.

Law, with two regiments, had opposed Hazen's landing on the

■ Col. John Bratton, 6th South Carolina, commanded the six regiments of Jenkins' brigade in its attack at Wauhatchie. As his skirmishers neared the Federals' flickering campfires, "a hasty observation showed that there was considerable commotion in their camp," Bratton reported. "Whether it was of preparation to receive or leave us I could not tell, but the hurrying hither and thither could be seen by the light of their campfires, which they were extinguishing."

Immediately after the affair Bratton wrote to his wife: "I have been spaired through another battle. Last night I was ordered over Lookout Mountain to attack and capture, if possible, a waggon train. We tried honestly and fought hard but did not succeed. Our first onslaught drove them from their train but we could not take possession of it. I know that they greatly outnumbered us, but how many it is impossible for me to estimate as I could only see the spurts of fire from their guns and not the men themselves. As we could not take the train we shot down a great many of the horses and mules. I was in the saddle from midday yesterday until sunrise today and my condition is decidedly feeble. I lost my haversack and India rubber cover in the fight. Fortunately the little prayer book was accidentally left under my pillow, so it was not lost with the haversack. But I am a broken merchant without the India rubber."

27th, and skirmished on the 28th with the advance of the 11th and 12th corps under Hooker, but had now withdrawn across Lookout Creek. From the mountains above, a fine view was afforded of the valley with Hooker's camp at the north end, and Geary's three miles behind it. Jenkins had been summoned before sundown to view it and get some idea of the topography. He returned after dark and joining Law discussed the enterprise, which Law strongly advised against. The orders, however, were peremptory and there was no superior at hand to appeal to. The moon was about full, and soon after dark Law moved with his brigade across the bridge and, after some time spent in exploration, took position on a ridge nearly parallel to the road between Brown's Ferry and Wauhatchie, and some 50 to 150 yards distant. It was about two miles below the camp of Geary's division, and less than a mile above the encampments of the 11th and 12th corps. The Texas brigade [Robertson] reporting to Law, he placed two of its regiments on his left and one on his right, and sent the fourth regiment to hold the bridge in his rear. Benning's brigade was sent to ambush the road farther ahead.

This effort to hold the road against efforts to reinforce Geary might have been much more effective had Law thrown his brigades boldly across the road, with perhaps two brigades in his front line supported by the third in a second line. He probably failed to adopt this policy only because he was too conscious of his weakness. His retreat was more assured and easier from the position which he took. And, in view of the risks attendant on the venture, and the small chances of success, it may have been the more prudent course.

In the placing of Law's command there had been a few picket shots about 10 o'clock, which had caused Geary's command to be put under arms and to be unusually alert. Soon after midnight their own picket challenged and was shot down, upon which the camp was alarmed, all lights extinguished, and the troops formed in line. The weather was somewhat cloudy, making the moonlight fitful. Jenkins endeavored to restrain his men from firing as they deployed before the camp, but it was in vain, and gradually the regiments extending on each side overlapped the Federal line and waited an attack on the Federal rear by Lt. Col. T.M. Logan, with a force of sharp-shooters, who had passed around to the rear. Their attack was to be a signal for a general charge. About an hour had now elapsed.

It was just at this juncture that Jenkins gave orders to withdraw. Law had notified him that the enemy had passed his position, which was a mistake. The road had been open all the while, but no troops had passed. On the opening of the attack upon Geary there had been a general alarm in all the camps below, and several brigades had been ordered to go to his relief. The first brigade passing Law's ambush received volleys which, in the darkness, did little harm but threw their lines into confusion. Forming then parallel to the road, the Federals charged Law's position but were at first repulsed. Re-forming, and extending their lines, Steinwehr's division made a second attempt, but [Orland] Smith's brigade, which struck Law's front, was again repulsed with heavy loss. The men, however, did not on this occasion fall back to the foot of the hill, but rallied in the darkness of the woods, near at hand, until a part of the 136th N.Y., which had overlapped Law's front, had appeared in his rear. The attack being then renewed was successful all along the line, and Law fell back toward the bridge, not being pursued. Robertson, who had eight casualties, and Benning, who had none, also withdrew, as the retreat of Law compelled.

Meantime, in the confusion of the night a column of two Federal brigades, ordered to go direct to Geary's help, had halted without orders, and was overlooked for nearly two hours.* Owing to this oversight, and the non-pursuit of Law, both he and Jenkins were able to cross the bridge before daylight.

The character of the attack by Jenkins' brigade had been excellent. The casualties were heavy, and included many officers distinguished among their comrades for conduct. Nothing less could have been expected, and nothing materially more could be hoped for, and such considerations should have forbidden this adventure. The guarding of the rear by Law proved a success, though due to a Federal mistake, not to his disposition. Only about half his force was engaged. It repulsed two attacks, but was swept away by the third. The enemy, however, made no advance and a free road, left open until after daylight, provided an escape for all four brigades from one of the most foolhardy adventures of the war.

## 'It was very difficult to prevent mistakes'

### Capt. James L. Coker
### Company E
### 6th South Carolina Volunteer Infantry

The enemy began to move from Bridgeport, Alabama, to open the railroad by way of Wauhatchie to Chattanooga, in order to supply food and strong reinforcements to Rosecrans' starving army. When this enterprising movement had reached Lookout Valley, General Jenkins, whose division was on the extreme left of our army, wished to be informed as to the movement and have a report of it made. It came about that the writer was called upon for this duty [as Bratton's acting assistant adjutant-general], and early on the morning of October 28th went over Lookout Mountain.

Large bodies of troops were seen marching up the valley towards Brown's Ferry, where a pontoon bridge had been thrown across the river, by soldiers from Chattanooga. After satisfying myself that it was a very heavy movement, I returned before dark to make my report. When I reached General Jenkins' headquarters about sunset, he was issuing orders for the division to get under arms. After receiving my report he seemed disturbed, and told me the purpose was to cross with the division over Lookout Creek, and with one brigade pass behind a hill up the valley to capture a large wagon train said to be there.

The report I gave him indicated that one brigade would be insufficient, that not only the large wagon train was behind that hill but also a heavy body of infantry, with artillery. Jenkins went to General Longstreet with my report, but it made no impression there, and the plan as originally made was insisted upon, and the

*Alexander was mistaken. The two brigades belonging to the XI Corps halted under direct orders from General Hooker.

■ Capt. James L. Coker of Company E, 6th South Carolina, was acting as Bratton's assistant adjutant general when he was wounded at Wauhatchie. Coker, seen here wearing a pre-war cadet uniform of the South Carolina Military Academy (later The Citadel), was very popular among the troops of Micah Jenkins' old brigade. Coker later wrote: "As I was borne through our camp on the next day after the battle, I requested that the litter be set down for awhile in order that I might take leave of my old company. For two years and a half we had been associated together under the trying experiences of a great war. I loved my comrades in arms, and valued the respect and affection they generously gave me, and never more so than on that day when our connection was severed."

■ Col. Martin W. Gary's Hampton Legion fought on the far right of Bratton's line at Wauhatchie. Flushed with the initial success of driving in Federal pickets on their front, Gary's South Carolinians soon ran into the 137th New York whose musket fire abruptly stopped the Legion. When the battle ended more than an hour later, "our men were getting out of ammunition," wrote Capt. Milo B. Eldredge of the 137th, which lost 90 men that night. "But, by sending to the hospital and cutting the cartridge boxes from the bodies of the dead, we were enabled to keep up a fire on the enemy until they retired; when they did so we did not have 200 cartridges in the regiment."

movement proceeded. It was said that both General Bragg and General Longstreet had been on the mountain, and had made up their minds from personal observation as to how the enterprise should be conducted.

Jenkins' brigade was chosen to go behind the hill to capture the wagon train, with the troops guarding it. The mountain was crossed after dark. Company E, 6th Regiment, had just been recalled from picket, and was designated as one of the companies to form a long skirmish line in advance of the line of battle. As it was night and the country very rough and wooded, it was very difficult to prevent mistakes and keep the direction for this skirmish line. This duty devolved upon Bratton's A.A. General.

The orders were to capture the pickets of the enemy, and press rapidly towards them and engage them, our battle line following the skirmishers as closely as possible. When the brigade came up, the skirmishers were ordered to fall in and fight with whatever regiment was nearest. The enemy were surprised when attacked by the skirmishers, but soon began to get into ranks and to return our fire. When Bratton got up with the brigade, he attacked them vigorously, aiming at the light of the discharging musketry in front. The enemy soon brought up their artillery and made good use of it until our fire grew too near and too hot for them.

The Confederates made progress, taking possession of the wagons and teams, and were pressing their advantage when orders came from General Jenkins for us to retire. This order was caused by a movement up the valley from Brown's Ferry, which seemed to be successful and would soon cut us off from our crossing at Lookout Creek.

I was sent in to bear this order to a part of the line, and while delivering it to Colonel Mart Gary on the right, was shot down. Gary directed those near to take me up and bring me off the field, but no one being designated by name, I was not taken up until Sergeant Nettles and others of our company, hearing my name, came up, and with the willing help of some of Gary's men, got me on a blanket and bore me to the rear after all our troops had retired.

The loss of Company E in this battle was not as heavy as in the remainder of the brigade, for the reason that they were most of them to the extreme right, deployed as skirmishers, and protected by large trees.

Bratton's brigade lost about three hundred and fifty men in this engagement, out of fifteen hundred engaged.

## 'Go, my little man!'

### Private Francis M. Mixson
### Company E
### 1st South Carolina Volunteer Infantry

At Chattanooga ... we had the hardest service of the entire war. The rainy season came on — cold, sleet and snow — and the creeks in our rear got so swollen that we were cut off from our supplies. We had a tough time getting something to eat. So scarce were rations that some men in our regiment tore down barns catching rats, which they would boil and put in "drop dumplings" and did have good stews. Finally Col. [Franklin W.] Kilpatrick

# 'To the level of any other general'

**Brig. Gen. Micah Jenkins took command of John Bell Hood's division after Hood lost a leg at Chickamauga. On October 28, Jenkins was ordered by Longstreet to attack Hooker's troops advancing into Lookout Valley. The attack was scheduled to begin at midnight.**

**Shortly after dark, Private Joseph B. Polley of Company F, 4th Texas, and two comrades were posted on Jenkins' picket line as part of J.B. Robertson's Texas brigade. Polley later related the ensuing incident:**

"I was lucky enough to be on picket duty with my friends Will Burges and John West, of Companies D and E of the Fourth. As the night advanced, it became cold enough to make a fire very acceptable, and, appropriating a whole one to ourselves, we had wandered from a discussion of the war and of this particular campaign that was little flattering to General Bragg, into pleasant reminiscences of our homes and loved ones, when someone on horseback said, 'Good evening, gentlemen.'

"Looking hastily up, we discovered that the intruder was General Jenkins, alone and unattended by either aide or orderly, and were about to rise and salute in approved military style, when, with a smile plainly perceptible in the bright moonlight, he said, 'No, don't trouble yourselves,' and, letting the reins drop on his horse's neck, threw one leg around the pommel of his saddle and entered into conversation with us.

"Had you been listening for the next half hour or so, you would never have been able to guess which of us was the General, for, ignoring his rank as completely as we careless Texans forgot it, he became at once as private a soldier as either of us, and talked and laughed as merrily and unconcernedly as if it were not war times. I offered him the use of my pipe and smoking-tobacco, Burges was equally generous with the plug he kept for chewing, and West was even polite enough to regret that the whisky he was in the habit of carrying as a preventive against snake bites was just out; in short, we were beginning to believe General Jenkins of South Carolina the only real general in the Confederate service, when, to our surprise and dismay, he straightened himself up on his saddle, and, climbing from 'gay to grave, from lively to severe,' announced that at midnight the picket line would be expected to advance and drive the Yankees to the other side of the creek.

"We might easily have forgiven him for being the bearer of this discomforting intelligence had that been the sum total of his offending; but it was not; he rode away without expressing the least pleasure at having made our acquaintance, or even offering to shake hands with us — the necessary and inevitable consequence of such discourtesy being that he descended at once in our estimation to the level of any other general.

■ Brig. Gen. Micah Jenkins

"But midnight was too near at hand to waste time in nursing indignation. Instant action was imperative, and, resolving ourselves into a council of war with plenary powers, it was unanimously decided by the three privates there assembled that our recent guest was an upstart wholly undeserving of confidence; that the contemplated movement was not only foolish and impracticable, but bound to be dangerous; and that, if a single shot were fired at us by the enemy, we three would just lie down and let General Jenkins of South Carolina do his own advancing and driving."

**During the battle of the Wilderness six months later, Jenkins was accidentally shot in the head and killed.**

■ Private Amos H. Dalton of Company F, Hampton Legion. Total Confederate losses at Wauhatchie were reported immediately after the battle as 356, with 31 killed, 286 wounded and 39 missing. Federal estimates placed the numbers much higher. Eighty-five casualties were sustained in the Hampton Legion (only the 5th South Carolina suffered more by losing 102 officers and men), including 12 missing. Among these was Dalton, who was captured. After surviving the battles of the Seven Days, Fredericksburg, Chancellorsville and Gettysburg, he did not live long in captivity. Confined at Camp Morton Prison near Indianapolis, Dalton died of dysentery on March 23, 1864.

had a detail of axmen to fell trees, out of which he had a large raft made, and sent a detail across the expanse of water and brought us in meal, bacon, salt and whatever there was. Ours was the only regiment so fortunate.

While here we one afternoon received orders to prepare for a reconnaissance. Our brigade was taken across the base of Lookout Mountain and about dark crossed Lookout Creek, into Wauhatchie Valley, where a heavy supply train had been discovered earlier in the day. Our object was to capture this train and bring the supplies in. After crossing Lookout Creek on a bridge, the only way this creek could be crossed, we were thrown into line of battle — Hampton Legion, Col. Gary, on the extreme right; Sixth South Carolina next, Fifth next, First next, Second next, with the Palmetto Sharpshooters on the extreme left. Capt. James Hagood's company, Company K, was deployed as skirmishers in front of our regiment. I was orderly for the colonel. We commenced the advance through these woods — underbrush, hills, hollows and holes — and kept as quiet as we could. But then we made considerable fuss. After advancing this way for perhaps two or three miles, Hagood's skirmishers struck them in front of us. At the same time the Fifth and Sixth and the Legion struck them. It was so that the Legion got right into the train before being discovered, and they went to turning loose the mules and raising Cain in general. In front of the Fifth, First, Second and the Sharpshooters there were no wagons. We had struck them but a few moments when they were ready to receive us, and lo and behold, we were in front of Hooker's army corps — one of the best corps of fighters in the entire Yankee army.

Here we were in a mess. In our advance we were so placed that the left of the First Regiment was resting on the railroad, the right of the Second resting on the same, the railroad between us. We advanced till our regiment got out of the woods and into a field. Fighting along the entire line was intense and heavy; we had advanced as far as we could and had lain down, continuing the heavy fighting.

After being here under one of the heaviest firing I ever saw for perhaps an hour, men being killed and wounded every second, I was lying down alongside Col. Kilpatrick, who was on his knees making observations — a minnie ball struck the colonel, killing him instantly, passing through his heart.

At the very moment this occurred I heard someone call Lieut. Clowney, and he, leaving me, responded to the call. Then I saw Col. Bratton, who was that night commanding the brigade, sitting on his old gray horse, smoking his old meerschaum pipe. He said, "Clowney, where is Kilpatrick?" Clowney informed him that he was just then killed. Col. Bratton said, "Get him off the field. We are going to fall back," and then said, "I want a man to carry some orders for me." Lieut. Clowney called out, "Come here, Mixson."

I went up to Col. Bratton and took hold of his horse's mane; he looked down at me and said, "My little man, all the staff are either killed or wounded. I want some orders extended. Can you do it?" I replied, "I can try, colonel." He answered, "That is all that any of us can do. You are very small, but I can trust you. You must run across the railroad and tell Col. Bowen of the Second that we are falling back. The Legion, Sixth and Fifth are now moving; your regiment will fall in behind the Fifth, and the Second will fall in behind the First; and you hear that heavy firing away over yonder? That is the Sharpshooters. Find Col. Walker and tell him we are all gone — to pull off and get back on our trail and save himself the best he can. *Go, my little man!*"

I went up on the side of the railroad embankment; stopping a moment or two until a shell had passed — they were making the railroad every half minute — between shells I ran across and down the embankment and right into the arms of Col. Bowen. Just then one of those shells bursted and knocked sand over us and knocked us both down. I delivered my orders to him and started across the open field to find Col. Walker with the Sharpshooters. I got up pretty close and stopped behind a persimmon tree; it being dark and raining, I could not see whom I was approaching — it might be Yankees — but I stopped and called out.

"What regiment is that?" and was told Palmetto Sharpshooters. Still, to make safe, I inquired, "Who is your colonel?" and was told Col. Walker. Then I ventured up and found Col. Walker, to whom I delivered the message. He made me tell him why I was carrying orders for Col. Bratton, and he was then satisfied that the orders were straight. On delivering these orders, and not realizing the length of time I had been at it, I ran back from whence I had come. I missed the Second Regiment, but took no notice of that; ran up and across the railroad embankment and down the other side. I ran into a spring about waist deep. On pulling out of this I discovered that the regiment had gone.

There being no more shelling on the railroad I took down it in the direction I knew was right. I had not gone more than two hundred yards when I ran up with two men. I asked who they were, and upon their giving me the number of a Yankee regiment I ordered them to surrender, which they did, throwing down their guns. *I had none.* I then relieved them of their haversacks, knives and whatever else they had, and then it was found out that the Yankees had advanced and we were in their rear. But with my two prisoners I continued down the railroad. We had not gone far when we were hailed from the side of the road, "Who's there?" I answered, "First South Carolina Volunteers," when a volley was fired into us. I rolled down the embankment on the opposite side and made tracks, then turned across toward where I had been to hunt the Sharpshooters. What became of my prisoners I never knew.

I finally got on the trail of the Sharpshooters, and when I struck Lookout Creek I found the brigade had recrossed and there were some of Company E at the bridge. They had cut the bridge away from the bank and had it on fire; this to prevent the Yankees from following us, as the creek was impassable except at the bridge. I was here again in a quandary. About ten or twelve feet of the bridge gone, the balance on fire. Darling Sprawls came to the end on fire and told me to take a running jump and he would try to catch me. I did so, and, as luck would have it, he caught me and pulled me in. This got me back within our lines and saved me from becoming a prisoner.

Our brigade, or the remnant of it, reached our quarters some time after sunrise, and then it was that we commenced to realize the loss that we had sustained during the night in the Wauhatchie Valley. We had lost in killed, wounded and missing over one-half of our number, and when we got back to quarters we looked "mighty scarce" and few.

■ 2nd Lieut. Joseph M. Adams of Company H, 2nd South Carolina Rifles, was struck in the right foot by a piece of shell at Wauhatchie while his regiment fired at Geary's troops from behind the railroad embankment. The fragment fractured Adams' foot, and he was left on the field. After his recovery in Federal hospitals at Bridgeport and Nashville, Adams was sent to Johnson's Island Military Prison, where he was among the last to be released on June 11, 1865.

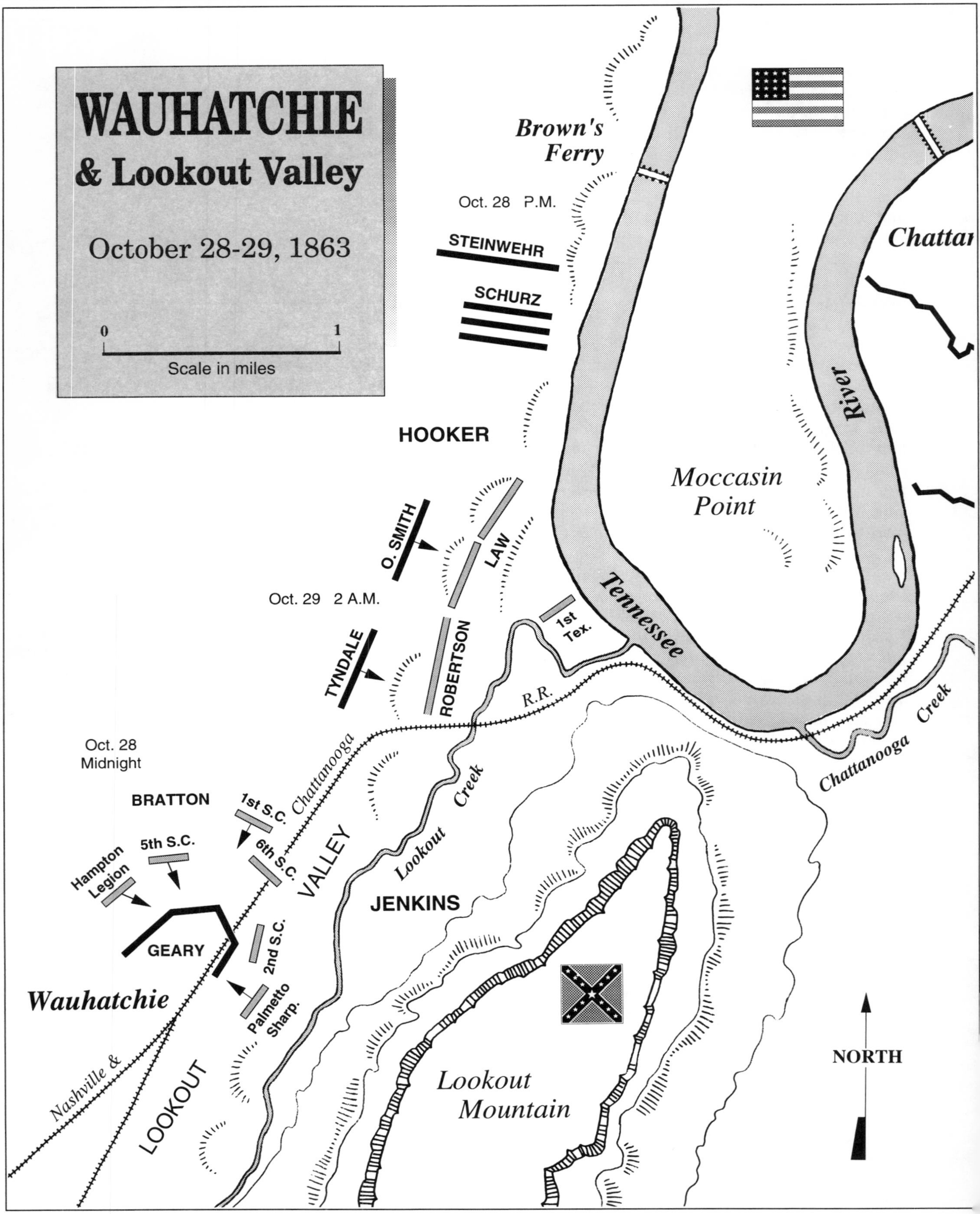
WAUHATCHIE
& Lookout Valley
October 28-29, 1863
0
1
Scale in miles
Brown's Ferry
Oct. 28 P.M.
STEINWEHR
SCHURZ
HOOKER
O. SMITH
LAW
Oct. 29 2 A.M.
1st Tex.
TYNDALE
ROBERTSON
R.R.
Tennessee
River
Moccasin Point
Chattan
Oct. 28 Midnight
BRATTON
1st S.C.
5th S.C.
Hampton Legion
6th S.C.
GEARY
2nd S.C.
Palmetto Sharp.
Wauhatchie
Chattanooga
Nashville &
LOOKOUT
VALLEY
Lookout Creek
JENKINS
Chattanooga Creek
Lookout Mountain
NORTH

## 'Camp-fires twinkling in the distance'

### 1st Lieut. Richard Lewis
### Company B
### Palmetto (S.C.) Sharpshooters

... We had an awful time in climbing the mountain, it being so steep and rocky it looked frequently like an impossibility to clamber up it all. We kept pushing ahead though, until we got in the valley; all there came to a halt for a while, thinking our night's work was done, when came orders in a few minutes: "The enemy must be driven off the steep hills towering above you."

The brigade was drawn out in regular array of battle, and soon the loud and sonorous voice of [Col. Joseph] Walker gave our regiment the command *"Forward!"* Then the whole line was seen moving with a steady and unwavering step, each soldier with a spirit of determination stamped on his brow. One hill after another in succession did we clamber over, still only a few flying Yankees to be found. At last though we began to come in sight of their camp-fires twinkling in the distance. All now began to realize that soon some Yankee picket would raise the battle cry. Sure enough, as we advanced nearer the camp a volley from them disputed our ground any further. After a very sharp contest between our line of skirmishers and the Yankees, the whole line raised a yell and moved up to within a few hundred yards of the enemy, and poured a tremendous volley into them, which was so terrific that everything was shrouded in silence for a time. But ah! only for the time, for it soon raged with more fury than ever.

Coker, the gallant captain of the Sixth, acting adjutant, came around about now with orders for us to bear on the enemy's flank. So we accordingly advanced beyond the skirt of woods we were in, out into open field, and there halted in front of a battery which was belching forth its iron hail of destruction into the regiments on our right. Here the Colonel commanded us to concentrate our fire on it; and with one murderous volley the sheet of flame and smoke was no longer to be seen gushing forth. Moving back but a short distance the thundering voice was to be heard again. We then laid down and exchanged long and continuous volleys with them, until we were ordered to cease firing and shelter ourselves. After lying for some time with the minies pegging away at us, we were commanded to retire as the enemy, in very heavy force, was trying to get in our rear.

We were moving all night long over the mountain and did not get back until seven or eight o'clock in the morning, the most completely broken down set you ever saw ...

## 'The woods are full of Rebs!'

### Private David Monat
### Company G
### 29th Pennsylvania Volunteer Infantry

**Oct. 28, 1863 —** ... After we had gone into camp and got our suppers, our Regiment was ordered on picket around the rest of

■ Sergeant Joseph Warford of Company A, 109th Pennsylvania. This regiment, numbering only 112 officers and enlisted men when it camped the night of October 28, lost nearly one-third of its strength at Wauhatchie. Of 32 casualties, two soldiers were killed, including one of Warford's company officers — 1st Lieut. James Glendening who was acting as the 109th's adjutant. Within three days Warford took up Glendening's former duties.

In this portrait, Warford wears a shoulder-tabbed jacket with unusual piping.

■ Corporal Alec Greiner of Company C, 29th Pennsylvania, was on the picket line of Geary's division when the Confederates attacked at Wauhatchie. As division officer of the day, Col. William Rickards Jr. of the 29th was with Companies C and G when they were driven back. Posting them to support Knap's Battery, he later took personal command of one of its guns after battery officer Edward R. Geary fell at his side with a bullet through the forehead.

our Division. Our Company G and Company C were sent out on the road leading across Lookout Creek and over the mountain towards Chattanooga. We went out about 3/4 of a mile, our Company posted on the right of the wagon and rail road in a woods above Lookout Creek and Company C on the left. Our post was in charge of Elisha Jones, acting Corporal, and along with Dan Kane, Jack MacLauchlan and myself we took our position.

Jack took first post and about 11 o'clock I relieved him. I had taken my place at a big tree about 10 or 12 yards away when I thought I heard troops moving. I called to Elish Jones to come up. We listened and nothing occurring he left me, saying "Keep a sharp look out." I had my gun cocked and shortly after heard the command towards my left of "Forward, guide center." A challenge was made by Jos. Strang of Company C whose voice I recognized of "Who goes there?" Sergeant Johnny Green of his company called out, "If they don't answer give it to them Strangy!"

A volley was immediately fired by the command in front in answer to Strang's shot. Strang was hit and managed to get away but died the next day. Sergt. Green had a tuft of hair taken from his head. I remained on post and shortly I heard Jack MacLauchlan come running up and say, "For God's sake, Dave, come on. The woods are full of Rebs!"

We ran down the slope to the Rail Road and up the embankment to the top where we could see on the other side of the road a large party of men. I shouted "Who are you?" They answered "Don't shoot, we's you'uns." I replied "You'uns be damned — come on Jack, they're Rebs." With that they let us have a volley but missed us. Jack and I got back on our side of the Rail road where we found our Captain and Captain Millison of Company C rallying the men together and moving back towards camp.

As our Captain was calling for Company G to fall in under his command and Captain Millison was calling for the pickets to fall in under him as senior Captain, I said to Jack, "Let us get back to the Division as soon as we can. Those damn fools will get us all captured and I don't want to go to Belle Island. I am going to take chances swimming the Tennessee if I can find the river."

We started back to camp and made quick time. When we reached the camp the boys was up and the 109th & 111th [Pennsylvania] were tearing down a rail fence at the edge of the woods and making breastworks in front of an old cornfield; on our right was the rail road embankment and beyond that the woods had been cleared for a short distance. The 4 pieces of the Battery were placed on a rise behind the men, 3 pieces fronting towards the corn field and 1 piece towards the woods on our right.

When we reached camp I heard Genl Geary say to Lieut. Col. Walker of the 111th, "What's all the trouble?" Walker replied "The pickets have been firing and I guess the enemy are coming." Geary replied "There's no Rebs there." I said "You'll damn soon find out" and then the shooting began.

Just inside our line was a log shanty and a number of us got behind that. The moon was shining bright and we could see the Rebs as they came across the stubble corn field while we were laying in the woods. As soon as they got close enough we let them have it. The battery opened, as they could only throw shell and case shot being Parrott guns. The fuses were cut very close and a few shells exploded over the 111th killing and wounding several. The Rebs suffered terribly, some of them being almost cut in half

where the shells had gone through them.

On the right a Reb Regiment came out of the woods into the open space and I heard their commander give the order "Halt! Front, ready, fire!" and then they dashed down to the Rail road bank and halted. If they had come on it would have been all up with us as we had no troops on our side of the track, only the 1 gun of the battery. This gun was in charge of Genl Geary's son, a Lieut. He had just raised from sighting the piece and had given the order to fire when the Rebs fired their volley and he fell shot on the right side of the forehead. Jack MacLauchlan and I stepped from behind the house and as we stooped to pick him up our Col. Rickards came along. I said, "Colonel, here's Geary's son." He said "My God, so it is; poor fellow, lay him down. We can't do anything for him now. I must get some of our fellows along the rail road."

He left us and shortly the 149th New York came dashing in on our side of the track and embankment. The men would crawl up the bank and shoot beneath the rails between the ties. One of them crawled up to the top and no sooner was his head above the Rails when he gave a yell and rolled down. The bullet just grazed his neck, and telling one of the men to cut his cartridge box off he rushed back to find the surgeon.

Pretty soon Capt. Millison came to the log shanty and ordered those of us who were there of Co. C & G of the 29th to drag the gun at which young Geary had been killed along the wagon road to where it crossed the Rail road track and ordered us to stay with the gun at all hazards. The Sergt. in charge said he would

■ A single field piece (at lower right) hurls case shot into advancing Confederate ranks as three other guns of Knap's Battery fire over the heads of Geary's infantry. With fuses shortened to two seconds, some of the shells burst in the midst of the 111th Pennsylvania, sheltered behind hastily-piled fence rails near the log cabin at center. One shell decapitated 2nd Lieut. Marvin D. Pettit of Company B, and another tore through both legs of 1st Lieut. Albert E. Black, Company K. During the engagement Knap's Battery fired 224 spherical shells at Bratton's South Carolinians.

# 'How dear it has cost me'

■ Brig. Gen. John White Geary

**"When the rays of the rising sun came over Lookout Mountain," wrote 1st Lieut. George K. Collins of the 149th New York, "they fell with a mellow light upon the tall and portly form of Gen. Geary, standing with bowed head on the summit of the knoll, while before him lay the lifeless form of a lieutenant of artillery. Scattered about were cannon, battered and bullet marked caissons and limbers, and many teams of horses dead in harness. And there were many other dead, but none attracted his attention save this one, for he was his son. The men respecting his sorrow stood at a distance in silence while he communed with his grief."**

**Brig. Gen. John W. Geary's 18-year-old son Edward was fatally shot in the head on October 29 when South Carolinians of Col. John Bratton's brigade nearly overran the field piece commanded by Edward Geary at Wauhatchie. On November 2, the elder Geary, former governor of Kansas and future governor of Pennsylvania, sorrowfully wrote to his second wife, Mary:**

"This day five years ago was the day of our union, when our hearts were united in one, as well as our destinies. That happy day is still vivid in my memory, and the joys and sorrows we each have had since then serve to remind us as of a beautiful fountain from which flows a crystal stream, but in its course here and there the foul soil muddys it and destroys its purity. The day is one which will never be forgotten by me, it is a source of unalloyed happiness to recognize its annual return.

"Were it not for the almost impenetrable gloom which hangs around me since the death of my

■ 1st Lieut. Edward R. Geary

beloved son, I would enjoy it. Poor dear boy, he is gone, cut down in the bud of his usefulness ... Oh, my God, I feel this chastisement for the pride I took in him, his rapid development and general character, and ability. None knew him who did not love him. His praise was on every tongue. He had been commissioned Captain in Hampton's Battery about one week previous to his death, and had he survived the action at Wauhatchie he would now be on his way to the Army of the Potomac. But, Alas! we are not alone in grief. Capt. Atwell of the same battery was mortally wounded, and died [today]. He leaves a weeping bride and a devoted father. There were but two sections of the Battery present and the killed and wounded were 22 in number. The number of horses lost were 33 out of 48.

"The Battle was fought on the same ground that Gen. Jackson once obtained a victory over the Indians. And now it was for a portion of my command numbering at 1200 men to be attacked at midnight by that celebrated Hood's Division of Longstreet's Corps, numbering over 5,000 men. They came upon us in three heavy columns with great rapidity, and with the most demoniacal yells. I instantly brought my men into line and received them as only long & oft-tried soldiers can do.

"At first they out-flanked my line on the left, and subjected us to a cross-fire from that side. I then turned my artillery upon them in the rear of my line of infantry, and drove them back with great loss in killed and wounded. Their next attempt was to turn my right, and for some time we were again subjected to a murderous cross-fire from that side. This was the time the battery suffered so severely. With well-directed artillery and rifles, they were again driven and thoroughly defeated. My entire loss is 34 killed and 184 wounded. The enemy's loss is 152 killed, as near as can be ascertained 763 wounded, and considerably over 100 prisoners. I have gained a great victory and there is none to share the laurels with me. But oh! how dear it has cost me ... my dear beloved boy is the sacrifice. Could I but recall him to life, the bubble of military fame might be absorbed by those who wish it."

■ Capt. Charles A. Atwell, commanding Battery E (Knap's), Pennsylvania Light Artillery, was mortally wounded at Wauhatchie and died on November 2. Battery 1st Sergeant David Nichol wrote to Atwell's wife Mattie six weeks after the battle: "It seems he had taken hold of No. 7 gun to assist in running it forward after the recoil and it was in this manner he recd the fatal wound, with an exclamation of pain falling to the ground. Corpl Volk (the gunner) offered to assist him off the field but he said he could walk himself, which he did. But I understand that William [Atwell, Charles' brother] met him and assisted him to the hospital ... He was heard to remark on the march the day preceding the Battle that he believed they were very hard on officers in this army, that the Rebs made it a point to pick them off on all occasions. Which remark has proved too true. We were all surprised to hear of his death."

stay and if the Rebs took the gun they would take him dead. We all promised to stay along. Soon they had the gun charged and sighted down the embankment where the Johnnies lay and they did not stop for another shot.

On the left of our line the 137th and 78th New York were stationed and the Rebs got so close and in their rear that it was reported our men had to about face and fight. The mules in the wagon train got loose and broke in amongst the Rebs, creating a panic after 3 hours of hard fighting as ever we had experienced. The Johnnies left leaving about 150 prisoners and 175 dead. Our Company lost John Gilbert taken prisoner & who died at Andersonville, Ga. and Bobby Buchanan & Henry Fisher wounded. Company C had 2 killed and 3 wounded.

The first thing some of the prisoners asked us was if we did not belong to the Army of the Potomac. When we told them "Yes," they said we knew damn well you did, "for these western fellows wouldn't have staid like you'uns." We laid on our arms till morning.

**Oct. 29, 1863** — Genl Hooker came in early and we were relieved by some of the 11th & 4th corps troops. One of the western fellows said to me, "You fellows must have had a tough fight down here last night." I said "Where?" He replied "Why here. Wasn't you in it?" I said "Oh, that was no fight, only a little kind of scrimmage." He says "Well, I don't know what you call a fight but it looks to me with all them dead Rebs as if one had been going on here and the shooting sounded as if all hell was loose."

I replied, "Oh, we're from the Potomac and we used to have those kind of rows nearly every morning to get up an appetite for breakfast."

## 'It was point-blank business'

### 1st Lieut. Albert R. Greene
### Company K
### 78th New York Volunteer Infantry
### Aide-de-camp, 3rd Brigade, 2nd Division, XII Corps

The wood in which we drew up joined a large open field in front of us, land which had been cultivated, and in that field was a loghouse of the poor class of dwelling. The field was perhaps one thousand feet square. On our right was a little hill with a railroad cut through it and then a railroad embankment; on our left we found a swamp with a thick growth of swamp brush. The wagon road passed through the right centre of our line. Back of a slight elevation beside this road the guns were placed in battery, and the caissons closed up.

Brigade headquarters were about seventy-five yards behind the left of the front line, and division headquarters were back on the road near the Seventy-eighth. No fires or lights were allowed [ignored or unenforced in other regimental camps], and we ate a cold supper in the dark. A pretty strong detail of pickets was sent out on the road in the direction of Howard, and also some to the rear and into the swamp on our flank in the direction of Kelley's Ferry.

General [George S.] Greene was strongly apprehensive of an

attack, and directed his staff to keep their clothes on and the horses to be kept saddled and bridled. At nine o'clock he sent me to Geary to ask whether the troops should sleep on their arms and not take their shoes off. I saw Geary himself and asked the question. He replied, "It is not necessary," and I reported this answer. Nevertheless the order was issued throughout the brigade and saved us from being captured, though [Col. David] Ireland's disobedience with respect to his regiment, the One Hundred and Thirty-seventh New York, caused some disorder a few orders later. I carried the order to Ireland in person, but he disregarded it.

A little before midnight we were aroused quickly by sharp firing of pickets in our front on the road in the direction of Howard. The Twenty-ninth Pennsylvania, One Hundred and Forty-ninth New York and the battery were in line facing the enemy. They were awake and ready in three minutes. The Seventy-eighth New York was faced about and put across the railroad in the rear of the cut through the hill. Our pickets came in and reported the approach of an attacking column.

Before the One Hundred and Thirty-seventh could get their shoes on to run up and fill the space on the right of the One Hundred and Forty-ninth, we could distinctly hear the tramp of men at the double quick across the open field in front of us. It was so dark that they could not be seen, but they seemed to know our position perfectly. We distinctly heard the command to those men, "By the left flank!" But before the command of execution was uttered, on our line was, "Battery! Fire!" and the flash of the four guns lighted up our whole front, showing for an instant the line coming toward us. Then in the darkness the flash of the rebel muskets marked their line and the bullets began to come. Our men replied, but the delay of the One Hundred and Thirty-seventh was making bad work, and the men began to cluster around trees and to carry wounded to the rear. Finally the One Hundred and Thirty-seventh was got into position and the men made amends for the misconduct of their regimental commander.

While General Greene was riding at the very front, urging the men to stand and encouraging them by his example, and getting the formation of his brigade orderly and steady, he was struck in the face by a rifle ball, which entered at the lower left corner of his nose and passed diagonally across his mouth, badly breaking his upper jaw and tearing out through his right cheek. He was assisted to his tent, not more than seventy yards in the rear, and his servant got him again on horseback and went with him to a house some distance back, where a hospital had been established.

A considerable pioneer corps attached to the brigade had been deployed across the rear about the distance of the headquarters tent to check and drive back men carrying the wounded and any stragglers. Field, line and staff officers kept the men in their places, and soon the men began to shout back in reply to the rebel yells. Then we breathed easier; we knew the line was safe.

Knap's battery had done its share at Gettysburg, but the way that battery was worked this night was enough to immortalize it if it had never on any other occasion fired a gun. Its flashes lighted up its own position and half the rebel line. We could hear the devils shout, "Shoot the gunners! Shoot the gunners!" It was point-blank business. The lines were not over two hundred yards apart, and the air was literally loaded with death. After the canis-

■ Brig. Gen. George S. Greene commanded the 3rd Brigade of Geary's division, XII Corps. At Wauhatchie, two of his five regiments were placed in line by Geary personally. "I had been twice along the line sending in a few stragglers that were in the rear," Greene reported, "when I was severely wounded in the mouth, and, from loss of blood and of voice, was unable to render efficient service in the field, and I retired to the hospital for attendance." He was replaced by Col. David Ireland of the 137th New York.

One month later Greene's son, Capt. Charles T. Greene (the brigade's assistant adjutant general), also suffered a severe wound. On November 27 at Ringgold, an unexploded shell passed through his horse and carried away the younger Greene's right leg below the knee.

■ Capt. Moses Veale, commander of Company F, 109th Pennsylvania, also served on Geary's staff as assistant commissary of musters. In the heaviest fighting at Wauhatchie, Veale and his company supported one of the guns of Knap's Battery, where he was struck in the right shoulder by a bullet and had his horse shot from under him. Refusing to go to the rear, he directed Company F's fire until the Confederates withdrew from the field. Veale's conduct, coupled with postwar political patronage, secured him a Medal of Honor "for gallantry in action [while] manifesting throughout the engagement coolness, zeal, judgment and courage."

ter was used up, shells were resorted to, and when an annoying fire came from men clustered around the log-house in the open, solid shot were put through that. With the infantry the officers stripped the dead and wounded of their cap and cartridge boxes and carried them to the line, for the brigade went into that wood with only sixty rounds and there was no reserve supply.

On the right the enemy got a line along the railroad embankment and opened a cross-fire. Rickard [Col. William Rickards Jr., 29th Pennsylvania] with some of his men dragged one of the guns up on to the embankment, doubled shotted it with canister, and ended that demonstration. On the left the rebels got around us in the swamp, but before they had done much their main line fell back, and some of the flanking party came in and surrendered. The firing lasted but a little over an hour, and at the close many of our men had but a single cartridge left. The attacking force went off, leaving their dead and all of their severely wounded.

This was the battle of Wauhatchie, and the first fighting in the west by troops from the Army of the Potomac. We had come to stay, and we stayed, but at a fearful cost.

## 'Two-o'clock-in-the-morning courage'

### Maj. Gen. Carl Schurz
### 3rd Division, XI Corps

In the afternoon of the 28th we arrived in Lookout Valley, near Brown's Ferry, about three miles from Chattanooga. The commanding form of Lookout Mountain frowned down upon us, with a rebel battery on top. We presumed that there must be a rebel force at its foot, but it was hidden from us by dense woods. There were with us two divisions of the Eleventh Corps, General Steinwehr's and mine, except some detachments, and part of General Geary's division of the Twelfth Corps, which, however, was left behind with a wagon train at a small hamlet called Wauhatchie, about three miles distant. The road from Wauhatchie to Brown's Ferry was bordered on the enemy's eastern side by steep ridges, intersected by gaps and ravines, through one of which ran a country road leading to Kelly's Ferry, and through another the track of the Memphis & Charleston Railroad. On the western side of the Wauhatchie road there was a valley about one-half mile wide, covered partly with cornfields, partly with timber and underbrush, and bordered by the Raccoon Mountains.

On our march we saw nothing of the enemy except little squads of cavalry, who vanished at our approach, and a small infantry force in the woods near Wauhatchie, which disappeared after having fired a few shots, when it saw some of our regiments deploy for attack. Besides, the rebel battery posted on the top of Lookout Mountain pitched some shells at us, without effect. But from the same height the enemy could easily observe every one of our movements, and it occurred to some of us that the separation by nearly three miles of bad road of Geary's small force from ours was really an invitation to an attack under circumstances very favorable to the enemy. However, such was the disposition made by General Hooker, and all we could do was to surround ourselves by strong picket lines, well thrown out, to guard against a surprise. So we went into bivouac.

All remained quiet until about midnight, when we were disturbed by a few shots fired on our picket line. Then profound stillness again, which, however, lasted only about half an hour. Then very lively firing was heard in the direction of Wauhatchie. This evidently meant something more serious. We could not doubt that the enemy was attacking Geary in order to overwhelm him, and thus to break the line of communication we had established. Prompt action was necessary. The troops abruptly waked from their first and best sleep, tumbled out of their blankets with alacrity, and were under arms in a few minutes, ready to march.

Night combats are apt to be somewhat uncomfortable affairs under any circumstances. Napoleon is quoted to have said that "the two-o'clock-in-the-morning courage" is the true test of the soldier's quality. To be called upon to fight when, as he feels, he ought to be permitted to sleep, and to fight, too, with a sensation of peculiar emptiness in his stomach, of dullness in his head, and of shiver in his back and limbs, and with a darkness surrounding him which prevents him from seeing the things he ought to see, and sometimes makes him see things which do not exist, is apt to make him surly, to confuse him, and to weaken his confidence in himself. However, our men were, on this occasion, in good spirits, indulging themselves in more or less jocose curses on the enemy who had disturbed them.

Soon General Hooker rode up — as it seemed to me in a somewhat excited state of mind — and ordered me to hurry my division to the relief of Geary. This was the order I had expected. Instantly I put myself at the head of Tyndale's brigade, which was the nearest at hand, and marched off on the road to Wauhatchie, sending my chief-of-staff to my other two brigades with the order to follow me. The moon shone brightly, only now and then obscured by passing clouds. We could see ahead on the open ground tolerably well. But the shadows of the dense woods we entered were all the darker. Having thrown out a skirmish line to the front, and flanking parties toward the hills, we pressed on with the utmost possible expedition on the road, which was very bad. The musketry fire ahead of us at Wauhatchie grew more lively and was punctuated with occasional discharges of artillery which, to judge from the sound, came from Geary's battery. Evidently, Geary was hard pressed, and we accelerated our speed.

We had advanced only a few hundred yards when we received a heavy volley of musketry from one of the darkly wooded hills on our left. One of my aides, riding by my side, was wounded and had to be carried to the rear. Several men in the marching column were also hit. Without orders some scattering shots were fired in reply from our side, which were promptly stopped, and we pushed on without delay, anxious as I was to reach Geary, and confident that our forces behind would at once take care of the enemy on my left and rear who had tried to molest us. This, indeed, was done by a brigade [Orland Smith's] of the second division which in splendid style stormed and cleared the hill from which the volley had come.

But it seemed probable that the whole row of hills along which the road to Wauhatchie ran, was occupied by rebel troops to guard the flank and rear of those who attacked Geary, and I reinforced my flanking parties. We soon struck a slight turn toward the hills in the road where it was especially muddy and difficult. I directed

■ Color Sergeant William C. Lilly, 149th New York, was mortally wounded as the regiment groped its way through the underbrush at Wauhatchie. "The enemy was so close at hand it was difficult in the darkness to distinguish friend from foe," wrote 1st Lieut. George K. Collins of Company I. "It was too dark to see more than a few feet away and the fire of the men was directed by watching the explosion of the enemy's muskets. The 149th occupied one side of the railroad embankment while the enemy occupied the other. The losses of the regiment were 1 killed, 1 missing and 11 wounded. Two of the badly wounded died a few days afterwards, one of whom was William C. Lilly, the color bearer. The men were comforted with the assurance that his injuries, though serious, were not necessarily mortal and they looked forward to his speedy recovery. [But] owing to excessive loss of blood his dissolution took place, much to the regret of the regiment."

■ Maj. Gen. Carl Schurz, a native of Liblar, Prussia, commanded the 3rd Division, XI Corps. Ordered to send a brigade to Geary's relief at Wauhatchie, Schurz and Col. Frederick Hecker found that their actions were criticized by Hooker. Recriminations forced Schurz and Hecker to request an investigation, and a court of inquiry convened in February 1864 to weigh Hooker's allegations. After 16 days of testimony and deliberation, both officers were exonerated.

In a lengthy statement made to the court, Schurz wrote: "Since the battle of Chancellorsville ... when, through newspaper articles dated at the headquarters of the Army of the Potomac, I was covered with the most outrageous slanders, which, although easily disproved were as easily repeated — since that time until the present day, I have had to suffer so much from the busy tongue of open and secret malignity, that even my well-tried patience was rather too severely tested."

the column to march straight ahead through what appeared to me an open field, expecting to reach Geary more quickly. But my advance skirmishers soon ran into a miry bog covered with low brush, which appeared to be impassable, and we were obliged to regain the road by a movement to the left. This was done without any loss of time. Until then General Howard had been with me off and on during the march. Now, accompanied by an aide, he rode on to Geary to tell him that help was near.

Then one of those confusing disarrangements occurred which occasionally will happen in campaigns or battles. I had hardly reached the road again, when through staff officers sent after me, I received the information that my second and third brigades which, according to my orders, were to follow Tyndale's, and which, therefore, I firmly expected to be at my heels, were not following me at all, but were kept back — one by General Hooker's personal direction, and the other by an order delivered by one of General Hooker's staff officers that it should accompany a lot of prisoners to Chattanooga. I was much surprised, but would have hurried on to Geary with Tyndale's brigade alone, had not at that moment one of General Hooker's aides-de-camp, Lieutenant Oliver [1st Lieut. Paul A. Oliver], come with an order from General Hooker that I should take and occupy with one brigade the hill on my left next to the railroad gap. I replied to Lieutenant Oliver that I was ordered by General Hooker personally to push through to Geary, that I had just been informed of my other two brigades having been stopped by General Hooker's direction, and that if I occupied the hill on my left with the only brigade I had on hand, I would have no troops at all to push on to Geary. Lieutenant Oliver answered that General Hooker wanted the hill on my left taken and he repeated the order. This was puzzling. However, it naturally occurred to me that circumstances might have changed.

The firing at Wauhatchie had for a while slackened and then died out altogether. It was evident that Geary, after a fierce fight, had succeeded in repulsing the rebel attack. But there was still more firing going on in my rear near the hill from which the volley had been thrown upon us. The enemy might perhaps have made a new movement, making it most important that the gaps in the row of hills be in our possession. Finally, although General Hooker had personally ordered me to push through to Geary, his last order, brought by his aide-de-camp, was that I should take and occupy with one brigade the hill immediately on my left, and according to all military rules, it was the last order that counted. I asked, therefore, General Tyndale to arrest the march to Geary, and to take and occupy the hill with his brigade.

This was done. Our skirmishers ascended the dark woods, silently. There was a moment of remarkable stillness. Then we heard about half way up a ringing voice calling out: "What regiment do you belong to?" Another voice, a little further away, responded, naming a Georgia regiment. Thereupon promptly followed a shot and then a rattle of musketry. Then three of our regiments rushed up after our skirmishers, the firing became more lively, and soon our men were on the crest and descended the opposite slope, the enemy yielding as our men steadily advanced. The affair occupied not much more than a quarter of an hour, but it cost us two killed, one of them a captain, and ten wounded.

The importance of our occupation of the hill consisted in its commanding one of the passes through that chain of ridges. Our troops had, therefore, to be put in proper position to sustain an attack, the immediate vicinity to be explored by scouts, pickets to be well thrown out on front and flanks, and a reserve to be properly placed — arrangements which require some time, especially in the dark and on densely wooded and uneven ground, not permitting anything to be discerned with certainty, even at a very short distance. While these things were being done, Lieutenant Oliver, who had left me soon after the fight, had ample time to report to his chief all that had happened, and General Hooker had ample time to send me further instructions if my doings were in any respect not in accordance with his wishes, or if he desired me to do anything beyond. But as I received no word from him I naturally believed that I had acted to General Hooker's entire satisfaction; and as the firing had ceased along the whole line, and everything seemed to be in the best of order, I hastened to report to General Hooker myself, and to look after my other two brigades held back by him.

I found General Hooker in the midst of my brigades, which stood there with grounded arms. Expecting a word of commendation in response to my salute, I was beyond measure astonished when in a harsh voice and in that excited manner which I had observed in him an hour or two before, he asked me why I had not carried out his order to march my division to the relief of Geary. Mastering my feelings, I quietly replied that I had tried to do so; that I had marched off at the head of my advance brigade; that I then had received his positive order while en route to take and occupy a certain hill with one brigade; that I had ordered my other two brigades to follow me, but that they had been held back by superior orders; that therefore I had no troops to take to Geary.

There was a moment's silence. He broke it by repeating that he had given me the order to march to Geary two hours before, and that I should do it now. I asked him whether my two brigades held back by his superior orders were now at my disposal again. He answered that they were, and rode away. I doubted, and my officers, too, doubted, whether he was in his senses.

At once we were in motion, Colonel Hecker's brigade leading. On the road Colonel Hecker told me what had happened. He had promptly obeyed the instruction brought to him by my chief-of-staff, to follow my second brigade, Colonel Krzyzanowski's, in marching to Wauhatchie. A little while after the head of our column had been fired upon from the hill on our left, he observed that Krzyzanowski's brigade halted, presumably by order. But he, Colonel Hecker, having received no such order, continued his march, passing by Krzyzanowski's brigade through an open field. He had hardly done so when Major Howard, of General Hooker's staff, brought him, too, a positive order to halt at the cross-roads, one branch of which led to Chattanooga, and to form his brigade front toward the hills. He had not time to do so when General Hooker himself appeared, and Major Howard said: "Here is General Hooker himself." General Hooker asked: "What troops are these?" Hecker answered: "Third Brigade, Third Division, Eleventh Corps." General Hooker asked further: "Where is General Schurz?" Hecker replied: "In the front, one of his aides has just been carried by here wounded."

General Hooker then instructed Hecker to form his brigade so

■ Maj. Gen. Oliver O. Howard, commander of the XI Corps after replacing Gen. Franz Sigel in April 1863, was unpopular with many of his men due to his religious activities. Lt. Col. William G. LeDuc of Howard's staff recalled: "The officers and soldiers of the XI Corps who had been accustomed to the alert, soldier-like ways of Gen. Sigel, did not approve of what seemed the attempt of Gen. Howard to make a Sunday School class of a military organization, and his conduct at Chancellorsville and Wauhatchie satisfied them that he was not fitted to command even a regiment in active duty against an enemy. He was always ready to encounter personal danger when duty required, but appeared more concerned with saving the souls of his men and of the enemy ... By officers and men he was regarded as a tin soldier; by the church people generally, he was thought to be a great hero."

■ Col. Frederick Hecker, 82nd Illinois, commanded the 3rd Brigade of Schurz's division, XI Corps. Due to conflicting orders from Hooker and Howard in Lookout Valley on October 29, Hecker's men were delayed relieving Geary at Wauhatchie for several hours. Hooker's after-action report did not censure Hecker by name, but implied disobedience to orders, which incensed the German-born officer. An 1864 court of inquiry eventually cleared his record, but he resigned his commission shortly thereafter.

During the revolution of 1848, Hecker led German democratic forces until their defeat forced his exile to the United States.

that it could easily change front toward the right — the valley — if necessary. He thereupon inquired about the troops standing nearest to Hecker, and was informed that it was the Second Brigade, Colonel Krzyzanowski's, of my division, and saying to Colonel Hecker: "You stay here!" he rode over to Krzyzanowski's brigade and remained with it a considerable time. Indeed, it was between it and Hecker's brigade, within speaking distance of both, where I found him when I returned from Tyndale's position. This was the report Hecker gave me. It was subsequently proved to be absolutely correct in every detail. It made the words addressed by General Hooker to me more and more inexplicable.

I could understand how the sudden appearance of the enemy on the range of hills between us and Chattanooga should have produced upon his mind the impression that the main action that night would have to be fought not at Wauhatchie, but in the immediate vicinity of our camp, and how that impression should have led him to throw into the hills or to keep in his own hand the troops he had ordered to the relief of Geary. But that he should not have appreciated what he had done in changing his dispositions, even after he had been informed of it, and that he should have blamed anybody for the confusion but himself, was not so easy to explain, except upon the supposition that he wanted a scape-goat for the mistake he had made in leaving Geary in so recklessly exposed a situation, which might have resulted in a very serious disaster, had the rebels attacked with a larger force. However, I consoled myself with the hope that when after a good sound sleep he reviewed the events of the night quite soberly, General Hooker would find it to be the best policy to recognize the truth and tell it.

As soon as I had free disposition of my two brigades again, both Hecker and Krzyzanowski were promptly dispatched to Geary, and the gap between him and Tyndale was properly filled.

## 'A veritable hornet's nest'

### 1st Lieut. Robert T. Coles
### Adjutant
### 4th Alabama Volunteer Infantry

General Longstreet sent orders to General Jenkins, commanding our division, to concentrate all of his command in Lookout Valley that night. Our brigade and the Texans and 3rd Arkansas were already on the west side of the mountain, in charge of General Law. The rest of the division, Jenkins' brigade (commanded by Colonel Bratton) and General Benning's Georgians, were on the east side of the mountain with the main army and could not reach us until after dark, at which time they would be concealed from the enemy's batteries while crossing the mountain. General Longstreet says he estimated our four brigades at five thousand men. Our other Virginia division (McLaw's) failed to put in an appearance as promised. General Bragg failed to send it, and General Longstreet omitted to countermand the order to attack after finding that it would not join in the proposed engagement.

The 4th Alabama received orders that evening to be ready to cross the bridge over Lookout Creek and take our position. The night of the 28th was beautifully moonlit, and as soon as our other two brigades from east of the mountain reached us, we moved out.

I suppose it was about midnight before getting fully under way. After crossing the bridge we were ordered to take possession of the ridge or "hogback" which ran parallel with the road from Brown's Ferry to Wauhatchie. Before reaching the ridge we threw out our pickets and were soon notified that it was unoccupied by the enemy; we then quietly climbed to the top and threw together a few chunks and logs for our protection. We secured here a prisoner who was very drunk, and the only information we could obtain from him was that he belonged to Howard's corps. As the other regiments arrived they formed on our right and left, the 4th Alabama in the center. The Texans and 3rd Arkansas were then brought up and placed on our left. General Law commanded both brigades. Colonel Sheffield of the 48th Alabama was in charge of our brigade.

Our position along the ridge overlooking the road was within about thirty yards of the road on our left and about one hundred and fifty or two hundred yards from it on the right. There was quite an interval, perhaps three-quarters of a mile, intervening between our right and the River. To protect us at this point, Colonel Sheffield placed a company of the 15th Alabama as videttes, and each regiment threw out in its front a picket line. We were supposed to be about midway between the force at Brown's Ferry and the supposed [Federal] rear guard up at Wauhatchie.

Our instructions were to hold this force near Brown's Ferry from reinforcing the rear guard at Wauhatchie while General Jenkins with his brigade, under Colonel Bratton, and General Benning's Georgians in reserve, were to either capture or disperse it. As the South Carolinians had never been on the west side of the mountain, Colonel Bratton requested Colonel Scruggs to furnish him a guide. Two or three of the best scouts in our regiment were furnished him.

We remained in our position for an hour or two patiently awaiting Colonel Bratton's attack on the rear guard. When he did open it, everything in the Union camp became busy. Our videttes reported a heavy force moving toward Wauhatchie from Brown's Ferry to the support of the rear guard. Our orders were not to fire until the head of the column had reached our left, when a volley was fired by the whole brigade, which created a great deal of confusion in the enemy's ranks and sent them back toward the River. In a short time they rallied and made a desperate effort to charge up the ridge, and were again driven off.

Other Union forces arrived on our left and the right of the Texans and 3rd Arkansas; these were also repulsed. There was an interval of several minutes and then another effort was made to push us back, but we were secure in our well protected position and the enemy failed. Colonel Sheffield, thinking his right not sufficiently secure, sent two more companies in that direction to be deployed — one from the 15th Alabama and the other from the 44th Alabama. Still finding that his right was not sufficiently protected, he informed General Law who sent the 4th Texas, which promptly took position on our extreme right and had scarcely reached there before a determined attack was made on the front of the 15th, 44th and 4th. The 15th and 4th succeeded in clearing their front, but the enemy rushed through the interval made by

■ Capt. Thomas H. Elliott, 28th Pennsylvania, served as assistant adjutant general of Geary's division. During the Wauhatchie fighting, a small number of Geary's ambulance and wagon train mules spooked and broke free. Crashing through the ranks of part of Bratton's Confederate line, the braying, frightened mules temporarily created the impression that a cavalry charge was in progress.

The Wauhatchie "mule stampede" soon became the subject of a poetic parody by Elliott, who was killed the following July at Peachtree Creek, Ga. "The Charge of the Mule Brigade" imitated Alfred Lord Tennyson's famous poem immortalizing the Light Brigade at Balaklava, and was written for the Philadelphia *Sunday Times.* It reads in part:

*"Forward the Mule Brigade!"*
*Was there a mule dismayed?*
*Not when the long ears felt*
*All their ropes sundered.*
*Theirs not to make reply,*
*Theirs not to reason why,*
*Theirs but to make Rebs fly.*
*On! to the Georgia troops*
*Broke the two hundred.*
*Mules to the right of them,*
*Mules to the left of them,*
*Mules behind them*
*Pawed, neighed and thundered.*
*Breaking their own confines,*
*Breaking through Longstreet's lines*
*Into the Georgia troops,*
*Stormed the two hundred.*

■ Brig. Gen. Adolph von Steinwehr, a native of the German duchy of Braunschweig (where his grandfather was a Prussian lieutenant general), commanded the 2nd Division, XI Corps. In the early hours of October 29, he was instructed to take the hill in Lookout Valley occupied by E.M. Law's brigade. The 73rd Ohio, 33rd Massachusetts and 136th New York from Col. Orland Smith's brigade made the assault. In the latter regiment, Private George P. Metcalf of Company D recalled: "Maj. Gen. Steinwehr, a German, had charge of us. He came to our front and in broken English said, 'Vhat regiment is dat?' He was told. 'Dat is a good line,' he said. 'We vant you to take dat hill. The Rebels are on top of it. You go up. Don't you fire a gun. If you do, dat vill give them the range to shoot you. Don't say one word until you get right onto them, and then holler like the tuyfel. They vill think the whole corps is behind you.' "

taking out the company from the 44th and broke its line. In an instant the 4th Alabama, seeing the perilous position in which we were placed, made a right wheel at charge bayonets (with a yell and rush through the thick undergrowth, losing nearly all of our head gear), re-establishing the line. This was the last attempt by the enemy to drive us from our position.

As it was impossible for our two brigades on the right to prevent, as instructed, the enemy from rushing reinforcements from Brown's Ferry by our front to the relief of their rear guard at Wauhatchie, General Law, fearing the South Carolina Brigade would be surrounded and captured, dispatched to Colonel Bratton notifying him of the fact, and suggested a withdrawal of his brigade, which he did in good order. General Law in the meantime sent the 1st Texas back to the Lookout Creek bridge to hold it in the event the enemy should follow us. Our two brigades then withdrew from the ridges and retired in an orderly manner across the bridge, the enemy making no effort to pursue.

We had emerged from a veritable hornet's nest of vastly superior numbers, and had it not been for our promptness in retiring before the enemy recovered from the surprise of the suddenness of our attack, every one of us would have been surrounded and killed or captured.

The casualties of the 4th Alabama were one man killed — Anderson of E Company — and not a man wounded or captured. The 4th, in the Lookout Valley expedition, accomplished more and inflicted greater damage to the enemy, with less loss to itself, than in any other campaign in which it participated during its four years' service.

## 'A regular Kilkenny cat fight'

### Private H. Howard Sturgis
### Company G
### 44th Alabama Volunteer Infantry

Law's and Robertson's brigades formed on the western slope of Lookout Mountain about nine o'clock at night [October 28]. They threw up a protection of logs and such other things as could be picked up. We were not allowed to cut any timber, as that would have disclosed our position.

We had little time to work for soon we heard the battle raging on our left about a mile distant. Soon the Yankees came hurrying to reinforce their line. Our pickets fired into them and we could hear their orders: "Halt! Left face! Forward!" Then we had a regular "Kilkenny cat fight," a very bad one. We got mixed up sure enough. We were driven from our insecure breastworks, Robertson failing to connect with our lines. The loss on our part of the line was small, but we were greatly outnumbered. Twice we recovered our works and drove them down the hill.

I was cut off and found myself surrounded with men calling for a New York regiment. I quietly made my way around till I heard others calling for Law's Brigade. Our lieutenant colonel was twice stopped, and the cape of his overcoat torn off in an effort to stop him. Once when we recaptured our works a Federal and Confederate were seen with their left hands in each other's collar, grasping their guns with their right hands, neither being willing to surrender. A lieutenant, seeing the predicament, ordered the Yank to surrender, which he refused to do, when the deadlock was broken with a bullet.

I saw a man roll down the mountain side, started by a ball from my gun when only a few feet distant from its muzzle. He had the first shot at me, his ball passing through my hat.

## 'We had to skedaddle'

### Sergeant Valerius C. Giles
### Company B
### 4th Texas Volunteer Infantry

At nine o'clock on the night of October 28, 1863, about five weeks after Chickamauga, without bugle call or the tap of a kettledrum, we were quietly ordered to "fall in," and silently moved westward in the direction of Raccoon [Lookout] Valley, Tennessee. After a rapid march of a few miles we were formed in line of battle on the crest of a hill, our right extending within one hundred yards of the Tennessee River. Off to our left we could see the flash and hear the roar of artillery and musketry. There was not a man among us who knew where he was or what he was there for. I don't believe the officers knew. The night was cold and clear, and the moon shone brightly. As far as my experience goes, it is always cold in the mountains of eastern Tennessee.

About two o'clock in the morning we discovered a solid line of infantry advancing up the hill. Owing to the manner in which we were deployed out on the ridge, we were little more than a strong skirmish line. When we saw that heavy column coming against our weak line, every private on the hill knew as well as the officers that we had to skedaddle. The muskets and bayonets of that advancing host flashed and gleamed in the cold moonlight. Our line opened fire on them and staggered them a little, but they rallied and came right on.

Colonel Bain [John P. Bane], commanding the regiment, gave the command to fall back in order. Major Winkler, on the right, either did not hear or understand the order. Some officious private sang out: "By the right flank." Major Winkler repeated the order: "By the right flank." It was not necessary for him to add the word march, for we were already going. My old regiment was not in the habit of running, but experience had taught the boys that it was folly to fight against such odds. We were going downgrade now, splitting underbrush and moonshine wide open.

The result was that those of us who were on the extreme right ran into the One Hundred and Thirty-sixth New York Regiment. They had completely flanked us by marching up the south bank of the Tennessee River. They appeared to be about as badly surprised and confused as we were, firing promiscuously in every direction. I ran squarely against a great, big, fat Dutchman and both of us came down in a heap, his gun going off in the air as we tumbled. While I lay sprawling on the ground, another big fellow sat down on me, either to hold me, or escape the bullets which were flying thick and fast.

After the confusion was partly over, the prisoners, twenty of us, were disarmed, gathered together and marched to the rear. I saw

■ Sergeant Valerius C. Giles of Company B, 4th Texas, belonged to Gen. Jerome B. Robertson's famed Texas Brigade, consisting of the 1st, 4th and 5th Texas, and 3rd Arkansas infantry regiments. Giles' regiment, under Col. John P. Bane, broke for the first time in its history during the fighting in Lookout Valley early on October 29. "As the rush to the rear came down the line like the swinging of a gate, the Fourth Texas couldn't resist the temptation," wrote Private Miles V. Smith of Company D. "If they were going to serve their country in the future they also had better right about face, and make a speedy march to the rear. Speedy does not express the velocity with which they went.

"The long slope of half a mile or more densely covered with large and small timber didn't seem to retard their motion much. The boys told it on Colonel Bane, that he struck a sapling about three inches in diameter with such force that he landed about the middle of it and climbed the balance of the way, and when he left its top he was fifteen or twenty feet further on his way."

■ A *Harper's Weekly* depiction of the 33rd Massachusetts and 73rd Ohio assault in Lookout Valley. Artist Theodore R. Davis wrote: "In many places the brave fellows had to drag themselves up by grasping shrubs and roots. When they reached the top of the ridge the explosions of musketry burned the contending troops. Captured rebels say that it was a disgrace to them that the place was taken, but they could not help it; for, said they, 'you kept coming, and the next we knew you were right among us.' "

but one man who could speak English. That was a Sergeant by the name of Charles Bedelle, who took charge of the prisoners ...

We were marched back and halted near General Hooker's headquarters. By that time it was daylight, and the whole earth appeared to be covered with bluecoats. I was a Sergeant at that time, and the only non-commissioned officer in our squad. I was ordered to report to General Hooker, and was escorted to headquarters between two muskets. Hooker was rather a pleasant-looking man, and returned my salute like a soldier. Then he began to interrogate me. He asked me a hundred questions and wound up by saying that I was the most complete know-nothing for my size he had ever seen.

That evening we were started to Chattanooga under a heavy guard. We crossed the Tennessee River about four miles below Lookout Mountain. Near the middle of the bridge we were halted and formed in one rank on each side, to let some General Officers and their escorts pass. General Grant and General Thomas rode in front, followed by a long train of staff officers and couriers. When General Grant reached the line of ragged, filthy, bloody, starving, despairing prisoners strung out on each side of the bridge, he lifted his hat and held it over his head until he passed the last man of that living funeral cortege. He was the only officer in that whole train who recognized us as being on the face of the earth. Grant alone paid military honor to a fallen foe.

## 'Don't fire on your own men'

### Private Andrew J. Boies
### Company E
### 33rd Massachusetts Volunteer Infantry

**Oct. 27.** We went marching along [from Bridgeport] in the following order: Pioneer company in front, followed by the 73d Pennsylvania, 134th, 154th and 136th New York regiments; next in order came the 33d Massachusetts, 73d and 55th Ohio, commanded by Gen. Steinwehr, "Fighting Joe" taking the lead of us all. We proceeded for seven miles, arriving at a place called Shellmound. Here we rested for an hour or more ... At the word "Fall in," we obeyed and went on; we marched slow and cautiously, up hill, down hill, across brooks, over rocks and upon the mountain sides, with overhanging crags high above our heads, presenting a fine view.

The country is rough with a few scattering log huts. The occupants were mostly women and children, looking out of the doors as we were passing along; not a man could be seen and we concluded that they must be in the army, for everything seemed to be in a state of demoralization; in fact, I thought to myself, how do they live? Thus we passed along until night overtook us, and having marched 15 miles we bivouacked for the night; made my bed upon four fence rails and had a good night's rest.

**Oct. 28.** At four o'clock this morning the drum announced to us to get ready for another day's march, and at daylight we were on our way with slow and cautious step, for we did not know what might be in store for us, as there were any quantity of Rebs and bushwhackers awaiting to receive us. We went on until noon, stopped for dinner and a rest. At the word "Forward" we proceeded on, but it was not long before the pioneers were ordered to the rear and an advanced guard was sent on ahead, followed by the 73rd Pennsylvania. About 3 p.m. they were received very coolly by the bursting of a shell over their heads, giving them to understand that something must be "did." We came on to a camp of Rebs, quite a sharp skirmish took place, which resulted in routing and driving them before us.

On we went, they still falling back; we killed a few, took some prisoners. As we were nearing the valley we were welcomed by solid shot and shells that came over our heads from the top of Lookout Mountain, and I am glad to say that no harm was done to us during the day with the exception of Sergeant Adams of Co. F, 33rd regiment, who was killed by a bursting shell. We succeeded in gaining the road which they (the Rebs) refused to give, and all praise is due to "Old Joseph." We proceeded on up the valley for about two miles where we surprised a force of the enemy; here we formed two lines of battle and drove them through the woods so fast that we hardly got an opportunity for a shot at them. They set on fire and destroyed the railroad bridge on their retreat.

We soon reached the foot of Lookout, which gave us a good sight of their "Long Tom," which was anything but pleasing, but its immense height at which it was placed rendered their shot and shell almost harmless. We still kept on for about two miles beyond and went into camp for the night, much fatigued by the

■ Col. Orland Smith (top), 73rd Ohio, led the 2nd Brigade of Steinwehr's division when two of its regiments attacked Law's entrenched Alabamians on October 29. The 73rd's commander, Major Samuel H. Hurst (bottom), reported four days later: "We were confronted by the enemy's whole line of battle sheltered behind formidable breastworks on the crest of the hill. As we came in sight of them in the clear moonlight they lowered their guns and poured into our ranks a most deadly fire. Our boys began to fall rapidly, but the ranks were instantly closed and steadily, in the face of death, our little battalion kept shouting and charging forward. One-half of my line officers and one-third of my men were either killed or wounded in this brief but desperate struggle ..."

■ Col. Adin B. Underwood, 33rd Massachusetts, was severely wounded in the upper thigh and groin while leading his regiment against Law's Alabamians. "He was called by the men an old maid," wrote 1st Sergeant John M. Cate of Company D, "and he was just a little fussy, but then he would do justice to all. No man could be unjustly punished while he commanded. He will never return to the regiment; his wound is a very bad one. The ball struck him in the rear just below the hip, passed through and entered his penis. The bullet was taken out almost at the end. The bone of the leg was badly fractured." After several operations Underwood's leg was shortened nearly four inches. He later was promoted to brigadier general, and in August 1865 to brevet major general.

Immediately after the battle, Surgeon Daniel G. Brinton, XI Corps medical director, personally tended many of the Lookout Valley injuries. "All the wounds recorded were by small-arms," he wrote, "except some contusions, and one shell wound. In such an action as this, if anywhere, we would look for bayonet wounds. Here was a charge — a hand-to-hand contest literally; some of the contusions were given by clubbed muskets. Not a bayonet wound is recorded. I looked for them, but neither saw nor heard of any. There was none."

march over the rough roads. We hoped for a good night's rest. Here we prepared our coffee and "tack," spread our blankets and lay down for the night in old Tennessee, among strangers and the enemy, expecting that on the morrow another hard day's work for us was in store. During all this time the Rebs had succeeded in gaining a foothold upon a ridge near the scene of our afternoon skirmish, and after dark threw up a line of rifle-pits which threatened us seriously.

About midnight we were awakened by the beating of the "long roll" and a cry made "To arms!" The enemy had attacked our pickets, and it was true a battle had commenced. It fell to the lot of [our brigade], which was immediately ordered out, and before 1 o'clock was marching back with orders to carry and hold the ridge at all hazards. Upon arrival it was found to be a steep declivity of nearly 200 feet, so thickly wooded and covered with underbrush as to almost render it impassable; but it must be done before daylight or the consequences would prove serious.

To the 33d Massachusetts and 73d Ohio was assigned this perilous duty of charging up that steep mountain side and driving the enemy from the top. The 33d regiment had only seven companies present, the other three having gone on a secret expedition. At the word "Forward" the boys took as quick a step as the nature of the ground would permit, and slowly worked their way up the steep side of the ridge, not knowing what might be in store for them upon their arrival at the top. The 33d was on the right, the 73d Ohio on the left. Arriving near the top and but a short distance from the pits, a few shots were fired by our men, when the Rebs commenced the old game, crying out, "Don't fire on your own men." It being so very dark, our boys did not know but such might be the case and the firing ceased. One of our officers inquired, "Is that the 73d?" "Yes," was the reply, "what regiment is that?" Upon being answered "the 33d Massachusetts," they poured into us a terrible volley from right to left. Our men gave them shot for shot, but the loss in our regiment was fearful. Adjutant Mudge fell dead at the first fire and Col. Underwood fell dangerously, and as we supposed, mortally wounded.

It being impossible to advance the regiment further in its disordered state, it fell back to the foot of the hill and quickly formed for the charge, and as we now knew what we had to contend with on our way up, and the disposition of the occupants at the top, we started slowly and cautiously, with orders not to fire, but drive the enemy out entirely with the point of the bayonet. Once more gaining our former position, we were received with a murderous fire. The men, with knapsacks on, kept pushing and climbing for the top which was finally reached, and then commenced a scene of heroism and bravery seldom equalled in this war.

Over the bank and into the pits with the enemy was but the work of an instant, and at it we went, charging with the bayonet, dealing each other blows over the head with the musket, slashing and cutting with swords, until the whole scene resembled a grand knock-down, our boys reaching over the pits and dragging out the Rebs by the collar. This was too much for them; they seemed amazed and confused, and finally gave way and started over the opposite side of the hill at a fast pace, our boys giving them the contents of their muskets as fast as possible, leaving the 33d in possession of the hill, about 100 prisoners, a large number of guns

# 'Forward, men, let us avenge our colonel!'

**In supporting Geary's troops at Wauhatchie, the 2nd Brigade, 2nd Division, XI Corps, assaulted Gen. E.M. Law's entrenched Confederates on a hill in eastern Lookout Valley. Among the attackers were two young officers of the 33rd Massachusetts, pictured here — 1st Lieut. Caleb Blood (seated) of Company F, and 1st Lieut. William P. Mudge, regimental adjutant who lost his life in the early morning darkness of October 29. Mudge's death was described by the 33rd's commander, Col. Adin B. Underwood:**

"An indistinct line is seen ahead, just made out in the glimmering moonlight. Then the old rebel trick, 'Don't fire on us.' Adjutant Mudge risks himself to save any fatal mistake, and steps before the line. 'Who is it?' he asks. 'Who are you?' comes down from the crest. 'The Thirty-Third Massachusetts' replies the adjutant. 'Take that,' replies the crest with a rebel yell, as the shower of lead falls ...

"Now to meet them with cold steel. 'Remember Massachusetts, fix ———!' I command. A bullet cuts short the order. I am one of the casualties and ... the adjutant is instantly at my side, and tenderly asks, 'Good God, colonel, are you wounded?' But time is too precious for such courtesies. 'Lead on the men,' is my answer. Gallantly and generously, but too fearlessly, the adjutant springs before the line. 'Forward, men, let us avenge our colonel,' is his impulsive battle cry. Instantly he is a mark for rebel bullets, and the pride and the idol of the regiment lies dead in the beauty of his young manhood ... How strangely his wish, so many times expressed to me, was fulfilled; if killed, that it might be when fighting under Joe Hooker."

**The 33rd Massachusetts suffered severely in Lookout Valley; of 238 officers and men who entered the fight, 35 were killed and 58 wounded. Lieut. Blood survived and replaced Mudge as adjutant.**

■ Commissary Sergeant Joseph L. Locke, 33rd Massachusetts, helped care for his regiment's wounded after its night assault in Lookout Valley. Two days later, Lt. Col. Godfrey Rider Jr., who assumed command after Col. Adin B. Underwood's wounding, reported the 33rd's casualties as 86 officers and men out of 230 taken into the fight. Rider wrote of the regiment's objective: "A crooked ravine some 20 feet deep [ran] parallel with the hill-side, the sides of which were almost perpendicular, slippery with leaves and clay, and covered with brush, and its appearance rendered still more formidable by the deceptive moonlight."

and all of their intrenching tools, which were speedily given into the hands of the pioneers, and in a short time we had a formidable line of pits thrown up on the other side of the ridge.

Out of 238 men and officers who went into action, the 33d regiment lost 87 killed and wounded, including eight commissioned officers — colonel, adjutant, two captains and four lieutenants. Our brave Colonel Underwood was dangerously wounded in the groin, and the thigh bone shattered; Adjutant W.P. Mudge killed instantly, shot through the head; Lieut. James Hill shot through the heart; Lieut. Jones shot through the back, spine broken. The other officers were wounded more or less serious. In Co. E, killed: Corporals John Mayo, Eliab Churchill, George L. Whitcomb and William Crockett. It was a fact, though remarkable, that these four had a strong presentiment that they would be killed. Previous to this, they had always been full of life and mirth, but on each occasion that I saw them during our march up the valley they appeared gloomy and despondent; and Crockett remarked to me that he thought some of them were going into their last battle. Poor fellows, their presentiment proved true, as I saw them the next morning lying nearly side by side as they had fallen. Privates T.J. Hutchins, Franklin Wright and David Wares also were among the killed. They were within 10 feet of the enemy's works.

One incident among the many was the heroic conduct of Sergeant John F. Buckley of Co. E. During the second charge of the regiment Corporal Jubb went over the rebel works and was collared by a stalwart Reb, who attempted to stab him with his knife, and while in the act, Buckley brought him (the Reb) a blow over the head with the butt of his gun, knocking him senseless; and, there being nine more in the pit, he demanded them to surrender, which they accordingly did and threw down their arms. He then collared his prisoner and ordered the others to follow. As he proceeded down the hill he met Major [William H.] Lamson, who ordered him to take them to the provost guard, which he did, and delivered them for safe keeping. The next morning, each one commenced telling of their midnight adventure to the boys, and after a little explanation it was found that Jubb was the man whose life had been preserved by Sergeant Buckley. When Buckley unrolled his blanket it was riddled with bullet holes.

## 'Changed by that one noble action'

### Commissary Sergeant Joseph L. Locke
### 33rd Massachusetts Volunteer Infantry

Lookout Valley, Tenn.

Dear Lem,

I believe I have never written to you about the desperate bayonet charge our Regt. was in, where we lost ⅓ of our men & some of our most valuable officers, but you undoubtedly saw accounts of it in the papers.

It was the first night after entering the valley, and the day before we had made a hard march and had a pretty sharp skirmish, and been shelled, hotly for some time, but thought we had got through with them, and went into camp late in the evening expecting a good nights rest. But a soldier never knows how long he can sleep when he gets a chance to rest, and about 12 midnight we were awakened by musketry not far off and were soon called out and hurried off double quick. We went about a mile when the Brigade was formed in line of battle and cautiously advanced along the side of a very steep hill. While marching in this manner the Rebs, who held the top and had thrown up breastworks, gave us a terrible volley, killing our Adjt., a splendid officer, and severely wounding our Col. and a number of other officers. This so staggered the Regt. and no officer taking command and rallying the men, they all fell back to the foot of the hill, but here every man rallied to his place.

Here our Brig. Gen. Smith took charge of the 33d and 73d Ohio (which had fallen back with us), had them load and fix bayonets, and then told them to take the hill — to reserve fire till close onto the enemy, and do the rest with cold steel — and the lines moved steadily forward.

As we advanced the Reb officers could be plainly heard telling the men to "Aim low, aim low and give 'em hell!" As our lines were within 4 rods of the breastworks the rebs poured a terrible volley upon them, and many fell and rolled over and over down the steep hill. The Regt. wavered and halted and was upon the point of again falling back.

This was the critical moment which was to decide the fate of the battle. Now we missed our brave Col. to lead us on and our beloved Adjt's voice was still in death. Our Major & Lt. Col. were not on hand, neither did any of our capts take any lead, but a young 2d Lieut. — Shepherd — seeing the want of a leader, sprang forward, waved his sword over his head and told them to come on. And now that body of men, wavering and silent a moment before, seemed changed by that one noble action into bloodthirsty fiends and sprang forward, every man with a yell as is never heard excepting upon a battle field. Nothing could withstand the force with which our boys threw themselves upon the Rebel lines, and although they were four to our one and behind breastworks 4 feet high, they were scattered in every direction, and the important position was ours.

Our 2 Regts which took the hill — the 33d & 73d Ohio — both had heavy details of men on picket that night so all the men in the fight did not exceed 500, and the Rebel prisoners all allowed that they had 2,000 men with them. The hill was some 300 feet high, very steep and filled with gullies, underbrush and fallen trees so that a man in the day time would have to pick his way along, and then get badly out of breath before getting to the top. But the men went up that night with knapsacks and haversacks on, and kept a good line over the ditches, logs & through the brush.

During the charge I remained at the foot of the hill — having no gun and no business where a fight is going on. But I always find enough to do and more than enough in helping the wounded to the rear and attending to their wants, and I have always in every fight we have been in, been with the Regt and found a chance to do a great deal of good, although I could keep as far away of bullets and shells as I pleased.

It was half past one o'clock when the fight was over and all the rest of that dark morning I worked hard in getting the wounded where they could be cared for, and the next day, in making head boards for our brave dead ...

■ Private Rufus F. Fisher of Company K, 33rd Massachusetts, was killed in Lookout Valley on October 29. Two days later Surgeon Robert Hubbard, XI Corps assistant medical director, detailed the casualties of Orland Smith's brigade: "Dearly they purchased a victory, for the 33rd lost out of 238 the fearful number of 101 and the 73rd about 50. I soon had my hospital in operation & in it 130 wounded. I have never seen in proportion to the number injured, men so severely wounded. Many will die & noble fellows too, particularly the 33rd Mass. with whom I am better acquainted. The men are decidedly of the better and more intelligent class. The severity of their wounds is owing to the short range at which the fire was received as is the case in most night attacks. The Inspector General of this army says that the charge of Smith's Brigade is one of the most gallant feats of the kind of the war."

CHAPTER 6

# Boys, they say we are going up there tomorrow

## Lookout Mountain: A life-and-death struggle amid fog-enshrouded boulders and tangled gullies

Despite Federal successes at Brown's Ferry and Lookout Valley, opening the Cracker Line had little immediate effect for many hungry soldiers manning Chattanooga's defenses. Increased rations only slowly appeared in Union camps through early November. Privation among companies detailed to picket duty remained a fact of life, as described by Private George M. Kirkpatrick of Company A, 42nd Indiana, in a letter to his sister written November 2:

"I take this opportunity to write you to let you know that I am still alive, but that is about all, for we get nothing to eat worth mentioning. I have got down so weak that I cant do my duty any more, and the horses and mules are dying off at the rate of two hundred a day. The rations I drew today were one cracker and a half, one half spoonful of coffee, and a little piece of meat for two days. That was all I got and I could sit down and eat all of it and not have half enough. Now when it gets down to that small rations, it seems to me the Army is pretty near gone up. Six mules, 60,000 men and six women comprise our force, and NOTHING to eat!

"Our regiment is on picket every day, but today I was not out. I had no shoes. I stood picket one night barefooted, and refused to do so again. They put me in the guard house with no one to guard me."

Another Westerner, Private George A. Cummins of Company F, 36th Illinois, complained in his diary on November 4: "All quiet along the lines, save cannonading occasionally by each side — the rebels mostly from Lookout & our forces from different points along the line. Rations very scarce. Having a hungry time of it, going without days at a time. Picket & fatigue is not in the least diminished, however, either day or night. Having a pretty hard time, especially privates. Oh, the meaning of *private* in the army! I shant be sorry when my time is out. I could give in detail an account of affairs but it is useless."

Cummins' and Kirkpatrick's cases may have been extreme,

**for *other* Federals began to see improvements in their situation. "Provisions are beginning to arrive freely," wrote Capt. Rodney S. Bowen of Company A, 100th Illinois, on November 5. "And the pressure is letting up. The enemy still hold Lookout, but there are indications of an attack upon the extreme right by Grant's and Hooker's forces." Six days later Bowen continued: "Boats are running regularly between Kelly's Ferry and Bridgeport, and rations are now coming in freely. Our communications are complete with Hooker's army and we have the inside track of Mr. Bragg." ***

## 'Hurrah for the bully little steamer!'

### Lt. Col. William G. LeDuc
### Chief Quartermaster
### XI Corps

The Eleventh and Twelfth Corps were detached [from the Army of the Potomac] to reinforce Rosecrans at Chattanooga. We were ordered to march to Alexandria and turn in the transportation to the depot Quartermaster, and prepare to take the cars with field baggage and equipment.

Officers' horses only were to be transported. This was an error of vital importance, and was objected to by me urgently as I had in the Eleventh Corps the best transportation in the army. The mules were all choice, well-broken animals accustomed to army work and army rations, and to the drivers. The harness and wagons were fitted to the animals and they were all shod and in good condition. The wagons, covers and harness were to be shipped with the troops. But in spite of my protest the mules and horses, except the artillery and officers' horses, were turned in at Alexandria and orders were given to seek supplies of the depot Quartermaster at Nashville, Tenn.

At Nashville I found a herd of unbroken mule colts and a lot of wornout mules and horses, crippled and diseased, the leftovers after supplying the Western armies.

When Gen. Hooker arrived at Stevenson and Bridgeport, Ala., he could go no farther until the transportation trains could be made up at Nashville and moved to the front over the mountainous roads to Bridgeport. This was a labor of the most discouraging kind, as the poor little mule colts and the broken-down horses were frequently unable to draw the empty wagons up some places on the rough mountain roads, and only by doubling teams could the teamsters get the trains through. The remnant that survived this ordeal was unable to draw more than half loads, and was wholly unfit for army business. We could not under these conditions supply one corps much less supply the whole army at Chattanooga, already on short rations.

Rosecrans had ordered five small sternwheel boats to be built at Bridgeport when he crossed the river at that place, anticipating the need of them in carrying supplies up the river. A Quarter-

■ Lt. Col. William G. LeDuc served as the XI Corps' chief quartermaster. In early October at Bridgeport, Ala., he took charge of construction of three small, flat-bottomed steamboats intended to carry supplies up the Tennessee River to Chattanooga. On October 29, the first of these boats, the *Chattanooga,* landed at Brown's Ferry with two pontoons full of rations lashed alongside. LeDuc later wrote of the reception: "Coming to the river bank [the soldiers] raised a shout: 'Hurrah for the bully little steamboat! Rations once more — hurrah!' When the pontoons touched the shore they jumped aboard and commenced to throw off the boxes of hardtack, bacon and the like, regardless of the commissary in charge, who shouted out: 'Don't do that, boys — I have to account for all this stuff!'

" 'All right, Captain, our commissary can give you receipts to burn. Pull down that fence and make a fire — here's coffee and sowbelly, and hardtack once more — hurrah for the bully little steamboat — rah, rah, rah!' "

* Two weeks later on Missionary Ridge, Bowen was severely wounded in the calf of his right leg while acting as regimental major. Eventually promoted to that grade, he was mortally wounded on November 30, 1864 in the battle of Franklin.

■ Private John Riddle of Company D, 18th Ohio, served during 1863 as a teamster and ambulance driver. Reduced rations sent teamsters and train guards foraging along wagon routes at the expense of local inhabitants. Livestock, fowls, and corn were prime targets. Wrote Brig. Gen. John Beatty: "What officers and privates [tell] me, teamsters and guards of forage trains are often furnished with but one day's rations of meat, with the understanding that they will supply themselves on the road for the other three or five days they remain out. This of course might be well enough ... without depriving a poor family of the cattle upon which they themselves rely for their winter support. On the road up the Tennessee Valley over Walden's Ridge, and near the foot of the mountain on the other side, almost every garden is found stripped and one will hardly discover a chicken or hog."

master named Edwards had been assigned the duty of building these boats. Edwards was a man past middle age who had been in the steamboat business on Lake Erie, and he sent for a shipwright named Turner who had been accustomed to building lake vessels — an excellent mechanic but one not familiar with flat-bottomed river boats. He had one little portable sawmill to cut the lumber needed for these boats from standing oak trees.

The enemy held the river at two points, one at the foot of Lookout Mountain, the other where the river forces its way through a ridge known as Raccoon Mountain. Rosecrans, one of the ablest strategists in the army, had planned to have Hooker advance up the river, drive away or capture the rebels at these points and make navigation safe. But Hooker could not move without transportation and the boats were not built, only begun, and the lumber with which they were to be constructed was still in the standing trees.

The horses and mules of Rosecrans' army could get no forage. More than 10,000 of them perished before the end of the siege. The artillery horses, when forage arrived, were long unable to move the guns. This was the result of the blundering order to turn in the transportation of the Eleventh and Twelfth Corps at Alexandria.

A half day's work on the steamer was lost after I was placed in charge at Bridgeport, by the command of Gen. Howard who ordered me to have no work done on Sunday.

"But," I said, "there are 50,000 men in Chattanooga starving."

"The Lord will provide," he replied.

His action was reported to Thomas and work went on night and day, Sundays included.

The hull of one boat was on the blocks and ready for caulking when it was found that the oakum necessary for caulking was not at hand and was probably at Stevenson, 12 miles distant. To Stevenson I rode to find and forward the oakum. The rain fell in torrents all day. I hastened back to Bridgeport the same day, and when I got to the boat yard Turner's men were piling pig iron (a carload of which for some reason or other had been dumped off at the station by the rebels) on the boat hull to prevent the rapidly rising river from floating her off the blocking. I saw this wouldn't do at all.

"Turner," said I, "if the bottom gets wet we can't caulk her until she dries, and that may be weeks or months at this season of the year, and you know that will cause the loss of Chattanooga."

I hurried to Edwards' tent and found him lying in his bunk, half crying and utterly despondent. Seeing that it was useless to talk with Edwards, I went to the river near where a pontoon bridge had been thrown across and there, tied to the bank, were several loose, empty pontoons. I started on a run for the boat yard, and had some men knock out a row of blocking from under the boat wide enough to receive one of the pontoon boats. I brought down the pontoons, half filled them with water (through auger holes bored in their bottoms). Then we dragged them under the boat, plugged up the auger holes and dipped out the water. The boat was thus lifted above the flood, dry and ready to caulk on the morrow.

Our little home-made steamer, the *Chattanooga,* was launched on Oct. 24 and on Oct. 29, with a barge lashed to her, was sent to meet a division of troops that had started out to hunt for rations.

They were to march through the country and forage as best they could toward Bridgeport until they met supplies coming on the boat. They were seen from the steamer, skirmishing through the fields for rabbits, squirrels and birds, and when the steamer landed the barge with the rations the soldiers, running to the bank of the river, shouted, "Hurrah for the little steamer!" As soon as the barge touched shore they rushed aboard and commenced to throw off the supplies, shouting, "Here's coffee, boys; here's sowbelly! Build a fire! Hurrah for the bully little steamer!"

The steamer left the barge and hurried downstream to catch onto two other barges that had been loaded while we had gone up the river. A part of a deckload was put on the boat, leaving room for the carpenters who were still busy at work on the little steamer putting on the upper deck and the unfinished pilot house. The barges, one on each side, were lashed fast, and the steamer started up river again on her 45-mile journey with 50,000 rations for the starving army.

I took charge of the boat myself, with a steersman named Williams who had run on a ferryboat from Cincinnati to Covington. A man by the name of Davis who had served as mate on a lake boat I put at the bow to watch for any drift. The engineer was familiar with the engines and we started up the river under a full head of steam. The carpenters were yet keeping on with their work, trying to finish up the boat.

After about five or six miles had been successfully accomplished, a hog chain broke and we floated down the current

■ After October 29, the steamers *Chattanooga* (shown here) and *Paint Rock* carried rations and supplies on the Tennessee River from Bridgeport to Kelly's Ferry. The *Paint Rock's* crew consisted of former Ohio River boatmen, including 2nd Lieut. Charles Grant of Company D, 18th Ohio. He later wrote: "At Kelly's Ferry were stationed one or two regiments, from which a detail of about 100 men were always at the landing ready to unload us the minute we got the boat landed. At Bridgeport the Quartermaster's Department had large gangs of 'contrabands' ready to load our boat with the utmost dispatch. For over two weeks we landed a cargo at Kelly's Ferry every 36 hours."

■ Before the Tennessee River from Bridgeport to Kelly's Ferry was opened to steamboats, the Federal supply line relied almost wholly on mule trains. *Harper's Weekly* artist Theodore R. Davis believed "the mule is *par excellence* the animal for this country. Up and down the steep mountain-sides he goes with certain step, where to take a horse would be almost impossible. The mail comes to us by pack-mules; so also do a large quantity of stores. My sketch (above) shows a train at a point on Waldron's[sic] Ridge at sunrise. The rebels call this arrangement of ours 'the cracker line.' "

while we mended it with a rope. The vibration of the steamboat hull was so great that I feared she would break the rope in two. We had spliced it as well as we were able, and I had ordered the engineer to use only steam enough to keep in slow motion up the river. Thus we merely crawled along.

The rain commenced falling and continued to increase with the darkness of the night. Finally it became so thick we could hardly see two boat lengths ahead, and Davis came back from his watch at the bow and said that if we didn't land somewhere we would be sunk. But we kept a sharp lookout for drift and forged ahead. We crawled up the rapid river, keeping as near mid-channel as possible. About 1 o'clock a campfire was seen on the north bank, and as we approached a sentry was visible against the firelight. We didn't know whether they were our men or rebs; if rebs, we were in a tight place for the river was not musket-shot across.

When within hailing distance I called to the sentry: "What troops are those? Who's your Colonel?"

"Fifth Tennessee Cavalry," came the reply. "Billy Stokes is our Colonel, and he's a good one, you bet."

"Col. Stokes is on our side," I shouted to my crew, and we brought her over toward the fire.

I asked the Tennessee boys how far it was to Kelley's Ferry from there, and they pointed to a campfire about a mile farther and said that was the Ferry. "They have been waiting for you all night," they added.

We pulled out again and the boat was soon made fast at Kelley's Ferry, where the barges with the precious rations were unloaded. I went ashore and into the arms of my excellent Assistant Quartermaster, Joe Shoeninger, who helped me up the slippery bank. A messenger was sent off at once to notify Gen. Hooker of our arrival. Then I took a pull at his canteen and lay down by the fire to dry myself. I was soaked through and tired to death. I slept until the sun came looking over the crest of Raccoon Mountain; then before noon I mounted and rode to Gen. Hooker's camp to report.

The orderly that carried news of my arrival with the *Chattanooga* to Gen. Hooker notified the different camps as he passed, and the soldiers cheered him and shouted, "Cracker line's opened, boys; full bellies again!" They made as great a hurrah as if we had won a great victory.

**Hooker's men in Lookout Valley continued work on breastworks and rifle pits under the morning shadow of Lookout Mountain. His pickets adopted a live-and-let-live attitude toward their Confederate counterparts across Lookout Creek, which separated the opponents at the mountain's western base. Fraternization was common during the first three weeks of November.**

**"While here the two picket lines at many places were not more than forty yards apart," wrote Private Robert A. Jarman of Company K, 27th Mississippi. "We could see and hear them relieving their pickets, and they could see us. We even met half way in the creek, where it was shallow and shoally, to swap newspapers, canteens and tobacco for coffee. And I have seen some swap hats and shoes, and talk for half an hour at a time, but this was only when no officer was present on either side."**

■ A *Harper's Weekly* version of Lookout Creek picket duty depicted Confederates camouflaged as bushes moving toward two wary Federal riflemen. In reality, "we were on very friendly terms with each other," wrote Private Henry M. Woodson of Company E, 34th Mississippi. "We had been stationed on the northwest slope of old Lookout for some two weeks doing picket duty. Exchanges of canteens, tobacco, coffee, etc., occurred daily. It was understood along the picket-line that if either side received orders to advance they would give us a signal, so the enemy could have time to get back to their breastworks."

**At night, however, picket duty was much more hazardous and frightening. For one young Texan spending his last night standing watch along the thickly wooded base of Lookout Mountain, the experience was unforgettable.**

## 'Always a strain on a soldier's nerves'

### Private Nicholas Pomeroy
### Company A
### 5th Texas Volunteer Infantry

One night I was again on the Picket Guard. Our line extended along the bank of a stream of water called Lookout Creek, and not more than a half mile from our encampment. We went on duty about 10 p.m. and we were not to be relieved till daylight. The stream of water ran along the foot of a low ridge in our front which was more or less covered with forest trees, our side being the lowest. Captain [D.C.] Farmer of my Company was in command of the Picket line. As usual he went along, placed each guard in such a position that he could see as far as possible across the stream, giving his instructions what to do in case the enemy made their appearance.

The place he posted me differed from any of the others. A large tree had fallen across the stream from the opposite bank. Its branches, sunk into the water, had been the means of stopping from time to time any drift-wood floating down the current towards it, so that it formed a big drift. The stream was deep and far too wide for a person to jump across, especially a soldier loaded with his accoutrements. Meanwhile the drift would make a convenient bridge for the enemy's infantry to pass over to our side dry-shod. Close to my left was a high knoll, and a few feet to my right the ground was marshy and covered with reeds, etc. Such was my position as I faced the drift.

■ Capt. D.C. Farmer commanded Company A, 5th Texas, from May 1862 until early 1864, when he became acting major. During that 21-month period he led his company at Seven Pines, Gaines' Mill, Malvern Hill, Second Manassas, Antietam and Gettysburg, but was absent at Chickamauga. Slightly wounded in the Wilderness on May 6, 1864, he commanded the regiment several days later at Spotsylvania.

The Captain first told me that it was reported that the enemy was to attack our part of the line some time during the night, and that the drift would be their main crossing over the stream. He then gave me the following orders, which are usually given on the Picket Line, to fire on any people approaching or attempting to cross the drift, or any part of the stream within my view, and keep firing and hold the enemy in check as long as I could, and when forced to fall back to load and fire as I retreated, so that our troops in camp would have timely warning to get under arms.

On top of the knoll near me was posted a little German Jew. He was one of the recruits who joined us at Yorktown, and one of those bad soldiers who always contrived to avoid dangers and hardships experienced by our soldiers at the front. He had been compelled to leave the hospital where he was feigning sickness, and had joined us two or three days previously. Captain Farmer told me he had purposely placed this man on the knoll so that he could be under my observance as he had a strong suspicion of his trying to desert during the night. He gave me strict injunctions to shoot him if he attempted to cross the stream to the enemy's side.

The night was fine but there was no moon, only a few stars in the sky which gave but a very faint light to see by, and my position was such that, in order to keep in view the man on top of the knoll and the drift across the stream at the same time, I would be compelled to move to the right a few steps, which would take me into the swamp of water which was anything but a comfortable station to remain in till daylight.

Captain Farmer often gave me credit for never failing to do my duty when called upon, and I was then ready and willing to execute any orders given me, but here I hesitated for a moment before accepting the arduous duty which I thought he was imposing on me. I asked why he chose me for the place. His reply was that he considered me the best and most reliable soldier in his command, and the position being of the utmost importance, were his reasons for placing me there. This had the desired effect, and so I cheerfully waded into the swamp and took up my position, the water reaching just beyond my knees. After cautioning me to be on the alert, the Captain left me.

A soldier on the Picket Line on a dark night, and expecting the approach of the enemy at any moment, is in a very trying situa-

# 'A trampoose on Lookout Mountain'

**When the weather was clear, Confederates atop Lookout Mountain's summit saw the above panorama of Moccasin Bend, surrounded by the looping Tennessee River. Chattanooga lies at the photograph's upper right, while the Cravens House and wagon road can be seen at center on the "bench" of the mountain's northern slope.**

**Many Southern soldiers stationed on or visiting the mountain marvelled at the spectacular view afforded from the craggy heights at Lookout Point. One of them, Private O.T. Hanks of Company K, 1st Texas, found excursions to the summit unlike anything he and his comrades experienced in the East while serving with the Army of Northern Virginia. In describing several different trips, Hanks wrote:**

"The night we arrived a detail of us was sent ahead to stand picket on Lookout. We climbed the cliffs to the top — a dangerous undertaking. Sometimes it seemed to me that it was all I could do to hold on to the crags of rock with my fingers.

"The clouds seemed to run extremely low. Occasionally you could hear a fellow bawl out: 'Look out, boys, we will have another shower! I see a cloud hung up in the trees.' Sure enough, the rain would come pouring down.

"Everything being quiet, we were allowed some liberties. Some of us took a trampoose on Lookout Mountain, three miles by the wagon road. On reaching the summit we found a beautiful little summering village [Summertown] nestled among the forest trees. Passing on towards Chattanooga the mountain ends abruptly with a precipice of considerable height, which no man dares walk up to and look over. We slid up to the edge of it on our stomachs and peeped down. Even then a kind of thrill would run through you. There you would feel like you would be safer a little further back.

"You can stand here and look in the distance as far as the eye can see. Chattanooga is in sight. There is the Tennessee River winding its way down to the Moccasin bend and on until it is lost in the mountains. We were on this mountain several times. At times there was a heavy fog or mist. On one of these occasions some of the boys suggested that we wash our hands and faces in the clouds. We went through the maneuver thinking we had accomplished a wonderful feat."

# 'In the height of their good humor'

**Major William D. Pickett, assistant inspector general of Hardee's corps, provided a staff officer's view of prevailing conditions along Lookout's picket line in mid-November:**

A short time before the battle of Missionary Ridge I was directed by General Hardee to make a night inspection of the picket line around the base of Lookout Mountain, fronting Moccasin Point and on Lookout Creek, which then separated our lines from Hooker's Corps. On account of the rough mountain side and the dense timber interfering with finding the various picket posts, those posts on Lookout Creek were not reached till after daylight, and probably after the boys had broken their fast. On approaching the picket post at the Nashville railroad bridge, loud laughing was heard, with every evidence of hilarity and good feeling. At that post was a sight to be remembered.

The bridge had been destroyed, but there was left the two stone abutments sixty or seventy-five feet apart. On one side were "the boys in blue" and on the other side "the boys in gray," each sitting flat on the abutment with their feet dangling below and, in the height of their good humor, striking the sides of the abutments. The boys had evidently been "swapping yarns" instead of tobacco and coffee. On inspecting the picket posts farther up Lookout Creek the same conditions were in evidence. On one side of the shallow creek was the Confederate post with the sentinel "in gray;" on the other side, one hundred to one hundred and fifty yards distant, was the sentinel "in blue" — each in sight of the other.

Before leaving corps headquarters nothing was told me of this truce. These partial truces were as they should have been. The few soldiers killed and wounded on the picket line cut no figure in war; it is the winning of battles and gaining possession of strategic points that control the results.

tion. Should he fail to give the alarm of the enemy's approach in time, the result to his own troops in the rear may be disastrous; and again, if he gives a false alarm he is censured. If he has the misfortune to be found asleep at his post, the penalty is death. With these things in his mind, added to the constant watching and listening, there is always a strain on a soldier's nerves. And should he be nervous, which is not always the sign of a bad soldier, he may imagine objects in front of him (such as bushes, tufts of grass, etc.) moving, and are people; and then the noise of the wind through the forest trees, or the falling of leaves he may fancy to be the sound of marching coming towards him, so he tries to steady his nerves and keep cool. Then these visions vanish for a while only to be renewed again in some other form.

My post was a peculiar one. I stood about 40 feet from the drift, and owing to the darkness I could only see a very short distance in front of me in the forest on the opposite side of the stream. So, should the enemy approach with the intention of crossing the drift they would almost reach the bank before I could see them and, according to my orders, fire upon them. On the next instant I was sure to expect a return fire sending a hail of bullets in my direction, and standing in the water without any protection my chances of escaping being killed or wounded would not be favorable. If I fell wounded and was unable to get up I would be drowned.

As to my watch on the man on the knoll, I could fairly well make out his figure through the gloom. He seemed restless, shifting his position from one place to another, and always looking down at me. This continued for some time, till at last he laid down and made himself comfortable. This last action of his led me to think he suspected me of watching him, so he gave up the notion which pleased me very much for the reason that I should have hated to fire on him.

So the night passed away and the enemy did not make their appearance. Neither did the man on the knoll try to desert, and at daylight we were relieved.

**On November 5, Pomeroy's regiment and the rest of Longstreet's corps pulled out of the line and headed for Knoxville — dispatched by Bragg to destroy, if possible, a small Federal army under Maj. Gen. Ambrose E. Burnside. The move rid Longstreet from the irascible Bragg's immediate presence, but it also weakened his forces by more than 10,000 men at a time when Grant's were growing stronger. Hooker's troops were up and four divisions from Maj. Gen. William T. Sherman's Army of the Tennessee were marching from the Mississippi and expected to arrive soon. Much of the Union battle blueprint depended on Sherman's XV and XVII corps soldiers, who were selected by Grant to strike and turn Bragg's right flank along the north end of Missionary Ridge at Tunnel Hill. Thomas, with the bulk of the Army of the Cumberland, would hold the Federal center and right, and attack only when Sherman rolled up the Confederate flank. On the far right end of the Union line, Hooker was ordered merely to demonstrate and threaten the Rebel left on Lookout Mountain.**

**Delays in bringing up Sherman's Westerners over mud-bogged roads from Bridgeport forced postponement of the assault, and troop dispositions were altered to conform to un-**

**forseen exigencies, including a break in the pontoon bridge at Brown's Ferry on November 23.* That same day, the battle of Chattanooga commenced — ironically, on Thomas' front where a line of fortified Confederate picket outposts at Orchard Knob was swallowed up in a surprise attack late in the afternoon.**

**Over on Lookout Mountain, Confederate infantry and artillerymen watched in awe as the spectacle unfolded below around Orchard Knob. Although there also was an unusual amount of Federal activity to their left in Lookout Valley, few Southerners stationed along the wooded, boulder-strewn northern slope realized that they, too, would soon be fighting for their lives.**

## 'Building a foot bridge'

### Lt. Col. Eugene Powell
### 66th Ohio Volunteer Infantry

After Howard's corps had been withdrawn from Hooker, Geary's division yet remained in Wauhatchie valley and at once extended its picket line to cover the space that had been occupied by the 11th Corps, in addition to its own. At that time I was attached to Geary's division in the capacity of Lieutenant colonel and commander of the 66th Ohio regiment, and it so happened that I came on duty as division officer of the day, the day before the demonstration was made by Hooker's forces upon Lookout Mountain.

After I assumed these duties, and while riding along the picket line close to Lookout creek at a point near the right of our line, far up that stream, I chanced to notice the knees of a dam that had been built across the creek to furnish power to drive a small grist mill that was situated on our side of the creek, the knees projecting quite a distance above the surface of the stream. The situation made quite an impression upon my mind as I rode off to continue my rounds of the picket line.

During the night following, while at my tent, I was awakened by the rapid riding of an orderly approaching, who, upon being halted by the sentinel at my tent, sang out, "I have orders for Col. Powell!" I immediately got up, stepped out and inquired as to what was wanted. The orderly stated that Gen. Geary desired to see me at his headquarters at once. I requested the orderly to wait a moment and we would ride over there together; but before getting there I noticed that the General's tents were lighted up, which to my mind indicated that a movement for us was at hand. Upon reaching Gen. Geary's headquarters I dismounted and went in; the General sat there, surrounded by a number of staff officers in addition to his own. These were from Grant's and Hooker's

■ Lt. Col. Eugene Powell, 66th Ohio, supervised Geary's "grand guard" between November 22-24. These 330 officers and men, drawn from five different XII Corps' regiments, bolstered Geary's defenses west of Lookout Creek.

Prior to service at Lookout Mountain, Powell commanded his regiment in three great battles fought by the Army of the Potomac. He was wounded by a musket ball in the face and neck at Antietam, where the 66th entered the fight with only two line officers and 120 men. With 362 effectives at Chancellorsville, the regiment lost 73 men (30 of them missing), and 18 more at Gettysburg. Powell was on duty in New York City following civil unrest there in July and August 1863. In March 1865 he was promoted colonel of the 193rd Ohio, which saw brief service in the Shenandoah Valley at the war's close, and was brevetted brigadier general to rank from March 13, 1865.

* Howard's XI Corps left Lookout Valley under orders on November 22, crossed the Brown's Ferry pontoon bridge, marched opposite Chattanooga and recrossed the Tennessee River, bivouacking near Fort Wood. His 6,000 troops were to reinforce Sherman, who had one of his divisions (commanded by Brig. Gen. Peter J. Osterhaus) stranded in Lookout Valley when part of the Brown's Ferry bridge washed away on November 23. Osterhaus' troops accordingly were attached to Hooker, and Sherman was reinforced further by one of Thomas' divisions under Brig. Gen. Jefferson C. Davis.

■ Metallic XII Corps pin worn by Private Thomas O. Jones of Company A, 66th Ohio. Shortly after the Chattanooga siege was lifted, the 66th reenlisted as veteran volunteers, and became the first regiment to return to Ohio early in 1864 for its 30-day furlough.

headquarters, and had undoubtedly brought Geary his orders and were waiting to see the movement begin.

It struck me, as I stepped into Geary's tent, that I had seldom looked upon a more silent, solemn party, but Geary broke the silence by saying, "Colonel, I have sent for you. I have orders to make a demonstration upon Lookout Mountain. I wish to know where and how I can cross that creek with my command."

It is not probable that Gen. Geary, in the presence of the staff officers who had brought him his orders, would have mentioned to me as to his having orders to make a demonstration on Lookout Mountain, if those orders were that he should assault and capture it. But Gen. Geary then added to what he had already said, as to what his orders were, that he intended to show the world what his ideas of a demonstration meant. So I think that Gen. Geary then, upon his own responsibility, resolved that he would make the most of his orders and push a demonstration to the utmost limits that a construction of that phrase would admit of, showing that in his own mind he had already turned a demonstration into an assault, and was going to make a reality of it.

That resolve of Gen. Geary, and the subsequent success of the reserve pickets in building a foot bridge across that creek, were very important factors in one of the most successful and brilliant assaults upon what was regarded as an impregnable position. And anyone today standing upon Lookout point, surveying the surrounding scenes, would say that any average body of soldiers could defend it against all of the soldiers that could be made to climb up against it. But the accidents and incidents of the moment turned in favor of Geary and against the Confederates, and these sometimes have as much to do in determining the results of warfare as does valor and endurance, as "Victory is not always to the strong, or the race to the swift."

Gen. Geary's inquiry of me as to where he could cross Lookout creek caused the situation at the dam to flash across my mind, and I described it to him and stated that I thought I could lash rails, boards, etc., to those knees and make a good foot bridge. Geary accepted the proposition at once, told me to return to my picket line, take the reserve pickets and build the bridge, and by that time he would be at the little mill just back of that point with his division, and would cross over upon Lookout Mountain.

I withdrew at once, mounted my horse and was soon moving with my pickets to carry out the orders. When I reached the open space at the dam, the moon was shining, making it quite light, but soon thereafter clouds of mist settled down upon the mountain side and it grew quite dark. I halted the pickets at the site of the proposed bridge and told the men what the orders were. I said that it was probable that as soon as we began building the bridge the Confederates would begin firing upon us, as we then could hear the enemy moving in the underbrush beyond. I said that I wanted half of my force to cross the creek by climbing from knee to knee, and when over to form a half circle for the protection of the bridge builders who necessarily would be unarmed and defenceless, and that the men who should go over must draw the fire of the enemy upon themselves and return such fire as effectually as possible and thus protect the men at work.

I called for volunteers to cross the creek; there was complete silence for a time, when a soldier stated he would go, then another, and it was evident that the whole command would go, so I divided my command as nearly equal as to numbers as I could and directed the right to sling their guns across their shoulders and climb across the knees. This was done, and soon a part of my force was on the enemy's side of the stream, being the first Union soldiers to reach there.

Then I placed a soldier on each knee and directed the others on our side of the stream to get rails, boards, etc., and pieces of rope from the mill. These were handed out to the soldiers on the knees and there tied securely, and soon we had a good solid foot bridge made, upon which men in single rank could move safely and rapidly across. This bridge was made without hammer, nails or saw, simply by lashing timbers to the knees, and as the boards had been torn off of the dam the water passed under the foot bridge without any resistance from it. During this time, much to our surprise, not a shot had been fired by the enemy.

Upon completion of the bridge I went back to the mill and found Gen. Geary there at the head of his division. I told him that I had completed the bridge; he said he would go to the bridge with me and examine it. We walked there together. As soon as Geary saw what a good solid foot bridge had been made and that some of my men were already on the other side, he thanked me heartily for the good work that the pickets had been able to accomplish, as until then he had no idea as to how or where he would be able to cross the creek.

Gen. Geary directed me to take my place at the bridge, and as his men came forward not to allow a foot of one of them to come up without another one should take its place, saying every second of time was of vital importance to us, that I should urge and press every man forward and direct that they push right up the mountain side to the foot of the palisades. Geary then returned to his division, and in a few moments, around upon the path from the mill, the head of the column came, crossed the foot bridge and went climbing up the mountain side as he directed, where we joined them, and at once moved forward, far above the heads of the Confederate pickets who yet remained (in ignorance of his movements) along the line of Lookout Creek watching our pickets upon the opposite side.

Our rapidly advancing troops drove in the outlying posts of the enemy, and this enabled Geary to come almost upon their main camps, which were situated near the foot of the palisades at the point of the mountain fronting Chattanooga, before the enemy had full knowledge that he had crossed the creek. After the enemy's pickets were aware of Geary's movements and knew that he had passed along above their heads, they fled from the line along Lookout Creek and sought to reach their tents.

Then another foot bridge was easily made by our pontooneers further down the stream, upon which Osterhaus' division and other troops crossed and joined Geary, thus making his force on the battlefield near the point of the mountain much stronger than that of the enemy.

[Two days later], after the battle of Chattanooga had been won, a Confederate picket party, some twenty in number, came in at the foot bridge from off of Lookout Mountain and gave themselves up as prisoners. They stated they saw the force building the foot bridge, but as that force was small they decided it was surely a scouting party and they would let us come over, then they would charge and cut us off from the bridge and capture our entire par-

■ Private John A. Patterson of Company I, 18th Tennessee, was captured November 24 on outpost duty along Lookout's western slope near Wauhatchie. Incorrectly listed as a deserter, he was shipped to Rock Island prison in Illinois and assigned to Barrack Number 9. In a letter written to his in-laws March 24, 1864, Patterson expressed hopes for exchange and mentioned he had a bad cold. "I hope that the time will soon come when I will return home to my family whear I know my support is needed ... It is my intention to come the first chance ..."

Patterson's wish was never realized. Less than three weeks later he died, leaving a wife and two infant sons. His remains lie today in Grave 1031 at Rock Island's Confederate cemetery.

■ Col. Charles Candy, 66th Ohio, commanded the 1st Brigade of Geary's division for the first six hours of the assault. His 1,010 Ohio and Pennsylvania troops formed the far left of Geary's line as they moved along the mountainside *en echelon,* scouring the broken ground for concealed Confederates. Shortly after 2 p.m., Candy slipped while clambering over a large rock. The resulting fall injured his hip, forcing him to relinquish brigade command to Col. William R. Creighton of the 7th Ohio.

ty. So they decided not to fire or molest us. But when the bridge was completed what was their surprise at seeing not the balance of our pickets coming over but instead Geary's division and on the run. Then they saw it was too late to fire or retreat, so they hid themselves in the bushes, being cut off from regaining their own camps or giving the alarm, and as the battle went against them they decided they would come in and surrender, which they did, crossing upon the foot bridge which they had allowed to be built.

Had that Confederate picket done its duty, and as soon as they saw that we were endeavoring to cross the creek and fired upon us, no bridge would have been built; at least not in the way or in the time that we built it, and the "battle above the clouds" might have resolved itself into what was intended — a demonstration on Lookout Mountain.

## 'Cry out, Forward the 1st Brigade!'

### Orderly Sergeant William H.H. Tallman
### Company E
### 66th Ohio Volunteer Infantry

Our picket detail was usually two days at this time. The distance we went from camp made it inconvenient to return the same day, as much time was taken up in going back & forth. My turn had come again [a few days before the battle of Lookout Mountain], and when we reached the reserve post we found the location changed from the point it was when last I saw it. It was nearer the foot of the mountain and not so far from Chattanooga, and not within hailing distance of our Johnny friends.

Col. Creighton of the 7th Ohio was chief officer of the day and we knew that much of the red tape business of turning out the guard every time he was in sight might be safely dispensed with, and we calculated on having an easy time and in that we were not disappointed. A short time after we had relieved the guards and returned to the reserve post, the Johnnies pitched a shell from up the mountain side and it landed in a stack of guns some distance away, but nothing was hurt but a gun or two. Col. Creighton visited the reserve but once in the two days, and then came up on us unobserved and loudly proclaimed that we need not turn out the guard. He came galloping through a railroad cut and then down an embankment that was almost perpendicular.

Our twenty-four hours having passed, we started for and arrived at camp but found it generally vacated, except for the noncombatants, and we began to congratulate ourselves on having escaped an expedition or march. But just then Col. Creighton came into our camp with the remainder of the pickets and we were ordered to join our commands. They had moved to the left about three miles and were occupying the line and works of the 11th Corps that had gone to Sherman over on the left of Chattanooga.

On our way to this place Col. Creighton said, "Boys, they say we are going to be going up there tomorrow (pointing to Lookout Mountain). I'd like to see a few American flags up there before we start." A good many of us felt the same way. But 'twas not the next day but two days afterward when we made the assault upon what was considered an impregnable position.

The works of the 11th Corps were much nearer the rebel line than our camp in Wauhatchie, but they were well protected by bomb proofs and other places of shelter. It had been raining very heavily for some days and the river was very high and the pontoon bridge was not in a safe condition. For that reason Osterhaus' division of the 15th Corps was on our side of the river.

On the morning of the 24th of November we were relieved by Osterhaus and started, as we thought, back to our old camp. But when the place was reached when we should have filed off, we didn't file but continued on past. We turned to the left and moved into a wood on the banks of Lookout Creek, where we were halted and told to unsling knapsacks. We knew what that meant. But we could hardly understand why we had come so far down and away from the rebel camp on the mountain. But the plan was for our division to come in upon their flank and rear while Osterhaus and Cruft's division of the 4th Corps would strike on the left and front.

Our division (Geary) crossed Lookout Creek on the remains of an old dam which had been prepared as a bridge. We formed our line, extending up to the mountain side and then advanced toward the point where the enemy was in an entrenched camp. Our brigade was last to cross Lookout Creek, but the advance had crossed so cautiously that they captured forty pickets at this point. Our march along the slope of the mountain was a difficult one. Over rocks and logs we went, pushing ahead as fast as possible. By this time the troops on our left had completed their bridge and were climbing up the mountain.

Gen. Geary was with our brigade which was on the left of our line, and an aide came down from the right and reported the Rebels on the run. I can hear the old man now. "Cry out, Forward the 1st Brigade!" and away we went, into and through their camp, among their sick, wounded and dead who had no time to get away or be removed. Then we struck a body of near two hundred prisoners captured just on our right, and this was the cause of a little episode that happened then and there between our Col. Candy, commanding brigade, and Gen. Geary, commanding division.

Geary ordered Major McConnell, commanding our regiment, to take charge of the prisoners, and Candy said, "Major McConnell, stay where you are." Geary says, "Col. Candy, I command this division," and Candy: "Gen. Geary, I command this brigade, and if you have any orders for my regiment give them through me. A part of the 5th [Ohio] is now guarding prisoners, and I shall send the rest of them with the prisoners." And it was done.

At this juncture the clouds came down upon us and we could not see which way to move. We halted for a while until the clouds rolled away, and they did; rolled down below us and shut out our view of Chattanooga and the valley. By this time it was growing dark and our brigade was thrown forward a few hundred yards into the rifle pits of the enemy that had lately occupied them. A sharp musketry firing was kept up for a while and the big siege gun on top of Lookout (that was on a point about a hundred and fifty feet high just above us) was sending shell, round shot and canister down the mountain side, cutting off tree tops and rattling among the big rocks. It made the situation very interesting.

■ Brothers Joseph M. (left) and John Wren served as privates in Company A, 66th Ohio. Joseph enlisted in October 1861, took part in all the 66th's campaigns, and mustered out as corporal in June 1865 at Camp Chase, Ohio. His younger brother's army service, however, was relatively short. Enlisting in January 1864, John died of disease in a Chattanooga hospital on July 7, 1864. This portrait, taken at M.L. Albright's gallery in Urbana, Ohio, during veteran furlough, shows Joseph wearing a small white XII Corps badge sewn on the front of his hat. Both soldiers are uniformed in commercially purchased sack coats.

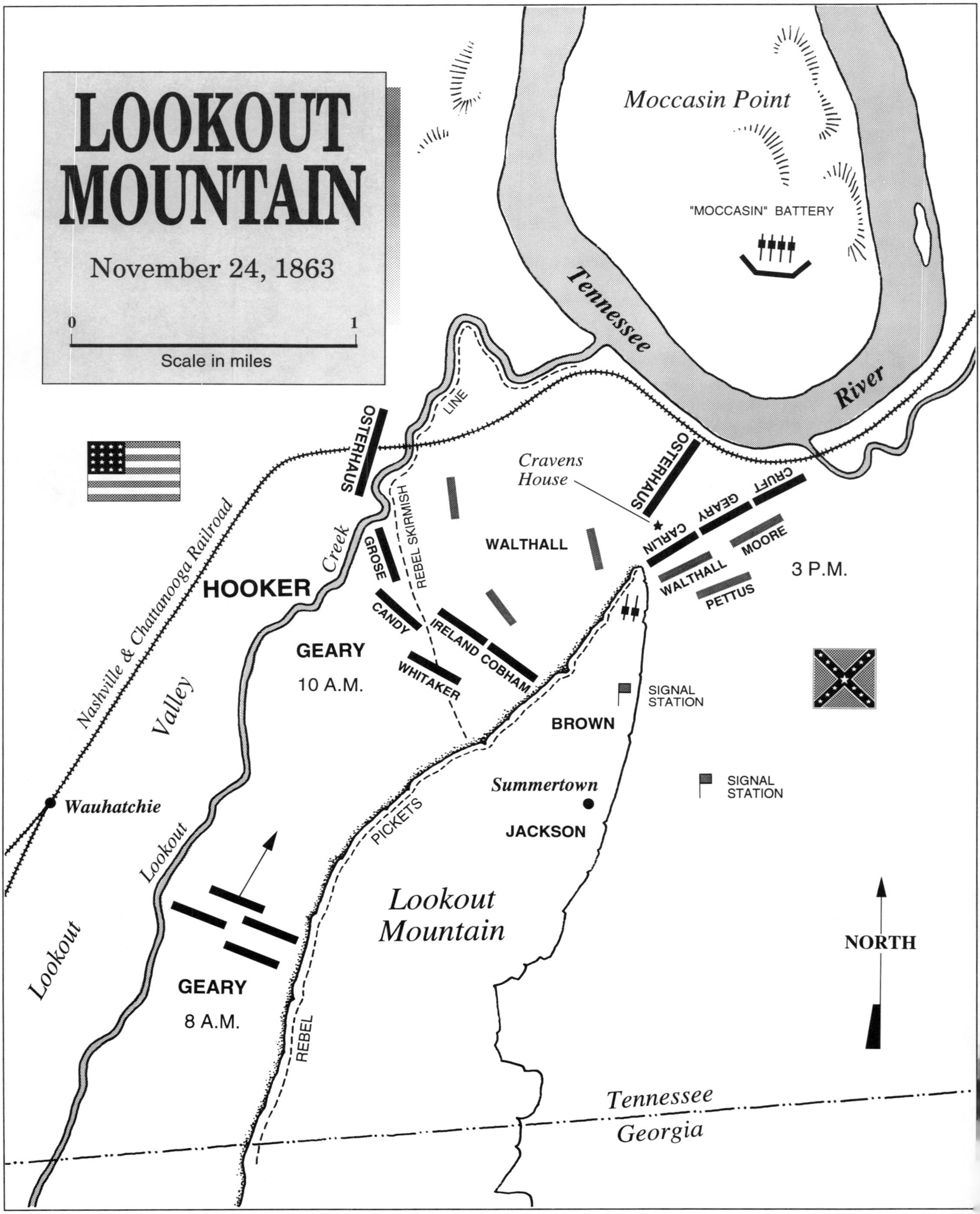
LOOKOUT MOUNTAIN
November 24, 1863
0
1
Scale in miles
Moccasin Point
"MOCCASIN" BATTERY
Tennessee
River
LINE
OSTERHAUS
Cravens House
OSTERHAUS
CRUFT
GEARY
CARLIN
MOORE
WALTHALL
PETTUS
3 P.M.
WALTHALL
REBEL SKIRMISH
GROSE
Creek
HOOKER
Nashville & Chattanooga Railroad
CANDY
IRELAND
COBHAM
WHITAKER
GEARY
10 A.M.
Valley
SIGNAL STATION
BROWN
SIGNAL STATION
Summertown
Wauhatchie
JACKSON
PICKETS
Lookout
Lookout Mountain
Lookout
GEARY
8 A.M.
REBEL
NORTH
Tennessee
Georgia

# 'Fall back, fighting over the rocks'

### Brig. Gen. Edward C. Walthall
### Brigade commander
### Cheatham's Division, Hardee's Corps

Early in November Gen. Longstreet was withdrawn and sent with his command to Knoxville, and Bragg's force was further weakened by sending other troops to join him. The Confederate line was so drawn in that no troops were left in Lookout Valley west of Lookout Creek, which was picketed by an outpost brigade. This command, on the 15th of November, I was ordered to relieve with a brigade less than fifteen hundred strong.

With this force it devolved upon me to occupy a picket line extending about a mile up Lookout Creek from a point near its mouth, and then up the mountain side to the cliff. From the creek up to the bench of the mountain [where the white-painted Cravens House was situated] the surface was so broken that the rapid or orderly movement of troops was impossible. The batteries on Moccasin Point commanded at easy range the only route by which troops could come to my support or my own could retire upon the main army. These batteries were trained to sweep the slope of the mountain from the wagon road to the palisades. Communication with my superiors on the mountain top was difficult and slow, the route by which messengers must travel being circuitous as well as rugged.

Such was the isolated and exposed position of this outpost brigade on the 23rd of November — with orders, if attacked by the enemy in heavy force, to fall back, fighting over the rocks. In view of the movements of the Union army on that day, this command was ordered under arms at daylight on the next, and through the night of the 23rd a working force was employed in deepening a rifle pit across the most exposed point near Cravens' house, to serve as a covered way, affording some shelter against the fire of the twenty-pounder Parrott guns on Moccasin Point.

On the morning of the 24th an infantry force crossed Lookout Creek a mile or more above the point where my picket lines turned up the mountain from the creek and formed across the western slope, with its right resting on the palisades. It was ready by nine o'clock to move upon my left flank and rear, the main body of my command being posted behind some rude breastworks of logs and stones, which the command that occupied the ground before me had constructed on the mountain side parallel to the creek. Batteries on the hills beyond Lookout Creek and several pieces in the valley opened fire on my position. An infantry column forced a passage across the creek, and soon my command was under a heavy fire in front and pressed on the left flank by a force of more than three times its own number. In the dispositions made for resistance two regiments were employed against the flanking force, but the slender lines along their whole length were overborne by the heavy masses which assailed them from two directions.

That the entire command, instead of the larger part of it, was not captured may be ascribed to the rugged field and the scattered condition of the troops, stretched out over a long, attenuated line; and that the remnant was able to retard the progress of such

■ Brig. Gen. Edward C. Walthall's Mississippi brigade occupied the west/northwest slope of Lookout Mountain on November 15, thinly deployed along Bragg's seemingly invulnerable left flank. One of Walthall's enlisted men, Private William Honnoll of Company D, 24th Mississippi, described their duties: "We have to stand picket every other day and go on fateege every other night to make brest works and doge the shells all day. The yankeys throwed at least 100 shell at us. You out to of seen us falling down and getting behind the rocks. The shells woud nock the dirt all over us and the peaces fell as thick as hale around us. One shell fell in ten foot of a large bunch of us but as it hapened it did not burst or it woud of made a perfect shucking of the crowd. In all the shelling that was done thare was but one man in the briggade hurt, he got his arm broke."

■ A Thomas Nast painting provided the basis for this 1864 engraving of Geary's assault. Unlike the depiction, Gen. Geary ordered his brigade commanders "to have their men put in light marching order. They had but one day's rations of hard bread in their haversacks. Thus scantily supplied, without overcoats or blankets, and most of them in ordinary summer blouses, the troops went out to the assault ..."

a force was chiefly due to the shelter the crags afforded the retreating troops while they kept up their fire upon the advancing columns. When these troops reached the ridge running down the northern slope of the mountain the guns on Moccasin Point soon rendered any further resistance impossible, and they made their way in confusion past Cravens' house under a sweeping artillery fire, some taking advantage of the covered way already described.

After passing Cravens' house about four hundred yards they were reformed in a strong position at a narrow point on the east side of the mountain, without the range of the guns on Moccasin Point, and there, about one o'clock, checked the advancing force. Gen. Pettus came to my support with three regiments of his brigade in time to save the position, which my depleted command whose ammunition was almost exhausted, would very soon have been forced to yield.

Whatever dispositions ought or ought not to have been made; whatever blunders, if any, were committed on the Southern side, on that day or before — it takes nothing from the credit of the gallant troops who attacked the forbidden position that during the two and a half or three hours which elapsed between the commencement of the firing and their occupancy of the point at Cravens' house they were confronted by no stronger force. About two hundred men picketing at the northern end of the mountain, without fault of their own or their commander, but because my troops could not hold the ground on their left and in their rear, were taken in reverse and captured before their position was approached in front. These men belonged to the brigade commanded by Brig. Gen. Moore, which gallantly held its ground on the right of the position where Pettus found me in the afternoon.

At nightfall the Confederates were still on this line, which covered the Summertown road, the only avenue of communication between the troops on the top of the mountain and the main army, and were never driven from it. About eight o'clock my brigade and two regiments of Pettus having been relieved by Holtzclaw's [Clayton's] brigade, were withdrawn to the Summertown road. During the night Bragg withdrew all his troops from the mountain, and in the morning the United States flag was floating at Lookout Point — the result of Gen. Hooker's demonstration.*

■ Private James Vandermark of Company G, 102nd New York. The regiment took only 130 enlisted men into battle on Lookout Mountain, suffering few losses despite leading Geary's 3rd Brigade as skirmishers. However, Confederate sharpshooters hit two of three regimental field officers — Lt. Col. Robert Avery lost a leg and Major Gilbert M. Elliott died, "the first one shot in the division on Lookout Mountain," Geary wrote.

In this photograph, Vandermark poses during veteran furlough proudly wearing two XII Corps badges.

## 'Every cover that nature afforded'

### Col. William F. Dowd
### 24th Mississippi Volunteer Infantry

About the 20th of November we were placed on picket duty on the north side of Lookout Mountain, below the great rock, between its base and Lookout Creek. Our videttes and pickets were thrown out on a line with this little stream. A large body of the enemy was encamped on the north side of the creek, and the pickets of both armies occupied its opposite sides. The enemy had threatened an attack on the western side of the mountain, and a large body of our forces was stationed on top of the mountain to meet this threatened attack. On account of the want of roads and the rough, rocky declivities of the mountain, our troops on top were separated by several hours' march from the post occupied by General Walthall's brigade.

Late at night on the 23rd of November I heard distinctly the tramp of a large body of the enemy on the march. By placing the ear to the ground I heard the sound which no soldier of experience can mistake.

Just at dawn I saw several batteries being moved out near the creek, as if threatening to attempt a crossing in our front. Lookout Creek, swollen by recent rains, was impassable. After daylight I saw the rear portion of the enemy's column moving up the creek in a westwardly direction. I sent a message to General Walthall, who was near us at the Cravens' House, with the information.

The enemy moved up the creek and crossed at its source, and moved down between the creek and the base of the high rock upon our left flank. Our whole brigade only numbered about fifteen hundred men, while the whole of Hooker's corps was rapidly advancing upon us. General Walthall was upon the ground early and changed our front, the right resting on the line of entrenchments which ran parallel with the creek, and our left on the base

* Walthall was struck in the foot by a minie ball on November 25, but remained in the saddle until the close of fighting on Missionary Ridge.

■ Brig. Gen. John C. Brown assumed command of C.L. Stevenson's division late on November 23, and directed operations the next day from the summit of Lookout Mountain. When Federal troops reached the Cravens House on the northern plateau below, Brown ordered his sharpshooters and two Napoleon guns of Capt. Max Van Den Corput's Georgia Battery to open fire. "I ordered rocks rolled down the mountain also," he reported. "The fog was so dense that we could not see the enemy, although we could hear his march, and guided by this and the report of his musketry ours was directed."

of the promontory of Lookout Mountain. We had a very strong position behind the fallen timber and rocks, but the enemy, in advancing, were quite as well protected, except for a comparatively open space of about eighty yards in our immediate front.

General Walthall appreciated to the fullest extent the situation, feeling that if his brigade gave way, the Federal forces could push round past the Cravens House and cut the large body of Confederates from the rest of the army on Missionary Ridge. I felt and knew that, if necessary, the brigade must be sacrificed to save the army. I knew, too, that it would take many hours to bring the Confederate forces from the top of Lookout Mountain to our support.

While General Walthall and I (as senior colonel of the brigade) were yet conversing, and as he was about to leave, our videttes were driven in and the fire became hot. General Walthall left the brigade in my command, and left to hurry the troops down from the mountain. I realized that everything depended upon the holding of this position until the descending troops could reach and support us.

I ordered my men behind rocks, trees and every cover that nature afforded, and instructed them not to fire until the enemy moved out in the open space in my immediate front. In the meantime the Federal troops advanced cautiously and carefully, yet following our videttes and pickets so closely, and driving them in so rapidly, that I was obliged to give the order to fire, thereby killing, I have no doubt, some of my own men. As soon as the enemy reached the open space a deadly and destructive fire was opened upon him, which soon drove him back under shelter of the rocks and trees.

The battle continued without a moment's intermission, at close quarters, until between 12 and 1 o'clock. Failing in his repeated attacks in front, the enemy moved a considerable force under cover of the rocks and trees close along the base of the rock, and before I discovered this movement, opened fire on my flank and rear, which killed and wounded several men. A powerful battery called Moccasin, and several others on the north side of the creek were pouring shot and shell into our right flank and rear. The slaughter was terrible on both sides. I saw our color-bearer shot down within a few feet of me, but the colors were immediately taken up and held by one of the color-guard. The battle-flag, rent and torn, was carried to Missionary Ridge the next day.

General Walthall had ordered me early in the morning "to hold my post till hell froze over," and thinking at this juncture that the ice was about five feet over it, I went up the line and ordered my regiment to retire slowly in a skirmish line, taking every advantage of the rocks, trees and other shelter, and to re-form in the rear of the Cravens House at the point where the roads from the house and mountain top intersected.

In the meantime, other brigades were formed in line of battle south of the Cravens House, extending from the base of the high rock to the foot of the mountain. Our brigade was formed behind this line as a reserve. The enemy advanced with inconceivable slowness and caution, but in the afternoon he began a severe attack on our line at very short range. Both lines were sheltered by the overhanging rocks. The battle raged without intermission until a late hour in the night, probably about 2 o'clock a.m.

There were two long lines of fire as far as the eye could reach up and down the mountain, but as far as my observation extended but little damage was done upon either side. About 2 o'clock the firing ceased, the Federals retiring to the Cravens House, or near there, and the Confederates moving off to join the main body on Missionary Ridge.

In the morning I had three hundred and fifty-six men and officers present for duty, of whom one hundred and ninety-nine were killed and wounded. A few, not many, were taken prisoners.

## 'Surrender! Hand over that toad sticker!'

### Private David Monat
### Company G
### 29th Pennsylvania Volunteer Infantry

**Nov. 24, 1863 —** When orders came to move we fell in and took the road towards Wauhatchie Jct. and after going a short distance halted in the road. Orders came to unsling knapsacks and the man in each company with the worst pair of shoes to remain on guard over them. George Thompson of our company was detailed from us. He was almost barefooted.

The 109th [Pennsylvania] Regt. of our Brigade were left in the works. Col. Cobham of the 111th Penna. commanding our Brigade rode past and said, "Boys, how would you like to have a fight this morning?" I said "It would be damn rough without any chance for breakfast." He replied "That's so, but I guess we'll get one." We then heard that one Regt. from each Brigade of our Division was to be left in the works we had vacated and that we were to assault Lookout Mountain.

It was a cold chilly day and a misty rain falling and we could not see very far up the mountain. Neither could the Rebs see us. After crossing the rail road and moving some distance down along Lookout Creek at the foot of the mountain we came to a halt near a mill. Genl Hooker & Geary with their staffs passed by in our rear. Shortly orders came for all the officers of our Regiment to report at the mill. They soon came back, our Captain looking very serious, and told us we were ordered to take the mountain and that our Regiment was to be the first to cross the creek. Our Chaplain came along and "God blessed us" and said "If any of you have any messages or valuables to send to your friends I will take them and see they are safely delivered." I said to Jack MacLauchlan, "Jack, I've got about 3 or 4 dollars. If I go, look out for them and if you get a chance take a drink and say 'here's to a good fellow.' "

The pioneers were then ordered forward to lay boards & planks across the mill dam and we started across the creek with orders to keep straight up the mountain till we reached the Palisades at the top, which looked like a wall on top of the mountain. The Rebs were up on the slope of the mountain towards Chattanooga where they had a line of breastworks around their camp.

When we reached the Palisades we halted and came to a front and passed the word down the line. Orders came to throw out Companies C & E as skirmishers and to move forward. It was hard travelling over the rocks & fallen trees & up & down gullies. We soon reached the Reb pickets when the firing commenced and

■ Col. George A. Cobham Jr., 111th Pennsylvania, commanded the 2nd Brigade of Geary's division. Two of Cobham's three Keystone State regiments stormed Lookout Mountain from the front line's far right, directly under the palisades. "The fighting was desperate," he wrote to his mother a few days later, "but we charged Bayonets on the Enemy and drove them out of their fortifications, and took more Prisoners than we had men engaged. The defeat of the Rebels was compleat and they lost the most formidable Stronghold in the South ... I have saved as a memento the metal tube of the friction primer that fired the *last shot* from this mountain on the Union forces. I will send that to you for a Christmas present, as I have nothing better to send you."

The following July, Cobham was fatally wounded in the battle of Peachtree Creek.

■ Capt. Jesse R. Millison of Company C, 29th Pennsylvania, commanded half the skirmish line covering the front of Cobham's brigade. After crossing Lookout Creek, Millison's company was the first to engage Confederate pickets about 7:30 a.m. During its advance along the base of Lookout's palisades, a bullet passed through Millison's arm and lodged in his right side. He survived the wound and was promoted to major in 1864, when this portrait was taken at A.S. Morse's Gallery in Nashville.

the skirmishers halted. Capt. Woeltge of the 111th on Cobham's staff shouted to Capt. Millison of Co. C in charge of the skirmish line to forward the skirmishers. Millison replied "The Rebs are in force in our front." Woeltge shouted "Damn it, dats what we want. Forward!" Millison gave the order to move forward and we had not gone far when he was shot in 2 places.

By this time we were all up with the skirmish line and kept on driving the Johnnies back and soon reached a position where we could look down the mountain at the Rebs in their works and they soon started to leave. The left of our line had some heavier fighting than us as that was where the main body of Johnnies laid. It appears they were so busy watching some of our troops who were making a show of crossing [at the foot of the mountain] that they had no idea we had gone down the creek and crossed there, and when we showed up above them they got demoralized and skedaddled.

We began to pick up prisoners at every step. An officer jumped up in front of me from behind a rock. I shouted "Surrender! Hand over that toad sticker!" He gave me his sword and as I raised my gun and shouted to some Johnnies who had started to run he said, "Don't shoot, the poor fellows are tired of the war." I said "All right, I'm only giving them a bluff. Damned if my gun is loaded. I ain't had a chance to load up since I fired the first shot." I told him he had better get to the rear as his own men might shoot him.

One Johnnie surrendered to me and I noticed on his cap a shield made from a muscle [mussel] shell with his Regiment on it. I asked him to give it to me and he said "Certainly," taking it off his cap. It had "27 Miss." in red sealing wax on it.

I gave the sword to Lieut. Bonner of our company. Jack Gallagher also took one from another officer and he gave his to Capt. Goldsmith.

It was impossible to detail men to guard the prisoners. There were so many so they were ordered back to the rear to a Brigade of the 4th Corps under Genl Whitaker who were following us as a support. He detailed men to guard the prisoners to the rear and reported that his Brigade had captured 2000 prisoners. It was reported that when Genl Hooker heard this he said "I'll let them know who captured these prisoners."

We kept on and drove the Rebs around to the face of the mountain overlooking Chattanooga. Just then the sun broke out and the mist lifted and our fellows over in the valley in front of Chattanooga saw us and gave such a shout and cheers as I never heard before. As Col. Rickards, Capt. Woeltge and several others joined us we took a drink from my canteen. As there were two brass cannon planted near a white house on the plateau below us on the road leading across the mountain, and the left of our line had not swung around yet, I said to the Colonel, "Let us go down and capture them." He said no, his orders were to keep close to the palisades, that the left would soon swing around which they shortly did, and it was not long before we saw them capture the 2 guns.

We reformed our line and piled up stones & rock & branches of trees for a breastwork and laid on our arms, being troubled a good bit by the Reb sharpshooters on top of the mountain. We remained here till about 10 o'clock in the night when our Regiment was relieved by the 33rd Ohio of the 14th Corps, and we were ordered to the road half way down the mountain so as to get some coffee & hardtack and fill up our cartridge boxes. During the night the Rebs left the top of the mountain by the other side, leaving behind a lot of rations and ammunition. The troops whom we fought belonged to Walthall's Brigade, Cheatham's Division of Hardee's Corps. Our Regiment lost 3 killed and 6 wounded.

## 'Rally 'round the flag, boys!'

### Private John W. Simmons
### Company E
### 27th Mississippi Volunteer Infantry

When the Yanks advanced on us in three lines of battle, we had but one thin line and no reserve, as a good portion of the brigade had been captured early in the morning while on picket duty by Lookout Creek, where the pickets had been carrying on a friendly exchange of papers, tobacco, coffee, etc.

Walthall's Brigade extended from the perpendicular cliffs near the top down the rugged mountain side, north toward the Tennessee River; and as the ground was covered with large rocks we were afforded fair protection, except from the artillery, which played on us incessantly from Moccasin Point across the river.

As the enemy would advance and drive us from one position, we would fall back a short distance, reform, get positions behind the rocks, and give it to them again. Many of our boys were captured that day on account of our line holding its position until the enemy were so near that it was almost certain death to run. This was one of the few times in battle that it took a braver man to run than it did to stand; because those who remained behind the rocks could surrender in safety, and those who ran would draw the fire of the heavy Yankee line.

It was near the noted Craven House that our line was formed, when the blue coats crowded us and came very close before our line gave way. Just as we started to fall back, the color bearer, who had bravely carried our regimental flag through many hot places, fell dead. One of the other boys, seeing this, turned back and grasped the colors when he, too, went down and fell across the former with the color staff under him. By this time the enemy was almost upon the flag, when a gallant youth from south Mississippi turned back and running to within a few steps of the enemy's line, seized the colors, breaking the staff off short, and ran after his regiment, waving the flag and hallooing at the top of his voice. It appeared that the entire Yankee line was shooting at him, but he soon regained his regiment and, with the short flag staff in his hand, mounted a large rock and waved it as high as he could reach, at the same time calling out that old saying so familiar to soldier boys: "Rally 'round the flag, boys!" which they were very prompt to do. The boys loved that old flag better after that than ever before.

That night we were relieved by other troops and the little handful of us that was left was moved down into the valley, and there in the shadow of Lookout Mountain that dim, moonlit night, that little short flag staff was stuck in the ground, and the boys crowded around it with saddened hearts and recounted the eventful and dangerous scenes of the day, some telling where Tom, Jack or Jim

■ Private James Simmons of Company L, 27th Mississippi, escaped the battle on Lookout Mountain unscathed, but many of his comrades were not so fortunate. "The contest was for awhile terrible," wrote Lt. Col. A.J. Jones of the 27th. "But the overwhelming numbers of the enemy enabled him to flank us right and left, and it was not long until we were entirely flanked on our right and nearly so on our left, and I gave the order to fall back, but so nearly were we surrounded in our front that 6 commissioned officers of the regiment and about half of the men were captured upon the spot."

The 27th lost 166 men captured, and Simmons' company commander, Capt. John L. Boyd, fell wounded.

■ Capturing Confederate works at the Cravens House, as published in *Harper's Weekly.* An officer in Pettus' brigade, 2nd Lieut. P.A. Cribbs of Company K, 20th Alabama, recalled: "Comrade Jess Davis and I were together, when a spent ball struck him on the stomach. He fell over a log, claiming that he was shot through and declaring it was fatal. I felt for the wound and found the ball flattened and lodged next to his skin, not having entered the flesh. 'Jess, you are not hurt very badly,' said I; 'here is the ball.' He revived quickly and, jumping up, declared that the Yank should lay his gun down, for he had 'caught him out.' The bullet passed through his blanket, which was rolled and worn over the right and under the left shoulder. The bullet made seven holes in the blanket, then passed through his coat and two shirts, and left a black spot about the size of a hand on his abdomen."

had fallen and others had surrendered. Many of them showed where minie balls had cut their hats, coats or blankets. The meeting at that flag was one never to be forgotten, and many of us joined hands around it and pledged that no Yank should ever lay hands on it without passing over our dead bodies, and they never did. Strong men unused to tears, although accustomed to the cruel scenes of war, cried like children.

## 'Run the gauntlet'

### Private James E. Reynolds
### Company K
### 30th Mississippi Volunteer Infantry

We had hardly gotten located on duty before we saw the Federal army maneuvering in and around Chattanooga, evidently preparing to attack and dislodge us. But a short time elapsed until their command crossed the creek [Lookout] and bore down on us in such numbers that it was folly to resist, so the brigade was compelled to capitulate. None but those who chose death to capture dared to take life in hand and run the gauntlet in attempting to escape.

We were under Lookout Heights, and to avoid surrendering

were compelled to go back over our own abatis work under heavy cannonading, which was playing on the mountain side to cut off our retreat. Four of my comrades — Henry C. Latham, Buck Humphries, Steve and Joe Hughes — and I unhesitatingly chose the latter alternative; and we made the break for liberty, the rest surrendering — at least, we saw no others escaping. My four comrades knew of a crevice in the mountain, which they made for, and were soon safe from the rattle of musketry and exploding of shells like hail about us.

Bearing as much as possible toward the top of the hill and next to the mountain, I took up my line of retreat. While falling back toward the point of Lookout, and after being disabled from a wound in my breast, my attention was called to frequent confusion in the enemy's ranks, the colors in their advance line frequently falling back on their massed columns as they pushed forward. I was facing the enemy in my retreat, and turned around to my right to see what caused the commotion and disorder, when, to my astonishment, I beheld some one hundred and forty-eight of our men who had been on picket duty the previous night, returning to their command. On discovering the situation they had formed in line of battle and were contesting every inch of ground that the enemy, numbering twenty-five to one, were taking. I forgot all about the rattle of bullets and cannon balls plowing the ground under me, and my eyes filled with tears when I saw them mashed to the ground. I saw them plainly using the butts of their guns and bayonets as they were being crushed underfoot, and not a Confederate's back did I see turned to the enemy.

## 'As if a million demons had been aroused'

### Private Henry M. Woodson
### Company E
### 34th Mississippi Volunteer Infantry

I do not know our numerical strength, but the brigade's regiments were tolerably full, having done no fighting since Chickamauga, and in that time had been recruited. The Thirty-Fourth Mississippi numbered nearly seven hundred.

The day before the battle our company was on picket near where the Nashville & Chattanooga railroad crosses the creek. Everything was quiet, the pickets were in plain view, and neither thought of shooting without giving notice. That night about twelve o'clock the pickets were relieved, Company F taking our place. Picket posts were always relieved at night.

The next morning, November 24, about sunrise, we heard several musket shots down on the picket-line, assuring us that "friendly" relations had ceased. In a few minutes a messenger came from the picket-line, calling for two companies from our regiment. By the time those two got to the front another messenger came, calling for the balance of the regiment. When we arrived at the foot of the mountain Lieut.-Col. McElwaine [Robert P. McKelvaine, 24th Mississippi], who was in command of the pickets, deployed the entire regiment as skirmishers. Had we remained in that position, the "battle above the clouds" might have resulted very differently, because the line of pickets covered nearly all that part of the western base of the mountain, and could not have been

■ Private Valentine Delmas of Company L, 27th Mississippi, was captured on Lookout Mountain along with a majority of his company, including commander 1st Lieut. Samuel W. Johnson, who fell badly wounded. Another member of the regiment recalled that when "the firing commenced between the enemy and our pickets, [the] enemy approached rapidly our position, seeming to force everything before them as though there was no resistance. One or two unsuccessful attempts were made to rally, but the incessant shower of shell and shot from the enemy's batteries and the rush of their heavy force of infantry gave no time for doing so ..."

Delmas was sent to prison at Rock Island, Ill., until March 13, 1865, when he was exchanged. This photograph was taken shortly after his October 1861 enlistment at Pascagoula, Miss.

■ Private Robert A. Jarman of Company K, 27th Mississippi, "skedaddled" when the Federals broke through Walthall's line. "The way they swarmed and crowded up Lookout Mountain that morning against only one brigade of Confederates was a sight to see," Jarman recalled. "We were simply crushed by numbers, and it was the tallest fighting I was ever in, for during the fight it was cloudy and a dense cloud settled down over us so we could not distinguish friend from foe over twenty steps. Some of the men that escaped scaled the face of the mountain and some escaped by way of a white house on the side of the mountain, called the Craven House. I came out by the house, and jumped over two cliffs nearly twenty feet high. During the day it was said the brigade lost more than nine hundred men either killed or captured on Lookout Mountain, and among the captured was Col. [James A.] Campbell of our regiment. Next day, November 25, we joined the main army on Missionary Ridge, but we looked like a regiment more than a brigade, and a small regiment at that."

successfully assailed by the enemy, and we could at least have skirmished with them until the remainder of the brigade could have formed and been ready for the fight.

But fate, or Col. McElwaine, decreed otherwise. He must have given the command, "Rally on the right!" for in a few minutes the whole regiment was assembled near where the railroad crosses the creek and formed in columns of companies. The western face of the mountain being thus left unguarded by pickets, the enemy had nothing to do but march up and find Walthall's brigade lying around with their guns stacked and depending on the pickets to give notice of the enemy's approach.

In the meantime our regiment was at the foot of the mountain, cut off from the rest of the brigade. Col. McElwaine ordered us to fall back, which we did. We fell back slowly, as the mountain was very steep and rugged. In all my war experience I never passed through just such a bombardment. It seemed that every battery in the Federal army was pouring bomb-shells and solid shot into the side of that mountain. The shells burst, knocking off thousands of pieces of rock and scattering them hither and thither. The whole face of the mountain was lurid with bursting shells and seemed to belch smoke from every crevice, while the mountain itself seemed to howl and shriek as if a million demons had been aroused in its caverns.

Slowly climbing and struggling up through all that awful storm of iron and smoke, we at last reached our former camp, to find it literally covered with Federal troops between us and our brigade, which was in line of battle farther east. In a moment our flag was down, and the Thirty-Fourth Mississippi Regiment had surrendered. Our lieutenant and J.M. Glenn, Bud Lowe and I happened to be together. The lieutenant said, "Boys, let's get out of this!" and in an instant we turned and, amid a perfect hail-storm of bullets, leaped down over a ledge of rocks which runs eastward almost parallel with the railroad, but some distance above it, and so made our escape. Two other members of Company E got away, making five who escaped, out of about eighty.

## 'A dense fog gathered'

### Brig. Gen. John C. Moore
### Brigade commander
### Cheatham's Division, Hardee's Corps

About the 1st of November I received orders to report to Gen. Bragg in the vicinity of Chattanooga. On arrival there I reported the almost helpless state of my command on account of [having] worthless arms, and was assured the matter would be attended to at once; but it was not done, and on the following day I received orders to proceed with my command to the eastern slope of Lookout Mountain and relieve the brigade on duty at that point.

We were without tents, having been ordered to leave these in our first encampment near the foot of the mountain. Many of the men were but scantily supplied with blankets, as well as provisions, which consisted principally of rice and beans. During the three weeks we occupied this position the men were frequently exposed to a cold north wind, the ground being sometimes covered with snow. When we secured ammunition we found the cartridges either too large or too small for a number of the guns. When too small they could at least be inserted in the barrel and held in place by ramming leaves on top as wadding; but when a snugly fitting cartridge was inserted into a gun with a worthless lock spring the soldier frequently discovered it had become permanently lodged in the barrel, and some of those guns may remain loaded to this day.

This position was a greatly exposed and badly protected key to Gen. Bragg's whole line of operation. This neglect of cautionary measures can only be satisfactorily accounted for on the supposition that the commanding general never believed the Federals would make this a serious point of attack, although it was the weakest and most dangerously exposed point in his whole line of investment. That the enemy were fully aware of both the weakness and importance of the position there is not a possible doubt, because the whole line of supposed defense was exposed to their full view and within easy range of their numerous field batteries.

These remarks may seem as "I told you so" after an event has occurred, but I repeatedly expressed that opinion days before the enemy assaulted and easily carried our lines. I made complaints to the corps commander, to Gen. Bragg's headquarters, detailing the condition of our arms, want of suitable ammunition, and protesting against the policy of a command thus armed being assigned to such an important and poorly protected position. All my efforts resulted only in an unfulfilled promise that the matter would be immediately attended to, and the fatal 24th of November found us in that pitiable condition.

At Point Lookout we had a field battery which seemed designed more for moral than physical effect, since it was never known to do any practical execution against the enemy, although it occasionally produced a "moral effect" at brigade headquarters, located just below on the mountain slope, by premature explosion of shells and scattering the fragments around. Just beneath the battery at Point Lookout was a residence known as the Craven house, and, being favorably situated for observation, was made brigade headquarters, though within plain view and easy range of the Federal battery at Moccasin Point. Federal shot and shell had done much damage to this house, but we decided to trust to luck and take our chances, as it afforded much protection against the snow and cold winds that swept down the river from the north; in fact, this consideration answered as a very effective spur to our apparently reckless display of courage and disregard for Yankee shells. But the commander of the Moccasin Point battery treated us with what we chose to regard as high consideration, as he left us in undisturbed possession until the day of the assault.

My brigade picket line extended from the mouth of Chattanooga Creek to a junction with that of Walthall's brigade, stationed on the northern slope of the mountain. The ascent in the immediate rear of our picket line was very steep and rugged; in fact, almost impassable, and therefore when the assault was made our whole brigade picket force of one hundred men was captured. Possibly one or two escaped.

As previously intimated, no serious effort had been made to construct defensive works for our forces on the mountain. It is true some of the timber in front of Walthall's brigade had been cut down and a narrow, shallow, but worthless, line of trenches (unworthily called rifle pits) extended from Walthall's left to the Cra-

■ Brig. Gen. John C. Moore commanded a brigade of three Alabama regiments on Lookout Mountain, losing 251 men killed, wounded and missing out of an effective force of 1,205 taken into the battle. Only eight weeks earlier his troops were exchanged, reorganized and re-equipped following their surrender at Vicksburg. At Demopolis, Ala., "my brigade was supplied with a lot of arms and accoutrements that had been condemned as unfit for service and piled up in an outhouse near the railroad depot," Moore wrote. "I was assured that this was merely a temporary supply, that it would answer for drill and guard duty, and that we would be supplied with serviceable guns before being ordered to the field. These arms were of many different calibers. Most of them, however, had the essential parts — lock, stock and barrel — but were in bad order."

■ Brig. Gen. John K. Jackson, temporarily in command of Cheatham's division, was criticized openly by three Confederate brigade commanders for his conduct on November 24. Remaining safely atop Lookout Mountain, Jackson was accused by Gens. Walthall, Moore and Pettus of contributing nothing beyond his messages to hold their positions. Walthall reported: "At no time during this prolonged struggle ... did I have the benefit of my division commander's personal presence ... After I was relieved, and while awaiting orders to move, I saw him for the first time on his way, as he told me, to see the general-in-chief."

Moore's criticism echoed Walthall's: "I had not seen Brigadier-General Jackson during the day. He gave me no orders during the engagement. I sent a staff officer to his headquarters to inform him of our condition, but he returned and reported he could not find General Jackson, who was absent. If we had been properly supported ... I believe we could have held the trenches, even with empty guns, but that support was not given us."

ven house, and from the extremity of a short line of stone fence at this point to the mouth of Chattanooga Creek a still more abortive pretense had been made. My brigade camp was established on the mountain bench road, about midway between the Craven house and division headquarters on the mountain resort road.

Our division commander, Gen. Cheatham, was absent on leave the day of the assault, and Gen. John K. Jackson, as ranking brigadier, was in command. I had not seen the division commander [Jackson] but once from the day we arrived until late on the night I was ordered to evacuate our position and after the movement had been accomplished. Up to the hour of assault I had never received a word of instruction as to the disposition of my command or the proposed line of defense, if any had even been determined, in case of attack.

The day preceding Gen. Hooker's assault on our lines we could see from our mountain perch great activity among the Federal forces on the open plain in front of Chattanooga — large bodies of troops apparently forming in masses, deploying in single, double or treble lines of battle, etc. They also planted a battery on an "Indian mound" situated on what had been treated as neutral ground lying between the Confederate and Federal picket lines. While these movements were going on we noticed that everything seemed perfectly quiet among the Federal forces north of Lookout Creek. These conditions led me to believe that preparations were being made to attack Gen. Bragg's lines on Missionary Ridge, but subsequent events proved that the whole movement was made as a feint to mislead us as to the intended point of attack, Lookout Mountain.

The day following the evolutions of the enemy in front of Chattanooga, November 24, was very cloudy, partially obscuring the sunlight, but clear enough in the lower atmosphere to observe with field glass the conditions of the enemy. I saw that their pontoon bridges had disappeared, which was evidence that the long-continued monotony of inaction would be speedily ended. As there was no evidence at Chattanooga of an intended attack on our Missionary Ridge lines, I hastened around to the northern slope of the mountain and found that the Federals were massing their forces in Lookout Valley, a half mile away. Hastening back to headquarters, I dispatched a staff officer to the division commander, asking for orders.

In the meantime I formed my brigade in line ready to move. My messenger soon returned and reported that he could find no one at division headquarters, only four or five hundred yards distant. By this time firing had commenced on the picket lines and I sent him again, with the same result. The firing soon became very heavy. Gen. Walthall and I had consulted, as neither had instructions as to disposition of forces in case of attack. It was agreed that my left should rest at the Craven house and my line extend to the mouth of Chattanooga Creek, unless otherwise instructed by the division commander when ordered into line, and Gen. Walthall's brigade would have charge of the line to the left and beyond the Craven house. Gen. Walthall remarked that he would hold his advanced position on the north slope of the mountain till forced back, and would still contest every inch of ground, and would then make connection with my left. This resolution was worthy of that daring and gallant officer, but, knowing his greatly exposed position and the narrow passage open for the withdrawal

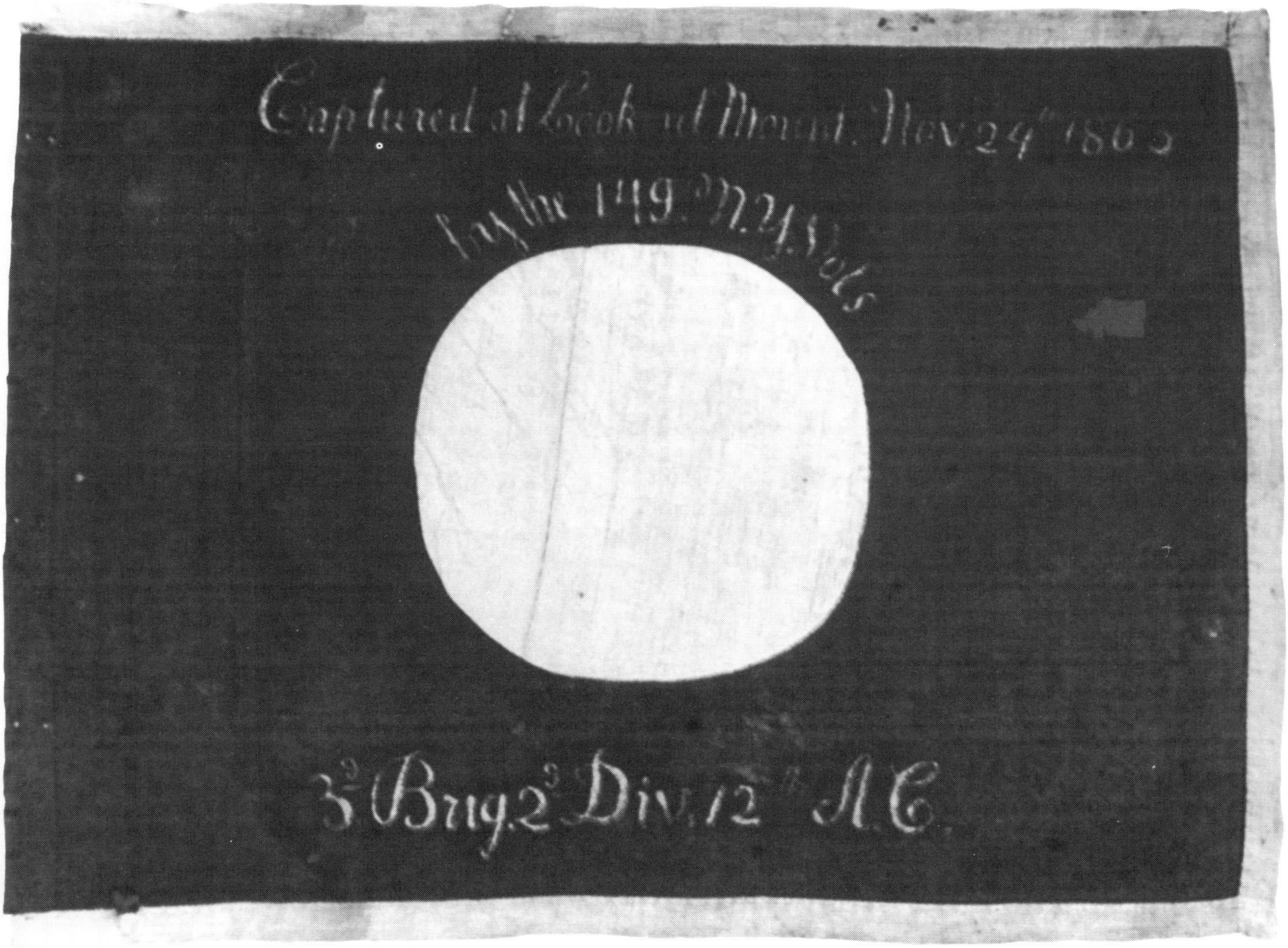


■ This Hardee-pattern battle flag belonging to an unidentified regiment of Walthall's brigade was captured on Lookout Mountain by Private Peter Kappesser of Company B, 149th New York. The German-born Kappesser rushed ahead of his regiment, tore the blue damascene silk and white cotton banner from its staff and shoved the bunting into his coat. He then ran to a wounded comrade, lifted him on his back and carried the injured man and flag back to his own ranks — actions for which he later received the Medal of Honor.

of his men, I greatly feared the daring effort might have a disastrous ending.

The firing had become very severe, both by small arms and the Federal battery on Moccasin Point and the ridge north of Lookout Creek. At this time a division staff officer dashed up, giving orders to place my men immediately in the so-called rifle pits. My brigade moved by flank at a double-quick, under heavy fire from the Moccasin Point battery. Soon after the assault began a dense fog gathered about the mountain and continued much of the day. The Federal gunners did some remarkably good guessing, however, as to about "where we were at." Just as our rear files turned out of the bench road near the Craven house we met the remnant of Walthall's brigade rushing to the rear in inextricable disorder. The officers seemed to be using every effort to arrest their flight, but the men rushed past them in spite of threats and even blows. Where or when they stopped I never learned.

Such incidents are too frequent in times of battle to be made a test of true courage, and all old soldiers experienced in war know that sometimes a body of men of well-tried and undoubted brav-

# 'Rebels behind every rock and tree'

**OPPOSITE PAGE: Troops of Geary's division climb over boulders under the north point of Lookout Mountain in this illustration taken from a painting by Capt. William L. Stork, 29th Pennsylvania. An acting aide on Geary's staff, Stork later wrote that "we were all on foot after crossing [Lookout] creek, it being impossible owing to the rough nature of the ground to ride a horse through the woods and over the rocks and felled trees. I followed, with the other members of the staff and the General, immediately behind the line of battle ..."**

**Private Robert Callahan of Company E, 29th Pennsylvania, was out in *front* of the battle line as a skirmisher. "The rebels seemed to be behind every rock and tree, and poured down lead like hail," he recalled. "But it was useless, for the boys kept them on the go and advanced without once wavering ... We clambered over rocks and tumbled into gulleys, but kept going and finally struck the last line [of rifle pits] that made a stand and scattered them like sheep, capturing hundreds and driving them to the rear, not taking the trouble to send a guard with them. Trusting to the troops behind to take care of them, we pushed on until we reached the nose of the mountain, which we found covered with a mist or fog. The rebels made a show of fighting, but most of them kept on going."**

ery become panic-stricken from really trifling causes, losing all presence of mind and self-control. These men had been placed in a dreadfully exposed position and assaulted by an overwhelming force, said to be a division and a brigade, and had lost over half their number, while there was open for possible escape but a single narrow passage. Under such circumstances who would not unhesitatingly decide "prudence to be the better part of valor." When the members of Walthall's brigade passed to the rear I had no idea that the balance had been killed or captured, but supposed them in line beyond the Craven house; but it soon became evident that such was not the case.

It was between twelve and one o'clock when we reached the trenches, and we were not a little surprised to find the enemy had preceded us at a few points; but they were not difficult to dislodge, perhaps due to the fact of having gotten a closer view of the miserable burlesque of our rifle pits they did not consider their possession worthy of a serious struggle.

By order of someone, two six-pounders had been placed at the Craven house, but were without horses, and the officer in charge abandoned them without firing a shot. When in possession of this house and vicinity the Federals were in position to enfilade the left of my line and in possession of the road leading to my rear. Why they delayed so long in taking advantage of this fact I could not understand. They pressed us very hard all along the line, while we had not one-fourth enough men to man it properly. On reaching our position, I sent messengers to the division commander, reporting the situation and asking for reinforcements, but none came.

About two o'clock they turned my left flank and opened a severe enfilade fire; and, as they were also pushing past my right flank, it became evident we must either fall back or be surrounded and captured. Orders to retire were at once given, and we reported to the division commander, again asking for reinforcements. Falling back some two or three hundred yards in good order, with line of battle well preserved, we took position along the crest of a ridge extending down the mountain slope and nearly parallel to our first line. In a short time Gen. Pettus arrived with three regiments of his brigade and formed on my left, extending his line to the base of the precipitous mountain slope at this point. In a few minutes the enemy threw a heavy force against our whole line, the most determined effort being made against Gen. Pettus' position; but that gallant officer nobly held his ground and successfully repulsed every assault made on his lines. He applied to the division commander for reinforcements, but none could be furnished.

The enemy kept up a more or less heavy fire during the day and until late at night. Our ammunition had become nearly exhausted; some men, in fact, had not a single charge. At the time we fell back my men were ordered to lie down, sheltering themselves as well as they could behind rocks, trees and fallen timber, and to reserve their fire until the enemy were near. We held our position until two o'clock that night, when I was ordered to withdraw my command, leaving out my line of pickets to conceal from the enemy our movements, and to follow the main force after its withdrawal.

We were directed to descend to Chattanooga Valley down the

■ Capt. John G. Harris of Company I, 20th Alabama. His regiment, part of Pettus' brigade, was thrown into the fighting after Walthall's decimated brigade fell back 300 yards from the Cravens House. The 20th bolstered the Confederate left closest to the mountain's bluff, and held its line well sheltered behind fog-shrouded rocks until relieved at 8 p.m. Harris, wounded two weeks before the fall of Vicksburg, was promoted to major in July 1864 and later resigned due to poor health.

mountain slope, over rocks and fallen timber. It being very dark, many a man received a stunning tumble during the descent. We crossed Chattanooga Valley, proceeded to Missionary Ridge, and were placed in line on the right of Cheatham's division. This march consumed the remainder of the night, and the reader can well imagine that we did not feel as frisky as a lot of schoolboys the following day, not even when the Federals decided to pay us another visit.

## 'Not unlike thousands of sparkling fire-flies'

**Capt. James W.A. Wright**
**Company H**
**36th Alabama Volunteer Infantry**

In the calm, bright beauty of a Sabbath morning, the 22nd [of November], all had been peaceful along our picket line just in front of the Watkins House, where was stationed the brigade of Alabamians to which my regiment, the Thirty-sixth — Gen. Henry T. Clayton's brigade — that I, then off duty, ventured for the only time during three years of active service, to exchange newspapers, by meeting a Federal officer midway between the picket lines, in this instance a lieutenant of the Tenth Illinois Infantry. Not a shot was fired near us during this brief handshaking and exchange of an Atlanta paper for a Chicago daily. But the pickets on both sides swarmed like ants from their rifle-pits to watch this impromptu walk and meeting of their two officers on neutral ground, a meeting brought on openly by the mere shaking of a newspaper, first on our side and then on theirs, and occupying scarcely ten minutes from the time each officer left his line until his safe return, for our picket lines there were only some four hundred yards apart.

But a few hours later the "long roll" called all of Bragg's troops except his reserves to their main line of trenches, immediately in front of the comparatively comfortable winter quarters which nearly every regiment had just finished out of pine slabs and oak clapboards, cut by our men in the neighboring woods. Sunday and Monday night we slept in the trenches to be ready for any emergency. Occasionally shells howled over us and some fell near our lines, without casualties, from Moccasin Point, Fort Wood and other Federal batteries.

Tuesday morning, November 24, broke upon our bivouac, cloudy overhead and foggy upon the surrounding mountains. Clouds and rolling mists obscured, like a white fleecy curtain, the upper three or four hundred feet of Lookout Mountain. Shells fell at intervals. An ominous silence reigned along the entire lines, unbroken till about 11 a.m. Then the heavy booming of artillery came from beyond Lookout and all eyes turned in that direction.

Our position at the Watkins House, midway across Chattanooga Valley, gave us a full view of the eastern and northern slopes of Lookout, including the Craven House and Bragg's line of intrenchments and picket-pits on the broad sloping terrace. About noon the sharp and continuous rattle of rifles was heard along those lofty slopes, and as the clouds and mists began to rise and sway to and fro we saw, all at once, through the rifts of this rolling curtain, a long narrow line of infantry moving steadily toward the mountain breastworks, now hidden by the changing mists, now fully exposed to view again. Occasionally the smoke of their own volleys would mingle with the surrounding mists.

General A.P. Stewart, who commanded our division, and Colonel J.T. Holtzclaw (afterward brigadier general), who was in command of our brigade in the temporary absence of General Clayton, and a party of their officers stood, field-glass in hand, watching with deep interest and astonishment this evident attack in heavy force along a line deemed so nearly impregnable that earthworks there seemed almost unnecessary. Suddenly, as a cloud rolled away, we saw our line of breastworks swarming with men for nearly half a mile and flags waving there. "What flag is that?" was asked. "Try the field-glass. There, it is plain enough: It is the Stars and Stripes!"

General Pettus, as soon as he was informed of the disaster, moved his two nearest regiments — one of them the Twentieth Alabama — at a double-quick to Walthall's relief. A strong position was then taken by the two brigades along a craggy spur, extending eastward from the base of the palisades. Here a sharp fusillade of rifles was maintained between the hostile lines till about ten o'clock at night. Late in the afternoon our (Clayton's) brigade was marched from the trenches across Chattanooga Creek by the bridge on the road from Rossville to Lookout, and, losing a few men by shell fire from Moccasin Point batteries as we were crossing the deep ravine, we relieved Pettus' and Walthall's wearied men about dusk, and together with Moore's brigade held their rocky ramparts till after midnight. The Thirty-sixth Alabama, my regiment, relieved our neighbors of the Twentieth Alabama, our left extending as their had done to the very base of the palisades. The right of our brigade connected with the left of Stevenson's division. Here we maintained a lively fire with the enemy's advance till after nine o'clock, losing some men even by the random shots in the darkness.

Friends who remained in the valley informed us next day that the rifle flashes at night along the waving lines of attack and defense, which extended eastward half a mile or more down the mountain slope from the palisades, presented a curious and beautiful sight, not unlike thousands of sparkling fire-flies on a midsummer's night. We were not, you may well suppose, in a position just then to appreciate such picturesque beauty. It was not safe to have fires, although after midnight it was cold, clear and frosty. Our position would have been revealed by fires, and a heavier fire would have been drawn to us.

A narrow escape from death by a ramrod deserves a record here as a real incident of this night on the slopes of Lookout. In the midst of a somewhat broken rifle firing, I heard an odd thud and a twang near me. I put out my hand in the darkness and, feeling around, found an iron ramrod vibrating there with its small end set firmly in a tree, evidently shot there by some Federal who had loaded too hastily.

The moon was full and in a partial eclipse at 3 a.m., when under orders our troops silently withdrew from the last line of defense on Lookout Mountain. A grim sight greeted the eyes of some of us as we left that rocky ridge in the dead of night. In the open ravine some of our poor fellows lay stark and cold, one with arms outstretched. Those pallid faces, those staring eyes, upturned to the bright moon, how startlingly distinct! No time to bury them,

# 'Unable to depress my guns'

**Seven hours before the Federal attack at Lookout Mountain, gunners of Capt. Max Van Den Corput's Cherokee (Georgia) Battery rolled two 12-pounder Napoleons to the summit's northern edge, barrels pointing west. Corput described his battery's role in the ensuing battle:**

About 10 a.m. the fog on the side of Lookout Creek had disappeared enough to show us the Federals moving in three different bodies from the foot of Raccoon Mountain toward Lookout Creek. The pickets had been firing from about sunrise toward the creek. We could hear very distinctly cutting of timber in the valley, but presuming that the pickets would give notice of any work going on on the side of the Federals, I took no notice of it.

The longest fuse that I had with my guns was 7, which time would carry my shells only 1 mile. The position of the Federals being far over that distance, I did not open fire on them then. After their first charge on our infantry — who instantly gave way, the enemy pursuing them — I opened fire on the Federals, having brought my section in position on the left of the mountain. I fired 33 shells, doing in many instances good execution. The Federals were, however, soon under cover of the rocks, [and I was] unable to depress my guns enough. The fog during all that time was very dense on the right and in front of the point. When the enemy made their charge I discovered two places over the creek where they had made bridges by cutting timber, which answered for the cutting that I heard in the morning.

At about 2 p.m. General Brown gave me orders to fire toward the Craven house if I could ascertain the direction, the enemy being reported in force in that direction. I obtained from the signal corps the position of the house, and fired about thirty times at intervals in that direction and toward the right. In the opinion of General Brown, then present, and according to my own judgment, I believe I did some good firing.

■ Col. William Grose, 36th Indiana, commanded a six-regiment brigade in the 1st Division, IV Corps, and was attached temporarily to Hooker's command at Lookout Mountain. At daylight November 24, Grose was ordered personally by Hooker to effect a crossing of Lookout Creek at a destroyed bridge near the railroad. "I immediately went forward in advance of the troops to make observations and learn the position," Grose wrote, "and found the enemy's pickets on the east bank and ours on the west, within 30 paces of each other, enjoying a friendship which was soon after broken and turned into wrath upon the approach of my forces."

By nightfall, "all my regiments had been in the front line during this engagement. The ground in front of the center of the line, in and about the white [Cravens] house, was the common stock of the skirmishers of all the commands engaged ... Our advancing lines completely enfiladed most of the enemy's works, which were poorly adapted to the defense of the position."

no time for weary men to bear bodies with them over the rugged rocky trail. It was all we could do to look after our wounded. How often since has that vivid scene come up in memory unbidden, as a type of utter desolation and loneliness, of death upon the battlefield.

## 'Principally Indian fighting'

### Private Elisha C. Lucas
### Company E
### 8th Kentucky Volunteer Infantry

Early on the morning of the 24th of November, our brigade [Whitaker's] moved up Lookout Valley into a dense forest where the enemy lost sight of us for a few hours. In the forest we piled our knapsacks, blankets and part of our rations, and left them under guard. We filed off to the left, crossed Lookout Creek on an old mill-dam, and commenced the difficult task of ascending the mountain through a thicket of cedars. Up, still up, meeting with no opposition except inanimate nature, pulling up by shrubs and projecting rocks. At last we reached the inaccessible walls of limestone, a perfect palisade several hundred feet high. This movement was still unobserved by the enemy, who were expecting us to attack them in front.

We faced north, the 8th Kentucky forming the extreme right wing of the [second] line. A heavy skirmish line was put forward. We moved forward, keeping well up with our skirmishers. Thus we swept along the steep, rugged mountain side over huge rocks, fallen trees and deep ravines, regardless of the scattering shot sent at us from the mountain top.

A heavy fog that hovered over the mountain enabled us to attack the enemy by surprise in the flank and rear of their works. Their evident confusion was so great that they made but a feeble, unorganized resistance — their defense being principally Indian fighting from behind trees and large rocks. We gleaned a large harvest of prisoners. Those of the enemy that were not captured fled around the nose of the mountain and took a strong position on the southeastern slope, just under a towering cliff. About this time two of our heavy guns on Moccasin Point opened fire, and were replied to by those of the enemy on the point of Lookout, almost immediately over our heads.

By this time, 3 p.m., a dense cloud enveloped the mountain. The enemy made a determined stand, as they were strongly reinforced in their fortified position. A good many of the 8th having been sent back to Lookout Valley, in charge of prisoners, we were left in reserve at the nose of the mountain. Being near the wall or palisade, the enemy not only shot at us whenever the cloud would lift, so as to enable them to see, but resorted to an awful mode of warfare — rolling down loose stones at us. Under cover of the fog a few of our sharpshooters, concealed behind trees and large stones, soon picked off every Johnny that dared show his head on the top of the cliff. Though their ordnance made a terrific noise, their heavy missiles passed harmlessly over our heads as their pieces could not be depressed to a sufficient angle to reach us.

B.F. Wood, an excellent shot, succeeded in silencing a particularly annoying sharpshooter who had secreted himself in a niche of the irregular crown of the precipice. The rapidity of his shots were only accounted for by his comrades behind loading for him. Ben maneuvered until he obtained a view of the annoying rebel's head. As the fog lifted from the mountain Ben's unerring rifle cracked. The rebel sharpshooter sprang forward and fell on the edge of a rock 20 feet below. His hat, with a bullet hole in it, came to the base of the cliff. Ben laid there a long while, but no other daring rebel showed his head at that point.

During the evening, and to a late hour of the night, a heavy battle was fought almost under our feet. Our forces succeeded in driving the enemy around the mountain to the Summertown road. Four of the 8th were wounded by balls, and several injured by rocks rolled at us from above. None were dangerous wounds.

## 'Fighting with the waker party'

### Sergeant Amos H. Miller
### Company B
### 13th Illinois Volunteer Infantry

Our division (General Osterhaus) was assigned to the left of the line along Lookout Creek. Here two batteries and a section of twenty-pounder Parrott guns were placed, so as to reach the enemy's works and camp on the mountain side. These batteries were hauled into their position by hand. The Thirteenth Illinois and Fourth Iowa, old and tried friends, were thrown together in support of the Fourth Ohio Battery, and the Twenty-fifth Iowa was in support of the New York battery [Battery I, 1st New York Light Artillery]. These were special details on the part of General Osterhaus; the Fourth Ohio always wanted the Thirteenth to support it if possible.

At 7:30 a.m. the division was reported all ready for duty. Our brigade was commanded by Gen. Charles R. Woods. He was soon ordered with all the brigade except our regiment to move to the right, and we did not get together again till the next day.

At 11 a.m. General Geary had commenced to move along the mountain side toward the point. Then all of our guns were opened and our skirmishers moved down the creek. The enemy were driven from the railroad embankment, and most of the pickets near the creek laid down in their pits ready to surrender as soon as our lines had gotten fairly to their rear.

Just after the artillery had opened, General Osterhaus rode up to the rear of our regiment on his bay bobtail horse, with the cape of his coat thrown back over his shoulders revealing a scarlet lining. One of the rebel pickets who saw him said, "Say, Yank, is that old U.S. [a reference to Gen. U.S. Grant] sitting on that horse yonder?" The nearest picket told him that he was right. It had been an understanding between the men who picketed on opposite sides of the creek, not three rods wide but deep, that they were not to fire at each other unless there was a battle on. When the battle opened, it was so one-sided at this point that the pickets were all captured before they got in a shot.

Just to the right of where our regiment was stationed supporting the battery, the wagon road ran along the creek for some rods, then crossed the creek and thence up the side of the mountain on the way to Chattanooga. Companies A and B of the regiment were

■ Col. Henry A. Barnum commanded the 149th New York at Lookout Mountain where he was wounded. His successor, Lt. Col. Charles B. Randall, reported: "Colonel Barnum, who had been previously unfit for duty, and was still scarcely able to march with the regiment from the effects of wounds [suffered in Virginia in 1862] yet unhealed, feeling unwilling that the regiment should go out to battle leaving him behind, had accompanied us and been in command of the regiment up to this time. While struggling forward greatly exhausted, a great portion of the time in front of the line inciting the men ... he received a musket ball through the right fore-arm, inflicting a severe wound, which, with his previous exhaustion and fatigue, totally disabled him from proceeding farther."

Barnum received the Medal of Honor for his action on November 24, as did Color Sergeant John Kiggins, 1st Sergeant Norman F. Potter (Company E) and Private Peter Kappesser (Company B). A fifth recipient, Private Philip Goettel (Company B), captured a flag and battery guidon three days later at Ringgold.

# 'The flag that gets there first'

**Near 8 o'clock on the morning of November 25, thousands of eyes focused on the northern nose of Lookout Mountain. Floating from the pinnacle of bare rock was the United States national colors. Waves of resounding cheers immediately erupted through the Federal lines.**

**Union veterans debated for years just who planted the first flag atop Lookout Mountain, but official credit was given to six soldiers of the 8th Kentucky Infantry — part of the IV Corps brigade commanded by Brig. Gen. Walter C. Whitaker. Capt. John Wilson, Company C commander who was in charge of the scaling party, later described the celebrated event:**

We were placed in one of the columns on the extreme right that marched around the palisades of Lookout Mountain on the 24th of November. We marched around to the nose or point of the mountain and lay that night above the Craven House. Just before daylight on the 25th, Gen. Whitaker came to our regiment and said [to Col. Sidney M. Barnes]:

"Col. Barnes, have you an officer that will volunteer to carry your flag and place it on the top of the mountain?"

I said, "General, I will go."

Turning to the regiment, he said: "How many of you will go with Capt. Wilson? I could order you up there, but will not, for it is a hazardous undertaking; but for

cautiously upward, clutching at rocks and bushes, supporting each other, using sticks and poles and such other aids as we could gather. At every step we expected to be greeted with deadly missiles of some sort from the enemy. But fortune favored us, and before sun-up I, in front, reached the summit and planted the flag on top of Lookout Mountain. It was the highest flag that was planted during the war. Soon other detachments came up and congratulated me and my party, and we were the lions of the day in the Union army.

**Shortly afterward, Wilson and his men were granted a special 30-day furlough by Gen. Thomas for their "gallant and heroic conduct." They also reenacted their feat for photographer Royan M. Linn. On the facing page, Wilson waves his slouch hat at the camera while the accompanying riflemen ascend the mountain's rocky face aided by scaling ladders. The lowest soldier, Sergeant Wagers, wears a rubber poncho.**

**At left, Wilson again doffs his hat while grasping the 8th Kentucky's silk colors, recently presented to the regiment by the ladies of Irvine, Estill County. Posing with Wilson are, from left, Wagers, Bradley, Davis, Witt and Wood.**

**Another soldier of Whitaker's brigade, Sergeant Charles A. Partridge of Company C, 96th Illinois, explained after the war why the Kentuckians were chosen for the honor over his own regiment: "[It was] state pride — Gen. Whitaker being a Kentuckian — and the fact that the 8th Ky. had a new and showy stand of colors ... while the flag of the 96th was hardly more than a pole, the staff being splintered by Chickamauga bullets and the silk torn from it in handfuls by the storm [of lead]."**

the flag that gets there first it will be an honor."

Five men went with me. I handed my sword to my Color-Sergeant to bring up, and I took the flag and started, accompanied by Sergeant James Wood, Company H; Private William Witt, Company A; Sergeant Harris H. Davis, Company E; Sergeant Joseph Wagers, Company B; and Private Joseph Bradley, Company I.

Those who have seen the awe-inspiring precipice at the top of the great mountain can realize what a serious undertaking was before us, not to mention our lack of knowledge concerning the Confederates, who the day before had held Hooker at bay. Dim daylight was dawning. We crept

■ Brig. Gen. Peter J. Osterhaus' 1st Division, XV Corps, was attached to Hooker's command at Lookout Mountain on November 24. Early that afternoon Osterhaus reached the Cravens House, which he called "the key to the whole Lookout, commanding alike its eastern and western declivities." With the 31st Iowa, and 3rd and 27th Missouri, he relieved troops of Geary's division who had exhausted their ammunition and momentarily were expecting a counterattack. "This had hardly been done," Osterhaus wrote, "when the rebels charged with great vehemence and attempted to regain the numerous intrenchments they had thrown up all around the white house. They were, however, signally repulsed and my regiments held this very important position during the following night."

pushed still closer toward the point where the road crossed the creek. This was in full sight of the rebel lines, but they were now so taken up with Generals Geary and Woods on their flank that they turned to them and did not fire at us at all, though we expected to receive their best respects in the shape of lead.

We then moved down to the bridge that had broken down, and under the direction of Major Douglas R. Bushnell of our regiment, set to work to construct a floating bridge out of the timbers. As soon as this was done, the prisoners in large numbers were brought over under charge of the Ninth Iowa, which had been detailed for that purpose.

While Major Bushnell was standing on the elevated roadside, an Irish lieutenant among the prisoners sang out, "How d'ye do, Major Bushnell?" After a sharp glance the Major recognized the man and in turn said, "Why Pat, what are you doing here?" The quick reply was, "Be jabbers, I am fighting with the waker party." The Major further asked, "Where is your brother John?" The answer was, "You fellows killed him down at Vicksburg."

Major Bushnell had been the surveyor in laying out the Northwestern Railroad in Whiteside County, Illinois, and the two Irish brothers had had the contract for grading the depot grounds at Sterling, Illinois. When the war broke out it found them in like occupation down in Mississippi. Being wide-awake fellows they made the most of the situation by accepting commissions in the Confederate army, perhaps caring little on which side they took arms, maybe having enough of the chivalrous in them to prefer to fight, if at all, "with the weaker party."

Pat went off to the rear while the gallant Major met his death just three days later.*

Later our regiment and the Fourth Iowa were ordered across the creek and up the wagon road over the mountain. General Geary had gotten possession of the point of the mountain at what is known as "Craven House." He then came down and led our two regiments up the mountain as reinforcements. He was a fine man, and walked up the mountain at our head gauging our strength by his own.

As we got up to the nose of the mountain it was almost dark. The mountain was in a dense fog. We soon passed through the works that the enemy had erected and past the two guns that had been captured. I saw one of our men standing on one knee as if about to shoot. That is probably what he had been in the act of doing when he was struck dead instantly, and all his muscles had become rigid and he remained in that position.

Our regiment moved into line as a support for the front line. We lost no men, though the missiles flew thick and the danger was great. I saw one of our musicians from Company D struck on the side of the head by a ball that had first struck a rock, and go down as if he were dead; but he was only stunned and had the tip of his ear cut off, and was on his feet again.

The thermometer began to go down and soon the weather was near the freezing point. As all of the men were wet, it made it hard to bear. The men made small fires behind some of the big rocks scattered over the mountain side and sought small comfort.

* Bushnell was shot through the head and killed on November 27 at Ringgold, Ga.

■ Tattered national and regimental colors of the 111th Pennsylvania, photographed in Pittsburgh before their retirement during veteran furlough late in 1863.

# 'We began to think about planting flags'

About the same time the 8th Kentucky scaling party climbed to Lookout Point, three soldiers from the 111th Pennsylvania decided to reach the mountain top on their own accord.

"The troops in the immediate front of Geary's Division were the 20th and 36th Alabama," wrote Orderly Sergeant Sheldon M. Moore of Company F. "They kept up a continuous firing until about 1 o'clock at night, when they apparently received orders to evacuate the position. The troops on the crest of Lookout left first, and by 2 o'clock in the morning there were no Confederates left on the mountain."

To make certain, Moore's three comrades began their ascent at dawn. "There were two approaches to the top of the mountain," recalled Sergeant Major Logan J. Dyke, "one at the nose or point, and the other around where we were encamped, under the bluff at a spring where the rebels came down for water. At this point a rude ladder of two poles, about 30 feet in length, with strips fastened on them for rungs, was the means of communication from the top to the spring.

"Just as day began to break, and long before the sun was up, not having heard any shots from above for some time, some of us decided to attempt a passage up that ladder. Sergeant Michael Gorman of Company F started up first, Private Guy [Frank Guy of Company E] second, and I was the third. We three passed up and on to the top of the mountain, at which time not a living soul was to be seen; but away in the distance, some 40 or 50 rods, were some tents still standing, and for these we went. After investigating the condition of the deserted camp, finding everything removed but a few old tents, we started to return, and as we did so espied Capt. Wilson coming up the point of the mountain with his flag. We then began to think about planting flags, and our own and other flags of our division we immediately brought up."

Of the three Pennsylvanians, two became casualties eight months later in the battle of Peachtree Creek, Ga. Gorman was killed, while Dyke lost an arm.

■ Capt. William L. Stork of Company I, 29th Pennsylvania, acted as aide-de-camp on Geary's staff during the battle. At daylight on November 25 he saw the 8th Kentucky's colors flying above Lookout's palisades, when he was ordered on a similar mission. Stork later wrote: "Gen. Geary turned to me and said, 'Captain, take our division flag and hurry up and plant it on the top.' Hastily calling an orderly and ordering him to bring the flag, I soon scaled the rocks and had our division flag waving on the same spot where I had first seen the Stars and Stripes."

As the enemy still had possession of the top of the mountain and could look down upon our lines, some few of the men were wounded near the fires by sharpshooters in the earlier part of the night.

Lieutenant Cuniffe of Company I of our regiment had been back to one of these fires. He was absent-minded and on his way back to the lines of the regiment, missed his way and walked over into the enemy's lines. It is said he looked up, and seeing a lot of the rebels about a fire, said, "What are you fellows doing here without being guarded?" They replied, "We will do the guarding," and they took possession of the young man. It is certain we never saw him with the regiment again.

## 'A dreary spot for a man to bleach his bones'

### Private Henry Gage
### Company G
### 96th Illinois Volunteer Infantry

On the 23rd we left camp at Shellmound and marched till ten o'clock and camped close to our cavalry pickets. That night there was a meeting of the generals, and General Whitaker said his brigade could just take that "little spur." Early the next morning we crossed Lookout Creek and pushed by the reb flank straight toward the summit.

Lookout is a long mountain, rocky and steep. The summit is capped with an insurmountable ledge of rocks that terminates at a point directly above the river. We were supposed to push forward to this ledge, then left face and march by the front of the mountain in battle line, then just pass clear of the mountainside until we passed the peak or "spur," then come up on the other side of the mountain, and then scale to the top.

Our brigade had the peak of the mountain for its part. We commenced four or more miles back and had a long ways to march and climb over rocks and fallen trees. The uncomfortable firing of our forward lines steadily drove the rebs from the first. We had the advantage after we once started driving them. Lots of the rascals hid in fissures in the rocks. They threw out their guns and waited for us, and then would throw up their hats and surrender. Some would sing out, "I say, Yanks, is it honorable?" If they were satisfied they would halloo to some comrade that "it's all right — come ahead." They came if they had a chance; some were shot by their own men, but most of them came safely. It was a dreary old spot for a man to have to bleach his bones. Few true blue lie there, but plenty of graybacks will miss being found.

We got to the point of the mountain and almost to a "fort" with two cannons. Our regiment was at the extreme right of the brigade, nearest the ledge. We could look right down on the entire force as the trees were all felled where we were. The 40th Ohio was opposite the hottest fighting. The rebs and the Ohio boys started for the fort, all crowded together. The Ohio boys were having a gay time, but could not follow the rebs because the rest of the brigade had stopped. This allowed the rebs to fire into the Ohioans from the cover of the breastworks.

From where we were we could see what was going on and knew what had to be done. Our right swung about and some other colonel than ours, who was on the left and could not tell what was up, ordered us back. However, our major sang out, "Forward 96th!" The other colonel swore and again ordered us to keep our place, but our Major Hicks sang out again "Forward 96th!" as if nothing had happened. We legged it down the hill keeping a good line as the nature of the rocks would permit. We astonished the rebels by a neat cross-fire that cut them up splendidly. Some of the rebels were close to the breastworks but we could rake them there, too. They threw down their arms and what was left of them surrendered. Some cut for the rear of their lines, some struck for the woods, and others down the hill only to get peppered by our forces on the left of the 40th Ohio. By this little operation we gained the fort, the cannon and ground, etc.

After we took the fort we advanced some ways, got to the edge of a ravine and stopped for the night. The rebels made some effort to charge us, but gave it up. Late in the night we were relieved and put on picket. About 2 a.m. an eclipse darkened the night so that firing ceased. Before daybreak, the brigade started to scale the wall. The 8th Kentucky of our brigade swung the first flag over the "spur" and old Whitaker was close behind to swing his hat. The boys yell some when they make a successful charge. The noise that rose from that side of the mountain was as artillery is to small arms. Now that we had the mountain, our regiment and the 8th Kentucky were given the honor of holding it, and the rest of the brigade went on.

■ Col. Thomas E. Champion commanded the 96th Illinois. After his regiment's fight on Lookout Mountain, Champion and Col. Sidney M. Barnes, 8th Kentucky, were chosen to garrison the peak which they held until December 2. Brig. Gen. Charles Cruft reported that "orders were received from Major-General Hooker [for] two regiments to be placed upon the point of the mountain, with instructions to intrench themselves and hold it at all hazards. These regiments were also further instructed to make proper details to explore the late battle-field, bury the dead and collect and secure all abandoned arms and property ..."

# CHAPTER 7

# Every effort was made to reach the enemy's works

## Tunnel Hill: Withering Confederate fire stymies Sherman's veterans

As fog and mist shrouded the fighting on Lookout Mountain, Sherman's troops on the Federal left hastily dug rifle pits and trenches on a series of small hills opposite the north end of Missionary Ridge. Their presence on the south bank of the Tennessee River early on November 24 completely surprised Bragg, who suddenly found his right flank jeopardized and his supply base at Chickamauga Station in danger. To complicate matters, he had just sent two more divisions by rail to aid Longstreet at Knoxville. One of these under Maj. Gen. Patrick R. Cleburne immediately was recalled, and by day's end was entrenched on the Confederate flank to oppose the new threat.

Sixty days earlier, Sherman's Vicksburg veterans marched east to reinforce the Army of the Cumberland via the overland route from Memphis through Tennessee, Mississippi and Alabama, taking nearly a month and a half. Along the way the Memphis & Charleston Railroad had to be repaired to keep supplies flowing, but the necessary work slowed forward progress. "The rebel cavalry, well led, active and bold, were scouring the whole region bordering the railroad between Memphis and Tuscumbia," wrote Capt. Henry S. Nourse of Company H, 55th Illinois. "The population left in this territory was for the most part bitterly hostile, and the problem of keeping over one hundred miles of track in good working order was a serious one indeed. Not only had every bridge and culvert to be carefully watched and protected, but single rails were often removed at night and concealed. Trains were therefore compelled to utilize daylight only, and to run slowly at that.

"By a singular accident," Nourse continued, "the regiment temporarily lost its colors during this trip. The flag, carelessly displayed on the top of the car, got caught in an overhanging telegraph wire, and was torn from the color-bearer's grasp. Fortunately it was recovered and forwarded to us the next morning."

**The journey was not without its dangers, as Sherman himself discovered on October 11. A special train taking him from Memphis to Corinth, Miss., came to a halt at Collierville, Tenn., when gunfire erupted around the station. Raiding Confederate cavalry gave Sherman and his escort a few tense hours, delaying their arrival in Corinth by a day.**

## 'I wanted some of the plunder'

### 1st Lieut. James Dinkins<br>Aide-de-camp<br>Chalmers' Division, Forrest's Cavalry Corps

We remained a few hours at Holly Springs[Miss., on October 10], then marched to Collierville. Major Mitchell [W.R. Mitchell, 18th Mississippi Battalion], with two companies of Major Chalmers' battalion [Alexander H. Chalmers, 18th Mississippi Battalion], was sent to cut the railroad east of Collierville, and Major Cousins [William H. Couzens], of the Second Missouri, with two companies, was ordered to do the same on the west side, to prevent any reinforcements from reaching the garrison.

We arrived within two miles of the station about daylight. Our advance guard captured the Yankee outpost and, as soon as the prisoners were turned over, made a dash at the inner guards who, however, discovered our men in time to escape and give the alarm. We moved forward at a gallop. Colonel McGuirk [John McGuirk, 3rd Mississippi State Cavalry], with the Third Mississippi, was ordered to go in the rear of the fort and attack from that point, while the balance of the command would advance from the south. McGuirk reached his place promptly and found that two Illinois regiments, Sixth and Seventh [Cavalry], had gone, leaving a lot of dismounted men in camp. These dismounted men, about one hundred, ran in every direction. It was just after daylight and the attack was a perfect surprise to them. Some of McGuirk's men began to chase the fugitives on foot, while others dismounted and began to go through the tents.

General Chalmers' plan was for McGuirk to charge the rear of the fort simultaneously with his attack in front. We formed line and moved through the woods to a point about four hundred yards from the fort, and waited for McGuirk. Our skirmish line was hotly engaged; the enemy, using artillery, threw shells high above and beyond us. General Chalmers, growing impatient, sent Lieutenant Banks [George T. Banks, staff officer] to order the Third Mississippi to the attack.

A moment afterward, a long train of freight cars rolled into the station from Memphis, from which the Thirteenth Regulars disembarked and ran into the fort. We knew, of course, that Major Cousins had failed to cut the road on the west as ordered, otherwise the train could not have passed him. General Chalmers knew that any further delay would be ruinous and, therefore, gave the order to charge. Our men moved forward in fine style, but were met by a hot fire. They charged within about sixty yards of the fort. We could see nothing of the enemy except the tops of their heads. General Chalmers saw it would be a great sacrifice to storm the fort and, therefore, withdrew under cover of the woods.

General Chalmers' plans were well laid, and had McGuirk

■ Brig. Gen. James R. Chalmers' Confederate cavalry ran into unexpected opposition at Collierville when a train carrying Sherman, his staff and a battalion of U.S. Regulars arrived, just as they attacked a nearby fort and cavalry camp. "The delay occasioned by the pursuit of the cavalry, who fled to [a] swamp, and in collecting the stragglers who were led from the ranks by the rich booty of the camp, was so great that the opportunity to take the town was lost," Chalmers reported. "Our artillery, which was principally directed against the fort and depot, was badly served and failed to do them any material injury."

Still, his troopers greatly damaged Sherman's train, and Chalmers claimed capture of 135 Federal soldiers, 13 wagons and a number of horses and mules. Thirty wagons, 200 tents and other quartermaster stores belonging to the 6th and 7th Illinois Cavalry were burned.

■ Lt. Col. Charles Ewing, XV Corps' assistant inspector general, served as a captain in the 13th U.S. Infantry before appointment to his foster brother's staff. Accompanying Sherman at Collierville, Ewing took refuge with the general and other staff members in the depot, leaving their personal baggage aboard the cars when Chalmers' troopers attacked. Wrote Private James P. Young of Company A, 7th Tennessee Cavalry: "Receiving orders to burn the train, the charge was again ordered, and the regiment sprung forward, recaptured the train and burned two cars, using the shirts of Gen. Sherman and his staff for kindling the fire. The other cars could not be fired for want of combustibles. Having accomplished this object right under the walls of the depot, which had been loop-holed and fortified, the regiment withdrew. The Confederates, being unaware that the famous Federal commander was concealed in the depot building, turned their artillery mainly upon the fort, thus enabling him to escape, as they could easily have blown the little depot into the air."

In April 1864 Ewing was promoted to assistant inspector general of the Military Division of the Mississippi. In this portrait he wears the Division headquarters medal designed in 1865.

charged the fort before the arrival of the Thirteenth Regulars, instead of halting in the cavalry camp, the garrison would, unquestionably, have been captured. Or had Major Cousins cut the road, as ordered, the Thirteenth Regulars could not have reinforced the garrison, and in that event we would have captured it.

After the line had fallen back and was resting in the woods, I was sent to find Lieutenant Banks and Major McGuirk. Arriving at the point where the rear of the train rested, I noticed a number of our men in the cars throwing out saddles, bridles, blankets and bundles. I dismounted, hitched my horse to a telegraph pole and boarded the coach at the end of the train. I wanted some of the plunder. The coach was empty, but on the seat was a handsome sword which I picked up. I ran out to where the men were busy getting saddles. In one of the cars were several horses. It had not occurred to the men that the horses could be gotten out. I said, "Make them jump out," and with that I pulled myself into the car, untied a fine horse and led him to the door. After much urging the horse jumped out. It did not require much time for the boys to get the others out. With their plunder, they all galloped off to catch the command which had retired about a mile back, where the general waited in vain for the Federals to follow.

Through the baggage taken from the cars, we discovered that General Sherman and staff were passengers on the train. We captured all their personal baggage. The sword which I found had the name of "Lieut.-Col. Ewing, Gen. Sherman's Staff" on the cover. It was a very handsome one. The horse which I captured was also a fine animal, and most likely was the one ridden by General Sherman. I was very proud of this horse, but my pride of ownership was short lived, for the general ordered the quartermaster to take charge of him, as well as the others captured.

As soon as we ascertained that General Sherman was in the fort, the failure was doubly regretted. Burton, one of my negroes, named the captured horse "Sherman," and often said his "marster captured Old Sherman."

## 'Who had the cake?'

### Capt. William L. Jenney
### Engineer officer
### Staff of Gen. W.T. Sherman

General Grant ordered General Sherman to report with his army with the greatest possible haste at Chattanooga. Sherman embarked on boats and landed at Memphis, where the march began. As the railroads were fully occupied in carrying supplies, the troops were forced to go on foot.

Sherman had a special train to take himself, staff and escort to Corinth. Just as we were leaving Memphis a German, with a large cheese box in his hands, appeared at the train, inquiring for Captain Jenney. I announced myself and asked him what he wished. "Oh, Captain, I told my wife what you had done for me, and she sent you this cake. Take it."

"What did I do for you?" I asked. "I don't remember anything."

"Yes, you did, here is the cake."

Just at this moment the train started. About noon we made

# 'The most enterprising of all in their army'

As Sherman's dusty, footsore veterans neared the midway point of their march to Chattanooga, gunfire echoed through the hills west of Tuscumbia, Ala. Five thousand Confederate cavalry and state troops from Mississippi and Alabama temporarily halted the leading Federal column, which returned the fire and held its attackers at bay. For six days the Federals were confronted by a skillful defense of Tuscumbia that delayed Sherman's entry until October 27.

The Confederates were led by Maj. Gen. Stephen Dill Lee (above), a 30-year-old South Carolinian who took command of the cavalry in Mississippi only two months before — and just six weeks after his capture at Vicksburg. In 1861, Lee was one of three men who called on Major Robert Anderson to demand the surrender of Fort Sumter. The following year he commanded an artillery battalion under Hood at Antietam. And in 1864, again under Hood, he commanded a corps at Atlanta, Franklin and Nashville, where he was wounded while protecting the Army of Tennessee's rear in its December retreat.

Sherman greatly respected Lee's military prowess at Vicksburg, calling him "the most enterprising [general] of all in their army." A month before the clash at Tuscumbia, Sherman wrote to Washington about his adversary's new command: "This class of men must all be killed or employed by us before we can hope for peace ... I have two brigades of these fellows to my front ... Stephen D. Lee in command of the whole ... Am inclined to think when the resources of their country are exhausted we must employ them. They are the best cavalry in the world ..."

■ Private Samuel M. McAnnally of Company I, 6th Illinois Cavalry. Detachments of this regiment and the 7th Illinois Cavalry reinforced Collierville, which was manned principally by 240 men under Col. DeWitt C. Anthony, 66th Indiana. Anthony's losses on October 11 were four killed, 15 wounded and 41 missing — exactly one-fourth of his six companies' effective force. Immediately after Chalmers' troopers left Collierville, Capt. Elijah T. Phillips, commanding the 6th Illinois Cavalry, telegraphed his brigade commander: "The attack on this place to-day was repulsed. General Sherman is here safe."

preparations for lunch and opened the box which contained a large, handsomely frosted cake. Just as we were about to cut it the train stopped and someone ran in and called to us: "Get out of here as quickly as you can. The road is cut ahead of us and we are stopped by Chalmers' cavalry."

We got out of the cars as quickly as we could. Directly above us on the bank was the redoubt of Collierville, of which we took possession. Sherman immediately stepped into the telegraph office and telegraphed to Corse [Brig. Gen. John M. Corse], who was some dozen miles away, stating the situation and ordering him to come to our relief double quick. Corse happened to be within easy reach and replied at once, "I am coming," so that we felt sure of relief ere long.

The enemy immediately commenced an attack on the redoubt and bombarded us with eight pieces of artillery for four hours. They had about 8,000 men and eight guns. We had some 600 men and no guns. Twice they got possession of our train when an assault from the ditch cleaned them out. On top of the cars we had brought a battalion of the Thirteenth United States Infantry. Numerous assaults were made by the enemy, which were always repulsed.

Two or three times one of the men would scream out: "There is a rebel who is trying to steal our knapsacks!" which were left on the top of the car, and would fire at him. "No," said the officer, "that is our man, Tom Smith, who is dead drunk and did not get off with us." As soon as the firing was over, some of his comrades climbed onto the car to see how many times Tom, who had been under the cross fire from both sides, had been shot. To their astonishment he was found to be entirely uninjured and woke up quite sober.

Our horses had not escaped so well. My own was wounded in the car and the train was generally riddled with bullets, broken glass, etc., and there was a cannon shot through the engine so that we were obliged to wait all night till a train could be sent for us from Corinth. I went down to our car which I found had been pretty well cleaned out by the enemy. Everything of any value had been taken — among other things, my cake. As I stood on the platform a soldier passed along with a large piece of cake in his hand. He called out, "Who had the cake?" I replied that I did, but it was all gone, and asked him where he had got that piece. "Took it out of the hand of a dead rebel — there under the fence. It is real good. He had his mouth full but I let him keep that."

I never was able to learn who presented me with that cake, nor could I recall the German nor anything that I had ever done for him.

**At Iuka, Miss. another kind of "fight" erupted — this time between soldiers and army sutlers. "The regiment received two months pay on October 24th," wrote Sergeant Henry H. Wright of Company D, 6th Iowa, "but it came too late to be of service to the horde of sutlers who had assembled with their goods. A general raid had been made by the troops on the establishments of the greedy vampires, and nearly every one of them suffered heavy loss. The men were mostly without money and the rich delicacies displayed in the stores were so tempting that they could not be restrained and the camp followers were unmercifully cleaned out, losing large quantities**

of provisions, and much wine and other liquor. A justified complaint had been made by the enlisted men on account of the exorbitant prices charged for goods and for unjust discriminations made against them by the sutlers. The men also took umbrage because the pay day had been deferred until they were far in the interior and a long distance from any trading point, and, because all the sutlers — by some strange intuition — were on the ground ahead of the paymasters, with all their wares.

"There was instituted a little spasm of effort to punish the men for the breach of discipline, but active campaigning and a lack of sympathy throughout the army for the injured parties — who had followed the army solely for gain and speculation — caused the affair to 'blow over' easily and no further action was ever taken."

Another XV Corps regiment in Iuka was detailed to unload supplies from a freight train when the soldiers discovered one car partly filled with a sutler's merchandise, which they promptly confiscated and distributed among themselves. A company commander who witnessed the scene later wrote:

"While the sutler was profanely remonstrating and trying to secure his property, General Sherman chanced along, and to him the angry man appealed for help. He received a characteristic response: 'Neither you nor your goods have any rights here. My orders were that only army stores should be shipped in these cars. You have stolen transportation belonging to these men, while they have had to make a forced march. You are served just right.' The general rode off while the welkin rang with cheers, and the crest-fallen sutler retired to figure up his profit and loss account, and make out his claim upon [the] government."

■ Col. Oscar Malmborg, 55th Illinois, was universally disliked by the regiment's officers and men, many of whom referred to him as "that damned old Swede." On October 11 he led the 55th in a fruitless day-long search for Chalmers' cavalry between LaGrange and Collierville. Three days later Malmborg's men marched through Holly Springs, Miss., where the Confederate raid on Sherman's train began on the 10th. A regimental member recalled: "A year before we had visited this locality for the first time, and remembered it as a beautiful town, with numerous tasteful residences, evidently the abode of cultured and wealthy people; while the region round about abounded in signs of prosperity. Now the whole face of nature seemed changed. The place was a slovenly ruin, and the fenceless fields far and wide were barren wastes."

Sherman reached Chattanooga on November 15. The following day he learned of his pivotal role in the coming battle and was shown the area of attack from an observation post on the west side of the Tennessee. Grant's plan detailed his troops to march up from Bridgeport, cross the river at Brown's Ferry, and move into concealed camps behind the hills north of Chattanooga before recrossing the Tennessee near Missionary Ridge's north end. "Pontoons for throwing a bridge across the river were built and placed in North Chickamauga [Creek], near its mouth, a few miles farther up, without attracting the attention of the enemy," Grant reported. "It was expected we would be able to effect the crossing on the 21st of November, but owing to heavy rains Sherman was not able to get up until the afternoon of the 23rd."

Grant was gambling heavily on the success of his friend's assault. One week earlier, Sherman studied the objective through a long-range glass and told chief engineer William F. Smith, "I can do it!" Given the same opportunity, many of his soldiers might not have shared their commander's confidence.

Just hours before the attack commenced, a 4th Minnesota line officer wrote home: "Sherman's corps ... is ordered to cross the river and carry and hold the end of Missionary Ridge. The undertaking is a difficult one to bring to a successful issue. The ridge is well fortified. The enemy is strong. Our regiment is to be in the advance as skirmishers, so you see that we shall have enough to do, and if by any mishap the en-

# 'Have you ever had a furlough?'

■ Maj. Gen. William T. Sherman, photographed in 1863 at the Memphis gallery of Bishop & Needles. Just eight days prior to leaving Memphis for Chattanooga, Sherman lost his nine-year-old son Willy to typhoid fever. On October 8 he wrote his wife: "Oh! that poor Willy could have lived to take all that was good of me in name, character and standing, and learn to avoid all that was captious, eccentric or wrong."

**Before its call to reinforce the besieged army at Chattanooga, Maj. Gen. William T. Sherman's XV Corps was camped along the Big Black River about 12 miles east of Vicksburg, Miss. An incident described by Capt. Henry S. Nourse, 55th Illinois, illustrated the general's sense of humor.**

One of Company F's men received notice that a son had been born to him at his home in Illinois, and wanted a name. He immediately wrote to his wife to call the boy William Tecumseh Sherman, and at the same time wrote General Sherman, informing him that he had a promising namesake.

The next day an orderly appeared with commands for Samuel Faas, private Fifty-fifth Ill. Vols., to report forthwith at army headquarters. The soldier with some trepidation obeyed the summons, saluted and awaited the general's pleasure. Sundry of the staff and other officers were present, and their faces wore an air of having enjoyed some joke, and of anticipating more amusement.

"Well," said the general, "I see by your letter, Mr. Faas, that your wife has presented you with a fine boy, and that you have done me the honor to name him for me. How long have you been in the service?"

"Two years, general," was the respectful reply.

"Have you ever had a furlough?"

Now it would have been strange if this question did not make the heart of the husband and father leap with hope of soon greeting his dear ones face to face. His general was surely proposing to allow him brief leave of absence for this purpose, reflected the soldier, as he feelingly replied: "No, general; I've never been absent from the regiment a day."

"Been two years in the service, and never had a furlough — and your wife has a bouncing boy! Why, really, Faas, I don't understand this."

The officers winked slyly at each other, enjoying the culmination of the strategy. The soldier's hopes sank; but his cheeks flushed, and his answer was prompt: "General, my wife last autumn made me a three weeks' visit when we were at Memphis."

Amid the laughter of all present, General Sherman owned himself for once outflanked, and told the father that when the boy should be ten years old he would gladly send him something to remember for whom he received his name.

**Sadly, the boy died a few years after the war. Faas himself was severely wounded at Atlanta on July 22, 1864, and discharged for disability in July 1865.**

**terprise should fail (which may the Lord forbid!) we shall be annihilated or captured."**

## 'No better place for throwing a bridge'

### Major Henry S. Dean
### 22nd Michigan Volunteer Infantry

One part of General Grant's plan for driving Bragg from Lookout Mountain and Missionary Ridge was for General Sherman to cross the Tennessee River at a point four miles above Chattanooga and attack and turn the enemy's right, which rested on the northern extremity of Missionary Ridge. This crossing was to be made by means of two pontoon bridges.

After the Brown's Ferry affair my regiment was transferred from Whitaker's to the Engineers Brigade, commanded by General Wm. F. Smith, who had been assigned duty as chief engineer of the Military Division of the Mississippi. With my regiment I was assigned the duty of taking the train for one of those bridges from Chattanooga to the point of crossing. In the performance of this duty I was enjoined to observe the utmost secrecy lest the enemy should discover what we were doing. I was directed to make myself thoroughly acquainted with the country and all the roads over which the train was to pass.

Capt. Preston C.F. West, A.A.G. on the staff of General Smith, went over the ground with me, and pointed out the roads over which the train could move, those over which General Sherman's forces would move into position, also the route each would take back to Chattanooga in case of disaster or failure to effect a crossing. I spent several days in making myself acquainted with the topography of the route selected [and] every little ravine and hill which furnished a hiding place for a wagon. As with the bridge at Brown's Ferry, Capt. P.V. Fox had charge of the construction and laying of this one.

The other bridge of regular pontoon boats, which had been picked up between Chattanooga and Bridgeport, was in charge of Lieut. George W. Dresser, Fourth Artillery, and was taken to the North Chickamauga above the point where the bridges were to be laid. The place selected for throwing the bridges was a little below the mouth of the South Chickamauga. On the south bank of the river at that point, a low hill rises a short distance back from the bank and gently slopes into the valley. On the north bank directly opposite this hill, a deep ravine comes down to the river, the hills on either side of which extend for some distance up and down the river, furnishing concealment for troops, and a position from which artillery can sweep the valley back of the hill on the south side. An experienced engineer could not have constructed a better place for throwing a bridge in the face of opposition, than nature supplied at this point. The road from Chattanooga over which the train must pass was in plain view of the enemy posted on Lookout Mountain. Heavy rains had rendered the roads almost impassible; the mules were so reduced in strength from lack of forage that when the poor creatures got down in the mud the men had to pull them out of the way.

At nine o'clock p.m., November 20th, Capt. Fox sent the pontoon train from under cover of Cameron Hill to the north side of

■ Major Henry S. Dean, 22nd Michigan, was relieved of staff duty at his own request and assumed command of the regiment on September 26. At Brown's Ferry the regiment helped secure the position after the successful landing early on October 27. Acting as pontoniers, his men also facilitated Sherman's Tennessee River crossing on November 24. Their proficiency won them assignment to the Engineer Brigade, headquartered at Chattanooga until May 1864, when they marched for Atlanta.

■ Capt. Perrin V. Fox, 1st Michigan Engineers and Mechanics, commanded the regiment's three companies serving at Chattanooga. According to a fellow Michigan officer, Fox's army reputation as a talented engineer was nothing compared to his prowess as a wrestler. "There was a grand day in Chattanooga," remembered 1st Lieut. Charles E. Belknap, 21st Michigan, "when another champion came up from [the] Fifteenth Corps to contest with Fox for the Belt. An amphitheatre was made from bridge planks and reserved seats sold to the Generals of the Army as well as the rank and file. It was also pay day and every Michigan man had twenty-six dollars with which to back their Wolverine against the Badger, who 'bane a Swede' standing six feet six, checked in at 240 pounds.

"Bets were arranged for 'best three in five.' The first fall came with the Swede on his back. The army went wild; when the pay-roll was up coats, watches and finger rings followed. When the second fall was won by the Wolverine there was a stampede and the backers of the big Swede, as they straggled away to their camps hatless, coatless and moneyless, looked like a defeated army."

the river, where it was delivered to me. At that time I did not know as much about pontoon trains as I did at the close of the war. That the train was to be taken to its destination without permitting the enemy to get sight of it we all understood, but of how it was to be arranged after it got there I was as ignorant as I child, so I asked Capt. Fox how he wanted it parked. He hesitated, and I repeated the question. Finally he said: "It is a delicate matter for an officer of inferior rank to give orders to a superior who is in command."

I looked squarely into that honest face of his and said: "I am the smallest major in the army. If you know how this train ought to be parked, tell me."

He said: "Place the balk here, the chess plank there, the spring lines so and so, the head line in such a place, and the anchors ..."

"Hold on," I said, "I know what an anchor is, but don't know anything about your balk, chess plank and spring lines. Show me what they are."

He did, and we started out with the train. It was raining and the night very dark. In many places the wagons would go down in the mud to the axletree. The poor, weak mules would get stalled in the mud and men would have to pull them out. Wagon wheels would give out, and the men supplied their places with wheels taken from General Palmer's [John M. Palmer, XIV Corps commander] ammunition train, which was parked on the north side of the river opposite Chattanooga. Wagons would upset and men, by means of ropes, would right them.

As the first grey of morning appeared in the east the wagons were quickly concealed in ravines and behind hills, or if they could not be gotten out of sight in that way, they were concealed by piling brush over them. The men and animals were moved behind the hills and not permitted to show themselves during the day. At 2 o'clock a.m., November 22d, we had the train parked in the ravine leading down to the river where the crossing was to be made, a thick growth of underbrush concealing it from the enemy's pickets on the other side of the river. On November 23d, concealed from view of the enemy, the men rested behind the hills. The strict guard established to prevent any of them from showing themselves was hardly necessary; they were completely worn out by three nights of labor, such as I have never seen performed by men before or since.

At midnight November 23d, one hundred and sixteen pontoon boats, with a brigade on board, started from their place of concealment in North Chickamauga Creek and floated down the Tennessee to the place selected for throwing the bridges. General Smith, standing on the bank close to the water, was anxiously awaiting their approach. A small boat in charge of an experienced oarsman was awaiting his orders. The man, looking along the surface of the water, reported that he could see the boats coming. General Smith ordered him to row across and place a range light close to the water on the opposite bank to indicate the point of landing.

The leading boat changed its course from the center of the river and headed toward the range light, each succeeding boat silently following its lead. The boats landed and the men disembarked so quietly that we did not hear a sound on our side of the river. The first indication that a landing had been effected was when the almost painful silence was broken by the sharp challenge of the rebel picket, as it rang out on the night air: "Who goes there?" Quickly came the response: "Grand rounds!" and the picket answered: "Advance, sergeant, with the countersign." The officer who made the rounds advanced, placed a pistol close to the ear of the guard, and in a low voice cautioned him not to make any noise, and passed him to the rear. This was repeated thirteen times. The fourteenth guard discharged his piece, fortunately without injury to anyone, and ran. When the guard fired, General Smith said: "Now we shall get it. Move your regiment down to the bank of the river and take your place with the train and await orders, which I shall send."

But he was mistaken. The enemy had regarded an attack in that quarter as so unlikely to occur that he had failed to place any force in the valley except a thin picket line along the river, which amounted to nothing as a resisting force, and it had failed to discover the slightest indication of what was going on within hearing distance of the guard composing it.

As soon as the men had landed from the boats which came down from the North Chickamauga, General Sherman's troops moved from behind the hills down to the river. The laying of the pontoon bridge was immediately started from both banks, the boats being used to ferry troops across until they were needed to place in position. General Smith ordered me to send enough boats and material from my train for a bridge two hundred feet in length, which was thrown across the South Chickamauga under direction of Capt. Fox. By daylight on the morning of November 24th, two divisions of General Sherman's troops had crossed to the south side of the river. While preparations for this crossing had been going forward, heavy rains had raised the river to such an extent that it was feared that a bridge could not be thrown at all, and if thrown that it could not be maintained as long as needed. The current was swift and the enemy were sending rafts and driftwood down to break the bridges at Chattanooga and Brown's Ferry. Under these circumstances it was decided not to attempt to throw the second bridge.

At 11 o'clock a.m. the bridge was completed, and General Sherman's forces crossed the Tennessee River to take their part in the battle of Missionary Ridge.

■ Col. Daniel McCook, 52nd Ohio, commanded the XIV Corps brigade that launched 116 pontoons in North Chickamauga Creek for Sherman's crossing of the Tennessee River. "To keep the expedition secret it was necessary to arrest all the citizens," McCook wrote a month later, "assigning a reason therefor that I had been bushwhacked." On November 18 "the pontoons began to arrive; strong guards were placed around them to keep even our own soldiers away. Captain [John] Kennedy, Company F, Eighty-fifth Illinois, was put in charge of the launching party. He so expeditiously conducted matters that he launched a boat every three minutes."

Seven months later McCook fell mortally wounded at Kennesaw Mountain, Ga. He died on July 18, 1864.

## 'Looks considerable like fighting'

### Journal of
### 2nd Lieut. James A. Woodson
### Company H
### 5th Iowa Volunteer Infantry

**Wednesday Nov. 19** This afternoon we march two hours and three fourths (a distance of 11 miles) to keep from resting in the camps of the Potomac Rats. From the way they run to see Western men and throw out their Eastern slang at us one would think the Western boys were monkeys. We passed Genl Joe Hookers Head Quarters. He was in front of his tent. He is quite a tall man, much more so than I had formed an idea he was. Has gray hair and whiskers — he is a very ordinary looking man, does not look like there was much fighting in him.

■ Chaplain Milton L. Haney, 55th Illinois, accompanied his regiment during the river crossing of Gen. Giles A. Smith's brigade. Haney later wrote: "There were some in those boats who were assured of protection, although engaged in one of the most hazardous undertakings of the war. Others were not so confident. I remember a surgeon fresh from the North who was with us. Before leaving the [North] Chickamauga his face blanched and his knees began to tremble as he said: 'As soon as we strike the river we shall be blown to pieces.' As his fears increased his body bent lower, until at length he lay prone with his face to the bottom of the boat. God's hand was over that expedition, however, and our boys landed in the face of the rebel army unnoticed and unhurt. Soon joy filled our hearts, as from boat to boat the news passed on that the rebel pickets had been captured without the firing of a gun. Hearing this, the terror-stricken man rose up and made a sickly attempt to yawn as though just aroused from refreshing slumber, and as his teeth ceased to chatter, said, 'Well, I've had quite a nap!' "

The following July, Haney, a native of Ohio, picked up a musket and voluntarily fought in the ranks during the battle of Atlanta. In 1896 he was awarded the Medal of Honor.

Just before dark we crossed the Tennessee River below Chattanooga and camped on the Bottom near the River about three miles below the town of Chattanooga. We cannot see Chattanooga from our camp as there is quite a little Mountain between us and it.

**November 20th** In quite a hurry this morning, for fear the Rebs will see our movements. We are up and on the move at 3 a.m. Went up the wrong valley, came to the Pontoon Bridge leading to Chattanooga; turned back, went up another valley and came around in view of Mission Ridge where we are to bivouac untill further orders. We are about 1½ miles from the Tennessee River 4 miles north east from Chattanooga. Received orders this forenoon that theirs to be no loud talking, laughing or hallooing. We will cross the river at some point close here. Raining at dark.

**November 21st** We got a good nights rest last night. Raining this morning. The boys suffer without tents from the rain and cold. At 3 p.m. orders came to be in readiness to cross the River and engage the Rebs. Men to carry eighty rounds Cartridges, three days rations in Haversacks and one Blanket. Looks considerable like fighting. General Sherman came up this morning and pitched his head quarters on the side of the mountain above our camp. There was four Divisions came up with him. Will not cross the river tonight.

**Nov. 22d** Did not move across the river last night as was ordered. The Sun is shining brightly this morning and is quite pleasant. From the top of the mountain we can see the Reble camp very plain. The Rebles appear to be making some kind of a move. Their tents are being taken down and the Supposition is that they are preparing for a fight on our crossing the river, or else to evacuate. Heavy firing at Chattanooga by our artillery (shelling the Mountain) but receive no reply from the Reble Batteries. Orders to move across the River to night. Two Divisions are to go across in Pontoon Boats and entrench. Then the Pontoon Bridge is to be thrown across and the main army will cross.

**Nov. 23d** Still as good luck will have it we are in camp yet. Nothing new to-day up to 12 M. 3 p.m. Genl Thomas advanced from his works and attacked the enemy. Had quite a little skirmish, drove the enemy from their first line of works. This throws the Rail Road in our possession. Our men occupy the works at dark. This was to draw the attention while we effect a crossing. We are to cross to night. I hope it will come off and then we will have some peace of mind.

**Nov. 24** We were woke up at a little after 12 M[idnight], got into line and marched to the river. We found Boats awaiting us. Morgan L. Smiths Division crossed first and captured the Picket Posts, finding them asleep. Also the officer of the day when he was making the grand rounds. When we got across we went to work entrenching. In less than fifteen minutes there was rifle pits over one mile in length sufficient to shelter us from the rebs, but as good fortune is on our side they have made no attack and the only shots I have heard yet is between the skirmishers. We could hold our ground pretty well. We advance about ¾ of a mile from the river and halted for a general rest. The Pontoon was thrown across the River and our artillery is across and in position.

3 p.m. In line and advancing into the timber without any opposition. Only a few shots along the skirmish [line] but we'll catch it when we go to ascend the mountain. We rest for the night on a

small ridge in the timber between the River and Mission Ridge. My Regt on Picket guard. No casualties in the Regt. yet. Cool and disagreeable. In front of General Sherman we may look for hard fighting tomorrow ...

## 'Like a rabbit through a rye field'

### Private John W. Dyer
### Company G
### 1st Kentucky Cavalry C.S.A.

On the morning of the 24th of November ... interest at once centered on Missionary Ridge and we knew that it would not be long till the struggle for its possession would begin. General Sherman moved up his whole force to the foot of the ridge and prepared for the onslaught.

Our brigade of cavalry, composed of the 1st, 2nd and 9th Kentucky regiments and the 2nd Kentucky (Dortch's) battalion, was on the extreme right of line near the foot of the hill skirmishing with Sherman's forces, who were trying to effect a crossing of a large creek which ran between us. We succeeded by hot work in keeping them on their side till about four o'clock in the afternoon when their whole line was advanced at a charge and broke through our position. We were holding in check the force in front of our brigade when without any warning the bullets began to rain down on us from our left and rear producing a very demoralizing effect. We didn't stay there any longer. It was hot enough with the bullets coming from one side, but when they came from both sides — well, I have never seen any men who could stand it long — we skeedaddled back over the hill, mounted our horses and prepared to follow the balance of our forces which were in full retreat, and cover the retreat to the best of our ability. Everything was in confusion among the Yankees as well as ourselves. Flushed with an easy victory they rushed on with very little order and as a consequence got some of themselves killed and gave us a better chance to get away.

Chickamauga Creek drains the valley in the rear of Missionary Ridge and is a stream that can be crossed only at certain places. There were a few fords and bridges, the latter built by the army, generally covered with logs and dirt and not easy to burn. Our line of retreat led over one of these bridges and as we neared it we found that a force of the enemy had slipped in between us and our infantry and was in possession. We knew if we hesitated we were lost. There was only one course to pursue and we took it. With the same old yell that could be heard when victory perched on our banners we went through those Yankees like a rabbit through a rye field. It was always against our principles, when on a retreat, to leave a bridge standing after we had crossed it, so we stopped and tried to burn this one, but it was so hard to set fire and the Yankees got so thick that we had to leave it. This was a source of regret all the balance of the war and stands out as our only failure in this line during our whole service. Night had now come on and gave us a rest till next day, which we were glad to take every advantage of, and we made the most of it for we knew there were squally times ahead and could form no idea of their magnitude.

■ Private Jesse H. Bean of Company H, 4th Minnesota. His regiment was first of the XVII Corps to cross the Tennessee River in pontoon boats early on November 24. Ordered to cover the front of Brig. Gen. John E. Smith's division, the 4th served as skirmishers (the colonel, adjutant and sergeant major all riding horses captured from Confederate scouts) and pushed into the valley below Tunnel Hill before nightfall. Relieved at 8 p.m. by the 48th Indiana, the Minnesotans withdrew to safety and counted only one casualty. The strenuous skirmish duty on the 24th kept Bean and his comrades in reserve the following day — sparing them from heavy losses suffered by other regiments in Sherman's command.

Brig. Gen. Hugh B. Ewing

Brig. Gen. Morgan L. Smith

Brig. Gen. John E. Smith

■ Sherman's Army of the Tennessee division commanders at Tunnel Hill were all Vicksburg veterans. From the XV Corps, Morgan L. Smith and Hugh B. Ewing (Sherman's foster brother) led the 2nd and 4th divisions, respectively. John E. Smith (no relation to Morgan) commanded the 2nd Division, XVII Corps, which was styled the 3rd Division, XV Corps, while at Chattanooga. A break in the Brown's Ferry pontoon bridge on November 23 prevented Osterhaus' 1st Division from joining Sherman at Tunnel Hill. Its replacement was Brig. Gen. Jefferson C. Davis' XIV Corps' division.

## 'A jam of infantry, artillery and ambulances'

### Diary of Private Jenkin L. Jones 6th Wisconsin Battery

**6 A.M. Nov. 24.** Two divisions were safely across [the Tennessee River] and a more beautiful scene I never witnessed. Through the gray dawn a long line of infantry could be seen drawn up on the opposite bank a mile long, while the waters were covered with boats busily going and coming, loaded with men, the regimental colors standing in the center of the boat. The [pontoon] bridge was now covered, boats brought up, anchored in line, and the floor laid without any delay, the 4th Division marching in the boats and the artillery covering the field. Fires were allowed to be built now and we soon had coffee. It commenced raining, as cold and disagreeable as the day could be. A steamboat was due at 4 a.m. to take us across, but did not come till 6:30 a.m. Taylor's Battery crossed the river first, and as we were not pressed we waited for the bridge to be built. It was very disagreeable, and I felt almost sick; late hours and irregular meals having brought on diarrhea, etc. A large constellation of stars were gathered on the bank, watching the progress of the bridge, among which were Sherman, Blair, W.F. Smith, etc. The line on the other side in one hour had a line of breastworks up and advanced out of sight to form another.

**12 M.** The bridge completed and we crossed it, being the second battery to do so. The dread of crossing had passed. Halted at a corn crib and the cannoneers got as much corn as they could, but the infantry was formed and advanced in column of division at secure arms, it raining very heavy. This savage-looking column moved forward with caution, crossed a forty-acre lot and halted.

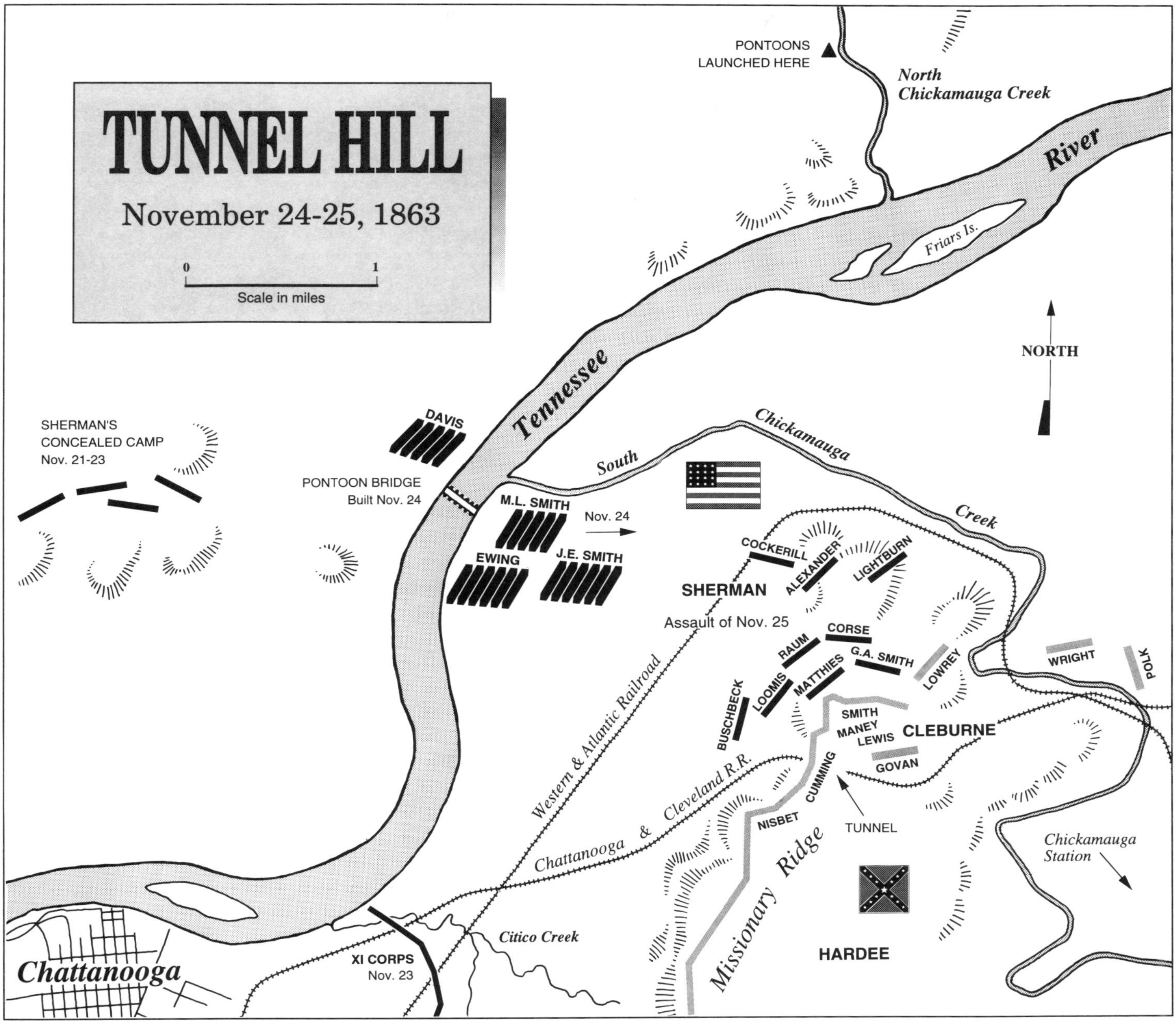


The skirmishers went out but not a gun was fired. Advanced again, the batteries were in column of sections. An occasional gun shot, but we advanced until we were directly under Mission Ridge. Not a reb seen and our infantry soon climbed it. Our line formed on the brow when the artillery moved up. Battery D, 1st Missouri was the first up and soon opened fire on them from the right. Our battery started for the left. The "smooth bores" were left on the other side of the river for want of horses, and we had four teams on a carriage, but the hill was too steep for us and two more teams were put on the pieces, and caissons left behind.

A detail of two hundred men was sent to our aid with axes, the enemy sending shells over us quite thick. 1st piece failed to advance with the horses. Ropes brought forward and it was hauled up by hand, we following with all haste. By this time a very brisk skirmishing was going on right to our left and rear quite close, and General Matthies came down at the head of his brigade at

■ Private Jenkin L. Jones, 6th Wisconsin Battery. While waiting to cross the Tennessee River early on November 24, he observed "a long line of snow-white ambulances which caused the anxious question — 'Who will be obliged to be borne in these from the field of battle?' " After the Tunnel Hill fighting 42 hours later, he noted in his diary: "The day closed, and the dark mantle of night was spread over the gory fields. We have gained nothing in the shape of ground all day, [and the] slaughter must be terrible ... But no man grumbled or complained as we thought of our wounded who lay on the field all night with no covering, and weak from loss of blood. Their groans could be heard by our men all night, and the friends in rebellion would not permit them to carry relief to them or bring them in. One, who had a brother lying on the field, started with the determination of relieving him or die in the attempt. True to his determination he was shot dead by the inhuman wretches who would not listen to his plea."

double quick, the old general on foot, making fine time. Captain Dillon ordered the howitzer section and Cogswell's Battery to the rear in all haste.* The extra teams were unhitched and the pieces unlimbered, and with great difficulty we made a left about, the hill being so steep that it shoved our horses down amongst the infantry that were pouring down. But the cannoneers fastened a rope to the axle-tree, and down we went in good earnest. Halted at the R.R. crossing in a complete jam of infantry, artillery and ambulances near General [John E.] Smith's headquarters, who knew nothing of our movements and demanded by whose orders we came down.

We stood there in the cold damp evening for half an hour, got a feed of shelled corn from an out-house close by, when we moved back into the first field above General Matthies, and came into camp alongside of Cogswell's Battery and the 2nd and 3rd brigades of our Division. Unhitched but did not unharness. Our rations were entirely out with the exception of coffee and some corn-meal picked up, so we ate hastily of unsifted mush and coffee.

Three drivers from each piece sent after sheaf oats for horses. I was on the detail and we rode back nearly three miles toward the river. Found the oats all gone, but plenty of good tame hay, of which we took as much as possible. Returned to camp by 9 p.m. I was nearly exhausted from cold and loss of sleep, having been up since 1 a.m. Lay down in cold and wet blankets.

**Mission Ridge, Wednesday, Nov. 25.** Called up before three in the morning to feed. Suffered very much from cold during the night. The blankets stiff with frost over us. Witnessed an almost total eclipse of the moon and again lay down, but no sleep.

**6 A.M.** McCook's Brigade of Davis' Division formed in line of battle facing to the left and supporting our artillery, should it be necessary. 1st Section (rifles) reported to be well fortified on the ridge.

**9 A.M.** Not much fighting as yet, the pickets advancing and skirmishing. A reb battery shells directly over and in rear. One twelve-pounder shell time-fused dropped ahead of our team and was dug up by the boys. A mule team came up and issued one day's rations of hard-tack.

**11 A.M.** The 2nd and 3rd Brigades went in on double quick followed by the 11th Corps with crescents flying, a fine looking body of men, but are looked on rather suspiciously by our sturdy veterans. They went in and advanced toward the rebels' works on Tunnel Hill, and musketry rattled very severe.

From that time [until] late in the evening a terrible struggle followed, wounded men coming back thick and fast. Our position was such that we could not witness the field and we were not permitted to leave the teams an instant. Our loss is very heavy especially in officers. The struggle on our side was for the occupation of Tunnel Hill and our line advanced up the steep side of the bluff time after time, but were obliged to fall back, the rebels being reinforced all the time and could pick them off with ease, the lay of the land being such that they succeeded in flanking the 11th

* Capt. Henry Dillon was artillery chief of the 2nd Division, XVII Corps. Artillery under his command were Capt. William Cogswell's Illinois Battery, the 6th Wisconsin Battery (1st Lieut. Samuel F. Clark) and the 12th Wisconsin Battery (Capt. William Zickerick).

Corps, and they fell back in disorder. But they were received by the 2nd and 3rd Brigade of our Division, and soon compelled to retire.

More desperate fighting, it is said by those who witnessed, they had never seen. Our line being for hours under the enemy they rolled stones upon us, wounding many. Three companies of the 5th Iowa were taken prisoners, having used up all their ammunition and would not run. Artillery could not be brought to much use, and my feelings as I staid under that hill listening to the noise and rattle of the fight, mingled with suppressed cheers of charging parties, and the groans of the wounded as they passed in the long trains of ambulances, or the lighter wounded hobbling back a-foot with bleeding and mangled limbs, I cannot describe in words. General Matthies was wounded in the head while leading his brigade on to the charge. I saw him ride to the rear covered with blood. Colonel Putnam of the 93rd Illinois was killed instantly while waving the colors in front of his men, a noble and much loved officer. The 90th Illinois and 73rd Pennsylvania were literally cut to pieces, and their officers all killed or wounded.

## 'Taking orders and dispatches'

### Private Theodore F. Upson
### Company C
### 100th Indiana Volunteer Infantry
### XV Corps scout

We went down the River road in the morning [of November 24] — Gen. Sherman and his staff and some of the scouts. We met General Grant and his escort. The two Generals stopped and talked for some time; when Gen. Grant came by us he turned and said, "By the way, Sherman, I see that some of your men have their overcoats on. These blue overcoats can be seen a long ways. They had better take them off after they cross the River. They might draw the enemy's fire." I believe General Grant sees every thing down to smallest details. He is a wonderful man.

We crossed the River on a little steamer and Chickamauga Creek on pontoons. I went with some of the others to General Ewing's Hd Quarters. I walked up on a hill where some of our men were planting a Battery. I have a good field glass I bought at Memphis. I could see the Confederate Batteries on Mission Ridge and a great many rifle pits lower down. I could even see arms stacked on the Ridge. While I was looking the Battery Captain came over by me and as I remarked about the stacks of arms he said he could not see any with his glass and took mine. After looking through it he wanted to trade and offered me ten dollars boot money. Just then General Ewing and one or two other officers came where we were and the General tried my glass and said it was the best he ever saw. I thought I would keep it so did not trade though the Battery Captain's cost 40 dollars while I paid 20 dollars for mine. The Battery Captain said there would be a hard fight there tomorrow. It seemed peaceful enough today. Our troops are coming across the River and camping out of sight behind the hills.

On the morning of Nov. 25 we — the scouts — were sent around to the right of our lines to see if others of our troops were

■ 1st Sergeant Eli J. Sherlock of Company A, 100th Indiana. When his regiment formed in line of battle at 8:30 a.m. November 25, Sherlock recalled: "We looked up through the fog and saw the thousands of bright gun barrels of the Rebel soldiers flashing in the sunshine as they moved in column after column from their center to their right. The polished brass cannons were seen by us glistening as they moved along the top of the ridge and also took position in our front, and so long did this continue that it seemed as if their entire force was being placed in position on the top and sides of the ridge in our front."

In the ensuing fight, Sherlock's company lost 16 men wounded, "but not a man was killed, although on that day it was the right color company in the line and had one-half of the number it took into the battle wounded. That none were killed is simply inexplicable."

# 'Exposed to a most galling fire'

**Major Ruel M. Johnson took command of the 100th Indiana at Tunnel Hill after Lt. Col. Albert Heath was taken from the field severely wounded. Johnson's actions that day earned him a Medal of Honor, the reverse of which is illustrated above. The award's citation described the 100th Indiana "pushing forward to the railroad in front of Tunnel Hill, through the most destructive fire of the enemy, where the whole Brigade was ordered to lay down, hold the ground gained and protect themselves as much as possible under cover of the embankment. This was done by the men but Johnson remained on his feet marching for four hours from right to left and from left to right along the battle line, cheering his men and urging them to stand fast to their duty, being all the time exposed to a most dangerous and galling fire of the enemy, only a few hundred feet away, four bullets passing through his coat and he receiving a wound in his right cheek by a fragment of shell."**

■ Major Ruel M. Johnson

there. We found them there all right and also drew a shell from a Johnny Battery up on the Ridge. About 8 o'clock our troops began to move forward in line of battle. My Regiment was at the right of our Division. When they got out in the open ground the Confederate Batteries opened up — so did ours — and there was a terrible racket for a while. Then our men moved up closer and the rifles began to rattle. It was grand! I stood on the hill where I could see. There was a good deal of fog along the lower part of the Ridge, but on the top I could see troops marching and catch the glint of the sun on the guns. It seemed as if the whole Confederate Army was coming to stand off our troops below.

The firing soon increased and the wounded began to come back. I saw many from my own Regiment. I was kept busy all day taking orders and dispatches either up on the firing line or back to the hospitals. My Regiment went into the battle with 320 men and officers. Out of that number we had one Captain and 14 men killed, 8 officers and 107 men wounded severely, besides many more slightly wounded. Other Regiments lost heavily too but a great victory was won. I almost escaped without a scratch but was struck on my left knee with a spent ball or piece of shell. And am glad I had a horse to ride for I should have been unable to walk. Gen. Ewing complimented all of his scouts and orderlies for their bravery and good conduct during the battle.

It looked pretty tough to see the poor fellows — many of whom I knew — being taken back to the field hospitals to be operated on. Once I went back after some ambulances and saw a pile of legs and arms as big as a haycock where they were amputating. There were a great many stretched on the operating tables and the groans of the wounded were terrible. Most of the wounded were plucky and some would joke and make light of their misfor-

■ While the Glass House burns at center, the 90th Illinois and 100th Indiana of Loomis' brigade, XV Corps, move to the assault at Tunnel Hill after enduring several hours of intense Confederate rifle fire. Private Henry Robinson of Company K, 100th Indiana, recalled: "We came under the cross-fire of their musketry here [and] were ordered to lay on the ground. Here we remained about twenty minutes and again we were ordered forward. Before we got up we lost four of our Company, one killed and three wounded. Then we marched about 200 yards across a meadow and again were ordered to lay down, but one more of our Company was shot dead and five more wounded. There we remained under the most galling and raking cross-fire the troops ever lay under. In that situation, we lay without firing a gun as we were ordered not to fire. When late in the evening we retreated from the field, we thought [we were] badly whipped for the day."

■ Private Samuel Jones of Company F, 26th Illinois. His regiment's colonel, John M. Loomis, commanded the 1st Brigade, 4th Division, XV Corps. Near the Glass House at Tunnel Hill Loomis' four Illinois and Indiana regiments suffered 386 casualties — 33 percent of all losses in the XV Corps on November 25. "Every color bearer in my brigade was shot down and four-sevenths of the entire color guard," he reported, "but men were thick to raise up and bear to the front the flags of their regiments."

tunes. I remember riding behind two Irishmen from the 90th Illinois. One said to the other: "It's a bad day for the 90th Illinois."

The other replied, "Indade it is, and the worst is our Colonel is kilt."

"No," said the first, "it's not so bad as that; he's badly wounded."

"Indade he is kilt," said the other; "I heard him say so wid his own mouth."

Brave Colonel O Marah [Timothy O'Meara]! He went into the battle dressed in his best uniform, his famous sword at his side, his crimson sash across his breast, a foreign medal won in some other war above it, and last but not least a little amulet or charm hung by a cord around his neck. This, he said, would keep him from all harm. But the bright sash was his undoing. Some sharpshooter's ball pierced his body; and after a few hours of suffering, while faithfully attended by the Catholic Chaplain of his Regiment, he gave his life for the country he called his own.

Beside him, wounded in the arm and shot through the body, lay Captain Charles Brouse of Company K of my Regiment who was on detached duty when the battle opened and could in honor have kept out of it but hastened to take his place at the right of his Company. Soon after he too was so severely wounded that at first the surgeons refused to do anything for him thinking it would only hasten the end. But 48 hours after the battle, finding him still alive, they dressed his wounds and we hope he may recover.*

Our brave Chaplain John A. Brouse who had been with us but a short time showed himself to be the right man in the right place. Without a thought of his personal safety he was up on the firing line assisting the wounded, praying with the dying, doing all that his great loving heart led him to do. No wonder our boys love our gallant Chaplain and sympathise with him in his anxiety in regard to his brave son, the Captain who was so desperately wounded.

## 'I never expected to see you come back alive'

### Capt. Ira J. Bloomfield
### Company K
### 26th Illinois Volunteer Infantry
### Acting Assistant Adjutant General
### Loomis' Brigade, XV Corps

Colonel John M. Loomis commanded a brigade consisting of the 12th Indiana, 26th Illinois, 90th Illinois and 100th Indiana. It formed in line near the edge of the woods early in the morning and advanced parallel to the railroad where it passed into the tunnel. The left was about opposite the tunnel or near the Glass house. There were about 1,200 men in line with 6 field officers. We advanced until we reached the earth work made by construction of the railroad track and there were halted and held down for

* Charles W. Brouse, the 100th's youngest captain, survived his wounds and was discharged for disability on January 16, 1865. For his actions at Tunnel Hill he was given the Medal of Honor in 1899.

several hours under fire of sharpshooters on the face of Missionary Ridge, but in a measure protected by this embankment.

I was on detached duty acting as Assistant Adjutant General of Loomis' brigade, General Ewing's division. Along about 4 or 5 o'clock in the evening Gen. Ewing motioned to the staff officers to approach him, and looking over them beckoned me to come to him and told me that I must go down and recall the troops. To do that I had to go down over the open field across three ditches and four rail fences. I reached the line and gave the order of recall, and was about starting to the 90th Illinois on the extreme left when Colonel Williams of the 12th Indiana said it was useless for me to attempt reaching it on horseback. He said he would send an officer to give the order to that regiment and dispatched two officers, but both were shot down and he then sent a third officer who succeeded in delivering the message.

I started back over the same ditches and fences, but the cannoneers of guns planted on the brow of Missionary Ridge had gotten the range so that they made it extremely warm for me. When I was coming to the last fence, which was a seven-rail Virginia worm fence and a little uphill, I thought my horse could not jump it, though I was well mounted, but I disliked to turn his broad side to the firing. However, when I was within three or four rods of the fence a shell burst near his side, frightening him so that he took the fence and went clean over it, but he jumped so high that he threw me out of the saddle. I had a blanket strapped on behind the saddle and caught to that and pulled myself back on. When I came back and reported to General Ewing, he said, "My God, I am glad to see you, sir! I never expected to see you come back alive."

Of the 1,200 men who started down into the field that morning, every third man was killed or wounded, and of the 6 field officers three were killed and two wounded.*

■ Col. Reuben Williams, 12th Indiana. Two of his lieutenants in charge of skirmishers on November 25 were lauded "for gallant conduct" by their brigade commander. But the conduct of Williams' second-in-command, Lt. Col. Elbert D. Baldwin, was chastised along with five other officers in Loomis' brigade. Without being specific, Loomis reported that Baldwin was "found out of place, in [a] position too doubtful to admit of explanation."

## 'I threw away my drum and went forward'

### Drummer John S. Kountz
### Company G
### 37th Ohio Volunteer Infantry

The 23rd [of November] was spent in camp, from which we had a splendid view of Chattanooga. That night we received three days' rations and marched to the Tennessee River, which at the time was swollen by rains and the current was rapid. Upwards of 100 flat boats had been floated into North Chickamauga Creek, about four miles above Chattanooga, designed for a pontoon bridge. Our Major [Charles Hipp] was placed in command of the detail, having in charge of the boats and was ordered to cross the river, secure a landing, continue to dispatch the troops over until two divisions had crossed, and then turn the boats over to the pioneer corps, under General "Baldy" Smith, which was to build the bridge.

The night was dark with a drizzling rain. About midnight all was ready and the signal given to cross, Major Hipp's boat leading

* Eleven days later, Bloomfield was cited for gallantry at Tunnel Hill in Col. Loomis' report.

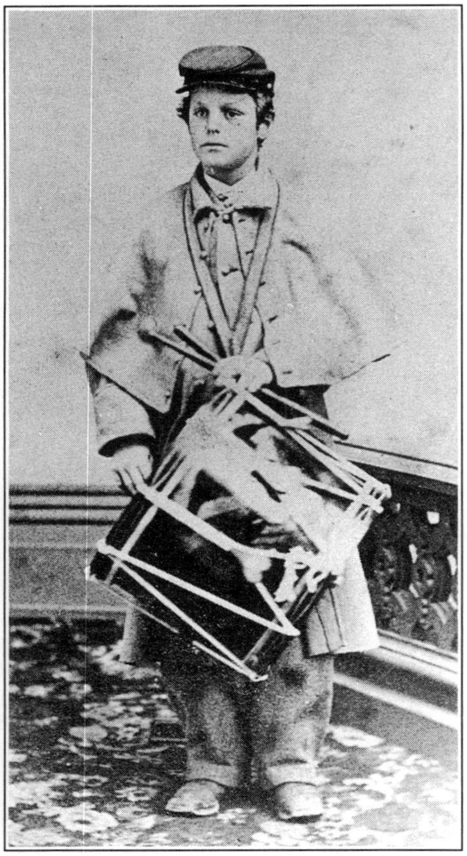

■ Drummer John S. Kountz of Company G, 37th Ohio, was 15 years old when he enlisted in that state's 3rd German Regiment in September 1861. "After considerable coaxing," Kountz recalled, "I finally obtained my father's permission to go. I bid adieu to home, to my father and sister. It was the last good-bye as both died while I was in the army. My mother had died a few years before."

Losing his right leg on November 25 ended Kountz's active field duty, but 21 years later he served as national commander of the Grand Army of the Republic when the veterans' organization enjoyed its largest membership. With the benefits of political patronage, he was awarded the Medal of Honor in 1895 for bravery at Tunnel Hill — the incident inspiring verses for "The Drummer Boy of Mission Ridge" by Kate Brownlee Sherwood.

the fleet, John Hess and others of Company E, 37th, being his companions. The Major pushed well into the river and, after awhile, headed straight for the south shore, and on nearing the point where it was proposed to land, a picket fire was discovered and our troops headed directly for it. The men hurried out of the boats and up the bank, surprising and capturing all of the Confederate pickets but one. The surprise was so complete that the "Johnnies" scarcely realized the situation. At this time a Confederate vidette came up at full speed, shouting "The Yanks are coming!" He was promptly dismounted and compelled to join his comrades just captured.

Major Hipp recrossed the river followed by the flat boats. On getting back the darkness made it difficult for him to find our troops and he shouted for the second division of the Fifteenth Corps, when he was immediately answered in suppressed voices to keep quiet or he would be arrested. Having no time for explanation and becoming impatient, the Major cried out, "Where is General Sherman?" The answer came promptly through the darkness from the General himself, who was not more than 50 feet away, "What do you want?" The Major answered, "I want a brigade, the boats are in waiting." The General at once asked, "Did you make a landing?" Major Hipp answered, "Yes, and captured the pickets." General Sherman, who was on horseback surrounded by his staff, was so pleased that he took off his hat and cheered.

At this time we embarked and after a short, though seemingly long ride, landed on the south bank of the river. Our Major continued the work of crossing and recrossing with fresh troops until morning, when two full divisions were on the east bank of the Tennessee. Meantime, our men put in splendid work digging entrenchments. General Sherman, who had crossed in one of the flat boats, personally superintended the work, and I well remember the General's remark, "Pitch in, boys; this is the last ditch," as he walked up and down the line. At the dawn of day a pontoon bridge was built over the Tennessee River and another over Chickamauga Creek near its mouth. That night's undertaking had been grandly accomplished and General Sherman was one of the happiest men in Grant's army.

At daybreak we were on the south side of the Tennessee River, strongly entrenched, prepared to meet any force General Bragg might pit against us. It must have been both a surprise and a mortification to the Confederate commander when he saw Sherman's army on the morning of the 24th securely fortified on the south bank of the Tennessee.

On the 24th we moved forward, with skirmishers in advance, over an open field to the hill near the railroad tunnel, where we fortified for the night. From our position we could see Hooker's men "above the clouds" on Lookout Mountain and also had a good view of the Army of the Cumberland on our right. Early on the morning of the 25th Sherman made his dispositions for the attack when we passed the valley which lay between us and the next hill, where the enemy had massed the corps of Hardee and other troops, the point of the ridge in our immediate front being held by that gallant Confederate General Cleburne.

General Corse attacked the enemy's position about 80 yards from his main line but it was so strong that but little headway was made, although the contest for an hour was very stubborn. During this time I saw the General carried off the field badly wounded.

While the fighting was going on to our right our brigade was under cover of temporary works, from which the enemy had been driven that morning. It was about 4 o'clock in the afternoon when the order was given to advance. As our men moved upon the enemy's works I became so enthused that I threw away my drum and went forward with the regiment. The assault lasted but a few minutes, the firing from the enemy's entrenched position being simply terrible — grape, canister, shot and shell rained upon us. The fire was so murderous that it fairly plowed up the leaves and made the very ground seem alive. Twice our forces charged upon the Confederate works, and twice our bleeding lines were compelled to fall back. So strong was General Cleburne's position in our immediate front that 1,000 men could hold it against ten times their number. In this assault my regiment lost thirty percent of its number in killed and wounded.

During the battle I was hit by a rifle ball just above the knee and the wound bled until the ground under me was covered with blood. I became very thirsty, but fortunately had two canteens of water. At my side lay [Private Christopher] Weber of Company A, who had been instantly killed. As I was not very far from the enemy's works and our men had fallen back to the point from which the advance was made, my position was not an enviable one as I lay between two fires. Captain John Hamm of Company A, who had always been very kind to me, having been told that I lay wounded in front of our line, walked over to my company and reported that Johnny Kountz lay in front, and asked, "Who will go and get him out?" William Schmidt promptly answered, "I will," and another comrade pointed out the direction in which I lay. Schmidt advanced some distance, then sprang forward and hurriedly placed me upon his back, and although there was much firing we were under cover of the hill to the left of our line.

I was then placed upon a stretcher and carried to the rear where the boys gathered around me expressing their sympathy. My leg was bandaged by Surgeon Billhardt of the 37th and I was carried to a log cabin in the ravine, below the point from which we made the advance. I remained upon the porch with other wounded until dark, when I was placed upon a stretcher and carried some distance over another hill and then put into an ambulance and taken to a point on the Tennessee River, near the mouth of Chickamauga Creek, where I was placed upon a rough table. After examination of my wound the surgeon informed me that my leg was so badly shattered that amputation was necessary, or words to that effect. I objected, but my objection was not heeded. I was then chloroformed and on awakening felt for my leg but it was gone. At this time I was 17 years of age.

## 'Who the hell are you shooting at?'

### Capt. Emory W. Muenscher
### Company I
### 30th Ohio Volunteer Infantry

The 30th Ohio belonged to the Second Brigade, Second Division, Fifteenth Corps. This corps, which had just arrived from Vicksburg, was hidden behind the hills on the north side of the Tennes-

■ Capt. John Hamm of Company A, 37th Ohio, acted as a surrogate father to John Kountz during the latter's army service. When Kountz was wounded at Tunnel Hill, Hamm asked for someone to bring him off the field. Seventeen-year-old Private William Schmidt, a school chum of Kountz and fellow member of Company G, volunteered. Schmidt later wrote: "I went to the left of our line, and, advancing some distance under cover of the hill, I sprang forward to the spot where he lay. The brave boy said to me, 'Save yourself! I am a goner anyhow.' I went to rescue him and was determined to do it if possible, so, hurriedly placing him upon my back, and, although there was much firing, I succeeded in getting him safely back to our lines. When I rescued him he was nearer the rebel works than any of the killed and wounded of our regiment."

Schmidt's selfless feat earned him the Medal of Honor.

■ Capt. Elijah Warner of Company E, 30th Ohio. At the start of his men's charge on the Confederate rifle pits, they were subjected to a burst of shellfire from Douglas' Texas Battery. Quick movement forward spared casualties, but Warner was not so fortunate evading enemy artillery seven months later. At Kennesaw Mountain, the Confederates plastered his regiment after its unsuccessful assault there on June 27, 1864. A fragment hit him in the foot as projectiles ripped into the 30th's ranks.

Warner served as Company E's commander through its entire three-year enlistment. He was promoted to major in November 1864, but never mustered at that rank.

see River on the evening of November 23, 1863. About midnight we marched down to the river where we found a number of pontoon boats, which had been hidden in North Chickamauga Creek and manned by a number of our First Brigade, who floated down the river, landed and captured all but one of the rebel pickets. We immediately commenced crossing and throwing up intrenchments to protect the landing.

At daylight I was ordered out on the skirmish line with my company. We advanced slowly to give time for the [pontoon] bridge to be built and the remainder of the troops to cross. The day was foggy and drizzly, and we could see but a short distance, though all day long we could hear the thunder of the battle which Hooker was fighting miles away [on Lookout Mountain]. Near sundown we reached the Atlanta Railroad which runs close around the point of the ridge. Here we halted to correct our lines, and a few minutes later I saw a column of troops approaching, which halted, and the commanding officer, Lieut. Col. Von Blessingh of the 37th Ohio, rode up and told me that he had been ordered to carry the ridge and asked if I would go ahead with my company as skirmishers. We had not seen any rebels and therefore felt very brave, and I replied that I thought we could. I gave the order and up we went on the run. We reached the summit just in time to meet a rebel line of skirmishers, who were advancing from the other direction. A few shots were exchanged, and they then fell back and we took possession. The troops moved up and we worked all night, part of the time by the feeble light of an eclipsed moon, throwing up earthworks which were occupied by Wood's Battery [Capt. Peter B. Wood, Battery A, 1st Illinois Light Artillery].

When the morning of the 25th dawned we found that the hill we had taken was not the main ridge, but a large isolated knob separated from the main ridge by a deep and narrow ravine through which ran a wagon track. Soon after daylight Gen. Sherman came up on the knob, and a few minutes later an order came to me and Capt. Warner of Company E to take our companies and carry the point of the main ridge, where the rebels had a line of rifle pits. The men were still digging when the order came, and they threw down their shovels, picked up their guns, formed their line and started. It was the understanding that they were to advance firing, then halt behind trees, load and advance again; but once started this was forgotten and they went on a dead run down one side of the ravine, across the valley and up the other side, driving before them or capturing a few skirmishers in the valley. In less than five minutes they had driven the rebels out of their rifle pits with the bayonet. One man was killed and one wounded in the charge. A Johnny raised his gun to shoot Capt. Warner, who yelled out, "Who the hell are you shooting at?" Either the fellow was a raw recruit or the Captain's voice had a peculiarly persuasive influence over him, for he immediately dropped his gun and surrendered.

I now moved my company forward in skirmishing order about 20 rods and lay down to await further orders. The ridge was very narrow at the point, but widened rapidly and rose with considerable rapidity toward the south. The timber was thin and scattered so that we could plainly see the entertainment which our friends, the enemy, were preparing for us. About 40 rods or less from where we lay they had thrown up a line of log breastworks clear across the ridge, and behind it lay part of Gen. Pat Cleburne's Texas and Arkansas troops, as stubborn fighters as the rebel army contained, and we could count the muzzles of 12 pieces of artillery. While we lay there we could see regiment after regiment coming down the slope at a double-quick and forming behind the works, until they were packed several lines deep. The point that we were threatening was a vital one, for if we succeeded in carrying these works Bragg's retreat would have been cut off, and he was weakening his center to protect his flank.

About 10 o'clock an order came to me to charge the rebel lines. I had been so absorbed in watching them that I had not observed what was going on behind me, and supposed that the order was to us alone. I exclaimed, "Thunder! Do they expect me to take those works with my 40 men?" But orders were orders and we started. Then the infernal regions seemed to break loose. Shell, grape, canister and bullets seemed to fill the air. Fortunately they all went over our heads, but we had advanced only a few rods when bullets began to whistle past our ears from behind.

Looking around to learn what the trouble was, I saw some 10 rods behind us our line of battle advancing and opening fire. The 40th Illinois, 46th Ohio, part of the 30th Ohio, and parts of the 103rd Illinois and 37th Ohio, probably not more than 1,000 men in all, were all that there was room for on the narrow ridge. I hurriedly moved my men by the left flank out of their fire and formed on the left of the line. Gen. John M. Corse led them on gallantly and they made a long and desperate fight against four or five times their number, until the General fell and was carried off the field. Then the line began to break up into groups and gather behind the trees, and finally a countercharge by the enemy drove the greater part of them down the hill.

Being the farthest away from the point, we were the last to reach it, and, disliking the idea of giving up all the ground we had gained, I halted my company at the rifle pits and we lay down. A number of men from different regiments stayed with us, and soon enough came back from below to present a front which the enemy did not attempt to disturb. The regiments engaged in this charge lost about one-fourth of their men. No more attacks were made by our division, but the Fourth Division (Ewing's) made a desperate assault on our right, which was repulsed as severely as our own. We did not succeed in breaking the enemy's lines.

## 'The enemy were running like wild cattle'

### 1st Lieut. R.M. Collins
### Company B
### 15th Texas Cavalry (Dismounted)

On the evening of November 23rd our division [Cleburne's] was put in motion moving in the direction of Cleveland. We marched about eight miles, went into camp and it is said were waiting for transportation by railroad to Knoxville. All night of the 23rd Gen. Bragg had details of men to keep up fires on that part of the line we had left, beating drums as if he had a big force on that part of the line. But Gen. Grant was too old a bird to be caught with that kind of chaff, and just kept on pressing.

■ Col. James H. Dayton, 4th West Virginia Infantry, led the only regiment from the newly formed "Mountain State" to serve in the Army of the Tennessee. Two companies under Capt. J.L. Mallernee were detached from the 4th during the Tunnel Hill operations, and loaned to a six-company force commanded by Lt. Col. George H. Hildt, 30th Ohio. "At about 3 a.m. [on November 24] we crossed the river on the pontoon boats," Hildt reported, "swimming our horses alongside holding their heads to the boats out of water, and, as it was icy cold, and they were forced to remain in it for nearly thirty minutes, they were so chilled and stiffened that they could scarcely ascend the bank to get out."

In the ensuing battle Dayton's regiment was lucky — losing only seven men wounded; the 30th Ohio suffered seven dead and 32 wounded.

■ Private William D. Swann served as a gunner in Douglas' Texas Battery at Tunnel Hill. His captain, James P. Douglas, commanded all the artillery of Cleburne's division on November 25 — four batteries of 16 guns — and lost 23 men killed and wounded. Ten days later Douglas wrote to his wife: "I have again mingled in the carnage of battle and marched for hours amid the deafening roar of artillery. On the right, the part of the field on which my division was posted gave the Yankees a terrible whipping, but this availed us nothing, as our center gave way and forced the entire army to retire ... We have not been as successful as we could desire, but still have no cause for despondency. The Vandals can never subjugate us. Our cause is just and will prevail."

While it was yet dark, on the morning of the 24th our division was moved back and took position just in rear of our old line, and east of the ridge. With permission I went to the top of the ridge, and from where we were we could see over the whole valley, and it was alive and working with long lines of blue infantry, bristling with bayonets. It was a fine view of the pomp and splendor of glorious war, and we felt it in our very bones that the ground was going to be torn up and lots of people hurt in the neighborhood before many days.

All at once, about 4:30 in the afternoon, we were put in line and started off at a double-quick to the right. We knew from the way couriers were dashing around, the serious expressions on the faces of those in high places, the haste with which we were being moved, and the old decks of playing cards the boys ahead of us were throwing away, that somebody was getting hurt or we were in a race with the Federals for some important point. Referring to the playing cards, it is strange that men will carry something in their pockets they are ashamed to be found dead with. I had seen this throwing of cards away before.

We crossed the mountain right over the Chattanooga & Cleveland Railroad tunnel, and formed in line in a valley between the mountain proper and a high point of mountain that seemed to jut down between Missionary Ridge and the river. We moved forward up the mountain but the Federals were already there; they had beaten us to the position. We fell back and took position on the main range, and formed a line with the left of our brigade resting over the tunnel already referred to, and extending along the mountain to the right, with Douglas' Texas Battery of Napoleon guns in the center and about 700 yards air line from the Federal battery on the point of the mountain already named.

It was now dark, the night cold and crisp, and being so close to the enemy we could have no fires and we had to just grin and bear it. As soon as the first streak of daylight began to paint the east, the crack of the skirmishers' rifles in our front rang out, and they sounded as loud as cannon. Capt. Rhodes Fisher was again in command of the skirmishers. During the night we threw up temporary works such as we could make of old logs, loose rocks, etc., from where we were. Chattanooga was on an exact line between us and the point of Lookout Mountain.

The morning of the 25th of November was bright and frosty. We could see the city and the valley. Long lines of infantry were moving up in our front. Now they are in range of our batteries; shot and shell were sent into their lines, they waver but on they come. Just now Maj. Gen. Cleburne comes up on foot in rear of our line. He ordered me to take one company of the 3rd and 5th Confederate [of Brig. Gen. Lucius E. Polk's brigade] and deploy them as skirmishers some forty yards down the mountain and in front of our line, and to remain until driven in by the enemy. I tipped my cap, formed the company and obeyed the command.

We were immediately under our own guns, and when the artillery duel opened between the Douglas battery and the Federal battery on the high point just in our front, ours and our company of Irishmen's position was a noisy one, and very dangerous. After getting the company deployed, I crouched down behind a very friendly chestnut tree. A big burly Irishman a few paces to my right said he was too busy to take a tree, when I reproached him for not protecting himself as much as possible. He was a fine sol-

# Cleburne's quiet humor

**Maj. Gen. Patrick R. Cleburne's division anchored the Confederate right flank at Tunnel Hill, hurriedly sent there late on November 24 to oppose Sherman. "I was determined to construct a slight work in front of my line," he wrote. "I was prevented for some time by an eclipse of the moon, which rendered the [early] morning very dark, but at length, distributing our few axes, we went to work."**

**One of the soldiers in Cleburne's line that night was Sergeant John M. Berry of Company I, 8th Arkansas, who recounted two earlier incidents in 1863 involving his commanding general:**

"When we were in camp at Wartrace, Tenn., our regiment was out drilling. After maneuvering a while we were halted at a front face. In a few moments Gen. Cleburne, who had been watching us, rode up and called 'Attention, battalion! By the right of companies!' He hesitated an instant, when Capt. Ellis of Company C sprang in front of his company and commanded, 'Company, right face!' when Cleburne called out: 'Hold on there, Captain, you don't know but that I was going to say by the right of companies into the moon.' The laugh was on Ellis, and the General finished the order by adding, 'To the rear into column.'

"On another occasion when at Bellbuckle, Tenn., one Sunday morning we were out for inspection and the General himself came slowly down the line. Everything went well until he came to Ben Stewart of my company. Ben was not noted for keeping a clean gun. The General took the gun, examined it critically, then handing it back he looked Ben in the face with a reproachful expression in his eyes and said: 'I hope I do you no injustice, my man, but I don't think you have washed your face for several days.' After that Ben's gun and face were always ready for inspection."

**The signed carte de visite of Cleburne, below, was taken in January 1864 at the Ben Oppenheimer Gallery in Mobile, Ala. Serving as best man for Gen. Hardee's marriage on January 13, Cleburne accompanied the wedding party to Mobile — his only furlough during the war.**

# Texas impetuosity

Just before noon on November 25, Federal brigades under Giles A. Smith and John M. Corse assaulted the precipitous, heavily wooded northern side of Tunnel Hill, occupied by Brig. Gen. James A. Smith's Texas brigade of Cleburne's division. Positioned on the crest above the Texans were four Napoleon guns of Swett's Mississippi Battery, its cannoneers fully exposed to enemy fire.

Private William J. Oliphant (left) of Company G, 6th Texas, helped defend the battery, observing the Federals rapidly advance, then charge Swett's guns. Oliphant carried scars from three slight wounds received at Chickamauga, including a broken jaw. His regiment, consolidated with the 10th Texas Infantry and 15th Texas (Dismounted) Cavalry, was ordered to counterattack when the enemy rushed within 150 feet of its position. A withering volley from the Texans smashed the assault, and the Federals then sought cover further down the hill. A heavy price was paid for the success. Oliphant's colonel, Roger Q. Mills, and brigade commander Smith were severely wounded while leading the counter-charge. Swett's gunners also suffered severely, losing all their officers and sergeants until command devolved upon a corporal.

Later in the afternoon the 6th Texas again counter-charged, carrying Oliphant and his comrades past the foot of the slope. Scores of Union soldiers and four stands of Federal colors were captured by nightfall.

dier, the balls were flying fast, but he would stand out in a clear place, take deliberate aim and then watch to see the effect of his shot. Like all others of his race he was a wit. We had been there for some time; he finally with a twinkle about his eyes, said, "Are you cold, Lieutenant?" I assured him that I was not. "Well," he said, "I didn't know, but thought ye were either cold or domed badly scared from the way yer trembling and shaking." He was a splendid specimen of manhood. Just before sundown a shot broke his neck and he fell dead not ten feet from where the conversation occurred in the morning.

About 10 o'clock we were run in and then our whole line sallied out and drove the enemy back. About 2 p.m. the fighting seemed to be general all along the line. Some two hundred yards in our front and near the Chattanooga end of the tunnel, there stood a dwelling, barn and some other outhouses, and right in the heat of battle three or four women came out and passed through our line. They did not seem to be alarmed nearly as much as I have seen a Texas woman get at a mouse.

Grant seemed to be concentrating his whole army on Cleburne's front. On they came line after line. I remember one brigade that had a green flag; they got up to within forty yards of our line. Things were getting pretty blue all around there. Gen. Cleburne came up on foot just in rear of our brigade and said in a very quiet sort of way, "Boys, take them in." That was enough. We sailed into them, captured many prisoners, six stands of colors and lots of guidons. I had unbuckled my sword, and as I went over the works left it, grabbed a rock and went in. A good many of the Yankees played dead that had not been touched. We captured a whole company that had taken shelter behind a big chestnut log; they were more than willing to surrender. Our regiment fought the 26th Missouri. We learned this from the wounded left on the field.

We thought we had gained the day when the truth of the matter was we had broke their line just the length of our brigade. Some of us were very much annoyed at a general charge not being ordered, as the enemy in our front were running like wild cattle. Merritt Mathews, Chris Gose and I and several others lit out after them on our own hook and must have gone three hundred yards inside of their lines, when all at once we discovered a full line of Federal infantry not more than forty yards to our right. They turned loose on us but we all made it out. Gose was shot in the back, but the ball struck where his two blankets, rolled up and worn like a shot pouch, crossed. The blankets saved his life. A brass button turned a ball that struck Major Sanders square in the breast; it broke his right arm.

After this everything was very quiet, and we thought we had gained a great victory. It was very natural for we had cleaned up everything that came against us that day in the charge. Gen. [James A.] Smith and Col. [Roger Q.] Mills, commanding the 6th, 10th and 15th Texas consolidated regiments, were wounded, and the command of the brigade fell on Col. Hiram B. Granbury of the 7th Texas Infantry.

Some time after nightfall, Col. Granbury ordered Capt. J.L. Leonard to take four companies and deploy them as skirmishers in front of our brigade, with orders to remain out until driven in. He had me detailed to act as adjutant, and the above orders were the first hint I had of things not being all right. The line of skir-

■ Brig. Gen. James A. Smith's Texas infantry and dismounted cavalry bore the brunt of fighting along Cleburne's front at Tunnel Hill. At midday, Smith — promoted to brigade command less than two months earlier — led a spirited counter-charge against the Federal XV Corps, and was seriously wounded when a musket ball pierced both thighs. Six months later he rejoined his brigade, but was again wounded on July 22, 1864 outside Atlanta. Following the Tunnel Hill fight Cleburne referred to Smith's brigade as a "band of heroes." One year later, Smith became division commander after Cleburne's death at Franklin.

■ Brig. Gen. Joseph H. Lewis commanded Kentucky Confederates known as the "Orphan Brigade." On November 25 his five regiments were detached from Bate's division to reinforce Cleburne at Tunnel Hill. "Cleyburn occupied the ridge just above us & occasionally I would go up to their line," wrote Sergeant Major John W. Green of the 9th Kentucky. "They had swept their front clean of Yankies ... the side of the ridge in their front was strewn with dead yankies & looked like a lot of boys had been sliding down the hill side, for when a line of the enemy would be repulsed they would start down hill & soon the whole line would be rolling down like a ball, it was so steep a hill side just there."

mishers was deployed about one hundred and fifty yards in advance of the line we had held all day.

About us and in rear of our line the dead and wounded were thick on the ground. We learned from the wounded that we had been fighting Missouri troops, especially the 26th Missouri Infantry. Lieut. Burris of Company B, 15th Texas Infantry, was personally acquainted with several of them. We rendered such assistance as we could to the wounded.

By 8 o'clock quiet prevailed in the valley of Chattanooga, the pale moon looked down into the faces of many Confederates and Federals whose life blood had baptized the hills and valleys in a cause which each thought was in the right.

## 'Now we give them fits'

### Capt. Samuel T. Foster
### Company H
### 24th Texas Cavalry (Dismounted)

About 3 o'clock in the night [early morning of November 25] I was ordered to take my Company and go forward and relieve the pickets. The night very dark and here along these high mountains and steep hill sides, and tall timber, and thick undergrowth of course it was very *very* dark — I went forward — found one end of the picket line and followed the line leaving one man every 10 or 15 ft as he could find a suitable tree to stand behind. I then made arrangements to pass any word *from,* or *to,* me, along the line from one to another — Stood perfectly still till day light — We then discover that the Brigd. is not behind us, where it was when we left it, but it has gone some where, and we don't know where. As soon as it is light enough to see anything one of my men (Theo Cullen) says "Capt. I see one. Can I shoot at him?" I told him wait till it was a little lighter and then blaze away.

He fired at him in a few minutes thereafter and in so doing fired the first gun for that day — As soon as the boys can see they open fire all along the line, which is replied to by the Yanks. I lost one man here — by the name of Geo W Woods. Shot in the throat and cut his windpipe. We keep up a brisk fire until 8½ or 9 o'clock a.m. when the Yanks charge us or rather they advance with their line of battle on our skirmish line. I passed the word down the line "to fall back slowly, but keep firing, from tree to tree as we fall back" — After falling back about 200 yards we come into an open ground; that is no undergrowth; but plenty large trees — so I could see nearly all my men at once — a thing I had not been able to do heretofore, and they are in a very good line — and going back from tree to tree — stop and load and shoot two or three times and go on again. The Yanks pressed us very hard, and we killed several that we could see fall. Our boys would see one of their men a little in advance, they would hide behind a big Oak and be nearly certain to get him, then he would move on, seemingly satisfied with what he had done. After going this way about ¾ of a mile, we find the Brigd. behind some temporary works made that morning of logs piled up on each other — I assemble my men, get over the works and take our place in line.

Then the fun commenced in good earnest. Now in a few minutes all is quiet — but soon a battery on a high place just on our left

■ Texans and Arkansans of Cleburne's division defend the crest of Tunnel Hill in this sketch by Alfred R. Waud. Early in the afternoon Federals charged the west slope, as described by Cleburne: "The enemy lay down behind trees, logs and projecting rocks, their first line not 25 yards from the guns [of 1st Lieut. Thomas J. Key's Arkansas battery], and opened fire. Tier after tier of the enemy, to the foot of the hill and in the valley beyond, supplied this fire and concentrated the whole on a space of not more that 40 yards, till it seemed like one continuous sheet of hissing, flying lead."

opens — a battery on top of the mountain in our rear opens. Shooting over our heads. In a few minutes the Yank line of blue coats come in sight at about 400 yards and our small arms, and theirs, all open, and they keep coming — but when they get about 100 yds closer they fall back in bad order — in other words they run — all of which I enjoy hugely — we just laugh and hollow.

By going just over the hill 500 yds they are out of sight of us. They reform and come again — and just to see them blue coats fall is glorious. We can see them dropping all along their lines, sometimes great gaps are made, they can't stand it, and away they go to find shelter from our bullets.

In a little while a fresh set comes. They have a flag. I told my men to go in for that flag and down it came, another one picks it up and down he went, then another — until away they all go leaving three dead in trying to carry that flag. They got in nearly 100 yds of us before they broke — and there are a great many dead left on the ground, and wounded ones crying for help — One man is helping another to get away and they are both shot down together. Now the fun of all this is that we are behind these logs and are not getting hurt one particle.

From the noise on our left they are charging all along the lines, for Artillery and small arms are making a constant roar all the time, but we don't notice it except when we happen to stop a little

■ Posed here at parade rest, Company C of the 56th Illinois saw action at Tunnel Hill in Col. Green B. Raum's brigade, J.E. Smith's division. Supporting Matthies' battered brigade, Raum was wounded as was the 56th's commander, Major Pinckney J. Welsh, during a Confederate counterattack that pushed the Federals downhill near the railroad tunnel.

In this photograph (probably taken at Corinth, Miss.), Capt. John E. Barker stands second from left next to his drummer, while 1st Lieut. John C. Lewis is in the rear at right. Their men are attired in a mixture of frock and sack coats, though all wear felt hats.

while. Our artillery keep up a continuous roar as fast as they can load and shoot them.

There are men bringing us ammunition and the men don't put it in their cartridge boxes but lay it upon the logs in front of them to be convenient — Here they come again for about the sixth time, and they come like they were going to walk right over us — Now we give them fits. See how they do fall, like leaves in the fall of the year. Still they advance, and still we shoot them down — and still they come. Oh this is fun to lie here and shoot them down and we not get hurt. Ark. Post was not like this.

This is business, we can see what we are doing here, when we kill a man we know it, we see him fall — They are now coming in a run stooping low to the ground but when they get in about 50 yards of us they halt, commence wavering, some keep coming, others hang back, some are killed [with]in 20 ft of our works, and finally, without any command our men commenced jumping over the works like sheep and Yelling like only Texans can, and charged into them killing a great many more, and run them back again. I was standing on top of the logs Yelling like an indian, when some poor deluded Yank — not having the fear of Confederates before his eyes, supposed to be a long way off, shot me in the right leg — the ball going cross ways under my knee, and just over the big leader. Several cried out, "Capt. you are hit. The Capt.s hit," and several came to help me down, at first I could not realize that I was shot. It felt like someone had struck my leg with the side of a ramroad, or a stick and benumbed it somewhat.

The boys soon ripped my pants open and there it was, bleeding very freely — No mistake I was wounded. The litter bearers are called. I am put on a litter and two men take it up and go in a trot until they get over the hill out of the range of the bullets, where I am put in an ambulance and carried to the field hospital.

When it comes my turn I am put on a table with all the instruments close by like I was to be carved up into soup bones. The Surgeon examined my wound, run his finger in the hole — but couldn't put it clear through so he put the other finger in the other side, then he run his fingers in and out, first one then the other, until as he said there was no foreign substance left in there to hinder it from healing up. After night I am put in an Ambulance and carried to the R.R. and from some cause or other the Train don't get off before morning.*

## 'My head roared for hours'

### Diary of Private Nelson Stauffer Company A 63rd Illinois Volunteer Infantry

**Nov. 25 —** Fighting began in good earnest about daylight and was kept up constantly until dark. We threw up one line of breast works on the bank of the river, and another about a half mile from it. Then the third line near the top of the ridge. After throwing up one line of works for our Regiment I was detailed to help throw up another to protect [a] battery — making four lines of works in which I took an active part, and there wasn't much fun in it, or if there was I couldn't see it, for two of them were built under fire.

The 80th Ohio charged the rebs several times, but were repulsed each time with considerable loss. At one time they were driven clear back to the valley — and one little fellow I guess went clear to never. He threw his hat one way and his gun another, then walled up his eyes like a scared cat and made a B line for the open space near the battery, and such a gettin up and goen I never did see. He started toward the tennessee River, but where [he] went is hard to tell. As he passed our regiment we gave him the right of way and all the encouragement we could by yelling at him, "Go it little one, they're after ye." The next Regt. took up the theme, and so on as far as we could see him. He seemed willing to take our advice and go.

Just as this little fellow passed out of view and the roar of our encouraging words ceased, and my coffee pot on the fire looked enticeing — the water was just beginning to siz and the coffee grounds blubber — when the rebble reserve came down the hill with a fiendish yell, and gave our men no chance to rally. Just then our colonel [Joseph B. McCown] yelled out "Attention 63rd, fall in — fall in — forward double quick!" I gave my coffee pot a glancing doleful look as if to say "Fare you well brother Watkins oh." But we saved the battery at our left which the Rebs expected to take, and while they beat a hasty retreat up the hill I beat one toward my coffee pot, and strange to say it was still there.

After saving the battery I was detailed to fill some canteens.

■ Private Nelson Stauffer of Company A, 63rd Illinois. His diary entries during the Chattanooga campaign are filled with references to short rations and attempts to alleviate hunger. "One of the boys picked up a piece of board about 6 inches wide and 2½ feet long. On this board, and on an old hoe, we baked the most of our bread for the company. We mixed water and meal without salt or grease, spread it on the board and braced it up to the fire. Some who could not wait their turn for the board rolled their dough up in a ball, and put it in the ashes and then piled coals on it. We filled up on this kind of bread until it went back on many of us."

On another occasion, Stauffer wrote: "Three of us saw a man with a sack of onions he had stolen from a sutler store. We bought about a peck of them, and sat down and ate them the same as if they were apples."

* Foster's wound healed and he returned to his regiment just before the Atlanta campaign started in May 1864.

■ Brig. Gen. Giles A. Smith commanded a XV Corps' brigade in the division led by his older brother, Morgan L. Smith. Giles Smith's six regiments spearheaded the Tennessee River pontoon landings early on November 24, and spent the day fortifying a spur of Missionary Ridge just north of Tunnel Hill.

Although not heavily engaged on November 25, Giles Smith's Illinois, Missouri and Ohio troops endured Confederate shell and musketry fire directed at Sherman's left flank. The fighting chaplain of the 55th Illinois, Milton L. Haney, later wrote: "As we were advancing upon the enemy's pickets through a region thickly covered with underbrush, I met General Giles A. Smith who had advanced beyond his post of duty. 'Chaplain,' said he, 'if I were you I would not go into that brush, for it is full of bullets.' I heeded his warning and he retired a little to the rear. Here he stood facing the enemy, when he was so severely wounded that he never fully recovered."

While at the spring my Regt. went on the skirmish line relieving the 80th Ohio. When I came back I asked a batteryman which way my regiment had gone. He pointed toward the mouth of his cannon, so I started toward them in the open space [in front of] the battery. Just as I got down the hill low enough for the cannon ball to go over my head the batteryman shot it off — I suppose to frighten me. It came very near knocking me down. My head roared for hours.

But on I went. My regiment deployed to the right of the battery-space, and being in that space — and the underbrush being thick, I missed them and began climbing the hill thinking they were still beyond me. I went until the minie balls whizzed around me so thick that I became suspicious that there was a mistake somewhere, so dodging behind a tree I looked back and saw my regt. several hundred yards to my left and below me, and if ever I ran crooked and dodged in all my life it was then. I reached the regiment without a scratch while I firmly believe 100 shots had been fired at me.

It now being near dusk the firing became less rapid. The word was passed along the line to prepare to charge at midnight but the rebs left about 10 o'clock, and we were not sorry. We had nothing to eat, and no prospect of getting anything until we took it from the enemy ...

## 'A mistake in orders'

### 1st Lieut. George W. Bailey
### Company E
### 6th Missouri Volunteer Infantry U.S.A.

On the 25th our brigade and division [of the XV Corps] were on the extreme left of our advance, which extended through timber and bottomland a considerable distance. Our first brush — with artillery accompaniment — was at [South Chickamauga] Creek. We drove the enemy back and captured his hastily abandoned camp. During this affair I was near Gen. Giles A. Smith, commanding our brigade, and saw him wounded by a rifle ball.

From what I understood at the time was owing to a mistake of orders, the 6th Missouri left the creek bottom to our left and swung clear around the north end of the Ridge to a very perilous and isolated position far in rear of the Confederate lines, and were still advancing, meeting no opposition, when we were hurriedly recalled. We were pretty tired when we returned and were assigned to a position to support our lines formed to assault Tunnel Hill. We were lying down at the west base of the Ridge just out of direct range of the Tunnel Hill guns. But shells and grape and canister-shot frequently tore through the tree tops over our heads.

I went forward to get a better view of the Confederate works, and came upon an officer who said he was Capt. Allison of an Iowa regiment that had been repulsed in the assault. Shortly thereafter a grape shot passed through his head and he fell dead.*

Late in the day the Confederate artillery seemed to have been

* Capt. Robert Allison commanded Company C, 6th Iowa.

entirely silenced by our batteries on the Ridge. After the repulse of the assault on Tunnel Hill the Confederates made a sally from their works and the 6th Missouri was ordered to check the same, which it did most effectively with a very accurate and destructive fire. This was the heaviest and only direct engagement of the 6th during the day. We all considered ourselves exceedingly lucky that a "mistake in orders" had probably kept us out of the assault.

## 'The sole of my shoe'

### Private John Potter
### Company I
### 101st Illinois Volunteer Infantry

November 25th was bright, the sun shining clear overhead. We drew rations and left the position we had held for nearly two days. The rebels appeared to be massing their forces against Gen. Sherman, who was seriously threatening their right. Howard's command was ordered to his support.

While we were on the "double-quick" to reinforce Sherman, the sole of my shoe gave way, turned back and tripped me up. I was considerably top-heavy, with three days' rations, a hundred rounds of cartridges, a blanket on my person, and gun at "right shoulder shift." The speed we were going it was impossible for me to recover, so I fell very hard, striking one of my knees on a small stump, bruising the cap severely and being very painful. However, I got up and went on with the command till we were halted for further orders. We rested half an hour or more. I was in great agony, and when I rose to my feet I found it impossible to proceed. I rolled up my pants and found my leg was greatly swollen and inflamed. The captain and orderly, seeing my condition, allowed me to drop out and they went on and left me to my fate.

As I lay there the battle continued to rage, but I was gratified to observe that it was moving farther away from me, indicating a victory for our forces. In spite of the din of battle and the hurrying past me of troops to the front, and the wounded to the rear and to the hospital, a feeling of lonesomeness came over me. No one paid me any attention and I could not help myself. Night was coming on and my comrades were all far away, following up the retreating Confederates.

Just at sundown an ambulance, with only two wounded men in it, approached. I hailed the driver, told him who I was and what was the matter with me. He said he only had orders to pick up the wounded of the 15th Corps and convey them to the hospital. I told him we had been detached from Thomas' army to reinforce Sherman; that I was far away from our own hospital and would have to remain there all night if I did not get help from him. At this he got out, and, with great difficulty, I was helped into the ambulance and conveyed to the field hospital of the 15th Corps.

The surgeons were very busy amputating limbs, extracting bullets from the wounded, and in other ways caring for them. The most needy cases of course received attention first. One of them came to me and examined my limb. Seeing I was helpless but not in danger, he remarked: "We'll attend to you after awhile." I never saw him again.

For a week I was unable to walk, but did crawl down to the

■ Major John B. Lesage, 101st Illinois. Taken at the end of the war, this photograph shows Lesage wearing a XX Corps badge on his commercially purchased sack coat, a garment favored by many officers for its comfort and utility. The XX Corps was formed in April 1864 by consolidating the XI and XII corps. The XII Corps star was retained as the XX Corps' badge.

■ Brig. Gen. John M. Corse, commanding a brigade in the 4th Division, XV Corps, pushed his troops within 30 yards of the Confederate breastworks on Tunnel Hill when he was hit in the leg by a spent ball. Soon after, regiments of the XI Corps were ordered forward to Corse's support. In one of these, Private John Potter of Company I, 101st Illinois, remembered: "We started double-quick to where the battle was raging fiercely on our left. We passed many wounded men, and the ambulances loaded with many more, hurrying to the Army of the Tennessee's field hospital that was near the mouth of South Chickamauga creek. We met an ambulance that was conveying Gen'l Corse who had been badly wounded in one of his limbs. He was regretting his misfortune very much, as I was told by [our captain] who heard him say: 'Can't a man have an extra leg or two, so when he loses one he can take up another,' mixing up his wandering talk with characteristic profanity."

Corse recovered from the wound, eventually received a division command and distinguished himself on October 5, 1864 in the battle of Allatoona, Ga., where he was again wounded.

river twice a day and bathed my bruised knee with cold water, which took out the inflammation and eased the pain, so that in a few days I could walk a little. My shoes were entirely worn out, and as I thought the men whose limbs were taken off would have no more use for shoes, I hobbled around to where the surgeons had performed their ghastly work, and there, among the mass of shoes, I found a pair. I do not think they belonged to the same man, but as they were right and left of the right size I appropriated them, although they were spattered with the blood of their late owners. If it had not been for the exigencies of war, I should have considered it very shocking to have worn them.

I got very tired of the hospital, and when I thought I could walk well enough to stand the trip, I went to Chattanooga and reported to the provost marshal there. He reported that the 11th Corps had gone with Sherman to reinforce Burnside at Knoxville and would likely be back before long, so he sent me to the soldiers' home to stay till they should return. I spent a couple of days there.

A German soldier of the 82nd Illinois Regiment was cooking what I took to be beef. As he seemed to have a good supply, I asked him if he could divide with me. We had had but a scant supply of pork for a long time, and I had had none of that since I was hurt. I had seen no beef for many weeks, and had been living on hard bread and coffee since leaving the regiment. The cooking beef was making my mouth water. The boy told me to help myself. I cooked and ate the meat with agreeable relish, and then asked my German friend where he had procured so much beef.

A broad grin spread over his countenance as he replied: "Yaw, it vas a beese of moole." I was a little taken back, but I had eaten it with such keen relish that I was not sentimental enough to "heave up Jonah," though I was sure the mule meat was taken from one of those unfortunate animals that had perished by starvation and been dead perhaps many days.

## 'You lead and we will follow'

### Private Henry H. Orendorff
### Company F
### 103rd Illinois Volunteer Infantry

**The 25th.** Before daylight we were up and ready for the coming conflict. Having taken our coffee and "hard tack," we did not have to wait long. Soon after 6 we advanced down the hill, crossed a narrow valley and began the ascent of Tunnel Hill, which was also very heavily timbered. Here our advance encountered the enemy's skirmish line and drove them back to their main line on top of the hill. This brought us in plain sight of their main fortified line, only about 400 yards distant, their first line being only half as far.

Our line was formed just below the crest of the ridge, and here we remained till about 11 a.m. while preparations were being made for the assault. The brigade was formed with the 103rd on the right, the 6th Iowa and 46th Ohio to our left, the 40th Illinois thrown forward as skirmishers.

Before we advanced, Gen. Corse ordered Maj. Willison to take 3 companies of the 103rd and deploy them about 30 paces in rear of the 40th Illinois, thus making a double skirmish line, with orders that when the "Charge" is sounded, to move rapidly to the front and halt for nothing, but go directly into the enemy's works, and that he would support him with the entire command.

The other regiments of the brigade having enlisted in 1861, and been in the battles of Ft. Donelson, Shiloh, Corinth and many other smaller ones in '62, had often suggested that the 103rd had only "come in to escape the draft, wear the uniform, eat the rations and walk along with *them,* but when it came to fighting, the old regiments would have to do that." Many of the 103rd thought when they were marched out to support the gallant "old 40th" that the time had now come when we could show them and all other "old soldiers" that the 103rd was composed of as good material as the 40th, or any other regiment in this or any other brigade.

The question was asked the men, shall we do it? and they answered, "You lead and we will follow." The bugle sounded the "Charge" and with a whoop and cheer our men sprang forward, receiving a terrible fire from the enemy, of both infantry and artillery as we passed through and beyond the 40th, carrying the outer line of the enemy's works and to within a few feet of their main line. Dropping behind trees, stumps, rocks or anything that would shield us from the enemy's fire, we there waited the promised support, which never came.

Finally the "Recall" was sounded, and we made our way down the steep hill as best we could, but leaving many of our comrades who had been killed or wounded. Below the crest of the ridge, Gen. Corse having been wounded in the first assault, Col. C.C. Walcutt [46th Ohio] assumed command of the brigade, and reforming it, advanced determined to break the line and carry the enemy's work, but it could not be done. This being a most important position in the enemy's line, Gen. Bragg had reinforced it to the depletion of his center.

The enemy outnumbering us nearly two to one, and being behind strong works and having two batteries of artillery bearing on the line of our approach, the attempt to take the hill was abandoned. The loss of the brigade had been very great in the two assaults, the 103rd suffering heavily. The three companies A, F and B, being on the skirmish line, of course suffered most. Many of the killed and wounded fell within 50 feet of the Rebel works, and some of them were riddled with canister and musket balls. A member of Company F, Joe S. Walters, getting a little too near, a lean, lank, hungry-looking Johnnie sergeant jumped over the works and demanded of him, "gimme that gun and come in hur, you damned yankee coward." Joe replied, "Here, take the gun, it ain't worth a cuss anyway." It had been hit with a bullet and was bent and spoiled. At this time a little corporal sprang over the works and grabbed Joe's other arm and with much bluster and many big oaths, ordered that "you come over here, you yankee coward," but Isaac Harn and another comrade were just at the right and heard the conversation. Harn gave the big sergeant the contents of his gun, bringing him to the ground, and Joe gave the little corporal a blow that brought him to the ground. Turning, he ran down the hill under a shower of bullets, escaping with the loss of one finger. Harn was killed soon afterward.

■ Major Asias Willison, 103rd Illinois, led Companies A, B and F as skirmishers partially covering Corse's brigade front during two separate assaults personally spearheaded by Corse until he was wounded. Willison's skirmish line, positioned directly behind that of the 40th Illinois under Major Hiram W. Hall, rushed through "a most terrific fire" of Confederate canister and musketry, that "it seemed almost impossible for any troops to withstand it." The 103rd lost 39 percent on the hillside. Skirmisher Henry Orendorff of Company F later wrote: "Of the 236 of the Reg't who went into the action (Cos. C and G being on duty in northern Ala.), 92 were either killed or wounded. Capt. [William] Walsh of Co. B was killed within 50 feet of the enemies' works, as were a number of men. The dead who fell near the works were all robbed of their watches and other valuables, as well as their shoes."

Commanding the 103rd the following May at Resaca, Ga., Willison was severely wounded by a shell fragment that killed his mount.

■ Major Hiram W. Hall, 40th Illinois, led the forwardmost skirmish line of Corse's brigade when it assaulted Tunnel Hill. Col. Charles C. Walcutt, who succeeded to brigade command after Corse was wounded in the charge, wrote three days later: "Being in easy canister and musket range, it seemed almost impossible for any troops to withstand it ... Every effort was made to reach the enemy's works, and only after repeated efforts had failed did the main portion of the men retire upon the ridge; some of the men yet remained in clusters on the opposite slope during the entire day, doing the enemy much damage; a few even reached the enemy's works, but were killed."

The three companies were recalled and those who were able formed on the color line, occasionally reminding the Rebs that we were still alive and in business at the old stand. We could hear the battle on our right and the cheers of our troops under Thomas as they drove the enemy from their works that they had left so thinly occupied, in order to strengthen their position on our front.

After dark we gathered up our dead and wounded, sending the last to the hospital. A trench having been prepared, we wrapped the dead in their blankets and tenderly laid them away.

## 'His dying gift'

### Private Victor H. Gould
### Company H
### 26th Illinois Volunteer Infantry

Mr. and Mrs. Clark

Dear friends,

It now becomes absolutely necessary for me to write you a letter in which I have sad, yea very sad news indeed, to tell you.

On the 25th of November we were called on to perform our duties on the bloody battlefield of Mission Ridge near Chattanooga. At 9 o'clock a.m. the battle opened and was quite severe, in which many of our brave fell wounded on the field.

At 12 o'clock midday George, your son, fell mortally wounded. He was struck with a shell, tearing his body most desperately, and also tearing both legs almost entirely off. He lived one hour, and then quietly fell asleep, leaving many true and loving and I trust christian friends to mourn his loss.

In the morning before going into the engagement he took from his pocket [the Bible] which he brought from home, and which he always carried wherever duty called him, and quietly read a few chapters which seemed to have a deep impression on his mind; and I trust had its desired effect. He seemed quite serious during the engagement, until he was struck by the fatal ball. His dying request I send you, but with serious and tender feelings do I attempt to write it: "Tell my parents," said he, "that I die a brave man and in defense of my country." He then took from his pocket the precious volume which he had been reading in the morning and gave it to me, requesting me to send it to Martha as his dying gift.

I was not permitted to take him off the field to bury his remains, for the battle was raging and becoming quite desperate on the left and also in our front, in which we lost a number of brave men. The battle lasted seven hours, and night coming on we retired back one mile for the night. Our dead lay on the field until the coming day ...

I will send George's testament as soon as I have an opportunity of so doing. George had four dollars in money, which the Captain will send you as everything falls into his hand to settle up. He requested me to write to you.

Finally fare you well,
V.H. Gould

## 'Something told me that I was doomed'

### 1st Lieut. Samuel H.M. Byers
### Adjutant
### 5th Iowa Volunteer Infantry

Our camp [north of the Tennessee River on November 23] was a concealed one in which no fires or lights were permitted — no noises allowed. In the darkness of the previous night the command had left bright fires burning in a wood, and had secretly marched to this hidden position. Close beside it, the broad and rapid waters of the Tennessee rolled off into the darkness. On the opposite bank numbers of rebel pickets kept guard, ignorant of our presence. Behind these pickets were the high hills known as Missionary Ridge, thoroughly intrenched and defended by a large rebel army. In a little creek close by lay secreted 116 pontoons. What were they there for? The silence, the secrecy, the mystery of the scene convinced us that there was work ahead — and that we had to do it.

Before sundown two great soldiers had quietly been inspecting the little camp and the banks of the river. They were Grant and Sherman. Other officers, strangers to us, had come and looked at the pontoons in the creek, and a great wagon-load of boat-oars had been quietly placed beside them. We were at supper when the order came to row over the river and assault at midnight. I laid down my knife and fork, and stopped eating. A strange sensation came over me. Certainly I had been in dangerous places before. The regiment had a record for gallantry. The names of five battles were already inscribed upon its banners. Within two years from enlistment half the men in the regiment had been killed, wounded or disabled. We already had our third colonel. Numerous of our line officers had been promoted to higher posts. My own red sash had been given me under the guns of Vicksburg. Yes, we had seen fighting, but I had always been a believer in presentiments, and, somehow, something told me that I was doomed — that some calamity was in store for me.

The critical situation and the vast consequences dependent on success or failure were known to us all as we lay in the shadows that evening, waiting the order to move over the dark river and assault the heights of Missionary Ridge.

Midnight came — but we still lay quiet; 2 o'clock, and we heard some gentle splashing in the water near us and the noise of muffled oars. Every man seized his rifle. "Quiet, boys — fall in quietly," said the captains. Spades were handed to many of us — we did not ask what for, we knew too well. Quietly the pontoon-boats had been slipped out of the little creek to our left and into the river, and quietly we stepped down the bank, two by two, into the rude craft. "Be prompt as you can, boys, there's room for thirty in a boat," said a tall man who stood on the bank near us in the darkness. Few of us had ever before heard the voice of our beloved commander. Sherman's kind words, his personal presence, his attention to every detail of the dangerous adventure, waked confidence in everyone. He was with us, and sharing the danger.

In a quarter of an hour a thousand of us were out in the middle of the river, afloat in the darkness. Would they fire on us from the opposite shore? — was our constant thought. Those were strange

■ Col. John M. Loomis, 26th Illinois, commanded a XV Corps' brigade that suffered the highest number of losses in Ewing's division — 37 killed, 342 wounded and 18 missing (40 wounded subsequently died). Artillery fire was responsible for many of the casualties, as Chaplain M.D. Gage, 12th Indiana, discovered a day later. Loomis placed Gage in charge of the brigade's burial detail, which the chaplain found to be "an arduous task and full of sadness. Thirty-five were buried where they fell, occupying the entire day till 9 o'clock p.m. Upon the hill-side, where the repeated charges had been repulsed, the dead thickly strewed the ground."

The chaplain found 10 officers and men from his regiment lying lifeless. At least half of them were killed by shellfire. Just hours before the battle Capt. Francis H. Aveline of Company B expressed to Gage a fatal presentiment, which proved true. Private Casper Miller, also of Company B, was struck by a shell and killed instantly; almost immediately another slammed into his prone body. Two others decapitated Corporal E.B. Copper of Company G and Private Henry Ridenbaugh of Company B. As Gage found, they "were not distinguishable except by a small remnant of hair at the back of the head, and by their clothing."

■ Col. Adolphus Buschbeck, 27th Pennsylvania, commanded the 1st Brigade, 2nd Division, XI Corps. These troops temporarily were assigned to assist Sherman at Tunnel Hill, and bivouacked the night of November 24 on the Sanderson farm. Advancing in support of Ewing's division the next morning, two of Buschbeck's three regiments suffered heavy casualties totalling 256 officers and men.

In this spring 1863 photograph taken near Sperryville, Va., Buschbeck is seated second from left, surrounded by members of his staff. Note XI Corps crescent on the brigade headquarters flag leaning against the tent.

feelings, we soldiers had, out in the middle of the river that night. We were not aware that a boat-load of our comrades in blue had crossed farther up the stream just at midnight, and had captured the rebel pickets on the bank without firing a shot. We met a boat in the water full of men — the captured pickets being rowed over to our side of the river. It was a fine ruse that had been played on them. The boys, crossing above, had got in behind them and then, calling out the "relief," deceived and captured all but one.

In half an hour we were up the opposite bank and creeping along through the thickets — a spade in one hand and a rifle in the other. What might happen any moment, we knew not. Where was the picket that had escaped? Why was not the whole rebel camp alarmed and upon us? Daylight came; but it found us two thousand strong, intrenched with rifle-pits a mile in length. What a sight for Bragg! Hand about, we worked and digged like beavers. An old Quaker came down to expostulate with us for ruining his farm by such digging. The scene was ludicrous and the boys gave a derisive little cheer for "Broad-brim." The noise drew upon us the shells from a hidden battery and cost us two wounded men. It very nearly cost our friend his life, as an exploding shell left a hole within a yard of him twice as broad as his big hat.

Still we dug on at our rifle-pits. Other regiments were ferried across. By noon the pontoon bridge was down behind us and soon the whole army corps was over.

All the afternoon we maneuvered and fought for position, chasing the enemy off one high hill-spur only to find him better intrenched behind another. These were the outlying hills between Missionary Ridge proper and the banks of the river. The real position was across fields and hollows, and farther up on the mountain. Sullenly and slowly the enemy gave way, preparing in his high position for the battle of the morrow. That night my regiment stood picket in the wood at the front. The ground was cold and wet, none of us slept a wink and we were almost freezing and starving. It had been one vast strain, and now a battle was coming on. All night long we could hear the rebel field-batteries taking position on Missionary Ridge.

The 25th of November dawned clear and beautiful, and with the sunrise came the bugle-sound for Corse's brigade at our center to advance on the enemy. All the morning the hills and woods in front of Missionary Ridge resounded with the crash of musketry. The battle raged for over an hour for the possession of a single hill crest. Once the hail of bullets became so heavy that a temporary halt was made. The enemy had the advantage of position and numbers everywhere. So close were they, and so protected behind rifle-pits, logs and boulders, that they could throw stones on the assaulting column and do almost as much harm with them as with bullets. More regiments were sent in to Corse, and the hand-to-hand assault was renewed till Corse himself was borne wounded from the field. Still his men fought on, retreating not a foot. Far off across Chattanooga Valley Hooker's men were driving in the left flank of the rebel army.

It was 2 o'clock when our division, my own regiment with it, was ordered to fix bayonets and join in the assault on the ridge. We had been concealed from the enemy all the forenoon by the edge of a wood; yet his constant shelling of this wood showed that he knew we were there. As the column came out upon the open ground and in sight of the rebel batteries, their renewed and concentrated fire knocked the limbs from the trees about our heads. An awful cannonade had opened on us. In front of us was a rail fence. Its splinters and fragments flew in every direction. "Jump the fence, boys; tear it down!" was the order, and never was a fence scaled more quickly. It was nearly half a mile to the rebel position and we started on the charge, running across the open fields. I had heard the roaring of heavy battle before, but never such a shrieking of cannon-balls and bursting of shells as met us on that run. We could see the rebels working their guns, while in plain view other batteries galloped up, unlimbered and let loose upon us. Behind us our own batteries were firing at the enemy over our heads till the storm and roar became horrible. The line officers screamed at the top of their voices, trying to repeat the orders to the men. "Steady, steady. Bear to the right! Don't fire! Steady, steady," was yelled till every one of us was hoarse, and until the fearful thunder of the cannonade made all commands unheard and useless.

Halfway over we had to leap a ditch, perhaps six feet wide and nearly as many deep. Some of our regiment fell into this ditch and could not get out; a few tumbled in intentionally and stayed there. I saw this, ran back and ordered them to get out, called them

■ Brig. Gen. Charles L. Matthies commanded the 3rd Brigade of J.E. Smith's division, XVII Corps. Ordered to assault the hill above the railroad tunnel, Matthies' four regiments double-quicked into "a hot place. Batteries plowed the ground around us," he wrote. "I was turning round to caution my men to fire low and sure [when] I was struck by a bullet in the head, which felled me to the ground."

Regaining consciousness, Matthies turned over command to Col. Benjamin Dean, 26th Missouri, who relinquished it to the 5th Iowa's colonel, Jabez Banbury. Dean's acting adjutant, 1st Lieut. William H. Mengel of Company H, recalled: "The regiment ... first walked, then crawled until we got so close to [the Confederate] line and cannon that neither side could venture to hold up their heads to shoot. The men commenced to throw rocks at each other, of which there was a good supply where our regiment was laying in line. We had two men severely wounded by rocks from the enemy."

■ Col. Jabez Banbury, 5th Iowa, had one-third of his regiment taken prisoner at Tunnel Hill. "Many of my men were compelled to submit," he reported, "including most of the color company and color guard. Those who escaped did so through a shower of balls, and yells from the enemy to halt."

Among those taken prisoner, Corporal Charles Fosdick of Company K later wrote: "To stay in an open field, contending with a superior force, strongly fortified, was more than men could stand. Gen. Matthies gave the order to 'Fix bayonets,' which was taken up by our Colonel, who shouted at the top of his voice: 'Fifth Iowa, fix bayonets, *charge!'* The brigade presses on up the steep hillside, only to be mowed down by canister and minie ball. They reach the rebel works and jump inside. The struggle is a hand-to-hand one; rebel and Yank go down together, pierced through with each other's bayonets. The rebels are reinforced, we are surrounded and ninety-five of the 5th Iowa are prisoners of war."

cowards, threatened them with my revolver. They did not move. Again I hurried on with the line.

In ten minutes the field was crossed, the foot of the ascent was reached and now the Confederates poured into our faces the reserved fire of their awful musketry. It helped little that we returned it from our own rifles, hidden as the enemy were in rifle-pits, behind logs and stumps, and trees. Still we charged and climbed a fence in front of them, and charged again. The order was given to lie down and continue firing.

That moment someone cried, "Look to the tunnel! They're coming through the tunnel!" There, on the right, pouring through a tunnel in the mountain and out of the railway cut, came the gray-coats by hundreds, flanking us completely. "Stop them!" cried our colonel to those of us at the right. "Push them back!" It was but the work of a few moments to rise to our feet and run to the mouth of the tunnel, firing as we ran. Too late! They were through by hundreds and a fatal enfilading fire was cutting our line to pieces.

"Shall I run over there too?" I said to the colonel. We were both kneeling on the ground close to the regimental flag. He assented. When I rose to my feet and started it seemed as if even the blades of grass were being struck by bullets. As I ran over I passed many of my comrades stretched out in death, and some were screaming in agony. For a few minutes the whole brigade faltered and gave way.

Colonel Matthies, our brigade commander, was sitting against a tree, shot in the head. Instantly it seemed as if the whole rebel army was concentrated on that single spot. For a few moments I lay down on the grass, hoping the storm would pass over and leave me. Lieutenant Miller, at my side, was screaming in agony. He was shot through the hips. I begged him to try to be still; he could not.

Now, as a second line of the enemy was upon us, and the first one was returning, shooting men as they found them, I rose to my feet and surrendered. "Come out of that sword," shrieked a big Georgian with a terrible oath. Another grabbed at my revolver and bellowed at me "to get up the hill quicker than hell." It was time, for our own batteries were pouring a fearful fire on the very spot where we stood. The rocks and the earth flew about us, and everything seemed to smoke. Not only this, our brigade was rallying to charge again and other brigades were climbing with them to the hill-top. Still more, Thomas was storming the center.

In a moment I reflected that I was a prisoner, and horrible pictures of Libby flashed through my mind*— and with them the presentiment of evil I had had the night before the assault. I took a blanket from one of my dead comrades lying near me, and at the point of the bayonet I was hurried on up the mountain, the fire from our own guns constantly increasing. I passed numerous

* Two weeks after the battle Byers entered Libby Prison in Richmond and was confined there until May 1864, when he was moved to an officers' prison in Macon, Ga. He escaped on July 15, walked to Atlanta wearing a makeshift uniform and masqueraded as a Confederate ordnance sergeant until discovered on July 23. Further confinement in Charleston and Columbia, S.C., ended on February 17, 1865, when Sherman's troops entered the city. A few days later Byers joined Sherman's

lines of the enemy standing or lying in the rifle-pits with which the whole mountain-side was honeycombed, both in front of Sherman and in front of Thomas. In a hollow back of the lines I was mustered with others of my brigade who had been captured. Three of [the previous] night's messmates were among them. We were relieved of our watches, our money, our knives, even our pocket-combs, by a chivalrous young officer of the guard.

## 'We could have repulsed them with stones'

### Col. James C. Nisbet
### 66th Georgia Volunteer Infantry
### Brigade commander
### Walker's Division, Hardee's Corps

The night after the Lookout Mountain fight, I was ordered to withdraw my brigade (Wilson's) quietly from the enemy's front on Chattanooga Creek and join the rest of the division in a march across the valley. Ferguson's Battery of six twelve-pounder Napoleon guns attached to our brigade had to be dragged up on Missionary Ridge.

Lieutenant R.T. Beauregard, commanding Ferguson's Battery, reported that his horses were too weak to pull the guns up. I detailed a company of infantry with each piece; some of the men pushed, others pulled with ropes, and at last we were all on top.

When we reached the crest it was still dark. We moved slowly to the right over a dim, wood-road. At several points we had to make a road for the artillery. Not long before daylight we arrived at our position in the new line, which was near and to the left of the tunnel, where the railroad from Chattanooga to Knoxville passes under Missionary Ridge. General Gist, commanding Walker's Division — General Walker, wounded at Chickamauga, had returned, but not to the command of his division — and myself assisted Lieutenant Beauregard in posting his guns on a high point in our rear, so that they could fire over our line of infantry.

The arrangement was that Stevenson's Division should touch Cleburne's Division which was just to the right of the tunnel, and the right of Walker's Division touch on Stevenson's left. But it was found that even after much space had been allowed between the men the line was not completely occupied. There was a gap right over the tunnel. I was ordered to fill it with one of my regiments. I detached from the brigade the 66th Georgia Regiment and the 26th Georgia Battalion for this purpose. As the movements of the enemy seemed to be against this point I remained here most of the day.

At daylight, November 25th, I saw the enemy approaching in line of battle below us through the Glass farm. I rode up to my battery and ordered Lieutenant Beauregard to commence firing.

■ Col. James C. Nisbet, 66th Georgia/26th Georgia Battalion, commanded Gen. Claudius C. Wilson's old brigade of Walker's division at Missionary Ridge. Before the battle, Nisbet's pickets were posted along Chattanooga Creek — not far from the camp of the 66th whose men possessed large Sibley tents. "I obtained the tents by requisition [in Florida]," Nisbet later wrote. "When we got them up, each company's in regulation order, our camp looked pretentious and was the envy of the old troops. Except [for] the general's headquarters, Bragg's whole army boasted no tents but our 'Indian wigwams.' "

While fighting progressed November 24 on Lookout Mountain, Nisbet's camp became a target for Union artillery. He continued: "The Federal batteries across the river were keeping up a terrific fusillade. My tents drew their fire. The inference was that they must be the headquarters of some 'big general.' Most of their shots were directed at my regiment and battalion. I was eating dinner when one of their shells, bursting overhead, came crashing right down on our camp chest, sending our dishes and dinner 'hell-west-and-winding.' "

---

staff at the general's invitation. He was impressed with a song Byers wrote during his Columbia imprisonment — "Sherman's March to the Sea."

Byers later wrote: "As to the eighty comrades who had been captured with me that 25th of November in the assault on Missionary Ridge, all but sixteen were dead [by war's end]. Nine of my old Company B of the Fifth Regiment were taken prisoners, and only one of them survived the horrors of Andersonville."

■ Brig. Gen. Alfred Cumming's four Georgia regiments from Carter L. Stevenson's division reinforced Cleburne at mid-morning November 25. Cumming's right rested above the railroad tunnel, and his troops immediately were drawn into battle. During the next five hours the Georgians were involved in ferocious fighting, charging downhill three times and engaging the Federals hand to hand. However, Cumming's success proved costly as all his regimental commanders became casualties. Three were wounded while the fourth, Col. J.T. McConnell, 39th Georgia, was shot through the head and killed.

He asked: "Have you an order to that effect?"

I said: "Commence firing, Lieutenant; what we see is order enough for me."

He opened with six pieces, and Captain Evan Howell, whose battery was there, also commenced firing. The enemy in my immediate front halted at the Railroad at the foot of the ridge and many went into the tunnel. Buschbeck's Brigade was advancing against the regiment on my right, just beyond the tunnel. I rode over there to see who they were and to tell them to be ready. I found that it was the 39th Georgia Regiment of Cumming's Brigade.

Some of the men broke ranks and came to where I was sitting on my horse. We shook hands. It was the first time we had met in two and a half years. They thought I was still in Virginia. I told them that my regiment was on their left and that my battery was firing on the regiments approaching. I ordered them to get into line and be ready to receive the enemy who would soon be on the spot. This was done. We repulsed several charges of Buschbeck's Brigade, with the help of Beauregard's and Howell's batteries.

A part of the 39th Georgia led by Captain Seaborn Daniels finally charged down the ridge and captured a good many prisoners in the Glass House. But they were ordered back to the top of the ridge. In the meantime, Cleburne's Division — attacked on two sides — was fighting fiercely still further to the right, defeating the assailants with great slaughter and driving them off the ridge. Cleburne's men were assisted by Cumming's Georgia Brigade who went to them as reinforcements and made a gallant and successful charge, but not without misfortune. Colonel Joe McConnell of the 39th Georgia was killed. His body was brought back on a litter, passing by where I was sitting on my mare watching the Federal regiments which had started up against my regiment.

These regiments reached the mouth of the tunnel, but halted. I suppose they decided the ascent was too steep to accomplish their undertaking and that the mouth of the tunnel was mighty tempting shelter from our canister, which was a fact.

With my flanks protected, the ascent of Missionary Ridge was too steep anywhere, for any regiment in any army, to have taken the position from my regiment or any other well organized command. We could have repulsed them with stones. The Yanks not venturing up, my brigade and division were not severely engaged with small arms. Our artillery and skirmishers were hotly engaged from daylight until about noon.

In the afternoon General Sheridan and others charged Bragg's center. Two Confederate brigades there acted disgracefully, running away on the approach of the enemy, then refused to be rallied on top of the ridge. This exposed the flanks of some good brigades who, after fighting gallantly, had to retire. In trying to stop the stampeded men, Bragg came very near being captured and it was regretted by Confederates that he escaped.

When darkness came on, and everything was quiet about the tunnel, except an occasional shot on the picket line down on the Glass farm, my men wanted to get supper as they had eaten nothing during the day. I was waiting orders from General Gist, whom I had not seen for several hours, supposing everything had gone well all along the line as it had with us, and expecting to renew the battle the next morning.

# 'Hold this position at all hazards'

**Due west of the railroad tunnel under Confederate defenses on Tunnel Hill, three regiments of Buschbeck's brigade, XI Corps, were thrown into the noon assault on the far right flank of Sherman's front. Leading the 73rd Pennsylvania was Lt. Col. Joseph B. Taft, loaned from the 143rd New York two days earlier when the Keystone regiment found itself without any able field officers. Among his line officers was Capt. John Kennedy, commanding Company H.**

**After dashing through a fusillade of heavy fire, Taft's 300 men occupied a line of abandoned rifle pits at the ridge's base. But their initial success turned to disaster, as described by Pennsylvania historian Samuel P. Bates:**

"This position the regiment held against every attempt to dislodge it. The ammunition was finally exhausted and Colonel Taft, who had thrice sent for a fresh supply, started himself to secure it and to ask for supports. He had scarcely moved from the works when he received a mortal wound. His last words were, 'Hold this position at all hazards.' 'He pressed my hand,' says Captain Kennedy, 'and kept repeating the words, Hold the position at all hazards.'

"A small quantity of ammunition was obtained from the bodies of the dead and wounded. At half-past four p.m. a brigade from the Western army [Matthies' brigade, XVII Corps] came to its support. In the most gallant manner it advanced, the brigade general at its head, each Colonel in front of his regiment, and as it passed at double-quick, on a left half-wheel, the men in the pits cheered loudly. But unfortunately it was almost immediately repulsed and came back in utter confusion, about three hundred of its number taking shelter behind the rifle-pits with the Seventy-third. Emboldened by this disaster, the enemy came out of his works, charged down the hill, flanked the position and captured nearly the entire party at its base. Only about twenty-five of the regiment escaped. Eight officers and eighty-nine men were taken prisoners.

"The captured party was hurried away to Atlanta and thence to Richmond, the officers being consigned to Libby and the men to Belle Isle. The flag, in the confusion of the surrender, was torn from the staff, taken by Captain Kennedy, concealed about his person, and through the long months of his imprisonment was studiously preserved from rebel eyes and brought safely home upon his release [in March 1864]."

■ Lt. Col. Joseph B. Taft

■ Capt. John Kennedy

■ Col. Holden Putnam, commander of the 93rd Illinois, was shot through the head and killed instantly while leading the regiment's assault at Tunnel Hill. The 93rd's adjutant, 1st Lieut. Harvey M. Trimble, later wrote: "The opposing lines were no more than sixty feet apart, so close together that large stones were hurled from each line at the other, over the crest of the Ridge. Several men were seriously injured by such rocks thrown from the enemy's lines. Six times the colors of [the] regiment went out of sight. Once, the life of the brave Colonel Putnam went out when the flag went down; twice, the spirits of brave sergeants took their flight when the banner fell; and three times, wounded and bleeding heroes relinquished it to other hands. The staff that supported its folds was splintered and shivered and shot in twain. The banner itself was riddled and tattered and torn into shreds. Not a twentieth part of it remained upon the broken staff."

The 93rd Illinois lost one-third of its officers and men who went into the battle.

I consented that the men should build fires and get supper and soon captured coffee was boiling in the camp kettles, and the meat frying in the pans.

I had ridden up to Beauregard's battery and was talking to him. It was getting dark. We saw some horsemen coming from the left. They halted. One of them asked: "What brigade is this?" Then he called out: "Is Colonel Nisbet there?"

I answered and rode down to where he was. I found it was General Pat Cleburne. He said: "Colonel Nisbet, what about these fires?"

I replied: "I have given the men permission to prepare some food, as they have not eaten anything during the day."

He then informed me of what had happened at Bragg's headquarters, and that the enemy was on the ridge; and if the line formed across the ridge should give way, the Yanks would swoop down on us. He said: "Have you no orders? Where's General Gist?"

I said: "I have received no orders; I don't know where General Gist is."

"Well," said he, "the whole army is in retreat. I give you orders to withdraw your brigade and battery to Chickamauga Station, Western & Atlantic Railroad; there you will find rations in the depot." The general and staff rode off to look after their own division.

As soon as I found the men had got something to eat, I issued orders to the regiments to prepare to march. Young Beauregard was much worried. He said he did not know of any road to get off the ridge; that his old, poor horses could hardly stand up on level ground; and that he was going to lose his fine Napoleons that had been captured at Chickamauga. In fact, he was so troubled the tears came in his eyes.

I said to him: "I will stand by you. I have some men hunting for torch-pine. We will have torches soon. I will keep my own regiment with your battery." I told him to get ready to move. In the meantime I ordered the senior officer to march the brigade to Chickamauga Station, stack arms and wait.

The men came with torches and soon reported they had found a "sorter-of-a-little old, blind wood-road" going down the east side of the ridge. I detailed a company to go with each gun, with orders to lock all the wheels with ropes or chains and to hold the carriages back by hand off the feeble horses.

A sleety rain was falling as we started. "Now," I said, "we are all right, if the Yanks don't advance and capture the whole shooting match." Lieutenant Beauregard got in better spirits when we arrived safely at the foot of the ridge.

But there we found a muddy branch. The six horses drawing the first gun were driven in, but after making one or two pulls laid down, and all the profanity and beating of their drivers could not move them. I ordered Captain Tom Langston of Company C to wade in with his company and set the horses up on their pins, push them and the gun out, and continue to push until they got to the top of the hill. This they did. From there, with a descending grade, the horses went in a gallop to the station. With each gun a company was detailed to help them across the branch.

At Chickamauga Station I ordered the regimental commanders to draw rations for their men out of the depot. As it was a grab game, I got some candles and stood on a barrel to see that my brigade got all they could. Sides of meat were strung on bayonets and sacks of hard-tack were packed out and distributed; but the men wanted syrup, and 'twas too thick to go in their canteens.

They knocked the head of a sorghum barrel in and scooped syrup in their hats. Soon the barrel was half emptied and they had to lean over to reach it. Some people will joke even at a funeral. There was a devilish fellow who would watch his chance and kick their feet from under those who in turn bent over the barrel. Down they would go in the sticky, saccharine fluid in the barrel. Then all hands would jerk the poor fellow out. All dripping with sweetness. When the fellow got out of the depot the soldiers would "sop" on him; he was very popular!

That barrel gave out and then another barrelhead was knocked in and contents half emptied — when the kicking and jerking out continued. But alas; alack a day! This was soft soap! So when *that* kind of a fellow got out and the "sopping" commenced, there was a howl of indignation.

My brigade marched into this station in good order, was halted, came to a front and stacked arms. But we found most of Bragg's army already there, a howling mob. They had set fire to an empty wooden storehouse whose lurid flames illuminated the country for miles around.

After two and a half years' service in Virginia, this was my first experience of the demoralization of defeat.

■ 1st Lieut. George H. Conant of Company C, 10th Iowa, was one of two regimental officers killed at Tunnel Hill. During Matthies' brigade assault, a large number of the 10th became intermingled with the 93rd Illinois and 26th Missouri. A company commander in the 26th, Capt. John W. Maupin, recalled: "Just in front of a Rebel battery ... we had climbed the hill to within 30 feet of these guns. You might say we had them and didn't have them. The smoke would go clear over our heads at every discharge, and if one of our men showed his head he was a goner."

# CHAPTER 8

# A splendid sight that sent the blood tingling

## Missionary Ridge: A spectacular Federal assault routs disbelieving Confederate defenders

**With Lookout Mountain on the right firmly in Hooker's hands and Sherman vainly battering away at Tunnel Hill to the left, Thomas' Army of the Cumberland troops in the center waited and wondered if their turn would come next. Two days before, on November 23, the battle of Chattanooga opened on Thomas' front when Brig. Gen. Thomas J. Wood's division, supported by Phil Sheridan's division and Howard's XI Corps, dashed forward midway between their lines and the foot of Missionary Ridge, and captured the fortified Confederate outposts centered at Orchard Knob. Preceded by a grand drill replete with unfurled flags, gleaming bayonets, beating drums and resonating bugle calls, the sudden attack caught the Rebels watching from their rifle pits in Chattanooga Valley by surprise. Musket fire crackled briskly at first, but the Confederate defenders soon were overpowered. The Federals immediately reversed the entrenchments, reinforced the new position's flanks and installed a six-gun battery on Orchard Knob where Grant moved his headquarters.**

### 'All remained silent spectators'

**Brig. Gen. Arthur M. Manigault**
**Brigade commander**
**Anderson's Division, Hardee's Corps**

My picket line occupied a front of about 800 yards, and a high and commanding eminence known as "The Cedar Hill" [Orchard Knob] was a part of the ground held. It was the most prominent point between the Ridge and Chattanooga, and one of much importance. The 24th and 28th Alabama regiments were on duty that day [November 23], and held the picket line. They numbered

■ Confederate prisoners (foreground) on their way into Federal lines as Baird's XIV Corps' division struggles up Missionary Ridge.

■ Skirmishers from Brig. Gen. August Willich's brigade, IV Corps, fire at Confederate-held Orchard Knob on November 23. The 8th Kansas covered Willich's front and "under a lively skirmish fire the brigade advanced in quick time," he reported. "The small loss, 4 killed and 10 wounded, is explained by the impetuosity of the advance, which did not permit the enemy to reform after being once broken by our skirmishers ... Under orders, I erected an epaulement on the crest of Orchard Knob, and breastworks in front and on both sides of it, under a heavy artillery fire from the enemy's guns, which was but little heeded by the men, and with all its terrific appearance did very little damage."

together about 600 men on duty, both of them being small regiments. The picket line was entrenched with a shallow ditch and low earthwork, with rifle pits a little in advance.

About 4:30 o'clock the enemy formed two lines of battle with a skirmish line in front, and began to move forward. About five o'clock their skirmishers came within range of ours, and the fight commenced. Our advanced troops were soon driven in by their line of battle, who moved steadily to the attack. Their first line was checked by our fire, but the second line coming to their assistance, together they moved forward in spite of our fire, which was not heavy enough to deter them, and came in contact with the reserve line of skirmishers. Both regiments behaved well, particularly the 28th, which resisted obstinately, and with great gallantry, many of them fighting hand to hand; but the odds against them were irresistible, and Lieut. Col. [W.L.] Butler, 28th Ala., commanding, in order to save his Regiment, was forced to give the order to retire. The other regiment, 24th Alabama, had already given way. Had they contended much longer, they would have been killed or captured to a man, as the lines to their right and left had broken, and the enemy were getting to their rear. The 28th lost a good many, the 24th fewer — in all about 175 men.

Having obtained possession of our picket line and the hill mentioned, the enemy seemed satisfied, and pushed forward no further. Our skirmishers retired about 350 or 400 yards and halted. Whilst the enemy advanced large numbers immediately in front of the hill to protect and hold it, he set large parties to work upon it, building breastworks and batteries for their artillery. In rear also was a large reserve force, and for the security of this point to which they seemed to attach much importance, they must have held in front at least 6,000 men, exclusive of the two lines in front.

Whilst this combat was going on, all remained silent spectators. No effort to reinforce our advance posts was made, and as our lines were very weak and we had not men enough to man them, and not knowing what was the ulterior intention of the enemy, I do not know that it would have been wise to risk more men to the front. Our skirmish line was lost and to recover it a general engagement would have to be fought.

## 'Their bright guns and bayonets sparkling'

### Journal of John S. Roper Civilian clerk Artillery headquarters, Army of the Cumberland

Nov. 23d, 1863.

About two o'clock this afternoon my attention was attracted by the more than usual firing from Fort Wood, which is on the left of our line, about a quarter mile from the river. On going out there I found that our Infantry, Genl. Gordon Grangers Corps (the 4th) was advancing in line of battle with their left, right in front of Fort Wood, while from the Fort, the thirty-two pounders and the little ten pound Rodmans were shelling the rebels out of the woods in front. The other forts along the line towards the right were also doing considerable firing, while the 14th army corps were lying about half a mile out beyond their breastwork. The 4th Corps had already advanced pretty well when I arrived at the Fort, while the 11th Corps were lying in a mass to the right of the Fort. I could hear our men cheering as they would make a charge, and the quick sharp cracking of the muskets showed they were having pretty warm work in the belt of woods which runs along at the foot of Mission Ridge.

In a few minutes a couple of horsemen come dashing furiously by Fort Wood, from the front, and ride along to the 11th Corps, then comes the order to "fall in" — and off they march — a solid mass of blue, their bright guns and bayonets sparkling in the occasional ray which old sol throws out. Oh, there's something magnificent[ly] grand about a body of Union troops. How finely they contrast with those Rebels (about 150 prisoners), that are being brought along from the front. There they have to stop in the road until the remainder of the 11th Corps gets by, the contrast in their dress is rather laughable while they are near together — the "Gray Back" and "Blue Back" joking with each other.

Now the 11th Corps begins to get into action in the front, they are in line of battle right in front and to the left of Fort Wood in an open field — skirmishers advancing slowly towards the woods, the line of battle following them. Their left just reaches the Knoxville railroad — ah, there goes two or three rebels across the track, they fire on our men (skirmishers) who return the fire and lay down to load. Now they're up and at them — standing right out in the open field — it takes nerve to stand up and be shot at in that way; now a part of them make for the strip of woods on

■ Maj. Gen. Gordon Granger took command of the IV Corps on October 10, 1863 after it was formed by consolidating the XX and XXI corps. His conduct between November 23 and 25 was criticized by a number of officers, including Gen. Philip Sheridan and Assistant Secretary of War Charles A. Dana, who witnessed the battle of Missionary Ridge and immediately reported to Washington, D.C.: "The rebels having sent the great mass of their troops to crush Sherman, Grant gave orders at 2 p.m. for an assault upon their lines in front of Thomas, but owing to the fault of Granger, who devoted himself to firing a battery instead of commanding his corps, Grant's order was not transmitted to the division commanders until he repeated it an hour later."

A similar incident occurred two days earlier. After the Federal capture of Orchard Knob, 1st Lieut. Michael V. Sheridan, an aide on his brother's staff, was ordered to report to Granger at Fort Wood. "I found General Granger enjoying himself hugely," Sheridan later wrote. "He always had the idea that he had a wonderful eye for artillery. So I now found him going from gun to gun of Fort Wood's great siege guns, sighting each at the ridge, and watching with much satisfaction the results of the shots. Just as I reached him, General Grant and General Thomas approached, and after watching for a moment, General Thomas very testily ordered: 'Pay more attention to your corps, sir.' "

■ Orderly Sergeant Isaac A. Kruson of Company A, 136th New York, was among 10 officers and men of his regiment wounded on November 23 during operations leading to the capture of Orchard Knob. After driving in Confederate pickets, "a spirited contest very soon commenced between his skirmishers and the skirmishers thrown out from the 136th," reported Col. James Wood Jr. "The enemy's skirmishers held a strong position in a brick house immediately in front of the line of our advance and between our forces and their line of battle." The house was carried, but Wood's troops found themselves dangerously exposed when the brigades on both sides of their own halted prematurely. "We were at this time within the enemy's line of pickets, and had we been supported could easily have driven him from and taken possession of his rifle-pits."

Kruson was discharged from Hospital No. 2 in Nashville on May 15, 1865. In this late-war photograph he sports a XX Corps badge pinned to his vest.

the left at double quick, the whole line following up rapidly. The men on their right at the white houses begin to advance into the woods, they are soon most all out of sight but the firing is rapid — occasionally a whole volley. Now the men who first went in (the right of the 11th Corps) are seen in the first open field in the woods, while the rebels open a brisk fire on them from a line of their rifle pits. I am not fortunate enough to have a glass now, and at the distance they have now got it is hard to tell much about their movements with the naked eye. But they have established a line, fully a mile beyond where our pickets were, and are maintaining it.

## 'Making myself as thin as possible'

### Private George P. Metcalf
### Company D
### 136th New York Volunteer Infantry

We were ordered to pack everything in our knapsacks and equip ourselves in light marching order. This meant that our guns, ammunition, canteens and haversacks were to be our only luggage. I securely packed away everything else in my knapsack, save my trusty frying-pan, coffee-pot, pint cup and a light rubber blanket. Our knapsacks were thrown into a huge pile, and the question was asked, who would stand guard over them? I felt like volunteering, but I was afraid the boys would make sport of me for not daring to take my chances with the rest. But I did not have time to accept or reject before old Otis Bigelow [a private in Company D] said he would go. So he started for the rear, some half-mile behind us.

Occasionally a shot from a stray picket would come whizzing over our heads. Hours before the army went into the general engagement, one of these stray bullets came along and, while Uncle Otis lay taking his ease on this pile of knapsacks and congratulating himself on having escaped going into this fight, struck him in the fleshy part of his hip or thigh. So the last was first and the first, last. We never saw Otis Bigelow again during the war. His injuries were not fatal, but painful, and enough to send him to a hospital.

In the afternoon [of November 23] the long column began to move toward Mission Ridge. Our regiment's position was almost opposite Fort Wood, and between that and the ridge shells could be sent from this fort onto the top of both Mission Ridge and Lookout Mountain. We soon reached the picket-line of the enemy, and they fled hastily to the top of Mission Ridge.

The long line kept steadily moving forward, and soon the bullets came flying over our heads from the skirmish-line of the rebels. As we steadily took our column toward the base of the hill, I could see long lines of soldiers keeping our brigade company. To the left and right, as far as the lay of the country would permit, men were seen marching forward. The bullets came now with more telling effect. Men were wounded here and there.

A little to our left was a large barn, and when a regiment of New Jersey Zouaves came marching in column, the center of their line came upon this barn. The soldiers in this regiment were all new men, and a cowardly set of fellows, too, although they looked

■ Col. George W. Mindil

■ Capt. William G. Boggs

# 'A very hot and lively contest'

**On November 22, Howard's XI Corps left Lookout Valley, crossed the Tennessee River at Brown's Ferry and marched to Chattanooga. Bivouacking 200 yards to the right of Fort Wood was the 33rd New Jersey — a new regiment facing its first campaign.**

**Commanded by Col. George W. Mindil, the 33rd tasted battle the following day when Federal forces captured Orchard Knob. The Jerseymen, part of Col. Adolphus Buschbeck's brigade, faced Citico Creek when firing began to their right along Gen. Gordon Granger's front. Ordered to unsling and pile knapsacks, Mindil's men moved out with Company A under Capt. William G. Boggs covering as skirmishers.**

**Confederates concealed in woods along the creek, behind a small railroad bridge and nearby buildings opened fire after the 33rd advanced barely 20 paces. Boggs fell mortally wounded in the first discharge. But Mindil immediately pushed Company F to the skirmishers' support, personally leading the attack to the creek's bank. "A very hot and lively contest ensued," he reported, "the contending parties being but 10 yards apart. Both having availed themselves of the shelter of the trees, but little loss was inflicted."**

**Capt. Thomas O'Connor with 160 men managed to wade the waist-deep creek and began flanking the bridge, but rebel sharpshooters soon pinned them down, killing Capt. Samuel F. Waldron of Company I. In the meantime, Mindil received new orders to merely hold the creek line. To communicate this to O'Connor meant passing over exposed open ground through a shower of bullets. Undaunted, Adjutant William H. Lambert mounted a horse and galloped for O'Connor's position — until the animal was shot from under him. Continuing on foot, Lambert reached O'Connor safely, delivered the order to withdraw, and all returned unhurt to the creek.**

■ Troops of the 33rd New Jersey. This regiment, clad in dark blue Zouave-style jackets, baggy trousers and leggings, was mustered into Federal service on September 3, 1863 — less than three months before its baptism of fire in the Orchard Knob operations of November 23. Two weeks earlier, four privates from the regiment drowned in a barge mishap near Kelly's Ferry, which included the loss of regimental baggage.

fearfully brave in their queer-looking pants, hats and tasseled belts. The soldiers, protected by this barn, stopped under its shelter and refused to move, and presently the whole of that regiment doubled up and packed themselves behind it like a flock of frightened sheep. Do all they could, the officers could not budge them. They refused to go further and the column on either side moved on without them, leaving a gap of some twenty rods open.

We hurried along, occasionally being frightened by a shell sent tearing through the air over our heads, either from our own force in the rear or the enemy on the ridge. We crossed a railroad-track and drove the skirmish-line before us back up the slope. Here we halted in an old corn-field from which the corn had been cut off the stalks. We were not told to lie down, but we knew enough to do that without orders. We did not get down any too quick either, as a shower of bullets went over our heads, quickly followed by another and another. We tried to see how close it was possible for one to lie on the ground. I tried making myself as thin as possible. But, do all I could, it seemed to me that every part of my body stuck up in plain view and would surely get hit by some of the many bullets that were flying over us. We soon found, however, that we were lying in a little depression, or sag, in the field, and if we only lay down flat no bullet could hit us. But a foot above our heads we could see the standing stubs of corn-stalks cut off by flying bullets.

We lay here over an hour. During all the time the bullets kept zipping over our heads, close to me lay a member of my company with his nose flattened on the ground. Out of sport I got hold of a dry stalk of a weed and hit him on his ear. He jumped as if shot and put his hand up to feel the blood that wasn't there. Others began to toss little stones, without exposing themselves to danger, onto the heads of their comrades that dared not look up and did not understand that we were safe if we only kept down below the range of the rebel rifles. I saw one of our officers lying with one foot purposely stuck up in the air, as I believe, hoping to be shot in this non-vital spot and so have an excuse not to go into the main fight.

Night soon came on, and we fell back a few rods and built a strong line of breastworks. I worked nearly all night carrying rails and logs and shoveling dirt. When morning came, we had a line of earthworks three feet thick and six feet high.

## 'Shoot me and I'll cut your head off'

### Capt. Joseph T. Patton
### Company A
### 93rd Ohio Volunteer Infantry

On Nov. 23d we issued sixty rounds of ammunition to the men and turned out as if for drill. The rebels from their position in our front were enabled to watch our every move; and supposing that we were turning out for a grand review, took no measure to meet the advance which soon followed.

The 93d was a part of the front line, and when the word "forward" was given, advanced in battle line without skirmishers. The rebel pickets fired and fled at our approach. When within charging distance of their line of breastworks, "Fix bayonets! Forward, double quick!" were the orders which followed in quick succession. The enemy were now fully alive as to the purpose of our movements, and opened fire from sixty pieces of artillery from Missionary Ridge; the infantry from behind their breastworks also opened a most destructive musketry fire, but the gallant boys pressed forward through this terrible storm of iron and lead which was rained upon them, without a halt or waver.

The rebel works were reached and over them the boys went, capturing many prisoners. Our [acting] Lieutenant Colonel, [Daniel] Bowman, was on the right of the regiment; as he passed around the end of the works he encountered a rebel with his gun aimed at him. With drawn sword the Colonel rushed at the fellow with the exclamation, "Damn you, you shoot me and I'll cut your head off." The force of the Colonel's remark had the desired effect as the reb dropped his gun and surrendered.

Orchard Knob and the first line of works were ours, but not without heavy loss, as more than one-third of our regiment were killed or wounded in the charge. Three color-bearers fell, the fourth planting *Old Glory* on the enemy's works.

As we started on the charge, I was turning toward the left of my company when a bullet struck a diary which was in the right breast pocket of my blouse, glanced downward and struck my sword belt-plate, which was bent until it was of no further use. Fortunately for my present usefulness, I had buckled my belt under my blouse before starting, which saved my life, as the diary stopped the bullet from passing through my right breast, and the belt-plate prevented it passing through my bowels.

The blow sent me to grass and left me insensible. When the stretcher bearers discovered me, they decided that I was dead and that they would first care for the wounded. (My name appeared in the newspapers as among the killed). How long I remained there I

■ Capt. Joseph T. Patton of Company A, 93rd Ohio, was the youngest company commander in his regiment when it stormed Orchard Knob on November 23. Knocked insensible by a bullet that first struck a pocket diary, then his belt buckle, he was left for dead on the field but soon recovered.

Rushing into the Confederate works, Capt. Daniel Bowman of Company D captured the 28th Alabama's colors and was slightly wounded. Two days later, Darius L. Sutphen, a sergeant in Bowman's company, captured another flag on the crest of Missionary Ridge.

■ 1st Lieut. John K. Shellenberger of Company F, 64th Ohio, was among his regiment's 18 officers and 208 men when they suddenly dashed from their works on November 23, completely overrunning a Confederate picket line near Brush Knob. The troops of Harker's brigade quickly fortified their new line and prepared for a counterattack that never materialized. "What a relief it was," exclaimed regimental Lt. Col. Robert C. Brown, "to get out of our old works where we had stood, like cattle in a stall, for two months."

have no means of knowing, but was finally removed to camp where I had comfortable quarters and my colored boy to care for me. The blow had broken my ribs and injured my spine. I thought from the pain which I experienced that the bullet had passed through my body, and was rather disgusted when an examination revealed the fact that I was knocked out without a scar to show for it.*

## 'Kicking up such a hell of a fuss'

### 1st Lieut. John K. Shellenberger
### Company F
### 64th Ohio Volunteer Infantry

On this 23d day of November, our pickets, who were to act as our skirmish line, had been carefully instructed, and when the bugles suddenly sounded the charge, they sprang forward with such a dash that they actually ran over some of the Confederate pickets before the latter had recovered from their astonishment. Their intrenched picket line was carried with a surprisingly small amount of resistance and with a correspondingly small loss to our side.

A little later, after the Confederates had recovered their self-possession, and the two skirmish lines were spitefully pecking away at each other, one of the Confederates called over:

"Hello, Yanks, what's got the matter with you all over there?"

One of our men called back: "We're out of wood." This was literally true; for not only all the timber inside our picket line had been cut off, but the stumps and the roots of the trees had been dug out of the ground in the growing scarcity of fuel. The Confederate called back:

"If you wanted wood why didn't you say so? We have more than we need out here, and if you had only asked us you might have sent out your teams and got all the wood you wanted without kicking up such a hell of a fuss about it."

Our battle line followed up the advance of our picket line until it reached the foot of the hill, where a halt was called. At this time heavy firing had broken out along the skirmish line, and the inference was that the main body of the Confederates had swarmed out of their camps and were advancing to drive us back. The position of the Sixty-fourth Ohio, where the line had halted, was a most unsatisfactory one. The ground ascended in our front for a couple of hundred yards, and this slope was nearly bare, while at the top of the rise the timber was heavy enough to afford good shelter. If the enemy should drive back our skirmish line and occupy this timber, they would have us at a great disadvantage.

The men were growling discontentedly and asking why we were not advanced to the top of the slope, when General Sheridan appeared upon the scene. He came dashing along from the left and immediately in front of our line, which was lying down, riding the same black horse which, with his rider, achieved such deathless fame nearly a year later at Cedar Creek. When he reached the front of the colors he pulled up so abruptly as to almost seat the

* Patton recovered from his injury and returned to duty on December 26.

horse on his haunches. His eyes were beaming as if he could scarcely refrain from bursting out laughing at some idea that was amusing him, and he leaned over toward us and began speaking in a suppressed sort of way, as if he was about to communicate in strict confidence something that we would find intensely funny.

He said: "Now, boys, lie low, you know, and let 'em come up close, you know, and then rise up and give 'em hell, you know."

It was probably the contemplation of the surprise of the enemy when we should unexpectedly "rise up and give 'em hell, you know," that was tickling him, and it certainly did seem an easy thing to do, the way he had of putting it. He paused an instant to flash his eyes along our line, the eyes of the men catching fire from his as they met, and then as if satisfied with his scrutiny, he nodded and smiled in a way that plainly said, "I know that I can rely upon you to do it," and dashed on to the next regiment.

It was a false alarm, for no enemy came, but if they had come, it is certain that the Sixty-fourth would have obeyed the general's instructions to the letter; for he was possessed of an extraordinary power of getting out of men the last particle of fight there was in them. We afterward took up a position that evening, connecting with Wood's division on the left, which was fortified by throwing up a light line of earthworks. We remained quietly behind these works until the afternoon of the 25th ...

■ 1st Lieut. Richard L. Walker of Company I, 19th Ohio, commanded one of four regimental picket outposts extending from the Tennessee River at Citico Creek to the left of Willich's brigade. On the afternoon of November 23, the 115 Ohioans manning three of these outposts, including Walker's, were deployed as skirmishers to assist in the general advance on Orchard Knob. Walker's men ran into stiff resistance on the left, where concentrated Confederate fire from across Citico Creek caught them in flank. Walker fell severely wounded and his men sought whatever cover available until they were relieved by troops of the XI Corps.

**As the afternoon of November 25 lengthened, Federal hopes of breaking Bragg's hold of Missionary Ridge and forcing him from its heights appeared to be sinking. Grant's primary aim of turning the Confederate right flank was stymied at Tunnel Hill. And a corresponding thrust into the Rebel left near Rossville Gap already was hours behind schedule. Obliged to repair or rebuild several bridges over Chattanooga Creek, Hooker's three divisions were delayed all morning in crossing.**

**However, an all-out assault on the center of the ridge was never planned. The previous day Grant informed Thomas that his movement forward would "be in cooperation" with Sherman's advance, and that Thomas' command should "either carry the rifle-pits and ridge directly in front of them or to move to the left [to Sherman's support], as the presence of the enemy may require." Grant clearly intended only a limited, complementary role for the main body of the Army of the Cumberland. But with Sherman making little headway, orders to be ready for action filtered down to division, brigade and regimental commanders. For some, the exact objective remained uncertain.**

**Along a 2¾-mile front facing Missionary Ridge, four divisions — two each from the IV and XIV corps, totalling nearly 20,000 men — prepared for battle. Six guns fired from Orchard Knob signalled the advance. Before day's end, Private James W. Riley of Company E, 42nd Illinois, recorded in his diary: "After our line was formed, an officer came and told us to charge the Rebels' line, and if any of us in the regiment didn't want to charge, we could step to the rear, for we were to lead a forlorn hope and it was a question if any of us would get across alive. But be it said to the credit of the boys, not a one stepped to the rear, and at the word 'Charge,' we went with a yell ..."**

■ 2nd Lieut. Edward Bromley of Company G, 55th Ohio, was instantly killed by a sniper's bullet just north of Orchard Knob on November 24. "We dug holes with our bayonets and tin cups — 'gopher holes' which were a good protection," recalled Sergeant Luther B. Mesnard of Company D. "We could see the rebs along a fence not far in front with colors flying, and as we commenced shooting they returned the fire, but we had better protection than they and soon the wounded from their lines began streaming to their rear. We yelled and fired and soon the colors and the whole line fell back to the foot of Mission Ridge. Soon after I sat talking with Lieutenant [Frederick H.] Boalt by a window in a little shanty back of the line when a ball passed between us and lodged in the opposite side of the room. This from a sharpshooter three fourths of a mile away. Lieutenant Bromley was soon after shot through the heart on our breastworks."

Note XI Corps crescent worn on Bromley's cap.

**"At the first sound of the guns we came to attention," wrote Private J.N. Stanford of Company A, 18th U.S. Infantry. "As the last one was fired we received the command 'forward.' We advanced through the woods in battle line. As we emerged from the timber the command was given 'Right shoulder shift, arms! Forward, double-quick!' and away we went for the foot of the ridge on a dead run."**

**On the summit of Missionary Ridge, 2nd Lieut. William A. Brown of T.J. Stanford's (Mississippi) Battery watched the pageantry from his post as section commander of two brass Napoleon 12-pounders. In his diary Brown wrote: "The scene spread before us from this position was truly magnificent ... Here we stood, idly looking at the splendid army of the enemy, maneuvering and forming below us, and in easy range of our guns. The preparations seemed better suited to a grand review than a battle."**

**Within the hour, Brown and his comrades were engulfed in a tidal wave of blue.**

## 'Beyond the pale of orders'

### Brig. Gen. Thomas J. Wood
### Division commander
### IV Corps, Army of the Cumberland

My headquarters had been on Orchard Knob since the afternoon of the 23d. Quite early in the forenoon of the 25th, General Grant, General Thomas and General Granger commanding the Fourth Corps, with their staff officers, took position on Orchard Knob. Mr. Charles A. Dana, the Assistant Secretary of War, General M.C. Meigs, quartermaster-general of the army, and other distinguished officials were also on Orchard Knob.

From Orchard Knob, the scene of General Sherman's attack was in full view, so that every movement of his command was easily and plainly discernible. About the middle of the forenoon, Sherman's command began the ascent of the northeastern flank of Missionary Ridge. The progress was steadily onward and upward, with heavy opposition, however, till the head of the assaulting column had advanced up the slope about two-thirds or three-fourths of its extent, when a polite gentleman was met, who said: "Thus far, Mr. Yanks, but no farther." In other words, the advance of General Sherman's command had butted its head against a heavy line of intrenchments held by Cleburne's division of the Confederate army.

Every eye on Orchard Knob was turned on General Sherman's operations, keenly watching his movements, and, in profoundest sympathy, ardently desiring success to crown his sturdy efforts. But all in vain! Assault after assault was repulsed. About half past two p.m. it was plainly and painfully evident to every beholder on Orchard Knob that General Sherman's attack, which, according to the plan of battle, was to be the dominant *coup* of the battle, had been hopelessly defeated, and was an irretrievable failure. It was evident that his further progress toward the crest of the Ridge was peremptorily stopped.

It chanced that at the moment of the repulse General Grant was standing near me. He approached and said: "General Sher-

# 'All acted like veterans'

Earmarked for the Missionary Ridge assault were four Army of the Cumberland divisions, whose commanders are pictured here.

Maj. Gen. Philip H. Sheridan, later to gain fame as commander of the Army of the Potomac's Cavalry Corps and Army of the Shenandoah, led the 2nd Division, IV Corps, and had a horse wounded beneath him. His three brigades attacked the ridge opposite the Thurman House, site of Bragg's headquarters. The battle was the only time during the war when four of the Union's most successful generals — Grant, Thomas, Sherman and Sheridan — served together on the same field.

Brig. Gen. Thomas J. Wood's three brigades of the 3rd Division, IV Corps, scrambled up the ridge to the immediate left of Sheridan. Two days earlier his troops were responsible for capturing Orchard Knob. Newspaperman B.F. Taylor of the *Chicago Evening Journal* wrote of Wood: "He went into battle in a shocking hat, a blouse 'hutched up' like a Norwegian woman's boddice, and his pistol thrust in his belt like a whaler's knife."

Walrus-whiskered Brig. Gen. Absalom Baird attacked on the far left with his 3rd Division, XIV Corps, after being recalled from supporting Sherman at Tunnel Hill. When the support order was countermanded, Baird's three brigades barely had time to reach their assault positions. "The ridge, more or less steep and difficult throughout, was particularly so in my front," he wrote, "but those striking the more accessible points ... soon passed to the front. Regimental organizations became somewhat deranged, and presented rather the appearance of groups gathering around the colors, which they pushed onward and upward through the storm of bullets."

On the far right, Brig. Gen. Richard W. Johnson commanded the 1st Division, XIV Corps. Only two of his three brigades participated in the assault — one of them containing six battalions of U.S. Regulars; the other with troops who had never been under fire. Despite this, Johnson reported that all under his command "acted like veterans. The hope for glory and distinction will account for the gallantry of officers, but how can we thank too much the private soldier who faces death without hope of future reward?"

■ Maj. Gen. Philip H. Sheridan

■ Brig. Gen. Richard W. Johnson

■ Brig. Gen. Absalom Baird

■ Brig. Gen. Thomas J. Wood

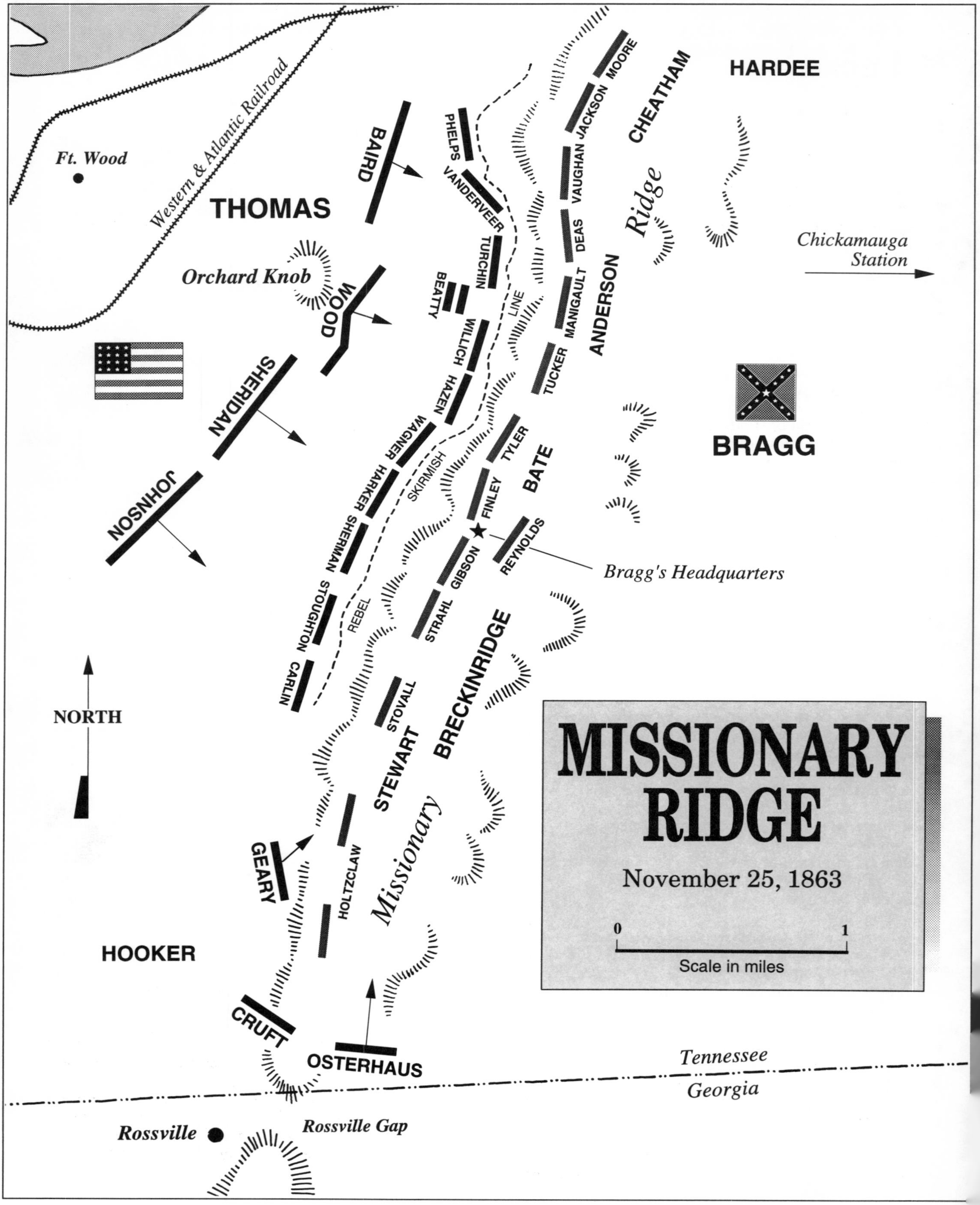
MISSIONARY RIDGE
November 25, 1863
0
1
Scale in miles
Western & Atlantic Railroad
Ft. Wood
THOMAS
Orchard Knob
BAIRD
WOOD
SHERIDAN
JOHNSON
PHELPS
VANDERVEER
TURCHIN
BEATTY
WILLICH
HAZEN
WAGNER
HARKER
SHERMAN
STOUGHTON
CARLIN
SKIRMISH
LINE
REBEL
MOORE
JACKSON
VAUGHAN
DEAS
MANIGAULT
TUCKER
CHEATHAM
ANDERSON
HARDEE
Ridge
Chickamauga Station
BRAGG
TYLER
FINLEY
BATE
REYNOLDS
GIBSON
STRAHL
Bragg's Headquarters
BRECKINRIDGE
STOVALL
STEWART
Missionary
HOLTZCLAW
GEARY
NORTH
HOOKER
CRUFT
OSTERHAUS
Tennessee
Georgia
Rossville
Rossville Gap

man seems to be having a hard time."

I replied, "He does seem to be meeting with rough usage."

To this General Grant said, "I think we ought to try to do something to help him."

I said, "I think so too, General, and whatever you order we will try to do."

General Grant continued, "I think if you and Sheridan were to advance your divisions and carry the rifle pits at the base of the Ridge, it would so threaten Bragg's center that he would draw enough troops from the right, to secure his center, to insure the success of General Sherman's attack."

I replied, "Perhaps it might work in that way; and if you order it, we will try it, and I think we can carry the intrenchments at the base of the Ridge."

General Grant walked immediately from me to General Thomas, distant about ten paces. I did not accompany him, though there would have been no impropriety in my doing so. Generals Grant and Thomas were in conversation a very short time, perhaps two or three minutes, when General Thomas called General Granger, who stood near to him. After perhaps two minutes conversation between Generals Thomas and Granger, the latter came to me and said: "You and Sheridan are to advance your divisions, carry the intrenchments at the base of the Ridge, if you can, and, if you succeed, to halt there."

He further said, "The movement is to be made at once, so give your orders to your brigade commanders immediately, and the signal to advance will be the rapid, successive discharge of the six guns of this battery."

I immediately sent for my brigade commanders, Hazen, Willich and Beatty, repeated to them the orders received from General Granger (who, on giving them to me, said they were General Grant's orders), and directed them to give the orders to their regimental commanders in person, who, in turn, were to give the orders to their company commanders in person. I was thus careful in having the orders transmitted, because I desired commanders of every grade in the division to fully understand what the movement was to be, and that there might be neither misconception nor confusion.

After a short interval, perhaps ten minutes, the guns on Orchard Knob boomed out the signal to advance; and ere the reverberation had died away my division was in rapid motion. As soon as the troops were in motion the enemy opened on them a terrific fire from his batteries on the crest of Missionary Ridge. These batteries were so posted as to give a direct and cross fire on the assaulting troops. But they pressed forward, and carried the line of intrenchments at the base of the Ridge. Having a shorter distance to pass over, the troops of my division were the first to arrive. When the intrenchments were carried, the goal for which we had started was won. The orders carried us no further.

We had been instructed to carry the line of intrenchments at the base of the Ridge, *and then halt.*

But the enthusiasm and impetuosity of the troops was such that those who first reached the intrenchments at the base bounded over them, and pressed on up the ascent after the flying enemy, without orders from any commander. The rank and file took in the exigencies of the situation and quickly adopted the only way out of the danger with which they were environed, namely, to

■ Brig. Gen. August Willich, a German-born brigade commander in Wood's division, IV Corps, ascended Missionary Ridge on foot with the 8th Kansas and reached the summit just minutes after his fastest men. One of these, Sergeant Samuel C. McKirahan of Company F, 15th Ohio, recalled: "Of course we had a jollification when General Willich came up. With hat in hand, as usual, and laughing, he said, 'Look! As I vas coming up the hill I saw a son-of-a-gun stopped behind a stump, and jumped on him and kicked him, and see, I broke all my spurs.' "

Moments later two other members of the 15th Ohio, Corporal Washington J. Vance, Company K, and Private Joseph C. McColley, Company G, rode up on two captured artillery horses and halted where Willich was surrounded by men of his brigade. "My poys, you kills me mit joy," he exclaimed. "You kills me mit joy."

■ Col. John A. Martin, 8th Kansas Infantry, led his 219-man regiment up Missionary Ridge on horseback. Also mounted amid the struggling troops of Willich's brigade was his regimental adjutant, 1st Lieut. Solomon R. Washer. Martin remembered Washer's bravery: "Wounded at Chickamauga, and not yet recovered from the effect of the wound, suffering from a severe sprain of the leg, which prevented his walking, he mounted his horse and rode through the whole battle ..."

At the base of the ridge "there was a break in the grey lines behind the rebel works; a few rushed to the rear, but nearly all, throwing down their muskets and holding up their hands in token of surrender, leaped to our side of the entrenchments and cowered behind them, for the hail of bullets raining down from the hill was as deadly to them as to us. The first line was won, but behind it there was not room for both forces, and seeing this Adjutant Washer dragged one of the prisoners from his place and ordered the whole of them to the rear. 'You have been trying to get there long enough,' he said, 'and now charge on Chattanooga!' Off the fellows scampered towards the lines we had left behind."

assault and carry the crest of the Ridge. The barricades at the base were no protection against the artillery on the summit. To remain at the base would be destruction; to retire would be both expensive of life and disgraceful. Officers and men all seemed impressed with this truth. In addition, the example of those who first bounded over the intrenchments and began the ascent was contagious.

Speaking for myself, I frankly confess I was simply one of the boys on that occasion. I was infected with the contagion of the prevailing enthusiasm. The troops did not halt to fire; to have done so would have been ruinous. Little more was left to the immediate commanders of the troops than to cheer on the foremost, to encourage the weaker of limb, and to sustain the very few who seemed to be faint-hearted.

Throughout the assault from the base of the Ridge to the crest, I rode immediately behind the center of the second line of my division. That was my proper tactical position. Being mounted, this position gave me a commanding view of the field of operations. Looking over my division, I took in the crest of the Ridge to the extent of, perhaps, a mile. I had also an unobstructed view to the right and right-rear; as, also, to the left and left-rear. I could thus determine accurately the relative position of divisions during the assault, as well as discriminate distinctly the order of precedence in the arrival of the divisions on the crest. I had the deepest interest in observing the relative position of divisions during the assault, not for the purpose of determining the question of precedence in reaching the crest, for in that moment of intense anxiety that thought did not occur to me; but for the much higher —indeed, to my division and myself — the vital object of seeing where support could come from, if the Confederates counter-charged.

The assault of Missionary Ridge, throughout its entire extent, from base to crest, imposed a very great strain on me. I was conscious from the moment the skirmishers of my division commenced the ascent of the steep acclivity, that the movement was in direct contravention of positive orders, and that nothing but success could excuse this palpable disobedience of orders. I did not need to be reminded, by message of inquiry, sent by General Grant through General Fullerton, asking whether I had ordered the assault, that I had gone beyond the pale of his orders, and that possibly dire consequences might flow from this disobedience. But the possible consequences, personal to myself, did not much trouble me in that perilous ascent. It was the result that I clearly saw would fall on my division, if the assault should be repulsed, that put the heavy strain on me.

What I feared was, that the Confederates, when the bulk of my division had arrived within about a hundred yards of the crest, would pour in a heavy volley, bound over their intrenchments, lower their bayonets, and come down on us at the double-quick, with that famous "rebel yell" with which we, who were at the front, were so familiar. This, by all the rules of battle, is what the Confederates should have done. Had they done it, practical annihilation would have been the fate of my division. Fagged and blown as the men were by the exhausting effort they had already made, they could have interposed but a feeble resistance to such a counter-charge. They would have been borne back, hopelessly and helplessly, by the impact of the counter-charge, down the steep

# 'Who ordered those men up the ridge?'

**Lt. Col. Joseph S. Fullerton, assistant adjutant general and chief of staff of Granger's IV Corps, was among the general and staff officers on Orchard Knob intently watching the Federal advance to the base of Missionary Ridge. When the troops of Baird, Wood, Sheridan and R.W. Johnson unexpectedly began ascending the precipitous slope, Fullerton noted the generals' stunned reactions:**

■ In a photograph taken at Hall's Gallery in Nashville late in the war, Lt. Col. Joseph S. Fullerton is seated at left. With him are Surgeon John T. Heard, right, IV Corps medical director, and Surgeon J.S. Bromley, IV Corps medical inspector.

"As soon as this movement was seen from Orchard Knob, Grant quickly turned to Thomas, who stood by his side, and I heard him say angrily: 'Thomas, who ordered those men up the ridge?' Thomas replied in his usual slow, quiet manner: 'I don't know; I did not.' Then, addressing General Gordon Granger, he said: 'Did you order them up, Granger?'

" 'No,' said Granger, 'they started up without orders. When those fellows get started all hell can't stop them.' General Grant said something to the effect that somebody would suffer if it did not turn out well, and then, turning, stoically watched the ridge. He gave no further orders.

"As soon as Granger had replied to Thomas he turned to me, his chief of staff, and said: 'Ride at once to Wood and then to Sheridan, and ask them if they ordered their men up the ridge, and tell them, if they can take it to push ahead.' As I was mounting, Granger added: 'It is hot over there and you may not get through. I shall send Captain Avery to Sheridan and other officers after both of you.'

"As fast as my horse could carry me I rode first to General Wood and delivered the message. 'I didn't order them up,' said Wood; 'they started up on their own account and they are going up, too! Tell Granger, if we are supported we will take and hold the ridge!'

"As soon as I reached General Wood, Captain Avery got to General Sheridan and delivered his message. 'I didn't order them up,' said Sheridan, 'but we are going to take the ridge.' He then asked Avery for his flask and waved it at a group of Confederate officers standing just in front of Bragg's headquarters, with the salutation 'Here's at you!' At once two guns — the 'Lady Breckinridge' and the 'Lady Buckner' — in front of Bragg's headquarters were fired at Sheridan and the group of officers about him. One shell struck so near as to throw dirt over Sheridan and Avery.

" 'Ah!' said the general, 'that is ungenerous; I shall take those guns for that!' "

■ Brig. Gen. Arthur M. Manigault and son A.M. Manigault II pose in an antebellum daguerrotype. Shortly after the war he wrote bluntly of the Missionary Ridge defeat: "We were beaten ... because of the great numerical disparity between ourselves and our opponents, and because the disposition of our forces was injudicious in the extreme. General Bragg was overconfident in the strength of his position, and underrated the number of his adversaries, and their fighting qualities ... He was completely outgeneraled by the Yankee commander.

"Panic seemed to seize upon all, and all order, obedience, and discipline, were for the time forgotten and disregarded. To stop the men in their mad flight, even after leaving the enemy hundreds of yards in their rear, was almost impossible. The officers generally seemed to lose their presence of mind. Threats and entreaties alike proved unavailing ... It was a long time before they got over the mortification of defeat, and the great majority earnestly longed for an opportunity of wiping out the disgrace."

descent, the Confederates following closely on their heels. Old, veteran and disciplined soldiers as they were, the Confederates were simply dazed, dumbfounded, by the very audacity of the assault. The successful assault of Missionary Ridge is a most pertinent illustration of the soundness of the old French military maxim — *l'audace, toujours l'audace.*

## 'Leave the gun, General, and save yourself!'

### Brig. Gen. Arthur M. Manigault
### Brigade commander
### Anderson's Division, Hardee's Corps

About four or four-thirty o'clock I was walking in rear of my line, talking with and encouraging the soldiers, when a rapid succession of shots from the artillery on Cedar Hill [Orchard Knob] gave the signal for the enemy to advance. It was followed by all their artillery in different works, and to a man, on both sides, I will venture to say that the meaning of it was perfectly understood. Our own artillery now commenced to play on the enemy's dark masses as they moved steadily forward, but not with the effect that I expected. A plunging fire against infantry is far less effectual than over a level plain or slightly undulating ground.

I watched with much anxiety the line below me. They stood firm, and when the enemy had arrived within about 200 yd., gave them their volley, and a well-directed and fatal one it proved; but then followed a scene of confusion rarely witnessed, and only equaled at a later hour on that day.

The order had been issued to retire, but many did not hear it in the excitement of the fight, and owing to the reports of their own pieces and the deafening roar of artillery. Others supposed their comrades flying and refused to do likewise. Some few feared to make the attempt to retire up the hill, exposed as they would be to a heavy fire in their rear, and as their movements would necessarily be slow, owing to the great steepness of the hillside, they felt certain that they would be killed or wounded before reaching their comrades above. All order was soon lost, and each, striving to save himself, took the shortest direction for the summit. The enemy seeing the confusion and retreat, moved up their first line at a double quick and went over the breastworks, but I could see some of our brave fellows fighting to the last, firing into the enemy's faces, and at last fall, overpowered by numbers.

Here the enemy opened heavily on our retreating forces and did some execution, but they soon got beyond their reach and then they began to reform their line, preparatory to an advance on our second line of works. During this delay our men opened a steady fire on them from their works above, and did much execution, delaying them some time in their movement by the confusion caused. The distance must have been about three or four hundred yards, varying according to the configuration of the ground. Our artillery could not be depressed sufficiently to strike the foot of the ridge, and could only be used in firing to the right or left where the ground admitted of it, and harassing the enemy in front of some other portion of the line.

The troops from below at length reached the works, exhausted and breathless, much the greater portion so demoralized that, breaking through their friends, they rushed to the rear bent on placing the ridge itself between them and the enemy. It required the utmost efforts of myself, staff and other officers to prevent this, which we finally succeeded in doing. Many threw themselves on the ground, broken down from over-exertion, and became deathly sick or fainted. I noticed several instances of slight hemorrhage, and it was fifteen minutes before most of these men were so recovered as to be made use of, or their nervous systems so restored as to be able to draw trigger with any steadiness. Soon, however, some order was restored to these regiments and they were got into position, although here and there the men of different commands were somewhat mixed up. Still, matters had assumed a very tolerable order in time to receive the Federals, who now began to advance against us.

A steady fire met them as they began the ascent, and before they reached half-way up their first line had crumbled and disappeared, and their second much broken and in some disorder. As a regular formation they did not advance more than fifty yards further, when they ceased to move forward, reeled and went back. Our men were now firing slowly and steadily, with great coolness and perfect confidence in themselves and in the security of their position. The third line now reached the ground, deployed, and a second effort was made with it, supported by such of the first two as could be got together to storm our works, but with no better success than on the preceding occasion.

I was now perfectly easy in mind as to my own situation, and turned my attention to General Deas' front, noticing that a large number of Yankees had succeeded in reaching a point within a few yards of his centre (perhaps 20 yards) where they were protected from his fire by some overhanging rock. I directed Captain [Stouten H.] Dent to turn two of his pieces on them, which he did, and also ordered one or two of my right companies to do the same. They were driven from our view, but it appears that beyond a turn of this same rock and beyond our reach, they also had obtained a lodgment in large numbers. I noticed also a short time before this that the enemy had made much progress in their advance on Tucker's brigade (Mississippians)* on my left, but as he had sent word to General Anderson that his position was secure, and that the enemy could not move him, I thought little more of it, regarding the danger on my right as being much more imminent.

Whilst thus employed, and happening to look towards the road that ran along the ridge, I noticed one of my regiments, the 34th Alabama, moving along it to my right. Surprised at so unexpected a movement, I immediately went to it and on enquiring the meaning of it, was informed by its commanding officer that by a special order from General Anderson, he had been withdrawn from the works and had been directed to reinforce General Deas, who was hard pressed and needed assistance. Immediately after, a staff officer reported to me the order of General Anderson, and I permitted the regiment to proceed, but was much annoyed at so unusual a proceeding and the want of courtesy shown me. My line was

■ Capt. Thomas P. Hodges of Company A, 41st Mississippi, watched helplessly as his men were among the first to break near the Confederate center on November 25. Col. William F. Tucker, Hodges' regimental and temporary brigade commander, wrote nine days later: "Unfortunately the works [on the crest] were so constructed as not to command a view of the front part of a high projecting point about the centre of the Brigade. Behind this the enemy massed their force, & secure from our fire, climbed the hill. When they suddenly appeared in front of our men at this unexpected point, seized with a panic, they gave way before them, & in spite of the efforts of their Officers, continued to break on each side of the point where the enemy entered our lines, until the whole Brigade fell back in disorder. I hastened back to bring up the reserve [part of his own regiment] only to find it stampeded with the rest. Nothing could now be done ..."

Hodges survived the battle but was killed in action the following July just west of Atlanta.

* Col. William F. Tucker, 41st Mississippi, was in command of James Patton Anderson's brigade while Anderson commanded Maj. Gen. Thomas C. Hindman's old division. Tucker's troops consisted of the 7th, 9th, 10th, 41st and 44th Mississippi Infantry regiments, and the 9th Mississippi Battalion Sharpshooters.

■ Capt. Cornelius I. Walker, 10th South Carolina, served on Manigault's brigade staff as assistant adjutant general. On November 25, three of Manigault's regiments — including the 10th — were at the base of the ridge when the Federals advanced. "It was a splendid sight," Walker recalled, "the valley swarming with the myriads of blue coats, all advancing in splendid order. The front line was abandoned, under the order to do so, and the Regiment dragged slowly up the tedious slope, under a terrible artillery fire, the men arriving at the summit completely exhausted. Men dropped as if shot, from sheer fatigue."

Walker, valedictorian of the South Carolina Military Academy's class of 1861, was promoted lieutenant colonel of the 10th South Carolina in June 1864. The following month (outside Atlanta), he was severely wounded in the neck at Ezra Church.

consequently much weakened, and the troops remaining had to be much stretched out to fill up the vacancy occasioned by the withdrawal of the 34th, by far the largest regiment in the brigade.

Again returning to the right of the command, I was watching with much interest and anxiety the progress of the fight on the right, when Captain Walker, the A.A.G., galloped to me and informed me that the enemy had broken the Mississippi Brigade on the left, were in possession of a great part of their line, together with the battery in their centre. From where we stood, the intervening rise in my own line prevented my seeing for myself, and going as fast as possible towards the left I soon found that Walker's report was correct. Two colors were plainly visible, and their troops were gathering in large numbers on the height near where the battery was located. Tucker's lines as far as I could see were entirely abandoned, and I saw only the rearmost of the men, making good their escape down the back slope.

My own left was now swinging in the air, and with a weakened line and no reserves that I knew of or saw, our position was critical in the extreme, and unless this force could be attacked and driven off at once, the day and our position were lost. I sent Walker with all speed to inform General Anderson of the disaster and made such arrangements as I could to save my left flank, now completely exposed. General Anderson's reply to Walker, when he informed him of the occurrence, was that it could not be so, the thing was impossible, the brigade was not broken. Walker, much provoked, answered that he had best satisfy himself, and could do so easily by riding a hundred yards to a point from which he could himself see the Yankees and their colors. This he did, and sent Walker back to me with orders to draw out half my force from the works and drive the Yankees off, but it is much more easy to give an order than to have it executed, and to do so with half a brigade what a whole one had a short time before failed to do — that is, to beat the Yankees under much less favorable circumstances — was not a thing so easily done.

At the same time, seeing the success attending their troops on their right, they were evidently preparing for another assault upon me. The incidents that succeeded passed in rapid succession. Deas' brigade now began to give way. The attacking force had obtained a foothold near his centre and all his efforts to drive them out failed. Whilst endeavoring to draw out a portion of my command with which to execute the orders of the division commander, the Yankees turned two of the captured guns on my line, completely enfilading it for some distance. At the same time they formed two lines of battle across the ridge, and at right angles with our line, at least 3,000 men at that point, and their numbers were momentarily increasing. Our left opened on them vigorously, also two pieces of our artillery at a range not exceeding 400 yards.

I had but little hope of being able to hold my position, and knew that nothing could save us but the timely arrival of reinforcements, which, hoping against hope, I trusted would yet make their appearance. I did not know that the division on our left, Breckinridge's [commanded by Brig. Gen. William B. Bate], was in pretty much the same condition as our own, and also that the extreme left of our army had been flanked, and that the Yankees in several lines of battle were carrying everything before them as they struck our lines in the most favorable manner possible for themselves.

I now began to observe a man here and there, sneaking, or going rapidly to the rear, and directed the Officer of the Provost Guard to order his men to shoot down all who attempted to pass to the rear, unless wounded, but in a moment I noticed that instead of an occasional individual, groups of four, five and ten were roving in like manner, and they almost all came from the centre, on which the two guns (captured) were playing. The firing was now heavy and furious. Every effort to check the fugitives in their mad flight proved abortive. My right and left, 28th Alabama (left) and 10th South Carolina (right) still stood their ground and were fighting manfully.

Deas' brigade was now going to the rear, broken and routed. Seeing that all was lost and that to check the fugitives was impossible, I directed the officers to halt and endeavor to rally their men on a ridge some four or five hundred yards in rear, and also sent two staff officers to do the same. I then turned my attention to the battery, with the view of saving it if possible. Captain Dent was already endeavoring to limber up and retire, but, being exposed to a heavy fire, he lost many men and horses. The enemy to our left was now advancing on us, the 28th firing on them as they did so; but still, onward they came and they, the 28th, finally gave way. Attacked now in front and flank, further resistance was useless ...

I was endeavoring to have one of the guns, which had become jammed between two trees, extricated, when Captain Dent called to me, "Leave the gun, General, and save yourself! The Yankees are on you!" Looking to the front, I saw them within fifty yards, pouring over the breastwork. Seventy or eighty men, including some artillerists, were scattered around me, some firing. Others had been assisting at the battery. I directed them to retire at once, and calling to Lieutenant Jannisson [1st Lieut. George A. Jennison, 24th Alabama adjutant], Acting Inspector General, told him we must now ride for it.

Many of those around me were shot down and the bullets whistled around me like a swarm of bees. I thought my chance of escape doubtful in the extreme, but determined not to be taken if I could possibly help it, and to run every risk to secure my safety. So putting spurs to our horses and separating from each other, we dashed down the rough and rugged slope at nearly full speed and at imminent risk of our necks, the balls pattering against the trees and rocks around me like hailstones. Riding as I was, straight from the enemy, I felt certain that I could not do so long without being hit by the many balls fired at me, and although I increased the distance I had to traverse more than one-half, I rendered their aim less certain and thought my chances better by changing my course. I therefore turned slanting to the left and had the satisfaction, after a ride of 300 or 400 yards, of placing an intervening ridge between myself and bloodthirsty foes. Here I was rejoined by Lieutenant Jannisson, who also had escaped. We literally ran the gauntlet, and as we were the conspicuous target for their fire, and several thousand shots must have been directed at us, it was only by God's mercy that we escaped. Our horses also were unhurt. Had they been killed, a like fate would in all

■ Private Calvin J.C. Munroe of Company G, 25th Alabama, managed to escape capture when Deas' regiments dissolved and fled down the ridge's east slope. Another brigade member, 18-year-old Private Samuel K. Vann of Company C, 19th Alabama, wrote home a week later: "I am sorry that some people are so down about the war, but the run we made at Missionary was enough to make them get out of heart, but we were overpowered so that we were compelled to run. They just came up line after line ... I fought as hard as any of them while we were fighting, and run as fast as any of them while we was running."

■ Private James G. Watson of Company I, 25th Illinois. Recovered from a shrapnel wound received at Chickamauga, he was among the skirmishers preceding Willich's brigade up Missionary Ridge. The next day Watson wrote to his father: "... after some hard fighting at close range for about 20 minutes, the rebels were completely routed and we had more fun laughing over it than we have had since the battle of Pea Ridge. They ran like sheep, and threw their guns, knapsacks and everything that would hinder them from running and lots of them run down hill and gave themselves up."

The 25th's commander, Col. Richard H. Nodine, reported the capture of "one James rifled cannon and seven caissons loaded with ammunition," as well as regimental losses of 67 officers and men out of 260 participating in the assault. The survivors bivouacked on the ridge's crest overnight. Wrote Watson: "We took off our equipment and rested for the first time in three days. We have been laying at our ease and have buried the rebel dead. I picked up a rebel haversack full of grub ... and had a good supper last night for once in a long while."

probability have befallen us, or at least a long and wearisome captivity.

Of those who were around me when I started in this race, only a few escaped. We saved two of our guns, the other two fell a prize to the conqueror.

## 'Every regiment formed in a V-shape'

### Lt. Col. Francis Erdelmeyer
### 32nd Indiana Volunteer Infantry

Before the order [was given] to advance upon the rifle pits at the foot of the Ridge, Willich's Brigade held the position on Orchard Knob. On the signal of six guns the Brigade moved forward. The 32nd held the right in the second line of battle. The ground in our front was one clear field and soon we got in the reach of the enemy's fire. The line moved double quick.

Arriving at the rifle pits the troops dropped behind the little earthworks which were an excellent range target for the enemies artillery and infantry fire. We then and there lost several men amongst which was Major Jacob Glass of the 32nd. Seeing the futility of staying in such a position with no chance of returning the fire, I called the attention of Gen. Willich's aide-de-camp, Lt. McGrath, and Col. Askew of the 15th Ohio, which was in the first line of battle. As the 15th Ohio and 32nd Indiana really laid on top of each other, I told them there was *no cover* this side of the Ridge and I proposed to move on the Hill for protection. Both seeing the condition as I did, I ordered my regiment forward. We soon were out of the range of fire and as every other command did likewise, we started up the Ridge in great earnest.

On going up the regiments grouped themselves with their colors, so every regiment formed in a V-shape with the colors in front. The 32nd took the right of the Brigade, the 15th Ohio to my left and the 49th Ohio next.

Over half way up we crossed a road running north ascending the Ridge. Myself and many officers and men lay under the bank of this road trying to rest and gain our breath from the exhausting strain of climbing. Laying there back to the hill, I noticed the formation of the ground. It looked like a trough or mould. We were on the south wall of it and there was a depression to the north and a north wall some distance away. I could plainly see our Brigade hanging and scrambling up the Ridge some fifty feet below. I could see Gen. Willich walking back and forth and swinging his cap in his hand. Forward we went again. On the next rest halfway from this to the summit my color sergeant fell with a ball in his forehead. At this point was sharp firing, but we continued to rush on and reached the Ridge where two pieces of artillery were located. Halting a moment for breath and to fix bayonets, my men rushed over the rifle pit, grappling for the guns. The enemy disappeared down the hill.

Standing on the crest of the rifle pit, I glanced to the left along the front. I there saw the 15th Ohio, 49th Ohio and 89th Illinois all scrambling over the rifle pit. The enemy gave little resistance. The line of breastworks seemed to curve around that same mould or crescent like the formation of the Ridge. Stepping off the rifle pit, making two steps, I heard cannons fire on the left and two balls coming down the Ridge ricochetting, passed three or four feet in front of my head. Was evidently a round shell as I could see the round hole in it.

Looking north and trying to organize my men, I perceived the lines on our left still hanging under the summit of the north wall of the mould, but soon the left of our Brigade became engaged in firing and the line in blue got over to the Ridge and the firing moved rapidly further north.

Then and there looking east — that is, on the other side of the Ridge — I saw artillery coming diagonally down the Hill trying to get on the road that ran east from our front. My men as well as the whole front at the regiment's left opened fire on them and horses and riders all tumbled into a heap. Our front being clear, the battle [now] was away to the north. We were ordered to remain there and we there bivouacked for the night.

## 'Such a confused mass I never saw'

### Capt. Charles B. Russell
### Company D
### 6th Ohio Volunteer Infantry

About 2 p.m. our regiment was relieved from the skirmish line by the One Hundred and Twenty-fourth Ohio, and ordered to the breastworks [on Orchard Knob]. As we knew nothing of the intended attack, we congratulated ourselves upon our good fortune in being relieved so soon. But the moment we reached our fortifications we saw that something was up.

The regiment was placed on the left of the first line of our brigade, and had not long to wait before the six signal guns were fired on Orchard Knob, and then came the order to advance. Over the breastworks moved the line, the rebels opening their artillery upon us almost immediately. We got through the woods and entered the cleared field, and then, with a yell, started on a run for the rifle-pits. It was a splendid and terrible sight. It reminded me of Tennyson's "Charge of the Light Brigade" — cannon to the right of us, cannon to the left of us, cannon in front of us, volleyed and thundered. We all knew that the sooner we took the ridge the better it was for us, and every man put in his very best. From what I could see, our regiment seemed to be the best runners; we distanced the other troops and were the first in the rifle-pits at the foot of the ridge.

Although our orders only required us to seize these works, we at once saw that we could not hold them, the rebel artillery and musketry from the ridge commanding them so closely that to stay there long would have been certain death. So we again led on for the summit. Such a getting up hill you never saw. We had to rest every few minutes, but gradually the troops moved up until nearly under the works, whence the enemy were still blazing away at us, and their batteries, in particular, working desperately.

As soon as we had recovered breath during our last halt, the command "Fix bayonets!" was given. This the rebels heard, and it scared them mightily. As we rose up to move forward again, a volley was poured almost into our very faces, and many of our boys fell. The next minute we cleared the works and jumped right in among the rebels. Such a confused mass I never saw, nor expect

■ Capt. Henry L. Rowell of Company H, 89th Illinois. Starting from the foot of Orchard Knob, he led his men unscathed through heavy Confederate rifle and cannon fire as the regiment dashed across the open plain toward the ridge. Once on its slope, Lt. Col. William D. Williams watched as his Illinoisans were cut down. He reported: "Capt. Rowell was seriously wounded near the crest of the ridge. Second Lieut. Erastus O. Young, commanding Company A, fell near the crest, shot dead, while shouting 'Forward and victory!' Three enlisted men were killed and 31 wounded during the advance up the hill."

Rowell's wound proved fatal; he died in Chattanooga on December 3.

# 'They fought like fiends incarnate'

**Harper's Weekly artist Theodore R. Davis sketched Federal troops surmounting breastworks on Missionary Ridge as Confederate artillerymen struggle to save their guns. During the assault of Hazen's brigade, the 6th Ohio under Lt. Col. Alexander C. Christopher confronted a battery whose fire cut down the regiment's major, Samuel C. Erwin. Fierce hand-to-hand fighting ensued when the crest was reached, as described by Sergeant Brian P. Critchell of Company A:**

About the hottest fight we ever got into was on Mission Ridge. We were close enough to the rebs to shake hands with them, and they fought like fiends incarnate. We were too close to each other to reload our guns, and the boys were using their weapons for clubs.

There was a tall, raw-boned Johnny gunner who was fighting like the very devil himself. He was laying about him with a heavy gun swab, and he seemed to me to be the biggest man I ever laid eyes on. A half-dozen of our boys went at him but he stood his ground. A heavy revolver, all the cartridges discharged, was thrown at him. It struck him full in the face with force sufficient to knock out a bull, but he only shook his head and went to work again. I threw up my sergeant's sword and cracked away at the swab ... and it shattered clear to the hilt. The big reb wouldn't yield an inch, and finally one of our boys, a Cincinnatian named Boyd [Sergeant William Boyd of Company C], caught him off his guard, and rammed a bayonet clear through him with such force that the barrel, too, passed out of the other side of the big fellow's body. Well, that man, mortally wounded, didn't give up, and as he lay there on the bloody turf, with his entrails hanging from the awful hole in his stomach, he grabbed a pistol and winged another boy in blue before he died.

to see again. Here were officers trying to rally their men, there a battery trying to limber up, and everywhere masses of running rebels — fellows "lighting out" for dear life — and our men popping them over as if they were quails. I saw many a poor fellow bayoneted, but it was all fair play.

As soon as we reached the summit, part of our regiment went for a battery, captured it, and compelled the gunners to work the pieces against their own men. A battery officer shot two of our men with a revolver, and would not surrender. He was quickly shot down. Hazen saw that the rebs on our left still held their ground, and were giving Willich some trouble, when he ordered our regiment to charge down on their flanks, which we did with a yell. Everybody seemed crazy with delight, doubling the rebels back and chasing them in every direction.

The rebels did not save many cannons they had on the hill. One gun that we took was marked "Captured from Rosecrans on the 31st of Dec., '62, at Stone River." Hazen (who was with us all the time) and the other generals were all in splendid humor, and complimented the troops greatly. Two of my company were killed and three wounded, one of my men being shot through with a solid shot ...

■ Lt. Col. E. Bassett Langdon, commander of the 1st Ohio Infantry, was seriously wounded as his regiment struggled up Missionary Ridge. According to regimental historian Albert Kern, "about half way up the Ridge Lieut. Col. Langdon, somewhat exhausted by the climb, placed his back to a tree on the side next to the enemy, and with his revolver in hand encouraged the men to proceed. A rebel soldier on top aimed his rifle at the colonel. The ball struck under the left eye, passed through and out of his lower jaw. The colonel fell, but raised himself and called out to the men, 'Boys! I'm not killed yet!' "

Langdon recovered sufficiently to rejoin the 1st Ohio in 1864, but died from the effects of his wound on May 30, 1867.

## 'When we started I commenced praying'

### Journal of Private William H. Huntzinger Company I 79th Indiana Volunteer Infantry

**November 25, 1863.** Before 12 midday the rebels ceased firing with their artillery in our front but our artillery kept up an occasional firing and the cannonading on the left was heavy and regular. One of our buglers reported having seen some of our troops marching to our left on our rear for an hour or more. At 12 M. there was not a cloud to be seen; the skies looked blue and the wind was blowing from the west. The same bugler said he saw all the generals on the knoll on our right. Gen. Grant was there; it was the best place to see his army and direct its movements.

At 12:45 p.m. the rebels got a good range on our rifle pits and sent their shells lengthwise, cutting limbs off trees right over us. From the sound on the left Gen. Sherman must be gaining on the rebels, as it sounds closer. We fell in at 2:30 p.m. and formed in close columns by division, stacked arms and waited for orders.

At 3:30 p.m. we deployed in line of battle, marched and formed a line outside the rifle pits. At 3:45 p.m. there were some cannons fired from the knoll and from the right as a signal and then we all started as hard as we could go for a little distance through the thicket and bushes. When we started I commenced praying. I felt as good as I ever felt. I did not think I would be hurt or wounded but I felt that James Hague, my messmate, would get killed or wounded. I heard the skirmishers firing in our front and I knew we would soon be engaged. We soon got out of the bushes in plain view of the rebels but they did not fire at us much from their rifle pits at the foot of Missionary Ridge.

We crossed two lines of their rifle pits and then started up the

■ Col. Frederick Knefler commanded the 79th Indiana at Missionary Ridge. One of his officers, Capt. Daniel W. Howe of Company I, later recalled: "When we reached the summit the men paused a few moments to get their breath. At this time we were but a few yards from the Confederate breastworks on the crest. I looked back and saw that the regiment was considerably in advance of the troops on our immediate right and left, although all were rapidly advancing. I was then standing beside Colonel Knefler and I called his attention to the fact. About the same time I saw a Confederate, a giant in size he seemed to me, standing on top of the Confederate works on the crest and firing loaded guns handed up to him by his comrades in the trenches behind. I could not help observing him for at one time I thought that he was aiming at Colonel Knefler or at me. He was undoubtedly a brave man for he persisted in standing until he was shot down. After the works were taken his body was found riddled with bullets."

ridge. The whole top of the ridge as far as we could see seemed to be full of artillery firing at us, most of the shells passing a few feet over our heads, for we were running as hard as we could all the way. The shells exploded in our rear and hurt some of the men who could not keep up. We could look up and down the valley and see whole lines of troops running toward Missionary Ridge. The shells were exploding all along the valley a few feet from the ground, some on the ground. It looked like a cloud of smoke. Our artillery was playing on their batteries stationed on top of the ridge.

We got to the rebel line of breastworks at the foot of the ridge and rested about three minutes, for we were nearly out of breath, some entirely given out. Some of the boys started on. I heard Col. Knefler say "Forward!" and we all started to charge the ridge. Grape and canister rained all around us. There was a high point just before our regiment and we charged for that point. The battery on that point, a battery to our left and two batteries to our right had a complete cross fire on us. The hill was very steep and rocky, with a few scrubby oaks growing on its side. Our two regiments (86th and 79th) were so far in advance of the other troops that the rebels shelled us from the right and left and from the point in our front. Their shells and the grape and canister plowed up the ground all around us and a good many were killed.

We reached within a few feet of their breastworks on top of the ridge and lay down, being so tired we could go no farther. We looked back and saw lines of troops coming to our support and the troops on our right and left were nearly up as far as our regiment, and being rested up a little we got up to go in their works, for we could see the troops to our right nearly ready to take the different points and the rebel battery. We could see our troops charge right up to the mouth of the cannons and take the batteries and turn them on the rebels, and I know the rebels could not have been very far down the mountain on the other side when our men turned their guns and fired at them as they were retreating.

We charged up and took the little outpoint that lay about 50 yards farther than the main straight line. A shell bursted close to James Hague, knocking him down senseless. He rolled down the hill a little ways and lodged against a tree. Someone took him back. I was not allowed to leave the line. I had orders not to shoot but I disobeyed and fired every good opportunity I had. Sergeant Michael R. Butler was wounded in the knee, and a shell passed so close to James P. Johnson that it bruised his arm. A few of the boys were missing when we got up to the main ridge. The rebels killed some of our men after we got clear up the ridge and were firing at them as they ran down the other side. We captured some prisoners, a few officers and flags. The 79th Indiana captured two guns; they were 12 pounder brass pieces. Several minutes of hard fighting took place after we got up on the ridge to our left about 400 yards.

It was a very hard fight and at sundown they were repulsed and driven clean off the ridge, and we could see them running off like rascals that they were. We could see off about 8 miles the smoke of cars they are burning or a train of wagons off to our left. We got wood, made fires and made some coffee for James Hague, for he had come to and had joined the regiment. We had crackers to eat. I went back to the place where we advanced up the hill and took a good view of the ground over which we had come up. The dead and wounded had all been cared for. We did not have many killed; the rebels shot too high. The shells did the most damage. We talked about the battle until 10:30 p.m. and lay down to rest. We were all very tired.

## 'Contest every inch of ground'

### Lt. Col. James J. Turner
### 30th Tennessee Volunteer Infantry

From our position on Missionary Ridge, Chattanooga, the Tennessee River, Lookout Mountain and the valley of some miles in length and breadth were in full view. By 10 a.m. we could see the Federal army crossing the river and moving into position with the intention of a forward movement and attack. By 3 p.m. they were in our front and marching in two lines of battle to the foot of the ridge, while Hooker's corps was flanking our position on the left. As soon as the Federals came within range our artillery opened on them, and continued the fire till they reached the ridge; but the fire was not effective, owing to the plunging shots. The Federal army gained the foot of the ridge in good order. As they commenced ascending, our muskets again opened fire upon them, but with little effect, as it was evident our troops were overshooting them to a great extent.

The position occupied by my command — the Tenth and Thirtieth regiments — was only a good skirmish line, and as we were heavily assaulted some three battalions and parts of regiments were sent to our assistance. We drove the enemy in our front and wings far down the ridge. I was pressing them when informed that Deas' and Manigault's brigades had broken on our left and right, and I then saw that the Federals occupied the ridge at these points and were turning our own artillery on us. I ordered an immediate retreat to the top of the ridge. I could then see our forces, except our brigade, retreating in great disorder.

Our brigade then consisted of the Tenth, Fifteenth, Twentieth, Thirtieth and Thirty-seventh Tennessee regiments, the Thirty-seventh Georgia and Caswell's battalion of sharpshooters. As we started to retreat from the ridge Col. Tyler was severely wounded, and I assumed command of the brigade as the senior officer. We fell back about fifteen hundred yards to where there was a considerable ridge, and where Gen. Bragg and staff were attempting to rally the army and make a stand; but he had lost the confidence of the army and officers and men dashed by without heeding his commands or appeals.

Our brigade was in good condition, and on reaching this ridge I halted it and in a few minutes had a line of battle formed across the road. Our division commander directed me to follow on to the pontoon bridge at Chickamauga Creek, the sun then being nearly an hour from setting. Men from Cobb's battery and a number of detached soldiers, numbering some five hundred, came up and fell into our line of battle. As all the generals had left and we were free to act independently, we concluded to stop the Federal forces at this point till darkness should arrest their advance. I directed

■ Col. George F. Dick commanded the 86th Indiana of Beatty's brigade, IV Corps. After two of the 86th's color sergeants were badly wounded, Capt. William S. Sims of Company F grabbed the flag and carried it over the Confederate works. Dick wrote: "The advance troops of our brigade turned quickly to the left, with my flag in front in command of Captain Sims. They soon came against a redoubt manned by the Forty-second Alabama, the commander of which saw our flag coming, and told his men to lie still and they would sally out and capture it when it came near. The commander of the Alabama regiment [Major W.S. Fergus] called to his men to leap over the works after him, but they arose and leaped out on the other side, leaving their commander to fall into our hands; and he did fall, hurting his face on the rocks at Sims' feet, who literally got on top of him and held him down. He took supper with us that night and told us all that I have described above."

■ Lt. Col. James J. Turner, 30th Tennessee, had been shot through the chest while attempting to rally a broken skirmish line at Chickamauga on September 19. His regiment lost half its number that day, but "the survivors all came out with new guns and cartridge-boxes which they had taken from the enemy."

At Missionary Ridge, Turner assumed command of Bate's brigade when Col. Robert C. Tyler was severely wounded. "Two-thirds of the army seemed to be disorganized and badly demoralized," he wrote, "and many had thrown away their guns in retreating."

Major Caswell to deploy his battalion of sharpshooters, consisting of five companies splendidly drilled and armed, and cover our front and feel for the enemy, and if forced to retire to do so slowly and contest every inch of ground. The order was executed to the letter. Soon they were hotly engaged and though compelled by force of superior numbers to retreat, they did so very gradually, holding a large force in check till dark, when they fell back and took position in our line.

As soon as the Federals came in range both sides opened with great spirit. We had the advantage of position and full knowledge of the ground, but were outnumbered by at least three to one. The Federals had advanced to close range, and the firing was very severe.

In the meantime the brigade was nearly out of ammunition, and it was quite dark, being at least an hour after sunset. At this juncture Gen. Breckinridge and a part of his staff came up from the rear and inquired what command it was and why [it was] remaining there. I informed him, and he said his entire command had been broken and were retreating, and that hearing the firing he came to it, but ordered me to retire at once as we were surrounded on all sides except the rear by overwhelming forces. I issued the order for a retreat, yet nothing but the darkness and our knowledge of the roads enabled us to get out.

## 'Three times over the same ground'

### Chaplain John J. Hight
### 58th Indiana Volunteer Infantry

**Wednesday, November 25 —** I did not get off so early as on yesterday. As I go out, an occasional gun could be heard on our left, but they were a long way off and some distance apart. The firing continued to increase. The most remarkable feature of the forenoon was the continual stream of rebel troops passing on the summit of the ridge to our left. Our batteries occasionally paid their respects to them, but with little effect. We could distinctly see infantry, cavalry and artillery. At one time we might see a rebel General accompanied by his staff. It was a lovely day, and objects were distinctly visible at a long distance.

Early in the afternoon our skirmish line became slightly engaged. We were then in the second line of battle, General Wood's division being in front, the flanks overlapping for a short distance. Besides the response from the rebel riflemen, the guns on the ridge fired several shots, some of which came so close that we all took to the ditches. I sat very contentedly on some leaves in a trench, just between the 58th Indiana and the 26th Ohio, but this cannonading was not very dangerous.

About 2 p.m. our lines advanced. Wood's men withdrew to the left to give the others room. The line of battle in our rear moved forward and occupied the trenches. The movements provoked quite a lively little firing from the rebel guns on the ridge. I tarried where I was until this firing lulled a little, when I rode over the brow of a hill and stopped at a line of rifle pits which had been dug for our skirmishers. The 58th was just a little in advance, lying flat on the ground. The rear line of battle now advanced and lay down just in the rear of the front. The 15th Indiana was behind the 58th. Wood's men continued to move off towards the left. My impression at this moment was that we were relieving some of Wood's men for the purpose of sending them to the support of our left under General Sherman.

It began to be whispered around that an advance was to be made. Dr. Adams came up and shared my pit. At length I heard someone in my rear give an order to an aide de camp, at a little distance, to tell someone to advance and take the works at the foot of the ridge. I did not distinctly hear all the words, but caught part of them and inferred that there was hot work ahead.

Major [Frank] White of the 15th rode up and down the line of that regiment, telling them to stand firm; if the first line gave way, to pass files to the rear and let them go, but not to go with them. General Wagner had called his regimental commanders a few minutes before and gave them some instructions. Colonel [Gustavus A.] Wood of the 15th seems to have misunderstood the order, which was to take the works at the foot of the ridge. He understood it was to take the ridge. Accordingly he came to Colonel Moore [Lt. Col. Joseph Moore, commanding the 58th Indiana] and told him that the order would soon be issued to take the ridge. Said he, "Have your men fix bayonets and move slowly to the top of the ridge."

At length the signal gun was fired from Orchard Knob, and long lines of men rose from the grass and began to advance. In a few minutes the 58th received orders to fix bayonets. At this time the front line of Wagner's brigade was composed of the 100th Illinois, 58th Indiana and 26th Ohio. The 57th Indiana was on the skirmish line, the 15th Indiana, 97th Ohio and 40th Indiana were in reserve. When bayonets were fixed there was manifested on the part of nearly all a disposition to go double quick.

First, there was a little belt of woods to pass. Here the men were checked again and again, but their impetuosity knew no bound. They continued to advance, faster and faster; already their shouts filled the woods and fields. The rebels were aroused by the charge, and from many points on the line the shots and shells were flying. Two batteries especially played on Wagner's brigade; one of these was in front of and a little to the right of Orchard Knob, and the other was at Bragg's headquarters. Twenty or twenty-five guns were firing at our brigade as fast as the ingenuity of the gunners would permit, and some of these shots came disagreeably near to where I was standing.

The regiment emerged from the woods in plain view of the enemy at the base of the ridge. As they advanced the speed of the men increased. The line was pretty well maintained until it came to a little water course. Here it was broken, but still it swept on. The 57th Indiana took the works and fell into the front line as it came up. Their line was but poorly defended, as the rebels had to reinforce their right during the day. The men were now in range of the rifles at the top of the ridge and a terrible hail of lead was poured down upon them. The artillery dealt out grape and canister, which seemed to "come in shovelfuls."

A blaze of fire now burst from the Union columns. Greek had met Greek and the tug of war had come. Wagner's brigade was the first of all to advance beyond the rebel works. It was but a moment's work to pass the rebel camps. An enfilading fire was poured upon our columns from right and left, and it was here that

■ Brig. Gen. George D. Wagner commanded a brigade in Sheridan's division, and sustained the largest loss of any Federal brigade commander in the fighting near Chattanooga between November 23 and 27 — 730 officers and men killed or wounded. More than 500 of these casualties were suffered by just three of Wagner's seven regiments at Missionary Ridge. The 97th Ohio lost 149, the 40th Indiana 158 and the 15th Indiana 199 — figures higher than in any other Union regiments engaged.

The 15th Indiana mustered only 125 officers and men immediately after the battle. Major Frank White, regimental commander and himself wounded, reported that "We captured the battle-flag of the Thirteenth Louisiana Regiment, but it was torn to pieces by the men for trophies before I could take it from them."

■ 1st Lieut. Daniel Royse, the 40th Indiana's adjutant, was serving on Wagner's brigade staff when his horse was killed beneath him. Royse's regimental commander, Lt. Col. Elias Neff, personally planted the 40th's flag on the crest after several color bearers were shot while struggling up the ridge. The regiment lost 20 men killed and 138 wounded (including eight officers) — nearly 45 percent of its strength.

many of our brave men fell. The troops on the right and left of us, seeing Wagner's men advancing, also went forward, and thus the whole line was moved. The taking of Missionary Ridge, therefore, was inaugurated not so much by the genius of commanders, or the bravery of soldiers, as by mistake. It was fortunate for us that this mistake was committed, as it would have been very disastrous to have remained long at the foot of the ridge.

When the line had reached one-third or perhaps one-half way up the ridge, the men were ordered to fall back to the works. By whom the order was given, or for what purpose, I can not tell, but it was attended with both good and bad results. It greatly exposed our brigade by causing them to pass three times over the same ground, and by placing them behind works that were not a protection. They were also much longer under fire than they would have been. But, on the other hand, our brigade was on an exceedingly rough piece of ground and immediately in front of a very strong position, so there would have been very great slaughter if the charge had been continued. The falling back drew the rebel fire on us, and this gave the other troops an opportunity to advance, which they did, and thus flanked the rebels and weakened their line on our front.

I maintained my position where it was at the beginning of the charge. It was at first designed to make that a place for the collection of our wounded, but there was a road a little to the right, leading to Chattanooga, and the wounded were principally collected along that way. A.R. Redman, severely wounded in the elbow, came to where I was, under the care of Jacob Gudgel. Some others came that way, but I did not remain long here. Most of the casualties of the 58th occurred in this part of the fight. Private William Riley Blythe of Company A was severely wounded and died in a few moments. Private Blackard of Company B was shot dead. Sergeant Howard remained on the hillside when the regiment went back. A few moments after they were gone he rose up from where he was lying behind a tree, and remarked to Ed. Carson who was near, "The regiment has gone, we had better go too." Just then he was pierced by a ball that passed entirely through him. He spoke of being shot and asked to be carried off. These were his last words, as his eyes were immediately closed in death. At the time of his death he was acting as lieutenant, though he had not yet been commissioned. As he lay on the field during the night his sword, jacket and boots were stolen from his body by some of the ghouls that infest the battlefield.

By this time the battle was gathering in more terrible earnestness than at any former period. Away to the left the contest was very sharp and I was exercised by fear of a failure. Our own brigade by this time was climbing the mountain side. I could distinctly see them working their way up, and could see that the rebels were running for dear life.

But my duties were with the wounded. I gave such aid as I could. At the breastworks I saw poor Robert Redman, the faithful and highly esteemed orderly, of Company F. He had been pierced by a grape shot through the back of the head while the troops were lying there. He was moving and struggling about, though he was entirely unconscious.

The rebel huts at the foot of the hill were filled with our wounded. I passed by Sergeant Howard and others of our dead. I went

# 'The last man to leave the trenches'

On November 25, Brig. Gen. Alexander W. Reynolds' brigade of 1,000 Virginia and North Carolina troops was attached temporarily to Patton Anderson's division, and held the line between Anderson and Bate's division. Located in the lower rifle pits, Reynolds' men were ordered up the crest when the assault began. Among the officers was Reynolds' young assistant adjutant general, Capt. J. William Mathews, who later served on Maj. Gen. Carter L. Stevenson's division staff.

Reynolds' extreme left, adjoining Bate, was commanded by Capt. James T. Weaver, acting major of the 60th North Carolina. Reynolds praised Weaver for "conducting the retreat of his command from the Riflepits to the top of the Ridge. He was the last man to leave the trenches ..." Within the hour, however, Weaver's men succumbed to the pressure, broke and streamed in disorder to the rear.

One year later as lieutenant colonel, Weaver was killed by a sharpshooter during the Confederate retreat from Nashville.

■ Capt. J. William Mathews

■ Capt. James T. Weaver

■ Capt. George W.F. Harper commanded Company H, 58th North Carolina. His regiment, with three others of Alexander W. Reynolds' brigade, was deployed on November 22 along a thin trench line at the foot of Missionary Ridge. Harper later wrote: "Here [we were] annoyed by the premature explosion of the shells from our batteries on the ridge in rear, firing upon the enemy in front. A veteran of Company H, with a grim sense of humor, suggested to his Captain that the command occupy the other side of the breastwork — a brisk musketry fire then coming from the enemy. The suggestion was not adopted. After three days in this position, with the larger part of the troops on duty day and night, the regiment ... was recalled to the top of the ridge, the charge of the enemy [Sheridan's division] being made as the last company moved out."

on up the road to Bragg's headquarters and found the First Brigade of our division there. I rode on to my regiment and found them still moving when I came to them. After remaining with the regiment for a short time I started on my return to the scene of recent battle.

The way was strewn with cast-off articles of the fleeing rebels. A person could pick up anything from a siege gun to a lousy shirt. I contented myself with a wooden stirrup which, however, proved of no value when I examined it in camp. I saw some parties of thieves prowling among the dead. I am in favor of leaving a detail of good men on such occasions to shoot down these cowardly scoundrels who remain behind to rob the dead.

The scene of suffering at the foot of the ridge, in the old camp,

■ Sergeant John M. Cassett of Company E, 100th Illinois. At Chickamauga this small regiment of Wagner's brigade lost 49 percent in casualties, including its two ranking field officers. With no line officers present, Cassett commanded his company in the assault. Lying at the ridge's base before making the ascent, the 100th nearly lost its remaining field officer when a bullet plowed into Major Charles M. Hammond's horse. Simultaneously, an exploding shell threw him to the ground, but he escaped unhurt. Wrote Capt. Rodney S. Bowen of Company A: "As soon as our advance commenced, the rebels opened on us a terrific fire. Had it been a veritable volcano, a burning mountain, it could hardly have surpassed the grandeur of the terribleness of the display now made. But the advance of our boys was hardly checked."

was terrible. In every direction could be seen fires which had been kindled, and about them was collected the wounded, trying to keep warm. The night was cold and many perished from suffering and exposure. It must have been midnight when I reached my quarters. My horse and myself were worn down. It seemed as if the experience of a month had been crowded into a day.

## 'His aim was a little too high'

### Color Sergeant George L. Banks
### 15th Indiana Volunteer Infantry

At Mission Ridge, when we first started in the charge, the Twenty-sixth Ohio was in our front but soon gave way, the Fifteenth taking their place. I was slightly wounded in the left thumb at the bottom of the Ridge. When the regiment reached the road well up the Ridge it was a perfect hail storm of bullets, and we went down on our faces in the road. It seemed for a moment as though we would stay there, when in my rear I heard someone say, "Men, for God's sake, forward!"

Looking around, I saw Major [Frank] White standing in that storm of bullets. I immediately got on my feet, raised the flag and started forward, calling on the boys to follow their flag. All company formation was broken, the boys from every company rallying 'round the flag. We had gone but a short distance when I was struck by a small ball, about one inch below the heart. It passed through a novel I had been reading which I thrust inside my blouse when called into line, also two letters, striking the rib but not having force enough to break through. It followed the rib to the right and lodged over the pit of my stomach. I had the ball cut out four days later.

I was knocked down and was senseless for a moment. While I was lying on the ground, four comrades raised the flag and were shot down — two killed and two wounded. When I got on my feet I saw the flag fall but a short distance up the hill. I found I was not disabled and reached the flag, raised it again, and with the boys rallying around me, we went on. When but a short distance from the works on the crest of the Ridge, we saw the Johnnies' guns being lowered over the works at us. We dropped to the ground and the volley passed over our heads without injury, and before they could reload we were on the works and killed or captured nearly all in our immediate front.

When I planted our flag on the works, the flag of the 13th Louisiana was flying on the works a few feet to my right. I fired six shots from my revolver over the works and dropped my hand on the log. A noise just then caused me to look down, and there was a Johnny leveling his gun at me. I turned my head, intending to jump off, but he was too quick for me. His aim was a little too high, his ball hitting me on the right side, just back of the crown of my head, plowing a furrow in my skull and the holes in my scalp being two or three inches apart. Second Lieutenant Thomas Graham seized my flag as I fell off the works backward, and carried it over the works. As soon as I was able to walk I was ordered to the rear by Major White, commanding the regiment, and

I obeyed orders very willingly. The flag was carried through the balance of the fight by Corporal Page.*

## 'We mowed them down by scores'

### Diary of Private Robert Watson Company B 7th Florida Volunteer Infantry

**Nov. 24th —** ... I drew 3 days rations at 10 p.m. and three of us went to work cooking them. At 11 p.m. just as we had got nicely started in baking the bread we were ordered to carry our cooking utensils to the top of Missionary Ridge, it being too steep for the wagons to go up loaded. Two of us carried them up and hard work it was, for the hill was very steep. By the time we got through it was nearly daylight.

**Nov. 25th —** At 7 a.m. some of the boys came in from the company to get the rations. The enemy were shelling our quarters at the time and some of their shells fell among our huts but hurt nobody. We carried the rations to the company who were then in the breastworks about ¾ mile to the right of us and issued it to them, the enemy shelling us all the time. We moved up and down the breastworks several times during the forenoon. At 2 p.m. the enemy advanced on us in 4 columns. They played us a Yankee trick by bring[ing] out their artillery covered with ambulance covers and we all took them to be ambulances until they opened fire on us.

They advanced on us in fine style. We held our fire until they were within about 300 yards of us and then poured a deadly fire into them and made many of them bite the dust; but [we] were very few in number, merely a line of skirmishers in single rank and scattered at that. I judged from the looks of their numbers that there must be all of 100,000 men. We mowed them down until they were within 30 yards of us and then we retreated up the hill and made a short stand at the second breastworks, but it was of no use for although we mowed them down yet they advanced on us and we were again forced to retreat, and then came the worst part of the fight for the hill was dreadful steep and the enemy kept up a continual fire and threw a continual shower of bullets among us and I only wonder that they did not kill all of us. Many a poor fellow fell exhausted and was taken prisoner.

I did not think that I should be able to reach the top for I had on a heavy knapsack and 3 days rations in my haversack and a canteen full of water. I stopped several times and took a shot at the damned Yankees and at the same time it rested me. The bullets flew around us so thick that it seemed impossible to escape unhurt. I would have thrown away my knapsack but could not get it off and it was lucky for me for a bullet struck my knapsack at

■ Private Thomas Bradford of Company C, 13th Louisiana, fell mortally wounded just south of Bragg's headquarters and died a prisoner in Chattanooga. Two days earlier his brigade commander, Col. Randall L. Gibson, warned a member of Gen. A.P. Stewart's staff: "It will take nearly half of the command to furnish the detail for picket in the morning. This will render the force on the left of the artillery, guarding the left flank of the division, very small; and posted, in consequence of the want of any spades or picks whatever, behind very inferior works."

Unequal numbers forced Gibson's Louisianans to retreat. Private A.D. Mason, a sharpshooter of Company D, 19th Louisiana, recalled: "We had stopped the Federal colors [a] seventh time when a very large, fair-complexioned officer, riding a roan horse, took the colors and started for the gap. We were so astounded by his gallantry that we allowed him to get within close range of our lines before firing on him. He fell from the horse, but the latter never broke his gait till suddenly he stumbled and fell. He also had received a bullet."

* Banks was awarded the Medal of Honor for his actions on November 25. Eleven months earlier he carried the 15th Indiana's flag in the battle of Stone River. He wrote: "The flag ... was pierced by fifty-two small balls and one cannon ball. The shaft was badly shattered, while I had two ball holes in my hat, four in my blouse, my canteen shot off me and haversack shot through. I escaped without a scratch."

■ 1st Lieut. Sanders Myers of Company B, 4th Florida, was wounded and taken prisoner on November 25. Regimental Quartermaster Sergeant Washington M. Ives Jr. described the Floridians' decimation: "... the Fla. Brig. gave way in the ditches and attempted to climb the ridge ... thus allowing the enemy to follow them partly up and getting higher up the hill or ridge than the Floridians, the latter were compelled after firing several rounds at the advancing foe, to climb the ridge under a terrible fire. The ridge was so long and steep and as all the underbrush and trees had been cut down for fire wood, our boys afforded fair marks for the Yanks and but forever reached the top. My reg't went in with 172 men and came out with 23 officers and men ..."

After medical treatment, Myers sat out the war in Federal prisons at Camp Chase, Ft. Delaware, Hilton Head and Ft. Pulaski.

the right shoulder and came out at the left shoulder, making 23 holes in my blanket.

When I reached the top of the ridge I was so much exhausted that I fell down and lay there for several minutes to recover breath. I then got behind a log and went to work with a will, shooting Yankees. They advanced slowly keeping up a continual fire. We mowed them down by scores when unfortunately for us our artillery got out of ammunition and retired but we held the ridge until the enemy were on the top and had their flags on our breastworks. We then retreated down the hill under a shower of lead, leaving many a son of the South dead and wounded on the ground and many more shared the same fate on the retreat. We retreated in great confusion, men from different companies all mixed up together. I arrived at Chickamauga Station at 8 p.m. and there the different brigades formed. After searching around for some time I found our Regt., that is a portion of it, for many of them were missing.

## 'Don't give up the field!'

### Orderly Sergeant Charles C. Hemming
### Company A
### 3rd Florida Volunteer Infantry

When we lined up on Missionary Ridge to meet Grant's tremendous array of men, our little army must have been somewhat intimidated; and yet I heard no expression of the kind. Just as we were getting our correct alignment, about one-half of the company was obliqued down the hillside and a battery placed in position just over us. I wished at the time that that hillside was in front instead of in the rear, because I saw I could not climb it, it was so steep, some twenty feet of sheer rock, and I could not get farther to the right because of other obstructions.

Our regiments, when in battle line, were conspicuous for our evidences of weakness. One file could scarcely touch another, and we discovered almost at once that in order to deceive the enemy, who could plainly see us on the crest of the hill, our commander was marching and countermarching for some time before the battle commenced, a constant stream of men moving toward our right and then circling back and the same men coming along in the rear.

It was somewhere about one-thirty when we heard the reverberation in the hills around of a tremendous gun, and over our heads screeched the large shells it was sending at us. Then we looked out on the plain, and with the precision of a dress parade their magnificent army came in view. The officers, all superbly dressed, pranced out on their high-mettled chargers; the bands played, and to the music came the most wonderful array of splendidly equipped soldiers I ever saw. The old flag waved beautifully at the head of each regiment and the smaller flags were in their places with the brigade and division commanders. The atmosphere was perfectly still excepting just breath enough to straighten out the banners.

I loved the old flag dearly when I was a boy, and when the Fourth of July came I had my miniature cannon lined up on small entrenchments in our game to cannonade the fort and salute the flag. When I looked upon the old flag at the head of that wonderful army, I confess that it drew my silent admiration, as I suppose it did that of many others of our Confederate soldiers.

However, we had a duty to perform and a new flag to serve; so we lay down on the top of the hill, waiting for the coming foe. We did not fire a gun until they got within two hundred yards, and the battery, which had been posted almost over my head, ceased to fire after they started to climb the hill.

When the order was given to fire it seemed to us that hundreds fell, and at first their line wavered, but brave officers held them to the work and, cheering wildly, they came at us again. All at once I heard someone shout, "For God's sakes, men, don't give up the field!" I looked and saw our line wavering in the center, and above the heads of our regiment, where our color bearer Charlie Ulmer was waving the flag and calling to the boys to hold steady, the commanding general of our army as well as that of our brigade, on their horses, were appealing to the wavering line.

The 3rd Florida had fallen back, but when such an order was given I do not know, for I did not hear it. Just where I was there were none left except Kernan and Livingstone.

We dashed out to try to make our escape. In what direction Kernan went I do not know, but I followed Livingstone as I thought him to be a good runner. There was only one way out and that was in front of the Federal line. I do not think I exaggerate when I say that from seventy-five to a hundred men of the Union army, just climbing the crest of the hill, were to my right not over twenty or thirty feet away. It seemed that they all fired at me at once. The blaze from their gun barrels scorched my face and one bullet barely reached my right cheek.

I was not frightened in the least. I held my gun and had my cartridge box, but I certainly was running faster than a young deer before the hounds. When I reached the decline of the hill on the other side, which could not have been more than two hundred yards from the crest upon which we fought, I saw there was no road leading down and, balancing my body with my gun, I sailed out into the air and lit at the bottom squarely upon my feet. Turning slightly to the right I ran into an old road and, when I got a little farther down, came across Sam Pascoe. The brave fellow was putting a tourniquet on his leg below the knee, and he cried out, "Charlie, don't leave me!" I saw the point from which the blood was running and knew he was not dangerously hurt. I answered jocosely, "It's no time to stop now," and pushed on. Livingstone was a little behind me.

About a hundred yards farther on I came to some thick brush — so thick I could not see through it — and as I rounded this little point of timber I heard the German command "Attention! Attention!" I looked and saw what I took to be two or three German regiments right together and to my left, about two hundred yards or so. I heard further orders given in German. Right then flashed across my mind: "We are fighting the world! Here on this battlefield are foreigners who do not speak English and yet are fighting for the American flag."

I looked over to the right of where I was and saw a little hut. In this Livingstone and myself took shelter. I peeked through the cracks at these same Germans, and I saw them shoot several men

■ Lt. Col. William T. Stockton, 1st Florida Cavalry (Dismounted). His small regiment, along with the 4th and 7th Florida, were skirmishers at the base of Missionary Ridge. Wounded in the face at Chickamauga, Stockton was captured on November 25. "My imperfect recovery had left me so weak," he wrote to his wife, "that I was unable from exhaustion to leave the field, when all was lost on our part of it. Our three little Regiments behaved well, but we were left alone. Two of my men were killed at my side while successively attempting to assist me."

Another member of the Florida brigade wrote: "The 1st Reg't Cav. had about 200 in the fight and brought out 33. Every field officer and captain of the 1st Cav. engaged in the fight was either killed or captured."

Stockton, a Philadelphia native and 1834 graduate of West Point, was sent to prison at Johnson's Island and released in July 1865. His brother Richard was killed at the Alamo in 1836.

■ Capt. Thomas L. Massenburg commanded the Jackson Artillery, a Macon, Ga., battery assigned to Major Felix H. Robertson's Reserve Artillery battalion. In the spring of 1863 Massenburg, a pharmacist by trade, was arrested for refusing to string up by the thumbs one of his men. Massenburg's close friend, Capt. Robert E. Park of the 12th Alabama, later wrote: "The care and protection which he gave to his splendid command of artillerists is explained by ... his love of justice and his unwillingness to inflict disgraceful punishment upon one of his command, though a violator of one of the regulations of the army."

with their hands up. All at once I made a decision, and that was to load up and fight it out.

Just then I saw a man coming toward us on a captured horse. He was a Union soldier and was making directly for the cabin door. I was ready and my gun loaded; I peeked through the cracks between the edge of the door and the casing on the logs; I looked at him closely. He was a handsome fellow and looked to be about twenty-two. He was not coming rapidly but steadily. I knew I could kill him as soon as he got close enough. I looked at him again. He had ruddy cheeks and dark brown hair, and was a soldier of whom either side would have been proud. I said to myself, "I cannot kill that boy!" I thought of his mother at once; a strange thing that she came into my mind, but that is just as it happened.

When he got within fifteen feet of the door, he sang out a violent oath and told us to come out. I am sure I surprised him more than he ever before was surprised in his life, for with my gun pointed at his breast I was within five feet of him in a moment and shouted, "Throw up your arms!" They went up, and his gun went down.

He said, "What do you mean? You are surrounded and cannot get away."

I answered, "I want to be treated as a soldier and not murdered, as your men have murdered all around us in the last few moments. Promise me that and I will surrender."

He said, "I will protect you," and I said, "Here's my gun." Livingstone then came out and we were both prisoners.

We walked back along the ridge on the same road we had pursued in getting away from it, but we did not see Pascoe where we had passed him earlier, and I suppose he had already been carried away as a prisoner in an ambulance. We climbed the hill and went over the very spot where our regiment had fallen. I saw Randolph Saxons lying there dead, and directly Livingstone called me and said, "Here is Ulmer." The dead lay just on the hilltop, and Ulmer's body was farther to the front than any other we saw.

Livingstone asked the Union soldier, our guard, if we could turn Ulmer over, as he was lying on his face with his face to the front where the battle had raged. The guard gave permission. There was no flag by Ulmer's side. Someone had saved it, but in his valor Ulmer had added glory and prestige to the courage of an American soldier.

I heard someone say, "Orderly Sergeant, come here!" I turned and looked up, and there was General Hazen of the Union army. He had called me. He was a very handsome man, and with his staff rode splendid horses. He said to me, "Where are all your people?" I said, "General," pointing in the direction of their retreat, "if you will go over in that timber you will find them." He laughed, and I followed the guard down the hill.*

---

* Hemming, 18, was sent to prison at Rock Island, Ill. Dressed in a makeshift Federal uniform, he escaped on September 28, 1864. He reached Canada and spent the next three months in disguise visiting Federal fortifications between Niagara Falls and Chicago, obtaining maps and charts for the Confederate consul in Canada. While doing so, Hemming was captured on three occasions but escaped each time. In January 1865 he was sent from Canada with dispatches to the Confederate War Department in Richmond — the successful journey being made via Nova Scotia, the West Indies, Cuba and Florida. After delivering the documents he rejoined his regiment in North Carolina just prior to the end of the war.

## 'Cut your traces and save the horses'

### Capt. Thomas L. Massenburg
### Battery commander
### Jackson (Georgia) Artillery

I was placed on the right of General Bragg's headquarters, and was supported by a part of Stewart's Division, and, as the enemy came out, we played on them until they got to our line of breastworks below, which had been previously abandoned. We then pulled our guns back, as we could not depress our fire any lower, and the infantry moved forward and received them as they came up the hill, charged and drove them back; they (the infantry) then fell back to their original position and I rolled our guns up again and engaged the second line, which was received by the infantry, when I could no longer fire.

Presently I saw our line broken and a Yankee flag floating over one of our batteries about a quarter mile on my right. Our infantry there was trying to rally a short distance back, and I was ordered up to their assistance. I immediately limbered up and galloped towards them, but before I could reach them they broke again and ran down the hill as fast as they could go. By this time the whole line on the left and centre was broken, and I had only to follow the infantry down the hill, which I did with all speed, being hurried considerably by the Yankee bullets which were flying thick and fast around us, but I reached the foot of the hill all safe and doubled my teams to get up the second hill.

The horses were so much worn down that it was impossible to get any of them to move the guns, so I reluctantly gave the order to take out the horses. It was here that Lieut. Foster fell [2nd Lieut. George B. Forster]; he was on foot trying to save the horses of his section when a shot struck him in the head and another in the breast. As he fell, he exclaimed: "Boys, I am killed, cut your traces and save the horses."

It is truly miraculous that no others were killed, for the fire above us was very hot and there were but few men in the gorge there besides ourselves. Several horses were shot while the drivers were getting them unhitched — altogether I lost thirteen. Three of the men were struck but not hurt sufficiently to disable them.

## 'A splendid sight that sent the blood tingling'

### 1st Lieut. John K. Shellenberger
### Company F
### 64th Ohio Volunteer Infantry

Until three o'clock of the 25th, we were listening with ears intent to the sound of the battle which General Sherman was waging on our left at the northern extremity of Missionary Ridge, and we could plainly see the columns of the enemy moving in that direction. During the night of the 24th General Bragg had called in all his forces from Lookout Mountain and from Chattanooga Valley, and it was the troops let loose by this shortening of his left that he was concentrating in front of Sherman. They all came

■ Brig. Gen. William B. Bate commanded two brigades of Breckinridge's division on November 25. When the assault began Bate's troops held the crest between the divisions of A.P. Stewart, and Patton Anderson, whose regiments were the first to break. Bate's extreme right fell back in confusion as the Federals scrambled over the top. While attempting to rally the defenders, Col. R.C. Tyler (commanding Bate's old brigade) was severely wounded, as was his successor, Col. A.F. Rudler of the 37th Georgia. Bate's assistant adjutant general was captured along with 590 others from the division.

"There was much difficulty in stopping the *debris* which had sloughed off from the first line," Bate wrote, "but through the personal exertions of General Bragg and staff and many subaltern officers, we formed a line about 1,000 yards from the one just abandoned ..." That night his division retired in good order via Chickamauga Station.

# 'We spiked the guns and hurled them down'

**As the fury of combat swept along the front of the Georgia and Florida brigades under Gen. William B. Bate, Confederate gunners of Capt. Cuthbert H. Slocomb's Louisiana Battery faced a desperate situation. These cannoneers belonging to the 5th Company, Washington Artillery of New Orleans, were near the center of the breakthrough on Missionary Ridge. One of Slocomb's subordinate officers, 1st Lieut. J.A. Chalaron, described his men's heroic but fruitless efforts to stem the Federal onslaught:**

The Federals never got up in front of our battery. Extending for 250 yards, it was kept clear by a rapid and well-sustained fire, from which the attacking lines diverged to the right and left, seeking shelter in the depressions between the abutments of the ridge, avoiding our direct fire.

My position was overlooking a gap in the ridge, facing Chattanooga, where at first I had two guns which I soon took outside, to the front of the [earth] work, that sufficient depression might be obtained to sweep the declivity in my front and to my right. The elevation to my right across the gap was occupied by two guns of Dent's Battery, and this point was the first one on the ridge to be carried by the Federal troops. I had turned my two Napoleons on this point as soon as I noticed its capture, and had fired two shots at the foe on and around the guns, when the limbers of these two Napoleons were exploded by a shell from a gun on Orchard Knob. I have read that Gen. Granger had sighted that shot. If he did so, it was a most opportune hit, for the next discharge of my guns would have played havoc with the small force of Federals that was forming to advance upon me from the point they had captured.

■ 1st Lieut. Joseph A. Chalaron

■ Private C.J. Barrow, 5th Company

Gen. Bragg sent Reynolds' brigade forward to retake the position. As this brigade reached my guns, coming from my left and rear, I started with a mounted Sergeant and a Corporal afoot, of my company and bearing its flag, to lead the column in a charge across the gap. The troops did not respond.

Failing to clear the only way by which my caissons could send me their limbers, I returned to my guns. The rifled gun that had been out of ammunition about the moment of the explosion of the Napoleons' limbers was ordered off to the hollow in the rear, and Capt. Slocomb and several of the men then ran to the left half-battery some 100 yards off, and returned bearing arms-full of ammunition. This we could not use, for we found ourselves without friction primers.

The close advance of the Federal sharpshooters, creeping up under cover of rocks and trees, and the movement of others to our rear from the gap, admonished us to save our men and what horses we had left. Under a pelting fire we spiked the guns and hurled them down the declivity towards the ascending enemy. My men were then told to save themselves.

■ Capt. Cuthbert H. Slocomb commanded an artillery battalion of three batteries (including his own) in Breckinridge's corps. As a first lieutenant Slocomb was shot in the chest at Shiloh. He recovered and on June 6, 1862, was promoted and given command of the 5th Company, Washington Artillery of New Orleans. Four other Washington Artillery companies served in the eastern theater.

At Missionary Ridge, all six of the 5th Company's guns were lost after the battery was abandoned by its infantry supports and most of the horses were killed. Two limbers were destroyed when Federal soldiers, after capturing Capt. Stouten H. Dent's Alabama battery, turned the guns on defenders of Bate's division.

This portrait and those on the facing page were taken just after the war at the gallery of Anderson & Turner, New Orleans.

■ Col. Charles G. Harker commanded the 3rd Brigade of Sheridan's division. "The difficulty and danger which the officers and men passed through from the foot of the hill to the summit baffles description," he reported. "Though officers and men were constantly falling, the command moved steadily forward, taking advantage of every depression in the ground — or tree, or stump — to rest for an instant, reload, and then move forward; thus, foot by foot and pace by pace, the crest was being reached to the admiration of all who witnessed it, and to the surprise even of those who participated in the perilous undertaking ... The crest thus gained, the most unbounded enthusiasm I had ever witnessed then prevailed throughout the entire command."

Harker was promoted to brigadier general four and a half months later. He was killed June 27, 1864 at Kennesaw Mountain.

from the direction of Rossville, marching in plain sight along the crest of the Ridge and across our front. I gave close attention to these movements, having nothing else to do, and I sat on our breastworks watching them with a good field-glass. I could see the marching troops so plainly that I could easily count the files, and I am confident not a man nor a gun was taken from the line that confronted us.

It was shortly after three o'clock when we began to move out from our breastworks to form for the assault. That part of the line where the Sixty-fourth had been posted faced diagonally up the valley in the direction of Rossville. In taking position, we advanced several hundred yards, making a left half wheel as we went forward, until we squarely confronted Missionary Ridge. This movement was executed by the regiments moving out successively from left to right. When a regiment arrived at its designated position and was properly aligned, it would lie down, leaving its general guides standing, by which the guides of the next regiment to come up could align themselves.

All the time the enemy was keeping up a slow fire with some of the guns posted along the crest of Missionary Ridge. Their range was poor and their shells did no execution that I saw; nevertheless, there was the harassing uncertainty as to where the next shell might explode, and our position while lying under this fire was an extremely uncomfortable one.

While waiting, Colonel [Alexander] McIlvain, commanding the Sixty-fourth, passed along the line and instructed his company commanders that in the coming advance the guide would be left, and that we must conform our movements to those of the line to the left of us. Nothing was said as to what it was expected we were to accomplish. The Sixty-fourth was in the front line on the left of Harker's brigade. The Third Kentucky occupied the position between the left of the Sixty-fourth Ohio and the right of Wagner's brigade, on our left. Colonel [Francis T.] Sherman's brigade was posted on the right of Harker's. A line drawn perpendicularly to the front of the Sixty-fourth would cross Missionary Ridge a short distance north of the house on the crest known as General Bragg's headquarters.

When all was ready, a battery stationed at Orchard Knob fired its six guns in rapid succession as a signal for the charge. Before the signal was fired, the quiet of expectancy had prevailed along our line, but, when it sounded, a scene of intense animation at once ensued. Far and near could be heard the bugle notes and the voices of the officers calling the men to attention, and as they sprang to their feet there was a great rustling of dead leaves and a snapping of dried twigs. I cast a hurried look to the right and the left, and on either hand as far as I could see stood two lines of blue coats with beautiful flags waving and bright arms gleaming in the pleasant afternoon sunshine. It was a splendid sight that sent the blood tingling to the finger tips. The moral effect which it produced upon the enemy must have contributed greatly to our success. We were standing in a stretch of open timber, but the leaves were all off the trees and we were in plain sight. As we advanced, every Confederate soldier along the crest of the Ridge in our front could take in our entire array with one sweeping glance; but while looking to the right or left along their own line, on account of the inequalities of the Ridge and other obstructions, he could see but a small number of his own comrades. He would naturally get the impression that they were being attacked by overwhelming numbers. Some of the prisoners afterward said it looked like all creation was charging on a few hundred of them.

The ground descended slightly in our front for a short distance to a small stream. We marched down this declivity at quick time, and on crossing the stream we emerged upon an open plain that stretched away without obstruction to the breastworks at the base of the Ridge nearly half a mile away. We could then see the yellowish streak of dirt that marked the line of these breastworks. It was back a short distance up the slope where the ground began to ascend at the base of the Ridge. Back of the breastworks the ground was clear for two or three hundred yards, and from thence, where the rugged ascent began, the face of the Ridge to the top was covered with a moderately heavy growth of timber.

On emerging upon the plain, all the artillery posted along the crest of the Ridge opened a rapid fire, and we then increased our pace to a double-quick. There were two guns which directed their fire at the Sixty-fourth, using spherical case. They got the range a little too high to begin with, and, as we approached nearer and they kept depressing their guns, they still maintained about the same relative elevation. I could hear the shells exploding, and on looking up could see, a little in front of us and twenty or thirty feet in the air, the round balls of smoke that marked the spots where the explosions had occurred. The missiles with which the shells were filled all passed harmlessly over our heads.

As we approached nearer the breastworks our pace increased with the increasing tension on our nerves until the whole line was sweeping forward on a run. I was commanding Company F, and was running a little in advance of my company with my eyes intently fixed upon the breastworks. We had approached near enough to see that there were no head-logs, and I was wondering why I could see no heads showing above the works, when I remembered what I had read of the orders given by General Putnam to his men at Bunker Hill, and almost with a groan I mentally exclaimed: "They are waiting till they can see the whites of our eyes." It was a tremendous relief to discover that the breastworks were not occupied. There had been a skirmish line behind them when we started, but the skirmishers had promptly run away when they first saw us coming, except those who lay still and surrendered when we came up.

When it was manifest that the breastworks would not be defended, I raised my eyes toward the crest of the Ridge and then saw the skirmishers falling back through the timber near the top. In our charge across the plain I did not see a single musket shot fired from the breastworks at the foot of the Ridge, nor did I see a single man hit by the fire coming from the artillery posted along the crest above. General Bragg certainly made a great mistake when he withdrew from the lower line. If the plunging fire which we encountered in going up the steep ascent, and which mostly overshot us, had been delivered from the breastworks below while we were crossing that level, open plain, it must inevitably have cut us to pieces.

All the dirt used in building the breastworks had been thrown from a ditch on the inside, in which the defenders would stand, and therefore the parapet on the outside was so low that we could run up over it without difficulty. As I leaped down into the ditch I

■ Col. Henry C. Dunlap, 3rd Kentucky, led his 271 officers and men up the ridge in the first line of Harker's brigade. "My loss [58 killed and wounded] was proportionately small compared to other battles," Dunlap wrote 48 hours later, "but it is not always those who lose the most men who do the most efficient fighting."

Along with Major John Brennan and Adjutant Gavine D. Hunt, Dunlap chose to ride into the assault on horseback. Brennan's mount was shot beneath him. Hunt, grasping the regimental colors, rode to within 50 feet of the summit when he toppled from the saddle, mortally wounded. Wrote Dunlap: "The color sergeant, who carried the national flag, fell exhausted upon the hill-side. Corporal Hayes, of the color guard, had not borne it but a few steps when he fell badly wounded. Being at his side, I took the flag and carried it to the crest of the hill, but had the staff shot in twain below the flag."

■ Capt. Henry H. Kling, commander of Company D, 64th Ohio, was killed instantly just before his men reached the crest of Missionary Ridge. The day after the battle the 64th's adjutant, 1st Lieut. Chauncey Woodruff, rode over the battlefield and noted: "Near the foot of the ridge I saw the remains of one from an Ohio regiment that showed how destructive had been the rebel shot. Evidently the soldier was lying down, his head toward the enemy, and his body on a line with the passage of the missile, for it struck him on the head and passed the whole length of the body and limbs. From appearances there were but few whole bones left. I think a bushel basket would have held all that remained."

paused there just long enough to take a look to the left. The line in that direction, having a little shorter distance to traverse, had already passed beyond the breastworks and was sweeping onward without halting. I then jumped out of the ditch, and calling "Forward!" to my company, pushed on up the hill.

When we arrived at these breastworks we had not come in contact with a battle line of the enemy, nor had we fired a single shot. The men, having listened for nearly two days to the sounds of the fighting which had been going on to the right and the left of them, naturally supposed that they had now been sent forward to take a hand, and not meeting with the expected opposition at the breastworks, they went on of their own accord, and without orders, to engage the line so plainly visible on the crest above.

After we crossed the breastworks, the cannoneers began to serve out canister to us, and the infantry line also opened fire. The bloody work now began in earnest; for the gunners had at last got down to a deadly range and the men went down before the canister fire like ten pins. We were so thoroughly "winded" by our rapid charge across the plain that our progress was now very slow, and most of the men were staggering on their feet in their efforts to get forward. The cannon above us would fire to the right and then to the left, so as to cover more ground. Three times, in crossing the space between the breastworks and the timber line, I seemed to be looking directly into the muzzle of one of these guns as it was discharged; and three times, as I saw the gunner pull the lanyard, I stopped still and, with chin dropped on my breast, eyes closed and teeth clenched, braced myself for the shock of an expected wound. I could feel the canister swish through the air close by me, but I remained unharmed.

On reaching the timber line, we threw ourselves flat against the face of the Ridge, panting for breath. Those of our men who had strength enough left to pull a trigger now opened fire on the enemy. On looking around I could see, by the way the bullets were striking the ground behind us and barking the trees above us, that while lying close the enemy could not reach us with their fire; and on rising up high enough to peep over the top of the stump behind which I had taken shelter, I could dimly see through the battle smoke some of the Confederates rising above their low breastworks and trying to search us out. These men made good targets, with their heads and shoulders outlined against the sky, for our men hugging close to the face of the Ridge. From the number of dead and badly wounded Confederates that I saw lying around inside their breastworks after we had taken them, I was convinced that we had inflicted more casualties upon them, while climbing the hill from the timber line up, than we had ourselves sustained. But this rule would not apply, by any means, to all parts of our line. Where the Sixty-fourth went up, we were under a direct fire only, while some of Wagner's regiments, a short distance to our left, were subjected to a raking flank fire, and the slaughter among them was terrible.

While lying there recovering our wind, Colonel McIlvain came walking along our line from the right, and as he came I saw the men rising up and running back in a straggling manner to the rear. When he reached me, he said: "Lieutenant, you must take your company and go back to the breastworks."

The order was so manifestly a blunder, and my social relations with the colonel were of such a character, that I ventured to violate the military proprieties by remonstrating against it. I pointed out how the enemy were overshooting us, and declared my decided conviction that we could inflict far more damage upon them, and with much greater security to ourselves, by remaining where we were; to which he replied, somewhat impatiently: "I know all that very well, but the orders are to go back to the breastworks, and we must obey orders."

When I got back to the breastworks I found them packed on the outside with our second line, which had stopped there, and with the men of the first line who had run back — all of them hugging the ground as closely as possible. When the front line fell back, all aggressive action on the part of Sheridan's division came to a standstill.

But it was soon evident that it would be intolerable to lie there doing nothing under the plunging fire of the enemy, and as Wood's division on our left could be plainly seen slowly but steadily pushing its way up the hill, Sheridan quickly decided to follow Wood's lead; for he came riding along the line, calling out: "As soon as you get your wind, men, we will go straight to the top of that hill."

The mistake was in ordering back the first line from the advantageous position which it had secured. It was a much safer place at the timber line to regain our wind than it was at the breastworks, to say nothing of the many brave men who were unnecessarily sacrificed in falling back and in advancing a second time over that dangerous belt of ground between the breastworks and the timber line, which was so thoroughly combed by that terrible canister fire, and where we met with our heaviest losses.

In going forward the second time, the two lines were intermingled without regard to regimental or company organization, the color bearers striving with each other as to which should take the lead. Where the Sixty-fourth went up, we were opposed by a Florida regiment, which broke away from the breastworks without waiting to come to a hand-to-hand encounter, while our advance was yet a few yards away. The breastworks were so low that it was easy to get over them; for if they had been built as high as usual they would have been a hindrance to the enemy in firing down the steep hillside. We captured two brass guns that had been firing at us ever since the charge began, and some of the gunners with them. One Irishman, who was handling a rammer, was at first inclined to fight at close quarters with it as a weapon, but when he saw it was no use he threw down the rammer and surrendered, bursting into tears as he did so, and bitterly exclaiming: "This battery was niver caphthured before."

The men went wild with joy over their splendid success. They shook hands and hugged each other, tossed their hats in the air, danced, sang, cheered, and some of them whooped and yelled like a lot of drunken demons. When the first ecstacy had somewhat subsided, on looking around we could see the enemy rapidly retreating through the woods to the east of the Ridge in great disorder; and especially a road which crossed the valley below, presented a scene of wildest confusion. It was filled with wagons, caissons, cannon and fugitives, mounted and on foot, all hurrying frantically to get away. As soon as the regiments could be re-

■ Private Joseph McGregor of Company A, 64th Ohio, assaulted the ridge in the front line of Col. Emerson Opdycke's demi-brigade. Catching their breath before ascending the 45-degree slope, these troops, Opdycke wrote, were "left to contemplate the unparalleled grandeur and sublimity of the scene. The second and third lines came up to the pits and took shelter in them. 'Forward' soon passed along the lines; then the whole moved up slowly in the face of an indescribable fire of all arms. My command captured Bragg's headquarters house and the six guns which were near there. One of these I ordered turned upon the enemy, which was done with effect."

In this portrait taken earlier in the war, McGregor holds a M1855 Springfield rifle with Maynard tape primer.

■ Private James C. Swassick of Company G, 65th Ohio. Temporarily commanded by Lt. Col. William A. Bullitt (3rd Kentucky), the 65th stormed the ridge as part of Harker's brigade. "The position in which my regiment found itself," Bullitt wrote, "was immediately in front of a battery, which belched forth a stream of canister upon us with terrible rapidity. In addition to this the enemy, when driven from other points, rallied around this battery and defended it with desperation. It cost a struggle to take it but we finally succeeded, and the colors of the Sixty-fifth Ohio were the first planted upon the yet smoking guns."

formed, Wagner's and Harker's brigades pushed rapidly forward in pursuit, but night had fallen before our advance could come up with them. The Sixty-fourth was now in the second line and did not become engaged. I saw only the flashes of the musketry as they lit up the darkness, and heard the sounds of the firing and the cries of the combatants.

## 'A dozen flags went over the works'

### Journal of Private Benjamin T. Smith Company C 51st Illinois Volunteer Infantry Orderly on Sheridan's staff

**Nov. 25th** I am on duty with the General. The day is bright and clear. Several Corps and Division commanders ride out together to an elevation [Orchard Knob] which gives a good view of Mission Ridge for miles up and down our front. The line of breastworks with their head logs strung along its top, and bristling with numerous black mouthed cannon, the steep sides of the ridge, with another line of works strung along its base, would seem to make the rebel defenses all but impregnable to a direct attack. Yet this is what is contemplated.

Genl. Sherman with the 15th & 17th Corps on our left has already begun an attack, and is pounding away on our extreme left. In front of the center where we are there is an open field some half to three quarters of a mile leading up to the ridge, bordered just in our front by a belt of timber, in front of which, in plain view of the enemy our troops are marching to the left, seeming with a view to reinforce Sherman. But this maneuver is only to deceive the enemy, for after marching some distance the troops go into the timber and countermarch back to their old position. We can see the rebels are moving some of their forces to their right, as they march along within their works.

When all is ready the order is given to advance, moving out in regimental or demi brigade front with intervals, and lapping each other. When our lines are well on their way the enemy open up their artillery all along their line, and the shot and shell is rained down upon the field. As our division is crossing through this hail of shot and shell I ride out with the General who has only one staff officer, Capt. [J.S.] Ransom, and two or three orderlies. I can see up and down the field as far as it extends, and owing to the formation of the troops it seems literally covered with them. The army appears much greater than it is. It's a most beautiful sight, but one can not contemplate it long.

As the troops finding the rebel shot are falling among them they break into a double quick to sooner gain the base of the ridge, as the enemy can not depress their guns enough for a direct fire. In crossing the field many of the rebel shots made gaps in some of the regiments. The lower line of works is captured with a rush, and all who occupy them are captured. If they tried to climb the ridge they were sure of being shot so they stayed in their trenches and surrendered.

Genl. Sheridan's horse was wounded in his forefoot and he told me to bring up his big black horse. I made a dash across the field and returned with his horse, which I rode as mine was nearly blowed. I exchanged again, and he sent one of the other orderlies back with the wounded animal.

The troops having rested, started to climb the steep sides of the ridge. An aide having been sent to Genl. Granger for further orders, came back with a suggestion that the troops be recalled if it was judged expedient. By this time they were half way up the ridge. Every regiment had lost its organization, and were all massed in a sort of triangle with the point upwards. About every flag of our division was struggling to reach the top first, every man for himself. Now and then a flag would fall, its bearer being shot, but it appeared in an instant held by the next soldier. The General said, "Let them go, they will be over in five minutes," and so it proved. A dozen flags went over the works, the men following. Nothing could stop their rush. The rebels deserted their guns and fled, hundreds of them staying a moment too long were captured.

An old log hut standing just to the left to where our division went over was occupied by Genl. Bragg and his staff. They had barely time to mount and ride away. Some of the rebel guns were turned upon their retreating ranks and shots sent after them. More than fifty guns were captured.

When we reached the top of the ridge my horse was about ready to drop from the unusual hard work he had done. So I took the harness off of a big white horse that had belonged to one of the rebel batteries, and put my saddle on him, turning mine loose to shift for himself. And that was the last I ever saw of my good old friend. But this animal is the tallest piece of horseflesh in four counties. I must look like a fly on a ridge pole, and feel as though I am astride of a small mountain.

Our troops are in full cry after the retreating enemy and it is growing dark. Lieut. Wyman is killed. He was a Sergt. in the old Powell's Scouts, but had recently received a commission. He lay half way up the ridge with his sword still grasped in his dead hand.

The wounded are being conveyed to Chattanooga. I ride back to headquarters on my big white horse. He gets over the ground in great shape with his long legs, but he won't do for my service. I took him to the Quartermaster who was glad to get the animal for artillery service, and he gave me one in exchange, one more suited for my work.

■ Corporal Thomas H. Maxwell of Company C, 42nd Illinois, was killed during the rush to capture Confederate rifle pits at the base of Missionary Ridge. The 42nd's commander, Col. Nathan H. Walworth, led a demi-brigade of four Illinois regiments and used his own as skirmishers. "They sent back about 100 prisoners," Walworth reported, but "lost heavily, particularly in officers." Maxwell and four other soldiers from the 42nd were killed while eight officers and 39 enlisted men were wounded.

## 'Fix bayonets and go ahead'

### Diary of
### Capt. Tilmon D. Kyger
### Company C
### 73rd Illinois Volunteer Infantry

**Wednesday, November 25, 1863. 3 o'clock p.m.** Orders came for a forward move at the firing of six shots from cannon on Orchard Knob, which was the signal for the whole line to move forward. We moved promptly on double-quick time. Our division had to charge across a sparsely wooded vale, then into an open lawn-covered space for nearly one mile and a fourth, until we came to

■ Missionary Ridge, as photographed by George N. Barnard in 1864 from Orchard Knob, looking southeast. Near this point, Private Edward Popplestone of Company D, 15th Indiana, reached the crest. He later recalled: "About 50 yards in front of the rebel breastworks the third man carrying our flag got knocked over. Serg'-Maj. [W.E.] Doyle said to me: 'Popplestone, go back and get those colors.' I told him if he wanted them worse than I did he could go back and get them, for I had passed through the hail of shot and shell, and felt safe in front of the enemy's lines."

the first rifle-pits at the foot of the ridge. This was done under a desperate fire from both artillery and infantry. Some fell on the lawn. Most of the shots were too high; shells burst directly over us.

General Sheridan rode up behind the 73d and remarked: "I know you; fix bayonets and go ahead." We were in the front line. We halted at the rifle-pits for a short time to rest and give the short-winded soldiers time to get up. Then we moved to the second line of works; rested again, after driving the rebels and taking many prisoners. Moved again, and under a terrific fire, reached the third line. Many fell. Started again; had to move up a hill at an inclination of about thirty degrees, exposed to bursting shell and a shower of grape, canister and minie-balls. The only shelter that we had was now and then a tree, a log or a stump. The flags moved up gradually; the color-bearers would stop and await the coming up of the men, who were pouring on the enemy a terrible fire; the enemy, having all reached the top of the ridge, except those who had been either killed, wounded or captured.

It was at this point that Stephen Newlin and Nathaniel Henderson were wounded. I left Sergeant Sheets to care for them, when we moved on again. This was our hardest time; we had to pass a more exposed point. From tree to tree, from stump to stump, and from log to log, we went until we came to a point where the slope was greater, the ascent steeper, perhaps about forty degrees elevation. Here we remained about twenty minutes, to get in readiness to make the final charge. General Sheridan came riding up, when we started and moved steadily on until we reached the top of the ridge. Just before we got there the rebels threw hand grenades and rocks at us. No matter for that, our flags and banners must be planted on top of the ridge. Hasty fell. I took the flag and moved forward, but soon became exhausted and fell. Hasty caught up and we went on together, and planted the colors on top the ridge at five o'clock p.m., about three paces in rear of the 88th Illinois.

Now came a time of rejoicing as those coming up the ridge would reach its crest. Yell after yell went up the whole length of the ridge. But with us this did not last long. We charged down the eastern slope, taking many prisoners and some artillery in the valley. Our losses were not heavy when compared to the work accomplished. The 73d lost three killed and twenty-two wounded. This was a great victory, something that, to look the ground over, would seem impossible to accomplish — charging a distance of two miles, about half the way at an average angle of thirty-five degrees.

## 'The boys were the generals'

### 1st Lieut. John M. Turnbull
### Company C
### 36th Illinois Volunteer Infantry
### Staff officer
### 1st Brigade, 2nd Division, IV Corps

I shall never forget the change of countenance exhibited by the men as they received the order [to charge Missionary Ridge] and nerved themselves for the conflict. The officers of the field and line, and the boys, were the generals ordering the advance; in other words, I think it was a necessity understood alike by officers and men, and acted on at once. This movement along the line was almost simultaneous, and it was done without any particular order as to lines or military movement. The crest of the ridge was now the objective point, and they started for it.

I had come forward with the skirmish line instead of returning and taking my place with the brigade staff. I now joined Col. [Francis T.] Sherman, ready for further duty, and after accompanying him part way up the ridge, was ordered back by him to the first line of works to urge forward any troops that might be there, to assist in the grand struggle at the top of the ridge. I did so, and on reaching the rifle pit, found it full of troops protecting themselves from the fire as best they could.

Just at this time two staff officers rode up and inquired for Col. Sherman. I pointed to where he was and told them he was leading his command up the ridge. One of them then told me that he belonged to Gen. Granger's staff; that he was sent to say the movement beyond the front line of works was contrary to orders, and asked me to communicate this to Col. Sherman. I declined to receive a verbal order from him, saying that he must communicate with the Brigade Commander himself, as I was now under orders from *my* commander that looked as though we intended to see the top of the ridge.

I then began in good earnest the task of urging forward laggards. On looking up the ridge I became alarmed. The column had

■ Col. James F. Jaquess commanded the 73rd Illinois which assaulted Missionary Ridge in the front line of Sheridan's division. Jaquess later wrote: "As we were in line, November 25, 1863, and about to move on the enemy's works ... I rode along the line and said jestingly to the men who were eager for the fray: 'Besides whipping the rebels thoroughly and paying them up fully for what they did at Chickamauga, I want you to capture, besides many prisoners, one horse — a good one — for me. The rebs got both of my fine horses at Chickamauga, as you know, and I want one now in return, and another later on.'

"As we passed over the last line of works where we captured many prisoners, one of my men [Private William Corzine of Company I] rushed out into the bushes in front and in a moment or two returned with a fine gray horse, and said: 'Here, Colonel, I have brought you your horse.' "

■ 1st Lieut. Arthur MacArthur Jr., 18-year-old adjutant of the 24th Wisconsin and future father of Gen. Douglas MacArthur, grabbed his regiment's national flag on the ridge's slope when the color bearer fell exhausted. Capt. Howard Green of Company B and 1st Lieut. Robert J. Chivas of Company I lay dead, with both officers of Company A wounded. Shouting "On, Wisconsin!" to his momentarily stunned comrades, the beardless youth carried the flag to the crest. "[I] had the honor of planting the colors of the 24th Wisconsin immediately in front of Bragg's old headquarters," he wrote the next day. "I showed the old flag to General Sheridan immediately upon his arrival on top of the ridge ... While I was carrying the flag a whole dose of cannister went through it, tearing it in a frightful manner. I only received one scratch and that through the rim of my hat."

Less than six weeks later MacArthur was promoted to major. He finished the war in command of the regiment, received lieutenant colonel and colonel brevets, and in 1890 was given the Medal of Honor for bravery at Missionary Ridge.

assumed a pyramidal or sugar loaf form. The brigade flags, I believe the colors of every regiment of the brigade, were grouped together and *were in advance* of the lines. I urged the men forward to help plant *their* colors on the ridge, and was meeting with only tolerable success when Gen. Sheridan, who had taken in the situation, dashed forward on his black charger to the foot of the ridge, dismounted, threw his cape to his orderly, and running forward among us, shouted, "Boys, we are going to take the ridge. Forward and help your comrades!" That settled the question, and there was no soldier who was not wounded or in some other way disabled that did not make every effort to be among the *first* to reach the top of the ridge.

The timber on the side of the ridge had been cut down and formed a kind of abattis. Some of the Rebels, on retreating, stopped about two-thirds of the way up and determined to sell their lives as dearly as possible. The 36th's color-guard lay down to rest behind a log, having got too far ahead of the troops. On commencing to rise, the Sergeant in charge saw a man with a musket leveled on them only a short distance away. "Lie down," he whispered sharply to the boys. They did so, and he coolly laid his musket over the log in front of him. "Now," said he, "show him your knapsack." The color-bearer, who had a full one on his back, rose carefully on all fours, exposing only his knapsack. The Sergeant's gun *went off.* "Lie down again," said he. He reloaded. "Do that again," said the Sergeant. The color-bearer did so, and the Sergeant's gun *went off again.* "Now," said he, "we can go."

One of the boys fished out a Mississippi captain among the logs. He had his bayonet fixed, and was calling on the captain to surrender. The captain was jumping first one way and then another, saying, "Call an officer." The soldier responded, "I'm officer enough for you; surrender, or I will put the bayonet through you."

I was passing along and said I would receive his sword. He very quickly gave it to me, remarking that we were certainly very rough to prisoners. I answered that the soldier ought to have put the bayonet through him. "Why sir," he said, "what do you mean? I have had prisoners in my charge and never treated them in this way."

"Then," said I, "take off that overcoat you have stripped from some of our shivering, wounded comrades at Chickamauga." The poor fellow threw it off quickly, saying that we attacked them so suddenly that he forgot to take it off. I made him take the coat with him to the rear, and told him to trade it for a blanket.

## 'The very air smelt of battle'

### Chief Musician William J. Worsham
### 19th Tennessee Volunteer Infantry

At the hour of one at night, the whole of Bragg's army could have been seen moving for the crest of Mission Ridge to form line of battle. Our brigade [Strahl's] left its ditches in the valley and formed line along the top of the ridge about one hundred yards from Gen. Bragg's headquarters. In forming our line we put one line as skirmishers at the foot of the ridge and had only a single line on top. The two lines were so deployed that neither formed a good skirmish line. To our right and in front of Bragg's headquarters was a knoll, which the Federals had covered with cannon, and from these batteries they shelled our brigade and regiment. Stanford's [Mississippi] battery was placed with our regiment.

While we lay in line of battle watching the busy maneuvering of the enemy's troops, one of the Old Nineteenth sat alone, seemingly holding communion with his own heart, utterly oblivious of what was going on, unconscious of the excitement that was moving and agitating Bragg's whole army. This was Lieut. Col. B.F. Moore, and such a state of mind and feeling was never observed before, at any time, much less at such a time as this. I believe that if Col. Moore had thought there was one drop of cowardice blood coursing his veins, he would have severed every artery to have let it out. If there be such a thing as premonition of coming danger, the soul of Col. Moore must have been heavily pressed by such an unseen power. About noon Col Moore's father came up to our regiment, and the Colonel gave him everything he had about his person, his knife, comb, money, watch, everything.

The battle had not yet opened, but the enemy's thousands were moving before and approaching the skirmish line of the Confederates. The very air smelt of battle, and the winds as they came sweeping the crest of Mission Ridge made sad music as if the precursor of the coming storm. Bragg had the heaviest part of his line on the right, while his left was strung out until it presented only a single and deployed line. About two o'clock in the afternoon the sound of musketry and cannon were heard on our extreme right, and grandly came on down the ridge to us and rolled across the valley like a wave at high tide. The enemy made a vigorous assault on our right but our men held their places not only against one but repeated attacks.

About three o'clock in the afternoon Thomas advanced on our left with, it seemed to us, ten thousand, where with our brigade we had only a skirmish line. We counted right in our front four double columns of the enemy, all moving directly against our brigade of a single line. These columns seemed to us to be not more than seventy-five or a hundred yards apart. In front of our regiment at the foot of the ridge was a small field not more than fifty yards wide. Across this these four columns had to pass. On the Federals came with that determined step that defied all opposition. Our men from the top of the ridge and from the foot who were behind works, while the enemy were crossing this field, poured so heavy a fire into them of both musketry and cannon, that after they had crossed there were left on the field men dead and wounded seemingly as thick as stumps in new ground. Several of our men who were at the foot of the hill never reached the top; whether they were killed or captured we never knew. Those who did reach the top came through a shower of bullets that plowed the ground and skinned the trees all around them.

The air between the ridge and Orchard Knob was filled with shot and shell. The ridge where we were was quite steep but the enemy came on, crawling up the steep ascent like bugs, and were so thick they were almost in each other's way. Our men fell back to a spur of the ridge, leaving the top under a most galling fire, going down the [east] slope and across an open field to our new position on this spur. As we descended the ridge, Tom Kennedy, an Irishman of Company C, did not stop to load his gun, but

■ Col. Francis M. Walker, 19th Tennessee, fought within sight of his home on November 25. A native Kentuckian and Mexican War veteran, he practiced law in Chattanooga for seven years prior to the war and raised an infantry company in 1861. In the weeks preceding the battle, Walker's regiment was swept by illness — claiming the lives of 10 privates, half of them from Company F. A member of the 19th recalled: "We had issued to us [in late October] what the boys called 'sick flour,' from which we made biscuits. Having no lard or grease of any kind, we worked up our bread with salt and water. These biscuits made a lot of sick boys. They were so hard, I saw several of the boys gouge holes in the biscuits, fill them with powder and blow them open, as they said, so they could eat them."

The following July, Walker was killed leading a brigade in the battle of Atlanta.

■ Maj. Gen. Alexander P. Stewart commanded a division of four brigades in Breckinridge's corps, consisting of Gibson's Louisianans, Strahl's Tennesseans, Stovall's Georgians and Holtzclaw's Alabamans. On November 25 Stewart's infantry was thinly deployed from Bragg's headquarters south to Rossville, where they were assailed by Hooker's command. Federal Brig. Gen. Charles Cruft reported: "So sudden and well conceived was [our] flank movement that it seemed to have taken the enemy wholly by surprise. Prisoners captured stated that the force of the enemy encountered upon the ridge was the division of General Stewart. Very many of the enemy were killed outright in this attack, and some 40 badly wounded were afterward cared for by our surgeons in the field. Two hundred and fifty-seven prisoners were captured and held during the assault. The whole ridge was swept of the enemy, who, in their retreat, ran down the east slope of it, and many fell into the hands of General Osterhaus' command. [My] men encamped along the ridge near the headquarters which the rebel general, Stewart, had occupied in the morning."

would turn around every now and then, take off his hat and shake it at the enemy while the minie balls were hissing all around him. Kennedy finally fell in line of battle the 22nd of July 1864 around Atlanta.

Gen. Strahl formed his men on the spur of the ridge opposite the one we had left, where we checked the enemy and held them for a while. They charged us from the front, at the same time sending a column to our left and rear. In this charge our lieutenant colonel, B.F. Moore, was killed and his brother was captured. Whether he was wounded or not we do not know; however, he remained with the Colonel, who fell on his father's place almost in sight and hearing of his home.

## 'Here's the way to gain your independence'

### Lt. Col. Luke W. Finlay
### 4th Tennessee Volunteer Infantry

About the hour of 4 p.m. the advance began; and as [the Federals] approached, under the inspiration of the siege pieces in their rear and the many field pieces, the fifty pieces on our side opened and joined in the continuous roar of the deadly conflict from the summit above.

At this place the Fourth with the Fifth was posted in the rifle-pits as a reserve skirmish force, about one hundred and fifty yards in rear of the Thirty-first and Thirty-third [Tennessee], who were deployed as skirmishers. The Federals, preceded by a skirmish line, advanced in three separate lines of battle. After driving back the skirmishers and breaking the first line of battle, Col. McNeill [Lt. Col. Henry C. McNeill] with the Thirty-first and Thirty-third retreated. As he passed the rifle-pits he said to me, "Why don't you open fire?" "I will," said I, "as soon as you uncover our front." This done, I said, "Ready! Aim! Fire!" and three hundred guns opened on the Federals again advancing with colors flying, and again they were broken.

In the midst of the firing a heroic Ensign [color bearer], rallying his men, was gallantly moving to the front, when Private W.C. King of the Fourth, noted for the accuracy of his shot, was directed to fire at him. At the crack of his rifle the brave man fell forward on the colors he bore so well. The forces in our front broken, six or seven Ensigns of broken regiments, assisted by their officers, were rallying their men off to our right and front. They covered a small space of ground in fine range. Then the order was clearly given, "Right oblique, fire!" and the guns were turned on them, and they too were dispersed.

At this juncture — not an organized body being in our front, the skirmishers as far as the eye could reach to the right being driven to the ridge, and the Federals being in hot pursuit — an order came to us to retreat to the top of the ridge. Accustomed to the skirmish fire, on their way to the top, from time to time they turned on the foe. Not one was badly hurt in the pits, but nearly one-third were disabled or killed in the ascent. Once on the summit, the boys falling in the attenuated line of battle, resumed the contest and continued until the Federals had gained the left center of our army, to our right, and were moving almost on us on our right flank; and then, Strahl's brigade being alone in the line of battle, and the last in that part of the field — both flanks being exposed — Gen. Strahl, in the presence of our division commander, Gen. A.P. Stewart, ordered a retreat to the opposite ridge. Private [D.J.] Goodloe [of Company B], intent on his work, did not hear the order, and seeing the soldier to his left — the extreme left of the regiment — moving to the rear, called out to him, "Here's the way to gain your independence;" and with the words loaded his piece, aimed and fired. The comrade turned and said the order was given to retreat. Goodloe rammed down another cartridge, emptied his gun once more, and looking to the right and left said, "I'll gain my independence that way too," and hurried from the field.

## 'As fast as their legs could carry them'

### Private William K. Poston Jr.
### Company A
### 4th Tennessee Volunteer Infantry

At the time of the battle of Missionary Ridge we were stationed near the extreme left of Bragg's army, which had been greatly weakened by sending reinforcements to his right to resist the fierce assault of Sherman with massed columns. The battle commenced in the early morning and continued through the whole day.

Our regiment had been marched the entire morning and early afternoon up and down and lengthwise the ridge to create the impression of strength on that part of the line. When the attack began on our front, about 3 to 4 p.m., our regiment was stationed behind a fairly good rifle pit about one-third the way up the ridge from its bottom. Just preceding the Federal charge, signal guns were fired from their position on Orchard Knob to our right, and very soon thereafter I saw three heavy lines of battle extending across our front and continuous to the right as far as I could see, advancing upon our position. These lines looked to me to be about 100 yards apart. It was a glorious sight to behold.

Having done much ditching and fortification-making before at Randolph, Fort Pillow, Island Ten and Columbus, with no previous opportunity of fighting behind them, a feeling of satisfaction glowed within me of how neatly and completely we were going to "do up" those foolhardy fellows. But on they came, apparently unaware of what direful fate awaited them.

There was a line of Confederate skirmishers at the foot of the ridge in our front. When the first Federal line got within 200 yards of the bottom of the ridge our skirmishers there opened fire on them, as also did our artillery on top of Missionary Ridge slightly to the right of our position. The first Federal line halted, wavered and began to break and run. Just then the second line came up and mingled with them, and very quickly the third line also reached and intermingled with them, and the entire mass then moved forward to the foot of the ridge.

We kept up a heavy fire on them and they on us for quite a while — probably half an hour. Our regiment was fairly protected by a good rifle pit. When the firing began Col. Finlay went in the

■ Brig. Gen. Otho F. Strahl commanded a brigade in A.P. Stewart's division. Positioned on Stewart's right flank, Strahl deployed his six Tennessee regiments in three defensive lines between the foot and crest of Missionary Ridge. In Strahl's middle line of rifle pits, 2nd Lieut. N.C. Howard of Company A, 5th Tennessee, watched the Federals advance: "When they got nearly to the foot of the ridge, we were ordered to fire. It was a deadly volley, and it seemed that every shot took effect as about half of the regiment in front of us went down. We continued firing with deadly aim for about twenty minutes, when the flanking enemy began to enfilade us and we had to retreat."

One year later, Strahl was killed at the battle of Franklin.

■ Col. Bernard Laiboldt, 2nd Missouri, commanded a demi-brigade in Sheridan's division and had two left-hand fingers shot away at Missionary Ridge. 2nd Lieut. Lucian F. Hemingway of Company E, 36th Illinois, remembered Laiboldt holding up the bleeding hand as the colonel struggled toward the summit. Hemingway recalled: "[Laiboldt exclaimed,] 'Shust see dat! I gives dree kegs lager peer if dem fingers shust comes back on mein hand again.' On he went, however, his hand dripping blood over his clothes and making him a most unsightly object. On reaching the top he spied a Rebel officer nearby and demanded his sword. The officer haughtily replied, 'Sir, I am a Colonel in the Confederate army and commander of a brigade, and desire to surrender my sword to an officer of equal rank. What rank are you, sir?' Col. L., who was covered with dirt and blood, and looked as rough as a private, replied, 'Ah, you bees a Colonel und commands von prigade, ha! Vel, I does dat peesness meinself sumdimes. You gives dat sword to me shust now, or I puts mein sword through your life so quick as von minnit.' He complied, of course, and was sent a prisoner to the rear."

# 'We lost half of our plucky little band'

**Halfway up Missionary Ridge, Tennesseans of Strahl's brigade pulled back musket hammers and sighted their weapons on Illinois, Missouri and Indiana troops in their front. Col. Jonathan J. Lamb, commanding the consolidated 4th and 5th Tennessee, stood unprotected behind the rifle pits and shouted "Fire!" as the Yankees ascended the slope. "The regiment took steady aim," wrote 2nd Lieut. Edwin H. Rennolds of Company K, "and poured in a volley, of which every ball seemed to find its mark, and tore great gaps in the Federal line."**

**Within 15 minutes the blue mass surged upward, and the Tennesseans were forced to make a choice. Rennolds continued: "Some of the men thought the chances too desperate to undertake to climb the ridge under such a fire as they knew they would receive, and remained in the trench and were captured. Others preferred to take any risk rather than go to a Yankee prison. When they emerged from the rifle pit they drew a concentrated fire from the front and both flanks."**

**2nd Lieut. Nathan C. Howard of Company A decided to withdraw. "We continued firing," he wrote, "when the flanking enemy began to enfilade us, and we had to retreat. Up to this time I don't think that a man of our three hundred had been struck by a shot. We had the steep ridge to climb, and it seemed that every Yankee in a mile was shooting at us. We lost about half of our plucky little band."**

**Two members of the 5th Tennessee who failed to reach the ridge's crest are pictured below. Private Marcus D. Milam of Company C was killed, while Capt. Joseph T. Kendall of Company K was mortally wounded and taken prisoner. He died in Chattanooga several days later.**

■ Private Marcus D. Milam

■ Capt. Joseph T. Kendall

rear of the center of our line, several steps higher up the ridge, mounted a stump or log, and for that long half hour stood there giving orders and encouragement to his troops, within point-blank range of 5,000 to 6,000 Yankees — the only rebel they could see — amid a hailstorm of bullets. Our skirmishers then retreated up the ridge. When they got into and behind our line, Col. Finlay gave us the order, "Ready, aim, fire!" and we opened on the foe.

Those in our front quickly shifted, under the stress of our fire, their position farther to the right of our front. Col. Finlay then gave the command, "Oblique, fire!" which was promptly obeyed. We maintained our position against great odds — probably ten to one — for about half an hour, when the Confederates to our right gave way, and the Federals were on our flank about as high up the ridge as we were. Col. Finlay then gave the order, "Men, fall back to the top of the ridge, but face the Yankees and fire as you fall back," which order those seasoned veterans of the Fourth and Fifth Tennessee, with some few exceptions, forthwith proceeded to disregard, and ran up that steep ridge as fast as their legs could carry them, under a tempest of balls, which conduct would be commended by anyone knowing how rough, rocky and steep the ridge was there.

Our Lieutenant Colonel hovered in the rear of our rabbit-footed boys, trying his level best to get them to face the Yankees and fire as they fell back, but without avail. About midway up the ridge, flying as nearly as I could, I was winged by a Yankee bullet through the left shoulder and knocked down. Seeing the impossibility of attempting to reach the top of the ridge in the hailstorm of bullets coming from above and below, I sought cover, found a friendly log behind which I took shelter and lay there, between the lines, which were firing heavily for about twenty-five or thirty minutes. The firing ceased on top of the ridge and very soon panting, perspiring Yankees came streaming up the ridge. The first one who hove in sight peeped at me in my snug cover behind the log and saluted: "Johnnie Reb, have you anything to eat?" On getting a negative reply, he pursued his way up the ridge.

Shortly afterward I was taken a prisoner to Chattanooga, thence to Rock Island, Ill., where I resided fifteen months.

■ 2nd Lieut. Edwin H. Rennolds of Company K, 5th Tennessee. Pictured here as orderly sergeant, Rennolds was elected to his lieutenancy on October 10, 1863, but found that he "felt still greener without a gun."

Two weeks before the battle, Bragg ordered a partial reorganization of his army. The 5th Tennessee, with the rest of Strahl's brigade, was transferred from Cheatham's to A.P. Stewart's division. "Cheatham's division, composed entirely of Tennesseeans, was regarded by General Bragg as too clannish," Rennolds wrote, "and it was decided to break it up by an exchange of brigades. While the men did not dislike serving under [Stewart], they did not want to leave 'Old Frank' or their fellow Tennesseeans, and much dissatisfaction ensued." On November 13 Rennolds wrote in his diary: "All the Divisions are being turned Topsy-turvy by the exchange of Brigades from one to another, and soon no one but Gen. Bragg will know anything of the organizations of other troops than those directly around him."

## 'My life passed before me'

### Corporal Joseph E. Riley
### Company K
### 33rd Tennessee Volunteer Infantry

The morning [of November 25] we marched around in front of Mission Ridge and formed near the extreme left of Bragg's battle line. We were sharpshooters and fought hard all day. When the break came I never reached the top of the Ridge. The enemy had come in between us and a battery near the center of our line. The guns trained on the enemy and a stray portion of a shell struck me in the left side.

I shall never forget my feelings when it struck. I felt the bullet, apparently, strike my left side just below my heart, pass through my body and out just under my right shoulder blade. I could not breathe, it seemed to me an age, but while I was conscious yet so stunned that I could not move, I felt that I was dying and the whole panorama of my life passed before me. Finally after a desperate struggle I caught a breath and revived enough to think, "Am I bleeding very fast?" I put my hand inside my shirt and to my pleasant surprise, instead of finding a hole in my side I found a knot protruding about the size of a goose egg. I caught my breath easier although two broken ribs made respiration difficult. I arose and looking back saw the Yankees about 100 yards from me. I tried to run but my legs would not carry me up the slope. They overtook me and I never fired another shot at the Yankees. However, the hardest service ever rendered by a soldier was to be my lot for the next sixteen months — Rock Island.*

■ Orderly Sergeant John Conklin of Company E, 74th Indiana. This regiment of Phelps' brigade, Baird's division, was armed with a mixture of Springfield and Austrian rifles, and fired nearly 8,100 rounds on November 25. Lt. Col. Myron Baker reported that his 237 enlisted men were "poorly clad, many of them being without socks, drawers, or blankets, and wholly destitute of overcoats."

Before reaching the crest the 74th had to negotiate a precipitous portion of the ridge "so steep that at some places it required all the strength one could put forth, together with what assistance might be derived from holding on to bushes and pulling one's self up by them. The men ... tugged up the hill as best they might, many of them at times, from exhaustion or the abrupt rise of the ground, being compelled to drag themselves along on their hands and feet toward the summit."

## 'Crawling on all fours'

### Private Nelson J. Letts
### Company H
### 74th Indiana Volunteer Infantry

The morning of the 25th dawned, and after a hurried breakfast Baird's division was ordered to the left to assist General Sherman in a charge. The 74th led the hurried tramping but was halted by staff officers with the news that Sherman had not room to operate the divisions already on hand. We were turned back to the left of the center, and with care kept out of sight of the enemy for our health until an open field had to be crossed to reach the desired position.

The 74th with the 10th Kentucky and the 10th Indiana on its right formed in the front line, the 14th and 38th Ohio, two large regiments, close behind us in the second line. We pressed forward until nearly at the top of a hill called Orchard Knob, and here we were ordered to lie down and wait for the signal of six guns from Fort Wood. While awaiting the signal, the Rebel artillery commenced to shell us. Sand and gravel was plowed up and thrown into our faces, but little actual damage was done. As we gazed upward toward the ridge and enemy, our thoughts were busy with the possibilities to come. Oh, for the signal for action!

At last it is given, the bugle sounds "Forward" and up we spring with loud hurrahs and yells, and start forward on the run. To stop or hesitate means death. A terrible fire came from the

* Riley reached the prison camp at Rock Island, Ill., about the middle of December 1863. He later recalled: "I was among the first to arrive and occupied Barrack No. 2. The day of our arrival was bitter cold. I was clad in a hickory shirt, a pair of cotton pantaloons and shoes without socks. Others were worse off so far as clothes were concerned, for they were ragged while mine were good enough to last me through my whole prison life.

"It was late in the afternoon when we reached the prison. Everyone had to be assigned his quarters. Out of doors we stood without fire or food until the roll was made out and assignments made. This took until late at night. We were kept busy pounding ourselves, walking, running and at any exercise to keep from freezing. Ever and anon we would notice one of the boys crouch down and begin to doze. Three of our comrades had done this and had frozen to death before we realized that this drowsiness was the precursor of certain death. After this when we would find a sleeper we would walk him, pound him and use whatever means at hand to arouse his fagging spirits and dormant circulation."

On March 2, 1865, Riley was exchanged and arrived home in Tennessee 36 days later.

enemy on the ridge as we passed the old Rebel camps at a lively speed. We could not halt here as ordered, for death-dealing missiles were coming thick and fast. A Rebel shell struck and exploded in an old vacated Rebel shanty, hurling the roof against Corporal James Pew, covering him so completely with debris that we had to extricate him as we passed. Harvey Wakefield was struck by a canister ball and his gun so bent that he was forced to pick up another.

But on, on, up, up, pell mell we went using our guns to aid us up the steep hillside, in some places crawling on all fours, proving the saying we got there just the same. When we reached the summit the bayonet in some cases was used, and soon the ridge was ours. Hardly had our colors been planted on the works when the Rebels attacked us on the flank. It was dark all around us and the flash of firearms alone guided us in our defense. Many a brave man went down. Colonel Phelps of the 38th Ohio, commanding the brigade, while standing by our regiment's flag urging his men to stand steady, fell dead; a Rebel bullet had pierced his heart.

Our company's casualties were fortunately light. Robert Warren was wounded and Orlando Light dropped as though killed, but on examination we found a bullet had passed through eight folds of his blanket and stopped at the ninth and last. It was a narrow escape but many close chances occur in war. However, we held the ridge and drove the Rebels away and commenced to protect ourselves immediately by preparing new works, anticipating a second attack, but it came not.

■ Col. Edward H. Phelps, 38th Ohio, commanded the 3rd Brigade of Baird's division, XIV Corps. The night before the assault he consulted two surgeons about a worsening illness. Though too sick to climb the ridge or ride a horse, Phelps followed his seven-regiment brigade up Missionary Ridge with the help of four men. While reorganizing his command on the summit, he was shot in the chest by a sharpshooter and killed instantly. Phelps was the only Federal officer above regimental command to die on November 25.

Before the war he practiced law in Defiance, Ohio.

## 'The undertaking looked like madness'

### Sergeant Jerome D. Gleason
### Company H
### 38th Ohio Volunteer Infantry

Chattanooga, Tenn. Dec. 8th 1863

Dear Brother,

I presume you would like to know something of the part taken by the 38th in the late campaign.

All the fighting we done was on the 25th of Nov. Early in the morning of that day the fight began on our left where the enemy were testing Sherman. They could plainly be seen marching along the crest of Mission Ridge in heavy columns and massing in front of Sherman. About eight a.m. we were relieved from the skirmish line and the 3rd division sent to reinforce him (Sherman).

It was about the same distance right back again, for when we got there we were informed that our services were not needed so we came back and formed on the extreme left of [Thomas'] line. A little less than half a mile in front of us were the formidable heights of Mission Ridge, upon the crest of which could plainly be seen a long line of Greybacks peering over a rude breastwork of logs and earth, with here and there a frowning battery surrounded by gunners ready to begin the slaughter of the Yankees. The undertaking looked like madness and it was some time before we really believed or began to comprehend what was to be done.

At length the word forward was given and away "we went" through a thicket of oak scrub and across an open field on double

■ Col. William H. Hays, 10th Kentucky, assumed brigade command after Col. Edward H. Phelps fell fatally wounded. "On reaching the top," Hays wrote, "we found the enemy in line 25 or 30 yards to our left, who delivered a murderous fire on our men as they ascended the crest ... We then strengthened our position by removing the logs from their works and placing them on the opposite side of the ridge."

Lt. Col. Gabriel C. Wharton, who succeeded to command of Hays' regiment, reported that the 10th's fight on the crest "did not last more than twenty-five minutes, yet for that time it was very hot. The officers and men behaved with great courage, many refusing to take cover when ordered to do so."

quick, till we reached the foot of a smaller elevation about half way to the main ridge. Here we layed down to rest a few moments. By this time the shells were flying as thick as blue jays in Autumn. And if ever I layed close to the ground I did it there. It was astonishing that no one was hurt for they bursted all around us and some of them came so close we could feel the wind caused by them.

We had yet a large open space to pass over before reaching the main ridge where we expected to be out of range of their guns. So the order was given for every man to reach the base of the mountain as best he could and then stop and reform. Away we went like a herd of buffalos. By this time the Grape and Canister began to come down like hail, and a few men were killed in crossing this space but none of the 38th. When we arrived at the stopping place we found they had a cross fire on us in place of being out of range. Consequently we could do no better than go on and formed the best we could going up.

When about half way up the Artillery ceased firing and the infantry began, but on we went returning the fire briskly. We charged right up to their works and when within about fifteen or twenty feet they skedadled down the other slope. Once they rallied and came back part way but we peppered the bullets into them so fast they broke and ran, keeping up a straggling fire from behind trees. We followed them down the slope part way. And here it was that our friend Noah Markel was killed. The firing had almost ceased before he was struck. He was shot through the right groin and left hip and did not live but a few moments. Henry Dellinger was struck in the head just before he reached their works and lived about twenty-four hours. Lieut. Joseph Newman was wounded in the knee and George Clark in the face while coming up the hill. Colonel Phelps was killed just inside of their works. One of the color guards (Russell McCoy) from Company I was killed. In all there was 38 wounded and 9 killed of the 38th.

We suffered more than most of the other regts. owing to being on the extreme left. They had a cross fire on us from a knob to our left. But we killed and wounded more of the rebs than they did of us, besides capturing most of their artillery and a great many prisoners ...

## 'When valor was in vain'

### 1st Lieut. Andrew J. Neal
### Section commander
### Marion (Florida) Light Artillery

Nov. 26th 2 o'clock A.M.

Dear Pa

All day until noon a steady stream of Yankees poured over towards our right & we doubled our lines to meet the shock. During the day they attacked our lines & were repulsed along the different points.

At 3 o'clock p.m. the grand assault commenced and hard & terrific was the struggle. Far below us in the Valley marched the invading hosts while our guns thundered & the mountain wilds resound with their awful roar. Still the Yankees advanced & were forced on — the front ranks pressed forward by the lines advanc-

ing from the rear.

I had my guns in position on the extreme left of the Battalion and was giving them fits — had the colors hoisted and waving, when a shower of balls came in upon us from the left. Looking in that direction I observed five heavy columns in a line perpendicular to ours on a hill one hundred yards to our left flank. I had noticed them when I first came up & called attention to it. Major [Llewellyn] Hoxton, Chief of Artillery on Gen. Hardee's staff, had observed them through his glasses as had several other field officers, but as they had given me no orders, I continued firing on those at our front. Soon as I saw the stars & stripes flashing along the line, I swung my guns around and brought them to bear on the flanking column — but the cannoneer ran the two left pieces too near each other to fire & before I could get the guns apart, Jackson's Brigade came rushing along through our Battalion in utter panic. My men stood steady as veterans, but in vain. The infantry rushed over us pell mell & we could do nothing.

The Battery mounted along side of my guns, seeing the danger, limbered up and ran away. Finding our support gone & that it was impossible to drive back the immense column, I determined to retire fighting. But the mountain ridge was too rough to manage the pieces by hand & I could not get the horses up to the

■ Wartime photograph of the 154th Tennessee's Stars and Bars pattern flag. Belonging to Alfred J. Vaughan's Tennessee brigade, the regiment (which traced its lineage to 1842 as state militia) was consolidated with the 13th Tennessee and fought on the ridge to the immediate right of Deas' brigade. After the latter gave way, Vaughan (inset) ordered the 13th/154th to block the breakthrough but, he reported,"before they could reach the point the enemy had been so heavily reinforced that it was impossible to dislodge him."

Note stencilled battle honors of Belmont, Shiloh, Richmond (Ky.), Perryville and Murfreesboro.

■ Col. Ferdinand Van Derveer, 35th Ohio, commanded a brigade in Baird's division. The color guard of his brigade skirmishers, the 2nd Minnesota, lost six of seven men killed or wounded in the assault. An eyewitness in Van Derveer's battle line later wrote: "The Second Minnesota owned several dogs during the great siege at Chattanooga, and as the Companies of the Regiment deployed we could see these dogs running in front of the lines of skirmishers upon a hunt for game. As soon as our skirmish lines emerged from the clump of woods into the cleared field beyond, the Confederate skirmishers from behind their breastworks and their Batteries on the crest of Missionary Ridge opened fire, which made the dogs of the Minnesota boys scatter in every direction."

guns, so I ordered the limbers away & retreated together.

I am proud of the conduct of my men, & believe they would have stood with me to the guns until we were bayonetted. I left only when valor was in vain, & of all that wing I brought up the rear. I lost two guns & one limber & had several men wounded & have myself a slight wound. A minie ball struck me on the shoulder cutting a great hole through my coat & shirt & bruising the flesh. It stung me some but did not disable the arm. I am in the field with two guns, which I hope may yet avenge the loss of their comrades.

We lost much property etc. by this mortifying affair. Everybody thinks our infantry did not stand up squarely. This thing never happened to Confederate soldiers before — God grant that it may never happen again.

## 'Like blue clouds by tens of thousands'

### Journal of Private Alfred T. Fielder Company A 12th Tennessee Volunteer Infantry

**Wednesday 25th —** The morning clear and quite cool. Health good. The moon was in eclipse last night and about 3 o'clock was very nearly total, not giving as much light as a large star. There was a scattering fire from the enemies batteries and between the enemies pickets and ours from about light until about 7 o'clock when the firing was more rapid and fierce and it was apparent that some move of the enemy was about to be made.

About 3 o'clock the enemy in our front was to be seen moving upon us in three lines of battle (besides their line of pickets) and steadily advanced toward us when at the designated point we fired upon them and fell back as ordered to the top of the Ridge and took our position in line of battle. The sight in the valley below was truly imposing — the enemy like blue clouds by tens of thousands were advancing while our artillery was playing upon them from every available point upon the Ridge and mowing them down by hundreds. Still on they came and when within range of our Enfields, we mowed them down with fearful havoc. But on they came and when within 100 yds. or less of the top of the Ridge, Deas' Brigade immediately on our left gave way and the enemy soon began to show his head upon the top of the Ridge. We were ordered to direct our fire at that point and right well the boys obeyed. The enemy faltered, staggered and fell back. There was an effort made to rally Deas' men, which was partially effected, but they again soon ran off in total confusion. The enemy again took courage, and renewing their fire at that point succeeded in gaining the top of the Ridge; hence they had an enfilading fire upon us which is always dangerous, yet we withstood them until our ammunition was greatly exhausted.

Having no support and being greatly outnumbered, we fell back a short distance and again rallied, shortly after which I received the third wound of the battle through the left hip, which disabled me and I was compelled to retire from the field. I had been wounded in the right foot and left knee, though comparatively slight. S.P. Rice of my company was shot through the leg about the time we first fell back. I carried him some distance on my back but had to leave him in the hands of the enemy, which I was very sorry to do. Lt. Lane [1st Lieut. M.C. Lane of Company E] was wounded in the back but got off. J.G. Furgason was shot in the leg and R.J. Gaulden in the left shoulder. All got off, I with Gaulden and Furgason — was put upon the cars about 12 o'clock that night (having been wounded about 4 o'clock) and started for Atlanta, Ga.*

## 'An awful thirst came over me'

### Private Samuel A. McNeil
### Company F
### 31st Ohio Volunteer Infantry

In the afternoon of November 25th, orders were given to prepare for business. Canteens were filled, blankets were folded closely and twisted rope fashion, the ends tied together making an oblong hoop, which was thrown over the head and rested on the shoulder.

It was late in the afternoon when the six cannon shots were fired in quick succession, and we moved rapidly toward the ridge sweeping the Confederate skirmishers and their reserves before us like chaff before the wind. Their artillery on the crest of the ridge, five hundred feet above the valley we were crossing, sent a perfect storm of shot and shell into our ranks, but the lines kept steadily on until the rifle-pits at the foot of the ridge were in our possession. We got the impression, somehow, that we were to stop there, but the firing from the crest above us was terrific; as if by impulse the boys in the ranks began to climb the west side of the ridge, shouting "Come on, boys!" and on we went without any orders, so far as I know, excepting our own. We were nearly exhausted by the race to the foot of the ridge, and we made slow progress. About half way up we encountered an enfilading fire from a force of the enemy who held a position north of a ravine on our left.

Among the many wounded was Cyrus Carter of the 31st. A ball went through the lower lip and smashed all the lower teeth on that side, passing out without serious injury to the jaw bone. Another ball, which had about spent its force, struck David McIlroy on the leather shoulder belt of his cartridge box, then bounced into a tin cup which was fastened on the belt strap of the man next in line.

Before the attack, D.J. Cheney insisted on having his blanket twisted to the limit, remarking that it might stop a rebel bullet. Strange to relate, a bullet did pass through his blanket, which prevented the ball from going through his body.

Farther up and to the right I saw a man waving a United States flag. He was too far away to see his uniform but I believed that he was a Confederate, tauntingly waving a captured flag at

■ Col. George W. Gordon's 11th Tennessee, part of Patton Anderson's division, suffered severely in hand-to-hand combat on the ridge. "Being overpowered by superior numbers from both front and flank, we were forced to give way and retreated in some confusion," Gordon wrote. "In this battle — a disaster to Confederate arms — the Eleventh Regiment had four different men shot down with its colors in hand, the fifth carrying them from the field, the staff of the colors being shot in two places. Five men fell dead in one pile in defense of our colors."

Gordon was promoted to brigadier general in August 1864. He was captured three months later commanding a brigade at the battle of Franklin.

* Gaulden died the next day before the train reached Marietta. Lane returned to the regiment on December 8. Fielder recovered and rejoined his company at the end of May 1864.

# 'No boy's play was before them'

**Douglas Putnam Jr. and William Beale Whittlesey graduated from Marietta College in Ohio two years apart — the former in 1859, the latter in 1861. In the fall of 1862 both were commissioned officers in the 92nd Ohio and soldiered together until November 25, 1863, when the 92nd attacked Missionary Ridge as part of Turchin's brigade, Baird's division, XIV Corps. Putnam, as lieutenant colonel, commanded the regiment in the assault and was wounded three times. Whittlesey, a newly appointed captain in command of Company F, was killed. Putnam later recalled their relationship and wrote of his friend:**

■ Capt. William B. Whittlesey

"For some reason, he, from the first, seemed to make [me] a confidant, and talked freely of his hopes and disappointments, as well as of his forebodings and fears.

"[At Chickamauga] he went into that battle and, in his earnestness, unnecessarily exposed himself — taking position in *front* of his Company, and directing their fire. He escaped without injury — was commended in the official report of the battle, and, afterwards a vacancy occurring, was made Captain.

"His humor was constant. During that awful Sunday afternoon of the Chickamauga battle ... the Union lines had been driven into the shape of a V, with the enemy on the two sides, and the Brigade of which the 92nd was a part, holding the apex, under a terrible fire of musketry from sharpshooters who were in the trees picking off all who were visible. The men were ordered to lie down and seek such shelter as the inequalities of the ground afforded, and there remained for some hours *waiting* and guarding, constantly under fire, yet with no opportunity of returning it. To my inquiry to General Turchin what we should do, the reply was, 'We will stay here until we are all cut to pieces.' Whittlesey lay with his Company and called to me: 'I am all right — look here — can't hit me!' The man in front of him wore No. 11 shoes, and as he lay on his face with his shoes on their toes, Whittlesey had placed his head behind them, thus forming a fine barrier.

"In the evening a line of the enemy had formed across the open end of the V; the Brigade was hurriedly ordered to drive them back, and did it, capturing many prisoners and opening connection with General Granger. In the excitement of this charge Whittlesey demanded the surrender of one of Granger's batteries — supposing it to belong to the enemy. His account of his chagrin on discovering his mistake was laughable, and made him the butt of many jokes."

"After the battle he talked freely to me of his feelings, and seemed to dread the next engagement. All doubts as to his ability to stand fire removed, he would say he never wanted to see another battle, and evidently lived in apprehension of the next one. Preparations soon began for the assault on General Bragg, securely posted on Mission Ridge and Lookout Mountain. From the summit of the latter shells were frequently thrown into our camp from a battery stationed there. It was not many days before the ominous order was issued to prepare three days cooked rations and one hundred rounds of ammunition. All soldiers knew its meaning, and were also well aware that no boy's play was before them.

"Whittlesey made the requisite preparations and then awaited the command to move — making his will first — in which he remembered the Psi Gamma Society, of which he was an enthusiastic member when in College. He expressed a wish that if struck by a ball, it might be through the heart. He led his company up that hill — so steep that it was no easy task to climb it when no enemy was on the top; and when near the top, a minie ball went crashing through his heart. Telling his men to go on, that he was killed, he breathed his last amid the smoke and carnage of that long to be remembered evening."

■ Lt. Col. Douglas Putnam Jr. was photographed on crutches while recovering from three wounds suffered at Missionary Ridge.

■ 1st Lieut. James K. Rochester of Company B, 31st Ohio, was in temporary command of Company D during the assault. "The nature of the ground being nearly precipitous and intersected by deep and narrow ravines, utterly precluded an attack in military formation," wrote the regiment's commander, Lt. Col. Frederick W. Lister. Noting the enemy's "furious and well-directed fire of artillery and musketry," Lister lost 10 enlisted men and one officer killed, the majority while ascending the ridge. The dead officer proved to be Rochester, who was shot midway up the slope.

During the fighting near Chattanooga between November 23-27, 40 Ohio officers were killed or mortally wounded — the most from any state whose troops were engaged.

our line. While looking up at the flag, a rebel musket ball, evidently fired from the point to our left, struck me just below the jaw bone, passing through my neck. Two streams of blood caused me to believe an artery was opened and that I would soon bleed to death. The first impulse was to get back down the ridge as far as possible before I should fall from the loss of blood. This I did and reached the rifle-pits at the foot of the ridge. A shower of shot and shell was falling around me as I lay where I really thought was my last resting place while in the flesh.

An awful thirst came over me and in my frantic efforts to get at the canteen strapped under my waist belt, I cut the canteen strap and got the water to my lips. That warm water was the best drink I had ever taken, and I thought perhaps it was my last. There was no fear of eternity, which seemed to me was very near. The thought of the possible failure of the assault, and that my body would be left within the enemy's lines, was worrying me more than anything else just at that time.

After resting a few minutes I found that the blood was not flowing so freely. In the pocket of my blouse was a silk handkerchief, a present from my mother. By pressing the soft silk into the wounds the flow of blood almost ceased. I was the happiest boy in the army. I started back toward Orchard Knob to find a surgeon, but became dizzy and was resting when a mounted officer came up, making a few remarks about stragglers and cowards. I never had much respect for officers who kept out of a battle for the avowed purpose of stopping stragglers. My Springfield rifle was loaded, and bringing it to a "ready" I told him to git. Doubtless he then saw the blood on my clothes, for he muttered a sort of apology and rode away, but not in the direction from which I had come.

During one of the frequent halts for a brief rest, I saw the flags of Turchin go over the works along the crest and heard the cheers of my comrades. Off to the south other flags were going over the Confederate works and "presto change," the thunder of the enemy's guns ceased. A military band on Orchard Knob struck up. I raised my hat to those boys of the army of the Cumberland and did my best to cheer them, but my voice wouldn't go off. Within a short time after witnessing the defeat of Bragg's army, I found a surgeon of Wood's division, who gave me a place in one of his ambulances in which I was taken to Baird's division hospital in Chattanooga.

## 'Without any kind of West Point alignment'

### Private Jacob H. Allspaugh
### Company H
### 31st Ohio Volunteer Infantry

On the afternoon of the 25th, ere the echoes of the signal guns had died away, we seized our arms with a firmer grip and found ourselves in line, moving with review-like precision across the plain in front of Mission Ridge, which had so long frowned defiance upon us and now seemed turning into a series of active volcanoes. We of the rank and file heard the command "Forward, men — Double-quick!" and the plain lay before us, with Mission

Ridge in the background and our old enemy pouring shot and shell into our ranks as we advanced to their rifle-pits at the foot of the slope.

Every man there knew that our position was untenable, and that we must make a retrograde movement across the plain or continue our advance until we had secured the summit. A few moments later we saw a brave color-bearer half way up the slope flaunting the old emblem of freedom in the very faces of the enemy, and we bounded out of the rifle-pits without any kind of West Point alignment, moving upward. It was left to the men who carried the musket to find a way across the rebel works the best they could, and it took some close hand-to-hand work at some points on the line to convince the rebel occupants that we had the better right there.

The rebel right had been strengthened by weakening his center, and the result was we of the left division (Baird's) found no boy's play before us. I do not pretend to give a description of the battle except so far as the front limited to the view of comparatively few would allow, but doubt not my experience was similar to that of thousands who took part in this enlisted men's battle.

As we neared the summit our line of battle did not present quite so review-like an appearance as when we were crossing the plain, but the portion nearest the rebel works seemed the most enthusiastic and vigorous, while those just a little behind were picking their way through, under, or over the obstructions and looking for a weak point in the rebel defenses. I was fortunate enough to be surrounded by men who represented a remnant of Chickamauga, and we had soon found or made a way across the rebel works and were sweeping to the north inside the rebel intrenchments, flanking or passing to the rear of such as were still intent on keeping our men from their portion of the front. To witness the astonishment, chagrin and disappointment of some of these men on their being invited to surrender from such an unexpected quarter would have been most amusing had it not been under such serious circumstances.

One heroic young Southerner I noticed turn from his front to find his company rods away, our irregular line in his rear, and his only chance of escape to run for it by passing along our left flank until reaching our front, and then in front of our column eastward. Strange as it may seem, he chose to make the attempt and, what may seem still stranger, he succeeded, although a score of shots were fired at him, some of them by parties not 75 feet distant. I never believed in downright murder, so held my fire, taking it for granted that some other wrathful Yankee would do the murderous work, and was rewarded a few rods farther on by having a loaded Enfield rifle to bring to bear on a piece of artillery that, full mounted some 300 feet to the northeast, was making its best time down the eastern slope.

"Shoot the leaders!" yelled a Sergeant, and half a dozen rifles brought down the leading team which caused the whole outfit to roll up into a conglomerate mass of men and horses, topped out by a fine piece of artillery that had done its last service in the interests of the Confederacy.

The style of gunning we enjoyed as we pushed northward on the ridge was brought to a halt a couple of hundred yards further on by the rebels meeting their reserve, which was approaching

■ Adjutant George B. Turner, 92nd Ohio (above), assumed regimental command on the crest following Lt. Col. Douglas Putnam's wounding. "With drawn sword [he] rallied the men about him and led them to aid in repelling ... the enemy," recalled Putnam. "He here received his mortal wound, a large minie ball striking him just behind the ear."

2nd Lieut. Hugh Townsend (below) of Company I fell dead near his colonel.

■ Brig. Gen. Charles R. Woods' brigade of Osterhaus' division, XV Corps, led Hooker's advance down the east side of Lookout Mountain early on November 25. When a wrecked bridge over Chattanooga Creek was under repair, Woods ordered the 27th Missouri under Col. Thomas Curly to cross on driftwood and advance toward Rossville gap as skirmishers. Before the bridge was finished and Osterhaus' division could come up, the 27th captured the gap — Bragg's extreme left position on Missionary Ridge. Curly reported: "We captured 160 prisoners, including 1 surgeon and 1 chaplain, making a total of 400 captured by the Twenty-seventh during the two days' engagement — 1 for each man in the regiment and 150 over."

from the north, and we soon found that our mixed-up line had its hands full. It had really the hardest part of the work of the day before it, and soon discovered too, that to fall back was the better part of valor. The advancing rebels were evidently in earnest for I still carry the evidence of somebody's marksmanship; for the moment we turned our backs to the foe I felt a shock, and an instant later a benumbed leg warned me that if I got out of that dilemma it must be by using my Enfield for a crutch.

A few rods further to the rear a line of our brigade (Turchin's) was forming across the ridge, and we gladly turned the enemy over to their tender care. We who had been in the way of rebel bullets, and were able, did not wait to see the balance of the little melee on Mission Ridge, but dragged our broken bodies down the west slope, speaking a cheering word to such as had fallen wounded before reaching the summit, and were hustled off to enjoy the sweets of hospital life by way of variety.

## 'So much noise and confusion'

### Lt. Col. John W. Inzer
### 32nd/58th Alabama Volunteer Infantry

Just before sunrise on November 25th, 1863, we were in line of battle on Missionary Ridge, near Breckinridge's Headquarters. We stacked and took a little breakfast. In a short time moved by the right flank about 700 yards in the rear of the top of the hill in an old field. Here I was called upon for the number of muskets. I had two depleted regiments, 376 men. At this place I had boxes filled with ammunition. Maj. [Harry I.] Thornton rejoined us this morning nearly exhausted.

Suppose it is some six miles from the positions we now hold to where we fought on the mountain [Lookout] last night. At the hour of two o'clock in the evening we were moved by the right flank in the rear of Bragg's Quarters. Halted, received, then distributed the mail. In a few minutes we moved off by the left flank on the ridge in the direction of Rossville. We had moved some half a mile when Col. [Bushrod] Jones joined the regiments. He had been absent some month or more in Mobile, Alabama, sick. We were halted — 18th, 32nd & 58th [Alabama] in an old field thick with "hogweeds" very high, the 36th and 38th were in the woods. Here we fronted. The 18th Alabama moved forward & took position on the ridge. I immediately took position on the left. I understood the balance of the Brigade moved down in the direction of Rossville some 3 or 4 hundred yards. In the course of some 40 minutes they began skirmishing with the enemy.

In obedience to orders, I sent one company (Capt. W.E. Lee's) to report to Maj. Ruffin, 18th Ala., for skirmish duty. Capt. Lee soon returned with his company — stated he was not needed. About the time skirmishing commenced, my regiment, also the 18th Ala., were moved by the left flank and to the engagement. Just as we commenced to file to the right we were fired into by the enemy. Immediately after this a large number of the men of the 36th & 38th came running out over us. This caused considerable confusion. Many of my men, instead of filing off to the left, attempted to seek shelter behind breastworks. I ran down the line,

■ 1st Lieut. Simeon T. Josselyn

# ‘Determined to have them at any cost’

As part of Brig. Gen. Charles R. Woods' nine-regiment brigade of Osterhaus' division, XV Corps, the 13th Illinois assaulted the weakened Confederate left flank on Missionary Ridge just north of Rossville, Ga. Its opponents were Alabamians of Clayton's brigade (A.P. Stewart's division), commanded on November 25 by Col. James T. Holtzclaw.

When the 270 men of the 13th ascended the ridge, 1st Lieut. Simeon T. Josselyn of Company C was in command of the regiment's skirmishers. "We had approached within a short distance of the enemy's line when they broke," Josselyn later recalled. "I caught sight of the rebel colors with the guard, who kept well together, and I determined to have them at any cost. My company was back of me and I knew that, although they were somewhat scattered, the men would follow me. I pushed on and captured a rebel, from whom I took a Springfield musket and cartridges, before ordering him to the rear as a prisoner.

"With the captured musket I opened fire on the color-guard, and brought down the color-bearer. When the flag came down the men disappeared in the tall grass and weeds. I reloaded quickly and rushed to the spot where I found nine men. I was about to fire upon them again, when they waved their hats and shouted: 'We surrender.'

"I seized the flag, which was that of the Eighteenth Alabama Infantry, and they handed me the belt and socket. Some of my men coming up at this moment, I placed them as guard over the prisoners. I then pushed forward in the direction of General Bragg's headquarters near the summit of the ridge, carrying the flag with me."

Josselyn's daring feat earned him a Medal of Honor. As for the Alabamians, Holtzclaw's command was decimated, losing 700 officers and enlisted men as prisoners alone. A note written on the original brigade report for November 24-25 flatly stated: "Of the number of men reported wounded in the 18th Alabama [48], 18 were left on the field. A number of others reported as missing are doubtless killed or wounded. No field or commanding officer being present with the 38th Alabama, nothing is known of them, and all are reported missing."

■ Maj. Gen. John C. Breckinridge of Kentucky commanded Gen. D.H. Hill's old corps, and in November was responsible for holding six miles of the Confederate left with only four weakened divisions. Late on November 24, following the evacuation of Lookout Mountain by his troops, Breckinridge favored having the Army of Tennessee remain on Missionary Ridge and stand its ground. He confided that night to one of Cleburne's staff officers: "I never felt more like fighting than when I saw those people shelling my troops off of Lookout today, and I mean to get even with them." But the next day Breckinridge was forced to defend nearly two-thirds of the entire Confederate line with only three divisions — Stewart's, Anderson's and Bate's — positioned behind poorly planned fieldworks. In the frenzy to evacuate the ridge, Breckinridge's assistant adjutant general, Major James Wilson, was captured, as was 1st Lieut. J. Cabell Breckinridge, an aide on his father's staff. Forced to surrender by two Iowa enlisted men, the younger Breckinridge was exchanged and resumed his staff duties in March 1864.

placed the colors and attempted to form the line here. But the line, I must say, was a poor one. A number of the men who passed the breastworks were seeking protection behind the trees, which were very thick. During all this time we were under a heavy fire.

We then commenced the fight in earnest. Before a great while I discovered the enemy was flanking us on the left. He was coming up a hollow some 100 yards from the left of our regiments, moving by the flank. I then attempted to rally my right and move by the left flank across the hollow for the purpose of checking this flanking column of the enemy. After repeated efforts, succeeded only partially in doing what I desired to do. In a few minutes more, the balance of the Brigade commenced giving away.

Moving up the ridge on the top, *I never worked so hard in my life* as I did at this time to rally my command. They may have heard the command "Retreat" given. I never did hear an order to fall back. I stood there until every man left me, begging them to come back and fight the enemy. I remained here until the men who had been with me were some 100 or 150 yards from me — near where Col. Holtzclaw was sitting on his horse. During this whole time I saw nothing of Col. Jones or Maj. Thornton, understood they were at the breastworks on the right of the regiment.

Seeing my men all gone, I moved up to where Holtzclaw was sitting on his horse. I went to him and begged him to rally the men. I told him most of the men knew him and I believed he could rally them at a point some 200 yards in our rear. Then asked him to send one of his staff. I was on foot. He declined to do so. In a few minutes more he told me the order was to face back in four ranks (column of squads). This was the first order I ever heard to face back. After the above conversation the Colonel put spurs to his horse and that was the last I ever saw of him.

I then moved back on the ridge in the direction of Gen. Breckinridge's Quarters, some 300 yards. Saw the men filing to the right down the ridge through a field. Here Col. Jones and Maj. Thornton passed me — both on the Colonel's mare. I turned down the hill trying to get the men to my left to follow me. After getting some 100 yards down the ridge, was fired into several times from my left. The hogweeds were so high and thick I could not see anyone. Believing this to be our friends, I hollowed several times to stop the fire, but without effect. Turned — saw several of my officers and men on top of the ridge waving their hats. Thought they were hollowing to the men on my left to stop shooting into us. There being so much noise and confusion I could not hear what they said.

Being so anxious to stop the firing, I went back to where my officers were but to my sorrow, saw when I got there they had surrendered, surrounded by thousands of the enemy. Seeing further resistance useless, I stuck my sword in the ground and became a prisoner. A large number of the officers and men of the 32nd, 36th, 38th and 58th Ala. regiments were captured at and near said point. This was about sunset. *Surrendered to the Second Ohio.* We were well treated. They took nothing from me. I had a lively conversation with the Colonel, then the General. The Colonel said he fought my regiment the night before on the Mountain — that we killed a number of his men. In some half an hour we were marched off for Chattanooga.

## 'That borderland between life and death'

### Capt. James W.A. Wright
### Company H
### 36th Alabama Volunteer Infantry

After an almost sleepless night of battle and exposure [on Lookout Mountain], with tiresome marching and counter-marching, our brigade reached its old camp near Watkins House before sunrise, Wednesday, November 25. Stacking arms long enough to get a hasty breakfast of boiled beef, cornbread and our celebrated Confederate coffee, made of pure parched cornmeal, we filled our haversacks with two days' rations and soon resumed our march with the rest of Bragg's left wing, its destination unknown to us, as was most frequently the case in such movements.

The boom of Sherman's guns on Bragg's extreme right near the tunnel at the north end of Missionary Ridge began to be heard at an early hour, but all was quiet along the center and left. At sunrise the relative positions of the two armies and their several corps were much the same as they had been the previous evening, except that Bragg had now evacuated Lookout Mountain. The changes which took place in the next few hours were as follows: Bragg merely swung back and contracted his center and left wing, and made the long crest of Missionary Ridge his main line of defense for a distance of at least six miles, from the tunnel [south] to Rossville Gap. Part of his picket line was near the western base of the ridge along his right and center, but was withdrawn entirely to the top of the ridge along much of his left wing.

Our brigade became, though not conscious of it then, the extreme left flank of Bragg's army and was isolated from the rest of Breckinridge's corps by half a mile or more. Marching by the left flank of Missionary Ridge on the neighboring road, just north of Rossville, we filed near a large farmhouse on the summit which we were told was Breckinridge's headquarters. We were posted some distance southeast of it, in line of battle facing west, or toward Lookout Mountain. We were near the end of the ridge where it overlooks to the southward Rossville and its mountain pass. Here our brigade, weary and footsore, was allowed to rest and we unrolled our blankets on the ground under the oaks that crowned the summit, and slept several hours under the lullaby of Sherman's guns — many of our poor comrades enjoying for the last time their dreams of home and loved ones.

Between one and two p.m. we were awakened by the deepening thunder of Sherman's artillery, answered by Hardee's on our right, as the fighting grew nearer along our line. An officer then acting on General John C. Breckinridge's staff rode up. We pointed out to him a large body of troops moving across the Chattanooga Valley with steady, rapid tread, southwest of us. They were evidently marching toward Rossville for a formidable flank movement. This was Hooker's corps [in reality, Osterhaus' division of the XV Corps, Cruft's division of the IV Corps, and a large part of Geary's division of the XII Corps]. On their march from Lookout they had been delayed three hours at Chattanooga Creek to rebuild the bridge which our men had destroyed after crossing it early that morning. One of our men remarked that we hoped General Bragg knew of that movement and would provide well for

■ Col. James T. Holtzclaw, 18th Alabama, commanded Clayton's Alabama brigade at Lookout Mountain and Missionary Ridge. Holtzclaw suffered from injuries sustained after falling from his horse at Chickamauga, where his son, James Jr., a lieutenant in Company G, was wounded.

On November 25, large numbers of Holtzclaw's command were captured. The prisoners presented a dirty and ragged appearance to their captors. Several weeks before the battle Orderly Sergeant Hiram T. Holt of Company I, 38th Alabama, wrote home: "I changed my clothing yesterday for the first time in nearly *two months.* You may guess they were some black. Many of our boys have not dressed or pulled off a garment in over two months."

■ Col. Lewis T. Woodruff's 36th Alabama surrendered nearly 120 officers and enlisted men on November 25. "We either had to take to our heels or be captured," wrote Private Smith Powell of Company C. "Every man was for himself in a helter-skelter race down Missionary Ridge. Everything I had was shot off of me — canteen, haversack, cartridge box. This stopped my shooting at my friends in blue, who gave me a close chase. Breaking my old Springfield against a tree, I trusted to my feet and came out unhurt. We risked everything rather than be captured."

Woodruff's regimental flag fell to the 88th Indiana, whose colonel, Cyrus E. Briant, described the Alabamians as "very badly torn up."

it. The staff officer said he felt sure it would be amply guarded against, and soon rode away.

As results proved, and as we soon learned to our sorrow, the only force provided to meet Joe Hooker's "fighting corps" that day was our one brigade of Alabamians, not more than two thousand strong. Nor had we a breastwork or a rifle-pit or a battery to strengthen our position, while there was no supporting force within half a mile. We afterward learned that a section of a Confederate battery — two guns — had been placed in Rossville Gap. But just before Hooker attacked our position he had the good fortune to surprise and capture these guns by some mismanagement of those in charge.

The storm of battle was steadily rolling nearer to our position. About this time some Federal sharpshooters had occupied a large farmhouse a mile or more beyond the right of our brigade. As they were annoying that part of Bragg's line by a galling fire, General Pettus called for volunteers from his brigade to dislodge them and burn the house. Part of the Twentieth Alabama made a gallant rush for the building. The sharpshooters abandoned it and in a few minutes black smoke was rolling up from its roof. Several houses near Bragg's line were also fired by our men during the afternoon.

Suddenly, not far from three o'clock, the order came for our brigade to "fall in." We were at once marched to a point still nearer the brow of the ridge overlooking Rossville. Our regiments were the Eighteenth, Thirty-sixth, Thirty-eighth, and Thirty-second and Fifty-eighth (consolidated) Alabama. The Thirty-sixth and Thirty-eighth were marched somewhat farther south than the others, and the Thirty-sixth being filed to the left, was faced south, forming an L with the rest of the brigade which faced west toward Lookout. No sooner was this position taken than four companies of the Thirty-sixth were rapidly deployed as skirmishers to our front and left toward Rossville. This skirmish line was commanded by Lieut. W.N. Knight of Company C, ably assisted by Lieut. John Vidmar of General Clayton's staff. General Breckinridge, our corps commander, also rode forward to supervise the posting of this skirmish line, then he rode back to his headquarters.

The moment our skirmishers reached the slight elevation along the end of the ridge, in full view of Rossville and the road through the gap, what was their surprise to see near them a long column of Hooker's men that had already passed far in rear of our main line and, facing northward, was preparing to move up our end of the ridge. Some of our men at first supposed them to be a part of Bragg's army. For this reason, when first ordered by Lieutenant Knight to fire upon the line, they hesitated until Hooker's men, apparently taking them for deserters, began calling out, "Come over, boys; we won't hurt you!" Our men, then recognizing the line of blue, opened fire at once and the fight began in earnest. Hooker's line advanced steadily up the slope against our skirmishers, who gradually fell back to our main line and the engagement became general.

Before our skirmishers reached us the Thirty-sixth and Thirty-eighth Alabama were withdrawn a hundred yards or more and were posted behind some low barricades of logs, which had been hastily made by Rosecrans' men to cover their retreat through this gap from Chickamauga two months previous. These really afforded our men little protection, for instead of facing Hooker's line of attack they extended diagonally toward it, thus exposing our right flank in this short line of defense to an enfilade fire from his left wing. In this unfortunate position, rallied as a "forlorn hope," our regiments maintained the best fight we could for half an hour or more, supported by the rest of our brigade which was posted about a hundred yards farther north on the ridge, their position being stronger than ours. After that time most of our number who were not killed or disabled fell back under a hot fire, suffering severely from it, to the stronger line of our other regiments.

General Breckinridge, at length seeing that such a contest was hopeless and that our brigade was in danger of being completely surrounded and cut off to a man, rode full speed on his fine dark bay horse to the line of battle, under a shower of bullets, and called out, "Who commands this brigade?" Being referred to Colonel L.T. Woodruff — colonel of our regiment — he gave the brief order, "Bring out your men and follow me!" This was done at a double-quick and just in time, by passing first up the ridge in a northeasterly direction and then down its eastern side.

It fell my share to be disabled by a minie-ball in the right hip early in the engagement, at the position first held by our regiment, and to lie there with our dead and wounded under a terrific crossfire of friend and foe during most of the remaining conflict. Who but such as have experienced it can fully realize the peculiar and painful sensation of lying wounded and disabled upon a battlefield, surrounded by dead and dying, with minie-balls whizzing and singing thick and fast around you, pattering like hail against the trees and rocks and ground, and into the living and the dead near you? How vividly then come thoughts of home and death and the mysterious hereafter. Nothing to do but listen and think on that very borderland between life and death. Then after a half hour or more of such extreme tension, how grateful the relief when the lull of battle follows, and the whistling bullets cease their deadly errands. Such was the experience of many of us on that exposed slope of Missionary Ridge near Rossville.

With the lull in this leaden storm came first the Federal skirmishers, and then the steady tramp of four lines of battle dressed to right as in an army review. Then what a feeling of hopelessness and desolation, a sense of sinking in our heart-throbs. Our friends were gone and we were prisoners! Our loved ones at home would be uncertain of our fate, and so they were, some of them not knowing for three months or more after the battle whether some of us were dead or alive.

Never can I forget the little episode when my sword had to be given up — a sword of Confederate make, its brass-mounted leather scabbard well battered and worn by rough service. Having bled profusely I was very weak and lay on the ground scarcely able to move myself. Several Federal soldiers of their advanced line had stopped and chatted with me a moment as they passed — in general speaking kindly, for they saw my weakened condition. My sword lay in its scabbard by my side. Sword belt, loaded revolver and field-glass were undisturbed upon me, being concealed by a light brown overcoat. Soon two boys in blue came by

■ Private William A. Chunn of Company I, 40th Georgia. Positioned near the Confederate far left flank, his regiment contested assaulting Federals of Carlin's brigade. "The yankees fell by scores," Chunn wrote his wife six days after the battle, "but still they moved on until they got within range of the rifles of our men on top of the ridge." Soon, however, "the Genl. [Marcellus A. Stovall] was made aware of the retreat & [that] the yankees were completely flanking our men. The firing was so terrible the men could no longer stand it & were ordered to retreat. Our line was only one column without reinforcements while that of the opposing forces was three."

# 'The rebs had no time to aim'

Capt. David F. Bremner (above) commanded Company E, 19th Illinois. This was the regiment's color company, and before it reached the crest of Missionary Ridge three color bearers were shot down. Bremner recalled: "We could not spare a rifle in that battle; if I ordered a man from the ranks to take up the Flag it would silence his musket; and as I carried only a sword, I took it up and bore it on. As my head was over the last entrenchment at the top of the ridge, the rebel officer in command pointed at me with his sword and shouted, 'Shoot that man!' But the guns of my own company were close at hand and the rebs had no time to aim."

His overcoat was pierced 14 times during the battle. In this postwar photograph, Bremner recreates his appearance on November 25, 1863.

in the pursuit and spoke to me. Seeing my sword, one of them took it, remarking, "I guess you'll have no more use for this." Two mounted officers were riding near. I called to one of them, "Are either of you a captain?" One answered that he was. I then told him that a man was taking my sword, and I preferred to surrender it to one of equal rank. The officer courteously received it and the faithful old blade went North as a "trophy." Its former wearer went to the Chattanooga and Nashville hospitals, and thence to the Nashville penitentiary, and last to Camp Chase at Columbus, Ohio.*

## 'You are cleverer fellows than we took you to be'

### Col. Benjamin F. Scribner
### 38th Indiana Volunteer Infantry

■ Col. Benjamin F. Scribner, 38th Indiana, returned from sick leave early on November 24 only hours before his regiment accompanied Brig. Gen. William P. Carlin's brigade to Lookout Mountain, where it assisted Hooker's attack. With Scribner assigned to command Carlin's second line, the 38th Indiana was commanded by Lt. Col. Daniel F. Griffin. The regiment captured the 38th Alabama's battle flag in the Missionary Ridge assault.

The enemy had thrown up earthworks a short distance in front of the ridge, and had dug rifle-pits on its side. We debouched from the woods and carried the earthworks, advanced a short way up the ridge with the skirmish line and there were halted. The enemy at the summit and extremity of the ridge extended beyond our right, and had a battery of six-pounders beyond our right. The Union lines extended upon our left for several miles, and the flags and glittering bayonets formed a grand and formidable sight. Situated thus, with our right in air, we did not expect to charge with the main line; of course, we would refuse our right and be assisted by a flank fire of troops on our left after they had reached the summit.

The earthworks were occupied on the reverse side by our men. The space between them and the base of the ridge had been the enemy's camp, from which they had just been driven. They had constructed shelters of clapboards loosely laid on sticks, and were made to crawl under for protection from the dew or sun, for they would shield them from nothing else.

There was slight, desultory firing kept up along the line. I had sent our horses to the woods in charge of a slightly wounded soldier, and had sought shelter from the observation of the enemy under one of the sheds, but the coming and going of the regimental staff officers drew attention to me from the rebels, and they directed their fire upon my shed and caused it to rattle as if in a hailstorm. Many of the bullets passed through the thin boards and routed me out of this trap. I sought refuge behind the earthworks with the men, and was followed by a solid shot from the rebel battery, which plunged into the earth in front of me, and had it been an explosive shell, this story would not have been written.

---

* Four months later Wright escaped confinement. "While being removed by rail with several hundred fellow officers in March 1864, to Fort Delaware for safer keeping, I escaped by jumping from the cars near Harrisburg, Pa. Befriended there by an old Princeton College chum, and afterwards by friends in Philadelphia, I made my way incognito by rail via Philadelphia, Princeton, New York, Vermont and Rouse's Point to Montreal; from Canada by the St. Lawrence River and by sea to the Bermuda Islands, thence by a blockade runner to Wilmington, N.C. in June 1864. Returning to my regiment at Atlanta, I fought with it to the crushing end of the strife."

■ Captured Confederates loiter near a siding at the Chattanooga railroad depot, awaiting transportation north. Within 30 minutes of being taken prisoner on Missionary Ridge, Lt. Col. John W. Inzer of the 32nd/58th Alabama and a "large number" of officers and men from Brig. Gen. Henry D. Clayton's brigade were marched to Chattanooga. "We were well treated," Inzer later wrote in his diary. "Before leaving my men I said some encouraging things. Told them I hoped we would soon meet again in Dixie to fight the enemy. The Yanks said nothing. We were marched first to the old depot building then ... confined in an old brick house. No blankets. Slept very little. Very cold."

Most of the enlisted men captured at Lookout Mountain and Missionary Ridge eventually were sent to Camp Chase (Columbus), Camp Morton (Indianapolis) and Camp Douglas (Chicago), while the officers were imprisoned on Johnson's Island in Sandusky Bay.

Gen. Carlin now hastily passed by and said that it was reported that the enemy were coming around our right, and ordered me to bring a company and follow him quickly to investigate the matter. The report was found to be untrue, but while we were examining the locality I happened to glance toward our lines and observed them in motion up the ridge. The whole line, as far as the eye could reach, was steadily climbing the hill. When I told Carlin, he exclaimed, with more emotion than he had ever before manifested to me: "My God, who will take the responsibility of this?" We both assumed that the charge had been ordered. Having sent the company back to its regiment, we hastened to the lines, but made no effort to restrain them; it was now too late for that. They were like a headstrong horse with a bit in his teeth, beyond holding in. The troops on the left had moved, and they did but keep up with the general movement. They had already shown emulation to dress up the lines in conformity with the general alignment, and to be as far in advance as the others. They were restive and impatient at the delay and were filled with confidence and ardor. They had not been ordered to advance, but the order seemed to have been taken for granted and to have been a spontaneous intuition. What else were they there for? This was their fight; their officers had nothing to do with the advance.

The movement began in two lines, but the second to get under the dip of the batteries had closed up to the first. Thus they charged up the hill in the wildest enthusiasm. They would spring into the rifle-pits before the rebels could get out and make their escape and would press onward and upward, and encourage each other. That brave soldier and kind-hearted gentlemen, Col. Carter [Major William L. Carter, 38th Indiana], waved his hat to me as we climbed, and as I caught his beaming joyous eye, he fell, suffering from a grievous wound then and there received.

But I did not share in this hopeful confidence. I had no misgivings about carrying the ridge, but in doing so the enemy would wrap his extended flank about us and we would be crushed and destroyed. And as I assisted myself over the obstacles of the way with my heavy sabre as a lever, I would exclaim to myself, "Good-by, my brave boys! Good-by; you will gain the top, but it will be your last success; it will be the last of the First Brigade!" I felt like a lamb led to the slaughter, helpless and hopeless.

It was now growing dusk, and still our lines pressed forward. We did not delay longer under the fire of the enemy than was necessary to overcome the obstructions of the ascent, and did not attempt to return shot for shot, but the enemy continued to pour into us an incessant fire, however overshooting us, partly in order to avoid shooting their own men whom we closely followed up the hill, and partly from errors in judgment. At length the summit was reached, and the enemy fell back and made no further resistance, and my forebodings came suddenly to an end.

Soon after the enemy gave way, Gen. Osterhaus opportunely came up from Rossville, and obliquely approaching our right, joined us, thus forming an acute angle within the area of which the enemy was huddled together in great masses. They were anxious to surrender for the protection it gave them. Many officers would deliver up their swords to an orderly, or to anyone who would take them. One of them claimed especial courtesy because the number of his regiment was thirty-eight [38th Alabama, of Clayton's brigade], the same as mine. Four hundred prisoners, including one hundred and seventy commissioned officers, were hastily collected and sent to the city in a body.

The joy of the men knew no bounds and shouts and cheers filled the air and reached up and down the lines. Even the prisoners caught the excitement and yelled and gesticulated in the general rejoicing, and clasping our hands would assert, "You are cleverer fellows than we took you to be." Gen. Osterhaus threw up his cap and exclaimed, "Two more hours daylight and we'll destroy this army!" I, too, caught the infection and joined in the universal exultation. I had come up from the "Slough of Despond" and now revelled in the bright realms of hope and success.

■ Brig. Gen. John C. Starkweather commanded the 3rd Brigade of R.W. Johnson's division, XIV Corps. Starkweather's eight regiments were left guarding Fort Negley on November 25, the soldiers viewing the Missionary Ridge assault from their entrenchments. "It was an anxious quarter of an hour for onlookers of every class," wrote a member of the 78th Pennsylvania. "The line moved onward and the top of the ridge was reached at a number of different points almost simultaneously. General Starkweather, commanding our brigade, was handed a dispatch, which he read in so loud a voice that the whole brigade could hear, 'The battery at Bragg's headquarters is captured and the whole ridge will be ours in fifteen minutes.' Then came such a shout as is seldom heard, and the enthusiasm was unbounded."

# CHAPTER 9

# The damned Yanks are everywhere

## Ringgold Gap: Retreating Rebels reach safety when Cleburne slams the door on Federal pursuit

Darkness veiled the despondent faces of Bragg's soldiers as they trudged and limped away from Missionary Ridge early on November 26. Trails of sweat streaked dirt- and powder-begrimed hands, lips and cheeks despite the night's dropping temperature. Stragglers were everywhere, some looking for their commands, some stumbling along weaponless, others searching for places to hide for the night.

Most Confederates, however, retained their regimental and brigade organizations in good order. Those in Cleburne's division and several others which held their positions on the right could not believe the battle was lost. Angry Texans, Arkansans, Tennesseans, Kentuckians and Georgians vented their feelings by cursing Bragg and the "shameful conduct" of comrades who broke and ran.

Missionary Ridge was a "sad affair," wrote Private Joel T. Haley of Company A, 37th Georgia, three weeks later. "I never felt more confidence in the anticipation of victory, nor did more to achieve it. We [each] expended nearly 60 rounds of cartridges ... An hour after dark [the regiment withdrew] sadly, silently to the rear. I trust that I may be spared such scenes in the future. For a time my spirits were below zero considerably."

The "Orphans" of Lewis' Kentucky brigade were especially dispirited as they tramped to Chickamauga Station after leaving Tunnel Hill. Sergeant Thomas Owens of Company I, 4th Kentucky Infantry, wrote:

"At Mission Ridge the Kentucky Battery (Cobb's), commanded by Lieut. Frank P. Gracey after Capt. Cobb's promotion to be chief of artillery for division, was detached from the brigade and placed in position near Bragg's headquarters. It was supported by troops that had hitherto conducted themselves well on every field, but were now among the first to give way before the Federal advance. The battery thus fell into the hands of the enemy, while the men who would have defended it as long as there was a charge to fire or room to

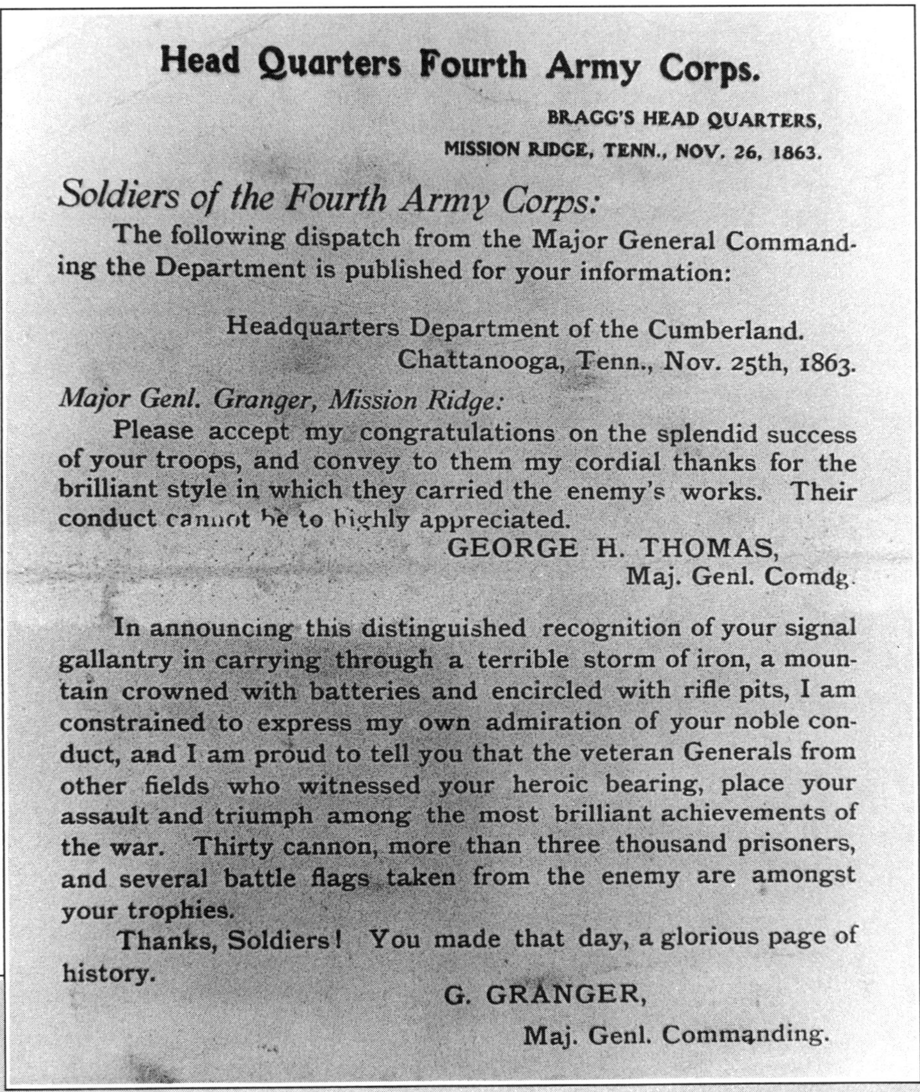

**Head Quarters Fourth Army Corps.**

BRAGG'S HEAD QUARTERS,
MISSION RIDGE, TENN., NOV. 26, 1863.

*Soldiers of the Fourth Army Corps:*

The following dispatch from the Major General Commanding the Department is published for your information:

Headquarters Department of the Cumberland.
Chattanooga, Tenn., Nov. 25th, 1863.

*Major Genl. Granger, Mission Ridge:*

Please accept my congratulations on the splendid success of your troops, and convey to them my cordial thanks for the brilliant style in which they carried the enemy's works. Their conduct cannot be to highly appreciated.

GEORGE H. THOMAS,
Maj. Genl. Comdg.

In announcing this distinguished recognition of your signal gallantry in carrying through a terrible storm of iron, a mountain crowned with batteries and encircled with rifle pits, I am constrained to express my own admiration of your noble conduct, and I am proud to tell you that the veteran Generals from other fields who witnessed your heroic bearing, place your assault and triumph among the most brilliant achievements of the war. Thirty cannon, more than three thousand prisoners, and several battle flags taken from the enemy are amongst your trophies.

Thanks, Soldiers! You made that day, a glorious page of history.

G. GRANGER,
Maj. Genl. Commanding.

■ **Below:** Trophies from Missionary Ridge — a display of captured Confederate cannon, limbers and caissons lined up in Chattanooga shortly after the battle. Capt. Thomas G. Baylor, Army of the Cumberland ordnance chief, reported that Confederate losses totaled 30 smoothbore field guns and howitzers, eight rifled field pieces and two siege guns; 38 field carriages, 26 caissons, four battery wagons, one traveling forge and 2,336 shells of varied calibers. Nearly 6,180 small arms, mostly Enfield rifles, were collected from the battlefield, as well as 1,911 cartridge boxes and 55,000 rounds of infantry ammunition.

The three large buildings immediately behind this ordnance park served as headquarters for Brig. Gen. John M. Brannan, Army of the Cumberland chief of artillery (left); Brig. Gen. William F. Smith, chief engineer (center); and Maj. Gen. George H. Thomas (right).

■ Private George A. Grammer of Swett's Mississippi Battery. Originally known as the Warren Light Artillery, the battery was attached to Cleburne's division and suffered heavy losses at Tunnel Hill. When all the officers and non-commissioned officers were killed, wounded or disabled, command of the first section (two 12-pounder Napoleon guns) devolved upon Corporal F.M. Williams. A lieutenant from Douglas' Texas Battery temporarily took command of the battery's other two-gun section.

handle a bayonet were far on the right, and ignorant of its peril. Lieut. Gracey stood to his guns, fighting till the whole line was abandoned, and then walked off, slow and sullen. The men of the brigade had regarded the cannons composing the battery, which had been with them so long, with a species of attachment amounting almost to affection, and had even bestowed upon two of them the pet names of Lady Buckner and Lady Breckinridge.

"The abuse that was heaped upon those who lost them was perhaps out of proportion to the offense. The Kentuckians believed themselves incapable of being routed from breastworks, even of the slightest kind, when their battery was to be defended, without leaving bloody evidence to show that there had been a fight. Bragg came in for his share of blame for entrusting it to other troops; they were so angered that as he passed a part of the command next day they hooted and otherwise manifested disrespect, and asked what he had done with their battery. A sight of those who had been placed to support, but had abandoned it, was sure to result in cries of 'Where's our battery?' and 'What did you do with our battery?' "

"Gen. Bragg has been outgeneraled," wrote Col. Newton N. Davis, 24th Alabama, to his wife. "We have lost a great many prisoners [and] over 40 pieces of artillery. There is no disguising the fact. We have been badly whipped this time & no mistake."

Accompanying the army, a correspondent for the *Savannah Republican* jotted his impression in a notebook just hours after the last of Bragg's men left Missionary Ridge: "The Confederates have sustained to-day the most ignominious defeat of the whole war — a defeat for which there is but little excuse or palilation."

At Chickamauga Station, rations were distributed — or stolen — before the Confederates marched on. In the decimated 27th Mississippi, Companies F and K "liberated" more food than the entire amount issued to the rest of the regiment. "We had as much as we could carry," wrote Private Robert A. Jarman of Company K, "enough to do a whole week, but as we had been on short rations about two weeks, the men packed all they could carry. I, for one, had my haversack full, and as much as five pounds of bacon and a half bushel of crackers in a sack besides."

Another Mississippian, Private George A. Grammer of Swett's Battery, found some soldiers at the depot ransacking army stores and destroying anything that could not be hauled away, including two 32-pound rifled siege guns. In his journal for November 26, Grammer wrote: "Early commenced evacuating. Before leaving, buried our dead near Station which had been brought from the field in a wagon. Buried them about 200 yards of station under a pine tree. After they were put in the grave, Corpl. Williams led in prayer. How solemn the scene as we paid the last respects due our comrades. No fond and loved ones were there to weep o'er their dead loved ones. Nothing but a wide board with name attached. Left and travelled ten miles and camped about one mile from Ringgold."

Bragg, relieved of command only four days later, was pushing his troops to Dalton, Ga., some 28 miles southeast of Chat-

**tanooga. Rearguard fighting against the pursuing Federals occurred over the next 30 hours as the Confederates desperately struggled to save their wagon trains and remaining artillery. "While I saw Gen. Bragg often," recalled Private Marquis L. Morrison of Company I, 26th Tennessee, "I remember him best as sitting upon his horse at the ford of Chickamauga Creek watching the infantry wade through the cold water on our retreat from Missionary Ridge. Most of the boys did not take off their shoes, but some of us knowing the bad effect on our feet of marching in wet shoes, sat down and removed both shoes and socks, taking time, also, to replace them on the other side of the creek. We halfway expected Gen. Bragg to rebuke us for the delay, but he did not."**

**Finally, on November 27, the leading Union divisions caught up with the Southerners at Ringgold. On Taylor's Ridge just east of town they ran headlong into Cleburne, whose stubborn defense bought enough time for Bragg's escape.**

## 'My motley crew'

### Lt. Col. Daniel F. Griffin
### 38th Indiana Volunteer Infantry

[By sundown on November 25] the summit was gained and the flying Rebs were scampering through the valley beyond. Quickly advancing our line and swinging to the left, we were soon met by Osterhaus' Division sweeping up from the Right, and between us we "gobbled up" 1 Lt. Col., 2 Majors, 25 Line Officers and 282 privates. As cheer after cheer arose along the Ridge we were told the day was ours; there was no mistaking the sound, 'twas not the sickly yell of the Rebs, but the clear, round cheers of thousands of happy Union boys.

My Regiment with the 76th Ohio of Osterhaus' Div. were detailed to take charge of prisoners, and in half an hour I was moving with my motley crew toward Chattanooga; of course the boys were in the best of spirits, for although Bragg yet held out at Tunnel Hill, still we felt sure that if he remained there until morning, he was ours.

Moved to town, deposited our prisoners in the big depot; had to furnish part of my Command to guard them and with the balance moved to our old camp where the men could have shelter, and myself a cup of coffee. The Major commanding and Adjt. of the 76th were my guests and their men, the guests of the Regiment. A happier lot of mortals you have never seen, for they had been lying out for four days and expected to bivouac that night out in the cold. Next morning at sunrise as we moved out, they saluted our boys with three hearty cheers for their Hoosier hospitality.

Joined our Brigade on the Ridge about 9 A.M. having four days rations on hand and ready for anything. Remained but a short time on the Ridge, when off started our Div. for Graysville and Ringgold, or at least in that direction; our Brigade in advance, the 38th in advance of the Brig.; with 2 companies as skirmishers, another as support, while the remaining 7 moved in line of battle. We advanced to Chickamauga River, picking up in that distance, say six miles, 1 Rebel Capt. and 27 stragglers, all of whom had their "rights" or were fast getting them. Here we found the bridge

■ Lt. Col. Daniel F. Griffin, 38th Indiana. After conveying some 300 Confederates captured on Missionary Ridge to Chattanooga's provost marshal, Griffin's Hoosiers joined the Federal advance toward Graysville on November 26 and bagged several dozen more prisoners before progress was halted just after midnight. Despite the darkness, the retreating Confederate column was followed by the noise it made. A member of the 38th recalled: "We marched through the woods until we at length came up to a road upon which the enemy were in full retreat. We proceeded quietly to form a line in the edge of the undergrowth which lined the road, and could hear the 'gee-ups' and cracking whips of the artillery men and teamsters, and the slang and ribaldry of the rebel soldiers as they with unconscious abandon trudged along."

■ Brig. Gen. William P. Carlin commanded the 1st Brigade of R.W. Johnson's division, XIV Corps. His brigade pursued the Confederates to the vicinity of Graysville, Ga., where resistance was encountered. Carlin reported: "The enemy escaped by forcing his men through Chickamauga Creek. In his haste to get away he abandoned a fine Napoleon gun, which fell into our hands. At Graysville, also, about 40 Georgia Militia were captured, and near 200 muskets. Here, Major-General Palmer called for a party of volunteers to scout the front, and they came forth immediately. Private James Bolin, Forty-second Indiana, one of these scouts, was captured, murdered and robbed by rebel cavalry."

burned, and two hours time consumed in effecting a crossing, when we were relieved of the advance by the 42nd Indiana and took position in the column.

Advanced very cautiously, now growing dusk, meeting but a few of the enemy's Cavalry, and about 9 P.M. quietly formed line of battle within a few hundred yards of the crossing of the Lafayette and Ringgold roads. The line formed, we could plainly hear the [Confederate] drivers and teamsters "cussing," yelling and making a noise generally, apparently with trains in the mud. Much time was consumed in preparation, as we had some ugly little streams to cross; and Hooker was at the same time to operate on the right. At last all was ready and through the woods we advanced on my first night attack, not knowing what we might run against.

But on we swept; then came a few hurried shots, a yell, a charge, and four pieces of artillery and quite a number of prisoners were ours. Our Div. then changing direction to the left, swept down upon Graysville on the banks of the east Chickamauga, capturing many of the unwary as they lay around their comfortable camp fires, on their beds or as they essayed an escape over the hills. Meantime, Hooker pressed on a few miles toward Ringgold, and we bivouacked at midnight in and around Graysville, appropriating without much ceremony the Rebel fires but not their beds, as we cared but little for the capture of that breed of "grayback."

## 'This beats Hell'

### Private Francis M. Carlisle
### Company D
### 42nd Indiana Volunteer Infantry

We made fires and cooked coffee and remained on the Ridge until morning [of November 26], when we took up the march after the remaining and retreating rebels. Our Brigade was led by Genl. Wm. P. Carlin.

We cut across the country through the woods, and headed the enemy off on the road just above Gray[s]ville, Ga., a little railroad town on the Chickamauga River. When we came close to the wagon road where the enemy's train and artillery was moving, we lay down and awaited until the 2nd Brigade came up on our right. While laying here three rebel soldiers came along by the road, which we were laying across. They were talking very loud and came right up to us before they knew that we were there. They were going to some of their old neighbors to stay all night. Two of them were going to talk to their girls, while the other was going to his home close by. Just as they had it understood — that the first two were to come by his mother's house and wake him up at four o'clock in the morning — they had come within twenty feet of us when we halted them, and they jumped like they had been shot and wanted to know who we were. We told them to surrender, that we were Yanks. They threw down their guns and came slowly. We told them that we disliked very much to keep them away from their girls, mothers and friends, but there was no choice in war, and we did not think that they could talk to their girls that night.

In a few minutes a signal was given for all to make a general charge, and we all went for the train and artillery and captured the whole train of fifty wagons, three pieces of artillery and a lot of ammunition. We then deployed across the road and scattered out through the woods and marched by a flank movement east to Gray[s]ville, about one-half mile. John Nixon, Ben. T. Simpson and myself were together. We came on to six rebels lying in the woods asleep; this was about ten o'clock in the night. We secured their guns and told them to get up, which they seemed to pay no attention to. We then kicked them a little and demanded them to get up, but they only said "Go to Hell." When we got them fully awake we told them that we were Yanks, and they soon realized the fact and said, "This beats Hell. We thought we would get one night's good sleep, but the damned Yanks are everywhere."

Our command in this way picked up several prisoners in their sleep that night. When we arrived at Gray[s]ville, we turned over our prisoners to the guard where the rest of the prisoners were kept, some five or six hundred of them. We here made coffee and camped until morning.

■ Capt. Lawrence Gates commanded Company H, 74th Indiana. His men had been fortunate on November 25; three privates were slightly wounded during Baird's assault. A fourth man dropped as though killed, but on examination his comrades found he was only stunned — a bullet had passed through eight folds of his slung blanket and stopped at the ninth and last fold. "It was a narrow escape but many close chances occur in war," recalled Private Nelson J. Letts. "We lay with our arms ready among the dead on the ridge that cold night. The next morning it fell to my lot with six comrades from Company H to assist in burying our own dead, also those of the enemy. Never can I forget the unpleasant and hurried way of the burial of those tall stiff men of the enemy on that side of Missionary Ridge. After burial duties had been performed we attempted to wash with but little water, had some hot coffee and hard tack, and left for Ringgold ..."

## 'The day had been lost'

### 1st Lieut. R.M. Collins
### Company B
### 15th Texas Cavalry (Dismounted)

While we were yet on picket duty after the great battle of Missionary Ridge, and during the few hours we were waiting and watching, we witnessed more of the horrors of cruel war.

Near where I was standing on the line of skirmishers [at Tunnel Hill], a wounded Federal was sitting on the ground with his back against a tree; he had been shot through the bowels. He seemed to be a very intelligent young man and spoke of the certainty of having to die very soon in a very quiet, dignified manner. He belonged to the 26th Missouri infantry. Another young man of powerful build, and I suppose from the same regiment, had been seriously wounded in the head; he was some distance higher up the mountain than the one already named. He would rise to his feet and then fall face foremost down the mountain, uttering cries and groans that pierced the hearts of old soldiers. We thought at first that it was a ruse he was playing to get through our line, but upon examination we found he was seriously wounded and was as crazy as a "march hare." But those surroundings were tame to our feelings compared to the effect of the huzza, huzza, huzza that commenced in the Federal lines to our left, and died away, away down yonder toward the base of Lookout mountain. "What does all this mean?" was the question asked in low tones, one of another. "I cannot tell, there is some mistake. I thought we had gained a great victory."

About 11 o'clock the order was passed down the line in a whisper, from post to post, for us to move out by the left flank, and to be careful as to making any sort of noise, not to allow saber or gun to strike with canteens, and not to tread on any sticks that might break and make a noise. We were old soldiers enough by this time to know what all this meant. I knew that the day had been lost; such thoughts as these passed through my mind in rapid succession: if we can't hold such a line as this against those

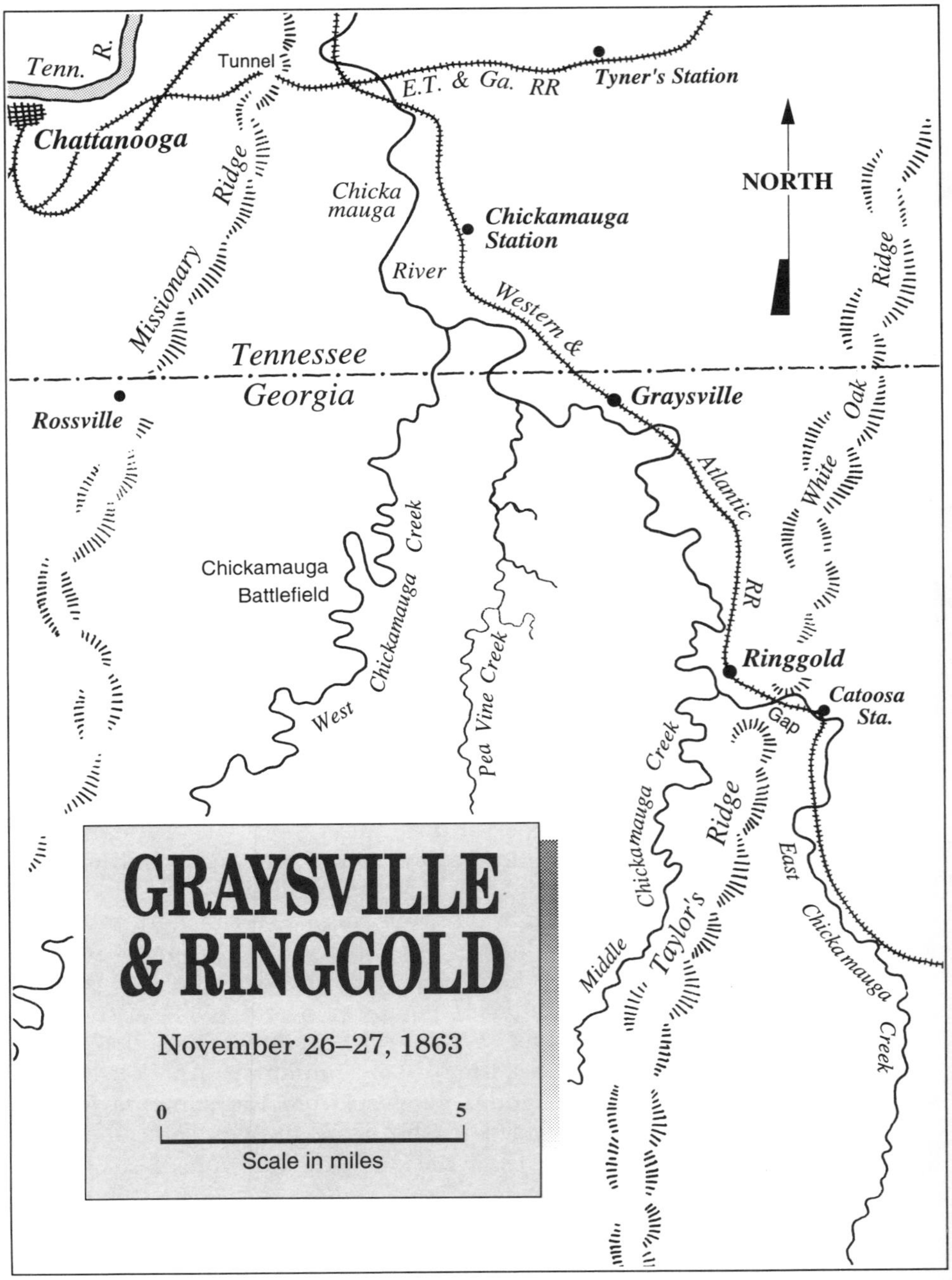


blasted Federals, where is the line or position between here and the coast of Georgia that we can hold?

We moved out as quietly as if there had been but one man only. Up, over the mountain and down through a deep gorge, wrapped in deep darkness inside and outside, not a word being uttered. Along with Capt. Jack Leonard, I was marching at the head of the column. The first words spoken was the following little speech I made to Capt. Leonard. "This, Captain, is the death-knell of the Confederacy, for if we cannot cope with those fellows over the way with the advantages we have on this line, there is not a line between here and the Atlantic ocean where we can stop them."

He replied by saying, "Hush, Lieutenant, that is treason you are talking." Doubtless such expressions in the presence of the men might have been wrong, but we thought it all right as be-

## Crackers, corncakes and 'empty' shoes

**Following Missionary Ridge's capture, food and other staples of soldiering remained uppermost in the minds of many enlisted men on both sides. Sergeant James P. Crane of Company K, 66th Georgia, wrote to his sister: "I had a very hard time on the retreat from Missionary Ridge. We marched from daybreak until midnight every day for a week. I lived on one dry cracker a day, every day ..."**

**Six days after the battle, Private Benjamin B. Mabrey of Company K, 82nd Indiana, confessed in a missive to his wife: "We have got Chattanooga as full of reb prisners as it Can hold. Thare was fore hundard came in this eavning ... i took a haver sack from one of them and had a good supper. I had Corn doger and sweat potatoes and meat for my supper."**

**Private Charles G. Phillips slept the night of November 25 near the crest of Missionary Ridge. The next morning he and his comrades of Company D, 104th Illinois, were awakened at dawn. "My breakfast was very slim that morning," Phillips remembered, "consisting as it did of one cracker and a little corncake which I captured on the way up the hill at the middle line of works. The Johnnies had sent a ball thru my haversack, which ruined my spoon, tin plate, corncake and all. We all got our coffee, and we were happy when we heard we were to draw rations for two days that morning."**

**It was not food but footwear that George H. Godden sought immediately after the battle. A private in Company B, 17th Ohio, Godden later wrote: "Being shoeless, I went over the battle field, looking for a shoe that would fit me. After walking around a good deal, where many rebels had fallen, I saw a shoe that looked pretty good and stooped to pick it up. I did not take it, however, for I discovered there was a foot already in it — the reb having been buried, all except his foot. I concluded I did not need a shoe very badly after all, so left it on the buried reb."**

tween officers.

Pretty soon we came to where our division was camped in a sort of straggling, irregular manner in a great woodland. We laid down and rested an hour or two. Some time before daylight we were up and put on the move, and about sunrise we arrived at Chickamauga station. This was on the Atlantic & Great Western Railway[sic], and had been General Bragg's main depot of supplies. Here we began to see and realize the situation and learn something of how the battle had gone. There were thousands of bushels of shelled corn, corn meal and some bacon scattered around the station.

We were halted, built fires and were broiling our bacon for breakfast. Off to our right, when facing Chattanooga, was a fort. I noticed some stragglers craning their necks over the parapets of the fort and looking in the direction the enemy would come. We looked down that way too, and not more than three hundred yards from us a line of Federal cavalry formed across the railroad. Their horses looked to be about sixteen feet high and each rider looked a regular Goliath, while the morale of Cleburne's division of Arkansas, Texas and Mississippi troops was not the best in the world, yet it was the best in the Army of Tennessee. We did not stand on the order of our going but moved out at once.

## 'The 'possum grins'

### Private Sam R. Watkins
### Company H
### 1st Tennessee Volunteer Infantry

When we had marched about a mile back in the rear of the battlefield, we were ordered to halt so that all stragglers might pass us, as we were detailed as the rear guard. While resting on the road side we saw Day's [Deas'] brigade pass us. They were gunless, cartridge-boxless, knapsackless, canteenless, and all other military accoutermentless, and swordless, and officerless, and they all seemed to have the 'possum grins, like Bragg looked, and as they passed our regiment you never heard such fun made of a parcel of soldiers in your life. Every fellow was yelling at the top of his voice, "Yaller-hammer, Alabama, flicker, flicker, flicker, yaller-hammer, Alabama, flicker, flicker, flicker." I felt sorry for the yellow-hammer Alabamians; they looked so hacked, and answered back never a word. When they had passed, two pieces of artillery passed us ... and they were ordered to immediately precede us in bringing up the rear. The whole rear guard was placed under the command of the noble, generous, handsome and brave General Gist of South Carolina.

Our army was a long time crossing the railroad bridge across Chickamauga river. Maney's brigade, of Cheatham's division, and General L.E. Polk's brigade, of Cleburne's division, formed a sort of line of battle, and had to wait until the stragglers had all passed. I remember looking at them, and as they passed I could read the character of every soldier. Some were mad, others cowed, and many were laughing. Some were cursing Bragg, some the Yankees, and some were rejoicing at the defeat. The prevailing sentiment was anathemas and denunciations hurled against Jeff

■ Maj. Gen. Benjamin F. Cheatham resumed command of his division in Hardee's corps late on November 24 after a three-week leave of absence. Following the Missionary Ridge debacle, Bragg looked to pin blame and hurled vitriolic accusations at Gens. Breckinridge and Cheatham. Bragg, who broke up Cheatham's former all-Tennessee division three weeks earlier, wrote to President Davis on December 1 that he could "bear to be sacrificed myself, but not to see my country and my friends ruined by the vices of a few profligate men who happen to have an undue popularity."

Nicknamed "Marse Frank," Cheatham was beloved by his troops, especially for the attention he paid to their welfare. One of them later reminisced: "General Cheatham was one of the most provident soldiers. He was always on the look-out for clothing, for shoes, and for all possible comforts of his command. The result was, that his division was the best equipped one in the Army of Tennessee."

■ Capt. Robert C. Williamson of Company D, 6th Tennessee. This regiment of Gen. George E. Maney's Confederate brigade was consolidated with the 9th Tennessee, and helped cover the retreat of Breckinridge's corps. Near Graysville the night of November 26, pursuing Federals were repulsed with few casualties, although Maney himself was severely wounded. Recalled Orderly Sergeant William H. Bruton of Company A: "The bridge across Chickamauga River at Graysville [was] burned, and that deep little stream swollen. The night was dark and bitter cold. Close in the rear could be heard the dull rolling of artillery carriages, and upon either side the enemy's cavalry could be heard taking positions on the rocky roads which ran parallel. Gloomier still, we could hear the splash and plunge of our own artillery as it was abandoned and rolled into the river. More gloomy than all this, we could hear men riding off on the artillery horses, evidently bent on escaping a pressing peril."

Wounded at Jonesboro, Ga. in August 1864, Williamson was promoted to major and commanded the decimated 6th/9th Tennessee during the war's closing days. He and seven others were all that remained of Company D's original 104 members.

Davis for ordering Longstreet's corps to Knoxville, and sending off Generals Wheeler's and Forrest's cavalry, while every private soldier in the whole army knew that the enemy was concentrating at Chattanooga.

When we arrived at Chickamauga Station, our brigade and General Lucius E. Polk's brigade were left to set fire to the town and to burn up and destroy all those immense piles of army stores and provisions which had been accumulated there to starve the Yankees out of Chattanooga. Great piles of corn in sacks, and bacon, and crackers, and molasses, and sugar, and coffee, and rice, and potatoes, and onions, and peas, and flour by the hundreds of barrels, all now to be given to the flames, while for months the Rebel soldiers had been stinted and starved for want of these same provisions. It was enough to make the bravest and most patriotic soul that ever fired a gun in defense of any cause on earth, think of rebelling against the authorities as they then were.

Most of our army had already passed through hungry and disheartened, and here were all these stores that had to be destroyed. Before setting fire to the town, every soldier in Maney's and Polk's brigades loaded himself down with rations. It was a laughable looking rear guard of a routed and retreating army. Every one of us had cut open the end of a corn sack, emptied out the corn, and filled it with hard-tack, and, besides, every one of us had a side of bacon hung to our bayonets on our guns. Our canteens, and clothes, and faces, and hair were all gummed up with molasses. Such is the picture of our rear guard.

## 'Into the icy water'

### Private Thomas J. Walker
### Company C
### 9th Tennessee Volunteer Infantry

I will never forget that night retreat. It was bitter cold way along in the night [when] our columns were halted. Pickets were thrown out on our right and orders came from Gen. Cheatham that when the march again commenced that we must march with as little noise as possible. As the enemy had cut us off from the rest of the Army, we had to make a detour and cross Chickamauga Creek lower down at a ford unbeknown to the enemy.

We marched pretty well all night over the roughest mountain road I have ever travelled. Just before day, the head of the column reached the ford. All the while, the enemy was passing parallel to our line of march on the main pike. General Cheatham stood on the bank and as each file passed going down the bank, he would say, "Boys, keep quiet! If you make the least noise, we are lost."

File after file plunged into that icy flood four feet deep, struggling to reach the opposite shore. The men held their guns and accoutrements on top of their heads. With bated breath and chattering teeth they waded waist deep in that ice cold water. Oh, how I dreaded my turn! As my file reached the edge of the water, we plunged in with clenched teeth for fear our breath would come out in such force that it would end in a scream. It proved to be too severe an ordeal for one of my file who was a great big fellow. As we stepped into the icy water to our waists, he hollered out at the top of his voice, "Jesus Christ! God Almighty!" However, with few exceptions, we passed over very quietly and struck the mountain trail and were soon on its top. We struck the main road with the enemy in our rear. Safe from capture at last!

We reached a safe place to camp about sunrise with our clothes frozen stiff upon us, after one of the most trying night marches I experienced during the war.

## 'It was impossible to make my escape'

### Journal of Private William H. Davis Company C 9th Tennessee Volunteer Infantry

**Thursday, Nov. 26th.** We reached Chickeymaugy Station at 2 a.m. Stayed here untill the Whole armey got in Motion and passed off on the difrent roads leading to Ringgold, Tunil hill [Ga.], Dalton. By this time we were made the Rear guard of the Whole Armey. It was 8 a.m. before we left the station which is only 2 miles from Mission Ridge. My Regt. was rear of the Brigade and our Brigade was rear of the Division. Skermishing began at 9 a.m. between there advance and 2 Companys of Cavalry which was in our rear. At twelve M. they drove them in and came within a few hundred yds of my Brigade and Seeing our strength halted for Reenforcements. We did not move untill 2 p.m. The Road was almost impasable from mud for artilery and Wagons.

About one Mile from Graysville we were halted. The Fedrals were pressing both flank and rear at 4 p.m. My Regt was thrown out as Skermishers. The yanks found out our Situation and began to execute a flank movement. At 5 p.m. we found a heavy force moving on us from Tiners Station. Gen. Manneys [George E. Maney's] Brigade was formed immediately to stop them and give our Artilery and Wagon train time to make there rounds. The yanks at this time were near graysville. A brisk fight ensued between Manneys and one Division of there advance for near one hour. In this time the armey had moved some Distance.

At six p.m. we were ordered to fall back and rejoin the Division. My Regt. fell back to join the Brigade. I thought that we were ordered back in a skirt of Woods to form again. We were under a very heavey fire at this time. Therefore we became some what scattered. Myself and a few Others halted near the first line and continued the fight not knowing that the Regt was gone. It was now about 7 p.m. I now found that my Regt was gone for the fighting had nearley Ceased. I started to overtake them but soon found to my Surprise that the Regt was more than a Mile [away] and the yank Cavalry was between the Regt and me. I immediately set about getting through their lines. I made my Way through 2 Pickett lines and then found myself on the banks of the East Chickeymauga. It was now two O'clock in the night and I thought it prudent to stop for the Night as I new nothing of the country. Therefore went to a tree in a bend of the River to bivauqe [bivouac] for the night. I did not build any fire for fear of being Captured. I then spread my Blanket on the ground and then humbled myself in silent Prayer. I dozed some just before

■ Brig. Gen. George E. Maney, whose two-brigade rearguard included his own command of Tennesseeans, covered the extreme right of Bragg's retreat. On November 26, "our progress was painfully slow," wrote a private in Company C, 1st Tennessee. "It was a broken march of one or two hundred yards and then a halt of five or ten minutes, to enable some wagon to get out of the mud."

Shadowed all day by Federal cavalry and cheering infantry, the beleagured Tennesseans fought at sunset near Cat Creek, where Maney was wounded. "Almost the entire attack seemed leveled at the First Tennessee regiment," continued the private. "The skirmish was hotly contested. The position was exposed — no particle of shelter, a plain, open field, with the enemy under cover of the woods. In the meantime, the order was given to fall back into the woods behind. This was done in reasonably good order. The moon, which had now risen, displayed the glistening bayonets of a still unbroken front. Every wagon was for the present in safety, and the only capture the enemy made from us was [my] gun," a new Bridesburg contract musket picked up two months earlier at Chickamauga.

■ Private Robert C. Thompson of Company H, 41st Tennessee. Late on November 26, his regimental commander, Col. Robert Farquharson, led a large portion of Maney's brigade to safety near Graysville. In the face of mounting Federal pressure, wrote regimental chronicler Robert Gates, "the men promptly resumed their arms, and stripping, placed their clothes on their bayonets, and thus quietly forded the river, the icy waters coming up to the necks of most of them, and forcing some to swim. But the brigade succeeded in crossing, and their fires on 'the hills beyond the flood' were the first notice the enemy had that their prey had escaped.

"At sunup the next morning the travel-worn, battle-begrimed brigade passed into the lines of its own army, through Cleburne's division drawn up at Ringgold ... Cleburne's men warmly greeted and cheered the gallant brigade as it marched safely through its lines. The successful retreat of Maney's brigade was a nine-days wonder, heightened as it was by the fact that the men bore every one of their wounded officers and comrades with them in safety to Ringgold. Col. Farquharson was the hero of the hour [during] this perilous and terrible retreat, in which the privates outgeneraled their own General and the enemy."

day. I got so cold that I could not lay any longer. I rose at 7 a.m.

**Friday, Nov. 27th.** I now found that it was impossible to make my Escape by the way of Ringold and went to an old Citizens quarters and inquired of him the best Way to make my way out. He directed me to cross the Chickeymauga and pass to the left or east of Lafayette [Ga.]. I then went down to the River and waided it and went up Peavine Creek nearley to where the Road leading from Chattanooga to Ringold crosses it. This Road was crowded. Yankee wagons, ambulances traveling to and from Ringold.

I saw it would be impossible for me to cross with out being seen. It was now 10 a.m. I waited untill four p.m. The road seemed to be worse crowded than it was in the Morning. At half past four I started. When I reached the Road it was vacant but I soon came in plain view of a cason [caisson] and some 10 or 12 yankees just off of the Road that I had not seen. The had already seen me. I could not hide and went boldly up to them. There was a few Words passed between us. I made the impression that I was tired of the War and was going to quit fighting. They told me the way to Chattanooga and I started as though I was going there. By this time it was getting dusk. I soon reached a turn in the Road which concealed me from view. I glided into the Woods in double quick time, and had gone some fifty yards when someone said halt. I quickened my pace when I was halted the second time by a Major within a few Steps of me with his Navy [revolver] drawn on me. I then Surrendered as I knew it was instant Death to procede any further.*

## 'Trying to squeeze ourselves into the ground'

### Private John W. Dyer
### Company G
### 1st Kentucky Cavalry CSA

On the morning after the retreat from Missionary Ridge, [the Federals] began to press us slowly in front and at the same time sent their forces around our flank in the endeavor to drive us from the railroad and away from our base of supplies. We skirmished with them and fell back to the range of hills at Chickamauga station where Bragg prepared to make a stand. After our lines were formed everything quieted down and not a gun was to be heard nor a Yankee seen. This silence was ominous and portended no good to anybody.

The Yankees had stopped somewhere out in the woods some two thousand yards in front of us or they might be sending their whole force around to our rear and we had to know what they were up to. So Lieutenant Sam Brooks of Co. D of our regiment was sent out with a half dozen of us to hunt them up and we rode out across a field to within two hundred yards of the timber before we saw any sign, when there they were and in my state of

* Along with 100 other prisoners, Davis reached Chattanooga on November 29. Two weeks later he arrived at Rock Island, Ill., and was imprisoned there until the end of the war. An older brother, Josiah Davis of Company A, 51st Tennessee, had been captured at Fort Donelson in February 1862, and died at Camp Butler, Springfield, Ill., on February 27, 1862.

feeling, there seemed to be at least a million. When we discovered them we made a gradual circuit to the left instead of turning square back in order to make them think we wasn't scared, but more especially because there was a skirt of woods not far off in that direction. This time they did not shoot at us and we got safely back nearly to our lines when they turned loose a shell at our squad which struck a stump right in our midst but did no damage further than to add to our scare. The enemy became restless and seemed spoiling for a fight so our regiment was dismounted, deployed as skirmishers and sent down on the face of the hill to meet them.

We were ordered to "ambush," which under the circumstances was an exceedingly grim joke. There was no more to hide behind on that hill than there is on a tin roof with no chimneys, and the blue coats were coming on in solid line of battle and they had their guns with them, too. It looked like they were coming to stay awhile. They unlimbered their artillery and began to shell us. They got our range very quickly and put their shells dangerously close.

We were lying down (in ambush) and trying to squeeze ourselves into the ground while the shells ploughed up the earth all around us but hit nobody. Captain Jeff Rogers of Co. D was looking down the muzzle of one of their pieces and concluded that it was aimed for him. He rolled over a few times to get out of the way when the shell struck almost exactly where he had been lying and tore a hole in the ground big enough to hide a man. With the remark that "lightning never strikes twice in the same place," the Captain jumped into the hole and was the only man of us who was fortified.

All this time we were lying there doing nothing, as they were out of range of our rifles, and we were anything but comfortable. Failing to shell us out they advanced their infantry line and pretty soon we began to pop away at them. They did not pay much attention to us but kept coming till within about eight hundred yards. They halted and let fly, scattering cold lead all about us. Just when things were growing interesting the order was given, "skirmishers, retreat!" and we were on our feet in an instant, falling back to the main line. We didn't run back but fell back gradually, skirmishing as we went. Several of the boys got hit, among the rest Philander Pool of our company. A ball struck Philander over the heart but was stopped by his sweetheart's picture, which he carried in his pocket. He dropped like a chunk and some of the boys ran to him to carry his — supposed — dead body off the field. Before they reached him he jumped up and then fell again, then up, then down, for all the world like a headless chicken, and finally started on a dead run toward the Yankees. He had gone fifty yards before the boys caught him and when they did they turned him about face and he kept going till he reached our line where he was cared for. He did not come to his senses for several hours afterward. On this account some of the boys always accused Philander of carrying his brains in his vest pocket.

Our next stand after Chickamauga station was at Graysville, a station a few miles to the south. In forming the line our brigade was on the left of a division of Tennessee infantry and occupied some breastworks that had been thrown up some time before. The Yankees charged our front and we repulsed them. For an hour or

■ Brig. Gen. States Rights Gist, temporarily in command of Gen. W.H.T. Walker's division, was responsible for covering the withdrawal of Breckinridge's corps from Missionary Ridge to Dalton. Riding with Gist's retreating troops, a *Savannah Republican* correspondent reported events of November 26: "The enemy had thrown forward a mixed column of mounted infantry, artillery and cavalry, which was harassing our rear guard, under command of Gen. Gist, considerably. General Gist was repeatedly pressed back against the wagons, but he managed finally, with the aid of his command (Walker's division) to save them all. At the time the enemy got in between him and the main column, but he took a neighborhood road and thus escaped destruction. Unfortunately, Ferguson's battery of four guns was captured. The horses were in very bad condition, and unable to keep up with the column. The greater part of the men and horses escaped. You will be astonished to hear that the horses in the artillery service — the most important in the whole army — are the most neglected — a fact, however, which quartermasters, and even artillerists, seem incapable of understanding."

■ Brig. Gen. Jefferson C. Davis' 2nd Division, XIV Corps, was not engaged at Missionary Ridge, but took part in the subsequent pursuit. Skirmishing ahead of the lead brigade, the 21st Kentucky entered Chickamauga Station amid buildings set ablaze by the Confederate rearguard. Davis recalled: "In this sharp encounter several of the enemy were wounded and captured, belonging to Kentucky regiments of the Confederate army. This fact was soon known to the Twenty-first Kentucky. Kentucky loyal was now meeting Kentucky rebel face to face. The enthusiasm it created ran through the lines like an electric thrill."

The 21st's commander, Col. Samuel W. Price, wrote that the Confederates "were forced to give way to the impetuosity of my men, who, without an order from me, charged the enemy, and it was with great difficulty that I kept the men at a reasonable rate of speed."

more there was no more fighting done, when suddenly a courier dashed up with information that the enemy was flanking us on the right and orders for us to mount our horses and go check the movement. We passed some fifty or sixty yards in the rear of the infantry on our right and just when we were exactly behind them the Yankees charged them, and for about forty minutes there was the hottest of hot times and we could not take a hand. We had to stand and take it. We could see everything that happened. Our infantry tumbling over like ten-pins, the minie balls flying thick among us, shells bursting all about us, limbs of trees falling on us and a general pandemonium reigned. After the scrap was over our brigade was marched back to its old position which it held till next morning.

We had several men and horses wounded, and it seems wonderful that the casualties were not greater as we sat on our horses in good range with nothing to shield us. John T. Quarles (known as "T") and I were beside each other when we were both struck. "T," with a groan, clapped his hand to his head and reeled over towards me. Supposing that he was shot through the brain, I caught and pulled him over in front of me and carried him down the hill to our field hospital where he was laid on the ground for dead. He began to show signs of life when an examination showed that the ball had entered the calf of his leg and ranged down the bone to his ankle where it was afterward cut out.

I did not know that I too had been hit till I got off my horse when I discovered that my foot and leg were asleep. An examination showed that a ball had hit me on the instep, but was glanced off by the hard rawhide shoe I was wearing. These shoes would soften and stretch in wet weather and draw up and get as hard as iron when they got dry. To one of these shoes, in the latter condition, I am indebted for the possession of two feet today.

## 'I never before heard such cheering'

### Journal of
### Acting Sergeant Major Levi A. Ross
### 86th Illinois Volunteer Infantry

**Nov. 26th.** Were called up at midnight and started in pursuit of the skedaddling Bragg, who began his retreat early last evening. We pressed the flying battalions and captured many prisoners. Genl. Sheridan distinguished himself in the pursuit of the enemy by a flank movement so skillfully executed that he gobbled in a large number of prisoners. "Phil" has much dash and skill in action.

Along the road side of the route of Bragg's retreat was scattered cornmeal, flour, salt, ammunition, caissons, broken wagons, exhausted mules and horses, and worn out soldiers as well as many deserters.

On we pushed singing: "We'll rally round the flag boys, down with the traitor and up with the stars," etc. A short time before sun set the enemy was pressed so closely that he had to either lose his train or fight for it. He chose the latter alternative, and accordingly made a stand, and poured upon our advance a volley of rebel lead. Our boys went into the fight with a yell, inspired by our great victory. This cheer ran back along the lines of the advancing columns like the mighty waves of the ocean. Every soldier shouted to the utmost strength he possessed. I never before heard such cheering. Really it was an appropriate manner for a soldier to spend this national Thanksgiving day.*

The 3rd Brigade was brought into line and ordered to fix bayonets. Gen. Davis just then rode along the line and shouted: "Go in boys, with a yell!" It was not necessary to say more to his Prairie boys. We *did* yell with a hearty good will and charged the Johnnies about three fourths of a mile through an open field and a skirt of woods along a small stream which we were obliged to ford. We pushed them through another field and finally they made a stand behind a high fence in the edge of some timber.

Night coming on put a stop to the fighting. The rebels continued their retreat and the Union army rested from its labors around large burning rail piles. A sublime scene today is worthy of note. We were deployed and marched by battalions with companies, right in front, deploying distance. The sun shone brightly upon the burnished guns and the buttons even seemed to partake of the brilliancy of the day as the army strode on ...

■ Capt. Allen L. Fahnestock, commanding Company I, 86th Illinois, bivouacked his men in line of battle near a swampy stream northeast of Graysville the night of November 26. Before drifting off to sleep, he scribbled in a pocket diary a short account of that day's chase from Chickamauga Station: "We pressed forward skirmishing all the way, the Rebbles throwing away Shot and Shell. The Road was lined with Wagons, caissons, everything that would lighten their load. At Sundown the Rebbles made 2 stands at Shepards Springs. We had orders to fix Bayonets and charge into the Fight. We done so crossing a open Field in Line of Battle. We had to pass over a deep Run, the men jumping in the water up to their waist. We then passed through a narrow strip of Timber to an open Field and formed a line and opened fire on the Rebbles, it being then so dark that we were compelled to fire in the Direction [of the ] flash of the Enemys guns."

## 'Plaintive cry of fifes, the moan of muffled drums'

**Benjamin F. Taylor**
**Correspondent**
***Chicago Evening Journal***

The day after the battle was Thanksgiving, and we had services in Chattanooga — sad, solemn, grand. The church-bells hung dumb in their towers, indeed, and you shall know why in its time, but for all that, there were chimes so grand that men uncovered their heads as they heard them.

At twelve o'clock the great guns at Fort Wood began to toll. Civilians said, "Can they be at it again?" and soldiers said, "The guns are not shotted, and the sound is too regular for work." I hastened out to the Fort, and the guns chimed on. A dim impression I had received before brightened as I stood upon the parapet and looked over the scene. What it was like flashed upon me in a moment: the valley was a grand cathedral, Fort Wood the pulpit of the mighty minister, and far down the descending aisle in front rose Orchard Knob the altar. The dead were lying there, far out to the eastern wall, and God's chandelier hung high in the dome. They were the accents of praise I was hearing; thirty-four syllables of thanksgiving the guns were saying ...

And the churches of Chattanooga had congregations. Those who composed them had come silent and suffering and of steady heart; had come upon stretchers; come in men's arms, like infants to the christening; ambulances had been drawing up to the church-doors all night with their burdens, and within those walls it looked [like] one great altar of sacrifice. The nearest of these edifices is

* On October 3, 1863, President Lincoln issued the first *national* Thanksgiving Proclamation designating the last Thursday in November as the day to be observed. Credit for this largely is given to Mrs. Sarah J. Hale, editor of *Ladies' Magazine* and *Godey's Lady's Book,* who began urging observance of a uniform day of thanksgiving throughout the United States in 1827. Her last editorial on the subject appeared in the September 1863 issue of *Godey's Lady's Book.*

■ Musician Loraine C. Cherington of Company D, 63rd Illinois. One of his comrades, a diarist in Company A, recorded impressions of November 26: "Early this morning I went over the battle field to see if I could find anything to eat, but found nothing. Dan Leppers found a couple corn pones in a dead rebs haversack. They were very bloody, but he cut out the bloody spots and had quite a feast. The battle field looked terrible on account of dead and wounded men. I passed one man sitting by the reb breast works with his gun in his hands. His eyes were open and he looked all right. As he gave me no look of recognition I did not speak to him. I thought [it] a little strange of him for not noticing me and wondered why he was sitting there. Presently I came back and saw a crowd of men standing around him. I pressed my way through the crowd and found that the man had been shot in the mouth and was dead. His mustash hid the wound. Another man had his head shot off from his mouth up leaving his under jaw. Of all I have yet seen in my army life, this battlefield was the most horrible. It almost made me sick. I hope I may never see the like again.

hardly a dozen paces from my quarters, and I go out and sit upon its step in the sun. It is the same building wherein the gifted Murdoch, only a few days before, had given his splendid renderings of drama and lyric. I do not hear the music of his voice, neither do I hear a moan. The doors are noiselessly opening and closing, and I see pale faces — bloody garments. Five still figures, covered by five brown blankets, are ranged on the floor beside me. Their feet are manacled with bits of slender twine, but a spider's thread could hold them. I lift a corner of the blankets and look at the quiet faces. By the gray coat I see that one is a dead rebel. Do men look nearer alike when dead than when alive? Else how could it have chanced that one of these sleepers in Federal blue should resemble him nearly enough for both to have been "twinned at a birth?" They are not wounded in the face, and so there is nothing to shock you; they fell in their full strength. Tread lightly, lest they not be dead, but sleeping. The silence within oppresses me; it seems as if an accent of pain from some sufferer in that solemn church would be a welcome sound.

Three or four little Africans are playing "hop-scotch" on the sunny slope at the corner of the church, gurgling like japanned waterspouts with laughter, and exploding now and then into an unmitigated "yah, yah." A couple of soldiers are going by, while several white-wood coffins are being borne up to the porch. They stop, give a glance, and one says to the other, "I say, Jack, our boys killed on Mission Ridge yesterday are thundering lucky, don't you think so?" "Why?" said his comrade. "Because they can all have wooden overcoats!" It was no heartless jest, but an old campaigner's way of putting things. Alas, for the battlefields to whose heroes the luxury of a coffin must be denied, and yet they sleep as sweetly close folded in the earth.

I go around the church; a soldier has his foot upon a spade, digging a hole. I ask him its purpose. He never looks up, but keeps crowding the rusty blade craunchingly into the red earth, and tosses the answer to me sullenly over his left shoulder: "buryin' legs!" I look down and see uncertain shapes beneath a blanket lying on the ground, go to the right-about, and walk gently away.

You wander down into Main street; hospitals there. You go up the hill by the Market House; hospitals *there.* You see thirty unarmed men drawn up on the sidewalk, a Lieutenant commanding. Four soldiers are bringing weapons strange to them across the street; their arms are full of shovels; you see the builders of the doomsday houses; it is the Shovel Brigade. An order is given, and away they move, up the hill, out of town, to the eastward. They are not sad men, but cheerful, if not smiling. Shall we follow them to the place of graves? There it is, the slope turned towards the setting sun, that even now is "promising a glorious morrow;" a strange piece of check-work; a spot already honeycombed with graves. And the Shovel Brigade begins to widen the breadth of the solemn tillage; doing for dead comrades what, for anything they know or think, somebody may do for them the next day or the next. There were seven hundred and forty-two graves in that one place, on Thanksgiving night.

Going slowly homeward we meet them coming. And what *is* them? The plaintive cry of fifes — it is almost a woman's wail — and the moan of muffled drums come up from the laps of the little valleys of Chattanooga. I have heard the splendid bands in great cities, and the sighing of organs over the dead, but that music among the mountains I cannot describe. There are tears in the tones, and will be till my dying day. An ambulance bearing the dead, and then a dozen comrades following after, two by two, another ambulance and more comrades; but no flags, no pomp, only those fifes. The ambulances are lightened. Dirge and "Dead March" are dropped into the graves, and back they go to a quick-step, here, there, everywhere; the fifes warble like birds in spring; life and cheer tread close on death and gloom. And so it went, Thursday and Friday and Saturday. And such was Thanksgiving at Chattanooga.

## 'There was something ahead of us'

### Private George Prets
### Company G
### 69th Ohio Volunteer Infantry

The night [of November 26] was a very dark one and there was a fine mist of rain. We were in pursuit of the retreating Johnnies. My regiment was in the rear of the brigade, and we discovered campfires ahead, about as many as would have been built to accommodate a brigade of troops. We Yanks began to feel as though we would soon go into camp for the remainder of the night and get some much needed rest. But not so. We marched some little distance to the right of said fires, then the word was passed along the line to move up as fast as the bad road and darkness would permit, and to do it silently, as there was something ahead of us and we wanted to capture it.

We moved along in that manner for some time and in single file, for we had gotten off of the road into the woods and each man must follow his comrade in front. Finally the foremost regiments halted and bunched up, and as we in single file came up, we took our places. It was not long after my company got into line until the brigade was formed, as my company was G, leaving only one more company to double up, which was Company H.

The order was then given to front, and when we did so and moved a few yards there was quite a bank looming up. It must have been fill for a railroad. It was about 25 feet at the base and about 14 feet high. We could see the reflection from fire on the opposite side. The order was given to charge and not fire unless ordered to do so, but when we gained the top of the embankment the temptation was too great for nearly one-half of the command, and they cut loose on the enemy.

It seems that in our immediate front there were three or four small fires which were surrounded by several chilly men in the gray garb of artillerymen. There was but one slight volley fired. Then everything was as still and calm as around some country farm-house where war had never been. Immediately after the firing our Colonel shouted, "Cease that firing." The result of our sneak was the capture of four pieces of artillery belonging to Ferguson's famous South Carolina battery and 110 prisoners. The 69th Ohio formed a square and marched the prisoners back some distance and went into camp for the balance of the night, which I thought was the smaller half, for I know we were all well worn

■ Private Robert M. McCoy of Company F, 69th Ohio. Provisioned with four days' short rations and 100 rounds of ammunition, the regiment started after Bragg's retreating columns early on November 26. That night about two miles from Graysville, word spread that Confederates were nearby. "Marching by the right flank," reported Major James J. Hanna, "the command was given to form rapidly and quietly into line with a view to attacking a portion of the enemy's train, which was reported a short distance ahead; this was done, and the regiment moved on in line of battle as well as the accidents of the country permitted.

"Suddenly, on debouching from the woods, the Sixty-ninth Ohio came upon a rebel camp immediately in front. The command to halt and dress was quietly given, and a well-directed volley poured into the camp. This was rapidly followed by a charge, and the regiment succeeded in capturing several prisoners (part of General Stewart's division, the rest escaping under cover of the night), 1 stand of colors, 3 pieces of artillery, and 1 caisson (part of Ferguson's battery), which was mired and abandoned by the rebels in their flight."

■ Capt. Andrew S. Burt commanded Company B, 1st Battalion, 18th U.S. Infantry. Six battalions of Regulars served in the Army of the Cumberland at Chattanooga — all of them in Col. William L. Stoughton's brigade of R.W. Johnson's division, XIV Corps. Four of these battalions led Stoughton's pursuit toward Graysville on November 26. Deployed as skirmishers that night to cover their battalion's front, Burt's men bagged a number of prisoners and captured a 12-pounder Napoleon gun belonging to Ferguson's South Carolina Battery, then commanded by 1st Lieut. Rene Beauregard.

Shortly after Chickamauga (where he won a gallantry citation), Burt requested reassignment to his company following distinguished service on the staffs of Robert L. McCook, Henry Halleck and William S. Rosecrans. Brevetted to major at Jonesboro in 1864, Burt continued with the army until his retirement in 1902 as a brigadier general.

out. The next morning the prisoners and guns were taken to the rear and then to Chattanooga.

Gam Pease, a comrade of my company who was left in the rear, told me there was a detail of the 69th with the battery. He was taken sick after the capture of Missionary Ridge and was sent back to camp to bring up our cooked beef rations, which he nobly did. He started from Cameron Hill with 63 pounds of cooked beef in company with a number of others who started on the same errand for their respective commands, and I think this man Pease was the only one who ever reached his command with the much desired food. We soon devoured his 63 pounds of cooked meat that he had toted for two days and nights. His comrades wanted him to throw it away, but he was a true comrade and said nay. He said that he would tote it until the regiment was found or until it became soured, and then he would knock the flies off of it a few hours in the hope that someone would still dare to eat it.

The brigade that captured the battery was composed of the 19th Illinois, 11th Michigan, 69th Ohio, and the 15th, 16th and 18th battalions of Regulars. We were in a woods clear of underbrush but the trees stood pretty thick. After the volley was fired the rebs came running up to us to surrender. One fellow, about seven feet and an ax handle tall, ran into me, and of course I halted him. He surrendered in the following language:

"You done got my brudder Ike, you done got my brudder Joe, and now you done got me." I replied, "If the ones you name are as tall as you we certainly have in our possession some length of the rebel army."

The ones who seemed to want to make their escape would jump from tree to tree. We could see them move and would command them not in the sweetest terms ever uttered to halt and come forth and throw up their hands and say "I am your prisoner," which in most cases they did. A negro boy about nine years old, quite small and the color of new leather, having a small brass snare drum, jumped up and sang out in a clear, boyish accent: "Massa, I's your prisoner, too." In the morning he was nowhere to be found. I think he made good his escape when we were marching them back, as we went through a piece of ground that had but recently been cleared and was full of stumps. I think it altogether likely that he sat down by one of those stumps and let us march by him.

## 'They took the hint'

### Sergeant Major John W. Green
### 9th Kentucky Volunteer Infantry CSA

**Nov 26th 1863.** We are still operating with Cleyburn's brigade[sic], covering the retreat. We camped at Chicamauga station last night. The roads are very heavy & the wagon trains are falling back very slowly.

Great quantities of commisary stores are being abandoned at this place [and] the boys are filling their haversacks with sugar & hard tack. We had a sharp skirmish with the yanks here. We had to keep them back until the wagon train got out of the way. We were deployed in line of battle on a wooded ridge & the yanks advanced across a wide field about one mile away. Our artillery opened on them & though they outnumber us ten to one we deterred them from advancing for an hour or more; finally they advanced against us in force & we, having delayed them as long as we could, fell back through an open field.

We had first to climb a high staked & rider fence. George Granger, a fat short leged boy in Co. H who was a good deal handicapped by a big supply of sugar & hard tack which he had just gotten at the station, was pressed pretty hard & had a close shave when he had to climb the fence. Before he had gotten well over a mr. yank fired at him but missed him. He was making his best speed across that open field when another yank blazed away at him which helped Granger along a good deal & enabled him to increase his speed by about double. When the second yank fired & missed him he yelled at him, "Run you scoundrel of a rebel!"

Granger called back at him, "You blamed fool you, dont you see I am doing my best."

We all made fine time across that field & had no body killed; but Granger over took one of the boys who was shot in the leg & though he had a decided longing for the cover afforded by the timber on the other side of that field he stopped & helped that poor wounded fellow along, and they both got safe across.

We had to form line of battle several times that day to give them a volley ... but we lost no men killed that day & only one wounded. The Yanks seemed determined to keep company with us just when we did not want to have them around, and it was determined by Genl Lewis to give them a hint. The road went up a wooded hill & then turning around followed its crest for a short distance. Our infantry was formed at the foot of the hill in the woods & the artillery was put in position on the top of the hill. The enemy could not see our line of infantry [and] when the artillery opened on them they made a rush for the battery. When they got near we surprised them by giving them a volley from our infantry & just then another piece of our artillery somewhat on their flank opened on them & they took the hint & hurried back out of the reach of our guns. We had only one man wounded.

This gave our wagon train time to get a good start but we now learned that there was another column of Yanks coming out from Rossville trying to cut us off where our road came into the Lafayette & Chattanooga road. Orders were sent to the wagon train & to the artillery to hurry up, but the road was terribly muddy & it seemed to us they were creeping along. It had grown dark & the road ran through the woods. We took no time to think of being tired. It was twelve o'clock at night & we were drawing close to the junction of the two roads where we expected the attempt would be made to ambush us. Videttes marched ahead of our column, flankers were thrown out on each side of us & instructions were given to load & no body was to speak a word. If we were fired upon the flankers from that side were to fall back immediately upon the regiment & the regiment was to face in that direction & wait for the flankers to come in & then fire at the flash of the enemies guns. We reached the junction without alarm save once or twice when a twig would break under the foot of one of the flankers who were walking through the woods.

Our course now turned at right angles to the left. Colonel John W. Caldwell riding at the head of the regiment had made the turn & the first company of the regiment had turned when crack,

■ Sergeant Luke Kennedy of Company H, 6th Kentucky. On November 26 his fellow Orphans of Lewis' brigade helped cover the retreat, and just below Graysville encountered Federals advancing on their heels in the dark. "The Yankees set up a most infernal howling, resembling a pack of wolves, which has succeeded in running down the prey," wrote 9th Kentucky private John S. Jackman. "They were in strong force, and lucky for us they did not reach the road in time to fire into our column."

Another Orphan, 1st Lieut. Lot D. Young of the 4th Kentucky, remembered that "the retreat that night was one of intense hardship and excitement. Passing so near one of their pursuing columns we could actually hear them talking and see them moving around the camp fires they were kindling. Had the Federals only known it, they had our retreating column cut in two and could have made a finish of the day's work and probably the Confederacy as well."

■ Capt. Irving A. Buck, assistant adjutant general on Cleburne's staff, marked his 23rd birthday three days before the battle of Ringgold. A native Virginian who enlisted in 1861 with the 17th Virginia, Buck rode as a courier for Gen. P.G.T. Beauregard at First Manassas. He served with Cleburne from December 1862 until September 1, 1864, when he was badly wounded at Jonesboro, Ga. Cleburne reportedly wrote to the surgeon tending him: "You must save Buck. He is the best adjutant general in the army."

crack, r-o-o-l came a volley of musket shots from a skirt of woods across an open field about fifty yards wide. Col. Caldwell's horse became unruly, being startled by a flesh wound. The Col. had his pistol in his right hand & his bridle reins in his left & the wound he had received at Chicamauga in his left elbow had so disabled him that it was with great difficulty that he could manage his horse who dashed across this open field directly towards the enemy.

Several more shots were fired directly at the Col. He finally stopped his steed within a few yards of the yanks & fired his pistol into the bushes from which their shots had come & they evidently believing that he was leading a charge against them skurried off to the rear. Our men had hurriedly formed in line facing the enemy but did not fire because the Col. was in front & we might have shot him. He rode back to the regiment & sent out the flankers on the skirmish line to see that the road was clear & finding it was we hurried on to Ringold ...

## 'Hold the position at all hazards'

### Capt. Irving A. Buck
### Assistant Adjutant General
### Cleburne's Division, Hardee's Corps

About midnight [November 26] an officer from General Bragg reached Cleburne, bearing him a verbal order that he take position in a pass of the hills a short distance in rear of Ringgold, and to hold it at all costs up to a stated hour the next day. Cleburne had less than 200 men in excess of 4,000, and knowing the great numerical superiority of the pursuing foe, and that he would be totally without support, stated these facts to the officer, and also his apprehension that it would mean the destruction of his division; but he added that he was accustomed to obey orders rigidly, though as a protection to himself in case of disaster he requested that the messenger put the order in writing, which was done. At 3 o'clock a.m. of the 27th, in addition to the order from the staff officer he received the following in writing:

Major-General CLEBURNE.

GENERAL: The General [Bragg] desires that you will take strong position in the gorge of the mountain and attempt to check pursuit of enemy. He must be punished until our trains and the rear of our troops get well advanced. The reports from the rear are meager and the General is not thoroughly advised of the state of things there. Will you be good enough to report fully?

Respectfully,
GEORGE WILLIAM BRENT,
*Assistant Adjutant-General.*

The troops were put in motion and staff-officers left to conduct them across the river and to the designated position, while Cleburne rode ahead, to see as well as he could, in the darkness, the ground he was to occupy and to form a plan of defense, at the same time sending an officer to General Bragg, with information as to starting of troops, and asking more specific instructions — this after the hasty examination he was able to make. General Bragg was found at Catoosa Station, and his instructions were: "Tell General Cleburne to hold his position at all hazards, and keep back the enemy, until the artillery and transportation of the

■ Looking slightly southeast, this view of Ringgold and the gap in Taylor's Ridge greeted Osterhaus' troops the morning of November 27 as his division led Hooker's pursuit. Hooker related that pro-Union citizens and a few "contrabands" confirmed Confederate passage through Ringgold, and that the enemy was "sorely pressed, his animals exhausted, and his army hopelessly demoralized. In a small portion of it only had the officers been able to preserve regimental and company formations, many of the men having thrown away their arms." Events that day showed these reports contained a good amount of exaggeration. Cleburne's defense of the gap and ridge badly bloodied the exultant Federals, and halted pursuit for seven hours.

army is secure, the salvation of which depends upon him." Such was the brief but comprehensive order in pursuance of which Cleburne with 4,157 effectives was to confront Hooker's confident veterans, and to do battle and risk sacrifice for the safety of the army.

Taylor's Ridge rises abruptly just east of the town of Ringgold and runs nearly due north and south, and is divided by a gap of just sufficient width of level ground for the passage of the Western & Atlantic Railroad, a wagon road, and a large branch of the East Chickamauga River. The gap is about half a mile in length. The creek in its winding was bridged at three points within the first half mile of the road leading to the rear or east entrance from Dalton, thus rendering the position hazardous in case of the turning of either flank. The western mouth of the gap widens out some towards the north. The ridge on the right or north of the gap facing the town rises gradually, while on the left or south it is abrupt and precipitous ...

In front of the hill were posted three companies of the Sixth and Seventh Arkansas (consolidated) of Govan's brigade, under charge of Lieutenant Dulin of his staff. For defense of the gap were placed the remainder of Govan's brigade. Skirmishers were thrown out in front of his line, and upon his front line was posted a section of Semple's battery — two Napoleon guns — commanded by Lieut. Richard W. Goldthwaite. These pieces were charged, one with canister and the other with shell, and both screened with bushes. The artillerymen were ordered to shelter themselves in a ravine close by. All of the other troops were directed to keep concealed from view. The few cavalrymen at Cleburne's disposal had been instructed to watch the crossing of the river, and as soon as the enemy appeared to fire upon him at long range, and retreat in haste through the town and gap to make the impression that only a weak force of cavalry confronted them.

These dispositions, hastily made, were barely completed when the cavalry discharged their guns, and in seeming panic rushed into the gap, followed soon after about 8 o'clock by the Federals marching in column of fours down the railroad, with skirmishers in front and on the flanks, but completely deceived and unsuspicious of the infantry and artillery concealed and awaiting them.

Cleburne, on foot, was on Govan's front line near Goldthwaite's section. The approaching column was allowed to come within short range, when Cleburne gave the order to Goldthwaite to throw down the mask of brush and open with both guns. This fire, striking the head of the column, caused it to stagger and recoil, and being kept up rapidly, and that of the infantry joined, forced the column to seek shelter under the railroad embankment from the flank fire which the conformation of Cleburne's line enabled him to deliver on their right. Notwithstanding the suddenness and surprise of the attack, the confusion in the enemy's ranks was but brief, and with admirable steadiness they deployed in front of the gap and opened a heavy fire, at the same time moving a force and making a vigorous attack upon the right of Cleburne's line at the foot of the ridge.

■ Brig. Gen. Mark P. Lowrey commanded five Alabama and Mississippi regiments on Taylor's Ridge. Placing the 16th Alabama at the gap, Lowrey led the rest of his brigade to Cleburne's right flank. There his troops sent volley after volley into the attacking Federal ranks. Six days later he wrote: "Our spirited fire ... and a terrific rebel yell combined to strike terror to the foe, and he fled in confusion. But as they continued to move to the right, it was necessary for our line also to move to the right and to leave a bare line of skirmishers to hold the crest of the hill on the left. When my ammunition was nearly exhausted and I had sent for more, my men and officers gave me assurance with great enthusiasm that they would hold the position at the point of the bayonet and with clubbed muskets if the enemy dared to charge them. My loss was slight, but 4 killed and 35 wounded."

Major [W.A.] Taylor [commanding the consolidated 17th, 18th, 24th and 25th Texas] had previously placed skirmishers up the hill at right angles to his line, and now, with three companies, he charged this flanking force and routed it, capturing 100 prisoners and the colors of the Twenty-ninth Missouri Regiment. Another body of the enemy moved beyond Cleburne's right to ascend the ridge. Information of this movement was sent to General [Lucius E.] Polk, in rear of the gap, with orders to meet and check it. General Polk had learned of it, and with good judgment and discretion had anticipated these instructions by sending to the proper point the First Arkansas Regiment, which encountered the enemy's skirmishers near the crest of the ridge, and with the assistance of the Seventh Texas Regiment drove them back after a stubborn fight, in which the officers used their pistols, and in some instances both officers and men used rocks, and so close was the fight that a number of the enemy were knocked down with these and captured.

Large masses were now seen passing to the Confederate right, and General [Mark P.] Lowrey was moved up to strengthen Polk and prolong the right along the top of the ridge. Moving rapidly ahead of his men, Lowrey found the First Arkansas heavily engaged, but holding its own against great odds. Assuring them that support was near at hand he encouraged them to renewed efforts. The Thirty-second and Forty-fifth Mississippi, being brought up at double quick and thrown into the fight at the critical moment, the enemy gave way and went down the hill in great confusion. The two other regiments of Lowrey's brigade were now brought up, as were the two remaining ones of Polk's. Constantly reinforcing, the enemy made another attempt to carry the hill at a point farther to the right. Favored by some ravines or depressions of the slope, he concentrated a heavy column in one of these. General Polk, assisted by General Lowrey, rapidly formed a double line opposite this force and at the same time the Second Tennessee was placed so as to enfilade the flank of any troops debouching from it. Again defeated in his attack, the enemy was sent fleeing down with loss of many killed, some prisoners and a flag of the Seventy-sixth Ohio Regiment.

Meanwhile, a force of the enemy, sent to menace the extreme left, was checked by the skirmishers of Dulin on the hill, and those of Govan on the bank of the stream and to left of the railroad. During all this time Govan's men at the gap had been subjected to a heavy and continuous fire, which was replied to with spirit and effect. Cleburne, with Govan, remained on the front line in the mouth of the gap and watched every movement.

The enemy effected a lodgment in some buildings near the line, from which he kept up a well-directed and annoying fire of sharpshooters. Finally concentrating a force under cover of these buildings they charged Govan's skirmishers, but were repulsed by canister from Goldthwaite's guns, which afterwards shelled the houses with such good effect that in a great measure the annoyance from that quarter was abated. In this charge upon Govan's skirmishers a stand of colors was left lying upon the ground within 50 yards of the line, and Captain McGehee of the Second Arkansas begged permission to charge with a squad and secure it. But Cleburne refused, saying he would not have a single one of his brave men killed or disabled for the honor of its capture, so the flag remained temptingly under the covetous eyes of the gallant McGehee, who could with difficulty be restrained from making the attempt alone, notwithstanding the General's prohibition.

It was now past noon, and for nearly five hours Cleburne had been battling against odds increasing every moment. Large masses of the enemy at this time in full view justified the belief that a great part of Grant's army was now at Ringgold or near there preparing to precipitate itself upon the flanks of the single small opposing division. Between 12 and 1 o'clock a dispatch was received from General Hardee to the effect that as the trains had now reached a safe distance Cleburne was at liberty to withdraw when, in his judgment, it was advisable. Up to 12:30 o'clock the enemy's fire had been exclusively of small-arms, but getting some guns up he now opened a rapid and heavy artillery fire, but did not again advance his infantry.

About 1 o'clock Goldthwaite's guns were remasked by brush and run back by hand, without loss, followed soon after by the main line of infantry, and only skirmishers were left along the front. These were withdrawn about 2 o'clock and the bridges across the creek fired. All of this was barely accomplished when the enemy advanced simultaneously over the ridge on the right and through the gap. Cleburne took up a position on a wooded hill about a mile in rear of the eastern mouth of the gap known as "Dick's Ridge," where some slight works were thrown up and preparations made for another contest; but the enemy declined further battle, and not advancing beyond the eastern outlet of the gap, abandoned the pursuit. The division carried into action 4,157 bayonets, and its loss in killed, wounded and missing — there were only 11 of the latter — was 221. With exception of the few cavalrymen before mentioned, who took no part in the actual battle, it

■ Col. Samuel Adams (in an early-war portrait) commanded the 33rd Alabama and 18th Alabama Battalion Sharpshooters at Ringgold. As part of Lowrey's brigade, "my men have never gone into a fight so eagerly as they did in this," Adams reported, "[although] I had several men engaged in the fight who had marched from Missionary Ridge to that place entirely barefooted."

The unequal contest was summed up succinctly by one of Adams' enlisted men, Private L.W. Bigbie of Company G: "... the Yanks cam up & then [we] gave them a Decent floggen."

■ Lt. Col. Frederick W. Partridge, commander of the 13th Illinois, lost his left hand at Ringgold gap where the fighting also claimed the life of his second in command, Major Douglas R. Bushnell. "I pressed forward the Thirteenth Illinois on the extreme right to some houses within 100 yards of the enemy's artillery," wrote Brig. Gen. Charles R. Woods the following day. "The fighting on the extreme right was severe, the Thirteenth Illinois firing 100 rounds of cartridges per man, besides taking all the ammunition from their killed and wounded in order to hold their position."

was fought by this division alone. For 6 hours it held at bay a large force of Grant's army. For this engagement and this splendid defense, Cleburne, his officers and men received a vote of thanks from Congress.*

## 'Facing a hailstorm'

### An unknown private
### Company C
### 13th Illinois Volunteer Infantry

On the 27th the pursuit was continued with our division and our brigade in the advance. We moved out of the camp at 6 a.m. We soon came upon the sights to be found in the wake of an army fleeing in haste. Broken-down gun-carriages, abandoned wagons, guns, ambulances, clothes, etc. For some reason, whether for good or bad, many rebels lingered in the woods. Forty or fifty were picked up as prisoners.

Captain [W.T.] House with his men mounted, some one hundred and seventy in number, led the way followed by the Seventeenth Missouri Infantry, as skirmishers. When they came to Chickamauga Creek, near the town of Ringgold, they found the ford and a covered bridge to the right of the ford, and further up the creek, guarded by about two hundred rebel cavalry. Captain House dashed at them and drove them into town. When the rebels saw the inferiority of numbers against them, they in turn drove him out of the town and back across the ford. The Seventeenth and Twenty-ninth Missouri hastened by a circuitous route to get possession of the covered bridge. This took time, but it was better than forcing the infantry through three feet of water. The roads were bad and for some reason the artillery was not up — a mistake; had it been the enemy could have been driven out with much loss of life and limb.

As our regiment came up, we passed to the right of the ford up the stream to the covered bridge over it, and through the town by flank. Just ahead of us were the Seventeenth, Twenty-ninth and Thirty-first Missouri regiments that had been skirmishing up to the foot of Taylor Ridge, where the enemy were strongly posted. The rebels pressed upon these and drove them back in some confusion. We then passed up near the depot and filed to the right into line squarely across the gap, into an open space. The boys were as chipper as could be, and hardly expecting so much danger so near at hand.

We had scarcely got faced to the front, when from a clump of young trees a masked battery of two pieces belched forth grape and canister. This passed through the right wing of our regiment. By it Captain Beardsley of Company D was wounded, John Dyke-

---

* On February 9, 1864, the Confederate Congress approved a joint resolution of thanks to Cleburne and those under his command at Ringgold. It read:

"*Resolved,* That the thanks of Congress are due, and are hereby tendered, to Maj. Gen. Patrick R. Cleburne, and the officers and men under his command, for the victory obtained by them over superior forces of the enemy at Ringgold Gap, in the State of Georgia, on the 27th day of November, 1863, by which the advance of the enemy was impeded, our wagon train and most of our artillery saved, and a large number of the enemy killed and wounded."

man of Company C had his thigh broken, and Martin Blair of Company A was bruised. Poor Dykeman, I stood near him as he went down with a groan. He lingered along till January 10th, 1864, and then died of his wounds.

This was a surprise and a severe test of our nerve and power of concession as a regiment. At a word from the officers, all the men lay flat on the ground but stayed in place.

Soon after this burst of canister upon us, the word came to advance some skirmishers to the front of the line. Lieutenant Colonel Partridge ordered forward Companies A and B, and went with them. The fire was directed toward the two pieces of artillery, so as to keep them from firing if possible. Among these skirmishers John D. Davis, of Company B, was wounded in the mouth before he got in a shot. He brought off his gun, went to the rear, had his wound dressed and came back to the front.

The order then came to advance the whole regiment. Major [Douglas R.] Bushnell gave the command, when the men arose and bending as though facing a hailstorm, moved most gallantly to the front. I am not prepared to say that the regiment understood just what was expected of it. I think if the command would have been given, they would have gone into the gap, and to the mouth of the guns. As it was, they went as far as a log-house located at the mouth of the gap and then sought shelter behind it and the barn, pig-pen and some old railroad ties near by.

But before we had reached this line the battery had opened upon us with canister sweeping through about where the colors were moving. Sergeant Patrick Reilly of Company K bore the colors and went down with a grape-shot through his breast. His life's blood soaked the Stars and Stripes and stained most of its folds. Of course, the colors went down with the brave man, but did not long remain. Corporal Joseph Sackett of Company C and a member of the Color-guard took up "Old Glory," now more sacred because it was drenched with patriotic blood, and bore it for some distance. As the regiment was no longer advancing, this brave man dropped the flag through the fork of an apple tree and cast himself upon the ground by it. It remained swinging under the eyes of the rebels during the rest of the fight.

The fight went on in the most determined way with constant losses to us. Colonel Partridge received a painful wound in his left hand while standing near the barn not far from the bank of the creek. Wishing to have it dressed, he asked one of Company B to seek Major Bushnell and ask him to take command of the regiment for a time. But the Major could not receive the word, for his ear was already heavy in death. With some others he had sought shelter behind some railroad ties, for unnecessary exposure was no virtue at such a time. A bullet from the enemy had grazed the end of a tie, and passing into his forehead lodged in the back part of his neck.

The command was given into the hands of Captain Walter Blanchard of Company K, who was located behind the log-house spoken of. Ere long, while he stood at the corner of the house, he was struck by a grape-shot that tore his knee all into pieces. He died from the effects of it about one week later. In this same house Charles Beckman, of Company K, was struck and had his right arm broken while in the act of shooting out of the window. He gave a little shriek as the bone snapped, and then was as brave as a man could be.

■ 1st Lieut. William E. Ware (top), 27th Missouri, served as a XV Corps' brigade staff officer in the battle. On the back of this portrait he inscribed: "On Nov 27th 1863 I carried the order to the 13th Ills. to make the charge at Ringgold, Ga. where Patrick Riley[sic] fell." Reilly (bottom), 13th Illinois color sergeant, was struck in the chest and instantly killed.

# 'I asked permission to amputate'

Stoically posed for the camera, four of the five Federal soldiers shown here lost limbs at Ringgold. Their faces show little of the excruciating pain endured, but empty sleeves and trouser legs bear mute testimony to their personal sacrifice.

In the photograph above, 1st Sergeant Joseph E. Goodman of Company D, 147th Pennsylvania, is flanked by Lt. Col. Robert Avery (left), 102nd New York, and Capt. Charles T. Greene. Avery was shot on November 24 in the lower right thigh at Lookout Mountain, shortly after regimental Major Gilbert M. Elliott was fatally wounded. At Ringgold, Goodman was struck above the left knee as his regiment attacked Taylor's Ridge near the 7th Ohio's left flank.

Greene served as assistant adjutant general of the 3rd Brigade, 2nd Division, XII Corps, formerly commanded by his father, Brig. Gen. George S. Greene, who also was badly wounded a month earlier at Wauhatchie. The elder Greene was succeeded by Col. David Ireland, who reported that his staff officer "was struck by an unexploded shell, which passed through his horse and carried away his right leg below the knee. The concussion was such that it threw him up about five feet, and on falling he was severely injured."

The 12th Missouri of Osterhaus' division suffered heavily at Ringgold, especially in officers. Six fell when this German regiment converged on the railroad gap, including Col. Hugo Wangelin, who lost his right arm at the elbow. Perhaps the worst injured of any soldier to survive the battle was Capt. Henry A. Kircher of Company E. After a bullet shattered his right arm and knocked him to the

■ Capt. Henry A. Kircher

■ Col. Hugo Wangelin

ground, a second ball smashed his left leg, splitting the tibia wide enough for a finger to be inserted into the fracture. Then, while being carried helpless to the rear, he was grazed by a third bullet, inflicting a flesh wound.

Still conscious, Kircher was taken to a nearby house, laid on a table and examined by regimental Surgeon Joseph Spiegelhalter. A short time later, the doctor recorded the scene in his letterbook: "The Capt. took it very easy & told me that I would have to cut off his arm. [I] informed him that I was going to put him under the influence of chloroform in order to examine his wounds closely & that I had as much fear for his leg, as for his arm; at the same time I asked his permission to amputate his leg also, if it should be necessary. This he gave me, by telling me to do whatever I thought best."

Spiegelhalter performed the double amputation, removing the captain's arm six inches below the shoulder and sawing through his leg "between the middle and lower third." Late on November 30 Kircher arrived by ambulance in Chattanooga, and eventually returned home to Belleville, Ill., where the photograph at left was taken in 1864.

■ Gen. Joseph Hooker (on white horse at center) and staff confer as XII Corps' troops march past Ringgold's railroad depot to join the battle on Taylor's Ridge. Col. Abel Godard's 60th New York arrived in time to relieve Osterhaus' hard-pressed troops. The 60th's chaplain, Rev. Richard Eddy, later wrote: "So terrible was the ordeal through which they had passed that, at its close, officers and men were, for a while, unable to speak, but clasped hands and embraced each other ... Few, if any, showed no marks of the strife. Colonel Godard, who, going before his men, gave the only order, 'Come on, boys!' had eleven bullet holes in his clothing and boot legs, his metallic sword scabbard was hit by a ball and considerably damaged while it was lying across his arm and partly against his side, yet, providentially, he was unhurt."

Robert Skinner was shot while passing from the pig-pen to the barn. I saw him fall. Seaman of the same company was shot and died from the effects of a hip amputation the next day. Charles V. Peck was struck on the top of his head, and with the brain open to the air, was living yet at the close of the battle. W.B. Howe of Company E had four fingers shot off of one hand and three off of the other. Ed Sheehey of Company H seemed not to have any sense of danger. He was in the house; he shuffled his feet and sang and swore in the thickest of the fight. Those who were either killed on the field, or died from wounds soon after, numbered twelve, while the killed and wounded were sixty.

After we had fought for some time and our ammunition was about all gone, some New York troops were ordered in as a support or relief. But they only came in to get many killed and wounded. We had fought our way in and could hold the ground with less loss than any other body of troops. We learned that the reason for crowding so closely and strongly on the gap was the hope of breaking through the lines before the enemy could get out of the way on the other side, and then be compelled to lose heavily in war materiel, if not in men. It failed. Another way would have been better; fewer men would have been sacrificed.

In this house in the gap a family lived. They were in the cellar while the battle was on, and made their appearance at the close of it. There was an able-bodied man in the number. He claimed to be innocent, but was counted among the prisoners and given a free ride North. The woman of the house scolded freely for making her feather bed bloody from Captain Blanchard's wound.

A graphic account is given of Captain Landgraber getting up his battery to our relief. [Capt. Clemens Landgraeber, commander of Battery F, 2nd Missouri Light Artillery]. He got within sound of our firing, but the road was filled so that he could not pass. But he was wild to go to the front. He dashed fiercely about until he got the order to give him the road. His men were mounted, and he was known as the "Flying Dutchman." As soon as he secured the right of way, he fairly flew along that stony road, bidding it to be cleared for his men. He said, "Oh my Gott, the Twelfth Missouri and Thirteenth Illinois are being killed, and I am not there to help them." These two regiments had won his special affection.

Then came the word "Forward." Spurs and whips were applied until those guns nearly flew to pieces as they went sounding over the rough road. Coming to Chickamauga Creek the speed was not slackened. As they passed through the creek the water flew as if a cyclone had gone by. A few moments more and some of the guns were in our rear and sending shells over our heads and into the enemy's lines that made music to us sweeter than the notes of the dulcimer.

## 'A lesson in good manners'

### Private William W. Gibson
### Company D
### 6th/7th Arkansas Volunteer Infantry

About daybreak on the morning of November 27, 1863, we were ordered to ford the Chickamauga River just west of the little town of Ringgold. The morning was dreadfully cold, and thin sheets and crystals of ice were dancing over the water. Many of the boys sailed in like horses with their harness on, while others, more thoughtful of their future comfort, disrobed themselves of their nether garments. I was among the latter, but had the misfortune, when about mid-stream, to stumble over a boulder and drop my pants in the water.

Crossing over, we were marched rapidly up through the town to a narrow gorge where the river had cut its way through the mountain, and through which ran the Western & Atlantic Railroad. Here we formed a line of battle, facing the town. To our right extended a long, high ridge; to the left, between the railway and the river, was a little narrow strip of wooded valley widening out in the direction of the town.

The ridge above mentioned was selected by Gen. Cleburne as his line of defense, and on which the division was at once formed. Company D, to which I belonged, and Company K of the Sixth and Seventh Arkansas Regiment were posted in the little valley to the left of the railroad; while Company E was sent across to the south side of the river where it took position on a high bluff. A skirmish line was thrown forward about one hundred or one hundred and fifty yards to the edge of the timber, while our two companies were ordered to lie down in line of battle. A blue cloud of Federals could be seen advancing through the town, preceded by a heavy skirmish line; they were soon engaged with our skirmishers and were driven to take shelter behind barns, houses, fences, etc., where they began a galling fire on our position.

■ Col. Daniel C. Govan, 2nd Arkansas Infantry, commanded the Arkansas brigade of Cleburne's division and defended Ringgold Gap proper in column of regiments. Positioned at the gap's mouth, the 5th/13th Arkansas supported two brush-masked Napoleon 12-pounders of Semple's Alabama Battery, commanded by 1st Lieut. Richard W. Goldthwaite. When the advancing Federal battle line approached within 150 yards, the artillerists fired solid shot and canister "with terrible effect," wrote Govan. "The line reeled and staggered and was finally driven back in confusion. Every attempt to force our line met with a similar repulse ..."

Goldthwaite's own report echoed Govan's: "So discouraged and dispirited were they by their defeat in every quarter that at one time, when attempting to cross, the mere sight of the piece and the cannoneers training it upon them (for the mask of brush had been blown away) made them break in confusion."

■ Brig. Gen. Lucius E. Polk commanded six Arkansas and Tennessee regiments, four of them consolidated, at Ringgold. Early on November 27 he was stationed in rear of the gap, but learned from a straggler that a Federal battle line was moving to flank Cleburne's right. Anticipating his commander's order, Polk rushed one regiment, then half his brigade, to the top of Taylor's Ridge just moments ahead of the Yankees, blocking their movement with rifle fire as each company arrived and found position in line. Eventually reinforced by several regiments from Lowrey's brigade, Polk's troops, numbering only 545 effectives, held off three successive Federal attempts to carry the crest.

Polk, a nephew of Gen. Leonidas Polk, was seriously wounded at Kennesaw Mountain the following June. This injury, his fourth in three years, incapacitated him from further service.

About this time Gens. Cleburne and Breckinridge came along our line on foot, observing the disposition of the enemy's forces in our front. They stopped just at the right of our company, where they remained a few minutes, sheltered behind a large tree. I saw a line of battle moving across our front to the left, and not exceeding three hundred yards from us. As their left wing reached the enfilading point a masked battery, just across the railroad on the spur of the ridge, caught them with double-shotted canister from all of the guns at once. Every man fell to the ground, and, from the way their hats, caps, guns and accouterments went flying in the air, I had not a doubt that the entire line was annihilated, and exclaimed: "By Jove, boys, it killed them all." Gen. Breckinridge and "Old Pat" smiled at my boyish credulity, while the latter said to me good-naturedly: "If you don't lie down, young man, you are liable to find that there are enough left for you to get the top of your head shot off."

In a little while our two companies were ordered forward to our skirmish line, each man taking such shelter as came his way. A good-sized white oak tree fell to my lot and did me good service for a couple of hours or longer, during which time I verily believe it was struck by a thousand balls, and only once was I touched — a mere scratch. While behind that tree I witnessed an incident never seen by me before or afterwards on any battlefield.

Hearing frequent reports near me resembling the discharge of a small pistol, I listened and watched to tell from where it came, and was not long in seeing small puffs of smoke in mid-air near me from which the reports came, and I knew at once that the enemy were shooting explosive bullets. I am sure there can be no mistake about this matter, for I saw and heard more than a dozen.

All this while there was "music in the air," and the earth was fairly trembling under the shock of battle up on the right. The boys afterwards told us that the enemy first came at them in a "rollicking" sort of way. In their first advance they came through the woods, whooping and yelling in imitation of driving cattle. They found the "cattle" all right, but somehow there was a hitch in the driving. Gen. Cleburne had formed the division in double line of battle, one immediately behind the other. As the enemy advanced to close range the front line would fire and lie down and load, the rear line firing over their heads. Time after time line after line of Federals charged up that ridge against Cleburne's lines, only to be shattered and hurled back in the valley.

Things were "distressingly interesting" behind my tree, the bare exposure of my hat brim or end of my gun barrel was greeted with a shower of balls. It was only a few yards on my left to the river, so I made a break in that direction and landed safely behind its protecting bank. Passing down the bank thirty or forty yards, I found my chum, Phil Turner, enjoying one of the softest snaps to be found on that battlefield. In a small washout near the top of the bank Phil had ensconced himself, with plenty of room to load and fire.

Joining him, we had a picnic firing at short range for some time, when I happened to notice that all firing had ceased along our line, and, what was more significant, there was not a "Reb" in sight. We learned afterwards that the order had been given for the command to draw off quietly a few at a time, and our failure to get this word was the cause of our being left. I called Phil's attention to the fact that our people were all gone, and that we two, for the moment, were enjoying the distinction of fighting the greater portion of Grant's army. Realizing the inequality of the contest, Phil suggested that we must get out of there, and get out at once. In order that we might not draw too heavy a fire, he proposed that we go one at a time, at the same time telling me to make the break. This I did, and after running some seventy-five or one hundred yards I felt like nothing but the swiftest of bullets could catch me; but about this time one did catch me on the thigh, and I thought myself a "goner," but looked around in time to see the bullet fall at my heel, proving conclusively that my movement up that gorge was so near in unison with the speed of that ball, coupled with the fact that it had first struck a tree and glanced to my leg, that the hurt amounted to a severe bruise only, and in nowise retarded my speed. Another run of two hundred yards or so took me to the railroad bridge over which the command had crossed, with Phil close at my heels.

This bridge was one of those old-style structures having a shingle roof over it and weatherboarded sides. To our dismay, however, we found that our people had set it afire after crossing, and it was then burning fiercely. Gens. Breckinridge and Cleburne were sitting on their horses on the opposite bank, watching it burn; they called and told us that there was a ford down to our right a hundred yards or so. Remembering our experience of the early morning, Phil said he could not wade that river again. "I am going to cross on this bridge or not at all," he said. I remonstrated, seized him by the arm, and tried to pull him with me in the direction of the ford, but, jerking loose, he hastily wound his blanket around his head and dashed into the burning bridge, leaving not a doubt in my mind that he had gone to an instant and horrible death. Running down to the ford, I waded over, the bullets splashing the water like hailstones around me as I did so.

Once over, my route led me near the point where the generals were still standing. As I passed Gen. Cleburne I said: "General, that battery didn't quite kill all of them this morning, but what was left have been taught a lesson in good manners." He instantly recalled the incident of the morning, and smilingly replied: "You are quite right, young man. I am proud of what you boys have done today, and I don't think they will bother us any more this evening." With such a compliment as this I felt that if I only had Turner out of that burning bridge I could go back and fight them again. By this time the bruise on my leg, caused by the glancing ball, was paining me so that I could not help limping, seeing which [Cleburne] very kindly inquired as to the nature of my hurt and congratulated me on my escape.

On going down the railroad Turner was one of the first men I came up with; and what a sight he was, to be sure! His blanket, of course, went up in the flames at the bridge, his hair below his hat was all singed off, his eyelashes, eyebrows and mustache were all gone, while his clothes were scorched and charred all over. Jack Williams, his bunkmate, said of him that night that he "looked like a cat that might have been pulled through Hades by the tail;" that he could interpose no valid objection to Phil's being sacrificed as a burnt offering upon the altar of his country, if the exigencies of the case demanded it; but did hate like blazes to lose that blanket, and thought that a detail should be appointed to

■ Private John Rulle of Company K, 2nd Tennessee Infantry, photographed early in the war heavily armed with musket, revolver and hunting knife. His understrength regiment belonging to Polk's brigade took 133 officers and men into the Ringgold battle, and assisted the 1st Arkansas in repulsing several Federal assaults on the Confederate right flank. The 2nd suffered only nine casualties (all wounded) in the uneven contest, including Col. William D. Robison, shot through the arm.

■ Major Willard Warner led the 76th Ohio almost to the summit of Taylor's Ridge when its ranks were riddled by Confederate musketry. For 20 minutes these Ohioans withstood bullets and flying rocks, their flanks bent back to oppose enfilading fire. "No better fighting was ever done," observed an Iowa colonel who witnessed the 76th's assault, "nor was fighting ever done under more hopeless circumstances. Major Warner did all that a brave and efficient officer could do — at one time seizing the colors from the fallen color bearer, going to the front and cheering the men forward."

Nine officers and men were killed or wounded carrying the regiment's colors. The regimental flag was lost to Confederates of Polk's brigade when Warner's exhausted troops were forced to retire. In May 1914 the banner was returned to the state of Ohio during a United Confederate Veterans' reunion in Jacksonville, Fla. Among the five commissioners accepting the flag were Capt. Charles H. Kibler and Corporal William C. Montgomery, who lost an arm carrying the 76th's national color at Ringgold.

"keep Phil out of the fire, as he did not seem to have sense enough to keep out himself."

The check of the enemy for a day gave Bragg's army ample time to reach a place of safety, and taught the Federals that "marching through Georgia" was not all smooth sailing.

## 'A terrific attack upon the colors'

### Capt. Charles H. Kibler
### Company D
### 76th Ohio Volunteer Infantry
### Assistant Adjutant General
### 1st Brigade, 1st Division, XV Corps

On the 26th, the Command started in pursuit of the retreating enemy, on the highway leading to Ringgold, Georgia, a station on the Railroad about 15 miles south of Chattanooga. This station was not reached that day, and the Division bivouacked, as was supposed for the night, about five miles from the station. In the night, however, the command was aroused from sleep and again marched south, arriving after daylight near the station.

It was found that a bridge over a considerable stream had been destroyed by the enemy. The circumstance necessitated a detour to the right, on the right bank of the stream, to reach another bridge to the west of the station. After crossing the bridge, the First Brigade, which was in the advance, proceeded on the highway to a point where it crossed the railroad track a short distance south of Ringgold Station. Other regiments of the Brigade had preceded the 76th Ohio and had been posted further south, and nearer the gap in the mountain, through which ran a rivulet and through which had been constructed the railroad track and the highway. The ridge on the east of the highway, called Taylor's Ridge, and the railway track, ran parallel, while the ridge to their west stretched in a course widening from the gap. Both were heavily wooded and were manned by rebel troops. A battery was located in the gap.

As the 76th Ohio arrived at the crossing mentioned, Major Willard Warner, in command, was ordered to take his regiment up the part of Taylor's Ridge nearest the crossing, and turn the flank of the enemy who were delivering a deadly fire upon the regiments of the Brigade which had been posted in the flat between the ridges. These regiments were helpless and were exposed to the fire of the enemy who were concealed in the woods, and to the artillery fire from the guns at the gap. The 76th Ohio was then small, with probably no more effective strength than 200 officers and men.

The order to advance up the ridge was a grave error, following the graver error of an attack in front upon the enemy who occupied the natural stronghold. It was evident that the enemy occupied in force the top and a greater part of the sides of that ridge. In fact, the ridges on each side of the gap, and the gap itself, were held by the division of Gen. Patrick R. Cleburne, one of the best fighting divisions, east or west, of the rebel armies. This fact ought to have been known by the General in command of that part of the Union Army which was in pursuit on that highway. To

send a small regiment up the ridge, no general advance being intended, was to invite disaster. It is true that after the advance of the 76th Ohio began, the 4th Iowa was ordered to follow and support the 76th, and some time afterward two regiments of the Second Brigade of the Division advanced a part of the way up the ridge, at a point further south and nearer the gap. By an unfortunate *contratemps* they did not reach the crest of the ridge. Only the 4th Iowa supported the 76th Ohio.

At about 9 o'clock a.m. the Regiment, in line of battle, commenced the ascent. The side of the ridge, often called a mountain, was rugged and steep, and covered for a great part with small, loose stones, or shale, which made the ascent slow and exceedingly toilsome. But it moved slowly up, meeting with little opposition until it was near the crest. There it encountered the enemy in great force, but notwithstanding, it pressed forward to the crest and halted. The view from the top of the ridge disclosed a large force of the enemy in front and others hurrying to oppose the 76th Ohio. Here the 4th Iowa, Lieut. Colonel George Burton in command, joined the 76th, and the two regiments thenceforth acted together. One account estimates the force of the enemy opposing the two regiments at a brigade. This force not only covered the

■ Creighton's brigade charges up Taylor's Ridge, from a sketch by *Harper's Weekly* artist Theodore R. Davis. The Pennsylvanians and Ohioans marched with parade-ground precision halfway up the steep slope before firing, but the ascent and enemy bullets quickly sapped the strength to maintain formation. When the 7th Ohio broke and fled downhill, the 28th Pennsylvania's left flank was exposed and Col. Thomas J. Ahl was helpless to keep order. "The men sheltered themselves behind trees and rocks as much as possible, being unable to move forward," Ahl wrote. "It was as much as a man could do to climb the mountain without any opposition, let alone in the face of double his own numbers pouring down heavy volleys of musketry on him."

# 'Senseless exposure of brave men'

■ Color Corporal William C. Montgomery of Company B lost his right arm at Ringgold. This portrait, showing the 76th Ohio's shot-torn national flag, was taken during veteran furlough at the gallery of Z.P. McMillen in Newark, Ohio, late winter 1864.

In the 76th Ohio, one of every four soldiers taken into the fight on Taylor's Ridge was killed, wounded or captured. Seven officers and men (including four color guards) were shot down carrying the 76th's flags.

"The regiment numbered about 250 effectives," wrote 1st Lieut. Charles D. Miller. "It was led by Major Willard Warner who had orders to go to the crest of the ridge. The fire was very destructive as the men climbed up from one rock to another; yet we could not hold against a superior number of the enemy in front. Major Warner ordered the men to fall back slowly with their faces to the foe and to keep up fire as well as they could. Both flags were carried to the top of the hill but so many of the color bearers were shot down that the Regimental or blue flag was lost. The national colors, however, were saved and carried back, but not until two officers and several of the color guards were killed or wounded. As one after another fell, the flag was picked up by yet another and held to the breeze."

Private Charles A. Willison of Company I remembered: "Our regiment was double-quicked through Ringgold at such a pace that, exhausted as I was from our long march, I was unable to keep up. In the confusion they were sent off to the left, while I, keeping straight on, got mixed up with the eastern troops in the thick of the fight directly in front. Men were being hit all around me and had I been instantly killed among these strange troops, it is doubtful my identity would have been ascertained ... From my position I could look back over the bottom land approaching the Gap and see our columns advancing in line of battle. It seemed like senseless exposure of brave men. They were in unobstructed and easy range of the battery posted on the ridge in the Gap, and were mowed down in swaths by the grape and canister that swept the field ..."

■ Capt. Beverly W. Lemert (left) lost eight men from Company A, including Private John W. Gardner (center), who was slightly wounded. 1st Lieut. John J. Metzger (right) of Company C suffered a severe arm wound. Note XV Corps badge worn by Metzger in this war's-end portrait.

...has been wiped out." "I die freely; Chicka-

KILLED AND WOUNDED OF THE 76TH OHIO, ON THE 27TH OF NOVEMBER, AT RINGGOLD, GA.

Company A—Sergt Jas W Howill, Corp Amos Porter, Joel D Hanley, killed; Lieut John Lemmert, dangerously wounded—left thigh broken; David Lloyd, dangerously wounded; S Rodgers, severely wounded; Sylvester Redmon, slightly wounded; John W Gardner, slightly wounded.

Company B—Captain Ira B French, killed, Lieut Jno R Miller, Corp Hiram Webb, Joseph Lyman, killed; Color Corp W Montgomery, severely wounded—right arm amputated; Corp Joseph Brooks, severely.

Company C—Corp Philip Wilson, Joseph Jennings, killed; Lieut John Metzgar, severely wounded, arm; Sergt Geo W Preston, dangerously wounded; Corp W F Bishop, severely wounded, foot; Warren Silvo, severely wounded, shoulder; Geo Wiley, dangerously wounded, lung.

Company D—Corp Wm Dilley, killed; Sergt George Grum, mortally wounded; Color Corp Johnson Haughey, severely, in hand.

Company E—Corp Jas G Mossman, Basil C Williamson, Jas Lalley, John Reef, John Wagoner, Charles A Oster, John Nolan, Thos Welch, killed; Sergt Frederick G Uhl, severely wounded, left shoulder; Corp Lawrence Schwenenger, slightly wounded; Corp Edward Arnold, dangerously wounded, right arm and left side; Color Corp Silas Priest, dangerously wounded, left lung; Joseph Meister, Joseph Brothers, severely wounded, Lewis Kline, dangerously wounded, right lung; Jacob Bowers, severely wounded, right wrist; Corp Timothy Sullivant, Charles Harvey, supposed to be wounded and prisoners

Company F—Thos Wilgard, slightly wounded, arm; Jas Patton, slightly, in face.

Company G—Corp Henthorn, slightly wounded; Corp Philip Evans, severely, thigh and scrotum; Corp Asias W Dicken, severely, shoulder; Corp C Disbinaett, severely, arm and knee; Philip Harting, slightly, arm and knee

Company H—Sergt Wm Baughman, killed; Lieut Simeon B Wall very dangerously wounded through lungs; Sergt C B Pendleton, severely, head; Amos P Williams, very severely, in right shoulder; David Cedars, slightly, in hand.

Company I—Chas Hart, very dangerously wounded in right side; Wm Lorimer, very severely in left shoulder and lung; Lawrence Roach, severely, in shoulder; Lyman Humphrey, slightly, in wrist; W H H Urier, slightly, in hand; Frank Jacobs, slightly

Company K—Eli Cavender, very dangerously wounded in lung; H B Goldsmith, severely, in left shoulder; Corp Wm Shiol, slightly, in face; Jacob Williams, slightly,

■ Casualty list published December 7, 1863 in the *Cincinnati Daily Commercial*.

■ 1st Lieut. John R. Miller of Company B was acting regimental adjutant when killed on November 27.

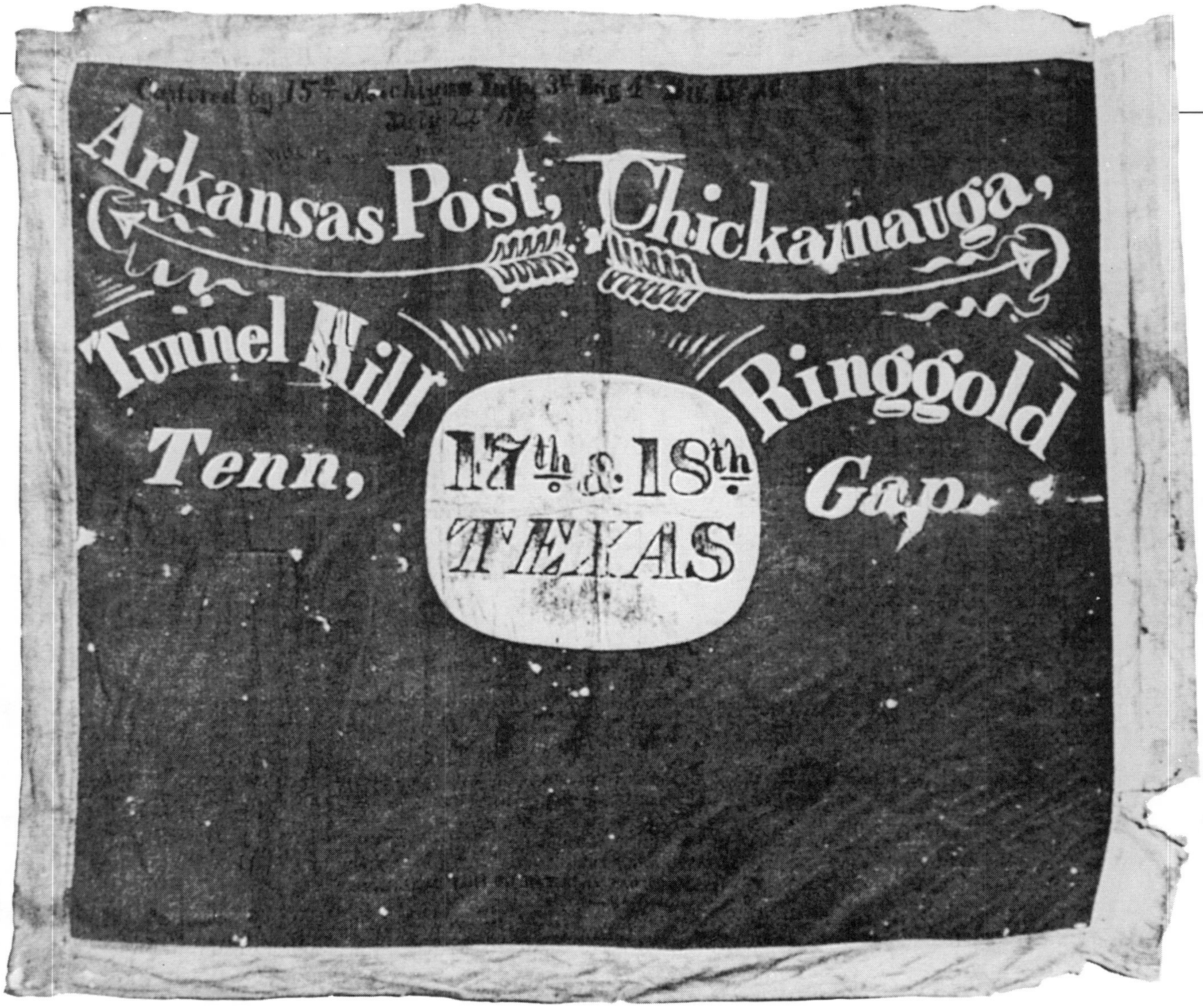


■ Hardee-pattern replacement flags of 1864 prominently display "Ringgold Gap" among battle honors won by two of Cleburne's veteran regiments. At right, the torn banner of the 33rd Alabama (Lowrey's brigade) was made of blue cotton flannel. The flag of the consolidated 17th & 18th Texas Dismounted Cavalry (Granbury's brigade), above, was captured in the battle of Atlanta, July 22, 1864, by Sergeant Major Andrew LaForge, 15th Michigan. The trophy was deposited in the Michigan state archives and remained there until 1914, when the flag was returned to Texas.

front of the two regiments, but also both flanks, so that their flanks were bent back to oppose the enemy. The two regiments met a hot front and enfilading fire. They held this line for about 10 minutes.

Here Capt. Ira D. French and Lieut. John R. Miller of Company B were killed, and Lieutenants John A. Lemert and Simeon B. Wall of Company A were mortally wounded. Here 10 of the men were killed and 40 officers and men were wounded. Here there was a terrific attack upon the colors of the 76th Ohio. Here eight of the color-bearers were killed and wounded. When the flag fell out of the hands of the killed or wounded bearer, another soldier seized and raised it to the "battle and the breeze." At one time Major Warner seized the flag from a fallen color-bearer, and raised it till he delivered it to another soldier. Captain French was killed while planting the flag. Lieutenants James M. Blackburn and John J. Metzger were wounded while bearing the flag. William C. Montgomery of Company C, the color-bearer, lost an arm. Joseph W. Jennings of Company C was killed while bearing the flag, and Corporal Johnston Haughey of Company D, and Sergeant George W. Preston of Company C, were wounded while holding the flag. It will be seen how dear the flag was to the men of the Regiment, and how unflinching was their determination to keep it afloat and retain it.

Gen. Cleburne, in his report of the operations at Ringgold, states that his troops "captured the colors of the 76th Ohio." This is not true of the [national] flag; but it is true of a banner, or shield of the State of Ohio, carried with the flag. It was a field of blue on which was inscribed a golden eagle and the number of the regiment. It fell into the hands of the enemy in this way:

It was carried by Silas Priest, a color guard. Receiving a grievous wound, he fell forward toward the enemy. In the fall the banner was projected further forward into the narow space of about 100 feet between the opposing lines. Several men rushed forward to recover it, but were wounded. Just then, the movement to the rear began, and the banner was left in the hands of the enemy. No valor could have rescued it. Later, the dead were buried on the crest of the hill near the place where they fell. The grief of the survivors was nonetheless acute, that they were vain sacrifices upon the altar of their country.

Seeing that the line at the crest could not be held against the superior force of the enemy on the front and flanks, or that the consequence of holding it longer would be annihilation or capture, Major Warner gave the order to retire down the hill to a more defensible position. This order was to retire slowly and fighting. It was an order full of peril. Would the men be firm, or would they interpret the order as a rout and give way to confusion and flight? They did not so interpret it. In line of battle, fighting, and in as good order as the conformation of the ground permitted, the regiment backed down about 150 feet and re-formed upon a line where the flanks were not endangered. They renewed the fight there under better auspices, and remained undislodged until the enemy retired. There is no record of more than a single act of poltroonery or skulking.

Pity it is that this splendid valor and endurance were in vain. It was not the fault of the regiment or its commanding officer. They were ordered into this dangerous place, and being there, stood as a rock against the assaults of an overpowering enemy.

■ Private James Beeson of Company H, 1st Arkansas Infantry. When Federal skirmishers attempted flanking the Confederate right, his regiment was rushed to that point and began firing by companies into the enemy only 20 yards away. After 30 minutes of obstinate fighting the Arkansans, commanded by Col. John W. Colquitt, drove the Federals to the foot of the ridge. Another late-morning assault also was repulsed within 20 paces of the summit, and Beeson's comrades captured the 76th Ohio's regimental flag. Colquitt later received the trophy from his father-in-law, Gen. Hardee.

Cleburne lauded the 1st Arkansas' stout defense, singling out the regiment "for its courage and constancy. In the battle the officers fought with pistols and with rocks, and so close was the fight that some of the enemy were knocked down with the latter missiles and captured."

# 'Roosters, walk right over them!'

■ Capt. Ernst J. Krieger

**No regiment on either side at Ringgold suffered heavier losses in officers than the 7th Ohio. Twelve of 13 who climbed Taylor's Ridge were hit — five of them fatally. In less than an hour, command of the regiment devolved upon Capt. Ernst J. Krieger of Company K, the lone officer to escape the battle unscathed. His after-action report described the 7th's ill-fated assault:**

When the first line reached the foot of the hill they halted to return fire. The rear line [composed of the 7th and 66th Ohio] continued its march, passed through the first line, and commenced ascending the hill. The Seventh ascended a ravine, which enabled the enemy to direct an effective fire on us from the front and both flanks, making us lose severely all along the line. The steepness of the ascent necessarily made our progress very slow, but the regiment persevered in its advance, not stopping to return the fire. The regiment nearly gained the crest of the hill, within a few yards of the rebel breastworks, when their fire became too heavy and effective for flesh and blood to withstand. Here Lieut. Col. O.J. Crane fell ... and as a mere handful only remained, and as there was no hope of carrying the hill, Colonel Creighton, commanding the brigade, ordered us to fall back to the foot of the hill, which we did, carrying as many of our wounded with us as possible.

On reaching the foot of the hill, finding that I was the only officer of the regiment not disabled, I took command, rallied the men and rejoined the brigade. Soon after reaching the foot of the hill, Colonel Creighton received his mortal wound, and soon after died from its effects.

The number of enlisted men who were in line at the commencement of the battle was 206, of whom [13] were killed, [48] were wounded, none missing. Most of the wounds are severe ones.

We were repulsed, but not disgraced; humbled, but not humiliated. All that men could do against superior numbers and the advantageous position of the enemy was done. We retired, upon orders from General Geary, from the hill with the consciousness that we had not dishonored our flag.

■ 2nd Lieut. Isaac C. Jones
Company C, killed

■ 2nd Lieut. Dwight H. Brown
Company A, wounded

■ 1st Lieut. Morris Baxter
Adjutant, mortally wounded

■ 2nd Lieut. Joseph Cryne
Company I, killed

In brigade command for only three days, the 7th Ohio's colonel, William R. Creighton (left), addressed his troops just before ascending the ridge: "We are ordered to take those heights, and I expect to see you roosters walk right over them!" Near the summit, Lt. Col. Orrin J. Crane (right) was shot dead. Creighton himself was fatally wounded minutes later.

Nicknamed "roosters" in the Army of the Potomac, many in the 7th wore metallic pins symbolizing their pride of reputation, as seen on Crane's chest at right.

■ Capt. Samuel McClelland
Company H, wounded

■ 1st Lieut. George Lockwood
Company D, wounded

■ Capt. William D. Braden
Company G, wounded

■ 2nd Lieut. Christian Nesper
Company K, wounded

■ Col. James A. Williamson, 4th Iowa, commanded a brigade of six Hawkeye State regiments in Osterhaus' division. Arriving at Ringgold about mid-morning on the 27th, Williamson sent the 4th Iowa forward to support the 76th Ohio's assault and personally led his remaining Iowans up the bullet-scarred slope to their left. Within 75 paces of the summit he was surprised to see three regiments of Creighton's brigade ascend the ridge in near-perfect order and pass through the ranks of his left flank. The Iowans cautioned the newcomers but, as Williamson reported, "they replied they would teach 'Western troops a lesson,' and advanced a short distance farther, when the enemy opened a terrific fire on them. They stood manfully for a minute or two, when they gave way, and came down like an avalanche, carrying everything before them, and to some extent propagating panic among my regiments. [Creighton's] regiments tried to go up as if on parade where [my] men could barely have gone up by clinging to the rocks and bushes."

## 'We placed them side by side'

### Capt. Henry G. Ankeny
### Company H
### 4th Iowa Volunteer Infantry

Ringold, Georgia
November 28, 1863.

My dear Wife:

I wrote to you a few lines while on the march the night before last, which I hope you will receive.

Yesterday morning, after marching all night, we came upon the enemy strongly posted on Taylor Ridge and Gap. Our division was in advance and first met the enemy. The 4th Iowa and [76th] Ohio charged up the ridge and took the crest, but in doing so we met with severe and irreparable loss — the bravest of the brave. These fell to rise no more, and Adams County again must mourn its dead and wounded. Sergeant Rufus E. Campbell who was acting as orderly was shot through the head and killed instantly. Corp. Moore was shot through the right breast and foot. Neither of these brave men knew what hurt them. They fell facing the foe and their friends can well be proud of them and their deeds. I sympathize deeply with Mother Campbell who is again called in old age to mourn for her second martyr, who have so nobly dedicated their lives to their country. You must tell her of Rufus' death as best you can, for I don't feel like writing to her. Doc Widner is severely wounded in the left thigh and arm. James Carnes in the left shoulder, severely; Anderson Young severely in the thigh, A.S. Thomas a slight bayonet wound in the hip. Sergt. J.B. Chaney a slight wound in the head and was taken a prisoner. This makes two killed and five wounded yesterday.

It is raining hard and we have no tents, and have very little to eat. Yesterday was as hard a fight as we were ever in. I hope never again to be called on to report another loss, but God's will be done.

I hope that we will now have some rest, for we are completely worn out from marching day and night, fighting three battles and living on short rations of crackers and coffee for ten days. Many of us have not had a blanket to lie on for a week. I have had no lieutenant to assist me all the time, one in command of the ambulance corps, the other sick. This makes my own work more severe, as you will see. Company H has lost more than its share. Of course it did its duty on every occasion, as has the regiment — whether it will receive full credit or not ...

Chattanooga, Tennessee
December 2, 1863.

My dear Wife:

... Inform Mrs. Campbell that I interred Rufus and Moore where they so nobly and unfortunately died on Taylor Ridge near Ringgold, Georgia; as they fell in life, so sleep they in death. We placed them side by side in one coffin, with a headboard to mark their last resting place on earth. Beside them are fourteen men of the 76th Ohio and Duncan, of the 4th Iowa. All of these men fell in a perfect line, as though they were on a dress parade, and their faces to the foe. I hope to God I may never see the like again, and then again some of our very best men appear to be the victims.

Rufus had with him $12.00, which I took from his pocket. This amount you will pay to his mother immediately. I understand that some of the men owe him. If so, I will collect and send to her, besides his Testament and some other things which I will send if possible. I now learn that there is $16.50 coming to him, which Clark Lawrence will collect and send to his mother. I will sell his blankets if possible. I also took from Moore's pockets $20.50, which you can pay to Ramsay, taking his receipt for same, he being Moore's business agent. I will communicate with his mother in Indiana about his affairs as soon as we are located. It will take me all day to arrange my company reports, etc.

Our wounded are doing finely. None of them will die. I hope not, as we have lost enough. Baker and Young have the most serious wounds. Widner feels well, considering his wound, and will soon be well again, as will all the rest, I hope ...

Henry

■ 7th Ohio metallic pin.

# 'The promises of men in authority'

**Following the 7th Ohio's bloody repulse at Ringgold, Private Theodore Wilder of Company C noted the lasting effect on the regiment's morale:**

It was a sad affair for the regiment. Its glory seemed to have departed. Of the twenty men in Co. C who entered the action, six were killed and eight wounded.

The army remained at Ringgold until December 1. It then fell back twenty miles to go into winter quarters at Chattanooga. Efforts were made at this camp to induce the men to re-enlist. A fine speech of Gen. Geary's was insufficient to cause the boys to forget their abuse and hard usage, which had so prejudiced their minds that they could not see it to be their duty to do further service. Besides, the General had not, by any means, made himself their favorite; and therefore, his protestations that "to lose the Seventh would be to lose the seventh star of the Pleiades," and that "they were dear to him as the apple of his eye," only served to disgust them.

Another effort was made by Gen. Slocum and all the [XII] Corps authorities to persuade the men to enter the veteran service; but they said, "We know the promises of men in authority, and how much care is exercised for the comfort of those under them. We love the society of our friends at home as well as the multitudes of young men who have never spent a day in the service. We will take our turn with them." These thoughts biased the men so that, again, they could not feel it their duty to re-enlist, and when the glad hour of their release came, they returned to their homes with clear consciences.

CHAPTER 10

# The future is pregnant with great events

## Epilogue

On November 28, while Cleburne slipped away to rejoin the main Confederate army retreating south toward Dalton, Grant called off the pursuit. Rations were low, forage in the barren country below Chattanooga was sparse, and the pressing need to relieve Burnside's besieged troops in Knoxville obviated an immediate excursion to battle Bragg in Georgia.

Granger's IV Corps already had been ordered north but, as the commanding general put it, "he moved with reluctance and complaints." Grant then called on Sherman to lead the relief forces to Knoxville, where Burnside was believed to be dangerously short of supplies. After a 90-mile forced march in cold weather, Sherman's cavalry vanguard arrived on December 3. The next day Longstreet's Confederates pulled out of their positions and headed east. The crisis was over.

"Our advance came up with the rear guard of Longstreet at Loudon," wrote Sergeant George W. Holmes of Company G, 100th Illinois, "but he raised the siege of Knoxville, and slipped away ... Some fault was found with Granger because the corps did not make better time, but I guess those who made the march thought they went fast enough. This march had been made by our corps after two months of short rations, the exhausting fighting in front of Chattanooga, and on Mission Ridge, and the chase after the enemy without any rest. The boys were many of them almost barefooted and all thinly clad, and much of the time on deficient rations. We had left with the expectation of returning soon and were allowed no transportation for extra baggage, only one wagon to a regiment, and hence were poorly prepared for a winter in East Tennessee. But this we soon learn is to be our lot."

While Granger's men remained at Knoxville, Sherman's troops and those belonging to Howard's XI Corps returned to Chattanooga. "We started on our way back towards Chattanooga on [December 7]," wrote Major Frederic C. Winkler to his wife. The 26th Wisconsin's commander continued: "We are

■ Posing in this rare half-plate ambrotype, IV Corps commander Gordon Granger (center) is flanked by the leader of his 2nd Division, Maj. Gen. Philip H. Sheridan (left), and Col. Charles G. Harker, 26-year-old commander of Sheridan's 3rd Brigade. Just as Granger's star waned after the battles for Chattanooga (he was relieved of IV Corps' command in April 1864), those of Sheridan and Harker were on the rise. Favorably impressed by "Little Phil's" energetic pursuit of fleeing Confederates from Missionary Ridge, Gen. Grant selected Sheridan in April 1864 to head the Army of the Potomac's Cavalry Corps, and that August the Middle Military Division, whose troops successfully fought in the Shenandoah Valley. Harker, promoted brigadier general to date from the battle of Chickamauga, became a favorite of Gen. Sherman. While leading his brigade in a charge at Kennesaw Mountain on June 27, 1864, Harker was shot from his horse and died before nightfall.

still wandering about without communication either with the rest of the army or the world. Our march is very slow, we rest at least one day in two; it is unprofitable rest though, as there has been nothing to make us comfortable. For the men it is hard. They are deficient in everything, food, blankets, and the shoes are giving out as well as salt; it is really hard on them, and therefore highly desirable that we get back to our lines of communication soon."

Private George P. Metcalf of Company D, 136th New York, recalled: "We were a motly-looking set of men. It could not be said we were uniformed, for scarcely a dozen were dressed alike. Old cast-off clothes, bags, coffee-sacks, army blankets, sheepskins or whatever would help to keep us warm, was worn on our return march during the last days of December. Our army was divided into three squads, as the boys called it: one called the well squad, another the bare-footed squad, and the other the invalid squad.

"From Athens [Tenn.] we moved directly to Lookout Valley, arriving about New Years Day. The weather was extremely cold, so cold that two men froze to death at Bridgeport. We found our knapsacks, and in the course of a week all the clothing came to us that we needed. We ... busily engaged in getting up good substantial winter quarters about a mile away in Lookout Valley. We went upon a ridge covered with large oak trees and cut and split these trees into slabs some four inches thick and a foot wide. Our little houses were made

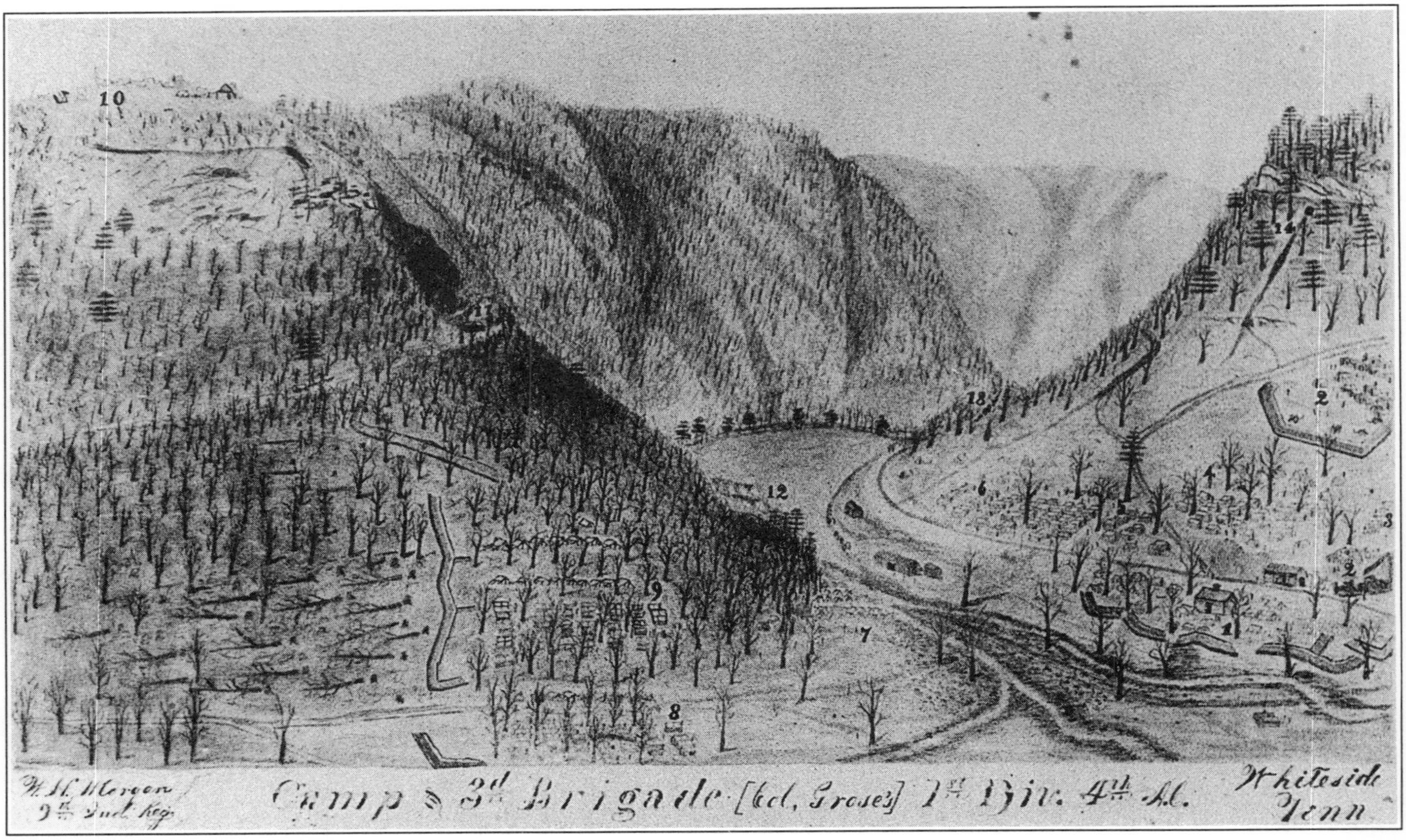


■ Illustration of Col. William Grose's brigade camp at Whiteside, Tenn., winter 1863-64, as drawn by Private William H. Morgan, 9th Indiana. Numbers seen in Morgan's sketch pinpoint the locations of: **1**, Grose's headquarters. **2**, Battery H, 4th U.S. Artillery. **3**, 84th Illinois. **4**, 36th Indiana. **5**, 59th Illinois. **6**, 75th Illinois. **7**, 77th Pennsylvania. **8**, 24th Ohio. **9**, 30th Indiana. **10**, 9th Indiana. **11**, 9th Indiana wagon park. **12**, wagon park. **13**, bridge rebuilding. **14**, coal hole and slide.

Instead of accompanying the bulk of Granger's IV Corps to Knoxville, Grose was ordered from Ringgold back to Whiteside, arriving there December 2. The previous day his troops buried the badly decomposed remains of 400 Federal soldiers still lying on the Chickamauga battlefield — a sight, he wrote, "I hope never to witness again."

**six feet by ten, and each would accommodate from four to six men. We built good substantial fireplaces with chimneys made of sticks and topped off with barrels."**

**Thirty miles away in the hills surrounding Dalton, the Confederates began constructing similar billets in which to spend the bone-numbing winter of 1863-64. "In close proximity to a running brook and nearby springs we built log huts," wrote Alabama artillerist James R. Maxwell. "Each mess was composed of individuals who associated at their own wills, without any interference of military rules or company officers." Mississippi infantryman Robert A. Jarman recalled: "The army gradually went into winter quarters. I say 'gradually' because axes for use in building huts were very scarce with us — about one axe to the company, so only one could be built at a time. It would have amused you at first to see men driving boards with a pole axe, for we had no frows until they could be made after the blacksmiths set up their forges. But quarters did not bother the men so much as short rations." Remembered Kentucky cavalry trooper John W. Dyer: "Our brigade was put on outpost and had to watch day and night. We had no rest and but little to eat. Our horses, ourselves, our clothing and equipments were run down to the ragged edge; in fact, Bragg's whole army was about in the same fix and was about as tough a looking lot of patriots as could be imagined."**

**Their leader of the past year, however, was gone. Four days after the debacle on Missionary Ridge, Braxton Bragg telegraphed to Richmond that "my first estimate of our disaster was not too large, and time only can restore order and morale ... I deem it due to the cause and to myself to ask for**

■ Federal soldiers throng Chattanooga's railroad depot yard, awaiting the next train north. In December 1863, the first veteran volunteer regiments began their 30-day furloughs home. The last of these troops returned for duty in May 1864, following the initial battles of Sherman's spring offensive in Georgia.

relief from command and an investigation into the causes of the defeat."

Reply from the Confederate capital was not long in coming, for on November 30 President Davis acceded to Bragg's request, and command of the Army of Tennessee fell to Hardee. He immediately issued a general order to the army, part of which read: "... there is no cause for discouragement. The overwhelming numbers of the enemy forced us back from Missionary Ridge, but the army is still intact and in good heart; our losses were small, and will be rapidly replaced. The country is looking to you with painful interest."

Before the year of 1863 was over Hardee, too, was superseded by Gen. Joseph E. Johnston. Under his new leadership, a rejuvenation of spirit and body swept through the Rebel ranks, but the army never fully recovered from the losses incurred at Chattanooga. With that city solidly in Federal hands, the door to the Deep South lay open and it proved only a matter of months before Northern military might came pouring through. As Bragg wrote on the day of his departure: "The future is pregnant with great events."

# Sources

## Text

***Sources to material quoted in introductory passages and the major accounts of each chapter.***

### Preface

**LEWIS E. JONES:** Letter of November 21, 1863, L.M. Strayer collection.
**4th TEXAS INFANTRYMAN:** V.C. Giles, *Rags and Hope, 199.*

### Chapter 1

**WILLIAM S. ROSECRANS:** "Tullahoma Campaign," *The National Tribune,* March 11, 1882.
**FEDERAL OFFICER:** C.C. Briant, *History of the Sixth Regiment Indiana Volunteer Infantry,* 201.
**JAMES A. GARFIELD:** *The Wild Life of the Army,* 278, 281-282.
**MICHAEL S. BRIGHT:** Letter of June 30, 1863, published in *Respects to All: Letters of Two Pennsylvania Boys in the War of the Rebellion.*
**ROBERT P. FINDLEY:** "A Story of a March," *G.A.R. War Papers,* vol. I, 352-353.
**DANIEL W. HOWE:** Letter of July 4, 1863, Smith Library, Indiana Historical Society.
**CHARLES C. BRIANT:** *History of the Sixth Regiment Indiana Volunteer Infantry,* 209-211, 213-214.
**MICHAEL S. BRIGHT:** Letter of June 30, 1863, published in *Respects to All: Letters of Two Pennsylvania Boys in the War of the Rebellion.*
**LYMAN WIDNEY:** Typed transcript of journal, KMNBP.
**GEORGE S. WILSON:** *Wilder's Brigade of Mounted Infantry in the Tullahoma-Chickamauga Campaigns,* 7.
**JOHN T. WILDER:** "The Battle of Hoover's Gap," *Sketches of War History,* MOLLUS-Ohio, vol. 6, 169-172.
**W.N. MERCER OTEY:** "Operations of the Signal Corps," *Confederate Veteran,* vol. VIII, no. 3, March 1900.
**SOLOMON M. DEACON:** Letter of July 16, 1863, CCNMP.
**JOHN A. WYETH:** *With Sabre and Scalpel,* 223, 224-226, 227-228, 232.
**JAMES TURNER:** "Jim Turner Co. G, 6th Texas Infantry, C.S.A." *Texana,* vol. XII, 1974, 161-162.
**HENRY M. CIST:** *The Army of the Cumberland,* 170-171, 174.
**GEORGE W. WILLIAMS:** Letter of August 12, 1863, Kyle Kelch collection, Urbana, Ohio.
**ROBERT P. FINDLEY:** "A Story of a March," *G.A.R. War Papers,* vol. I, 360-362.

> ## Abbreviations
>
> **CCNMP — Chickamauga and Chattanooga National Military Park, Ft. Oglethorpe, Ga.**
>
> **KMNBP — Kennesaw Mountain National Battlefield Park, Kennesaw, Ga.**
>
> **Mass. MOLLUS — Massachusetts Commandery, Military Order of the Loyal Legion of the United States.**
>
> ***Official Records* — *The War of the Rebellion: A Compilation of the Official Records of the Union and Confederate Armies.***
>
> **USAMHI — United States Army Military History Institute, Carlisle Barracks, Pa.**

**ALVA C. GRIEST:** Typed transcript of diary, Smith Memorial Library, Indiana Historical Society.
**JOHN S. McGRAW:** Letter of August 23, 1863, John S. McGraw Papers, Manuscript Section, Indiana Division, Indiana State Library.
**NEWTON N. DAVIS:** Letter of August 22, 1863, Newton N. Davis Papers, Alabama Department of Archives and History.
**ASBURY L. KERWOOD:** *Annals of the Fifty-seventh Regiment Indiana Volunteers,* 202-204.
**FRANCIS W. PERRY:** "Chickamauga. Toilsome March of the Fourteenth Corps over the Mountains," *The National Tribune,* June 28, 1883.
**JAMES A. CONNOLLY:** "Major James Austin Connolly," *Publications of the Illinois State Historical Library No. 35,* 281.
**ROBERT P. FINDLEY:** "A Story of a March," *G.A.R. War Papers,* vol. I, 363.

### Chapter 2

**JOHN T. COXE:** "Chickamauga," *Confederate Veteran,* vol. XXX, no. 8, August 1922.
**D. AUGUSTUS DICKERT:** *History of Kershaw's Brigade,* 263-264.
**NEWTON N. DAVIS:** Letter of September 16, 1863, Newton N. Davis Papers, Alabama Department of Archives and History.
**WILLIAM W. STOKEY:** M. Yeary, *Reminiscences of the Boys in Gray, 1861-1865,* 727.
**LEROY S. MAYFIELD:** "A Hoosier Invades the Confederacy," *Indiana Magazine of History,* vol. XXXIX, 1943.
**PETER KEEGAN:** *The Diaries of Peter Keegan,* 27.
**ALFRED PIRTLE:** "Lytle's Last Sacrifice," unpublished typescript, The Filson Club, Louisville, Ky.
**JOHN T. BOOTH:** "A Night March," *The Ohio Soldier and National Picket Guard,* vol. III, no. 11, January 4, 1890.
**JOHN B. TURCHIN:** *Chickamauga,* 65-66.
**OHIO PRIVATE:** S.A. McNeil, "At Chickamauga," *The National Tribune,* April 14, 1887.
**JACOB H. ALLSPAUGH:** "Chickamauga. The Struggle of Sunday as Seen by an Enlisted Man," *The National Tribune,* October 7, 1886.
**VALERIUS C. GILES:** *Rags and Hope,* 199-200.
**ISRAEL B. WEBSTER:** "Chickamauga. Going into Action with Hands Full of Bacon and Coffee," *The National Tribune,* July 2, 1891.
**GEORGE W. MILLER:** "The 31st Ohio at Chickamauga," *The National Tribune,* February 21, 1907.
**WILLIAM W. LYLE:** *Lights and Shadows of Army Life,* 288-291.
**LUCIUS G. MARSHALL:** J.B. Lindsley, *The Military Annals of Tennessee, Confederate,* 820-823.
**JAMES F. MELINE:** E. Hannaford, *The Story of a Regiment,* 462-465.
**JAMES L. COOPER:** Typescript of journal and reminiscences, Tennessee State Library and Archives.
**LEWELLYN A. SHAVER:** *A History of the Sixtieth Alabama Regiment, Gracie's Alabama Brigade,* 14-16.
**SHERMAN HENDRICKS:** "Chickamauga. The Part Taken in the Great Battle by Battery C, 1st Ohio L.A.," *The National Tribune,* November 5, 1891.
**ISRAEL B. WEBSTER:** "Chickamauga. Going into Action with Hands Full of Bacon and Coffee," *The National Tribune,* July 2, 1891.

**JAMES H. FRASER:** Letter of September 26, 1863, reprinted in the *Alabama Courier,* September 20, 1905.
**AUSTIN E. STEBBINS:** "A Daring Movement," *The National Tribune,* October 19, 1899.
**ALFRED PIRTLE:** "Lytle's Last Sacrifice," unpublished typescript, The Filson Club, Louisville, Ky.
**THOMPSON P. FREEMAN:** F.M. McAdams, *Every-day Soldier Life, or A History of the One Hundred and Thirteenth Ohio Volunteer Infantry,* 371-372.
**ILLINOIS ARTILLERYMAN:** "Gen. Steedman. His Brilliant Services at Chickamauga," *The*

■ Immediately after the battle of Missionary Ridge, photographer Royan M. Linn left Marion, Ohio, for Chattanooga, taking with him camera and equipment. The enterprising Linn (left, on Pulpit Rock), was struck by the scenic grandeur of Lookout Mountain. He quickly recognized a business opportunity and purchased a small house close to the mountain's Point Lookout. A tiny photographic gallery was built nearby, perched precariously among the rocks. With scores of Federal soldiers ascending the peak daily to see the sights, Linn was furnished with a steady stream of eager customers.

He soon sent for his brother, J. Birney Linn, to assist him, and together their Point Lookout Gallery became famous for its cliffside views. Between December 1863 and the end of the war, the Linns photographed literally thousands of soldiers — from privates to major generals.

After R.M. Linn's death in 1872, J.B. Linn maintained the business until 1886, with help during the last six years from Royan's son, George, who was born on Lookout Mountain in 1866. A Michigan concern, Hardie Brothers, operated the studio between 1886 and 1899, but the following year George Linn returned to the Point and remained for nearly four decades. The studio was razed in 1939.

*National Tribune,* August 4, 1887.
**HENRY H. EBY:** *Observations of an Illinois Boy in Battle, Camp and Prisons – 1861 to 1865,* 98-99, 103, 105-107, 111-113, 119-122, 123-124, 124-126.
**JOHN T. COXE:** "Chickamauga," *Confederate Veteran,* vol. XXX, no. 8, August 1922.
**ISAAC CUSAC:** S.S. Canfield, *History of the 21st Regiment Ohio Volunteer Infantry in the War of the Rebellion,* 135-137.
**WILLIAM M. OWEN:** *In Camp and Battle with the Washington Artillery of New Orleans,* 282-284.
**ISAAC H. BAILEY:** *Histories of the Several Regiments and Battalions from North Carolina in the Great War 1861-'65,* vol. III, 449-453.
**WILLIAM B. HAMILTON:** A. Gracie, *The Truth About Chickamauga,* 431-432, 435, 436.
**J.M. WEISER:** "Trigg's Brigade at Chickamauga," *Confederate Veteran,* vol. XXXIV, no. 12, December 1926.
**EDWARD S. SCOTT:** 1863-1864 journal, Firelands Historical Society, Norwalk, Ohio.

## Chapter 3

**JOHN SNOW:** Letter of September 30, 1863, Perkins Library, Duke University.
**WILLIAM R. TALLEY:** Typescript of reminiscences, CCNMP.
**O.T. HANKS:** Unpublished typescript, "History of Captain B.F. Benton's Company 1861-1865," Confederate Research Center, Hill Junior College, Hillsboro, Texas.
**WILLIAM J. WORSHAM:** *The Old Nineteenth Tennessee Regiment, C.S.A.,* 95.
**SAM R. WATKINS:** *Co. Aytch: Maury Grays, First Tennessee Regiment or A Side Show of the Big Show,* 118-119.
**BENJAMIN F. SCRIBNER:** Letter of September 21, 1863 (copy of typescript), CCNMP.
**WILLIAM B. MILLER:** Typescript of journal, CCNMP.
**AUGUSTUS C. FORD:** "Midnight on Missionary Ridge," *War Papers,* MOLLUS-Indiana, 240, 241-244.
**D. AUGUSTUS DICKERT:** *History of Kershaw's Brigade,* 286-287.
**FRANCIS M. CARLISLE:** Typescript of reminiscences, CCNMP.
**AURELIUS M. WILLOUGHBY:** Typescript of diary, CCNMP.

■ The first Point Lookout Gallery, little more than a wooden shack, with Linn assistant and camera near its cliffside perch.

**GEORGE W. ROUSE:** G.H. Woodruff, *Fifteen Years Ago; or the Patriotism of Will County,* 295.
**HEZEKIAH RABB:** Letter of October 9, 1863 (typescript), CCNMP.
**LEVI A. ROSS:** Typescript of journal and reminiscences, Illinois State Historical Library.
**ISAAC H.C. ROYSE:** *History of the 115th Regiment Illinois Volunteer Infantry,* 168-171.
**GEORGE BARKHAMER:** "On Picket Before Chattanooga — A Wild Cavalry Charge," *The National Tribune,* July 26, 1883.
**JOHN D. FLOYD:** Letter of October 8, 1863 (typescript), Tennessee State Library and Archives.
**WILLIAM J. WORSHAM:** *The Old Nineteenth Tennessee Regiment, C.S.A.,* 96.
**CLINTON M. WINKLER:** Letter of September 27, 1863, published in A.V. Winkler, *The Confederate Capital and Hood's Texas Brigade,* 145-146.
**ROYAL W. FIGG:** *Where Men Only Dare to Go! or the Story of a Boy Company (C.S.A.),* 155-158.
**JOSEPH T. GIBSON:** *History of the Seventy-eighth Pennsylvania Volunteer Infantry,* 122-123, 124-125.
**THOMAS J. McCALL:** "Capture of our Wagon Train in Sequatchie Valley, Tennessee," *History of the Fifteenth Pennsylvania Volunteer Cavalry 1862-1865,* 303-306.
**GEORGE B. GUILD:** *A Brief Narrative of the Fourth Tennessee Cavalry Regiment: Wheeler's Corps, Army of Tennessee,* 35-39.
**THEODORE PETZOLDT:** Typescript of reminiscences, CCNMP.
**JOHN M. PALMER:** *Personal Recollections of John M. Palmer: The Story of an Earnest Life,* 190-194, 196, 198.
**WILLIAM W. MACKALL:** Letters of October 5, 9, 10 and 12, 1863, published in W.W. Mackall, *A Son's Recollections of his Father,* 181-186.
**GEORGE W. HOLMES:** G.H. Woodruff, *Fifteen Years Ago; or the Patriotism of Will County,* 297-301.
**DAVID G. BLODGETT:** "The Tenth Indiana Battery at Moccasin Point," *The National Tribune,* August 9, 1883.
**GEORGE T. TODD:** *First Texas Regiment,* 19.
**JAMES R. MAXWELL:** G. Little and J.R. Maxwell, *A History of Lumsden's Battery C.S.A.,* 19-21, 24-25.
**ESAU BEAUMONT:** H.H.G. Bradt, *History of the Services of the Third Battery Wisconsin Light Artillery,* 51-53.
**ALEXANDER R. THAIN:** C.A. Partridge, *History of the Ninety-sixth Regiment Illinois Volunteer Infantry,* 249-251, 252, 253-256.
**JAMES R. CARNAHAN:** *The Eighty-Sixth Regiment Indiana Volunteer Infantry,* 214-216, 217, 218-219, 221, 222-223.
**R.M. COLLINS:** *Chapters from the Unwritten History of the War Between the States,* 167-170.
**CHAUNCEY C. BAKER:** "And a Little Child Shall Lead Them," *Confederate Veteran,* vol. XXVIII, no. 12, December 1920.
**DANIEL O'LEARY:** Letter of October 24, 1863 (transcription), KMNBP.

## Chapter 4

**WILLIAM F. SMITH:** *Official Records,* series 1, vol. XXXI, part 1, 77.
**WILLIAM B. HAZEN:** *A Narrative of Military Service,* 154-155, 156-158.
**ROBERT T. COLES:** Unpublished typescript "History of the Fourth Regiment Alabama Volunteer Infantry," Alabama Department of Archives and History.
**WILLIAM C. OATES:** *The War Between the*

■ With camera mounted on a tripod, a photographer at right (possibly J.B. Linn) prepares to make an exposure on an overcast day during the winter of 1863-1864. Patches of snow appear on the ground, while soldiers loiter between Umbrella Rock and the large stone formation at center. Note scratched caption in the emulsion at bottom: "Crest of Lookout. Sweeny," indicating that Cleveland, Ohio, photographer Thomas T. Sweeny recorded this unusual scene. Sweeny was close on the Linn brothers' heels, and quickly established a field gallery at Cleveland, Tenn.

*Union and the Confederacy and its Lost Opportunities,* 275-280.
**WILLIAM C. JORDAN:** *Some Events and Incidents during the Civil War,* 55-61.
**LAUNCELOT L. SCOTT:** "Brown's Ferry Expedition," *The National Tribune,* January 25, 1912.
**ALBERT G. HART:** Letter of October 27, 1863, published in *The Surgeon and the Hospital in the Civil War,* 278-282.
**ARNOLD BRANDLEY:** "The Cracker Line," *The National Tribune,* May 28, 1885.
**WILLIAM A. MORGAN:** "Brown's Ferry," *War Talks in Kansas,* MOLLUS-Kansas, 345-349.

## Chapter 5

**92nd ILLINOIS TROOPER:** *Ninety-Second Illinois Volunteers,* 115.
**ROBERT L. KIMBERLY:** *The Forty-First Ohio Veteran Volunteer Infantry in the War of the Rebellion 1861-1865,* 64.
**HENRY S. NOURSE:** *The Story of the Fifty-Fifth Regiment Illinois Volunteer Infantry in the Civil War 1861-1865,* 280.
**WILLIAM BAKHAUS:** "Jottings by a 15th Corps Boy," *The Ohio Soldier and National Picket Guard,* vol. II, no. 16, December 1, 1888.
**GEORGE K. COLLINS:** *Memoirs of the 149th Regt. N.Y. Vol. Inft.,* 188, 189.
**ROBERT HUBBARD:** Letters of October 5 and 11, 1863 (typescripts), Manuscript Division, USAMHI.
**DAVID MONAT:** Unpublished reminiscence, Historical Society of Pennsylvania, Philadelphia.
**EDWARD P. ALEXANDER:** *Military Memoirs of a Confederate,* 467-471, 471-472.
**JAMES L. COKER:** *History of Company G, Ninth S.C. Regiment, Infantry, S.C. Army and of Company E, Sixth S.C. Regiment, Infantry, S.C. Army,* 130-132, 134-135.
**FRANK M. MIXSON:** *Reminiscences of a Private,* 44-50.
**RICHARD LEWIS:** Letter of October 30, 1863, published in *Camp Life of a Confederate Boy of Bratton's Brigade, Longstreet's Corps, C.S.A.,* 64-66.
**DAVID MONAT:** Unpublished reminiscence, Historical Society of Pennsylvania, Philadelphia.
**ALBERT R. GREENE:** "From Bridgeport to Ringgold by way of Lookout Mountain," *Personal Narratives of Events in the War of*

■ On Christmas Day 1863, Gens. Joseph Hooker and John W. Geary went sightseeing on Lookout Mountain. Among those accompanying them were members of Geary's XII Corps' division staff, six of whom posed while picnicking near R.M. Linn's photography shack. Standing from left: Capt. Henry H. Wilson (ordnance officer); Capt. Thomas H. Elliott (assistant adjutant general); and Capt. Reuben H. Wilbur (aide-de-camp). Seated from left: Capt. James Gillette (commissary of subsistence); unidentified orderly; and Capt. William T. Forbes (acting assistant inspector general). Note metallic XII Corps badges.

*the Rebellion,* 20-25.
**CARL SCHURZ:** *The Reminiscences of Carl Schurz,* vol. III, 59-66.
**ROBERT T. COLES:** Unpublished typescript "History of the Fourth Regiment Alabama Volunteer Infantry," Alabama Department of Archives and History.
**H. HOWARD STURGIS:** "Hard Fighting by Lookout Mountain," *Confederate Veteran,* vol. XVII, no. 3, March 1909.
**VALERIUS C. GILES:** *Rags and Hope,* 214-215, 216-217.
**ANDREW J. BOIES:** *Record of the 33d Mass. Volunteer Infantry,* 46-49.
**JOSEPH L. LOCKE:** Letter of January 9, 1864, Joseph L. Locke Papers, Illinois State Historical Library.

## Chapter 6

**GEORGE M. KIRKPATRICK:** Letter of November 2, 1863, published in *The Experiences of a Private Soldier in the Civil War,* 47, 48.
**GEORGE A. CUMMINS:** Diary, Illinois State Historical Library.
**RODNEY S. BOWEN:** G.H. Woodruff, *Fifteen Years Ago; or the Patriotism of Will County,* 307.
**WILLIAM G. LeDUC:** "Opening Up the Cracker Line," *The National Tribune,* September 5, 1912.
**ROBERT A. JARMAN:** "The History of Company K, 27th Mississippi Infantry," *The Aberdeen Examiner,* March 7, 1890.
**NICHOLAS POMEROY:** Typescript of reminiscences, Confederate Research Center, Hill Junior College, Hillsboro, Texas.
**EUGENE POWELL:** "An Incident of the Capture of Lookout Mountain," *Historical and Philosophical Society of Ohio Publications,* part II, 47-51.
**WILLIAM H.H. TALLMAN:** Handwritten memoir, Charles Rhodes III collection, USAMHI.
**EDWARD C. WALTHALL:** "Walthall on the Battle of Lookout," *Confederate Veteran,* vol. VI, no. 12, December 1898.
**WILLIAM F. DOWD:** "Lookout Mountain and Missionary Ridge," *The Southern Bivouac,* vol. I, no. 7, December 1885.
**DAVID MONAT:** Unpublished reminiscence, Historical Society of Pennsylvania, Philadelphia.
**JOHN W. SIMMONS:** "Heroic Mississippians," *Confederate Veteran,* vol. V, no. 2, February 1897.
**JAMES E. REYNOLDS:** "Heroism of Walthall's Mississippians," *Confederate Veteran,* vol. XV, no. 8, August 1907.
**HENRY M. WOODSON:** "Battle on Side of Lookout Mountain," *Confederate Veteran,* vol. VI, no. 1, January 1898.

**JOHN C. MOORE:** "Battle of Lookout Mountain," *Confederate Veteran,* vol. VI, no. 9, September 1898.
**JAMES W.A. WRIGHT:** W.S. Hoole, *A Historical Sketch of the Thirty-Sixth Alabama Infantry Regiment, 1862-1865,* 21-22, 23-24.
**ELISHA C. LUCAS:** "Lookout Mountain," *The National Tribune,* June 10, 1886.
**AMOS H. MILLER:** *Military History and Reminiscences of the Thirteenth Regiment of Illinois Volunteer Infantry in the Civil War in the United States 1861-1865,* 372-375.
**HENRY GAGE:** Undated letter published in *Kiss Clara For Me: The story of Joseph Whitney and his family, early days in the Midwest, and soldiering in the American Civil War,* 119-123.

## Chapter 7

**HENRY S. NOURSE:** *The Story of the Fifty-Fifth Regiment Illinois Volunteer Infantry in the Civil War 1861-1865,* 273.
**JAMES DINKINS:** *1861 to 1865 by an Old Johnnie: Personal Recollections and Experiences in the Confederate Army,* 112-115.
**WILLIAM L. JENNEY:** "With Sherman and Grant from Memphis to Chattanooga – A Reminiscence," *Military Essays and Recollections,* MOLLUS-Illinois, vol. IV, 211-213.
**HENRY H. WRIGHT:** *A History of the Sixth Iowa Infantry,* 223.
**XV CORPS COMPANY COMMANDER:** H.S. Nourse, *The Story of the Fifty-Fifth Regiment Illinois Volunteer Infantry in the Civil War,* 274.
**ULYSSES S. GRANT:** *Official Records,* series 1, vol. XXXI, part 2, 32.
**4th MINNESOTA OFFICER:** A.L. Brown, *History of the Fourth Regiment of Minnesota Infantry Volunteers during the Great Rebellion 1861-1865,* 268, 269.
**HENRY S. DEAN:** *The Relief of Chattanooga,* MOLLUS-Michigan, 8-14.
**JAMES A. WOODSON:** Diary, James A. Woodson Papers, Illinois State Historical Library.
**JOHN W. DYER:** *Reminiscences; or Four Years in the Confederate Army,* 133-135.
**JENKIN L. JONES:** *An Artilleryman's Diary,* 139-142.
**THEODORE F. UPSON:** *With Sherman to the Sea: The Civil War Letters, Diaries & Reminiscences of Theodore F. Upson,* 83-87.
**IRA J. BLOOMFIELD:** Letter of November 21, 1907, CCNMP.
**JOHN S. KOUNTZ:** Typed transcript of reminiscences, L.M. Strayer collection.
**EMORY W. MUENSCHER:** "Missionary Ridge," *The National Tribune,* April 8, 1909.
**R.M. COLLINS:** *Chapters from the Unwritten History of the War Between the States,* 174-183.
**SAMUEL T. FOSTER:** *One of Cleburne's Command: The Civil War Reminiscences and Diary of Capt. Samuel T. Foster, Granbury's Texas Brigade, CSA,* 59-65.
**NELSON STAUFFER:** *Civil War Diary,* copy at Illinois State Historical Library.
**GEORGE W. BAILEY:** Letter of December 10, 1907, CCNMP.
**JOHN POTTER:** *Reminiscences of the Civil War in the United States,* 64, 66-69.
**HENRY H. ORENDORFF:** *Reminiscences of the Civil War from Diaries of Members of the*

■ Orderly Sergeant Wilmon W. Blackmar of Company K, 15th Pennsylvania Cavalry, stands pointing in the distance with an unidentified regimental comrade. In March 1864, Blackmar was promoted to lieutenant and transferred to the 1st West Virginia Cavalry, which served during the war's final four months in Gen. George A. Custer's cavalry division. On April 1, 1865, Blackmar, without orders, led a successful charge at Five Forks, Va. — for which he later received the Medal of Honor. He served as Grand Army of the Republic national commander in 1904.

*103d Illinois Volunteer Infantry,* 26-29.
**VICTOR H. GOULD:** Letter of December 22, 1863, Illinois State Historical Library.
**SAMUEL H.M. BYERS:** *Battles and Leaders of the Civil War,* vol. III, 712-713; *With Fire and Sword,* 202-203.
**JAMES C. NISBET:** *Four Years on the Firing Line,* 156-159, 160-163.

## Chapter 8

**ARTHUR M. MANIGAULT:** *A Carolinian Goes to War,* 131-132.
**JOHN S. ROPER:** Letter of November 23, 1863, published in *Journal of the Illinois State Historical Society,* January 1914, 497-498.
**GEORGE P. METCALF:** Typescript of reminiscence, Ohio Historical Society, Columbus.
**JOSEPH T. PATTON:** *Personal Recollections of Four Years in Dixie,* MOLLUS-Michigan, 18-20.
**JOHN K. SHELLENBERGER:** "With Sheridan's Division at Missionary Ridge," *Sketches of War History,* MOLLUS-Ohio, vol. IV, 53-55.
**ULYSSES S. GRANT:** *Official Records,* series 1, vol. XXXI, part 2, 44.
**JAMES W. RILEY:** Diary entry of November 25, 1863, published in the Dowagiac (Mich.) *Daily News,* November 12, 1963.
**J.N. STANFORD:** "The Charge Up Mission Ridge," *The National Tribune,* May 27, 1886.
**WILLIAM A. BROWN:** Typescript of diary, Greenwood (Miss.) Public Library.
**THOMAS J. WOOD:** "The Battle of Missionary Ridge," *Sketches of War History,* MOLLUS-Ohio, vol. IV, 33-38, 39-40, 40-41.
**ARTHUR M. MANIGAULT:** *A Carolinian Goes to War,* 138-142.
**FRANCIS ERDELMEYER:** Undated letter, CCNMP.
**CHARLES B. RUSSELL:** E. Hannaford, *The Story of a Regiment: A History of the Campaigns and Associations in the Field of the Sixth Regiment Ohio Volunteer Infantry,* 507-509.
**WILLIAM H. HUNTZINGER:** Typescript of journal, Smith Memorial Library, Indiana Historical Society.
**JAMES J. TURNER:** J.B. Lindsley, *The Military Annals of Tennessee, Confederate,* 452-453.
**JOHN J. HIGHT:** *History of the Fifty-Eighth Regiment of Indiana Volunteer Infantry,* 216-219, 220, 221-224.
**GEORGE L. BANKS:** *Indiana Battle Flags,* 122-123.
**ROBERT WATSON:** Typescript of journal, CCNMP.
**CHARLES C. HEMMING:** "A Confederate Odyssey," *American Heritage,* vol. 36, no. 1, December 1984.
**THOMAS L. MASSENBURG:** Letter of November 29, 1863, published in the Macon (Ga.) *Telegraph,* December 5, 1863.
**JOHN K. SHELLENBERGER:** "With Sheridan's Division at Missionary Ridge," *Sketches of War History,* MOLLUS-Ohio, vol. IV, 55-60, 61-66.
**BENJAMIN T. SMITH:** Handwritten journal, Benjamin T. Smith Papers, Illinois State Historical Library.
**TILMON D. KYGER:** *A History of the Seventy-third Regiment of Illinois Infantry Volunteers,* 265-266, 267.
**JOHN M. TURNBULL:** L.G. Bennett and W.M. Haigh, *History of the Thirty-sixth Regiment Illinois Volunteers during the War of the Rebellion,* 525, 527-528, 531-532.
**WILLIAM J. WORSHAM:** *The Old Nineteenth Tennessee Regiment, C.S.A.,* 99-101.
**LUKE W. FINLAY:** J.B. Lindsley, *The Military Annals of Tennessee, Confederate,* 188-189.
**WILLIAM K. POSTON JR.:** "Missionary Ridge Reminiscences," *Confederate Veteran,* vol. IX, no. 9, September 1901.
**JOSEPH E. RILEY:** Typescript of reminiscences, CCNMP.
**NELSON J. LETTS:** "Company H, 74th Ind. at Missionary Ridge," *The War for the Union, 1861-1865. A Record of its Defenders, Living and Dead, from Steuben County, Indiana,* 94-95.
**JEROME D. GLEASON:** Letter of December 8, 1863, Chris Magewick collection, Redford, Mich.
**ANDREW J. NEAL:** Letter of November 26, 1863 (typed copy), CCNMP.
**ALFRED T. FIELDER:** Copy of journal, Tennessee State Library and Archives.
**SAMUEL A. McNEIL:** *Personal Recollections of Service in the Army of the Cumberland and Sherman's Army,* 27-30.
**JACOB H. ALLSPAUGH:** "Mission Ridge," *The National Tribune,* June 2, 1887.
**JOHN W. INZER:** *The Diary of a Confederate Soldier,* 43-46.
**JAMES W.A. WRIGHT:** W.S. Hoole, *A Historical Sketch of the Thirty-Sixth Alabama Infantry Regiment, 1862-1865,* 25-26, 27, 29-30, 31-33, 34, 36-37.
**BENJAMIN F. SCRIBNER:** *How Soldiers Were Made,* 178-184.

## Chapter 9

**JOEL T. HALEY:** Letter of December 17, 1863, Tennessee State Library and Archives.
**THOMAS OWENS:** E.P. Thompson, *History of the First Kentucky Brigade,* 231.
**NEWTON N. DAVIS:** Letter of November 29, 1863, Newton N. Davis Papers, Alabama Department of Archives and History.
**CORRESPONDENT:** Dispatch of November 25, 1863 to the *Savannah Republican,* reprinted in *The Charleston Mercury,* December 2, 1863.
**ROBERT A. JARMAN:** "The History of Company K, 27th Mississippi Infantry," *The Aberdeen Examiner,* March 7, 1890.
**GEORGE A. GRAMMER:** Typescript of journal, CCNMP.
**MARQUIS L. MORRISON:** *The Tennessee Civil War Veterans Questionnaires,* vol. IV, 1594.
**DANIEL F. GRIFFIN:** Letter of December 4, 1863, published in "A Hoosier Regiment at Chattanooga," *Tennessee Historical Quarterly,* vol. XXII, no. 3, September 1963.
**FRANCIS M. CARLISLE:** Typescript of reminiscences, CCNMP.
**R.M. COLLINS:** *Chapters from the Unwritten History of the War Between the States,* 184-188.
**SAM R. WATKINS:** *Co. Aytch: Maury Grays, First Tennessee Regiment or A Side Show of the Big Show,* 127-128.
**THOMAS J. WALKER:** "Reminiscences of the Civil War," *Confederate Chronicles of Tennessee,* vol. I, 1986.
**WILLIAM H. DAVIS:** Journal typescript, Woodruff Library, Emory University.
**JOHN W. DYER:** *Reminiscences; or Four Years in the Confederate Army,* 137-140, 142-144.
**LEVI A. ROSS:** Typescript of journal and reminiscences, Illinois State Historical Library.
**BENJAMIN F. TAYLOR:** *Mission Ridge and Lookout Mountain with Pictures of Life in Camp and Field,* 79-84.
**GEORGE PRETS:** "That Battery Again. The Part taken by the 69th Ohio in Capturing those Rebel Guns," *The National Tribune,* February 11, 1892.
**JOHN W. GREEN:** *Johnny Green of the Orphan Brigade: The Journal of a Confederate Soldier,* 111-114.
**IRVING A. BUCK:** *Cleburne and his Command,* 176-177, 179, 180-184.
**13th ILLINOIS PRIVATE:** *Military History and Reminiscences of the Thirteenth Regiment of Illinois Volunteer Infantry,* 383-388.
**WILLIAM W. GIBSON:** "Reminiscences of Ringgold Gap," *Confederate Veteran,* vol. XXII, no. 11, November 1904.
**CHARLES H. KIBLER:** *76th Ohio at Ringgold or Taylor's Ridge,* 1-7, HCWRT-Gregory Coco collection, Manuscript Division, USAMHI.
**HENRY G. ANKENY:** Letters of November 28 and December 2, 1863, published in *Kiss Josey For Me!,* 194-197.

---

■ **Opposite:** Capt. James D. Robinson (far right) and enlisted men of Company C, 1st Michigan Engineers and Mechanics. As part of Capt. Perrin V. Fox's detachment, this company took part in the October 1863 Brown's Ferry operations. At times under Confederate artillery fire, the Wolverines hurriedly laid the Tennessee River pontoon bridge without the loss of a man. Engineer castles are worn on many of their hats.

■ Col. P. Sidney Post (holding field glasses), 59th Illinois, commanded brigades in the XIV and IV Corps during 1863-1864. Pictured here with members of his brigade staff in February-March 1864, Post was severely wounded nine months later at the battle of Nashville. Leading an assault December 16 at Overton's Hill, "a canister shot just missed the top of his hip bone," a comrade wrote, "and came out before reaching his backbone, opening up his side with a great gaping wound." Post survived and later was awarded the Medal of Honor for his actions that day.

# Photographs, sidebars & illustrations

***Sources to quotations in sidebars and captions of photographs and illustrations.***

## Chapter 1

**'BUSY AS BEES':** B. Morse, *Civil War Diaries & Letters of Bliss Morse,* 61; C.A. Mosman, *The Rough Side of War,* 57.
**BRAXTON BRAGG:** W.P. Johnston, *The Life of Gen. Albert Sidney Johnston,* 547-548; P.D. Stephenson, "Missionary Ridge," *SHSP,* vol. I, 19; typescript of J.W. Harris letter of October 13, 1863, Tennessee State Library and Archives.
**EARL VAN DORN:** *Official Records,* series 1, vol. XXIII, part 1, 92.
**WILLIAM MURPHY:** *Official Records,* series 1, vol. XXIII, part 2, 351.
**WILLIAM S. ROSECRANS:** T.H. Jones quoted in G.W. Sunderland, *Five Days to Glory,* 89; M. Holmes Jr., *A Soldier of the Cumberland,* 155; W.D. Bickham, *Rosecrans' Campaign with the Fourteenth Army Corps, of the Army of the Cumberland,* 29-30; J.D. Cox, *Military Reminiscences of the Civil War,* vol. I, 111, 112, 127.
**J. MONROE STOOKEY:** Letter of July 14, 1863, published in *The Civil War Letters written by James Monroe Stookey,* 21; C.A. Mosman, *The Rough Side of War,* 60.
**THEOPHILUS E. HILL:** L.S. Widney, typescript of journal, KMNBP.
**WILLIAM J. HARDEE:** N.C. Hughes Jr., *General William J. Hardee: Old Reliable,* 82, 84.
**ST. JOHN R. LIDDELL:** *Official Records,* series 1, vol. XXIII, part 1, 590.
**HIRAM CHANCE:** *Official Records,* series 1, vol. XXIII, part 1, 497; *The Journal of Francis A. Kiene 1861-1864,* 157.

## Chapter 10

**ULYSSES S. GRANT:** *Official Records,* series 1, vol. XXXI, part 2, 35.
**GEORGE W. HOLMES:** G.H. Woodruff, *Fifteen Years Ago; or the Patriotism of Will County,* 313.
**FREDERIC C. WINKLER:** *Letters of Frederic C. Winkler 1862-1865,* 105.
**GEORGE P. METCALF:** Typescript of reminiscence, Ohio Historical Society.
**JAMES R. MAXWELL:** G. Little and J.R. Maxwell, *A History of Lumsden's Battery C.S.A.,* 29.
**ROBERT A. JARMAN:** "The History of Company K, 27th Mississippi Infantry," *The Aberdeen Examiner,* March 7, 1890.
**JOHN W. DYER:** *Reminiscences; or Four Years in the Confederate Army,* 145.
**BRAXTON BRAGG:** *Official Records,* series 1, vol. XXXI, part 2, 682.
**WILLIAM J. HARDEE:** *Official Records,* series 1, vol. XXXI, part 3, 776.
**BRAXTON BRAGG:** *Official Records,* series 1, vol. XXXI, part 2, 683.

**JOHN T. WILDER:** "The Battle of Hoover's Gap," *Sketches of War History,* MOLLUS-Ohio, vol. VI, 169.
**WILLIAM N. ROGERS:** J.T. Wilder, "The Battle of Hoover's Gap," *Sketches of War History,* MOLLUS-Ohio, vol. VI, 173; B.F. Magee, *History of the 72d Indiana Volunteer Infantry of the Mounted Lightning Brigade,* 121.
**JOHN A. WYETH:** *With Sabre and Scalpel,* 237.
**NATHANIEL DELZELL:** W.H. Davis letter of August 2, 1863, Woodruff Library, Emory University.
**GEN. McCOOK & STAFF:** J. Beatty, *The Citizen Soldier; or, Memoirs of a Volunteer 1861-1863,* 295.
**CHARLES T. QUINTARD:** *Doctor Quintard, Chaplain C.S.A.,* 87.
**SOLDIERS THREE:** General Order No. 174, Department of the Cumberland, Winchester, Tenn., July 25, 1863; H. Richards, *Letters of Captain Henry Richards,* 15.
**PONTOON–TRESTLE BRIDGE:** A. Silsby letter of August 20, 1863, CCNMP.
**LUCIUS H. DRURY:** W.E. Doyle, "Recollections of Chattanooga," *The National Tribune,* June 22, 1899.
**JOHN BEATTY:** *The Citizen Soldier; or, Memoirs of a Volunteer 1861-1863,* 244.
**ROBERT H. SPENCER:** F.W. Perry, "Chickamauga. Toilsome March of the Fourteenth Corps over the Mountains," *The National Tribune,* June 28, 1883.
**'WRETCHED FIASCO':** S.J.R. Liddell, *Liddell's Record,* 139; J.B. Turchin, *Chickamauga,* 40.
**HENRY M. CIST:** *The Army of the Cumberland,* 215, 216.

## Chapter 2

**LONGSTREET'S DISEMBARKATION:** Letter of October 13, 1863, published in J.C. West, *A Texan in Search of a Fight,* 111.
**SIMON B. BUCKNER:** E.P. Thompson, *History of the First Kentucky Brigade,* 296.
**JAMES LONGSTREET:** G.M. Sorrel, *Recollections of a Confederate Staff Officer,* 192-193; J. Longstreet, *From Manassas to Appomattox,* 437.
**ALFRED PIRTLE:** "Lytle's Last Sacrifice," unpublished typescript, The Filson Club, Louisville, Ky.
**THOMAS J. STANLEY:** A.R. Phillips,

■ Col. Timothy R. Stanley (third from right), 18th Ohio, fellow officers and ladies admire the breathtaking view. Brigade commander John Beatty remembered his subordinate: "Father Stanley ... presides over the swing ferry [on the Tennessee River], in which he takes especial delight. He has in his time been a grave and reverend senator of Ohio; he never loses sight of this fact, and never fails to impress it upon those with whom he comes in contact."

*Fighting with Turchin,* 106.
**ISAAC SKINNER:** *Official Records,* series 1, vol. XXX, part 1, 923.
**JOHN T. CROXTON:** "In Memorium. John T. Croxton," *Society of the Army of the Cumberland Eighth Reunion 1874,* 174.
**JOSEPH B. NEWTON:** Diary, L.M. Strayer collection.
**CHARLES H. STOCKING:** *Official Records,* series 1, vol. XXX, part 1, 224, 226.
**GABRIEL C. WHARTON:** *Official Records,* series 1, vol. XXX, part 1, 424.
**OSCAR N. WHEELER:** S.A. McNeil, "At Chickamauga. The Fighting and Maneuvering on the First Day," *The National Tribune,* April 14, 1887.
**WILLIAM W. LYLE:** *Lights and Shadows of Army Life,* 291-292.
**WILLIAM W. CARNES:** J.H. Mathes, *The Old Guard in Gray,* 66.
**CONFEDERATE GUNNERS:** T.L. Massenburg, "Capt. W.W. Carnes' Battery at Chickamauga," *Confederate Veteran,* vol. VI, no. 11, November 1898.
**JOHN C. CARTER:** *Confederate Veteran,* vol. XXXIII, no. 4, April 1925.
**'DRIFTWOOD IN A SQUALL':** B.L. Ridley, *Battles and Sketches of the Army of Tennessee,* 220, 225.
**TERRY H. CAHAL:** Letter of September 30, 1863, Tennessee State Library and Archives.
**HENRY H. TINKER:** E. Hannaford, *The Story of a Regiment,* 460, 481.
**JAMES L. COOPER:** Typescript of journal and reminiscences, Tennessee State Library and Archives.
**'FINGERS ON THE TRIGGER':** J.P. McGuire quoted in J.B. Lindsley, *The Military Annals of Tennessee, Confederate,* 475.
**JOSEPH J. LANDRAM:** *Official Records,* series 1, vol. XXX, part 1, 427.
**BATTERY A, 1st OVLA:** H.M. Davidson, *Fourteen Months in Southern Prisons,* 14, 15; *Official Records,* series 1, vol. XXX, part 1, 553-554.
**ISRAEL B. WEBSTER:** "Chickamauga. Going into Action with Hands full of Bacon and Coffee," *The National Tribune,* July 2, 1891.
**ORVILLE T. CHAMBERLAIN:** *The Congressional Medal of Honor: The Names, The Deeds,* 742.
**THOMAS ON SNODGRASS HILL:** J.H. Allspaugh, "Chickamauga. The Struggle of Sunday as Seen by an Enlisted Man," *The National Tribune,* October 7, 1886.
**JAMES B. STEEDMAN:** F.W. Gates, "Chickamauga. The Important Services of the Reserve Corps on the Second Day," *The National Tribune,* April 14, 1887; J.G. Mitchell quoted in undated notes on Chickamauga by Major Arnold McMahon, 21st Ohio, L.M. Strayer collection.
**'THE OTHER SIDE':** J.H. Allspaugh, "Chickamauga. The Struggle of Sunday as Seen by an Enlisted Man," *The National Tribune,* October 7, 1886.
**ZACHARIAH C. DEAS:** *Official Records,* series 1, vol. XXX, part 2, 336, 331-332.
**WILLIAM J. PHILLIPS:** *Official Records,* series 1, vol. XXX, part 2, 334.
**THEODORE WEST:** *Official Records,* series 1, vol. XXX, part 1, 587.
**WILLIAM H. LYTLE:** Typescript of John K. Ely journal, CCNMP; W. Reid, *Ohio in the War,* vol. I, 881.
**LYTLE STAFF OFFICERS:** *Official Records,* series 1, vol. XXX, part 1, 585; L.G. Bennett and W.H. Haigh, *History of the Thirty-sixth Regiment Illinois Volunteers,* 472, 473.
**SILAS MILLER:** Letter of October 30, 1863, Silas Miller Papers, G.A.R. Memorial Hall, Aurora, Ill.

■ Color Sergeant John Geddes of Company C proudly displays the 105th Ohio's national flag, which he carried from January 1863 until war's end. A regimental officer remembered Geddes' service: "The colors were literally shot to rags, the staff struck by bullets several times and his clothes cut more than once, [but] he was never once touched."

**10th OHIO OFFICERS:** *Official Records,* series 1, vol. XXX, part 1, 63.
**LYTLE GUARD OF HONOR:** A. Pirtle, "Lytle's Last Sacrifice," unpublished typescript, The Filson Club, Louisville, Ky.
**GATES P. THRUSTON:** "Chickamauga," *The Southern Bivouac,* December 1886.
**113th OHIO INFANTRYMEN:** J.N. Hall quoted in F.M. McAdams, *Every-day Soldier Life, or A History of the One Hundred and Thirteenth Ohio Volunteer Infantry,* 269.
**GEORGE WEBER:** F.M. McAdams, *Every-day Soldier Life, or A History of the One Hundred and Thirteenth Ohio Volunteer Infantry,* 42-43.
**A. PIATT ANDREW III:** *Some Civil War Letters of A. Piatt Andrew III,* 82.
**CONFEDERATE BATTLE LINE:** J.H. Martin, "Longstreet's Forces at Chickamauga," *Confederate Veteran,* vol. XX, no. 12, December 1912; J.M. Sloan, "A Most Worthy Plea for Help," *Confederate Veteran,* vol. II, no. 2, February 1894.
**JOHN M. PALMER:** *Personal Recollections of John M. Palmer, 184-185.*
**H.C. CUSHING–F.L.D. RUSSELL:** *Official Records,* series 1, vol. XXX, part 1, 783.
**JOHN M. SUTPHEN:** *Official Records,* series 1, vol. XXX, part 1, 758.
**KELLY HOUSE & FIELD:** *Official Records,* series 1, vol. XXX, part 2, 403.
**JOHN T. COXE:** "Chickamauga," *Confederate Veteran,* vol. XXX, no. 8, August 1922.
**GEORGE T. EISELE:** *Official Records,* series 1, vol. XXX, part 2, 324, 325.
**ISAAC CUSAC:** A. Gracie, *The Truth About Chickamauga,* 421.
**ISAAC N. DUNAFIN:** "The Journal of Sergt. William J. McKell," *Civil War History,* vol. III, no. 3, September 1957.
**ARNOLD McMAHON:** J.H. Bolton quoted in S.S. Canfield, *History of the 21st Regiment Ohio Volunteer Infantry,* 144; A. McMahon, undated manuscript (circa 1885) entitled "Suggestions," prepared for Joseph T. Woods, L.M. Strayer collection.
**COLT RIFLES:** E.G. Wetmore, "21st Ohio at Chickamauga," *The National Tribune,* October 2, 1884; J.S. Mahony quoted in S.S. Canfield, *History of the 21st Regiment Ohio Volunteer Infantry,* 139; A. McMahon, undated manuscript (circa 1885) entitled "Suggestions," prepared for Joseph T. Woods, L.M. Strayer collection.
**WILLIAM M. OWEN:** *In Camp and Battle with the Washington Artillery of New Orleans,* 281-282.
**WILLIAM PRESTON:** W.M. Owen, *In Camp and Battle with the Washington Artillery of New Orleans,* 269, 270-271.
**ISAAC H. BAILEY:** *Official Records,* series 1, vol. XXX, part 2, 446.
**JOHN L. CLEM:** W.W. Carter, "Little Johnny Clem, the Drummer Boy of Chickamauga," reprinted from *Grand Army Journal,* April 8, 1871; J.L. Clem, "From Nursery to Battlefield," *Outlook Magazine,* July 4, 1914; A.H. Quint, *The Potomac and the Rapidan,* 391-392.
**JESSE J. FINLEY:** *Official Records,* series 1, vol. XXX, part 2, 436.
**ROBERT C. TRIGG:** W.J. Vance, "On Thomas' Right at Chickamauga," *Blue and Gray,* vol. I, no. 2, February 1893; *Official Records,* series 1, vol. XXX, part 2, 432.
**CALEB H. CARLTON:** A. Gracie, *The Truth About Chickamauga,* 428.
**STEPHEN V. WALKER:** "The Journal of Sergt. William J. McKell," *Civil War History,* vol. III, no. 3, September 1957.
**THEODORE T. FOGLE:** Letter of September

■ Well armed with smoking pipes, these 105th Illinois line officers posed in the spring of 1864. Front row, from left: 1st Lieut. George A. Bender, Company I; 1st Lieut. John W. Burst, Company C; Capt. Charles G. Culver, Company C; and Capt. Theodore S. Rogers, Company B. Back row, from left: 2nd Lieut. Willard Scott Jr., Company B; 1st Lieut. Albert C. Overton, Company E; Capt. James S. Forsythe, Company H; and Capt. Seth F. Daniels, Company F.

■ A company from the 78th Pennsylvania crowds together for a distinctive portrait sometime in early 1864. Its commander appears at upper left, staring directly at the camera. This regiment camped at Summerville on Lookout's summit from early December 1863 through April 1864 — a time, recalled one member, of "our most delightful army experiences," in spite of sudden, often violent weather changes. With winter winds reaching 50 miles per hour, standing picket at night was a dreaded exception to the otherwise light duty.

20, 1863, Woodruff Library, Emory University.
**'FRUITLESS SACRIFICE':** R.H. Hannaford, "On the Field at Chickamauga," *Military Images,* vol. IV, no. 3, November-December 1982; L.A. Shaver, *A History of the Sixtieth Alabama Regiment,* 18, 19.
**CORNELIUS A. O'CALLAGHAN:** Alonzo H. Wood letter of February 26, 1909, CCNMP.
**HANS C. HEG:** *The Civil War Letters of Colonel Hans Christian Heg,* 245; A. Skofstad letter, *Milwaukee Sentinel,* October 20, 1863.
**REUBEN V. KIDD:** *Reuben Vaughan Kidd, Soldier of the Confederacy,* 336.
**JOHN H. MARSH:** W.L. Scott quoted in J.B. Lindsley, *The Military Annals of Tennessee, Confederate,* 793.
**GUSTAVUS A. WOOD:** *Marietta Register* article reprinted in the Gallipolis (Ohio) *Journal,* October 29, 1863.
**JOHN GREGG:** "Diary of Private W.J. Davidson," *The Annals of the Army of Tennessee,* vol. I, no. 7, October 1878.
**10th WISCONSIN:** W.W. Day, *Fifteen Months in Dixie; or, My Personal Experience in Rebel Prisons,* 4, 5.
**DANIEL H. GILMER:** W.E. Patterson diary, CCNMP.
**WILLIAM R. SMITH:** V.C. Giles, *Rags and Hope,* 203.
**DANIEL L. SOWER:** Letter of February 18, 1913; "On Leaving Rebel Prisons," copy of unpublished 1867 Sower essay, Frank Crawford collection.
**ISAAC P. RULE:** Typescript of J.M. Raymond letter of October 18, 1863, Firelands Gallery, Bellevue, Ohio.

## Chapter 3

**CHATTANOOGA VALLEY:** N.B. Grant, *The Life of a Common Soldier 1862-1865,* 19.
**'GIVE THEM A DARE':** J.A. Wyeth, *That Devil Forrest,* 235.
**GEORGE E. FLYNT:** *Official Records,* series 1, vol. XXX, part 3, 778; *Ibid.,* vol. XXX, part 1, 160.
**FRANCIS M. HATFIELD:** *Official Records,* series 1, vol. XXX, part 1, 736, 742.
**WILLIAM D. GALE:** W.M. Polk, *Leonidas Polk, Bishop and General,* vol. II, 281; J.H. Parks, *General Leonidas Polk, C.S.A.,* 341.
**'LEG TAKEN OFF':** T.T. Keith letter of October 7, 1863, CCNMP.
**OFFICER'S MASQUERADE:** A.L. Waddle, *Three Years with the Armies of the Ohio and the Cumberland,* 55.
**LEVI A. ROSS:** Typescript of journal and reminiscences, Illinois State Historical Library.
**ISAAC H.C. ROYSE:** *History of the 115th Regiment Illinois Volunteer Infantry,* 168-169.
**JOSEPH GORE:** J.M. Waddle quoted in I.H.C. Royse, *History of the 115th Regiment Illinois Volunteer Infantry,* 285.
**SAMUEL C. ALEXANDER:** J.H. Moore quoted in I.H.C. Royse, *History of the 115th Regiment Illinois Volunteer Infantry,* 258.
**JAMES A. GARFIELD:** *Official Records,* series 1, vol. XXIII, part 1, 409; letter of September 23, 1863, published in *The Wild Life of the Army,* 296-297.
**KATE CUMMING:** *A Journal of Hospital Life in the Confederate Army of Tennessee,* 95.
**CLINTON M. WINKLER:** Letter of October 22, 1863, published in A.V. Winkler, *The Confederate Capital and Hood's Texas Brigade,* 147.
**THEODORE C. HOWARD:** R.K. Krick, *Parker's Virginia Battery C.S.A.,* 325.
**LOOKOUT MOUNTAIN'S SLOPE:** D.A. Dickert, *History of Kershaw's Brigade,* 293, 294.
**AUGUSTUS B. BONNAFON:** A. Blakeley quoted in *Pennsylvania at Chickamauga and Chattanooga,* 226.
**HARVEY S. LINGLE:** W.M. Palmer quoted in

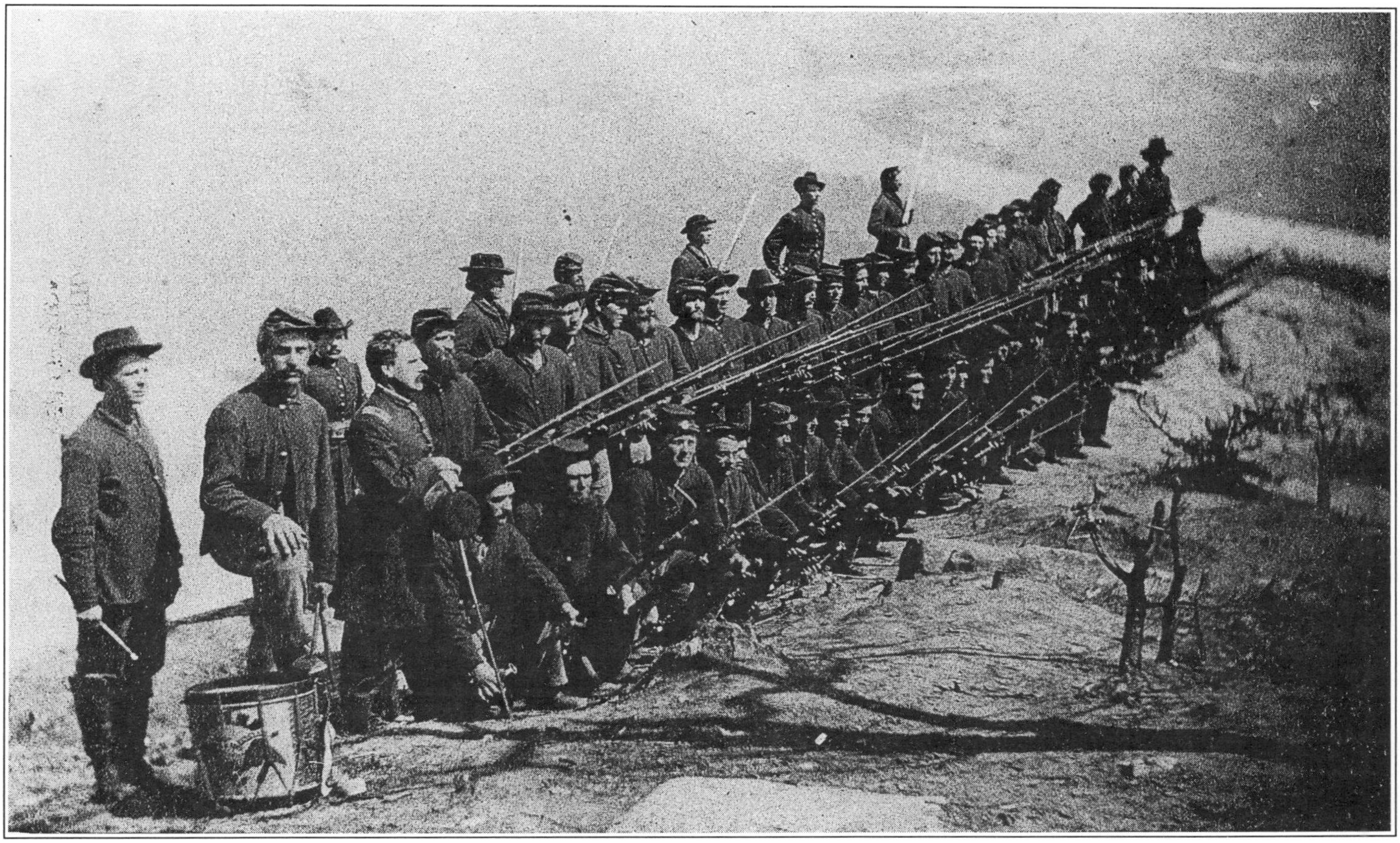

■ An infantry company at "charge bayonet." Set against the background of Moccasin Bend, this is among Linn's most dramatic photographs. File closers pose in the rear rank at "present arms," a position used to discourage straggling from the ranks. Little is known about the identity of this group, but it is probably part of the 78th Pennsylvania, which spent four months atop the mountain in early 1864.

C.H. Kirk, *History of the Fifteenth Pennsylvania Volunteer Cavalry,* 358, 359.
**COMLEY J. MATHER:** T.H. Smith quoted in C.H. Kirk, *History of the Fifteenth Pennsylvania Volunteer Cavalry,* 212.
**'GOOD THINGS TO EAT':** *Official Records,* series 1, vol. XXX, part 2, 696, 697; W.F. Colton quoted in C.H. Kirk, *History of the Fifteenth Pennsylvania Volunteer Cavalry,* 656, 307.
**FEDERAL WAGON TRAIN:** I.W. Avery quoted in "Wheeler's Raid – Unwritten History of the War of the Rebellion," undated *Cincinnati Enquirer* clipping in Henry Campbell Scrapbook, Wabash College Archives, Crawfordsville, Ind.
**GEORGE B. GUILD:** *A Brief Narrative of the Fourth Tennessee Cavalry Regiment,* 50.
**'CHEESE AND CRACKERS':** *Official Records,* series 1, vol. XXX, part 2, 723; J.A. Wyeth, "The Destruction of Rosecrans' Great Wagon Train," *Miller's Photographic History of the Civil War,* vol. IV, 160-164; J.A. Wyeth, *With Sabre and Scalpel,* 284.
**WILLIAM T. MARTIN:** *Official Records,* series 1, vol. XXX, part 2, 725.
**EDWARD M. McCOOK:** *Official Records,* series 1, vol. XXX, part 2, 819, 820.
**ALEXANDER McD. McCOOK:** *Official Records,* series 1, vol. XXX, part 1, 204.
**THOMAS L. CRITTENDEN:** *Official Records,* series 1, vol. XXX, part 1, 202.
**GEORGE H. THOMAS:** J.T. Gibson, *History of the Seventy-eighth Pennsylvania Volunteer Infantry,* 126.
**WILLIAM W. MACKALL:** W.W. Mackall, *A Son's Recollections of his Father,* 186.
**JEFFERSON DAVIS:** E.H. Rennolds diary, Special Collections, University of Tennessee Library, Knoxville; T.T. Fogle letter of October 16, 1863, Woodruff Library, Emory University.
**RODNEY S. BOWEN:** Journal quoted in G.H. Woodruff, *Fifteen Years Ago; or the Patriotism of Will County,* 306.
**MICHAEL H. FITCH:** *Echoes of the Civil War as I Hear Them,* 178, 179.
**JAMES R. MAXWELL:** G. Little and J.R. Maxwell, *A History of Lumsden's Battery C.S.A.,* 19.
**BEHIND THE GUNS:** *Official Records,* series 1, vol. XXXI, part 2, 553; typescript of W.G. Putney memoir, KMNBP.
**FORT WOOD:** Typescript of P.T. Vaughan diary, Alabama Department of Archives and History.
**JOHN D. GALLOWAY:** E. Beaumont quoted in H.H.G. Bradt, *History of the Services of the Third Battery Wisconsin Light Artillery,* 54.
**'BEAVERS FELLING TIMBER':** *Ninety-Second Illinois Volunteers,* 116.
**MICHAEL J. KELLY:** T.R. Davis quoted in *Harper's Weekly,* December 12, 1863.
**CHARLES C. ALESHIRE:** *Official Records,* series 1, vol. XXX, part 4, 217.
**'SACRIFICES MADE':** Typescript of J.L. Cooper journal and reminiscences, Tennessee State Library and Archives; J. Brigham letter of November 24, 1863, Tennessee State Library and Archives; H.W. Henry, "Little War-time Incidents," *Confederate Veteran,* vol. XXII, no. 7, July 1914; J.C. West letters of October 24 and 31, 1863, published in *A Texan in Search of a Fight,* 123, 125-126.
**'DARKEST BEFORE DAY':** October 1863 letters of J. Whitney published in *Kiss Clara For Me,* 112-113, 114.
**27th ILLINOIS INFANTRYMEN:** H.M.F. Weiss letter of October 16, 1863, CCNMP.
**WILLIAM STRAWN:** W.W. Calkins, *The History of the One Hundred and Fourth Regiment of Illinois Volunteer Infantry,* 364.

**'RESIGNED TO MY FATE':** Copies of M.J. Simonds letters of October 8 and 27, 1863, and G.H. Wright letter of October 30, 1863, Illinois State Historical Library.
**BROTHERS UNTO DEATH:** W.F. Hinman, *The Story of the Sherman Brigade,* 446; B. Morse, *Civil War Diaries & Letters of Bliss Morse,* 90.
**57th INDIANA CAMP:** A.L. Kerwood, *Annals of the Fifty-seventh Regiment Indiana Volunteers,* 211-212, 215.
**ON EQUAL TERMS:** I.H.C. Royse, *History of the 115th Regiment Illinois Volunteer Infantry,* 180-181.
**NARROW WINDING PASSAGES:** I.C. Doan, *Reminiscences of the Chattanooga Campaign,* 10, 11, 12.
**'WATER'S EDGE':** S.F. Horrall, *History of the Forty-Second Indiana Volunteer Infantry,* 196-197.

## Chapter 4

**WILLIAM F. SMITH:** *Official Records,* series 1, vol. XXXI, part 1, 77.
**WILLIAM B. HAZEN:** *A Narrative of Military Service,* 162, 163, 164.
**ULYSSES S. GRANT:** O.O. Howard, "Grant at Chattanooga," *Personal Recollections of the War of the Rebellion,* 245-247.
**TIMOTHY R. STANLEY:** *Official Records,* series 1, vol. XXXI, part 1, 79, 80.
**4th ALABAMA SHARPSHOOTERS:** Typescript of T. Vaughan diary, Alabama Department of Archives and History.
**ROBERT T. COLES:** Unpublished typescript "History of the Fourth Regiment Alabama Volunteer Infantry," Alabama Department of Archives and History.
**LAWRENCE H. SCRUGGS:** *Official Records,* vol. LI, part 2, 764.
**EVANDER M. LAW:** *Official Records,* series 1, vol. XXXI, part 1, 225.
**WILLIAM C. OATES:** *The War Between the Union and the Confederacy and its Lost Opportunities,* 272.
**WILLIAM H. SURLES:** T.J. Bond, "About Brown's Ferry," *The National Tribune,* October 10, 1912.
**AQUILA WILEY:** *Official Records,* series 1, vol. XXXI, part 1, 91.
**THOMAS QUIRK:** J.A. Wyeth, "Trials with Gen. John H. Morgan," *Confederate Veteran,* vol. XIX, no. 3, March 1911.
**LAUNCELOT L. SCOTT:** C.M. Heaton, "Hazen's Midnight Excursion," *The National Tribune,* December 20, 1906.
**CHARLES A. CABLE:** *Official Records,* series 1, vol. XXXI, part 1, 80.
**ROBERT A. GAULT:** "Capturing Brown's Ferry," *The National Tribune,* November 18, 1915.
**OTIS A. SHATTUCK:** R.A. Gault, "Capturing Brown's Ferry," *The National Tribune,* November 18, 1915.
**ROBERT L. KIMBERLY:** *The Forty-first Ohio Veteran Volunteer Infantry in the War of the Rebellion 1861-1865,* 64.
**JAMES C. FOY:** *Official Records,* series 1, vol. XXXI, part 1, 86, 87.
**LAYING PONTOON BRIDGE:** C.E. Belknap quoted in *Society of the Army of the Cumberland 26th Reunion 1896,* 135.
**JOHN B. TURCHIN:** T.D. Osborne, "Capture of Brown's Ferry," *The National Tribune,* May 2, 1901.

## Chapter 5

**JOSEPH HOOKER:** W.G. LeDuc, *Recollections of a Civil War Quartermaster,* 119.
**HORACE BOUGHTON:** M.G. Young, *A Condensed History of the 143rd Regiment New York Volunteer Infantry,* 21-22.
**'REOPEN THIS ROAD':** Typescript of W.M. Clark letter of October 28, 1863, CCNMP.
**29th PENNSYLVANIA PRIVATE:** G.W. Holmes quoted in G.H. Woodruff, *Fifteen Years Ago; or the Patriotism of Will County,* 300.
**SAMUEL M. ZULICH:** *Official Records,* series 1, vol. XXXI, part 1, 124.
**'RESPONSIBILITY IS IMMENSE':** *The Life and Services of Major-General Henry Warner Slocum,* 140, 141-142; *From the Cannon's Mouth,* 272.
**E. PORTER ALEXANDER:** *Fighting for the Confederacy,* 310-311.
**JOHN BRATTON:** *Official Records,* series 1, vol. XXXI, part 1, 231, 232.
**JAMES L. COKER:** *History of Company G, Ninth S.C. Regiment, Infantry, S.C. Army and of Company E, Sixth S.C. Regiment, Infantry, S.C. Army,* 135.
**MARTIN W. GARY:** *Official Records,* series 1, vol. XXXI, part 1, 132.
**MICAH JENKINS:** J.B. Polley, *A Soldier's Letters to Charming Nellie,* 142-144.
**CHARLES A. ATWELL:** Typescript of D. Nichol letter of December 10, 1863, Dr. William Glenn Robertson collection, Leavenworth, Kan.
**GEORGE S. GREENE:** *Official Records,* series 1, vol. XXXI, part 1, 127.
**GEARY'S GRIEF:** G.K. Collins, *Memoirs of the 149th Regt. N.Y. Vol. Inft.,* 199-200; typescript of J.W. Geary letter of November 2, 1863, CCNMP.
**MOSES VEALE:** *The Congressional Medal of Honor: The Names, The Deeds,* 935.
**WILLIAM C. LILLY:** G.K. Collins, *Memoirs of the 149th Regt. N.Y. Vol. Inft.,* 198, 200.
**CARL SCHURZ:** *Official Records,* series 1, vol. XXXI, part 1, 201.
**OLIVER O. HOWARD:** W.G. LeDuc, *Recollections of a Civil War Quartermaster,* 98.
**ADOLPH VON STEINWEHR:** *Official Records,* series 1, vol. XXXI, part 1, 102.
**VALERIUS C. GILES:** M.V. Smith, *Reminiscences of the Civil War,* 43.
**LOOKOUT VALLEY ASSAULT:** *Harper's Weekly,* November 28, 1863.
**ORLAND SMITH–SAMUEL H. HURST:** *Official Records,* series 1, vol. XXXI, part 1, 108, 109.
**ADIN B. UNDERWOOD:** *Official Records,* series 1, vol. XXXI, part 1, 100-101; J.M. Cate letter of November 15, 1863, Jean M. Cate collection, Rancho Santa Fe, Calif.
**'AVENGE OUR COLONEL':** A.B. Underwood, *Three Years' Service with the Thirty-Third Mass. Infantry Regiment,* 160-161, 170.
**JOSEPH L. LOCKE:** *Official Records,* series 1, vol. XXXI, part 1, 104.
**RUFUS F. FISHER:** Typescript of R. Hubbard letter of October 31, 1863, Robert Hubbard Papers, Manuscripts Division, USAMHI.

## Chapter 6

**WILLIAM G. LeDUC:** *Recollections of a Civil War Quartermaster,* 103.
**JOHN RIDDLE:** *Official Records,* series 1, vol. XXX, part 4, 368-369, 367.
**STEAMER *CHATTANOOGA:*** C. Grant, "The Cracker Line," *The National Tribune,* October 30, 1884.
**MULE SUPPLY TRAINS:** *Harper's Weekly,* December 12, 1863.
**LOOKOUT CREEK PICKET DUTY:** H.M. Woodson, "Battle on Side of Lookout Mountain," *Confederate Veteran,* vol. VI, no. 1, January 1898.
**LOOKOUT MOUNTAIN:** Typescript of O.T. Hanks memoir, Confederate Research Center, Hill College, Hillsboro, Texas.
**'THEIR GOOD HUMOR':** W.D. Pickett, "Dead Angle – Rules for Burial of Dead," *Confederate Veteran,* vol. XVI, no. 5, May 1908.
**JOHN A. PATTERSON:** Typescript of letter of March 24, 1864, courtesy Dr. B.D. Patterson, Hillsboro, Texas.
**EDWARD C. WALTHALL:** W. Honnoll letter of November 18, 1863, Woodruff Library, Emory University.
**THOMAS NAST PAINTING:** *Official Records,* series 1, vol. XXXI, part 2, 407-408.
**JAMES VANDERMARK:** *Official Records,* series 1, vol. XXXI, part 2, 407.
**JOHN C. BROWN:** *Official Records,* series 1, vol. XXXI, part 2, 726.
**GEORGE A. COBHAM JR.:** Typescript of letter of November 29, 1863, Warren County Historical Society, Warren, Pa.

---

■ **Opposite:** Twenty-three members of Company D, 21st Wisconsin, clambered atop the mountain for this Linn Gallery photograph taken April 20, 1864. 2nd Lieut. John H. Otto stands third from left in the top row, with Sergeant Lyman C. Waite to his immediate left. Musician Harold Galpin poses with his drum in the front row. All three were residents of Appleton, Wis.

**JAMES SIMMONS:** *Official Records,* series 1, vol. XXXI, part 2, 700.
**CRAVENS HOUSE:** P.A. Cribbs, *Confederate Veteran,* vol. VI, no. 8, August 1898.
**VALENTINE DELMAS:** *Official Records,* series 1, vol. XXXI, part 2, 700.
**ROBERT A. JARMAN:** "The History of Company K, 27th Mississippi Infantry," *The Aberdeen Examiner,* March 7, 1890.
**JOHN C. MOORE:** "Battle of Lookout Mountain," *Confederate Veteran,* vol. VI, no. 9, September 1898.
**JOHN K. JACKSON:** *Official Records,* series 1, vol. XXXI, part 2, 695-696, 705.
**'BEHIND EVERY ROCK':** W.L. Stork, "Lookout Mountain," *The National Tribune,* May 19, 1887; R. Callahan, "They Kept Going: A 29th Pa. Man Tells How the 'White Star' Shone on Lookout Mountain," *The National Tribune,* December 23, 1886.
**'DEPRESS MY GUNS':** *Official Records,* series 1, vol. XXXI, part 2, 728.
**WILLIAM GROSE:** *Official Records,* series 1, vol. XXXI, part 2, 169, 171.
**HENRY A. BARNUM:** *Official Records,* series 1, vol. XXXI, part 2, 448.
**8th KENTUCKY FLAG:** J. Wilson, "He Put It There," *The National Tribune,* March 31, 1887; J. Wilson, "Lookout Mountain," *The National Tribune,* June 11, 1891; C.A. Partridge, *History of the Ninety-sixth Regiment Illinois Volunteer Infantry.*
**PETER J. OSTERHAUS:** *Official Records,* series 1, vol. XXXI, part 2, 600.
**111th PENNSYLVANIA FLAGS:** S.M. Moore, "The 111th Pa.," *The National Tribune,* May 5, 1887; L.J. Dyke, "Lookout Mountain," *The National Tribune,* September 22, 1887.
**WILLIAM L. STORK:** "Lookout Mountain," *The National Tribune,* May 19, 1887.
**THOMAS E. CHAMPION:** *Official Records,* series 1, vol. XXXI, part 2, 146.

## Chapter 7

**JAMES R. CHALMERS:** *Official Records,* series 1, vol. XXX, part 2, 760.
**CHARLES EWING:** J.P. Young, *The Seventh Tennessee Cavalry,* 70, 71.

■ A distinguished group of staff officers from Department of the Cumberland headquarters. From left: Capt. Henry Stone (assistant adjutant general); Major Gates P. Thruston (assistant adjutant general and acting judge advocate); Col. Joseph P. Burke, 10th Ohio (commanding headquarters guard); Capt. Hunter Brooke (aide-de-camp and acting judge advocate); unidentified; Major Charles S. Cotter (commanding artillery in the Chattanooga garrison); and a newspaper correspondent, who bears a strong resemblance to Theodore R. Davis of *Harper's Weekly.*

**STEPHEN DILL LEE:** H. Hattaway, *General Stephen D. Lee,* 100, 101.
**SAMUEL M. McANNALLY:** *Official Records,* series 1, vol. XXX, part 2, 748.
**OSCAR MALMBORG:** H.S. Nourse, *The Story of the Fifty-Fifth Regiment Illinois Volunteer Infantry,* 274.
**WILLIAM T. SHERMAN:** H.S. Nourse, *The Story of the Fifty-Fifth Regiment Illinois Volunteer Infantry,* 267; *Home Letters of General Sherman,* 275-276.
**PERRIN V. FOX:** C.E. Belknap quoted in C.R. Sligh, *History of the Services of the First Regiment Michigan Engineers and Mechanics,* 74-76.
**DANIEL McCOOK:** *Official Records,* series 1, vol. XXXI, part 2, 503.
**MILTON L. HANEY:** *The Story of the Fifty-Fifth Regiment Illinois Volunteer Infantry,* 457.
**JENKIN L. JONES:** *An Artilleryman's Diary,* 138, 142, 143.
**ELI J. SHERLOCK:** *Memorabilia of the Marches and Battles in which the One Hundredth Regiment of Indiana Infantry Volunteers Took an Active Part,* 54, 59.
**RUEL M. JOHNSON:** E.J. Sherlock, *Memorabilia ...,* 245-246,
**GLASS HOUSE:** H. Robinson, typescript of undated wartime letter, CCNMP.
**SAMUEL JONES:** *Official Records,* series 1, vol. XXXI, part 2, 634-635.
**REUBEN WILLIAMS:** *Official Records,* series 1, vol. XXXI, part 2, 634, 635.
**JOHN S. KOUNTZ:** *The Ohio Soldier and National Picket Guard,* November 9, 1889.
**JOHN HAMM:** W. Schmidt, *The Ohio Soldier and National Picket Guard,* August 24, 1895.
**JAMES H. DAYTON:** *Official Records,* series 1, vol. XXXI, part 2, 781.
**WILLIAM D. SWANN:** J.P. Douglas, *Douglas's Texas Battery, CSA,* 77, 78.
**PATRICK R. CLEBURNE:** *Official Records,* series 1, vol. XXXI, part 2, 749; J.M. Berry, "The Quiet Humor of Gen. Pat Cleburne," *Confederate Veteran,* vol. XII, no. 4, April 1904.
**JOSEPH H. LEWIS:** J.W. Green, *Johnny Green of the Orphan Brigade,* 110.
**FIGHTING ON TUNNEL HILL:** *Official Records,* series 1, vol. XXXI, part 2, 750.
**NELSON STAUFFER:** Entries of November 27 and December 5, 1863, *Civil War Diary,* copy at Illinois State Historical Library.
**GILES A. SMITH:** M.L. Haney, *The Story of the Fifty-Fifth Regiment Illinois Volunteer Infantry,* 457-458.
**JOHN M. CORSE:** J. Potter, *Reminiscences of the Civil War,* 64-65.
**ASIAS WILLISON:** *Official Records,* series 1, vol. XXXI, part 2, 636; *Reminiscences of the Civil War from Diaries of Members of 103d Illinois Volunteer Infantry,* 29.
**HIRAM W. HALL:** *Official Records,* series 1, vol. XXXI, part 2, 636.
**JOHN M. LOOMIS:** M.D. Gage, *From Vicksburg to Raleigh; or, a Complete History of the Twelfth Regiment Indiana Volunteer Infantry,* 142-143, 146.
**CHARLES L. MATTHIES:** *Official Records,* series 1, vol. XXXI, part 2, 652, 653; W.H. Mengel letter of January 11, 1908, CCNMP.
**JABEZ BANBURY:** *Official Records,* series 1, vol. XXXI, part 2, 655; C. Fosdick, *Five Hundred Days in Rebel Prisons,* 7-8.
**JAMES C. NISBET:** *Four Years on the Firing Line,* 143, 152.
**'AT ALL HAZARDS':** S.P. Bates, *History of Pennsylvania Volunteers 1861-5,* vol. I, 867-868.
**HOLDEN PUTNAM:** H.M. Trimble, *History of the Ninety-Third Regiment Illinois Volunteer Infantry,* 77-78.
**GEORGE H. CONANT:** J.W. Maupin letter of December 16, 1907, CCNMP.

## Chapter 8

**WILLICH'S SKIRMISHERS:** *Official Records,* series 1, vol. XXXI, part 2, 263.
**GORDON GRANGER:** *Official Records,* series 1, vol. XXXI, part 2, 68; M.V. Sheridan quoted in A. Cope, *The Fifteenth Ohio Volunteers and Its Campaigns,* 388.
**ISAAC A. KRUSON:** *Official Records,* series 1, vol. XXXI, part 2, 377, 378.
**'HOT AND LIVELY CONTEST':** *Official Records,* series 1, vol. XXXI, part 2, 362.
**JOHN K. SHELLENBERGER:** *Official Records,* series 1, vol. XXXI, part 2, 240.
**EDWARD BROMLEY:** L.B. Mesnard unpublished memoir, Firelands Historical Society, Norwalk, Ohio.

■ Col. Charles H. Grosvenor, 18th Ohio Veteran Volunteer Infantry, and ladies. At Chickamauga, Grosvenor led a successful counterattack to the crest of Horseshoe Ridge with "about eighty men of my regiment, which was a pretty good-sized crowd for any regiment on that battlefield on the afternoon of Sunday, September 20th," he later wrote. As the line neared the top, the Palmetto flag of the 7th South Carolina became a conspicuous mark inside the breastworks. Just then Gen. John Beatty called out: "Colonel Grosvenor, there is a brigadier-general's commission for the man that will capture that flag." Several men sprang for the color just as Ensign Alfred D. Clark of the 7th suffered a fatal wound. "As he fell," his messmate recalled, "he threw the flag backwards over his head and landed it safely in the hands of his comrades, he falling dead."

**'ALL ACTED LIKE VETERANS':** B.F. Taylor, *Mission Ridge and Lookout Mountain with Pictures of Life in Camp and Field,* 133; *Official Records,* series 1, vol. XXXI, part 2, 509, 461.
**AUGUST WILLICH:** S.C. McKirahan quoted in A. Cope, *The Fifteenth Ohio Volunteers and Its Campaigns,* 383, 382.
**JOHN A. MARTIN:** *Official Records,* series 1, vol. XXXI, part 2, 274; J.A. Martin, *Military History of the Eighth Kansas Veteran Volunteer Infantry,* 64.
**'ORDERED UP THE RIDGE':** J.S. Fullerton, "The Army of the Cumberland at Chattanooga," *Battles and Leaders of the Civil War,* vol. III, 725.
**ARTHUR M. MANIGAULT:** *A Carolinian Goes to War,* 142, 143.
**THOMAS P. HODGES:** W.F. Tucker after-action report in *The Confederate Collapse at the Battle of Missionary Ridge,* 71.
**CORNELIUS I. WALKER:** *Rolls and Historical Sketch of the Tenth Regiment, So. Ca. Volunteers,* 105.
**CALVIN J.C. MUNROE:** S.K. Vann, *Most Lovely Lizzie: Love Letters of a Young Confederate Soldier,* 13.
**JAMES G. WATSON:** Typescript of letter of November 26, 1863, CCNMP.
**HENRY L. ROWELL:** *Official Records,* series 1, vol. XXXI, part 2, 270.
**'FIENDS INCARNATE':** B.P. Critchell, "A Wicked Fight," *The National Tribune,* October 6, 1887.
**E. BASSETT LANGDON:** A. Kern, *History of the First Regiment Ohio Volunteer Infantry,* 27.
**FREDERICK KNEFLER:** Typescript of D.W. Howe memoir, Daniel W. Howe Papers, Smith Memorial Library, Indiana Historical Society.
**GEORGE F. DICK:** J.A. Barnes, J.R. Carnahan and T.H.B. McCain, *The Eighty-sixth Regiment Indiana Volunteer Infantry,* 274.
**JAMES J. TURNER:** J.B. Lindsley, *The Military Annals of Tennessee, Confederate,* 451, 453.
**GEORGE D. WAGNER:** *Official Records,* series 1, vol. XXXI, part 2, 216.
**'THE LAST MAN':** A.W. Reynolds after-action report in *The Confederate Collapse at the Battle of Missionary Ridge,* 77.
**GEORGE W.F. HARPER:** *North Carolina Regiments,* vol. III, 436-437.
**JOHN M. CASSETT:** R.S. Bowen quoted in G.H. Woodruff, *Fifteen Years Ago; or the Patriotism of Will County,* 308.
**THOMAS BRADFORD:** *Official Records,* series 1, vol. XXXI, part 2, 676; *Confederate Veteran,* vol. XXIV, no. 7, July 1916.
**SANDERS MYERS:** W.M. Ives Jr., *Civil War Journal and Letters of Washington Ives 4th Fla. C.S.A.*
**WILLIAM T. STOCKTON:** Letter of December 1863, William T. Stockton Papers, Florida State Archives, Tallahassee; W.M. Ives Jr., *Civil War Journal and Letters of Washington Ives 4th Fla. C.S.A.*
**THOMAS L. MASSENBURG:** *Confederate Veteran,* vol. XVI, no. 12, December 1908.
**WILLIAM B. BATE:** *Official Records,* series 1, vol. XXXI, part 2, 742.
**'SPIKED THE GUNS':** J.A. Chalaron, "At Missionary Ridge," *The National Tribune,* May 4, 1899.
**CHARLES G. HARKER:** *Official Records,* series 1, vol. XXXI, part 2, 230-231.
**HENRY C. DUNLAP:** *Official Records,* series 1, vol. XXXI, part 2, 239.
**HENRY H. KLING:** C. Woodruff quoted in W.F. Hinman, *The Story of the Sherman Brigade,* 462.
**JOSEPH McGREGOR:** *Official Records,* series 1, vol. XXXI, part 2, 234.
**JAMES C. SWASSICK:** *Official Records,* series 1, vol. XXXI, part 2, 242.
**THOMAS H. MAXWELL:** *Official Records,* series 1, vol. XXXI, part 2, 246, 247.
**ORCHARD KNOB–MISSIONARY RIDGE:** E. Popplestone, *The National Tribune,* May 4, 1899.
**JAMES F. JAQUESS:** W.H. Newlin, *A History of the Seventy-third Regiment of Illinois Infantry Volunteers,* 267.
**ARTHUR MacARTHUR JR.:** N.J. Monson, "The 24th Wisconsin's gallant Boy Colonel, Arthur MacArthur, planted the colors on Missionary Ridge," *America's Civil War,* March 1992.
**FRANCIS M. WALKER:** W.J. Worsham, The Old Nineteenth Tennessee Regiment, C.S.A., 97.
**ALEXANDER P. STEWART:** *Official Records,* series 1, vol. XXXI, part 2, 147-148.
**OTHO F. STRAHL:** N.C. Howard, "An Incident of Missionary Ridge," *Confederate Veteran,* vol. XXI, no. 6, June 1913.
**BERNARD LAIBOLDT:** L.F. Hemingway quoted in L.G. Bennett and W.M. Haigh, *History of the Thirty-sixth Regiment Illinois Volunteers,* 531.
**'PLUCKY LITTLE BAND':** E.H. Rennolds, *A History of the Henry County Commands which served in the Confederate States Army,* 66; N.C. Howard, "An Incident of Missionary Ridge," *Confederate Veteran,* vol. XXI, no. 6, June 1913.
**EDWIN H. RENNOLDS:** *A History of the Henry County Commands which served in the Confederate States Army,* 64; typescript of diary, CCNMP.
**JOHN CONKLIN:** *Official Records,* series 1, vol. XXXI, part 2, 545, 544.
**WILLIAM H. HAYS:** *Official Records,* series 1, vol. XXXI, part 2, 541, 548.
**154th TENNESSEE FLAG:** A.J. Vaughan after-action report in *The Confederate Collapse at the Battle of Missionary Ridge,* 51.
**FERDINAND VAN DERVEER:** D.B. Floyd, *History of the Seventy-Fifth Regiment of Indiana Infantry Volunteers,* 233.
**GEORGE W. GORDON:** J.B. Lindsley, *The Military Annals of Tennessee, Confederate,* 298.
**'NO BOY'S PLAY':** D. Putnam Jr. quoted in *Marietta College in the War of Secession, 1861-1865,* 35, 36-37, 38.
**JAMES K. ROCHESTER:** *Official Records,* series 1, vol. XXXI, part 2, 521.
**GEORGE B. TURNER:** D. Putnam, *History of Washington County, Ohio,* 251.
**CHARLES R. WOODS:** *Official Records,* series 1, vol. XXXI, part 2, 611.
**'AT ANY COST':** S.T. Josselyn quoted in *Deeds of Valor,* 285-286; *Official Records,* series 1, vol. XXXI, part 2, 745.
**JOHN C. BRECKINRIDGE:** I.A. Buck, *Cleburne and his Command,* 166.
**JAMES T. HOLTZCLAW:** H.T. Holt quoted in R. Partin, "A Confederate Sergeant's Report to His Wife During the Campaign from Tullahoma to Dalton," *Tennessee Historical Quarterly,* vol. XII, no. 4, December 1953.
**LEWIS T. WOODRUFF:** S. Powell, "A Boy Soldier of Alabama," *Confederate Veteran,* vol. XXIX, no. 1, January 1921; *Official Records,* series 1, vol. XXXI, part 2, 472.
**WILLIAM A. CHUNN:** Letter of December 1, 1863, William A. Chunn Papers, Special Collections Library, Duke University.
**DAVID F. BREMNER:** J.H. Haynie, *The Nineteenth Illinois,* 278.
**CAPTURED CONFEDERATES:** J.W. Inzer, *The Diary of a Confederate Soldier,* 46.
**JOHN C. STARKWEATHER:** J.T. Gibson, *History of the Seventy-eighth Pennsylvania Volunteer Infantry,* 135-136.

## Chapter 9

**DANIEL F. GRIFFIN:** B.F. Scribner, *How Soldiers Were Made,* 186.
**WILLIAM P. CARLIN:** *Official Records,* series 1, vol. XXXI, part 2, 464, 465.
**LAWRENCE GATES:** N.J. Letts quoted in W.F. Peddycord, *History of the Seventy-fourth Regiment Indiana Volunteer Infantry,* 125.
**CRACKERS, CORNCAKES:** J.P. Crane letter of December 29, 1863, Atlanta Historical Society; B.B. Mabrey letter of December 1, 1863, published in *Benjamin Benn Mabrey, Yankee Soldier;* C.G. Phillips, "Lookout and Mission Ridge," *The National Tribune,* February 1, 1912; G.H. Godden quoted in C.T. Develling, *History of the Seventeenth* [Ohio] *Regiment,* 113.
**BENJAMIN F. CHEATHAM:** C. Losson, *Tennessee's Forgotten Warriors,* 130; "General B.F. Cheatham," *The Southern Bivouac,* vol. II, no. 4, December 1883.
**ROBERT C. WILLIAMSON:** W.H. Bruton quoted in J.B. Lindsley, *The Military Annals of Tennessee, Confederate,* 217.
**GEORGE E. MANEY:** "Maney's Brigade After the Battle of Missionary Ridge," *The Southern Bivouac,* vol. II, no. 8, April 1884.
**ROBERT C. THOMPSON:** R. Gates quoted in J.B. Lindsley, *The Military Annals of Tennessee, Confederate,* 218.
**STATES RIGHTS GIST:** *Savannah Republican,* reprinted December 4, 1863 in

■ 1st Lieut. Hiram P. Marston of Company D, 33rd Massachusetts, points his sword toward Missionary Ridge while Capt. Anzi S. Taylor (left) of Company C, 33rd New Jersey, and Capt. James F. Rowe of Company E, 33rd Massachusetts, look on. Camped at the foot of Raccoon Mountain in log huts covered with tent flies, the 33rd Massachusetts, veterans of Chancellorsville, Gettysburg and Wauhatchie, "spent the winter in quiet retirement, free from the excitements of active campaigns, with no one to molest them ...There were occasional festivities at Sutler Trainer's, where that new beverage known as 'wooden hoop beer' chased dull care away, sometimes rapidly. Other things occupied attention. A skillful nine selected from Hooker's body guard, challenged the regiment to match them in a manly game of base ball, and [their] nine got worsted. A New York regiment threw down the glove with a like result. The champion Sharon boys knew a thing or two about base ball ..."

*The Charleston Mercury.*
**JEFFERSON C. DAVIS:** *Official Records,* series 1, vol. XXXI, part 2, 492, 498-499.
**ALLEN L. FAHNESTOCK:** Diary, Allen L. Fahnestock Papers, Illinois State Historical Library.
**LORAINE C. CHERINGTON:** Entry of November 26, 1863 from N.Stauffer's *Civil War Diary,* copy at Illinois State Historical Library.
**ROBERT M. McCOY:** *Official Records,* series 1, vol. XXXI, part 2, 486.
**LUKE KENNEDY:** J.S. Jackman, *Diary of a Confederate Soldier,* 96; L.D. Young, *Reminiscences of a Soldier of the Orphan Brigade,* 71-72.
**IRVING A. BUCK:** *Cleburne and his Command,* 65.
**RINGGOLD GAP:** *Official Records,* series 1, vol. XXXI, part 2, 321.
**MARK P. LOWREY:** *Official Records,* series 1, vol. XXXI, part 2, 769.
**SAMUEL ADAMS:** *Official Records,* series 1, vol. XXXI, part 2, 771; typescript of L.W. Bigbie letter of December 3, 1863, CCNMP.
**FREDERICK W. PARTRIDGE:** *Official Records,* series 1, vol. XXXI, part 2, 608.
**'PERMISSION TO AMPUTATE':** *Official Records,* series 1, vol. XXXI, part 2, 439; J. Spiegelhalter quoted in H.A. Kircher, *A German in the Yankee Fatherland,* 146-148.
**HOOKER AT RINGGOLD:** R. Eddy, *History of the Sixtieth Regiment New York State Volunteers,* 312.
**DANIEL C. GOVAN:** *Official Records,* series 1, vol. XXXI, part 2, 763, 760.
**WILLARD WARNER:** *Official Records,* series 1, vol. XXXI, part 2, 613.
**CREIGHTON'S CHARGE:** *Official Records,* series 1, vol. XXXI, part 2, 414.
**'SENSELESS EXPOSURE':** Typescript of C.D. Miller memoir, Tennessee State Library and Archives; C.A. Willison, *Reminiscences of a Boy's Service with the 76th Ohio,* 78-79.
**JAMES BEESON:** *Official Records,* series 1, vol. XXXI, part 2, 756.
**ROOSTERS:** *Official Records,* series 1, vol. XXXI, part 2, 418, 419; T. Wilder, *The History of Company C, Seventh Regiment, O.V.I.,* 39.
**JAMES A. WILLIAMSON:** *Official Records,* series 1, vol. XXXI, part 2, 616, 617.
**'PROMISES OF MEN':** T. Wilder, *The History of Company C, Seventh Regiment, O.V.I.,* 39, 40-41.

## Chapter 10

**GROSE'S BRIGADE CAMP:** *Official Records,* series 1, vol. XXXI, part 2, 173.

## Sources

**P. SIDNEY POST:** C.A. Mosman, *The Rough Side of War,* 322.

**TIMOTHY R. STANLEY:** J. Beatty, *The Citizen-Soldier,* 355, 158.
**JOHN GEDDES:** A.W. Tourgée, *The Story of a Thousand,* 280.
**78th PENNSYLVANIA:** J.T. Gibson, *History of the Seventy-eighth Pennsylvania Volunteer Infantry,* 139-140.
**CHARLES H. GROSVENOR:** A. Gracie, *The Truth About Chickamauga,* 309-311.
**33rd MASSACHUSETTS:** A.B. Underwood, *The Three Years' Service of the Thirty-Third Mass. Infantry Regiment 1862-1865,* 198, 199.
**9th PENNSYLVANIA CAVALRY:** W. Thomas quoted in J.W. Rowell, *Yankee Cavalrymen,* 188.

# Acknowledgments

***The authors wish to thank all the individuals whose invaluable assistance and contributions were instrumental in completing this book.***

***A debt of sincere gratitude is owed to the following people for providing a variety of written and photographic material, as well as giving unselfishly of their time:***

**ALABAMA:** Douglas R. Cubbison, Madison; Norwood A. Kerr, Alabama Department of Archives and History, Montgomery.
**ARKANSAS:** Bobby Roberts, Central Arkansas Library System, Little Rock.
**FLORIDA:** Rich Chojnacki, Winter Park; Warren Hitt, Clearwater; Joan Morris and Jody Norman, Florida State Archives, Tallahassee.
**GEORGIA:** Dennis Kelly, Kennesaw Mountain National Battlefield Park, Kennesaw; Kathy Knox, Woodruff Library, Emory University, Atlanta; Richard W. Nee, Atlanta; James H. Ogden III, Chickamauga & Chattanooga National Military Park, Ft. Oglethorpe; Brad L. Pruden, Marietta; G.W. Sheppard Jr., Warner Robins; Dale S. Snair, Atlanta.
**INDIANA:** Craig Dunn, Kokomo; Fred Jolly, Muncie; Mick Kissick, Albany; John Sickles, Merrillville; Mark Weldon, Ft. Wayne.
**ILLINOIS:** Franklin Brandt, Stewardson; Harvey Cash, Clay City; Frank Crawford, Caledonia; Mary Michals and Cheryl Schnirring, Illinois State Historical Library, Springfield; Karl Sundstrom, North Riverside; Mrs. Pat Talsma, Belvidere; William J. Warner, Ashton; Ray Zielin, Chicago.
**IOWA:** Roger Davis, Keokuk; W. Clark Kenyon, Iowa City; Mark Warren, Bloomfield.
**KANSAS:** Al L. Camblin, Topeka.
**KENTUCKY:** Thomas Fuller, Dawson Springs; Ken Hamilton, Lexington; Jerry Raisor, Georgetown.
**LOUISIANA:** Larry Chapman, Trout; George C. Esker III, Metairie.
**MARYLAND:** Gil Barrett, Laurel; Roger D. Hunt, Rockville; Craig T. Johnson, Towson; Dr. Richard A. Sauers, Westover; Bill Turner, La Plata; Courtney B. Wilson, Catonsville; David Zullo, Gaithersburg.
**MASSACHUSETTS:** Steven J. Adolphson, West Newbury; Henry Deeks, Acton.
**MICHIGAN:** Robert M. Coch, Flat Rock; Jerry Everts, Adrian; Chris Magewick, Redford; Michael Waskul, Ypsilanti.
**MISSISSIPPI:** Frances Evans, Tupelo; Vann R. Martin, Jackson.
**NEW JERSEY:** Joseph Fulginiti, Haddonfield; C. Paul Loane, Cherry Hill.
**NEW YORK:** Michael Albanese, Kendall.
**NORTH CAROLINA:** John R. Peacock, High Point.
**OHIO:** Bob Albertini, Olmsted; Matthew Burr, Bellevue; Timothy R. Brookes, East Liverpool; Richard F. Carlile, Dayton; Ron Chojnacki, Medina; Gary Delscamp, Dayton; Stephen Fryburg, Bellbrook; John P. Gurnish, Mogadore; Edwin G. Hibarger, Cincinnati; Mike Hilber, Lakewood; Greg Hitt, Bowling Green; Christopher Jarvis, Dublin; Dennis Keesee, New Albany; Michael G. Kraus, Creston; Dr. Kenneth Lawrence, Orwell; Roger Long, Port Clinton; David V. McCullough, Leipsic; Tom Molocea, Boardman; David A. Neuhardt, Yellow Springs; Larry Stevens, Newark; David W. Taylor, Sylvania; Robert Van Dorn, Findlay.
**PENNSYLVANIA:** Herb Brown and Van Nitz, Fields of Glory, Gettysburg; Ronn Palm, Kittanning; Harry Roach, Henryville; Wes Small, The Horse Soldier, Gettysburg; Ken C. Turner, Ellwood City; Michael J. Winey, Dr. Richard J. Sommers, Randy Hackenburg and David A. Keogh, U.S. Army Military History Institute, Carlisle Barracks.
**TENNESSEE:** Ann Alley, Doreen Brown and Marilyn Hughes, Tennessee State Library and Archives, Nashville; Tim Burgess, White House; Thomas Cartwright, Carter House Museum, Franklin; Neal Coulter and Bill Prince, Lupton Library, University of Tennessee-Chattanooga; Phillip George, Murfreesboro; Paul Gibson, Blountville; Charles S. Harris, Ooltewah; Mike Miner, Sevierville; Herb Peck Jr., Nashville; Bill Rasp, Jackson; Paul Reeder, Germantown; Debbie Smith and Clara Swann, Chattanooga-Hamilton County Bicentennial Public Library; George F. Witham, Eads.
**TEXAS:** Lawrence T. Jones III, Austin; B.D. Patterson, Hillsboro; Paul Petree, Ft. Worth; L.E. Smith, Austin.
**VIRGINIA:** Scott C. Patchan, Centreville.
**WEST VIRGINIA:** Charles Hale, Richard King and John Walters, *The Herald-Dispatch,* Huntington; Dr. Kenneth T. Slack, Blake Library of Confederate History, Marshall University, Huntington.
**WISCONSIN:** William Brewster and Lynnette Wolfe, Wisconsin Veterans Museum, Madison.

# Photograph & illustration credits

## Preface

**3:** Mass. MOLLUS, USAMHI.

## Chapter 1

**5:** Illinois State Historical Library, Springfield. **6:** Bill Turner collection. **7:** Tennessee State Library & Archives, Nashville. **8:** Richard F. Carlile collection. **9:** Smith Memorial Library, Indiana Historical Society, Indianapolis. **10:** Kennesaw Mountain National Battlefield Park. **11:** Cumberland Gallery Collection. **12:** E.W. Payne, *History of the Thirty-fourth Regiment of Illinois Infantry.* **13:** courtesy Kenneth C. Thomson Jr., Bowling Green, Ky. **14:** E.J. Warner, *Generals in Gray.* **15:** Cumberland Gallery Collection. **16:** C. Paul Loane collection. **17:** Cumberland Gallery Collection. **18:** Illinois State Historical Library. **19:** J.A. Wyeth, *With Sabre and Scalpel.* **20:** Herb Peck Jr. collection. **21:** map by Richard A. Baumgartner. **22:** Mass. MOLLUS commandery series, USAMHI, Carlisle Barracks, Pa. **23:** Tennessee State Library and Archives. **24:** A.W. Tourgée, *The Story of a Thousand.* **25:** Mass. MOLLUS, USAMHI. **26:** Cumberland Gallery Collection. **27:** Gil Barrett collection. **28:** Mark Weldon collection. **29:** Craig T. Johnson collection. **30, top:** Mass. MOLLUS, USAMHI; **bottom:** E.J. Warner, *Generals in Gray.* **31:** Mass. MOLLUS, USAMHI.

## Chapter 2

**33:** J.M. Brown, *The Mountain Campaigns in Georgia.* **34, 35:** Mass. MOLLUS, USAMHI. **36:** The Filson Club, Louisville, Ky. **37:** Cumberland Gallery Collection. **38:** courtesy Phillip George, Murfreesboro, Tenn. **39:** Mark Weldon collection. **40:** Mass. MOLLUS, USAMHI. **41:** Cumberland Gallery Collection. **42, 43:** Gary Delscamp collection. **44:** Cumberland Gallery Collection. **45:** Gary Delscamp collection. **46:** J.H. Mathes, *The Old Guard in Gray.* **47:** map by Richard A. Baumgartner; **inset:** National Archives. **48:** W.M. Owen, *In Camp and Battle with the Washington Artillery of New Orleans.* **49:** courtesy John R. Peacock, High Point, N.C. **50, left:** Mike Miner collection; **right:** B.L. Ridley, *Battles and Sketches of the Army of Tennessee.* **51:** *Confederate Veteran.* **52:** Cumberland Gallery Collection. **53:** Carter House Museum, Franklin, Tenn. **55, 56:** Cumberland Gallery Collection. **57:** Gary Delscamp collection. **58:** Mark Weldon collection. **59:** *The Soldier in Our Civil War,*

■ Two unidentified soldiers chat in the shade provided by Umbrella Rock.

Frank Leslie's Columbian Memorial Edition, vol. II. **60:** Gary Delscamp collection. **62:** Alabama Department of Archives and History. **63:** *Confederate Veteran.* **64:** Wisconsin Veterans Museum, Madison. **65:** Mick Kissick collection. **66, upper left and center, bottom:** Cincinnati Historical Society; **upper right:** Franklin Brandt collection. **67:** Franklin Brandt collection. **68-71:** Cumberland Gallery Collection. **72, 73:** Dennis Keesee collection. **74:** A.P. Andrew, *Some Civil War Letters of A. Piatt Andrew III.* **75:** *Battles and Leaders of the Civil War,* vol. III. **76:** Mass. MOLLUS, USAMHI. **77, top:** Mass. MOLLUS, USAMHI; **bottom:** A. Gracie, *The Truth About Chickamauga.* **78:** Cumberland Gallery Collection. **79:** *Indiana at Chickamauga.* **80:** *Confederate Veteran.* **81:** Mississippi Department of Archives and History, Jackson. **82:** A. Gracie, *The Truth About Chickamauga.* **83:** Robert Van Dorn collection. **84, left:** Cumberland Gallery Collection; **right:** courtesy Warren Hitt, Clearwater, Fla. and Greg Hitt, Bowling Green, Ohio. **85:** Dr. Glen C. Cangelosi collection. **86:** Karl Sundstrom collection. **87:** *North Carolina Regiments.* **88:** Ken Turner collection. **89:** Mass. MOLLUS, USAMHI. **90:** Brockenbrough Library, Museum of the Confederacy, Richmond, Va. **91:** *Confederate Veteran.* **92:** Gary Delscamp collection. **93:** A. Gracie, *The Truth About Chickamauga.* **94:** Cumberland Gallery Collection. **95:** Woodruff Library, Emory University. **96:** Franklin Brandt collection. **97:** L.M. Strayer collection. **98, left and upper right:** Cumberland Gallery Collection; **lower right:** Lawrence T. Jones III collection. **99, upper left:** Dennis Keesee collection; **lower left:** *Confederate Veteran;* **right:** A. Gracie, *The Truth About Chickamauga.* **100, top:** Craig T. Johnson collection; **lower left:** Cumberland Gallery Collection; **center:** Tom Fuller collection; **lower right:** Frank Crawford collection. **101, left:** Dale S. Snair collection; **right:** courtesy G.W. Sheppard Jr., Warner Robins, Ga. **102, left:** Tim Burgess, courtesy Carter House Museum; **right:** Library of Congress. **103, upper left:** John Gurnish collection; **lower left and right:** Cumberland Gallery Collection. **104, left:** Valentine Museum, Richmond; **right:** Bill Turner collection. **105, left:** Frank Crawford collection; **right:** Craig T. Johnson collection. **106, upper left:** Illinois State Historical Library; **right:** R.A. Moore, *A Life for the Confederacy;* **bottom:** courtesy L.E. Smith, Austin, Texas. **107, upper left:** Dale S. Snair collection; **lower left:** Karl Sundstrom collection; **right:** Frank Crawford collection. **108, upper left:** courtesy Mrs. Pat Talsma, Belvidere, Ill.; **lower left:** courtesy Mike Hilber, "The People's Dealer," Lakewood, Ohio; **right:** *History of Jerome Township, Union County, Ohio.* **109, top:** Hayes Presidential Center,

Fremont, Ohio; **bottom:** courtesy Firelands Gallery, Bellevue, Ohio.

## Chapter 3

**111, top:** Charles S. Harris collection, photographed by R.A. Baumgartner; **bottom:** Richard F. Carlile collection. **112:** *Confederate Veteran.* **113, right:** Karl Sundstrom collection; **bottom left:** Cumberland Gallery Collection; **bottom right:** Confederate Museum, New Orleans. **114:** Craig Dunn collection. **115:** Vann R. Martin collection. **117:** Cumberland Gallery Collection. **118:** Illinois State Historical Library. **119, 120:** I.H.C. Royse, *History of the 115th Regiment Illinois Volunteer Infantry.* **121:** Illinois State Historical Library. **122:** Cumberland Gallery Collection. **123:** Mass. MOLLUS, USAMHI. **124:** K. Cumming, *Gleanings from Southland.* **125:** A.V. Winkler, *The Confederate Capital and Hood's Texas Brigade.* **126:** W.A. Albaugh III, *Confederate Faces.* **127:** H.V. Boynton, compiler, *Dedication of the Chickamauga and Chattanooga National Military Park.* **128:** Ronn Palm collection. **129:** C.H. Kirk, *History of the Fifteenth Pennsylvania Volunteer Cavalry.* **130, 131:** Ronn Palm collection. **132:** *Frank Leslie's Illustrated History of the Civil War.* **133:** J.B. Lindsley, *Military Annals of Tennessee, Confederate.* **134, left:** Dale S. Snair collection; **right:** George C. Esker III collection. **135:** Cumberland Gallery Collection. **136:** George C. Esker III collection. **137:** David Neuhardt collection. **138:** Gary Delscamp collection. **139:** Cumberland Gallery Collection. **140, top:** Tennessee State Library and Archives; **bottom:** Mass. MOLLUS, USAMHI. **141:** E.J. Warner, *Generals in Gray.* **142:** Wisconsin Veterans Museum. **143:** Mass. MOLLUS, USAMHI. **144:** map by Richard A. Baumgartner. **145:** A. Gracie, *The Truth About Chickamauga.* **146:** courtesy David Zullo, Gaithersburg, Md. **147:** W.E. Mickle, *Well Known Confederate Veterans and their War Records,* vol. I. **148:** George F. Witham collection. **149, top:** Dale S. Snair collection; **bottom left:** Cumberland Gallery Collection; **bottom right:** George F. Witham collection. **150:** *Battles and Leaders of the Civil War,* vol. III. **151:** Craig T. Johnson collection. **152:** Illinois State Historical Library. **153, left:** *Harper's Weekly;* **right:** *Society of the Army of the Cumberland, 36th Reunion 1908.* **154:** A. Gracie, *The Truth About Chickamauga.* **157:** Craig Dunn collection. **158:** courtesy Courtney B. Wilson, Catonsville, Md. **159:** W.W. Calkins, *The History of the One Hundred and fourth Regiment of Illinois Volunteer Infantry.* **160:** Illinois State Historical Library. **161:** Cumberland Gallery Collection. **162:** Michael Waskul collection. **163:** State Historical Society of Wisconsin, Madison. **164:** Mass. MOLLUS, USAMHI. **166:** C.W. Bennett, *Historical Sketches of the Ninth Michigan Infantry.* **167:** Craig Dunn collection.

## Chapter 4

**169, top and bottom:** C.E. Belknap, *History of Michigan Organizations at Chickamauga, Chattanooga and Missionary Ridge;* **inset:** Mass. MOLLUS, USAMHI. **170:** Illinois State Historical Library. **171:** Gary Delscamp collection. **172:** Cumberland Gallery Collection. **173:** *Harper's Weekly.* **174, 175:** Alabama Department of Archives and History, Montgomery. **176:** *Confederate*

■ With haversacks slung from shoulders, this group of 113th Ohio officers evidently brought a meal along for the visit to Lookout Mountain. Chaplain Joseph Morris stands at far left. The others include Capt. Toland Jones, Company A; 1st Lieut. John S. Skeels, Company C; Capt. Alvan L. Messmire, Company G; Capt. Otway Watson, Company H; and Surgeon Albert Wilson.

*Veteran.* **177:** W.C. Oates, *The War Between the Union and the Confederacy and Its Lost Opportunities.* **178:** Cumberland Gallery Collection. **179:** Chicago Public Library, courtesy Steven J. Adolphson. **180:** map by Richard A. Baumgartner. **181:** David Neuhardt collection. **182, 183:** *Confederate Veteran.* **184:** *Harper's Weekly.* **185-188:** Cumberland Gallery Collection. **189:** Mass. MOLLUS, USAMHI. **190:** W.B. Hazen, *A Narrative of Military Service.* **191:** *Harper's Weekly.* **192:** Michael Waskul collection. **193:** Mass. MOLLUS, USAMHI.

## Chapter 5

**195:** Karl Sundstrom collection. **196:** M.G. Young, *A Condensed History of the 143d Regiment New York Volunteer Infantry of the Civil War.* **197:** Ronn Palm collection. **198, 199:** Joseph Fulginiti collection. **200, left:** Wisconsin Veterans Museum; **right:** Karl Sundstrom collection. **201:** Tulane University Library, New Orleans. **202:** *Confederate Military History,* vol. V. **203:** Elizabeth B. Coker, courtesy *Military Images.* **204:** Library of Congress. **205:** J.P. Thomas, *Career and Character of Gen. Micah Jenkins C.S.A.* **206:** courtesy Lake Ray, Jacksonville, Fla. **207:** Ed Cohen, courtesy Confederate Calendar Works, Austin, Texas. **208:** map by Richard A. Baumgartner. **209:** Ronn Palm collection. **210:** Joseph Fulginiti collection. **211:** J.R. Boyle, *Soldiers True, the Story of the One hundred and eleventh Regiment Pennsylvania Veteran Volunteers.* **212:** Karl Sundstrom collection. **213:** M.D. Geary, *A Giant in Those Days.* **214, 215:** Mass. MOLLUS, USAMHI. **216:** Ronn Palm collection. **217:** G.K. Collins, *Memoirs of the 149th Regt. N.Y. Vol. Inft.* **218:** Karl Sundstrom collection. **219:** Mass. MOLLUS, USAMHI. **220:** C. Schurz, *The Reminiscences of Carl Schurz,* vol. III. **221:** Ronn Palm collection. **222:** Karl Sundstrom collection. **223:** F.P. Todd, *American Military Equipage 1851-1872,* vol. II. **224:** *Harper's Weekly.* **225, top:** Karl Sundstrom collection; **bottom:** Ross County Historical Society, Chillicothe, Ohio. **226, 227:** Mass. MOLLUS, USAMHI. **228:** Illinois State Historical Library. **229:** Amy C. Barry collection, USAMHI.

## Chapter 6

**231:** Ron Chojnacki collection. **232:** Rich Chojnacki collection. **233:** Cumberland Gallery Collection. **234:** *Harper's Weekly.* **235:** *Frank Leslie's Illustrated History of the Civil War.* **236:** J.B. Polley, *A Soldier's Letters to Charming Nellie.* **237:** Mass. MOLLUS, USAMHI. **239:** Frederick H. Meserve Historical Portraits, courtesy New York State Library. **240:** Ken Hamilton collection, photographed by R.A. Baumgartner. **241:** courtesy B.D. Patterson, Hillsboro, Texas. **242:** Gary Delscamp collection. **243:** Cumberland Gallery Collection. **244:** map by Richard A. Baumgartner. **245:** Marshall County Museum, Holly Springs, Miss. **246:** Mass. MOLLUS, USAMHI. **247:** Michael Waskul collection. **248:** Alabama Department of Archives and History. **249:** Douglas R. Cubbison collection. **250:** Tom Fuller collection. **251:** Vann R. Martin collection. **252:** *Harper's Weekly.* **253:** George C. Esker III collection. **254:** courtesy Frances Evans, Tupelo, Miss. **255:** courtesy Paul Reeder, Germantown, Tenn. **256:** *Confederate Military History,* vol. VI. **257:** Museum of the Confederacy. **259:** *Battles and Leaders of the Civil War,* vol. III. **260:** Bill Turner collection. **262:** Craig Dunn collection. **263:** Mass. MOLLUS, USAMHI. **264, 265:** Cumberland Gallery Collection. **266:** Mass. MOLLUS, USAMHI. **267:** Michael Kraus collection. **268:** Joseph Fulginiti collection. **269:** Karl Sundstrom collection.

## Chapter 7

**271:** Southern Historical Collection, University of North Carolina, Chapel Hill. **272:** Cumberland Gallery Collection. **273:** Karl Sundstrom collection. **274:** John Sickles collection. **275:** Ray Zielin collection. **276:** Illinois State Historical Library. **277:** Michael Waskul collection. **278:** C.R. Sligh, *History of the Services of the First Regiment Michigan Engineers and Mechanics during the Civil War.* **279:** Cumberland Gallery Collection. **280:** Mass. MOLLUS, USAMHI. **281:** Cumberland Gallery Collection. **282, left:** Cumberland Gallery Collection; **center:** Mass. MOLLUS, USAMHI; **right:** Bob Albertini collection. **283:** map by Richard A. Baumgartner. **284:** J.L. Jones, *An Artilleryman's Diary.* **285:** E.J. Sherlock, *Memorabilia of the Marches and Battles in which the One hundredth Regiment of Indiana Infantry Volunteers Took an Active Part.* **286, left:** Mark Weldon collection; **right:** E.J. Sherlock, *Memorabilia.* **287:** E.J. Sherlock, *Memorabilia.* **288:** Karl Sundstrom collection. **289:** Craig Dunn collection. **290-293:** Cumberland Gallery Collection. **294:** J.P. Douglas, *Douglas's Texas Battery C.S.A.* **295:** Karl Sundstrom collection. **296:** Austin History Center, Austin Public Library, Austin, Texas. **297:** *Miller's Photographic History of the Civil War.* **298:** Edwin G. Hibarger collection. **299:** J.M. Brown, *The Mountain Campaigns in Georgia.* **300:** courtesy Robert Gormley. **301:** Ray Zielin collection. **302:** Bill Rasp collection. **303:** Ken Turner collection. **304:** Cumberland Gallery Collection. **305, 306:** Illinois State Historical Library. **307:** Roger D. Hunt collection. **308:** courtesy David W. Taylor, Sylvania, Ohio. **309:** Roger Davis collection. **310:** State Historical Society of Iowa, Des Moines. **311:** J.C. Nisbet, *Four Years on the Firing Line.* **312:** *Confederate Military History,* vol. VI. **313, top:** M.G. Young, *A Condensed History of the 143d Regiment New York Volunteer Infantry of the Civil War;* **bottom:** Mass. MOLLUS, USAMHI. **314:** Robert M. Coch collection. **315:** Roger Davis collection.

## Chapter 8

**317, 318:** *Harper's Weekly.* **319:** Mass. MOLLUS, USAMHI. **320:** Cumberland Gallery Collection. **321, left:** Mass. MOLLUS, USAMHI; **right:** USAMHI. **322:** W.C. Davis, editor, *The Image of War,* vol. V. **323:** Gary Delscamp collection. **324:** W.F. Hinman, *Camp and Field, Sketches of Army Life.* **325:** Mass. MOLLUS, USAMHI. **326:** Cumberland Gallery Collection. **327, top left:** courtesy Fields of Glory, Gettysburg, Pa.; **top right:** Cumberland Gallery Collection; **bottom:** Mass. MOLLUS, USAMHI. **328:** map by Richard A. Baumgartner. **329:** Cumberland Gallery Collection. **330:** Tom Fuller collection. **331:** Cumberland Gallery Collection. **332:** A.M. Manigault, *A Carolinian Goes to War.* **333:** *Confederate Veteran.* **334:** Confederate Museum, Charleston, S.C. **335:** courtesy Paul Petree, Ft. Worth, Texas. **336:** courtesy William J. Warner, Ashton, Ill. **337:** Tom Fuller collection. **338:** *Harper's Weekly.* **339, 340:** Cumberland Gallery Collection. **341:** Craig Dunn collection. **342:** *Confederate Veteran.* **343:** Cumberland Gallery Collection. **344:** Mass. MOLLUS, USAMHI. **345, left:** George C. Esker III collection; **center:** Library of Congress; **right:** John Bernhard, courtesy *Military Images.* **346:** Illinois State Historical Library. **347:** courtesy Larry Chapman, Trout, La. **348, 349:** Florida State Archives, Tallahassee. **350:** *Confederate Veteran.* **351:** Bill Turner collection. **352, 353:** George C. Esker III collection. **354:** Richard W. Nee collection. **355:** Mass. MOLLUS, USAMHI. **356:** Cumberland Gallery Collection. **357:** Timothy Brookes collection. **358:** Cumberland Gallery Collection. **359:** Illinois State Historical Library. **360:** G.N. Barnard, *Photographic Views of Sherman's Campaign.* **361:** Illinois State Historical Library. **362:** State Historical Society of Wisconsin. **363:** W.J. Worsham, *The Old Nineteenth Tennessee Regiment, C.S.A.* **364:** Valentine Museum, Richmond. **365:** *Confederate Veteran.* **366, top:** *Proceedings of the 23rd Annual Reunion of Survivors of the 73rd Illinois;* **bottom left:** Dale S. Snair collection; **bottom right:** E.H. Rennolds, *History of Henry County Commands.* **367:** E.H. Rennolds, *History of Henry County Commands.* **368:** Mark Weldon collection. **369:** Cumberland Gallery Collection. **370:** Gary Delscamp collection. **371:** Bill Rasp collection; **inset:** Mass. MOLLUS, USAMHI. **372:** Cumberland Gallery Collection **373:** Edwin G. Hibarger collection. **374:** I.W. Andrews, *Marietta College in the War of Secession.* **375:** Special Collections, Dawes Memorial Library, Marietta College,

Marietta, Ohio. **376:** Cumberland Gallery Collection. **377, top:** Special Collections, Dawes Memorial Library, Marietta College; **bottom:** Cumberland Gallery Collection. **378:** Cumberland Gallery Collection. **379:** W.F. Beyer and O.F. Keydel, editors, *Deeds of Valor.* vol. I. **380:** Library of Congress. **381:** *Miller's Photographic History of the Civil War.* **382:** Alabama Department of Archives and History. **383:** Dale S. Snair collection. **384, left:** Ray Zielin collection; **right:** J.H. Haynie, *The Nineteenth Illinois.* **385:** B.F. Scribner, *How Soldiers Were Made.* **386:** Cumberland Gallery Collection. **387:** Craig T. Johnson collection.

## Chapter 9

**389, top:** Montgomery County Historical Society, Dayton, Ohio; **bottom:** Mass. MOLLUS, USAMHI. **390:** Mississippi Department of Archives and History. **391:** Mass. MOLLUS, USAMHI. **392:** Richard W. Nee collection. **393:** Cumberland Gallery Collection. **394:** map by Richard A. Baumgartner. **395:** Library of Congress. **396:** J.H. Mathes, *The Old Guard in Gray.* **397:** Mass. MOLLUS, USAMHI. **398:** *Confederate Veteran.* **399:** Bill Rasp collection. **400:** Richard W. Nee collection. **401, 402:** Illinois State Historical Library. **403:** Cumberland Gallery Collection. **404:** Dennis Keesee collection. **405:** Kentucky Military Museum, Frankfort. **406:** I.A. Buck, *Cleburne and his Command.* **407:** Mass. MOLLUS, USAMHI. **408:** courtesy Al L. Camblin, Topeka, Kan. **409:** Alabama Department of Archives and History. **410, 411:** Illinois State Historical Library. **412:** Mass. MOLLUS, USAMHI. **413, left:** Illinois State Historical Library; **right:** Mass. MOLLUS, USAMHI. **414:** J.M. Brown, *The Mountain Campaigns in Georgia.* **415:** Alabama Department of Archives and History. **416:** Mass. MOLLUS, USAMHI. **417:** Herb Peck Jr. collection. **418:** Cumberland Gallery Collection. **419:** *Harper's Weekly.* **420:** Richard F. Carlile collection. **421, top from left:** Robert M. Coch collection; Larry Stevens collection; Robert M. Coch collection; **lower left:** L.M. Strayer collection; **lower right:** Robert M. Coch collection. **422, top:** *Confederate Veteran;* **bottom:** Alabama Department of Archives and History. **423:** W.E. Mickle, *Well Known Confederate Veterans and their War Records.* **424:** Richard F. Carlile collection. **425, top row:** L. Wilson, *Itinerary of the Seventh Ohio Volunteer Infantry, 1861-1864;* **center row:** Cumberland Gallery Collection; **bottom row:** L. Wilson, *Itinerary of the Seventh Ohio Volunteer Infantry, 1861-1864;* **bottom far right:** Cumberland Gallery Collection. **426:** Roger Davis collection. **427:** Charles S. Harris collection.

## Chapter 10

**429:** Ross County Historical Society, Chillicothe, Ohio. **430:** Herb Peck Jr. collection. **431:** Cumberland Gallery Collection.

## Sources

**433-434:** Cumberland Gallery Collection. **435:** Mass. MOLLUS, USAMHI. **436:** courtesy Henry Deeks, Acton, Mass. **437:** Mass. MOLLUS, USAMHI. **438:** Cumberland Gallery Collection. **440:** Mass. MOLLUS, USAMHI. **441:** Cumberland Gallery Collection. **442:** Ken Lawrence collection. **443:** Gary Delscamp collection. **444:** Cumberland Gallery Collection. **445:** Michael G. Kraus collection. **447:** State Historical Society of Wisconsin, Madison. **448-449:** Cumberland Gallery Collection. **451:** Mass. MOLLUS, USAMHI. **453:** Cumberland Gallery Collection. **454:** Mick Kissick collection. **459:** Cumberland Gallery Collection.

# Bibliography

## Manuscript materials


Armstrong, Charles J. (33rd Alabama), diary, Alabama Department of Archives and History, Montgomery.

Bailey, George W. (6th Missouri US), letter of December 10, 1907, CCNMP.

Banbury, Jabez (5th Iowa), diary typescript, Civil War Miscellaneous Collection, Manuscript Division, USAMHI.

Barron, James F. (6th South Carolina), typescript of letter of November 5, 1863, CCNMP.

Bigbie, L.W. (33rd Alabama), typescript of letter of December 3, 1863, CCNMP.

Bloomfield, Ira J. (US staff officer), letter of November 21, 1907, CCNMP.

Bratton, John (6th South Carolina), typescript of letters of October 29 and November 3, 1863, Woodruff Library, Emory University, Atlanta, Ga.

Brigham, W. Joseph (50th Tennessee), letter of November 24, 1863, Brigham Family Papers, Tennessee State Library and Archives, Nashville.

Brown, William A. (Stanford's Battery), diary typescript, Greenwood, Miss., Public Library.

Cahal, Terry H. (CS staff officer), letter of September 30, 1863, Tennessee State Library and Archives.

Cate, John M. (33rd Massachusetts), letter of November 15, 1863, Jean M. Cate collection, Rancho Santa Fe, Calif.

Chunn, William A. (40th Georgia), letter of December 1, 1863, Special Collections Library, Duke University, Durham, N.C.

Clark, William M. (147th Pennsylvania), typescript of letter of October 28, 1863, CCNMP.

Cobham, George A. Jr. (111th Pennsylvania), typescript of letter of November 29, 1863, Warren County Historical Society, Warren, Pa.

Cooper, James L. (20th Tennessee), journal typescript, Confederate Collection, Tennessee State Library and Archives.

Crane, James P. (66th Georgia), letter of December 29, 1863, Atlanta Historical Society Library.

Crowder, James P. (47th Alabama), typescript of letter of September 27, 1863, Woodruff Library, Emory University.

Cummins, George A. (36th Illinois), diary, Illinois State Historical Library, Springfield.

Davis, Newton N. (24th Alabama), letters of August 22, September 16 and November 29, 1863, Alabama Department of Archives and History.

Davis, William H. (6th/9th Tennessee), diary typescript, Woodruff Library, Emory University.

Deacon, Solomon M. (87th Indiana), typescripts of letters of July 16 and September 8, 1863, CCNMP.

Ely, John K. (88th Illinois), journal typescript, CCNMP.

Fahnestock, Allen L. (86th Illinois), diary, Illinois State Historical Library.

Erdelmeyer, Francis (32nd Indiana), undated letter, CCNMP.

Fielder, Alfred T. (12th Tennessee), copy of journal, Confederate Collection, Tennessee State Library and Archives.

Floyd, John D. (17th Tennessee), letter of October 8, 1863, Confederate Collection, Tennessee State Library and Archives.

Fogle, Theodore T. (2nd Georgia Infantry), letters of September 20 and October 16, 1863, Woodruff Library, Emory University.

Geary, John W. (US division commander), typescript of letter of November 2, 1863, CCNMP.

Gleason, Jerome D. (38th Ohio), letter of December 8, 1863, Chris Magewick collection.

Gould, Victor H. (26th Illinois), letter of December 22, 1863, Illinois State Historical Library.

Grammer, George A. (Swett's Battery), diary typescript, CCNMP.

Griest, Alva C. (72nd Indiana), diary typescript, Smith Memorial Library, Indiana Historical Library, Indianapolis.

Haley, Joel T. (37th Georgia), letter of December 17, 1863, Confederate Collection, Tennessee State Library and Archives.

Hardee, William J. (CS corps/army commander), document: "Statement of the strength of the Army of Tennessee in the engagements before Chattanooga, the losses in those engagements, the strength of the Army on its arrival at Dalton, its strength on the 20th [December 1863], and the increase of effective strength since the retreat and to the 20th December," Confederate Collection, Tennessee State Library and Archives.

Harris, John W. (CS staff officer), letters, Confederate Collection, Tennessee State Library and Archives.

Honnoll, William (24th Mississippi), letter of November 18, 1863, Woodruff Library, Emory University.

Howe, Daniel W. (79th Indiana), letter of July 4, 1863, Smith Memorial Library, Indiana Historical Society.

Hubbard, Robert (US medical officer), letters of October 5, 11 and 31, 1863, Manuscript Division, USAMHI.

Huntzinger, William H. (79th Indiana), diary typescript, Smith Memorial Library, Indiana Historical Society.

Jones, Lewis E. (36th Ohio), letter of November 21, 1863, L.M. Strayer collection.

Keith, Thomas T. (24th Wisconsin), letter of October 7, 1863, CCNMP.

Locke, Joseph L. (33rd Massachusetts), letter of January 9, 1864, Illinois State Historical Library.

Marion, Frederick (31st Ohio), letter of December 1, 1863, Illinois State Historical Library.

Marsh, George (104th Illinois), diary and scrapbooks, George Marsh Papers, Illinois State Historical Library.

Maupin, John W. (26th Missouri), letter of December 16, 1907, CCNMP.

McGraw, John S. (57th Indiana), letters, Manuscript Section, Indiana Division, Indiana State Library.

McMahon, Arnold (21st Ohio), undated written statements, Joseph T. Wood Papers, L.M. Strayer collection.

Mengel, William H. (26th Missouri), letter of January 11, 1908, CCNMP.

Miller, Silas (36th Illinois), letter of October 30, 1863, G.A.R. Memorial Hall, Aurora, Ill.

Miller, William B. (75th Indiana), journal typescript, CCNMP.

Monat, David (29th Pennsylvania), letter of November 11, 1863, The Historical Society of Pennsylvania, Philadelphia.

Neal, Andrew J. (Marion Light Artillery), typescript of letters of November 26 and 29, 1863, KMNBP.

Newton, Joseph B. (14th Ohio), diary, L.M. Strayer collection.

Nichol, David (Knap's Battery), letter of December 10, 1863, Dr. William Glenn Robertson collection.

O'Leary, Daniel (15th Kentucky US), letters of October 3 and 24, 1863, KMNBP.

Patterson, John A. (18th Tennessee), typescript of letter of March 24, 1864, Dr. B.D. Patterson collection.

Patterson, William E. (38th Illinois), copy of diary, CCNMP.

Rabb, Hezekiah (33rd Alabama), typescript of letter of October 9, 1863, Michael Musick Collection, Manuscript Division, USAMHI.

Rennolds, Edwin H. (5th Tennessee CS), diary, Special Collections, University of Tennessee Library, Knoxville.

Robinson, Henry (100th Indiana), typescript of undated 1863 letter, CCNMP.

Roseberry, Isaac (1st Michigan Engineers), diary, Woodruff Library, Emory University.
Scott, Edward S. (89th Ohio), diary, Firelands Historical Society, Norwalk, Ohio.
Scribner, Benjamin F. (38th Indiana), typescript of letter of September 21, 1863, CCNMP.
Silsby, Amandus (24th Wisconsin), typescript of letter of August 20, 1863, CCNMP.
Simonds, Merritt J. (42nd Illinois), diary, Northern Illinois University Historical Archives, DeKalb, Ill.; October 1863 letters, Illinois State Historical Library.
Slack, Albert L. (121st Ohio), letter of December 19, 1863, Woodruff Library, Emory University.
Smith, Benjamin T. (51st Illinois), journal, Illinois State Historical Library.
Snow, John (Lumsden's Battery), letter of September 30, 1863, Special Collections Library, Duke University.
Sower, Daniel L. (49th Ohio), letter of February 18, 1913, Frank Crawford collection.
Stockton, William T. (1st Florida Cavalry), undated December 1863 letter, Florida State Archives, Tallahassee.
Vaughan, P. Turner (4th Alabama Infantry), diary typescript, Alabama Department of Archives and History.
Watson, James G. (25th Illinois), typescript of letter of November 26, 1863, CCNMP.
Watson, Robert (7th Florida), journal typescript, CCNMP.
Weiss, Henry M.F. (27th Illinois), letter of October 16, 1863, CCNMP.
Widney, Lyman S. (34th Illinois), journal typescript, KMNBP.
Williams, George W. (121st Ohio), letters of August 12 and September 15, 1863, Kyle Kelch collection.
Willoughby, Aurelius M. (39th Indiana), typescript of diary, CCNMP.
Wood, Alonzo H. (14th Ohio), letter of February 26, 1909, CCNMP.
Woodson, James A. (5th Iowa), diary, Illinois State Historical Library.
Wright, George H. (42nd Illinois), letter of October 30, 1863, Illinois State Historical Library.

## Published diaries & correspondence

Andrew, A. Piatt III, *Some Civil War Letters of A. Piatt Andrew III,* Gloucester, Mass.: privately printed, 1925.
Ankeny, Henry G., *Kiss Josey For Me!* edited by Florence Marie Ankeny Cox, Santa Ana, Calif.: Friis-Pioneer Press, 1974.
Bright, Michael S., *Respects to All: Letters of Two Pennsylvania Boys in the War of the Rebellion,* edited by Aida C. Truxall, Pittsburgh: University of Pittsburgh Press, 1962.
Connolly, James A., "Major James Austin Connolly," *Publications of the Illinois State Historical Library No. 35,* Springfield: Phillips Bros., 1928.
Cumming, Kate, *A Journal of Hospital Life in the Confederate Army of Tennessee,* Louisville: John P. Morton & Co., 1866.
Garfield, James A., *The Wild Life of the Army,* edited by Frederick D. Williams, Lansing: Michigan State University Press, 1964.
Green, John W., *Johnny Green of the Orphan Brigade: The Journal of a Confederate Soldier,* edited by A.D. Kirwan, Lexington: University of Kentucky Press, 1956.
Griffin, Daniel F., "A Hoosier Regiment at Chattanooga," edited by Arville L. Funk, *Tennessee Historical Quarterly,* vol. XXII, no. 3, September 1963.
Hannaford, Robert H., "On the Field at Chickamauga," edited by Robert F. Russell, *Military Images,* vol. IV, no. 3, November-December 1982.
Hoffmann, John, *The Confederate Collapse at the Battle of Missionary Ridge: The Reports of James Patton Anderson and his Brigade Commanders,* Dayton: Morningside, 1985.
Holt, Hiram T., "A Confederate Sergeant's Report to His Wife During the Campaign from Tullahoma to Dalton," by Robert Partin, *Tennessee Historical Quarterly,* vol. XII, no. 4, December 1953.
Inzer, John W., *The Diary of a Confederate Soldier,* edited by Mattie Lou Teague Crow, Huntsville, Ala.: The Strode Publishers, Inc., 1977.
Ives, Washington M. Jr., *Civil War Journal and Letters of Washington Ives 4th Fla. C.S.A.,* Tallahassee: privately published, 1987.
Jackman, John S., *Diary of a Confederate Soldier: John S. Jackman of the Orphan Brigade,* edited by William C. Davis, Columbia: University of South Carolina Press, 1990.
Jones, Jenkin L., *An Artilleryman's Diary,* Madison, Wis.: Democrat Printing Co., 1914.
Jones, Tighlman, *Five Days to Glory,* edited by Glenn W. Sunderland, Cranbury, N.J.: A.S. Barnes & Co., 1970.
Keegan, Peter, *The Diaries of Peter Keegan, from the Original Notebooks,* Indianapolis: privately printed, 1938.
Kiene, Francis A., *A Civil War Diary: The Journal of Francis A. Kiene, 1861-1864,* compiled by Ralph E. Kiene Jr., Shawnee Mission, Kan.: privately published, 1974.
Kircher, Henry A., *A German in the Yankee Fatherland: The Civil War Letters of Henry A. Kircher,* edited by Earl J. Hess, Kent, Ohio: Kent State University Press, 1983.
Kirkpatrick, George M., *The Experiences of a Private Soldier in the Civil War,* The Hoosier Bookshop, 1973.
Lewis, Richard, *Camp Life of a Confederate Boy of Bratton's Brigade, Longstreet's Corps, C.S.A. Letters Written by Lieut. Richard Lewis of Walker's Regiment to his Mother during the War,* Charleston, S.C.: The News and Courier Book Presses, 1883.
Mabrey, Benjamin B., *Benjamin Benn Mabrey, Yankee Soldier,* edited by Verle Proctor Sutton, San Bernardino: Crown Printers, 1978.
Mayfield, Leroy S., "A Hoosier Invades the Confederacy: Letters and Diaries of Leroy S. Mayfield," edited by John D. Barnhart, *Indiana Magazine of History,* vol. 39, 1943.
McKell, William J., "The Journal of Sergt. Wm. J. McKell," edited by Watt P. Marchman, *Civil War History,* vol. III, no. 3, September 1957.
Moore, Robert A., *A Life for the Confederacy as Recorded in the Pocket Diaries of Pvt. Robert A. Moore, Co. G, 17th Mississippi Regiment,* edited by James W. Silver, Jackson, Tenn.: McCowat-Mercer Press, 1959.
Morse, Bliss, *Civil War Diaries & Letters of Bliss Morse,* edited by Loren J. Morse, Wagoner, Okla.: privately published, 1985.
Mosman, Chesley A., *The Rough Side of War,* edited by Arnold Gates, Garden City, N.Y.: The Basin Publishing Co., 1987.
Polley, Joseph B., *A Soldier's Letters to Charming Nellie,* New York: The Neale Publishing Company, 1908.
Roper, John S., "Letter Written During Battle of Missionary Ridge," *Journal of the Illinois State Historical Society,* vol. VI, no. 4, January 1914.
Sherman, William T., *Home Letters of General Sherman,* edited by M.A. DeWolfe Howe, New York: Charles Scribner's Sons, 1909.
Stauffer, Nelson, *Civil War Diary,* California State University, Northridge Libraries, 1976.
Stookey, James M., *The Civil War Letters written by James Monroe Stookey to his brother Daniel Stookey 1861-1865,* compiled by Mary E. Stookey Owen, privately printed, n.d.
Tourgée, Albion W., "A Civil War Diary of Albion W. Tourgée," edited by Dean H. Keller, *Ohio History,* vol. 74, no. 2, Spring 1965.
Upson, Theodore F., *With Sherman to the Sea: The Civil War Letters, Diaries & Reminiscences of Theodore F. Upson,* edited by Oscar O. Winther, Baton Rouge: Louisiana State University Press, 1943.

■ On August 29, 1864, Private William Thomas and 27 comrades of Company B, 9th Pennsylvania Cavalry, "had our Photograph taken on one plate on Point Look out." Thomas, a three-year veteran, noted the occasion in his diary upon returning to the regiment's camp at the foot of the mountain. Just two days later his company, augmented with a number of new recruits, was sent to chase Confederate cavalry raiding in the Sequatchie Valley. Note Starr carbines and the mixture of jackets, sack coats, hats and caps.

Vann, Samuel K., *Most Lovely Lizzie: Love Letters of a Young Confederate Soldier,* Birmingham: privately printed, 1958.

West, John C., *A Texan in Search of a Fight, Being the Diary and Letters of a Private Soldier in Hood's Texas Brigade,* Waco: Press of J.S. Hill & Company, 1901.

Whitney, Joseph, *Kiss Clara For Me: The story of Joseph Whitney and his family, early days in the Midwest, and soldiering in the American Civil War,* edited by Robert J. Snetsinger, State College, Pa.: The Carnation Press, 1969.

Williams, Alpheus S., *From the Cannon's Mouth: The Civil War Letters of General Alpheus S. Williams,* edited by Milo M. Quaife, Detroit: Wayne State University Press, 1959.

Wills, Charles W., *Army Life of an Illinois Soldier: Letters and Diary of the Late Charles W. Wills,* compiled by Mary E. Kellogg, Washington, D.C.: Globe Printing Co., 1906.

Winkler, Frederic C., *Letters of Frederick C. Winkler,* edited by William K. Winkler, privately published, 1963.

## Memoirs, reminiscences & recollections

Alexander, E. Porter, *Fighting for the Confederacy: The Personal Recollections of General Edward Porter Alexander,* edited by

Gary W. Gallagher, Chapel Hill: University of North Carolina Press, 1989.

———, *Military Memoirs of a Confederate,* New York: Charles Scribner's Sons, 1907.

Allspaugh, Jacob H., "Chickamauga. The Struggle of Sunday as Seen by an Enlisted Man," *The National Tribune,* October 7, 1886.

———, "Mission Ridge. The Story of the Charge Told by an Enlisted Man," *The National Tribune,* June 2, 1887.

Baker, Chauncey C., "And a Little Child Shall Lead Them," *Confederate Veteran,* vol. XXVIII, no. 12, December 1920.

Bakhaus, William, "Jottings by a 15th Corps Boy," *The Ohio Soldier and National Picket Guard,* vol. II, no. 16, December 1, 1888.

Banks, George L., "Storming the Ridge," *The National Tribune,* July 20, 1899.

Barkhamer, George, "On Picket Before Chattanooga – A Wild Cavalry Charge," *The National Tribune,* July 26, 1883.

Beatty, John, *The Citizen-Soldier; or, Memoirs of a Volunteer,* Cincinnati: Wilstach, Baldwin & Co., 1879.

Belknap, Charles E., "That Cracker Line. The Opening of the Tennessee River," *Society of the Army of the Cumberland, Twenty-sixth Reunion 1896,* Cincinnati: The Robert Clarke Company, 1897.

Berry, John M., "The Quiet Humor of Gen. Pat Cleburne," *Confederate Veteran,* vol. XII, no. 4, April 1904.

Blodgett, David G., "The Tenth Indiana Battery at Moccasin Point," *The National Tribune,* August 9, 1883.

Bond, Thomas J., "About Brown's Ferry," *The National Tribune,* October 10, 1912.

Booth, John T., "A Night March. From Pond Spring to Crawfish Spring on Night of September 18th and 19th, 1863," *The Ohio Soldier and National Picket Guard,* January 4, 1890.

Brandley, Arnold, "The Cracker Line," *The National Tribune,* May 28, 1885.

Buck, Irving A., *Cleburne and his Command,* Wilmington: Broadfoot Publishing Company, 1991.

Byers, S.H.M., *With Fire and Sword,* New York: The Neale Publishing Company, 1911.

———, "Sherman's Attack at the Tunnel," *Battles and Leaders of the Civil War,* vol. III, New York: Thomas Yoseloff, 1956.

Carlisle, Francis M., typescript of unpublished recollections, CCNMP.

Chalaron, Joseph A., "At Missionary Ridge," *The National Tribune,* May 4, 1899.

Coker, James L., "Battle of Lookout Valley or Wauhatchie," *Confederate Veteran,* vol. XVIII, no. 10, October 1910.

Collins, R.M., *Chapters from the Unwritten History of the War Between the States,* St. Louis: Nixon-Jones Printing Co., 1893.

Cox, Jacob D., Military *Reminiscences of the Civil War,* 2 vols., New York: Charles Scribner's Sons, 1900.

Coxe, John T., "Chickamauga," *Confederate Veteran,* vol. XXX, no. 8, August 1922.

Critchell, Brian P., "A Wicked Fight," *The National Tribune,* October 6, 1887.

Cumming, Kate, *Gleanings from Southland,* Birmingham: Roberts & Son, 1895.

Davidson, Henry M., *Fourteen Months in Southern Prisons,* Milwaukee: Daily Wisconsin Printing House, 1865.

Day, William W., *Fifteen Months in Dixie, or My Personal Experiences in Rebel Prisons,* Owatonna, Minn.: The People's Press, 1889.

Dean, Henry S., *The Relief of Chattanooga,* MOLLUS-Michigan, Detroit: Winn & Hammond Printers, 1893.

Dinkins, James, *1861 to 1865 by an Old Johnnie: Personal Recollections and Experiences in the Confederate Army,* Cincinnati: The Robert Clark Co., 1897.

Doan, Isaac C., *Reminiscences of the Chattanooga Campaign,* Richmond, Ind.: J.M. Coe's Printery, 1897.

Dowd, William F., "Lookout Mountain and Missionary Ridge," *The Southern Bivouac,* vol. I, no. 7, December 1885.

Doyle, William E., "Recollections of Chattanooga: The Capture and Holding of a Gateway of the Rebellion," *The National Tribune,* June 22, 1899.

Dyer, John W., *Reminiscences; or Four Years in the Confederate Army,* Evansville, Ind.: Keller Printing & Publishing Co., 1898.

Dyke, Logan J., "Lookout Mountain," *The National Tribune,* September 22, 1887.

Eby, Henry H., *Observations of an Illinois Boy in Battle, Camp and Prisons – 1861 to 1865,* Mendota, Ill.: privately published, 1910.

E.N.N., "Gen. Steedman. His Brilliant Services at Chickamauga," *The National Tribune,* August 4, 1887.

Figg, Royal W., *Where Men Only Dare to Go! or the Story of a Boy Company (C.S.A.),* Richmond: Whittet & Shepperson, 1885.

Findley, Robert P., "A Story of a March," *G.A.R. War Papers,* vol. I, Cincinnati: Fred C. Jones Post No. 401, 1891.

Fitch, Michael H., *Echoes of the Civil War as I Hear Them,* New York: R.F. Fenno & Company, 1905.

Ford, Augustus C., "Midnight on Missionary Ridge," *War Papers Read Before the Indiana Commandery Military Order of the Loyal Legion of the United States,* Indianapolis: 1898.

Fosdick, Charles, *Five Hundred Days in Rebel Prisons,* Chicago: Chicago Electrotype & Stereotype Co., 1887.

Foster, Samuel T., *One of Cleburne's Command; The Civil War Reminiscences and Diary of Capt. Samuel T. Foster, Granbury's Texas Brigade, CSA,* edited by Norman D. Brown, Austin: University of Texas Press, 1980.

Fullerton, Joseph S., "The Army of the Cumberland at Chattanooga," *Battles and Leaders of the Civil War,* vol. III, New York: Thomas Yoseloff, 1956.

Gates, Frank W., "Chickamauga. The Important Services of the Reserve Corps on the Second Day," *The National Tribune,* April 14, 1887.

Gault, Robert A., "Capturing Brown's Ferry," *The National Tribune,* November 18, 1915.

Gibson, William W., "Reminiscences of Ringgold Gap," *Confederate Veteran,* vol. XII, no. 11, November 1904.

Giles, Valerius C., *Rags and Hope: The Recollections of Val C. Giles, Four Years with Hood's Brigade, Fourth Texas Infantry 1861-1865,* edited by Mary Lasswell, New York: Coward-McCann Inc., 1961.

Grant, Charles, "The Cracker Line," *The National Tribune,* October 30, 1884.

Grant, Nicholas B., *The Life of a Common Soldier 1862-1865,* Adamsville, Tenn.: J. Gillis, n.d.

Grant, Ulysses S., *Personal Memoirs of U.S. Grant,* 2 vols., New York: Charles L. Webster & Company, 1885.

Greene, Albert R., "From Bridgeport to Ringgold by way of Lookout Mountain," *Personal Narratives of Events in the War of the Rebellion,* Providence: Rhode Island Soldiers and Sailors Historical Society, 1890.

Hanks, O.T., "History of Captain B.F. Benton's Company 1861-1865" [Company K, 1st Texas Infantry], typescript of unpublished recollections, Confederate Research Center, Hill College, Hillsboro, Texas.

Hart, Albert G., "The Surgeon and the Hospital in the Civil War," *Papers of the Military Historical Society of Massachusetts,* vol. XIII, 1902.

Hazen, William B., *A Narrative of Military Service,* Huntington, W.Va.: Blue Acorn Press, 1993.

Heaton, Charles M., "Hazen's Midnight Excursion," *The National Tribune,* December 20, 1906.

Hendricks, Sherman, "Chickamauga. The Part Taken in the Great Battle by Battery C, 1st Ohio L. A.," *The National Tribune,* November 5, 1891.

Henry, H.W., "Little War-time Incidents," *Confederate Veteran,* vol. XXII, no. 7, July 1914.

Holmes, Mead, *A Soldier of the Cumberland, Memoir of Mead*

*Holmes Jr., Sergeant of Company K, 21st Regiment Wisconsin Volunteers,* Boston: American Tract Society, 1864.

Hood, John Bell, *Advance and Retreat,* Philadelphia: Press of Burk and McFetridge, 1879.

Howard, N.C., "An Incident of Missionary Ridge," *Confederate Veteran,* vol. XXI, no. 6, June 1913.

Howard, Oliver O., "Grant at Chattanooga," *Personal Recollections of the War of the Rebellion,* MOLLUS-New York, 1891.

Howe, Daniel W., typescript of recollections, Smith Memorial Library, Indiana Historical Society.

Jenney, William L., "With Sherman and Grant from Memphis to Chattanooga – A Reminiscence," *Military Essays and Recollections,* vol. IV, MOLLUS-Illinois, Chicago: Cozzens & Beaton Company, 1907.

Jordan, William C., *Some Events and Incidents during the Civil War,* Montgomery, Ala.: The Paragon Press, 1909.

Kibler, Charles H., *76th Ohio at Ringgold or Taylor's Ridge,* n.p., n.d.

Kountz, John S., "The Battle of Missionary Ridge," typescript of reminiscences, L.M. Strayer collection.

LeDuc, William G., "Opening Up the Cracker Line," *The National Tribune,* September 5, 1912.

———, *Recollections of a Civil War Quartermaster,* St. Paul: The North Central Publishing Co., 1963.

Liddell, St. John R., *Liddell's Record,* Dayton: Morningside, 1985.

Longstreet, James, *From Manassas to Appomattox,* Philadelphia: J.B. Lippincott Co., 1896.

Lucas, Elisha C., "Lookout Mountain," *The National Tribune,* June 10, 1886.

Lyle, William W., *Lights and Shadows of Army Life: or, Pen Pictures from the Battlefield, the Camp, and the Hospital,* Cincinnati: R.W. Carroll & Co., 1865.

Mackall, William W., *A Son's Recollections of his Father,* New York: E.P. Dutton & Company, 1930.

"Maney's Brigade After the Battle of Missionary Ridge," *The Southern Bivouac,* vol. II, no. 8, April 1884.

Manigault, Arthur M., *A Carolinian Goes to War: The Civil War Narrative of Arthur Middleton Manigault, Brigadier General, C.S.A.,* edited by R. Lockwood Tower, Columbia: University of South Carolina Press, 1983.

Martin, John H., "Longstreet's Forces at Chickamauga," *Confederate Veteran,* vol. XX, no. 12, December 1912.

Massenburg, Thomas L., "Capt. W.W. Carnes' Battery at Chickamauga," *Confederate Veteran,* vol. VI, no. 11, November 1898.

McNeil, Samuel A., "At Chickamauga. The Fighting and Maneuvering on the First Day," *The National Tribune,* April 14, 1887.

———, *Personal Recollections of Service in the Army of the Cumberland and Sherman's Army,* privately published, 1909.

Mesnard, Luther B., typescript of unpublished memoir, Firelands Historical Society, Norwalk, Ohio.

Metcalf, George P., typescript of reminiscences, Ohio Historical Society, Columbus.

Miller, Charles D., "A Narrative of the Services of Brevet Major Charles Dana Miller in the War of the Great Rebellion 1861-1865," unpublished typescript of recollections, Tennessee State Library and Archives.

Miller, George W., "The 21st Ohio at Chickamauga," *The National Tribune,* February 21, 1907.

Mitch, John L., "Croxton at Chickamauga," *The National Tribune,* November 5, 1925.

Mixson, Frank M., *Reminiscences of a Private,* Columbia, S.C.: The State Company, 1910.

Monat, David, unpublished reminiscences, The Historical Society of Pennsylvania, Philadelphia.

Moore, John C., "Battle of Lookout Mountain," *Confederate Veteran,* vol. VI, no. 9, September 1898.

Morgan, William A., "Brown's Ferry," *War Talks in Kansas,* MOLLUS-Kansas, Kansas City: Franklin Hudson Publishing Company, 1906.

Muenscher, Emory W., "Missionary Ridge," *The National Tribune,* April 8, 1909.

Nisbet, James C., *Four Years on the Firing Line,* edited by Bell I. Wiley, Jackson, Tenn.: McCowat-Mercer Press, 1963.

Osborne, Thomas D., "Capture of Brown's Ferry," *The National Tribune,* May 2, 1901.

Otey, W.N. Mercer, "Operations of the Signal Corps," *Confederate Veteran,* vol. VIII, no. 3, March 1900.

Owen, William M., *In Camp and Battle with the Washington Artillery of New Orleans,* Boston: Ticknor & Company, 1885.

Palmer, John M., *Personal Recollections of John M. Palmer: The Story of an Earnest Life,* Cincinnati: The Robert Clarke Company, 1901.

Patton, Joseph T., *Personal Recollections of Four Years in Dixie,* MOLLUS-Michigan, Detroit: Winn & Hammond Printers, 1892.

Perry, Francis W., "Chickamauga. Toilsome March of the Fourteenth Corps over the Mountains," *The National Tribune,* June 28, 1883.

Petzoldt, Theodore, typescript of recollections, CCNMP.

Phillips, Alfred R., *Fighting with Turchin,* privately printed, 1924.

Phillips, Charles G., "Lookout and Mission Ridge," *The National Tribune,* February 1, 1912.

Pickett, W.D., "Dead Angle – Rules for Burial of Dead," *Confederate Veteran,* vol. XVI, no. 5, May 1908.

Pirtle, Alfred, "Lytle's Last Sacrifice," unpublished typescript, The Filson Club, Louisville, Ky.

Polley, Joseph B., *Hood's Texas Brigade: Its Marches, Its Battles, Its Achievements,* New York: The Neale Publishing Company, 1910.

Pomeroy, Nicholas, typescript of reminiscences, Confederate Research Center, Hill College, Hillsboro, Texas.

Poston, William K. Jr., "Missionary Ridge Reminiscences," *Confederate Veteran,* vol. IX, no. 9, September 1901.

Potter, John, *Reminiscences of the Civil War in the United States by Rev. John Potter,* Oskaloosa, Iowa: The Globe Presses, 1897.

Powell, Eugene, "An Incident of the Capture of Lookout Mountain," *Historical and Philosophical Society of Ohio Publications,* part II, Cincinnati: The Caxton Press, 1926.

Powell, Smith, "A Boy Soldier of Alabama," *Confederate Veteran,* vol. XXIX, no. 1, January 1921.

Preston, J. Earl, "Battle on Lookout Mountain," *Confederate Veteran,* vol. VI, no. 3, March 1898.

Prets, George, "That Battery Again. The Part Taken by the 69th Ohio in Capturing those Rebel Guns," *The National Tribune,* February 11, 1892.

Putney, William G., typescript of recollections, KMNBP.

Quintard, Charles T., *Doctor Quintard, Chaplain C.S.A. and Second Bishop of Tennessee, Being his Story of the War (1861-1865),* edited by Rev. Arthur Howard Noll, Sewanee, Tenn.: The University Press, 1905.

*Reminiscences of the Civil War from Diaries of Members of the 103d Illinois Volunteer Infantry,* Chicago: J.F. Leaming & Co., 1904.

Reynolds, James E., "Heroism of Walthall's Mississippians," *Confederate Veteran,* vol. XV, no. 8, August 1907.

Riley, Joseph E., typescript of reminiscences, CCNMP.

Rosecrans, William S., "Tullahoma Campaign," *The National Tribune,* March 11, 1882.

Ross, Levi A., typescript of journal and reminiscences, Illinois State Historical Library.

Schurz, Carl, *The Reminiscences of Carl Schurz,* vol. III, New York: Doubleday, Page & Company, 1909.

Scott, Launcelot L., "Brown's Ferry Expedition," *The National Tribune,* January 25, 1912.

Scribner, Benjamin F., *How Soldier Were Made,* Huntington, W.Va.: Blue Acorn Press, 1995.

Shanks, William F.G., *Personal Recollections of Distinguished*

*Generals,* New York: Harper & Brothers, 1866.
Shellenberger, John K., "With Sheridan's Division at Missionary Ridge," *Sketches of War History 1861-1865,* vol. IV, MOLLUS-Ohio, Cincinnati: The Robert Clarke Company, 1896.
Sherman, William T., *Memoirs of General William T. Sherman,* 2 vols., New York: D. Appleton and Company, 1875.
Simmons, John W., "Heroic Mississippians," *Confederate Veteran,* vol. V, no. 2, February 1897.
Sloan, John M., "A Most Worthy Plea For Help," *Confederate Veteran,* vol. II, no. 2, February 1894.
Smith, A.B., "Reminiscences of the War," *The National Tribune,* July 15, 1882.
Smith, Miles V., *Reminiscences of the Civil War,* n.p., n.d.
Smith, William F., *Brown's Ferry. 1863,* parts I-II, privately published, 1901.
Sorrel, G. Moxley, *Recollections of a Confederate Staff Officer,* New York: Neale Publishing Company, 1905.
Sower, Daniel L., "On Leaving Rebel Prisons," unpublished 1867 essay, Frank Crawford collection.
Stebbins, Austin E., "A Daring Movement," *The National Tribune,* October 19, 1899.
Stephenson, Philip D., "Missionary Ridge," *Southern Historical Society Papers,* vol. I, April 1914.
Stork, William L., "Lookout Mountain," *The National Tribune,* May 19, 1887.
Sturgis, H.H., "Hard Fighting by Lookout Mountain," *Confederate Veteran,* vol. XVII, no. 3, March 1909.
Talley, William R., "An Autobiography of Rev. William Ralston Talley," typescript, CCNMP.
Tallman, William H.H., handwritten memoir, Charles Rhodes III collection, USAMHI.
Taylor, Benjamin F., *Mission Ridge and Lookout Mountain with Pictures of Life in Camp and Field,* New York: D. Appleton & Company, 1872.
*Tennessee Civil War Veterans Questionnaires,* vol. IV, Easley, S.C.: Southern Historical Press, 1985.
Thruston, Gates P., "Chickamauga," *The Southern Bivouac,* vol. II, no. 7, December 1886.
Turchin, John B., *Chickamauga,* Chicago: Fergus Printing Company, 1888.
Turner, James, "Jim Turner Co. G, 6th Texas Infantry, C.S.A. from 1861 to 1865," *Texana,* vol. XII, no. 2, 1974.
Vance, Wilson J., "On Thomas' Right at Chickamauga," *Blue and Gray,* vol. I, no. 2, February 1893.
Waddle, Angus L., *Three Years with the Armies of the Ohio and the Cumberland,* Chillicothe, Ohio: Scioto Gazette Book and Job Office, 1889.
Walker, Thomas J., "Reminiscences of the Civil War," edited by Russell B. Bailey, *Confederate Chronicles of Tennessee,* vol. I, 1986.
Walthall, Edward C., "Walthall on the Battle of Lookout," *Confederate Veteran,* vol. VI, no. 12, December 1898.
Watkins, Sam R., *Co. Aytch, Maury Grays, First Tennessee Infantry, Or a Side Show of the Big Show,* Jackson, Tenn.: McCowat-Mercer Press, 1952.
Webster, Israel B., "Chickamauga. Going into Action with Hands Full of Bacon and Coffee," *The National Tribune,* July 2, 1891.
Weiser, J.M., "Trigg's Brigade at Chickamauga," *Confederate Veteran,* vol. XXXIV, no. 12, December 1926.
Wetmore, Elbridge G., "21st Ohio at Chickamauga," *The National Tribune,* October 2, 1884.
Wilder, John T., "The Battle of Hoover's Gap," *Sketches of War History,* MOLLUS-Ohio, vol. VI, n.p., n.d.
Willison, Charles A., *Reminiscences of a Boy's Service with the 76th Ohio,* Huntington, W.Va.: Blue Acorn Press, 1995.
Wilson, George S., *Wilder's Brigade of Mounted Infantry in Tullahoma-Chickamauga Campaigns,* MOLLUS-Kansas, 1891.
Wilson, John, "He Put It There," *The National Tribune,* March 31, 1887.
———, "Lookout Mountain," *The National Tribune,* June 11, 1891.
Winkler, A.V., The Confederate Capital and Hood's Texas Brigade, Austin: Eugene von Boeckmann, 1894.
Wood, Thomas J., "The Battle of Missionary Ridge," *Sketches of War History 1861-1865,* vol. IV, MOLLUS-Ohio, Cincinnati: The Robert Clarke Company, 1896.
Woodson, Henry M., "Battle on Side of Lookout Mountain," *Confederate Veteran,* vol. VI, no. 1, January 1898.
Wyeth, John A., *With Sabre and Scalpel: The Autobiography of a Soldier and Surgeon,* New York: Harper and Brothers, 1914.
———, "Trials with Gen. John H. Morgan," *Confederate Veteran,* vol. XIX, no. 3, March 1911.
———, "The Destruction of Rosecrans' Great Wagon Train," *The Photographic History of the Civil War,* Francis T. Miller, editor, vol. IV, New York: Thomas Yoseloff, 1957.
Yeary, Mamie, compiler, *Reminiscences of the Boys in Gray 1861-1865,* Dayton: Morningside, 1986.
Young, Lot D., *Reminiscences of a Soldier of the Orphan Brigade,* Louisville: Courier-Journal Job Printing Co., n.d.

## Newspapers & periodicals

Atlanta *Southern Confederacy,* December 3, 1863.
*Cincinnati Daily Commercial,* issues of October 8 and December 7, 1863.
Avery, Isaac W., "Wheeler's Raid – Unwritten History of the War of the Rebellion," clipping, *Cincinnati Enquirer,* n.d.
Fraser, James H., letter of September 26, 1863, printed in the *Alabama Courier,* September 20, 1905.
Gallipolis (Ohio) *Journal,* October 29, 1863.
*Harper's Weekly,* issues of November 7 and 28, 1863, December 12, 19 and 26, 1863, and January 2 and 9, 1864.
Hemming, Charles C., "A Confederate Odyssey," *American Heritage,* vol. XXXVI, no. 1, December 1984.
Jarman, Robert A., "The History of Company K, 27th Mississippi Infantry," *The Aberdeen Examiner,* Aberdeen, Miss., March 7, 1890.
Massenburg, Thomas L., letters of November 28 and 29, 1863, published in the *Macon Telegraph,* Macon, Ga., December 1 and 5, 1863.
Monson, Nels J., "The 24th Wisconsin's gallant Boy Colonel, Arthur MacArthur, planted the colors on Missionary Ridge," *America's Civil War,* March 1992.
Riley, James W., "Civil War Diary," *Dowagiac Daily News,* Dowagiac, Mich., November 11, 1963.
*The Charleston Mercury,* Charleston, S.C., issues of December 1, 2 and 4, 1863.
*Tiffin Tribune,* Tiffin, Ohio, October 30, 1863.

## Official records

Davis, George B.; Perry, Leslie J. and Kirkley, Joseph W., Board of Publication. Compiled by Capt. Calvin D. Cowles. *Atlas to Accompany the Official Records of the Union and Confederate Armies,* Washington, D.C.: Government Printing Office, 1891-1895.
United States War Department. *War of the Rebellion: A Compilation of the Official Records of the Union and Confederate Armies,* 128 vols., Washington, D.C.: Government Printing Office, 1891-1902.

## Regimental histories

Barnes, James A., Carnahan, James R. and McCain, Thomas H.B., *The Eighty-sixth Regiment Indiana Volunteer Infantry,* Crawfordsville, Ind.: The Journal Company Printers, 1895.
Bennett, Charles W., *Historical Sketches of the Ninth Michigan*

*Infantry,* Coldwater, Mich.: Daily Courier Print, 1913.
Bennett, Lyman G. and Haigh, William M., *History of the Thirty-sixth Regiment Illinois Volunteers during the War of the Rebellion,* Aurora, Ill.: Knickerbocker & Hodder Printers, 1876.
Bishop, Judson W., *The Story of a Regiment, being a Narrative of the Service of the Second Regiment, Minnesota Veteran Volunteer Infantry, in the Civil War of 1861-1865,* St. Paul: 1890.
Blackburn, Theodore W., *Letters from the Front: A Union "Preacher" Regiment (74th Ohio) in the Civil War,* Dayton: Morningside, 1981.
Boies, Andrew J., *Record of the 33d Mass. Volunteer Infantry from Aug. 1862 to Aug. 1865,* Fitchburg, Mass.: Sentinel Printing Co., 1880.
Boyle, John R., *Soldiers True, the Story of the One Hundred and Eleventh Regiment Pennsylvania Veteran Volunteers,* New York: Eaton & Mains, 1903.
Bradt, Hiram H.G., *History of the Services of the Third Battery Wisconsin Light Artillery in the Civil War of the United States,* Berlin, Wis.: Courant Press, 1902.
Briant, Charles C., *History of the Sixth Regiment Indiana Volunteer Infantry,* Indianapolis: William B. Burford Printer, 1891.
Brown, Alonzo L., *History of the Fourth Regiment of Minnesota Infantry Volunteers during the Great Rebellion 1861-1865,* St. Paul: The Pioneer Press Company, 1892.
Calkins, William W., *The History of the One Hundred and Fourth Regiment of Illinois Volunteer Infantry, War of the Great Rebellion, 1862-1865,* Chicago: Donohue & Henneberry Printers, 1895.
Canfield, Silas S., *History of the 21st Regiment Ohio Volunteer Infantry in the War of the Rebellion,* Toledo: Vrooman, Anderson & Bateman, Printers, 1893.
Clark, Walter, editor, *Histories of the Several Regiments and Battalions from North Carolina in the Great War 1861-'65,* vol. III, Goldsboro: Nash Brothers, 1901.
Coker, James L., *History of Company G, Ninth S.C. Regiment, Infantry, S.C. Army, and of Company E, Sixth S.C. Regiment, Infantry, S.C. Army,* Charleston, S.C.: Press of Walker, Evans & Cogswell, 1899.
Coles, Robert T., "History of Fourth Regiment Alabama Volunteer Infantry, C.S.A.," unpublished typescript, Alabama Department of Archives and History.
Collins, George K., *Memoirs of the 149th Regt. N.Y. Vol. Inft., 3rd Brig., 2d Div., 12th and 20th A.C.,* Syracuse: privately published, 1891.
*Condensed History of the 143d Regiment New York Volunteer Infantry, of the Civil War 1861-1865,* Newburgh, N.Y.: Newburgh Journal Printing House, 1909.
Cope, Alexis, *The Fifteenth Ohio Volunteers and its Campaigns, War of 1861-65,* Columbus: Press of the Edward T. Miller Co., 1916.
DeVelling, Charles T., *History of the Seventeenth* [Ohio] *Regiment, First Brigade, Third Division, Fourteenth Corps, Army of the Cumberland,* Zanesville, Ohio: E.R. Sullivan Printer, 1889.
Dickert, D. Augustus, *History of Kershaw's Brigade,* Newberry, S.C.: Elbert H. Aull Co., 1899.
Douglas, Lucia R., editor, *Douglas's Texas Battery, CSA,* Waco: Texian Press, 1966.
Eddy, Richard, *History of the Sixtieth Regiment New York State Volunteers,* Philadelphia: privately published, 1864.
Floyd, David B., *History of the Seventy-fifth Regiment of Indiana Infantry Volunteers,* Philadelphia: Lutheran Publication Society, 1893.
Gage, M.D., *From Vicksburg to Raleigh; or, a Complete History of the Twelfth Regiment Indiana Volunteer Infantry,* Chicago: Clarke & Co., 1865.
Gibson, Joseph T., editor, *History of the Seventy-eighth Pennsylvania Volunteer Infantry,* Pittsburgh: Press of the Pittsburgh Printing Co., 1905.
Guild, George B., *A Brief Narrative of the Fourth Tennessee Cavalry Regiment: Wheeler's Corps, Army of Tennessee,* Nashville: 1913.
Hannaford, Ebenezer, *The Story of a Regiment: A History of the Campaigns and Associations in the Field of the Sixth Regiment Ohio Volunteer Infantry,* Cincinnati: privately published, 1868.
Haynie, J. Henry, editor, *The Nineteenth Illinois,* Chicago: M.A. Donohue & Co., 1912.
Hight, John J., *History of the Fifty-eighth Regiment of Indiana Volunteer Infantry,* Princeton, Ind.: Press of the Clarion, 1895.
Hinman, Wilbur F., *The Story of the Sherman Brigade,* Alliance, Ohio: Press of Daily Review, 1897.
*History of the Organization, Marches, Campings, General Services and Final Muster Out of Battery M, First Regiment Illinois Light Artillery,* Princeton, Ill.: Mercer & Dean, 1892.
*History of the Seventy-third Regiment of Illinois Infantry Volunteers,* Springfield: W.H. Newlin, 1890.
Hoole, William S., *A Historical Sketch of the Thirty-Sixth Alabama Infantry Regiment, 1862-1865,* University, Ala.: Confederate Publishing Company.
Horrall, Spillard F., *History of the Forty-second Indiana Volunteer Infantry,* Chicago: Donohue & Henneberry Printers, 1892.
Hunter, Alfred G., *History of the Eighty-second Indiana Volunteer Infantry,* Indianapolis: William B. Burford Printer, 1893.
Kern, Albert, *History of the First Regiment Ohio Volunteer Infantry in the Civil War, 1861-1865,* Dayton: privately published, 1918.
Kerwood, Asbury L., *Annals of the Fifty-seventh Regiment Indiana Volunteers,* Dayton: W.J. Shuey Printer, 1868.
Kimberly, Robert L. and Holloway, Ephraim S., *The Forty-first Ohio Veteran Volunteer Infantry in the War of the Rebellion, 1861-1865,* Cleveland: W.R. Smellie, 1897.
Kirk, Charles H., *History of the Fifteenth Pennsylvania Volunteer Cavalry,* Philadelphia: 1906.
Krick, Robert K., *Parker's Virginia Battery C.S.A.,* Berryville, Va.: Virginia Book Company, 1975.
Lindsley, John B., *The Military Annals of Tennessee. Confederate,* Nashville: J.M. Lindsley & Co., 1886.
Little, George and Maxwell, James R., *A History of Lumsden's Battery C.S.A.,* Tuscaloosa, Ala.: R.E. Rodes Chapter, United Daughters of the Confederacy, 1905.
Magee, Benjamin F., *History of the 72d Indiana Volunteer Infantry of the Mounted Lightning Brigade,* Huntington, W.Va.: Blue Acorn Press, 1992.
Martin, John A., *Military History of the Eighth Kansas Veteran Volunteer Infantry,* Leavenworth: Daily Bulletin Printing House, 1869.
McAdams, Francis M., *Every-day Soldier Life, or A History of the One Hundred and Thirteenth Ohio Volunteer Infantry,* Columbus: Chas. M. Cott & Co., 1884.
McCaffrey, James M., *This Band of Heroes: Granbury's Texas Brigade C.S.A.,* Austin: Eakin Press, 1985.
*Military History and Reminiscences of the Thirteenth Regiment of Illinois Volunteer Infantry,* Chicago: Woman's Temperance Publishing Association, 1892.
*Ninety-Second Illinois Volunteers,* Freeport, Ill.: Journal Steam Publishing House, 1875.
Nourse, Henry S., et. al., *The Story of the Fifty-fifth Regiment Illinois Volunteer Infantry in the Civil War 1861-1865,* Huntington, W.Va.: Blue Acorn Press, 1993.
Oates, William C., *The War Between the Union and the Confederacy and its Lost Opportunities, with a History of the 15th Alabama Regiment and the Forty-Eight Battles in which it was Engaged,* New York: The Neale Publishing Co., 1905.
Osborn, Hartwell, *Trials and Triumphs, the Record of the Fifty-fifth Ohio Volunteer Infantry,* Chicago: A.C. McClurg & Co., 1904.
Partridge, Charles A., editor, *History of the Ninety-sixth Regiment Illinois Volunteer Infantry,* Chicago: Brown, Pettibone & Co., 1887.

Peddycord, William F., *History of the Seventy-fourth Regiment Indiana Volunteer Infantry,* Warsaw, Ind.: Smith Printery, 1913.
Perry, Henry F., *History of the Thirty-eighth Regiment Indiana Volunteer Infantry,* Palo Alto, Calif.: F.A. Stuart Printer, 1906.
Rennolds, Edwin H., *A History of the Henry County Commands which served in the Confederate States Army,* Jacksonville, Fla.: Sun Publishing Company, 1904.
Rowell, John W., *Yankee Cavalrymen: Through the Civil War with the Ninth Pennsylvania Cavalry,* Knoxville: University of Tennessee Press, 1971.
Royse, Isaac H.C., *History of the 115th Regiment Illinois Volunteer Infantry,* Chicago: Windsor & Kenfield Publishing Co., 1900.
Shaver, Lewellyn A., *A History of the Sixtieth Alabama Regiment, Gracie's Alabama Brigade,* Montgomery: Barrett & Brown, 1867.
Sherlock, Eli J., *Memorabilia of the Marches and Battles in which the One Hundredth Regiment of Indiana Infantry Volunteers Took an Active Part,* Kansas City: Gerard-Woody Printing Co., 1896.
Simpson, Harold B., *Hood's Texas Brigade: Lee's Grenadier Guard,* Waco: Texian Press, 1970.
Sligh, Charles R., *History of the Services of the First Regiment Michigan Engineers and Mechanics during the Civil War, 1861-1865,* Grand Rapids: White Print Co., 1921.
Thompson, Edwin P., *History of the First Kentucky Brigade,* Cincinnati: Caxton Publishing House, 1868.
Todd, George T., *First Texas Regiment,* Waco: Texian Press, 1963.
Tourgée, Albion W., *The Story of a Thousand, being a History of the Service of the 105th Ohio Volunteer Infantry in the War for the Union, from August 21, 1862, to June 6, 1865,* Buffalo, N.Y.: McGerald & Son, 1896.
Trimble, Harvey M., *History of the Ninety-third Regiment Illinois Volunteer Infantry,* Chicago: Blakely Printing Co., 1898.
Underwood, Adin B., *The Three Years' Service of the Thirty-Third Mass. Infantry Regiment 1862-1865,* Huntington, W.Va.: Blue Acorn Press, 1993.
Walker, C. Irving., *Rolls and Historical Sketch of the Tenth Regiment, So. Ca. Volunteers, in the Army of the Confederate States,* Charleston, S.C.: Walker, Evans & Cogswell Printers, 1881.
Wilder, Theodore, *The History of Company C, Seventh Regiment, O.V.I.,* Oberlin, Ohio: J.B.T. Marsh Printer, 1866.
Wilson, Lawrence, *Itinerary of the Seventh Ohio Volunteer Infantry 1861-1864,* New York: The Neale Publishing Company, 1907.
Woodruff, George H., *Fifteen Years Ago: or the Patriotism of Will County,* Joliet: Joliet Republican Book and Job Steam Printing House, 1876.
Worsham, William J., *The Old Nineteenth Tennessee Regiment, C.S.A.,* Knoxville: Press of Paragon Printing Company, 1902.
Wright, Henry H., *A History of the Sixth Iowa Infantry,* Iowa City: The State Historical Society of Iowa, 1923.
Young, J.P., *The Seventh Tennessee Cavalry (Confederate). A History,* Nashville: Publishing House of the M.E. Church, South, 1890.

## Bibliographies & reference works

Albaugh, William A. III, *Confederate Faces,* Solana Beach, Calif.: Verde Publishers, 1970.
Barnard, George N., *Photographic Views of Sherman's Campaign,* New York: Dover Publications, Inc., 1977.
Bates, Samuel P., *History of Pennsylvania Volunteers 1861-5,* 5 vols., Harrisburg: B. Singerly, 1869.
Boatner, Mark M., *The Civil War Dictionary,* New York: David McKay Co., 1959.
Cole, Garold L., *Civil War Eyewitnesses: An Annotated Bibliography of Books and Articles, 1955-1986,* Columbia: University of South Carolina Press, 1988.
Davis, William C., editor, *The Image of War 1861-1865,* vols. IV and V, Garden City, N.Y.: Doubleday & Company, Inc., 1983.
*Deeds of Valor from Records in the Archives of the United States Government: How American Heroes won the Medal of Honor,* vol. I, edited by W.F. Beyer and O.F. Keydel, Detroit: The Perrien-Keydel Company, 1906.
*Dictionary of American Biography,* vols. I-X, edited by Allen Johnson, New York: Charles Scribner's Sons, 1964.
Dornbusch, C.E., *Military Bibliography of the Civil War,* vols. I, II and III, New York: The New York Public Library, 1975.
Douglas, George W., *The American Book of Days,* New York: The H.W. Wilson Co., 1937.
Dyer, Frederick H., *A Compendium of the War of the Rebellion,* Dayton: Morningside, 1979.
Foster, John Y., *New Jersey and the Rebellion: A History of the Services of the Troops and People of New Jersey in Aid of the Union Cause,* Newark: Martin R. Dennis & Co., 1868.
Fox, William F., *Regimental Losses in the American Civil War 1861-1865,* Albany, N.Y.: Albany Publishing Co., 1889.
*General Orders, Department of the Cumberland, 1863,* Nashville: John T.S. Fall Printer, 1863.
Georgia. *Roster of the Confederate Soldiers of Georgia 1861-1865,* 6 vols., Hapeville, Ga.: Longino & Porter, Inc., 1958.
Heitman, Francis B., *Historical Register and Dictionary of the United States Army, from its Organization, September 29, 1789, to March 2, 1903,* vol. I, Washington, D.C.: Government Printing Office, 1903.
Hoobler, James A., *Cities Under the Gun: Images of Occupied Nashville and Chattanooga,* Nashville: Rutledge Hill Press, 1986.
Hunt, Roger D., and Brown, Jack R., *Brevet Brigadier Generals in Blue,* Gaithersburg, Md.: Olde Soldier Books Inc., 1990.
Illinois. *Report of the Illinois Adjutant General containing Reports for the Years 1861-66,* 8 vols., Springfield: Phillips Bros. State Printers, 1900-1902.
Indiana. *Report of the Adjutant General of the State of Indiana,* 8 vols., Indianapolis: W.R. Holloway, State Printer, 1865-1868.
Iowa. *Roster and Record of Iowa Soldiers in the War of the Rebellion Together with Historical Sketches of Volunteer Organizations 1861-1865,* 5 vols., Des Moines: Emory H. English, State Printer, 1908.
Kentucky. *Report of the Adjutant General 1861-1866,* 2 vols., Frankfort: John H. Harney, Public Printer, 1866-1867.
*List of Staff Officers of the Confederate States Army 1861-1865,* Bryan, Texas: J.M. Carroll & Company, 1983.
Louisiana. *Records of Louisiana Confederate Soldiers and Louisiana Confederate Commands,* 3 vols., New Orleans: n.p., 1920.
Massachusetts Adjutant General. *Record of the Massachusetts Volunteers 1861-1865,* 2 vols., Boston: Wright & Potter, 1868-1870.
McAuley, John D., *Civil War Breech Loading Rifles: A Survey of the Innovative Infantry Arms of the American Civil War,* Lincoln, R.I.: Andrew Mobray Inc., 1987.
Michigan. *Alphabetical General Index to Public Library Sets of 85,271 Names of Michigan Soldiers and Sailors Individual Records,* Lansing: Wynkoop Hallenbeck Crawford Co., 1915.
Miller, Francis T., editor, *The Photographic History of the Civil War,* 10 vols., New York: Thomas Yoseloff, 1957.
*National Cyclopaedia of American Biography,* New York: James T. White & Co., 1954.
Ohio. *Authors and Their Books. Biographical Data and Selective Bibliographies for Ohio Authors, Native and Resident, 1796-1950,* edited by William Coyle, Cleveland: World Publishing Co., 1962.
Ohio. Roster Commission. *Official Roster of the Soldiers of the State of Ohio in the War of the Rebellion, 1861-1866,* 12 vols., Akron, Cincinnati, Norwalk: 1886-1895.
Phillips, Stanley S., *Civil War Corps Badges and Other Related Awards, Badges, Medals of the Period,* Lanham, Md.: S.S.

Phillips and Associates, 1982.
Phisterer, Frederick, compiler, *New York in the War of the Rebellion 1861 to 1865,* 5 vols., Albany: J.B. Lyon Company, 1912.
Sauers, Richard A., *To Care For Him Who Has Borne the Battle: Research Guide to Civil War Material in The National Tribune,* vol. I, 1877-1884, Jackson, Ky.: History Shop Press, 1995.
Sears, Stephen W., editor, *The American Heritage Century Collection of Civil War Art,* New York: American Heritage Publishing Co., 1974.
*Society of the Army of the Cumberland, Eighth Reunion 1874,* Cincinnati: The Robert Clarke Company, 1875.
*Society of the Army of the Cumberland, 26th Reunion 1896,* Cincinnati: The Robert Clarke Company, 1897.
*Society of the Army of the Cumberland, 29th Reunion 1900,* Cincinnati: The Robert Clarke Company, 1901.
*Society of the Army of the Cumberland, 36th Reunion 1908,* Chattanooga: MacGowan-Cooke Printing Company, 1909.
*Sons of Confederate Veterans Ancestor Album,* Houston: Heritage Publishers Services, 1986.
*Tennesseans in the Civil War: A Military History of Confederate and Union Units with Available Rosters of Personnel,* 2 vols., Nashville: Civil War Centennial Commission, 1964-1965.
*The Congressional Medal of Honor: the Names, the Deeds,* Forest Ranch, Calif.: Sharp & Dunnigan, 1984.
*The Soldier in Our Civil War,* Frank Leslie's Columbian Memorial Edition, vol. II, New York: Stanley Bradley Publishing Co., 1890.
Todd, Frederick P., *American Military Equipage 1851-1872,* vol. II, Chatham Square Press, Inc., 1983.
United States. Adjutant General's Office. *Official Army Register of the Volunteer Force of the United States Army for the Years 1861, '62, '63, '64, '65,* parts I-VIII, Gaithersburg, Md.: Olde Soldier Books Inc. 1987.
Warner, Ezra J., *Generals in Gray: Lives of the Confederate Commanders,* Baton Rouge: Louisiana State University Press, 1959.
———, *Generals in Blue: Lives of the Union Commanders,* Baton Rouge: Louisiana State University Press, 1964.
Welsh, Jack D., *Medical Histories of Confederate Generals,* Kent, Ohio: Kent State University Press, 1995.
Wilson, Mrs. Mindwell C., *Indiana Battle Flags and A Record of Indiana Organizations in the Mexican, Civil and Spanish-American Wars,* Indianapolis: Indiana Battle Flag Commission, 1929.
Wisconsin. *Roster of Wisconsin Volunteers, War of the Rebellion, 1861-1865,* 2 vols., Madison: Democrat Printing Company, 1886.

## Biographies

Hattaway, Herman, *General Stephen D. Lee,* Jackson: University Press of Mississippi, 1976.
Hughes, Nathaniel Cheairs Jr., *General William J. Hardee: Old Reliable,* Baton Rouge: Louisiana State University Press, 1965.
Johnston, William Preston, *The Life of Gen. Albert Sidney Johnston,* New York: D. Appleton and Company, 1878.
Losson, Christopher, *Tennessee's Forgotten Warriors: Frank Cheatham and His Confederate Division,* Knoxville: University of Tennessee Press, 1989.
Mathes, J. Harvey, *The Old Guard in Gray,* Memphis: Press of S.C. Toof & Co., 1897.
Mickle, William E., *Well Known Confederate Veterans and their War Records,* vol. I, New Orleans: privately printed, 1907.
Parks, Joseph H., *General Leonidas Polk, C.S.A.,* Baton Rouge: Louisiana State University Press, 1990.
Pierrepont, Alice V.D., *Reuben Vaughan Kidd, Soldier of the Confederacy,* Petersburg, Va.: privately published, 1947.
Polk, William M., *Leonidas Polk: Bishop and General,* vol. II, New York: Longmans, Green & Co., 1915.
Slocum, Charles E., *The Life and Services of Major-General Henry Warner Slocum,* Toledo: The Slocum Publishing Company, 1913.
Stickles, Arndt M., *Simon Bolivar Buckner,* Chapel Hill: University of North Carolina Press, 1940.
Thomas, John P., *Career and Character of General Micah Jenkins, C.S.A.,* Columbia, S.C.: The State Company, 1903.
Wyeth, John A., *That Devil Forrest: Life of General Nathan Bedford Forrest,* Baton Rouge: Louisiana State University Press, 1989.

## Local histories

Beach, D.E., *Marietta College in the War of Secession, 1861-1865,* Cincinnati: Peter G. Thomson, 1878.
Clark, William H.H., *History in Catoosa County* [Ga.], privately published, 1972.
*History of Defiance County, Ohio,* Chicago: Warner, Beers & Co., 1883.
*The War for the Union, 1861-1865. A Record of its Defenders, Living and Dead, from Steuben County, Indiana,* 1889.

## Military histories

Belknap, Charles E., *History of the Michigan Organizations at Chickamauga, Chattanooga and Missionary Ridge 1863,* Lansing: Robert Smith Printing Co., 1899.
Bickham, William D., *Rosecrans' Campaign with the Fourteenth Army Corps, of the Army of the Cumberland,* Cincinnati: Moore, Wilstach, Keys & Co., 1863.
Brown, Joseph M., *The Mountain Campaigns in Georgia,* Buffalo, N.Y.: Matthews, Northrup & Co., 1890.
Cist, Henry M., *The Army of the Cumberland,* New York: Charles Scribner's Sons, 1882.
Connelly, Thomas L., *Autumn of Glory: The Army of Tennessee, 1862-1865,* Baton Rouge: Louisiana State University Press, 1971.
Cozzens, Peter, *This Terrible Sound: The Battle of Chickamauga,* Urbana, Ill.: University of Illinois Press, 1992.
———, *The Shipwreck of Their Hopes: The Battles for Chattanooga,* Urbana, Ill.: University of Illinois Press, 1994.
Daniel, Larry J., *Soldiering in the Army of Tennessee,* Chapel Hill: University of North Carolina Press, 1991.
Gracie, Archibald, *The Truth About Chickamauga,* Boston: Houghton Mifflin Co., 1911.
Horn, Stanley F., *The Army of Tennessee: A Military History,* New York: The Bobbs-Merrill Co., 1941.
Korn, Jerry, *The Fight for Chattanooga: Chickamauga to Missionary Ridge,* Alexandria, Va.: Time-Life Books, 1985.
McDonough, James L., *Chattanooga – A Death Grip on the Confederacy,* Knoxville: University of Tennessee Press, 1984.
*Pennsylvania at Chickamauga and Chattanooga,* Harrisburg: William Stanley Ray, 1897.
Reid, Whitelaw, *Ohio in the War: Her Statesmen, Her Generals and Soldiers,* 2 vols., Cincinnati: Moore, Wilstach & Baldwin, 1868.
Ridley, Bromfield L., *Battles and Sketches of the Army of Tennessee,* Mexico, Mo.: Missouri Printing & Publishing Co., 1906.
Strayer, Larry M. and Baumgartner, Richard A., *Echoes of Battle: The Atlanta Campaign,* Huntington, W.Va.: Blue Acorn Press, 1991.
Sword, Wiley, *Mountains Touched with Fire: Chattanooga Besieged, 1863,* New York: St. Martin's Press, 1995.
Tucker, Glenn, *Chickamauga: Bloody Battle in the West,* Indianapolis: The Bobbs-Merrill Company, Inc., 1961.
Vale, Joseph G., *Minty and the Cavalry. A History of Cavalry Campaigns in the Western Armies,* Harrisburg: Edwin K. Meyers, Printer, 1886.
Van Horne, Thomas B., *History of the Army of the Cumberland, its*

*Organization, Campaigns, and Battles,* vol. I, Cincinnati: Ogden, Campbell & Co., 1875.

Walker, Robert S., *Lookout Mountain Battles and Battlefields,* Chattanooga: Kingwood Publishers, 1946.

---

***The authors gratefully acknowledge the following publishers for permission to reprint copyrighted material from these works:***

Samuel T. Foster: *One of Cleburne's Command: The Civil War Reminiscences and Diary of Capt. Samuel T. Foster, Granbury's Texas Brigade, CSA,* edited by Norman D. Brown, copyright 1980, reprinted with permission from the University of Texas Press, P.O. Box 7819, Austin, Texas 78713.

John W. Green: *Johnny Green of the Orphan Brigade: The Journal of a Confederate Soldier,* edited by Albert D. Kerwin, copyright 1956, reprinted with permission from The University Press of Kentucky, 663 S. Limestone St., Lexington, Ky. 40506.

Arthur M. Manigault: *A Carolinian Goes to War,* edited by R. Lockwood Tower, copyright 1983, reprinted with permission from the University of South Carolina Press, Columbia, S.C. 29208.

James C. Nisbet: *Four Years on the Firing Line,* edited by Bell I. Wiley, copyright 1987, reprinted with permission from Broadfoot Publishing Company, 1907 Buena Vista Circle, Wilmington, N.C. 28405.

# Index

***Page numbers appearing in boldface indicate photographs or illustrations.***

# C

# D

## E



## F



## G

## H

# I



# J

# M

## N



## O

# P



# Q



# R

## S

## T



## U

## V



## W

## Y



## Z

# About the authors

**Richard A. Baumgartner** is a former journalist who worked between 1975 and 1991 for Gannett and Knight-Ridder newspapers in West Virginia and California as a feature writer, artist, designer and graphics editor. A native of Wisconsin, he is a graduate of the University of Missouri School of Journalism. A 1967 visit to Perryville battlefield in Kentucky sparked his special interest in the Civil War's western theater. Baumgartner's published works include a number of articles for *Military History* magazine, editing *Blood & Sacrifice: The Civil War Journal of a Confederate Soldier,* and the illustrated First World War narratives *Fritz: The WWI Memoir of a German Lieutenant* and *The Passage.* He currently is writing a book about Col. John T. Wilder's mounted infantry brigade in the battle of Chickamauga. A full-time researcher and writer, he lives in Huntington, W.Va.

**Larry M. Strayer,** a native of Toledo, Ohio, dates his interests to the Civil War centennial, when he began reading about the conflict and collecting artifacts. His focus eventually gravitated toward soldier narratives, regimental histories and photographs. Involved with living history since the early 1970s, he has reenacted and researched at most major battlefields and archives throughout the country. During his college years, he was a Confederate interpreter at Chancellorsville National Battlefield. Earning a history degree from Ohio University, Strayer attended Capital University Law School and presently is employed by Lexis-Nexis research services in Miamisburg, Ohio. Married to Katherine H. Lessuck, they have four children.

First meeting in Gen. William T. Sherman's Ohio hometown of Lancaster in 1972, Baumgartner and Strayer have compiled an archive of nearly 6,000 photographic negatives and more than 2,000 personal accounts of the Civil War. Integrating first-person primary sources, wartime photographs and illustrations, their initial joint publication *Echoes of Battle: The Atlanta Campaign* received the 1994 Richard B. Harwell Award, presented by the Atlanta Civil War Round Table. This was followed by *Yankee Tigers: Through the Civil War with the 125th Ohio,* and 10 other enhanced reprintings of rare soldier memoirs and regimental histories. Both are serving as consultants for Time-Life Books' *Voices of the Civil War* series.

# Echoes of Battle: The Atlanta Campaign

Rocky Face Ridge, Resaca and New Hope Church. Pickett's Mill, Kennesaw Mountain, Peachtree Creek, Ezra Church, Jonesboro: battles on Georgia soil in which thousands were killed or wounded — and overshadowed for decades by attention paid to the Civil War in the East. But the war in the West was equally important, more so strategically, and is the subject of the first ***Echoes of Battle*** volume focusing on Gen. William T. Sherman's 1864 offensive to defeat the Confederate Army of Tennessee and capture Atlanta.

This highly praised book offers a brutally realistic portrayal of the pivotal Atlanta Campaign through the words of 265 Union and Confederate soldiers. Hundreds of letters, diaries, memoirs and reminiscences were compiled by editors Larry M. Strayer and Richard A. Baumgartner to provide an essence of war's reality experienced by these fighting men. And more than 330 photographs (over half of them previously unpublished), illustrations and maps complement the illuminating narratives.

**Hardcover $39.95**
ISBN 0-9628866-1-0

**Softcover $29.95**
ISBN 0-9628866-0-2

1994 Richard B. Harwell Award recipient

"This handsome folio-sized volume ... makes for absorbing reading, for the narratives contain literally hundreds of vivid, memorable anecdotes that make the various battlefields all too real. ***Echoes of Battle*** is a very significant contribution to the history of the Civil War's western theater."
***The Georgia Historical Quarterly***

"... a unique and not to be missed treasury of information and insight into one of the critical episodes of the Civil War."
***The Wisconsin Bookwatch***

"***Echoes of Battle*** [is] sprinkled with magnificent illustrations — both drawings and photographs. [They] are especially interesting for the rich details that many of them provide about such matters as weapons and uniforms."
***Atlanta History: A Journal of Georgia and the South***

"Strayer and Baumgartner have put together an outstanding collection of accounts, anecdotes and photographs of the ordinary men who shouldered muskets and the officers who led them. It will delight any Civil War buff."
***Small Press Reviews***

"... an excellent collection ... much valuable material about the soldiers' food, sleeping conditions, the vermin that plagued the men, the fatigue, the weather, and other details about the soldiers' lot that helps to humanize the campaign and makes it more meaningful to the modern reader. This well-edited book is a highly commendable attempt to ensure that those who fought and suffered in the Atlanta campaign will not be forgotten."
***The Journal of Southern History***

"The journals, letters and written accounts ... supplemented with hundreds of vintage war photos, make for lively coverage which should involve even reluctant American history readers. The first-person journal and diary entries are edited and organized for maximum impact."
***The Midwest Book Review***

"... an insightful and absorbing chronicle of soldiers' experiences. Strayer's and Baumgartner's intent is to get us into the soldiers' ranks, and they do so very effectively."
***Blue & Gray Magazine***

"Collections of first-person narratives concerning various Civil War battles and campaigns are increasingly popular. One of the best is this volume from Blue Acorn Press. [The] extensive use of soldier images is uncommon in books, and is sure to delight readers ... ***Echoes of Battle*** is extremely well done."
***Military Images***

**BLUE ACORN PRESS**
P.O. Box 2684 • Huntington, West Virginia 25726 • (304) 733-3917

# How Soldiers Were Made

THE WAR AS I SAW IT UNDER BUELL, ROSECRANS, THOMAS, GRANT and SHERMAN.

**By Benjamin F. Scribner**

New reprint of 1887 memoir by Colonel Benjamin F. Scribner, 38th Indiana and 14th Corps' brigade commander. Scribner began his military career in the Mexican War and experienced bloody combat during the Civil War at Perryville, Stones River, Tullahoma, Chickamauga, Lookout Mountain, Missionary Ridge, Rocky Face Ridge, Resaca and Kennesaw Mountain. His narrative vividly describes personalities and events in the war's western theater, and provides perceptive insights into how officers and enlisted men under his command from Ohio, Wisconsin, Indiana, Illinois, Kentucky and Pennsylvania evolved into veteran soldiers. A very rare title for many years, ***How Soldiers Were Made*** is among only a few book-length accounts written by Army of the Cumberland brigade commanders.

**Hardcover $27.50**

**History of the 72nd Indiana: Wilder's Lightning Brigade.**
Sergeant Benjamin F. Magee's excellent chronicle of a distinctive Hoosier regiment, part of Col. John T. Wilder's famous mounted brigade armed with Spencer repeating rifles. This massive history is based on Magee's diary plus dozens of his comrades, highlighting hundreds of events and experiences of the common soldier.

*800 pages, 61 photos, full regimental roster.*

**Hardcover $43**

**With the Western Sharpshooters.**
Michigan boys of Company D, 66th Illinois, as profiled by Sergeant Lorenzo A. Barker, with additional regimental history by R.A. Baumgartner and L.M. Strayer. Armed with Dimick target rifles and later with Henry repeating rifles, the Western Sharpshooters were the western-theater counterpart to Berdan's Sharpshooters.

*192 pages, 68 photos, Company D roster.*

**Hardcover $23.95**

**A Narrative of Military Service.**
William B. Hazen's memoir of service as brigade and division commander at Shiloh, Stones River, Chickamauga, Chattanooga, Atlanta, Fort McAllister, the Carolinas.

*576 pages, 96 photos, engravings, maps.*

**Hardcover $35**

**33rd Massachusetts.**
By Adin B. Underwood. 11th Corps service at Chancellorsville, Gettysburg, Chattanooga; 20th Corps service in the Atlanta and Carolinas campaigns.

*420 pages, 72 photos, full regimental roster.*

**Hardcover $30**

**The 55th Illinois 1861-1865.**
One of the Army of the Tennessee's hardest fighting regiments, with exemplary service at Shiloh, Vicksburg and the Atlanta campaign. Foreword by Edwin C. Bearss.

*620 pages, 73 photos, full regimental roster.*

**Hardcover $35**

**A Boy's Service with the 76th Ohio.**
Private Charles A. Willison's narrative provides a humorous but realistic picture of a teen-aged soldier's hard campaigning and fighting with the 15th Corps, Army of the Tennessee.

"Willison's honesty sets his memoir apart from many soldiers' accounts of the war. [He] refused to place himself at the head of every charge, nor was he always the last to retreat. This book, with its solid descriptions of soldiering in the western campaigns, an area most buffs tend to overlook, deserves a sizeable audience."
***Civil War Magazine***

*200 pages, 26 photographs, 4 appendices, index.*

**Hardcover $24.95**

**BLUE ACORN PRESS**

P.O. Box 2684 • Huntington, West Virginia 25726 • (304) 733-3917